SAIPAN

*The Battle That Doomed Japan
in World War II*

JAMES H. HALLAS

STACKPOLE
BOOKS

Guilford, Connecticut

Published by Stackpole Books
An imprint of The Rowman & Littlefield Publishing Group, Inc.
4501 Forbes Blvd., Ste. 200
Lanham, MD 20706
www.rowman.com

Distributed by NATIONAL BOOK NETWORK
800-462-6420

British Library Cataloguing in Publication Information available

Library of Congress Cataloging-in-Publication Data available

ISBN 978-0-8117-3843-9 (hardcover)
ISBN 978-0-8117-6843-6 (e-book)

♾™ The paper used in this publication meets the minimum requirements of American National Standard for Information Sciences—Permanence of Paper for Printed Library Materials, ANSI/NISO Z39.48-1992.

Printed in the United States of America

Contents

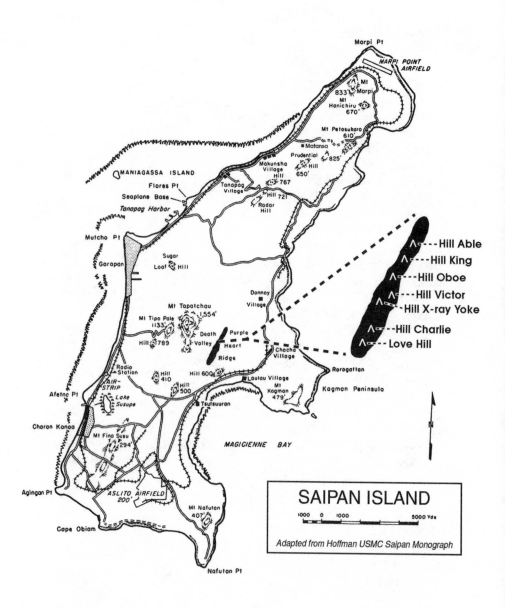

Marpi Pt

MARPI POINT
AIRFIELD

Mt
833' Marpi
Mt
Hanichiru
670'

Mt Petosukara
610'

Matansa
Prudential
825'
Hill

Makunsha
Village
Hill
767

650'

MANIAGASSA ISLAND

Flores Pt

Tanapag
Village

Seaplane Base

Hill 721

Tanapag Harbor

Radar
Hill

Mutcho Pt

Sugar
Loaf Hill

Garapan

∧---Hill Able
∧---Hill King
∧---Hill Oboe

Donnay
Village

∧---Hill Victor
∧---Hill X-ray Yoke

Mt Tapotchau
1,554'

Mt Tipo Pale
1133'

Death
Valley

Purple
Heart
Ridge

∧---Hill Charlie
∧---Love Hill

Hill 789

Chacha
Village

Radio
Station

Hill
410

Hill 600'

Rorogattan

AIR-
STRIP

Hill
500

Laulau Village
Mt
Kagman
479'

Kagman Peninsula

Afetna Pt

Lake
Susupe

Tsutsuuran

Charan Kanoa

MAGICIENNE BAY

Mt Fina Susu
294'

N

Agingan Pt

ASLITO AIRFIELD
200'

Mt Nafutan
407'

Cape Obiam

SAIPAN ISLAND

1000   0   1000   5000 Yds

Adapted from Hoffman USMC Saipan Monograph

Nafutan Pt

INTRODUCTION

BY EARLY 1944, IT HAD BECOME CLEAR THAT JAPAN WAS LOSING THE WAR. As the United States brought its immense military and industrial power to bear, the seemingly invincible Japanese juggernaut had sputtered and begun to recoil under a succession of defeats. Though the Japanese public remained largely oblivious, high-ranking military officers and knowledgeable government officials—even the emperor himself—were all too aware of the decline in Imperial fortunes. Victory, once seemingly so close at hand, had begun to slip inexorably away.

In response, Japanese military and political leaders decided to bet the fate of their nation on a calculated roll of the dice. Carefully husbanding its resources, the Imperial Navy would wait until the moment was right, then sally forth for a decisive confrontation with the U.S. fleet. The powerful force of carriers, battleships, and land-based aircraft would then inflict a defeat of such magnitude on the American devils that their stunned enemy would agree to a negotiated peace.

The much-awaited opportunity arrived in mid-June 1944 when U.S. forces began to land on the island of Saipan in the southern Marianas. While Japanese soldiers mounted a tenacious defense on the ground, a powerful naval force set out to destroy the U.S. Fifth Fleet. The ensuing sea battle took place over two days, while the ground fighting on Saipan dragged on into July. When it was all over, Japanese hopes for victory lay entombed with thousands of navy pilots and seamen beneath the waves of the Philippine Sea and other thousands of Imperial infantrymen moldering among the burned cane fields and rugged hinterlands of once tranquil Saipan.

It may seem presumptuous, given the nature of the war in the Pacific, to single out any one action as "the battle that doomed Japan." Victory in the Pacific was cumulative, marked by any number of "turning points" or milestones such as the Coral Sea, Midway, and Guadalcanal in the long march toward peace. The American victory at Saipan did not end hostilities. Peleliu, the Philippines, Iwo Jima, Okinawa, and a host of other bloodbaths, large and small, still lay ahead, claiming the lives of many more thousands of Americans and Japanese. But it was the defeat of the Imperial Navy in the waters off Saipan in June 1944 and the fall of the island itself in July that emphatically demonstrated to the Japanese that the war was lost.

The ramifications of the confrontation at Saipan—to include the naval battle of the Philippine Sea—were both varied and far-reaching. The inexorable American advance had shattered the much-vaunted Absolute Defense Sphere, brushing aside a Japanese navy that had once seemed virtually invincible and eradicating Japanese naval airpower as a significant threat to U.S. operations in the Pacific. The emperor himself began to press his advisors to search for an honorable exit from the war that had begun so auspiciously and now, only two and a half years later, threatened his nation with destruction.

The disaster forced the resignation of prime minister Gen. Hideki Tojo, whose Cabinet had led Japan since late 1941, and encouraged a nascent peace movement in some of the highest military and government circles. To the man in the street, the loss of the supposedly impregnable island bastion—home to a substantial Japanese civilian population—was incontrovertible proof that the Americans were closing in on the homeland. That proof would soon be clearly visible overhead. American air bases on Saipan, Guam, and Tinian brought the Japanese home islands within range of the newly developed B-29 Superfortress bombers, which would proceed to lay waste to city after city in a firestorm that would culminate in mushroom clouds over Hiroshima and Nagasaki.

Events at Saipan were also to have a more subtle—but no less significant—impact as they helped shape American and Japanese thinking and decision-making over the next thirteen months. Higher than anticipated American casualties in the ground battle for the island left planners brooding over potential losses in any invasion of the Japanese home islands. The so-called "Saipan ratio" suggested that U.S. casualties would be enormous—500,000 at a minimum and quite probably higher.[1] Those concerns were not eased by the highly publicized suicides of what were said to be thousands of Japanese civilians on Saipan as defeat loomed. If even the civilian population on Saipan embraced an orgy of self-annihilation, what would happen when American forces invaded Japan with its many millions, each man, woman, and child a potential enemy?

Saipan also gave rise to two controversies that linger to this day. Historians continue to debate Adm. Raymond Spruance's handling of the Fifth

Fleet during the battle of the Philippine Sea. Though his carrier pilots won a stunning victory, Spruance was criticized for what many perceived as a lack of aggressiveness—a failure that may have cost him the opportunity to destroy the Imperial Navy in one fell swoop. Meanwhile, the ground campaign for Saipan spawned one of the most toxic interservice controversies of World War II when Marine lieutenant general Holland Smith relieved U.S. Army major general Ralph Smith of command of the 27th Division. The disparaging allegations involving Ralph Smith and the 27th Division's performance on Saipan and the counterclaims against Holland Smith and their potential effect on interservice cooperation reached such proportions that it threatened to hinder the prosecution of the war in the Pacific.

Ironically, considering its significance, Saipan has been called "the bloodiest battle you never heard of."[2] Overshadowed by the Allied landings in Normandy the week before, the campaign has only recently been explored in any detail by historians writing for a more general audience. That recognition is long overdue. As a simple matter of logistics, the execution of the operation, simultaneously with the Normandy landings half a world away, was an unparalleled show of American military and industrial might as well as a stunning demonstration of the evolution of the amphibious assault and the lethal reach of naval task forces built around the new queen of the seas: the aircraft carrier. The D-Day landings on the coast of France were conducted over 20 miles of water separating England from the Continent. The assault on Saipan moved 535 ships and over 70,000 men some 3,200 nautical miles across the vast Pacific to land on a hostile shore only 1,250 nautical miles from Tokyo.

Saipan was also the first multidivisional amphibious assault in Marine Corps history; the first to tackle a limited land mass; the first to encounter Japanese civilians in substantial numbers; and the first where Marines had to deal with street-to-street fighting in an urban area. It was the setting for the largest carrier battle in history; scene of the largest enemy tank assault of the Pacific war; the largest mass "*banzai*" attack; and one of the great tragedies of the war as hundreds of civilians chose to leap to their deaths from Saipan's towering cliffs rather than accept capture by the hated Americans.

Saipan was no pushover. Observed the 2nd Marine Division historian later, "Take all the Pacific battles that had gone before, from the fall of Corregidor to Eniwetok. Take Tulagi and Guadalcanal, and Tarawa and Attu, and Lost Negros and Buna and Gona. Stir them all together, and add a little European seasoning—perhaps from Sicily—and pour them out on a flat blue sea under a blue bowl of sky, and you'll have something that looks and smells and feels and hurts like Saipan. For Saipan had everything: caves like Tulagi; mountains and ridges like the 'Canal; a reef nearly as treacherous as Betio's; a swamp like Buna; a city to be conquered, like those of Sicily; and death-minded Japs like the defenders of Attu. A lot, for so small an island. But Saipan never seemed small, though it was only [47] square miles."[3]

U.S. planners had hoped to have the situation on Saipan in hand within three days. For a variety of reasons—faulty intelligence and fierce Japanese resistance prominent among them—it took two Marine divisions and a U.S. Army division more than three weeks to push their way up Saipan's 12-mile length. They had expected to face about 15,000 Japanese. There were actually at least 30,000, well equipped with tanks and plenty of artillery. It was a tough, sanguinary fight that boded ill for what was to come during the long slog toward the Japanese home islands. But none of that was yet evident the morning of June 15, 1944, as the men of the 2nd and 4th Marine Divisions clambered into their amphibious tractors and began circling off the smoking shore of a place most had never heard of until a couple of weeks before. They thought they were ready. They expected to win and they did. But it didn't come cheap.

The price, as always, was borne by young men in green dungarees. Twenty-four-year-old Lt. John H. Magruder would never forget the scene by a Saipan roadside after a night of heavy enemy mortar fire inflicted numerous casualties on his outfit. The dead were being loaded into trucks for transport to the 2nd Marine Division cemetery. Magruder looked to see if there was anyone he recognized among the half-dozen or so Marines stretched out next to one of the trucks, some on their backs, some face down. "One of the latter was a young, fair-haired private who had only recently arrived as a replacement, full of exuberance at finally being a full-fledged Marine on the battle front," he recalled. Sticking out from the youngster's back pocket was a yellow pocket edition of a book he had evidently been reading in his spare moments. Only the title was visible—*Our Hearts Were Young and Gay*.[4]

War is cruel in unimaginable ways and Saipan would be no exception. "None of us ever thought we were going to die," remarked an aging former corporal many years later. "But a lot of us did."[5]

CHAPTER 1

Fateful Decisions

Tokyo: February 1944

LT. GEN. KENRYO SATO WAS A REALIST. IT WAS A QUALITY THAT DID NOT always endear him to his fellows, as when he advocated caution about going to war with the United States in 1941 or recommended abandoning the losing struggle for Guadalcanal in 1943. Nevertheless, he remained one of Prime Minister Hideki Tojo's most trusted advisors and confidantes.

Now, as Japan embarked on a third year of war, General Sato was preparing to test that relationship with a controversial recommendation that was likely to determine the future of his nation. He believed Japan should abandon plans to defend the Mariana Islands and instead pull back and retrench in the Philippines. The question was, would anyone listen? The military situation in the Central Pacific was not going well—that was clear to any objective observer—yet all too many of Japan's military leaders stubbornly refused to make the unpleasant choices that were now so necessary.

This reluctance to confront present realities was perhaps more understandable when viewed through the lens of Japan's astonishing successes earlier in the war. As part of the military hierarchy, General Sato had shared in the elation of victory after victory in the months following the surprise attack on the U.S. Pacific Fleet at Pearl Harbor on December 7, 1941. But over the course of the next two years that nationwide euphoria had ebbed along with Japan's military fortunes. The disastrous naval battle at Midway in June 1942 had been followed by a string of defeats at Guadalcanal, the Aleutians, New Guinea, Bougainville, and Tarawa. American Marines and naval forces seemed unstoppable in the Central Pacific, while in the Southwest Pacific U.S. Army troops under Gen. Douglas MacArthur advanced inexorably from island to island toward the Philippines.

This turn of fortune prompted Japanese strategists—with the emperor's consent—to go on the defense. Instead of expanding the war in hopes of victory, the new plan, settled upon in late September 1943, was to regroup and build up an "Absolute Defense Sphere." Reorganizing behind a bulwark of fortified islands, the Imperial forces would draw the enemy into a decisive battle that would halt the American advance and bring about a negotiated peace.[1] According to this plan, Rabaul and the Marshall Islands would serve as a screen to the main line. Behind this sacrificial outer shell, a second, inviolable inner defense line would extend from the Marianas to the Palaus to western New Guinea. Located only 1,250 to 2,000 miles from Tokyo itself, this line was to be held at all costs. Possession of the Marianas was particularly crucial as their loss would put Japan within reach of the new American long-range B-29 bomber.

These island bases were also key to what Japanese leaders envisioned as a sort of giant trap to destroy the U.S. fleet as it approached Japan. First, Japanese aircraft operating from unsinkable island bases would punish the American fleet, inflicting heavy losses before the enemy ever came within gun range of a Japanese ship. Any warships that survived the land-based attacks would be destroyed as the main fleet engagement unfolded. Reeling from the magnitude of the naval disaster, the United States would readily agree to a negotiated peace, leaving Japan with most of her wartime spoils, or so the thinking went.

Unfortunately for Japan, the theoretical beauty of the plan did not reflect the ugly reality on the ground. As of early 1944, the so-called National Absolute Defense Sphere was more of an optimistic grease pencil mark on the map than a practical barrier against enemy attack. The weakness of the Japanese position was duly noted as early as October 1943 when Capt. Mitsuo Fuchida of the *1st Air Fleet*, and Vice Adm. Chuichi Nagumo, who had directed the air attack on Pearl Harbor on December 7, 1941, toured the Mariana Islands bases. (Note: Japanese military units such as *1st Air Fleet* are italicized throughout to distinguish them from Allied units.) Nagumo, who was scheduled to take command of the Marianas naval area at Saipan on March 4, 1944, was not encouraged by what he saw there. The main islands—Saipan, Tinian, Guam, and Rota in the southern Marianas—all had airfields, but they were not sufficient for what planners envisioned. A massive influx of air forces and construction of associated facilities would be needed if the Japanese strategy was to succeed. Fuchida recommended building ten new air bases in the southern Marianas to accommodate the required reinforcement.

At the time of Admiral Nagumo's visit in October, it appeared there would be ample time to accomplish the buildup. In actuality, the window of opportunity was about to narrow dramatically. U.S. forces seized Makin and Tarawa in November, then followed with a stunning amphibious strike deep into the Japanese-held Marshall Islands. The bold gambit seized Roi-Namur, Kwajalein, and Eniwetok and shattered Japanese complacency along with the outer defense ring intended to blunt an attack toward the home islands. Alarmed, the emperor scolded his naval chief of staff. "The Marshalls are part of Japan's territory," he complained. "Why can't you do anything when it has been taken by the enemy?"[2]

It was this ominous turn of events that led General Sato to reconsider the wisdom of making a stand at the Marianas. His conclusion was not likely to please his offensively minded peers, but it was time to face reality. Under the present circumstances, any defense of the Marianas was unwise, decided Sato. Better to abandon the islands and fight the decisive naval engagement around the Philippines, which offered more defensive advantages as well as better access to crucial fuel.

Sato approached Prime Minister Tojo with his proposal. Nicknamed the "Razor" for his administrative efficiency, the fifty-nine-year-old army officer had been transformed by Allied propagandists into the face of the Japanese war machine. With his close-cropped bullet head, sparse mustache, and round black-rimmed glasses, Tojo was an easy caricature, but in fact he was more bureaucrat than warrior. As a general officer, he had served briefly in a combat command in China, but his career had been mainly in administrative posts. His political perspicuity and close relationship with the army had encouraged his appointment as prime minister in 1940. As such, he was expected to ensure coordination between the individual armed services as well as between the military in general and the government. In 1941 he had leaned heavily toward the march to war, but those heady days were rapidly becoming a distant memory.

Sato was blunt. "We should withdraw to the Philippines and there gamble on the final decisive battle," he advised the prime minister.

"Is that the opinion of the General Staff?" inquired Tojo skeptically.

"No, it is my personal opinion," replied Sato.

"Did you consult the General Staff?"

Sato said he had done no such thing because he knew the General Staff would bitterly oppose his suggestion. Nevertheless, he was convinced

3

that Japan's best hope was to abandon the Marianas and Carolines and fall back to the Philippines, seized from the Americans in the early months of the war.

His face reddening with annoyance, the prime minster snapped, "Last year at an Imperial conference we made the Marianas and Carolines our last defense line! Do you mean to say that six months later we should give them up without a single fight?"

Sato refused to be cowed. He observed that the few airfields in the Marianas and Carolines could be knocked out with relative ease by powerful U.S. air and naval forces. By contrast, the Philippines offered hundreds of islands that could be used as "air-borne fortresses"—too many to be effectively neutralized. The ground for the coming decisive encounter must be chosen wisely, he pointed out, as it would be the last throw of the dice. "This should be the last battlefield of the war," he insisted, "since if that battle is lost, we won't be able to fight another." Having dealt the enemy "a heavy blow," Japan could then move toward negotiating an honorable conclusion to the war.[3]

The two men came to no decision, but Sato left the meeting hopeful that Tojo would accept his suggestion. Despite his outburst, the prime minister had appeared receptive to the logic of Sato's argument. His spirits rose when, only days later, Tojo assumed the post of army chief of staff in addition to his responsibilities as prime minister, army minister, and munitions minister. Thinking this latest power grab would enable them to override any objections from the General Staff, a much-heartened Sato immediately commenced planning for a decisive battle in the Philippines.

A few hours later, the general's telephone rang. It was Prime Minister Tojo. "I am going to defend the Marianas and Carolines," he informed Sato bluntly. The emperor himself had already been assured that the inner defense line running through the Marianas would be held, he reiterated. There would be no change of plan, no action that might displease his imperial majesty.[4]

About 1,270 nautical miles southeast of Tokyo, thousands of soldiers and civilians on Saipan—at 47 square miles[5] the second largest of the Mariana Islands, as well as the governmental seat—remained oblivious to the machinations that would determine their future. Saipan's transformation from idyllic isle to strategic pawn had begun over 400 years earlier with the "discovery" of the Mariana Islands by Ferdinand Magellan in 1521. Entranced by the exotic rigging on native boats, Magellan named his discovery the "Islands of the Lateen Sails." His less poetically inclined crew dubbed the islands "Los Ladrones," or "Islands of the Thieves," in a nod to the light-fingered inhabitants who considered property—including any odds and ends left unwatched by their Spanish visitors—to be communal. The islands were renamed Las Marianas in 1568 in honor of Queen Mariana, widow of Spain's Philip IV, but as late as World War II, sailors continued to refer to them as The Ladrones.

Extending some 425 miles in a northeast-southwest arc, the largest of the chain's fifteen islands lie in the south and include Guam, Saipan, Rota, and Tinian, which were to become military assets in 1944. Most of the rest are uninhabited volcanic specks of no particular interest. Approximately 12.5 miles long and up to 5.5 miles wide at its broadest, Saipan is surpassed in size only by Guam, which is nearly five times bigger, making it the largest island in Micronesia. Tinian, only three miles to the south of Saipan, is about 39 square miles and Rota, about 70 nautical miles south of Tinian, is smaller still at 33 square miles.

Shaped roughly like a child's drawing of a lobster claw with a substantial bite out of the lower, meaty side to accommodate Magicienne Bay, Saipan was home to about 30,000 civilians, the bulk of them Japanese who had settled there to work in the sugar cane industry. The topography was relatively flat and open on the extensively cultivated southern third of the island—a patchwork of rectangular sugar cane fields bordered by lines of trees and dotted with farmhouses and carefully tended vegetable plots. To the north, the ground rose into a rocky spine, becoming more rugged, dominated by 1,554-foot Mount Tapotchau, the highest point on the island. Average year-round temperature was 84 degrees, with an average humidity of 79 percent. Annual rainfall averaged 120 to 125 inches—twice that of New Orleans, the wettest U.S. city. The two main towns were Garapan, the capital of Japanese holdings in the Marianas, and Charan Kanoa.[6]

The Japanese presence on Saipan was relatively recent, following Spanish and then German possession. Spain's main interest in the Marianas in the 300 years following Magellan's arrival was to convert the inhabitants to Catholicism—a process that, with the assistance of war and disease, managed to reduce the native population from 45,000 to about 5,000 by 1693.[7] The conversion was successful, but Spain's long rule over the islands ended with the Spanish-American War. The victorious United States appropriated Guam to serve as a naval coaling station in 1899. Spain then sold the rest

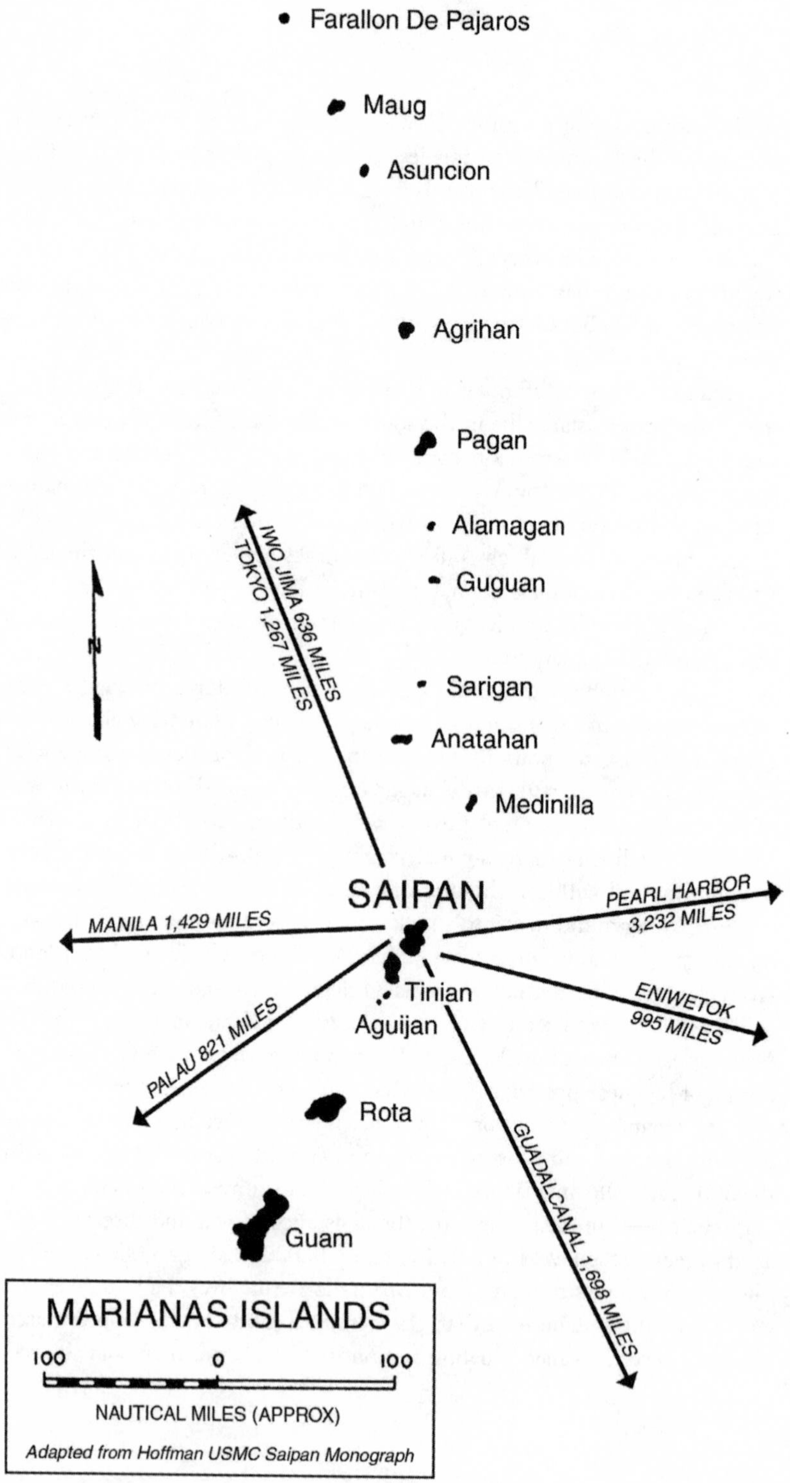

- Farallon De Pajaros
- Maug
- Asuncion
- Agrihan
- Pagan
- Alamagan
- Guguan
- Sarigan
- Anatahan
- Medinilla

IWO JIMA 636 MILES
TOKYO 1,267 MILES

N

SAIPAN

MANILA 1,429 MILES

PEARL HARBOR
3,232 MILES

PALAU 821 MILES

ENIWETOK
995 MILES

Tinian
Aguijan

Rota

GUADALCANAL 1,698 MILES

Guam

MARIANAS ISLANDS

100   0   100

NAUTICAL MILES (APPROX)

Adapted from Hoffman USMC Saipan Monograph

of its holdings in the Carolines, Marshalls, and Marianas to Germany for $4.5 million. The United States could have bought them, but the McKinley Administration thought the price was too high. As it turned out, the price would be a lot higher forty-five years later.

In any case, Germany's tenure was brief. When World War I broke out in 1914, an opportunistic Japan came in on the side of the Allies and promptly seized the German possessions. That seizure was legitimatized after the war when Japan was granted mandate over the Marianas by the League of Nations. While Guam remained a U.S. possession, Saipan, Rota, and Tinian came under formal Japanese control, as did the Carolines and Marshall Islands. As the administrative seat, Saipan became Japan's most important holding in the Marianas. Over the next twenty years, the Japanese accomplished more on Saipan than the proselytizing Spanish had in three centuries. The key to their success was a decision to focus on sugar cane production as a major industry.

In 1920, Haruji Matsue, a graduate of the sugar chemistry program at Louisiana State University, arrived on Saipan to oversee the fledgling efforts. By 1938 over 3,200 tons of sugar cane was being produced per day in the Marianas. By 1944, approximately 70 percent of Saipan's acreage was devoted to sugar cultivation, providing a livelihood for large numbers of Japanese, particularly Okinawans, who flooded in through the South Seas Development Company to work in the burgeoning industry.[8]

By 1941, the island had become a thoroughly Japanese enclave. Of the approximately 30,000 inhabitants, less than 4,000 were native Chamorros and Caroline islanders—the rest were Japanese settlers. The town of Garapan on the western coast evolved into an impressive administrative center, home to some 10,000 residents. Nicknamed "Little Tokyo," the bustling town was the image of a typical coastal Japanese settlement with four main streets lined with two-story business and government offices, numerous shops, private residences, a hospital, agricultural school, and picturesque parks, one of which boasted a statue of that father of local prosperity, "Sugar King" Haruji Matsue. Japanese religious shrines took their place alongside the Catholic church left by the Spanish and still a center of Chamorro worship.

There was a clear pecking order. Japanese residents sat firmly atop the social pyramid, followed by Okinawans, Koreans, and lastly the easygoing Chamorros and Carolinians. Many of the Chamorros lived in towns such as Garapan, but also maintained small farms in the countryside. "The Japanese worked harder," recalled Chamorro Antonieta Ada. "The Chamorros were more relaxed; Japanese more businesslike."[9] Higher education was reserved for native Japanese, though the brightest Chamorro children were encouraged to study at the specialized agricultural training school. Children were also required to learn Japanese in the lower schools.

The activity in the Marianas and other mandates, while largely benign to begin with, raised concerns in the West due in large part to the Japanese penchant for secrecy. Under the terms of Article 22 of the Covenant of the League of Nations, Japan agreed to refrain from "the establishment of fortifications or military and naval bases" in the Marianas. However, after gaining control, the Japanese severely restricted access to the islands by Westerners, raising fears that the islands were being fortified in violation of the mandate. Concerns deepened when Japan formally withdrew from the League of Nations in March 1935.

The suspicions were not completely unfounded. Much of the money poured into the Marianas went toward infrastructure work, at least some of which offered military benefit. A narrow-gauge railroad was constructed to link Saipan's cane fields to the sugar mills in coastal Charan Kanoa. Dredging of Tanapag Harbor north of Garapan began in 1927. A seaplane base at nearby Flores Point was completed in 1935. Aslito Airfield materialized in 1933 as a rudimentary airstrip among the cane fields on Saipan's southern plain, but within four years the Japanese navy began to upgrade the field into a modern facility with a 3,600-foot coral-concrete runway. The Japanese insisted Aslito was a civilian field, intended for "rescue work in case of shipwreck" and "to assist fishermen in locating schools of fish," but the type and quantity of the facilities under construction suggested otherwise.[10] Considerable funding was devoted to construction of barracks, storage buildings, offices, water-supply facilities, ammunition-storage facilities, and communications stations, few of which had a practical civilian application.[11]

By late 1940 there was no more pretense. The *5th Defense Force* arrived on Saipan in December and began digging trenches along potential landing beaches, building gun positions, and upgrading roads and harbor facilities. In June 1941, the 500-man force was directed to prepare for the seizure of Guam in the event of war with the United States. Seaplanes based at Flores Point began making reconnaissance flights over Guam, 125 miles to the south, in October and November. Bombs had already fallen on Pearl Harbor when, on the morning of December 8, planes from the *18th Naval Air Group* lifted off for an airstrike on Guam. The bombing raids were followed by an amphibious assault by several thousand Japanese troops the night of December 9–10. The small U.S. garrison was quickly overwhelmed and Guam joined the rest of the Marianas as a Japanese possession.[12]

Over the next two years, as Japanese forces swept across the Pacific, Saipan served as a rear-area supply and staging area. Tanapag Harbor saw service as a fueling station for Japanese shipping. Part of the naval task force that conducted the ill-fated operation against Midway assembled there in May 1942 before sailing to disaster. Naval patrols guarding Marianas shipping routes were also based at Saipan, while Aslito Airfield and the seaplane base provided links in an aircraft ferry route between Japan and points south.

Despite the war, life on the island could seem almost idyllic. Arriving in late 1943 with 1,500 men of the *1st Yokosuka Special Landing Force*, Pvt. Genkichi Ichikawa observed in his diary: "It is four o'clock on Sunday. I am writing a letter at the quiet barracks in the Southern Islands. I am at the corner of a balcony. Two palm trees are slowly moving by the wind. Beyond the trees, the flag of naval ensign shines brilliantly in the southern sky. Music is coming from somewhere. Songs with many memories are heard, one after another from a gramophone."[13]

But as 1944 arrived, there were signs that all was not well in the outside world. Radios were forbidden among the Chamorro community and news was strictly controlled, but the natives could not help but take notice when the Japanese started to ration food items. "Chamorros and Carolinians could not buy shoes, milk, rice, canned goods, even if we had the money—only the Japanese could buy those things," observed Juan Diaz.[14] The Garapan church was closed down for use as a storehouse. The Catholic priest and handful of nuns were accused of being spies and placed under house arrest.

Military units stepped up preparations for battle. "I swear an oath that I will get the heads of American and British this year," Private Ichikawa, a naval paratrooper, confided to his diary. "[T]raining was extremely hard today. Evening, we stayed in the trenches . . . This morning, we are overhauling weapons . . . We are on the battlefield of Saipan. I prayed this day would come soon! We exercised bayonets at the airfield in hot sunshine. We trained hard to the extent of hurting my body . . . The commander made a speech and he explained the seriousness of the war. No mail is allowed until further notice. Now, the Mariana Islands become the battlefields. We are all working hard to defend the island. . . ."[15]

Work intensified on new airfields on the west coast and north at Marpi Point. "The Japanese would tell us Chamorro people nothing about the war and I couldn't read kanji," recalled Escolastica Cabrera. "People were very quiet, but when they started building the [new] airfield I knew something was coming."[16]

Though Gen. Kenryo Sato could not know it, U.S. thinking regarding the Marianas was also in flux. While long on the table—the prewar Orange and Rainbow plans had called for seizing the Marianas as stepping stones to the Philippines—not all U.S. planners thought invading the islands made strategic sense.

The loudest voice in favor of an operation to seize the Marianas was Adm. Ernest J. King, the sixty-five-year-old U.S. chief of naval operations. The son of an Ohio railway worker, King could be personally difficult, but was brilliant at his trade, having graduated fourth in the Class of 1901 at the Naval Academy. In contrast to many of his peers, he had long been convinced that the Marianas were key to victory in the Western Pacific. King argued that occupation of the Marianas would sever enemy lines of communication between Japan and bases to the south in the Caroline Islands and Bismarck Archipelago and threaten Japanese routes to the Philippines and Southeast Asia, provide bases for the continued Allied advances toward China and the Philippines, and cut the Japanese home islands off from access to vital raw materials in the Southwest Pacific.

As early as the Casablanca Conference between Allied war leaders on January 14, 1943, King proposed an advance through the Marshall Islands to Truk to the Marianas and then the Philippines. King continued his lobbying at the Trident Conference in May and at the Quebec Conference in July.[17] He found an ally in Army Air Corps chief Hap Arnold, who saw the Marianas—with their proximity to Japan—as a potential base for America's new long-range B-29 bomber.

However, a powerful opponent emerged in Southwest Pacific commander Gen. Douglas MacArthur. The egotistical MacArthur viewed King's proposal as a threat to his theater of operations and—perhaps equally important—to his personal stature in the war against Japan. "From a broad strategic viewpoint I am convinced that the best course of offensive action in the Pacific is a movement from Australia through New Guinea to Mindanao," he advised the Combined Chiefs of Staff.[18] In an appeal to Secretary of War Henry L. Stimson, he promised, "Give me central direction of the war in the Pacific, and I will be in the Philippines in ten months . . . Don't let the Navy's pride of position and ignorance continue this great tragedy to our country."[19]

At the Cairo Conference in November, the Combined Chiefs of Staff tried to placate both sides, endorsing a two-pronged assault across the Pacific. MacArthur would continue his advance along the New Guinea–Mindanao axis in the Southwest Pacific, while Adm. Chester Nimitz pressed forward with his island-hopping campaign through the Central Pacific. The Combined Chiefs tentatively called for the recapture of Guam and seizure of the Marianas in October 1944, not quite a year in the future. The two-pronged advance of Nimitz and MacArthur would eventually converge on the Luzon-Formosa-China triangle. With that objective in hand, the Japanese home islands could be bombed, blockaded, or invaded as proved necessary.[20]

In early January, Admiral King flew to Pearl Harbor where Nimitz's staff apprised him of their work on plans for the Central Pacific drive. Titled "Granite," the plan called for capture of Kwajalein and Eniwetok in the Marshalls, followed by an assault on the Carolines. Seizure of the Mortlock Islands would take place about August 1, concurrent with or followed by the seizure of Truk. Saipan, Tinian, and Guam in the Marianas would be captured almost simultaneously, if possible, on or about November 1.[21]

Admiral King had ample reason to assume his views had prevailed, but MacArthur was not yet ready to fold up his tent. Arrogant and demanding, he continued to press for abandonment of the Central Pacific push and the diversion of resources to his own advance toward the Philippines. Nor was he alone in his argument. The would-be American Caesar found considerable sympathy for his views at a conference of senior officers held at Pearl Harbor on January 27 and 28, 1944. While MacArthur did not personally attend the conference, he was represented by a delegation consisting of his chief of staff, Maj. Gen. Richard K. Sutherland; his air force commander, Maj. Gen. George C. Kenney; and his naval chief, Vice Adm. Thomas C. Kinkaid—all of whom came prepared to argue for a single axis of advance via New Guinea and the Philippines.[22]

They managed to sway the one man King might have expected to remain firm to the end: Admiral Nimitz himself. Nimitz was a generally congenial man. He could be utterly ruthless when necessary, but he remained haunted by the U.S. experience at Tarawa in November 1943. That seventy-six-hour assault against 5,000 Japanese on heavily fortified Betio atoll in the Gilberts had cost the U.S. 2nd Marine Division a staggering 3,381 dead, wounded, and missing, all for a piece of ground less than 1 square mile in area. What would happen, he asked himself, when U.S. troops engaged tens of thousands of Japanese on larger land masses such as Guam or Saipan in the Marianas?[23]

Nimitz's apprehensions were echoed by some of his staff, who had come to doubt the need to seize Saipan, Guam, and Tinian, none of which offered particularly good harbors. One key opponent was Adm. John H. Towers who, with some prescience, had forwarded a memo criticizing the Marianas operation for fear it would be vulnerable to enemy air attacks leapfrogging through airfields on Iwo Jima and Chichi Jima. The admiral also questioned the value of Saipan as a potential U.S. bomber base, pointing out that fighters did not have sufficient range to escort the B-29s on the long flight to and from the Japanese home islands. Nimitz's own chief of staff, Adm. Charles H. McMorris, and plans officer, Rear Adm. Forrest Sherman, were also opposed.[24]

As was to be expected, MacArthur's delegation harped on the same refrains at the strategy conference at Pearl. Previous suggestions that bombing missions by the new long-range B-29 Superfortresses flying from the Marianas would provide a key strategic advantage were dismissed out of hand. Kenney scoffed that bombing Japan with B-29s from the Marianas would be "just a stunt."[25] McMorris expressed skepticism that a bombing campaign would force the Japanese to give up. Admiral Sherman said seizure of Guam, Saipan, and Tinian would result in high casualties and provide harbors of only limited value. Kinkaid declared that "any talk of the Marianas for a base leaves me entirely cold."[26] All agreed on prioritizing seizure of the Philippines. Arguments in favor of concentrating resources for an advance along the New Guinea coast to the Philippines were well received on all sides. No one spoke up in favor of a push into the Marianas.[27] "The morning finished with everyone feeling good and ready to work together and get the war over," wrote Kenney. Admiral Nimitz designated Admiral Sherman to present the consensus to the Joint Chiefs of Staff in Washington. It appeared the Marianas would be spared and MacArthur's monumental ego would be sated.[28]

The participants in this mutual love fest failed to reckon with Admiral King and the Joint Chiefs of Staff. The Joint Chiefs had already decided on the Marianas and no one was going to thwart King. He immediately fired off a scathing letter to Nimitz. The strategy of moving along the New Guinea coast and up through the Philippines was "absurd" and "[n]ot in accordance with the decisions of the Joint Chiefs of Staff," he informed Nimitz.[29] Furthermore, an advance on that axis would leave the Marianas as an unacceptable threat. "I assume that even the Southwest Pacific advocates will admit that sometime or other this thorn in the side of our communications to the western Pacific must be removed," he wrote. "In other words, at some time or other we must take out time and forces to carry out this job."[30]

King also made his case to U.S. Army chief of staff Gen. George Marshall. The Combined Chiefs had decided on two simultaneous, mutually supporting advances in the Pacific (Southwest and Central), he reminded Marshall. However, it had also been agreed that when conflicts in allocation of means arose, "due weight should be accorded to the fact that operations in the Central Pacific promise at this time a more rapid advance toward Japan and her vital lines of communication." Now was not the time to revise that strategy, declared King, pointing out that MacArthur, despite his braggadocio, had yet to demonstrate any particularly long or rapid strides of his own.[31]

Marshall recommended reexamining Pacific strategy and suggested asking the Joint Strategic Survey Committee (JSSC) for advice on the matter. The committee replied on February 16 that it remained convinced "the primary effort against Japan should be made from the East, across the Central Pacific" with an eye to "the early seizure of the Formosa, Luzon, China coast area, as a base from which to attack the citadel of Japan." In a followup, the JSSC added that "a fundamental strategic prerequisite is our control of the Marianas, Carolines, Palau Ocean Area."[32]

In the interim, in early February, Nimitz launched a bold amphibious assault into the heart of the Marshall Islands. Conducted against the advice of many of his staff, the attack bypassed more heavily defended outer islands and caught the Japanese completely by surprise. Kwajalein, Roi-Namur, and Majuro fell quickly with light U.S. casualties. Emboldened, Nimitz pushed on to seize Japanese-held Eniwetok as well. A massive carrier raid on the much-feared Japanese bastion at Truk that same month devastated the enemy base and revealed it to be a tiger without claws. These successes represented a quantum leap in the advance across the Central Pacific and put the specter of Tarawa largely to rest.

The Joint Chiefs issued a final decision on March 12, just over a month after Nimitz's brilliant Marshall Islands campaign. They came down squarely on King's side. The "most feasible approach to the Formosa-Luzon-China area is by way of Marianas-Carolines-Palau-Mindanao area," they decreed. Hollandia was to be seized April 15, 1944. Truk would be neutralized, not invaded. The southern Marianas would be invaded on June 15. "The objective is to secure control of sea communications through the Central Pacific by isolating and neutralizing the Carolines and by the establishment of sea and air bases for operations against the Japanese homeland."[33] King had won the argument. The course was set.

The Japanese were slow to recognize the immediacy of the threat to Saipan and the Marianas. Following the loss of Eniwetok, they anticipated the next U.S. blow would fall on the Palaus in the Western Caroline Islands and gave those garrisons priority for shipment of construction material for defense works. However, their complacency received a jolt on February 22 when U.S. carrier forces under the command of Adm. Marc Mitscher, returning from a sweep at Truk, paused to work over the Japanese garrisons on Saipan, Guam, Tinian, and Rota. It was the first bombing attack of the war on the Marianas.

Mitscher launched his aircraft at 0745 on February 22 from about 100 miles off Saipan's western coast. American intelligence knew so little about the island that pilots could not even be briefed on the location of the enemy airfields. They found them anyway, roaring in under heavy cumulus clouds to destroy 168 aircraft, two freighters, and a scattering of smaller vessels. U.S. losses were five fighters and one torpedo bomber (TBF).

While the American airstrike on February 23 did not persuade the Japanese that Saipan was next on the invasion list, it did emphasize that the base facility could no longer be considered a safe rear area. Toward the end of February, preparations got underway to evacuate large numbers of Japanese civilians—mostly wives and children—to Japan. "Even the wife of the civilian chief of police was preparing to leave," recalled Manual T. Sablan, who lived in Garapan. There were two ships, observed Sablan: the *Santos Maru* and the *Amerika Maru*. The *Amerika Maru* was for "the hotshots' wives," he added. "All of the ordinary civilians were put on board the *Santos Maru*."[34]

At the same time, the Japanese *29th Division*, then located in Manchuria, was ordered to the Marianas. Transported by train to Pusan, Korea, the troops boarded ships for Ujina, Japan, where they exchanged their winter uniforms for tropical clothing. On February 26, four transports set sail, shepherded by three destroyers. Among the troops aboard the *Sakito Maru* was twenty-nine-year-old Capt. Sakae Oba, a former teacher who had charge of a 270-man medical company. Though his parent unit, the *18th Infantry Regiment*, had spent the past three years in China, many of the men were new. The first morning at sea, the regimental commander called a meeting of all officers. They were heading to Saipan, he told them. They had been ordered to reinforce that island's garrison, though it seemed unlikely the Americans would attempt a landing there. Estimated time of arrival was March 4.

That could come none too soon for the troops packed into the *Sakito Maru*'s stifling hold. Due to restricted deck space, only limited numbers of men were allowed topside for fresh air at one time and then for only an hour. The others remained deep in the ship's hold impatiently awaiting their hour-long reprieve. The doctors and enlisted medics assigned to Oba's company were kept busy, first treating men for seasickness and then for respiratory ailments and other complaints brought on by the stifling living conditions.

By February 29 the convoy was about 100 miles east of Formosa. Oba had just settled down to lunch—the usual monotonous rice and soup, along with some spinach and a diced sweet potato masquerading as dessert—when a violent explosion threw him to the deck. The ship had been torpedoed. As the *Sakito Maru* went dead in the water, Oba could see flames through a pillar of smoke and steam erupting from the aft hatch. The main deck was in chaos as survivors streamed from below. Panicked troops began swarming down rope nets lowered over the side of the stricken ship. Some men, too frightened to wait, jumped into the sea. Bamboo rafts were tossed overboard, some of them crashing down on men struggling in the water below.

Oba strapped his sword onto his back underneath his life jacket before clambering over the rail and starting down the net. A glance below showed several bodies already floating face down in the water, bumping gently against the steel side of the ship. He dropped the final short distance into the icy water and swam toward the ship's bow, joining several dozen other survivors. Behind him, oil from the stricken vessel caught fire, spreading toward the stern of the ship and engulfing anyone still in the vicinity.

All that night, Oba floated in the icy water. The excruciating cold eventually subsided into numbness. Twice during the night he bumped into other survivors. One man mumbled, "Be strong." The other did not speak and when Oba reached out for him, the man's shoulder sank away beneath his touch. Sometime after dark, the *Sakita* exploded, sending shockwaves through the water. The wreckage burned fiercely for several minutes, then slid stern first beneath the waves. Somewhere in the distance Oba could hear men singing—it was an army song, he realized—but the sound gradually faded away as the survivors tired or died.[35]

Though he did not know it, the crew of the submarine that had inflicted this misfortune on him—the USS *Trout*, a veteran boat on her eleventh patrol—was already dead. The three Japanese destroyers escorting the convoy had gone after the *Trout* immediately after the attack. The destroyer *Asashimo* got a sonar fix and dropped nineteen depth charges. Oil and debris bubbled to the surface and *Asashimo* dropped a final depth charge on that spot. Skippered by thirty-three-year-old Lt. Cmdr. Albert H. Clark of Norway, Maine, *Trout* went down with all eighty-one hands.[36]

Drifting in and out of consciousness, Oba was picked up early the next morning by a soldier paddling around on a bamboo raft designed to float machine guns ashore during amphibious landings. Later that day they were plucked from the water by one of the escort destroyers. Oba was lucky. Of the 3,080 troops aboard the torpedoed transport, less than 1,800 were rescued. Days later, the survivors were put ashore on Saipan—alive, but with virtually no equipment.

Oba had lost more than half his company in the sinking. Somewhat to their surprise, the disheveled survivors found themselves greeted as saviors by Saipan's Japanese civilian population. As Oba climbed out of a truck at Garapan, a kimono-clad woman broke away from a group of respectfully bowing civilians. Dropping to her knees before him, she touched her head nearly to the ground and expressed her thanks to Oba and his companions for coming to protect the island from the enemy. In the coming days and weeks, Oba would have reason to wonder if that confidence was well placed.[37]

CHAPTER II

Sharpening the Spear

As Capt. Sakae Oba shed his oil-soaked clothes and recovered from his ordeal, U.S. plans to seize Saipan were beginning to take definite form. Admiral Nimitz assigned the highest priority to the Marianas operation, codenamed *Forager*, on March 13. The plan called for the seizure of Saipan, followed almost immediately by landings on Guam and Tinian. Saipan was given priority because of its status as a Japanese command center and to preclude its use as a staging area for air attacks against the amphibious landing on Guam.

A Joint Staff Study designated V Amphibious Corps (VAC) and III Amphibious Corps (IIIAC) to execute *Forager*. VAC, composed of the 2nd and 4th Marine Divisions, would seize Saipan (codenamed *Tattersalls*) on June 15, followed by Tinian (*Tearaway*). The complete organization and attached units built around V Amphibious Corps would be designated Northern Troops and Landing Force (NTLF). The Southern Troops and Landing Force (STLF) would be built around IIIAC, fielding the 3rd Marine Division and 1st Provisional Marine Brigade. STLF would assault Guam (*Stevedore*) once Saipan was in hand—hopefully within three days. The 27th Infantry Division would be in Expeditionary Troops reserve, available to either NTLF or STLF as needed.

It would not be easy. The time, distance, and materiel involved in *Forager* dwarfed any previous operation. Saipan was 3,232 nautical miles from Pearl Harbor and 1,000 miles from the nearest U.S. forward base area at Eniwetok. Over 500 ships would be required for as long as three months. The ships would sail at different times depending on their speed. If scheduling calculations worked out as they were supposed to, all ships—fast and slow—would converge as they neared the target. A total of 71,000 troops would sail from Hawaii; another 58,000 would be drawn from the Guadalcanal area.

The command structure for *Forager* was complicated both by the scale of the operation and by the high level of interservice cooperation required. Admiral Nimitz retained overall command. Directly under him was Fifth Fleet commander Vice Adm. Raymond A. Spruance. Subordinate to Spruance, Vice Adm. Richmond Kelly Turner was to command the Joint Expeditionary Force (Task Force 51), executing the actual amphibious assault on the islands. Turner was also in command of the Northern Attack Force (later designated Task Force 52) which was comprised of all the amphibious elements assigned to the attack on Saipan and Tinian. Southern Attack Force (Task Force 53), commanded by Rear Adm. Richard L. Conolly, would conduct the landings on Guam.

Tactical command of all troops ashore during *Forager* was assigned to Marine Corps lieutenant general Holland M. Smith, a bespectacled, sixty-one-year-old Alabaman. Known to his friends as "Hoke," Smith looked more like a rather paunchy small-town pharmacist than a fighting Marine, but he was considered an expert on the subject of amphibious assaults. During the prewar years he had been a prime mover behind the Marine Corps' specialization in modern amphibious landings. He had pushed hard for more sophisticated tactics and specialized equipment such as the ramped Higgins landing craft. Now his foresight was paying off in the island-hopping campaign across the Pacific. "No one ever accused him of brilliance," observed Adm. Harry W. Hill, "but everyone learned quickly that he had many positive ideas of his own. . . ."[1]

The down side of Smith was his difficult personality. Widely known as "Howlin' Mad," he was stubborn, intemperate and tactless, quick to express anger or opinions without concern for feelings or the nuances of a situation. Army historian Col. (later general) S. L. A. Marshall, who encountered Smith during the Makin Island campaign, considered him an obnoxious bully and "tactically a chowder head."[2] Admiral Hill, who knew Smith better, was somewhat more circumspect. "He was basically a great show-off," remarked Hill. "A great talker, he liked to dominate the conversation—and usually did so in a rather loud voice."[3] Completely devoted to the Marine Corps, he distrusted the motives of the other armed services and was quick to respond to slights, real or perceived, against "his" Corps. "He loved to complain," recalled Spruance's chief of staff, Capt. Charles J. Moore, of the Marine general. "He loved to talk and he loved to complain and he would come and sit on my desk and growl . . . 'All I want to do is kill some Japs. Just give me a rifle. I don't want to be a commanding general. Just give me a rifle. I'll go out and shoot some Japs. I want to fight the Japs.'"[4]

Holland Smith would command Northern Troops and Landing Force (NTLF), exercising tactical control of all troops ashore during the capture of Saipan. His selection came over the objections of Lt. Gen. Robert C. Richardson Jr., commander of all U.S. Army forces in the Central Pacific. Howlin' Mad's personality aside, friction between Smith and Richardson was practically inevitable thanks to Richardson's low regard for Marine officers—a disdain wholeheartedly reciprocated by Smith, who referred to the dapper Richardson as "Nellie," as in "Nervous Nellie." Like many senior Army officers, Richardson did not believe the Marines—being such a small service—were up to the job of managing large troop formations in field operations. Such commands should be reserved for Army officers, he contended. He proceeded to express that opinion in an "eyes only" letter to Admiral Nimitz, not neglecting to express his low regard for Holland Smith in particular.[5]

For their part, there was a growing feeling among many Marines that U.S. Army troops were second rate—poorly led and cautious to the point of timidity. This view was based in part on the past performance of the 27th Infantry Division, a federalized New York National Guard outfit that was the designated Expeditionary Troops reserve for the upcoming Marianas operation. The division's 165th Infantry Regiment landed at Makin in November 1943 against light resistance, then spent three long days clearing the atoll of about 400 Japanese. An unimpressed Holland Smith criticized their performance as "infuriatingly slow."[6] In fact, it was not the Army's most shining moment. Naval and Marine Corps officers were similarly critical of what they considered the 106th Infantry Regiment's lackluster performance in the seizure of Eniwetok three months later.

Richardson's recommendations were ignored, but Holland Smith and the Army general were destined to butt heads again. That clash would become highly public and contribute to years of acrimony between the Army and the Marine Corps.[7]

As American plans took shape, the Japanese were pressing forward with belated efforts to reinforce the Marianas. A new organization, the *31st Army*, had been formed on February 18, 1944, built around the *29th* and *43rd Infantry Divisions*, and given responsibility for defense of the Marianas, Bonins, Marshalls, and Carolines. Named to lead the *31st Army* was fifty-three-year-old Lt. Gen. Hideyoshi Obata, who had served in Burma in 1942. A naval counterpart described him as "extremely intelligent and, for an Army officer, of extremely broad vision."[8]

Obata established his headquarters at Garapan on Saipan's western coast and began to prepare for the influx of troops. The most significant army organization assigned to the defense of Saipan was the *43rd Division* (the *29th Division* was destined for Guam), which was scheduled to sail from Japan in May. With the arrival of the *43rd Division*, Obata intended to have Saipan's defenses in place by November—ironically, November had been the original U.S. target date for the invasion—and was optimistic about his ability to defeat any landing attempt.[9] His confidence was echoed by the Imperial General Staff. "More than once I was told by the officers of the General Staff that Saipan was absolutely invincible," observed Toshikazu Kase, a high-ranking official with the Foreign Ministry.[10]

Those assurances notwithstanding, the defense of the Marianas faced a number of obstacles, one of them being an insidious weakness in the Japanese command structure. On March 10, 1944, following the loss of the Marshalls, a new *Central Pacific Area Fleet* was formed to exercise direct authority over all Imperial Navy and Army forces in the Marianas, Bonins, and Western Carolines. Despite the "fleet" designation, the new command organization was essentially an administrative effort to coordinate operations. The man in charge of this paper command was Vice Adm. Chuichi Nagumo. The former hero-leader of the attack on Pearl Harbor in 1941, Nagumo had fallen from grace following the defeats at Midway and the naval battles around Guadalcanal. He did little to redeem himself in his new position. When *31st Army* command bristled at the thought of answering to a naval officer, Nagumo failed to assert his authority. After some argument, he and Obata agreed that they would operate as equals, a decision which essentially left the defense of the Marianas in the hands of a committee.[11]

The average Japanese soldier knew no more about such high-level disputes than his American counterpart did about U.S. interservice bickering, but at least some of the men arriving on Saipan were sobered by the reality on the ground. Assigned to oversee about a hundred men building gun positions overlooking Garapan, Capt. Sake Oba was stunned by the primitive state of the construction effort. Equipment and materials that had been readily available in China and Manchuria were not to be found. Heavy tractors, explosives, cement, and steel were unavailable. Most work was done by hand.[12]

In a desperate effort to speed construction, the Japanese military impressed Chamorro men to work on trenches, revetments, shelters, and improvements to the airfields. Juan Atalig DeLeon "Tang" Guerrero was put to work on the emergency airstrip near Charan Kanoa. Provided with hand tools, the men lined up and inched slowly along, digging to the specified depth with picks and shovels. They then compacted the dirt and rocks. Guerrero's crew worked from 6:00 P.M. to 6:00 A.M., then rested while other groups worked the day shift.[13]

Fourteen-year-old Ryoko Okuyama and her fellow students at the Girls School of Saipan also traded in their books for hand tools and went out to work on airfield construction. Their schoolhouse was turned into a naval hospital.[14] As a Japanese, Ryoko did not need to be coerced, but the forced labor parties reflected a hardening attitude toward non-Japanese civilians. Workers making improvements on Aslito Airfield were not allowed to return home at night and the punishment for infractions could be severe. Just how severe was discovered by Felipe Iguel Ruak's father, Jesus Ruak, who was drafted to work on the airfield. When Jesus ran away, the Japanese beat him so badly they broke his ribs. "When he breathed, they could see that something in his side was moving in and out, so they let him go," recalled Felipe. Some relatives brought Jesus home where he lingered in agony for several days before he finally succumbed to his injuries.[15]

Back in Hawaii, V Amphibious Corps staffers assigned to duty with NTLF had begun to choreograph the complicated dance that would deliver U.S. Marines onto Saipan's unfriendly shore. Their biggest headache—one that would plague *Forager* right up to and beyond the landings themselves—was a lack of information about the island. Saipan had been closed to Western visitors for nearly thirty years and little was known about the terrain, beaches, or defenses. The first trickle of intelligence was gleaned from photographs taken during the February 22–23 carrier raids on the island. Unfortunately, Saipan's typically heavy cloud cover, the small scale of the photos (generally 1:10,000), and the carrier pilots' inclination to devote more attention to destroying the enemy than on snapping pictures resulted in very spotty coverage.

NTLF pleaded for more comprehensive photos of the target area, but to no avail.[16] The decision to limit coverage derived in part from the long distance to the target area and a lack of resources to get there. Also a factor was a calculated decision by Fifth Fleet commander Ray Spruance to limit photographic overflights of the Marianas for fear they would alert the Japanese to the pending invasion. Some additional photographic coverage was belatedly provided by a mission from Eniwetok on April 18 in what was also the first land-based air attack on Saipan. Five Navy PB4Ys, escorted by B-24s from the 392nd Squadron, ventured out to snap verticals of the island's terrain. Again, heavy cloud cover and the 1:10,000 scale limited the value of the photos, though the mission was not without excitement. The B-24s dropped bombs and fought off eighteen or more Japanese interceptors. One B-24 was forced to make a water landing. A PB4Y that attempted rescue was also stranded. Both crews were eventually picked up by a U.S. destroyer.[17]

Also disappointing were photos taken by the U.S. submarine *Greenling*, which spent several days prowling through the Marianas snapping photos of Guam, Tinian, and Saipan. The obliques of Guam proved useful, but the photographic coverage of Saipan failed to include the preferred landing beaches. The *Greenling* photos were probably the views referred to by the 4th Marine Division in its subsequent summary of *Forager*. "Unfortunately, the only portion of the shoreline omitted in the coverage was our landing beaches," observed the intelligence section. The division added, with admirable grace—or perhaps thinly veiled sarcasm—that the photos did provide evidence of the type of sea, surf, and coastline and an appreciation of the profile of the island.[18]

Working from this spotty photographic coverage and Japanese charts captured in the Marshall Islands campaign, NTLF compiled a 1:20,000 scale map of Saipan. Intelligence identified three airfields. The main field was Aslito on the southern flats. Assumed to be fully operational, it was 3,600 feet long with numerous facilities. A second airfield appeared to be under construction on Saipan's northern plateau near Marpi Point, an area known to the Japanese as Banadera. The third was a rudimentary strip that ran along a straight stretch of beach road parallel to the coast just north of Charan Kanoa in what would subsequently be the 2nd Marine Division landing area. Built crossways to the prevailing winds, it was suitable only for small planes.

Intelligence was right about the airfields, but the rest of the map was severely flawed. The depiction of Lake Susupe behind Charan Kanoa greatly underestimated the size of the surrounding swamp, as the Marines would later learn firsthand. The maps also failed to adequately reflect the island's topography—particularly the northern two-thirds of the island,

which was characterized by a rugged, overgrown limestone spine dominated by 1,554-foot Mount Tapotchau. Elevations were based on 20-foot
contours, described as "logical" contours, adapted from captured charts and
partially revised from photographs.[19] Unfortunately, in this instance "logic"
failed. "In actual use, it was ascertained that these 'contours' were not only
inaccurate but that they offered a misleading representation of the basic
features of Saipan Island, representing, as examples, sheer cliffs as slopes,
and box canyons as ravines or draws," reported intelligence officers with
some bitterness.[20]

The island's 54 miles of coastline was rightly recognized as being largely
cliffs, leaving only about 12 miles suitable for amphibious assault. Most of
that lay behind a protective reef on the western coast. The rest was inside
heavily defended Magicienne Bay on the east. Relying on tracked vehicles
capable of crawling over the reef, planners decided to land the 2nd and 4th
Marine Divisions abreast over a 6,000-yard front on Saipan's southwestern
coast. The beaches there appeared less heavily defended than Magicienne
Bay and offered the shortest practicable route to the Aslito airfield, a key
objective of the operation. Should the preferred beaches prove to be too
heavily defended or inaccessible due to heavy surf, the 2nd Marine Division
would go ashore north of Tanapag Harbor, to be followed later by the 4th
Marine Division.

High in the mountains of Hawaii, temporary home of the 2nd Marine
Division, resided several thousand experts in all the things that could go
wrong trying to cross a fringing reef under enemy fire. Six months before,
lacking enough water to float their landing craft over the reef at Tarawa, the
exposed Marines had been shot to pieces when they were forced to wade
hundreds of yards to shore.

Returning to Hawaii in December, the survivors were trucked out to
Camp Tarawa on the extensive Parker Ranch, 65 miles from Hilo, over "the
world's most snakelike roads," observed the division historian.[21] Located on
a lofty saddle between the volcanic peaks of Mauna Loa and Mauna Kea,
the camp was a remote place, swept by chill winds, fog, and mist. According
to scuttlebutt, the higher-ups had stuck the division well out in the boondocks for fear the Tarawa survivors had been so brutalized by combat that
they now posed a danger to the civilian population. Actually, the reasons
were more logistical than social. The isolated camp had the benefit of fewer
distractions, as well as plenty of training room. Finally, being well above sea

level, the cooler climate—many Marines would have said "freezing"—benefited the division's numerous malaria sufferers.

The term *camp* initially turned out to be a bit of a euphemism. "All we found were wood platforms and stacks of canvas tents; nothing had been erected," recalled Sgt. Mike Masters.[22] The men accepted their situation philosophically. Averaging between nineteen and twenty years old, they had volunteered for the Marines and most figured they had no one to blame but themselves. "[We] were young, stupid and, above all, resilient, so little things like freezing our cans off and being otherwise uncomfortable hardly fazed us," recalled George L. H. Cooper. "In retrospect I believe that most of us were happy just to be alive [after Tarawa], and felt that, from here on out, everything was free."[23]

Some observers had wondered if the 2nd Marine Division could be restored to front-line battle efficiency after the gaping hole Tarawa had torn in the organization. Replacements soon trickled in to share the chill of Camp Tarawa with the veterans. There were plenty of gung ho teenaged volunteers fresh out of boot camp, but now, for the first time, there were also large numbers of men who had come into the Corps through Selective Service. Most had freely chosen the Marines and despite some initial skepticism from the old hands, they were eventually assimilated. One consolation came when the sergeant called names for working parties and the new men ended up with most of the shit details.

Among the more exalted arrivals was a new commanding general. Fifty-two-year-old Thomas E. Watson replaced Gen. Julian Smith, who had led the division through the Gilberts campaign. Known as "Terrible Tommy" for his ferocious temper, Watson was sarcastic, demanding, and, by most accounts, thoroughly disliked by his officers and men. Watson had enlisted in 1912, was commissioned in 1916, and had served in a variety of assignments in the Caribbean, China, and the United States through the years. Most recently he had overseen the seizure of Eniwetok in February. His performance earned him a second star and command of the 2nd Marine Division. The division would find him quite a change from quiet-mannered Julian Smith.[24]

The training program at Camp Tarawa initially emphasized physical conditioning, but as spring approached, the regimen became more specific. Assault teams practiced taking out fortifications built by Army engineers on the training range. One addition that would save many lives in the 2nd Marine Division at Saipan was the widespread distribution of rocket launchers, more familiarly known as bazookas. The F-series Table of Organization, effective from May 5, 1944, authorized 172 bazookas in a Marine division, including three per rifle company. These weapons could be issued as the company commander saw fit based on the tactical situation.

The directive for *Forager* came down to the 2nd Marine Division on April 10. While the average enlisted Marine remained oblivious to the specifics, the sudden appearance of a guard outside Division Intelligence indicated that something was in the works. During field exercises, the Marines began conducting maneuvers through canebrakes on one of the many Hawaii plantations. They had been receiving information on several different islands, but most of them didn't have canebrakes, observed the division historian.

Two that did were Saipan and Tinian in the Marianas.

On March 6, the USS *Nautilus* was on the thirteenth day of her eighth war patrol, prowling the waters about 420 nautical miles north-northwest of Saipan. At 0549, almost an hour before sunrise, she spotted two ships and began to maneuver for an attack. Closing to 5,000 yards, Capt. William Davis Irvin saw there were three ships in an irregular column. At 0607, at a range of 2,000 yards, *Nautilus* fired tubes 1 and 2 at the leading ship, which Irvin described as similar to a "HOKKI MARU." The second ship in the column appeared closer than the first and as its bow overlapped the stern of Irvin's first target, *Nautilus* fired tubes 3 and 4. The after-action report continued:

> 0609 . . . Observed two hits through periscope on nearer ship. First ship hit between after stack and after mast which enveloped it in flames. The second hit at the stern, broke off the mast and blew the entire stern off. I don't see how he could stay afloat. 0611 . . . with an escort destroyer smoking heavily and bearing down on us . . . took her down and rigged for depth charge attack. Heard two more hits which sounded more distant than the first two. Sound reported crackling all over the dial.[25]

The ships attacked by *Nautilus* were the *Amerika Maru* and the *Santos Maru*, which had left Saipan days before, bound for Japan with civilian evacuees. *Santos Maru* was badly damaged but managed to limp away and reach Japan. The 6,000-ton troop transport *Amerika Maru*, carrying the more privileged civilians—including the wife of Saipan's police chief—went down in just two minutes. As many as 1,700 people may have been aboard. How many perished is unknown, but there were few survivors.[26]

Ten days after the sinking of *Amerika Maru*, the USS *Seahorse*, skippered by thirty-two-year-old Lt. Cmdr. Slade Cutter, left Pearl Harbor, bound for Saipan. Cutter was a big bear of a man, a standout Naval Academy boxer and football player who, somewhat incongruously, had once aspired to be a flutist with the Chicago Symphony Orchestra. He ended up at Annapolis instead and subsequently in the small elite of the submarine service.

In two previous patrols as captain of *Seahorse*, Cutter had wreaked such havoc on enemy shipping that he had been awarded the Navy Cross with Gold Star. But this third patrol had a slightly different twist. A couple of weeks earlier, Cutter had been summoned to a meeting with sub force commander Vice Adm. Charles A. Lockwood Jr. "The admiral told me that we were going to invade Saipan in late May 1944, and that the amphibious people wanted to know whether the beaches on the south coast were mined or had underwater obstacles," recalled Cutter. To answer those questions, the sub USS *Greenling* had been directed to survey the coastline. Cutter's role was to raise some hell in the waters off Saipan to draw anti-submarine forces away from *Greenling* as she operated close to shore.

"The admiral said the area was very 'hot' and that previous submarines had been driven off due to intensive anti-submarine activity by the enemy," recalled Cutter. Oh, and by the way, the information regarding the invasion of Saipan was top secret and Cutter was not to share it with his crew, and he was not to allow himself to be taken prisoner should things go bad. "It was a rather sobering briefing, but stimulating," Cutter observed wryly.[27]

Seahorse arrived off Tanapag Harbor on Saipan's west coast on March 27 and immediately had a run-in with a twin-engine Japanese patrol bomber. The plane dropped three depth charges that shook up the crew but caused no damage. Cutter sighted enemy shipping over the next few days, but had no opportunity to attack until the afternoon of April 7. Spotting three fat freighters shepherded along by a pair of destroyers, he worked his way into position, waited until dark, then launched six torpedoes—three at each freighter. Within seconds an explosion pulsed through the water as the first ship took a hit, followed by another as the second ship was struck.

Cutter raised the periscope—painted a most unwarlike pink in the theory that the color would better reflect the changing hues of sky and ocean—and saw that the first ship had been hit just under the bridge. "A brilliant mass of flame shot high into the air, and the water on both sides of the ship, for several hundred yards, was sprayed with debris," he noted in his patrol report. The second ship was on fire amidships. "Sound reported the destroyers coming in, and we went deep." *Seahorse* spent the next three hours dodging depth charges, but finally eluded her pursuers.[28]

Two days later *Seahorse* spotted another convoy heading toward Tanapag Harbor. The convoy was uncharacteristically large for the Japanese: fifteen or more merchant ships accompanied by numerous escorts and at least four destroyers. Cutter loosed four torpedoes, all of which missed when the convoy suddenly changed course. Undeterred, he readjusted and fired two more fish at one of the merchant ships. Two explosions in quick succession indicated hits, but any celebration was cut short as the sonar operator excitedly reported an incoming torpedo. One of *Seahorse*'s previous four fish had malfunctioned and circled back on the sub. Cutter took the boat down deep and the torpedo narrowly missed, continuing to circle until it ran out of fuel.

Cutter played tag with Japanese destroyers and aircraft into the early morning hours, before the pressure eased and *Seahorse* raised periscope to find the remnants of her victim drifting on the waves. "The debris consisted of many different items such as life rafts, one life boat with oars sticking over the side, part of a deck house, many large latticed crates, boxes, wooden buckets, several blunt-nosed cylindrical objects that appeared to be detachable gasoline tanks for aircraft, and a large oil slick," observed the sub's log, all the remains of the 4,667-ton naval transport *Mimasaka Maru*.[29]

Seahorse's run continued on April 20, Easter Sunday. Cutter was patrolling west of the main entrance to Tanapag Harbor, charting depths and the sea bottom, using his periscope to triangulate bearings on the smokestack of the Charan Kanoa sugar mill, a lighthouse and a prominent cliff. Relieving the lookout on the search periscope, the skipper was astonished to see a Japanese submarine, complete with rising sun emblazoned on the conning tower, motoring toward the harbor on the surface, its deck crowded with white-uniformed sailors.

Seahorse sent two wakeless electric torpedoes toward the enemy sub at a range of 1,600 yards. Two minutes later a tremendous explosion shook the deck plates. The blast was so intense that Electricians Mate Sheldon Stubbs thought a bomb or a depth charge had been dropped on the American sub. One of *Seahorse*'s fish had apparently struck the Japanese submarine—later identified as RO-45 though it may have been I-174—in the torpedo room, setting off its warheads.[30]

Seahorse claimed her last victim on April 27. The sub was submerged 45 miles west of the harbor that morning when the lookout spotted smoke. An investigation revealed a slow-moving convoy consisting of three large freighters, a smaller freighter, a destroyer, and three anti-submarine escorts. *Seahorse* sent four torpedoes at a 5,244-ton naval transport. The first struck the ship just forward of the bridge, the second blew a huge hole in the side just aft of the bridge, and a third tore into the stern. As *Seahorse* submerged to avoid the enemy escorts, the stricken ship was already going down by the stern.[31]

Seahorse's rampage was no aberration. Sitting out on the end of the supply and troop pipeline, the defenders of the Marianas were feeling the pinch as U.S. subs took their toll. In March a convoy carrying reinforcements to the Marianas—including the *1st, 5th*, and *6th Expeditionary Force* and naval troops—ran afoul of USS *Sandlance*. The *Kokugyo Maru*, carrying 1,029 reinforcements for Guam's *54th Naval Guard Force*, was sunk. The light cruiser *Tatsuta* was also sunk and a third ship was damaged.[32]

In April the Japanese implemented a regular convoy service, the so-called Matsui Transport, in a concerted effort to deliver critical war materials to the Marianas, especially high-priority cement and reinforcing steel needed for defensive works. Three of those convoys ran afoul of *Seahorse*, with disastrous results. The hemorrhage continued into May. On May 10 *Silversides* sank the *Okinawa Maru, Mikage Maru*, and the converted gunboat *Choan Maru II*. A few days later *Silversides* continued her rampage, sinking the *Shosei Maru* off Guam. Two fuel tankers, the *Skoken Maru* and *Horaizan Maru*, were sent to the bottom May 29 as they neared Saipan. On May 31 a convoy loaded with building materials was caught by USS *Pintado*, which sank *Toho Maru*. Operating between the Marianas and the Carolines, *Silversides* sank six Japanese merchant ships totaling 14,150 tons between May 10 and May 29.[33]

As desperately needed cement, steel, and building materials intended for the Marianas went to the bottom of the Pacific in the holds of sunken ships, Maj. Gen. Keiji Igeta, the *31st Army* chief of staff on Saipan, expressed his frustration in a message to the *Central Pacific Area Fleet*:

> *We cannot strengthen the fortifications appreciably now unless we can get materials suitable for permanent construction. Specifically, unless the units are supplied with cement, steel reinforcements for cement, barbed wire, lumber, etc., which cannot be obtained in these islands, no matter*

how many soldiers there are they can do nothing in regard to fortifications but sit around with their arms folded, and the situation is unbearable . . . I would like this matter of supply of construction materials dealt with immediately.[34]

The rampage was not without cost. *Trout* went down with all hands on February 29, the victim of Japanese convoy escorts. *Tullibee* was lost in the Palaus in March when she attacked an enemy transport and one of her own errant torpedoes apparently circled around and hit the sub. The lone survivor from *Tullibee*'s crew ended up in a Japanese prison camp. *Gudgeon*, on her eighth war patrol, disappeared in the Marianas area in mid-April. Enemy documents uncovered after the war revealed that a Japanese aircraft sighted a submarine 166 miles off the island of "Yuoh" [possibly Maug in the northern Marianas] on April 18. The aircraft attacked with bombs. "The first bomb hit bow. Second bomb direct on bridge. Center of the submarine burst open and oil pillars rose," reported the Japanese. *Gudgeon* and her seventy-eight-man crew joined the forty-eight U.S. submarines and 374 officers and 3,131 enlisted crewmen lost during World War II directly or indirectly to enemy action.[35]

One byproduct of the U.S. submarine campaign in the Marianas was an unscheduled influx of reinforcements to the Saipan garrison. Japanese survivors of U.S. submarine attacks flooded in, many with only the clothes on their backs. The strays came from all sorts of organizations. About 1,500 survivors of the *9th Expeditionary Force*, originally bound for Yap, were stranded on Saipan when their ship was sunk. Another unexpected arrival was the *15th Infantry Regiment*, which had been on its way to Koror. Many smaller units and fragments of units also ended up on the island where they would later create a major headache for U.S. intelligence personnel trying to compile an enemy order of battle.

In early May, transports carrying the Japanese *43rd Division* departed from Japan to reinforce Saipan. Activated in June 1943, the division had recently been reorganized along the lines of a regimental combat team, dropping its field artillery component. Headquartered in Nagoya, a large industrial city on Honshu, the newly organized division was composed of the *118th*, *135th*, and *136th Infantry Regiments* along with engineer, signals, ordnance, transport units, and a field hospital. Total strength was 12,239 officers and men, many of them recent draftees.

As the division prepared to leave for Saipan, it received a new com-mander, fifty-three-year-old Lt. Gen. Yoshitsugu Saito. A long-faced former cavalryman sporting a carefully arched moustache and largely undistin-guished career, Saito's most recent post had been head of the War Ministry Military Administration Bureau Horse Administration Section in Japan. He replaced the former division commander, Prince Kaya Tsunenori, who happened to be a cousin of the emperor's wife. As a member of the royal house, he would not be sent to the front with the division. Division staff officer Maj. Takashi Hirakushi, who inherited Saito after the departure of Prince Kaya, was unimpressed with his new commander, considering him indecisive and not particularly competent. Major Hirakushi would come to know General Saito well and would find little reason to amend that initial assessment.[36]

General Saito's division, codenamed *Homare* or "Honor Division," sailed in two separate convoys in hopes of avoiding U.S. submarines. Twenty-three-year-old Sgt. Takeo Yamauchi, a former Russian language student now serving with the *136th Infantry Regiment*, sailed with the first convoy, which managed to avoid interception. Even so, the voyage was no luxury cruise. "We were laid out on shelves like broiler chickens," recalled Takeo. "You had your pack, rifle, all your equipment with you . . . You kept your rubber-soled work shoes on continually, so your feet got damp and sweaty. Water dripped down on you, condensation caused by human breath-ing. The hold stank with humanity." In the event of a torpedo attack, they would have little chance of escape. "A few rope ladders and one narrow, hurriedly improvised stairway, were the only ways out," he remembered.[37]

Despite all fears, Takeo reached Saipan on May 19 without incident. The second contingent, which sailed later in the month, was not so lucky. Leaving for Saipan on May 30, the eleven-ship convoy was six days out when they were sighted by USS *Shark*, which sent *Katsuya Maru* to the bot-tom. "On 5 June, we were attacked again from two sides and *Takaoka Maru* and *Tamahime Maru* were sunk," reported convoy commander Tadao Kuwa-hara. "On 6 June we were attacked once more on two sides, simultaneously. *Kashimazan Maru*, carrying aviation gasoline was hit during this attack and exploded. About an hour later, another attack sank *Havre Maru*." Hundreds drowned, including the commander of the *118th Infantry*, Col. Tsuyoshi Ito, who went down with the *Takaoka Maru*.

"Of the troops of the three troop transports . . . 80 percent were saved . . . ," reported Kuwahara.[38] However, those survivors lost their heavy equipment, guns, and ammunition. Major Hirakushi, who had safely reached Saipan with the first convoy, saw two destroyers pull in, their decks crowded with survivors. "When they came closer, I saw men, almost all wounded, burned. Some died after being picked up," he recalled.[39] The sinkings added to the continuing litany of bad news, including the arrival of the "shipwrecked" survivors of the *3rd* and *4th Independent Tank Companies, 14th* and *17th Independent Mortar Battalions*, and assorted aviation units. The new arrivals were of "no use as fighting troops," observed the dispatch from Saipan, noting that "the infantry are without hats and shoes and are in confusion."[40]

Over 3,000 miles away, the 2nd and 4th Marine Divisions, which would form the point of the U.S. spear aimed at Takeo Yamauchi, Major Hirakushi, and their comrades, continued to hone their deadly skills in the Hawaiian boondocks. When finally brought up to strength, the 2nd Marine Division (reinforced) would field 21,746 men for Saipan, the 4th Marine Division (reinforced) would number 21,615, and the 27th Infantry Division (reinforced) would number 16,404 men.

Like the 2nd Division at Camp Tarawa on the Parker Ranch, the 4th Marine Division was relegated to the hinterlands, encamped on Maui 1,300 feet up the slopes of Mount Haleakala. The division was commanded by fifty-seven-year old Gen. Harry Schmidt. A Marine since 1909, Schmidt had experience ranging from service in the Far East and shipboard duty to a stint as assistant commandant. A heavyset Dutchman, he was considered stolid, rather unimaginative, and thoroughly reliable.[41] Under Schmidt, the division had been blooded in February, participating in the seizure of the Marshall Islands where the Marines escaped serious casualties. They would later remember Maui mostly for rain and red mud.

"Maui, at first glance, seemed to be a paradise," recalled Lt. Paul Harper. "The fields were full of pineapple and sugar cane. The two volcanoes were high and handsome. The empty beaches stretched for miles. But Maui had a dry side and a wet side, and our tent camp was on the wet side. The daily rains washed down the mountain slopes and turned our camp into a muddy swamp."[42] Al Perry recalled, "The first night we were there we put our shoes under our bunks. The next morning all our shoes were found at the bottom of the company street. They had floated down during a downpour. The company streets were red mud and the showers were ice cold."[43]

The men lived in tents equipped with wooden decks and a bare electrical lightbulb, nine tents to a row. "At the far end of these rows, about a hundred feet from the last tent, was an outside toilet or crapper, as we called them," noted Sgt. Harry "Hap" Pearce. "These crappers were nine-holers, or room for nine guys to sit at one time."[44] A long sheet-metal urinal adorned one wall. These were supplemented at the end of each company street by "what the French would call a pissor—a funnel attached to a pipe driven into the ground," recalled John E. Lane.[45] Showers consisted of ten or twelve spigots that emitted "the coldest water this side of the North Pole," observed Carl Matthews.[46]

"There was a long line to everything," recalled Matthews, including a line to eat at the field mess, which hardly seemed worth the wait. "We used our own mess gear . . . aluminum top and bottom plate, canteen cup, knife, fork, and spoon. When we were finished with a meal there was another long line to the 'Dishwasher' . . . several fifty-five gallon oil drums cut in half, filled with water, and heated with gasoline burners that sounded like blow torches. After several hundred Marines had dunked their kits in the first drum the liquid began to look a lot like chicken soup, but the barrels became progressively clearer and the final wash was . . . usually . . . clear liquid with a rolling boil."[47]

Some amenities were available at the regimental post exchange, recalled Lane. There was "pogey bait," ice cream, candy, gum, toiletries, and GI beer that came in olive green cans the same color as ammunition cans. Cigarettes were only five cents a pack or fifty cents a carton. For some reason, there was also plenty of Aqua Velva aftershave. Carl Matthews found one of his buddies in a tent drinking this stuff with a Marine by the name of Lee Marvin, who some years later, now with a Purple Heart and Honorable Discharge, would find his way to Hollywood. "They were having a real party . . . laughing, telling dirty stories, and drinking Aqua Velva," recalled Matthews. "They had a special technique of wiggling the bottle to extract the liquid that appeared to make them happy. I had a bottle back in my tent that my Aunt Kitty had sent me for Christmas and I tried it when I returned to our area. It wasn't very good."[48]

There was little time for goofing off. Emphasis was placed on individual and small unit training, infantry-tank-engineers cooperation, and maneuver of battalions, regiments, and entire divisions as units. The heart of the division was its three infantry regiments, each numbering about 3,200 men. An infantry regiment was composed of three battalions, each with a headquarters company and three rifle companies for a total of about 920 men. Each regiment had a Weapons Company with 37mm guns and four self-propelled 75mm guns. The division also included an artillery regiment and a tank battalion. The 2nd Marine Division fielded the 2nd, 6th, and 8th Marine Regiments (infantry), the 10th Marines (artillery), and the 2nd Tank Battalion. The 4th Marine Division fielded the 23rd, 24th, and 25th Marines (infantry), the 14th Marines (artillery), and the 4th Tank Battalion. These were the units that would shoulder the bulk of the direct combat.

As they approached combat on Saipan, Marine units were more lethal than ever. A reorganization of rifle squads into three four-man fire teams headed by a squad leader provided a more flexible assault element. It also upped the number of Browning Automatic Rifles (BARs) per squad from one to three—increasing the number in a division from 558 to 853. Special assault squads were armed with bazookas and flamethrowers—with the number of flamethrowers in a division increased tenfold, from twenty-four to 243. Experimental Canadian flamethrowers made by Ronson were also fitted to a company of light tanks, which the Marines promptly dubbed "Zippo tanks" in honor of the famed cigarette lighter.

The 2nd Marine Division wrapped up its stay at Camp Tarawa in May with a "walk through" rehearsal based on the scheme of maneuver to be employed at Saipan. The successive phase lines from the landing beaches to the Force Beachhead Line were laid out on the ground to scale. "In front of the staked-out beaches were marked the adjacent water areas over which the ship-to-shore movement was to take place off Saipan," explained division commander Gen. Thomas Watson. The entire division moved over this giant game board according to the timetable calculated for the actual assault. "In this manner every officer and man learned the part he was to play in the landing and came to appreciate the time and space factors involved," observed Watson. "Yet only a few commanders and staff officers of the thousands of men who participated in this rehearsal actually knew the real name of the target."[49]

One other who did know was Dick Bailey, a twenty-four-year-old corporal in Watson's own division. A veteran of Guadalcanal and Tarawa, Bailey learned that his younger brother Jim, a Navy chief petty officer, was stationed at Pearl Harbor and he obtained permission to go visit him. As it turned out, Jim Bailey had a high security job with JINPOA (Joint Intelligence Pacific Ocean Area) tracking Japanese merchant ship movements. After passing through various sets of armed guards, Jim took Dick into his office. One wall bore a large map of the Pacific Ocean with all the islands depicted and ship positions marked. "Do you know what's next for you?" asked Jim. Dick replied in the negative. Jim took a pointer and touched Saipan.

"You didn't do that," replied Dick. "I don't want to know."[50]

While combat Marines trained, logistics experts worked on ensuring they got to the target, over 3,000 miles from Hawaii, with everything they would need. The distances involved, the numbers of men, and the sheer amount of materiel that had to be transported were staggering.

Forager would involve 166,000 troops; 71,000 of that total were assigned to the Saipan assault. The operation would involve 535 ships, including battleships (7), heavy cruisers (6), light cruisers (5), carriers (11), destroyers (86), destroyer escorts (16), minesweepers (44), attack transports (43), attack cargo ships (13), fast transports (13), transports (17), cargo ships (10), merchant transports (9), merchant cargo ships (12), landing ships, dock (8), landing ships, tank (91), landing craft, infantry (50), landing craft, tank (36), auxiliary transport-hospital (1), auxiliary coastal transport (1), as well as a variety of repair ships, patrol craft, net layers, sixteen submarine chasers, and six tugs. Crucial to the landing were the amphibious tractors needed to get the assault Marines over Saipan's fringing reef. At Saipan, more than 700 amtracs from eight Marine and U.S. Army amphibious tractor battalions—the 2nd, 5th, 10th, 534th, 715th, 773rd, 2nd Armored, and 708th Armored—would help ensure there would be no repeat of the bloodbath at Tarawa.

The assault forces would bring a thirty-two-day supply of rations; sufficient fuel, lubricants, chemicals, ordnance, and engineer and individual supplies for twenty days; medical supplies for thirty days; seven days of ammunition for ground weapons; and ten days of ammunition for antiaircraft guns. Men wounded in the early hours of the landings would be collected on three specially equipped "hospital" LSTs [Landing Ships, Tank] for initial treatment. They would then be transferred to medical wards located aboard designated transports. Hospital ships would arrive three days later (D plus three) or when directed.

As the timeframe narrowed, NTLF held a full-scale landing exercise on May 17 at Maalaea Bay on Maui. According to Lt. John C. Chapin, it was "the same old stuff" with "the interminable hours of circling, meanwhile getting wet, hungry and bored . . . Some of the men got seasick, and all of us were soaking wet and cold." They finally went ashore, "wading through the surf, getting your only pair of shoes and socks wringing wet, and then onto the beach where all the sand migrated into your shoes. A series of conflicting and confusing orders flowed down through the chain of command: halt and move on, go here, go there."[51]

On May 19 another exercise was conducted at Kahoolawe. Troops boarded LVTs [Landing Vehicles, Tracked] and approached to within 300 yards of the beach under live naval bombardment and aerial support. This time Chapin avoided getting his boondockers wet, but otherwise the exercise received little praise. "The rehearsals as a whole were very ragged and poorly conducted due in large measure to the late issue of rehearsal plans, the wide separation of all participating units and the inability to brief personnel in advance," observed an official review.[52]

The rehearsals were also marred by an operational accident involving three specially adapted LCTs [Landing Craft, Tank] assigned to the 2nd Marine Division. The 120-foot-long barge-like LCTs, originally designed to bring tanks ashore, had been equipped as gunboats with six 4.2-inch mortars with the idea of employing them as mobile firing platforms to pound beach positions. The modified LCTs were secured to the decks of the big troop-carrying LSTs [Landing Ship, Tank]. Supported on long wooden beams and secured by huge cables, the space underneath and in the LCTs themselves provided a handy spot to bunk down the overflow of Marines.

It was also more dangerous than anyone realized. On the night of May 14, Corp. Roy Roush awoke to shouts as the LST—not a very stable vessel in the best of weather—began to roll violently in the heavy seas. "Cots and men tumbled towards the railing which I saw was actually dipping water," he remembered. "I really thought that we were going to roll over, especially when the LCT above began to move several feet sideways like it was going to launch itself." The LST made a few more rolls before stabilizing. "Men and equipment were strewn everywhere," said Roush. "Many of the men had been thrown out of their cots when they overturned. It was utter chaos...."[53]

Roush later learned he had been lucky. A number of Marines sleeping in an LCT lashed to the deck of LST 485 had gone overboard when the cables securing the LCT gave way in the early morning darkness. Hit by a trailing LST, the LCT sank within minutes. Similar accidents occurred aboard LST 71 and LST 390 as LCTs went overboard. A search for survivors continued through the night, but few were found. Two men were known dead, seventeen missing, and sixteen injured. An investigation later determined that the LCTs had been insufficiently—or possibly improperly—secured. Heavy loads of water and ammunition stored aboard the LCTs may have contributed to the failure of securing lines as the LSTs rolled in the heavy seas.[54]

Another casualty of the maneuvers—though not part of the official record—was a dog adopted by one of the companies in Col. Justice Chambers's battalion and taken along aboard ship. The mascot came to the attention of the division chief of staff—a man Chambers held in low regard. "He sent for me and told me to find that damn dog and throw it over the side," recalled Chambers.

Chambers refused. "I wasn't about to throw that dog over the side," he observed. "The boys loved him and that was that." He told the officer he would see that the dog was left behind on the beach during the upcoming landing exercises. Back aboard ship as the exercise wound down, Chambers could see one of his men standing on the beach with the dog as the Marines got back in the landing craft. "The last thing I remember on Maui, on this particular trip, was that poor damned little dog sitting there where his friends had all left him," Chambers remarked years later.[55]

Chapter III

Acts of Man or God

WHILE THE MARINES GIRDED FOR BATTLE, ONE OF THE GREAT INTELLI-
gence coups of the war was playing out like something dreamed up by a pulp
fiction writer. Through a series of unlikely circumstances, guerrilla forces in
the Philippines had come into possession of the Japanese plan for decisive
battle.

The plan was the brainchild of Adm. Mineicha Koga, who had assumed
command of the *Combined Fleet* after the legendary Adm. Isoroku Yamamoto was killed in an aerial ambush in the skies over Bougainville the year
before. Unlike his more colorful predecessor, Koga was cool and conservative, a pragmatic and logical man with considerable staff, administrative,
and seagoing experience. He also firmly believed that Japan's best hope lay
in drawing U.S. naval forces into a decisive engagement and smashing them.
"From the very beginning, he insisted on the one decisive action, first with
ships and later with shore-based planes," recalled then *Combined Fleet* chief
of staff Vice Adm. Shigeru Fukudome. "Under the circumstances, this strategy seemed to be the only logical one." Fukudome added that both he and
Koga agreed that defense of the Palaus-Marianas line was "absolutely indis-
pensable." Loss of that "last line of defense," believed Koga, would doom
Japan's hopes of emerging from the war with any semblance of victory.[1]

Koga outlined his battle strategy in a document codenamed *Z Plan*.
According to Z Plan, a U.S. advance into the Philippine Sea by way of
the Marianas, the Palaus, or New Guinea would bring the *Combined Fleet*
forth for the decisive confrontation. The admiral planned to operate from
Saipan in the event of an American push toward the Marianas or Western
Carolines. If the threat materialized farther to the south, he would exercise
command from Davao in the Philippines.[2]

In the meantime, he moved his headquarters to Truk, but U.S. carrier
sweeps over that once-feared bastion in February persuaded him to relocate

to the Palaus in the Western Carolines, about 1,500 miles to the east. There he refined his Z Plan. A final draft version, *Combined Fleet Secret Operations Order No. 73*, was issued on March 8 alerting the fleet that all remaining Japanese naval airpower would be committed to meet the expected American naval offensive and destroy the U.S. Pacific Fleet.[3] The plan called for overwhelming the enemy with mass aerial attacks launched from carriers and island land bases. As many as 450 planes would be embarked on carriers supplemented by the approximately 1,200 land-based fighters, bombers, and torpedo planes available in the Western Pacific. Another 200 aircraft could be flown in from bases in Japan.[4]

Unlike some other high-ranking officers, Koga did not believe he had the luxury of time. In his estimation, the Americans could strike any time after April 1. He immediately began concentrating his forces, accumulating more aircraft, and training replacement pilots. The biggest unknown was just where the great battle would be joined. Koga received a scare on March 29 when Japanese scout planes reported that U.S. warships were approaching the Palaus. U.S. carrier planes struck the next day, but there was no invasion. Fearful he would be isolated at Palau, he decided to move his headquarters to Davao in the Philippines, 600 miles to the west. On March 31, he and his staff boarded two big four-engine Kawanishi flying boats sent from Saipan and lifted off from Koror Harbor for the three-hour flight to Mindanao.[5]

As Koga and Vice Admiral Fukudome were ferried out to the aircraft, Koga displayed some pessimism about the turn the war had taken for Japan and perhaps for his own future as well. "Yamamoto died at exactly the right time," he remarked to his chief of staff. "Let us go out and die together."[6] They shook hands and then, for security reasons, boarded separate aircraft for the flight to Davao. Admiral Koga's remark about death turned out to be a premonition. En route, the big Kawanishis, known to the Allies as "Emilys," encountered a severe tropical storm front. Koga's plane disappeared. No trace of the admiral or crew was ever found.[7]

Vice Admiral Fukudome, accompanied by fourteen staff officers and guarding a small wooden box containing a bound copy of the top secret Z Plan, very nearly joined Koga. His pilot spent hours attempting to skirt the storm. Finally running low on fuel at about 0230 that morning, the exhausted pilot decided to attempt an emergency landing. He put the seaplane into a steep approach, but misjudged the altitude. Fukudome, an experienced pilot, reached over and yanked on the control in an effort to pull the plane out of its dive. The results were disastrous. The big flying boat over-responded and smashed into Bohol Strait, about 2½ miles off Cebu. "When the plane crashed, I sank and when I came up the gasoline on the surface of the sea was burning," remembered Fukudome. "Fortunately I was outside of the burning area, and those who came up outside the burning area were saved." Thirteen passengers and crew survived; twelve others were killed.[8]

Grabbing onto a seat cushion, Fukudome paddled away from the flames. He swam and floated for eight and a half hours just offshore before some natives finally approached in canoes. Exhausted, he allowed himself to be dragged aboard. Two other survivors from the crashed plane made their way to a Japanese garrison on the coast. Fukudome and the remaining ten were hustled inland by Filipino guerrillas, leaving the badly burned corpse of one of their comrades on the beach where it was soon eaten by dogs. One prisoner was killed when he tried to escape, but the others were delivered a week later to Lt. Col. James Cushing, a hard-drinking former American mining engineer who had taken charge of the guerrilla movement on Cebu.[9]

The morning of April 3, Pedro Gantuangoko, a shopkeeper from Perilos, a village down the beach from the crash site, spotted an object floating off shore. His neighbor, Oopoy Wamer, took his boat out and pulled an oil-covered wooden box from the water. Inside, he found a sodden red leather portfolio embossed with a large gold naval seal, a pouch containing an assortment of kernel-sized gold nuggets, and a cloth sack containing about a dozen condoms. Realizing the documents were probably important, the men hid the box. Days later, fearful as hundreds of Japanese troops swarmed the area in search of the missing naval officers and demanding the return of any papers that may have floated ashore, they passed the portfolio—as well as the pouch of gold nuggets—on to a local guerrilla, who brought it to Cushing.[10]

Fukudome and his comrades told Cushing they were low-level staff officers on a routine inspection of the area, but the guerrillas became suspicious when they noticed that Fukudome was treated with considerable deference by the others. The importance of their prisoner was confirmed when a couple of thousand Japanese army troops descended on the area, burning villages, executing hundreds of civilians, and demanding the return of the captured officers. Cushing messaged General MacArthur's Southwest Pacific Area (SWPA) headquarters that he had captured a "general." Elated at the possibility of having an enemy general officer to interrogate, headquarters sent a submarine to pick up the prisoners, but Cushing could not wait. As Japanese troops closed in on him—and continued to exact retaliation on local villagers—he released Fukudome and the others in exchange for a promise that the Japanese would cease their campaign of terror against the civilian population.

MacArthur's chief of staff, Lt. Gen. Richard K. Sutherland, was livid at missing out on a high-ranking officer, but SWPA was about to get a consolation prize. As the furor subsided, Cushing got around to examining the documents Pedro Gantuangoko had found floating in the water. Immediately recognizing their importance, he radioed SWPA on April 13. At sunset on May 11, the U.S. submarine *Crevalle* surfaced just north of Basay, Negros, and took aboard forty-one American citizens and the copy of Koga's Z Plan. By midday on May 19, the top secret plans were in the hands of MacArthur's intelligence chief. Translators quickly identified one document as copy six (of 550) of "Secret Combined Fleet Order No. 73," issued on March 8, 1944, and signed by Admiral Koga. The preamble was stunning, stating:

> *The Combined Fleet is for the time being directing its main operations to the Pacific Area where, in the event of an attack by an enemy Fleet Occupation Force, it will bring to bear the combined maximum strength of all our forces to meet and destroy the enemy, and to maintain our hold on vital areas. These operations will be called "Z Operations."*[11]

Translation of the "Z Operation Orders" was completed by May 22. The first copy went to Army chief of staff Gen. George C. Marshall by special courier. The second went to MacArthur. The twenty-two-page copy of the Japanese operation orders was quickly followed by a translation of "A Study of the Main Features of Decisive Air Operations in the Central Pacific." At the urging of Capt. Arthur McCollum, a naval liaison officer with MacArthur's headquarters, copies of the translated documents were hastily forwarded to the Joint Intelligence Center Pacific Ocean Area (JICPOA) at Pearl Harbor. The documents were flown to Pearl by an Army bomber that covered nearly 5,000 miles in forty-eight hours with refueling stops along the way.[12]

Despite frantic efforts to recover any documents that might have survived the air crash, the Japanese apparently had no inkling that the material had indeed fallen into American hands. Japanese tidal and current experts were sure that if the box had survived the crash, it would have ended up somewhere near Pedro Gantuangoko's village. They set similar boxes adrift at the crash site to verify their calculations and all floated in near the village. Villagers were assembled and asked about the box. No one spoke up. Obviously suspicious, the Japanese burned the village. When threats failed, they offered a 50,000 peso (about $25,000) reward, but to no avail. With no leads and no evidence to the contrary, the authorities finally decided the top secret plan must have been destroyed in the plane crash.[13]

On May 5, the Japanese publicly announced Admiral Koga's death, stating he had been killed in action in March while directing naval operations from a plane. The announcement named Adm. Soemu Toyoda as Koga's replacement as *Combined Fleet* commander. Hard-driving and abrasive—he reportedly had driven subordinates to nervous breakdowns—the fifty-nine-year-old former Naval Academy instructor was known for his brains, but had little wartime saltwater experience. In addition to his new title, the admiral inherited Imperial Headquarters Directive No. 373: the Z Plan.

Toyoda fully realized a pivotal moment was drawing near. In a message to commanding officers upon assuming command, the admiral observed, "The war is drawing close to the lines vital to our national defense. The issue of our national existence is unprecedentedly serious, an unprecedented opportunity exists for deciding who shall be victorious and who defeated. This autumn we will make this great task our responsibility . . . we will carry out the decisive operations which mean certain enemy defeat."[14]

May 21 was a Sunday. Hundreds of ships in the Saipan invasion fleet lay at anchor at Pearl Harbor. Many sailors had liberty. A few lucky Marines also managed to get ashore, wearing uniforms they had pressed by placing them under the mattress on their sleeping racks. About half the LSTs remained at Maalaea Bay on Maui due to lack of facilities at Pearl. "While there, we were tied up near to and downwind of the Dole pineapple cannery," recalled Corp. Dick Bailey. "Our ship smelled of pineapple for the rest of the trip. It was years before I could eat pineapple again."[15]

Tucked away in Pearl Harbor's West Loch, twenty-nine other LSTs had been combat loaded with a volatile mix of ammunition and gasoline for the *Forager* operation. Nearly 350 feet long with a 54-foot beam and bow doors that could open to launch landing craft at sea or cargo on shore, an LST ordinarily carried a crew of 119 men and up to 200 assault troops. Now, trucks, jeeps, and weapons carriers crowded main decks in readiness for the upcoming battle. Artillery and mortar shells and small arms ammunition were stowed below and on decks crowded with Marines who would live aboard during the long haul to Eniwetok and Saipan. Each LST also carried eighty to one hundred drums of high-octane fuel on the forecastle—gasoline that would be needed to fuel the LVTs bringing the Marines ashore at Saipan. More ammunition, DUKW amphibious trucks, field guns, and landing craft were crammed below. The LSTs also had their own ammunition magazines and a fuel capacity of 200,000 gallons. Drums of lubricating oil, fog oil smoke pots, and floats were carried on the fantail. Due to a shortage of regular ammunition ships—only six were available in the whole Pacific area—sixteen LSTs had been transformed into seagoing ammunition dumps.[16]

Crammed with gasoline and ammo, the LSTs were floating bombs, just awaiting a spark. Lt. Cmdr. James B. Hoyt, commanding LST Group 39, Flotilla 13, observed that the loading procedure violated every safety precaution the U.S. Navy had required for the past 300 years. "However, when you have to do it, you do it," he remarked.[17] Adding to the danger, the LSTs in West Loch were moored side by side—practically gunnel to gunnel—close enough for men to jump from one to another—in "nests" at seven different tares or pier areas. The number of vessels ranged from only two LSTs at Tare 3 to eight at Tare 8. One of Lieutenant Commander Hoyt's LST captains expressed concern that the combination of close mooring and volatile cargo would result in the loss of the entire nest should a serious fire break out, but there wasn't much the crews could do about the arrangement except be careful and hope for the best.[18]

While many of the men enjoyed a day of rest, a group of GIs was busy on LST 353 moored toward the end of the row at Tare 8, seventh of the eight LSTs in the nest. The outermost vessel was LST 49, then 353, followed by LSTs 179, 43, 69, 274, 225, and finally LST 205 about 75 yards from shore. Following the loss of the modified LCTs during rehearsals the week before, the plan to provide mobile mortar support for the Saipan landing had been canceled. The Army work detail had been sent out to LST 353 to remove the mortar ammunition from the LCT still secured to the tank deck. The GIs boated a truck out to the LST and began loading the boxes of shells. One truckload had already been filled and the work detail had another about two-thirds full by about 3:00 P.M.[19]

Motor Machinists Mate First Class Vernon D. Nichols was sitting on the LCT's port 20mm ready rack idly watching the working party. The GIs were passing boxes of ammunition from man to man over the ramp of the LCT and onto the bed of the truck which stood on the LST elevator when there was a bright flash that seemed to emanate from some drums of gasoline stored by the elevator. The flash was accompanied by an explosion that blasted Nichols from his perch and sent him sprawling to the deck.[20]

LST 43 commander Lt. William H. Zuehke was standing in the conning station when the explosion occurred. It seemed relatively minor. Flames shot about 15 feet into the air by his calculation, as if a gasoline drum had exploded. A smattering of debris rained down on 43's deck. But as Zuehke sounded general quarters, there was a second, larger explosion followed by a massive blast as the barrels of gasoline stored on LST 353's forecastle exploded. Flames shot 75 to 100 feet into the air, showering LST 49 and the other ships in the nest with burning debris. LST 353 was an inferno within a matter of minutes.

Zuehke was trying to cast off when there was yet another huge explosion, apparently from ammunition stored on the stricken LST. The explosion blew off Zuehke's clothes and knocked him momentarily senseless. When he gathered his wits, he saw that LST 179, located between his ship and 353, was on fire from the stern to the superstructure. His own LST's main deck was also on fire and all of the firefighting crews on deck had been leveled. Zuehke gave the order to abandon ship.[21]

Marine rifleman James T. Cobb was lying on his cot below decks on LST 225, just one ship removed from shore, when he heard a muffled explosion. He went topside and saw that an LST farther out in the loch was burning briskly. The fire was punctuated by numerous small explosions. In what seemed like a matter of minutes, the flames began leaping from ship to ship in his direction. Confusion mounted as injured and panicked sailors and Marines retreated across Cobb's vessel from the outboard LSTs. What firefighting efforts were underway seemed uncoordinated and not very effective.

Cobb and his fellow Marines went over the side and swam to shore. As they fled inland through a sugar cane field, one of the LSTs exploded. The force of the blast was so great that an entire Higgins boat was hurled into the air, plummeting down into the field beside him. Flying debris took off one man's legs at the knees.[22]

Marine Harold E. Boulware, stationed as a guard at the West Loch ammunition dump, was walking down the hallway on the second floor of his barracks when all the glass blew out of the windows. Something hit Boulware in the side and fell to the floor with a clinking sound. Boulware bent over and picked up the object. It was a silver dollar, apparently blown all the way from the LST nest. Another explosion sent a huge fragment of an LST over the barracks and into the front yard area. The mass of twisted metal was still too hot to touch the next day and so big it had to be cut up with torches before being hauled away in trucks.[23]

An investigation later determined that the first explosion took place on LST 353 at 3:08 P.M., quickly followed by two more blasts, including one as the ammunition on LST 353 detonated, sending flaming debris raining down on the seven other LSTs moored at Tare 8 and starting more fires. At 3:11 P.M. a second LST exploded. Another massive explosion occurred at 3:22 P.M.[24] The captain of LST 69 estimated that his own deck was engulfed in flame within five minutes of the initial explosion. Like the other ships, LST 69 had a considerable quantity of ammunition stored in the open, including hundreds of 5-inch shells. Water hoses were turned onto the ammunition, but the fire was too hot and out of hand. The wooden ammunition boxes started to burn. All the life rafts on the bridge were on fire.

"The LCT [secured on deck] was on fire inside," recalled Lt. (j.g.) Albert N. Gott. "All those cots and bedding were a blazing inferno and underneath the LCT where we had bunked Marines, all of those cots and bedding was on fire and the ways of the LCT back aft was blazing and we saw it around the boxes that the ammunition was in...."[25]

The crew abandoned ship just before the gasoline went up. Some men sought safety in the water only to die as oil and gasoline spilled into the loch and caught fire. Chief Bosun's Mate Clyde V. Cook was aboard LST 272 in the relative safety of Tare 6 off to the southeast. A few minutes after the first explosion, he noticed large numbers of men in the water. Only their heads were showing; the sight reminded him of a flock of ducks. Then the gasoline and oil on the water ignited. The conflagration swept over the heads in the water and when the flames finally receded, there was no one to be seen. Other men simply drowned or were dragged into the screws of LSTs that started their engines in an effort to escape the holocaust.[26]

On LST 39, Pvt. Harry Pearce had been blown out of his cot by the explosion. Clad in his skivvies and a steel helmet, he was surrounded by bedlam. Men were clinging to the sides of the ship. There were men in the water with no life preservers. "These men were bobbing like corks in the water. They couldn't swim and were going up and down. Some men were drowning. A Navy lieutenant cut loose a metal donut life raft on the side of the LST. It dropped into the water on top of six or eight men. They disappeared and never came back up," remembered Pearce.[27]

The response of the LST crews ranged from heroic to inept. Some sailors deserted their ships. Efforts to battle the conflagration were generally disorganized. Fleeing Marines and sailors added to the chaos and disrupted firefighting efforts. But there were also incidents of great courage. After the second explosion, Marine Harry Seehode saw sailors heading forward with a hose to fight the fire. Suddenly there was a third explosion and the sailors disappeared in a wall of fire.[28] Aboard LST 273, Seaman 1st Class Bill Gourlay looked over at one of the burning LSTs to see a lone sailor with a hose trying to get the fires under control. The fires seemed to be getting the better of him, but the sailor stayed with it. Then something exploded. Gourlay saw huge billows of smoke flame and debris soar into the air, along with the fire hose. The sailor was gone.[29]

Survival was often just a matter of luck, a whim of fate. Marine Frank T. Thompson, a Navajo code talker, was aboard LST 179 right next to LST 353 that afternoon. Most of the men aboard were playing cards, napping, reading, just lying in the sun or cutting each other's hair. A couple of Thompson's friends were playing cards on a stack of ammunition in the center of the deck. They invited Thompson to join them, but he declined and walked on down the deck. He looked over toward LST 353 and saw Army personnel loading ammunition. Before he could take another dozen steps, a tremendous explosion blew him off his feet and toward a gun mount. When he recovered he looked back and saw gasoline and ammunition on fire and exploding. The stack of ammo where his friends had been playing cards was gone. Screams and cries arose from all directions. Mobs of men fled over the nearby LSTs heading shoreward in an effort to escape. Others jumped into the water.

Thompson made it to the last LST in the row, about 75 yards from shore. It was crowded with fleeing men. "By now, everyone was trying to get away," he observed. "Some of the men were jumping into the water while others were trying to escape by going from ship to ship inboard. Some men were screaming for help even though they were wearing lifebelts or jackets." The water was full of people. "Some had drowned, some were drowning, and others were trying to swim to shore or just floating while waiting to be picked up." He saw a handful of small boats circling with lines dragging in the water, hauling men closer to shore. Thompson took to the water, grabbed onto a raft, and eventually made it to shore.[30]

PFC Elester Clements was also aboard LST 39, which had arrived late in West Loch and tied up next to 353 on the outboard side at 11:00 A.M.

that same morning. Clements and his best friend, James Weber, had just finished lunch and were sacked out on cots on the forward port side. Clements decided to go play cards amidships, a decision that probably saved his life. He left Weber reading a book. After the explosion, he waited uncertainly by the rail since he couldn't swim and had no life jacket. Finally a small boat came along. Clements jumped in the water and the crew dragged him aboard. As they pulled away, LST 39 exploded. Jeeps and other equipment rained down in the water around them. Clements survived. His friend Jim Weber was never found.[31]

Harry Pearce also made it off of LST 39. He got to shore and turned to see the oil and gas on the water had caught fire. He began pulling men to shore. "One Navy boy came to me with a kapok life preserver on and asked me to help him take it off," recalled Pearce. "When I went to pull it loose from his back, the meat off his back was coming loose and attached to the kapok lifesaver. I told the man, 'Just leave it on until we get you to the hospital.'"[32]

Seaman Henry Schramm watched from the deck of his minesweeper, which was anchored farther away in the harbor. A truck, then a jeep rose above the blast, seemed to hang forever, then tumbled back into the inferno. "The explosions continued, each new burst of flame accompanied by a distinctive boom, reaching us several seconds later," Schramm recalled. "More and more of the northern sky was blotted out by the thick, oily clouds. Fireboats and seagoing tugs with high-pressure hose mounts proceeded up the channel with sirens going, cutting fierce wakes as they roared forward."[33]

Coast Guardsman William L. C. Johnson was leaving on a mail run in a small boat when the explosions began. The crew immediately set out to pick up survivors in the water. "Men were jumping into the water from all the ships and the fires were spreading to all the ships like wildfire," he recalled. "Things were really hot there. No one had time to get helmets or life belts, so many of the fellows drowned as soon as they hit the water. The thing happened so quickly that most of the ships didn't even get their small boats working. I didn't see any life rafts. Ours was one of three or four boats picking up swimmers. I saw one guy blown about forty yards straight into the air, only to come back down into the fire. We made two trips taking survivors from the water to shore. I took care of one fellow who had most of one arm blown off."[34]

Boatswains Mate Bernard Hillman was aboard LST 126 about 300 yards away from Tare 8 when the explosions began. An ensign ordered Hillman and Seaman Steven "Sack" Sacoolidge to man the ship's LCVP

[Landing Craft Vehicle, Personnel] and help rescue survivors. The LCVP had most recently been used for garbage detail. "As we headed in, fiery debris rained all about us," recalled Hillman. "Sack hurriedly tossed overboard the garbage cans that crowded our VP's deck. He no sooner threw the last can over than we began to pull in men that were in the water. Once everyone in the water was aboard, we moved alongside LST 39's starboard quarter. In spite of the height, sailors and Marines jumped directly into our boat. I'm sure many suffered broken arms or legs, but at the time, no one seemed to care. They were safe and that's all that mattered."

Hillman headed across West Loch to the ammo wharf to offload the injured men. "We all turned and looked at what we had escaped," he said. "Even from that distance, I could see more men jumping off the LSTs we had just left. Realizing that certain death awaited them in the flaming, oil-soaked waters, I asked several of the men we had pulled from the water if they would stay and help us rescue them. No one refused."

They guided the LCVP back among the burning LSTs and began pulling men from the water. By now oil had spread across the bay making it difficult to get the survivors into the boat. Hillman noticed another LCVP had lowered its bow ramp to the level of the water, allowing the crew to stand there and literally scoop men out of the water. It looked like a good idea to Hillman and he quickly lowered his own ramp.

For the next twenty-five minutes he continued to pluck men from the water, but as the oil around them began to catch fire the crew finally headed away toward safety. "As we left the area, I saw one poor fellow hanging off the stern anchor on an LST 100 feet away," recalled Hillman. "Everyone in the boat yelled for him to jump and swim, but before you could blink your eye, the oil around the ship caught fire and he disappeared into the flames. There was nothing more we could do." Hillman later estimated he had helped save thirty to forty men.[35]

The 2nd Marine Amphibious Truck Company had previously brought its vehicles ashore for service. As the magnitude of the disaster became clear, the DUKW drivers took to the water to rescue swimmers and transport the injured to the hospital. One of the DUKW men, Arthur W. Wells, saw a Navy tug come up against a burning LST and begin pouring water on the flames. A massive explosion on the interior tank deck suddenly blew the LST's doors open and devastated the superstructure of the tug, sweeping away anyone on deck. Wells's DUKW crew scoured the water for survivors, but could find no one.[36]

Ashore when the explosions began, Coast Guardsman Lindel C. Jones was ordered to take a fireboat into West Loch. Numbers of LSTs were adrift in the loch. Jones helped push one ashore, then had to pause because so much drifting clothing had become entangled in his screws. Crewmembers took turns diving into the water to cut the clothing away until the screws again turned freely. An officer in a small boat told Jones to pull his fireboat onto the lowered ramp of a burning LST. He did and began directing foam and water into the interior of the tank deck. Small arms ammunition was exploding and slugs were ricocheting around the tank deck but miraculously none of his crew was hit. Once the fire had been beaten down, the sailors ventured in to rescue any survivors. There was no one left alive. They found the corpses of some men who had sought refuge from the fire in the chain and rope lockers only to suffocate there.

By nightfall, the flames were under control, but Jones continued to pick up survivors from ships and the water all night long, transferring them to tugs and other craft. At one point he had so many men crammed onto his 15-foot forward deck that the stern was literally lifted out of the water. Finally, at about 7:00 A.M., he was released from duty and told to get some chow.[37]

The sun rising over West Loch on Monday, May 22, revealed a scene of devastation as the fire-wracked LSTs at Tare 8 continued to smolder. Coast Guardsman Jones ventured back aboard one of the ships he had tried to save the day before. It was completely gutted and there were dead bodies everywhere.

Six of the LSTs were a total loss: LST 353, LST 179, LST 43, LST 480, LST 39, and LST 69. Also lost were the supplies and equipment they had carried, including the personal gear and weapons of the Marine units on board. Some of those Marines would never need a weapon again: 163 men were listed as dead or missing in the disaster, another 396 were listed as injured. The 2nd Marine Division lost 95 men and the 4th Marine Division lost 112. The rest were sailors, along with the handful of Army stevedores in the initial working party on LST 353.[38]

John R. Garner, a seaman with Mobile Hospital #11, recalled that bodies were taken to Alea Heights Naval Hospital overlooking Pearl Harbor and stored in reefers until identification could be made. Other bodies floated to the surface of West Loch for several days afterward. Many were buried at Redhill near the Army hospital. Clearing stations were established and survivors were routed either to hospitals for medical treatment or to the Transient Center, V Amphibious Corps.[39]

Military authorities quickly clamped down on any loose talk about the disaster for fear it would tip off the Japanese about the pending Saipan operation. Survivors were warned not to discuss the incident. A one-paragraph statement was released to the press a few days later. It stated only that an explosion had caused "some loss of life, a number of injuries and resulted in the destruction of several small vessels." Some families would not learn the true circumstances of their loved ones' deaths for years.[40]

An investigation into the disaster failed to establish a definitive cause. Various possibilities were considered, including sabotage, sparks from welding conducted earlier on LST 353, unauthorized smoking, and the explosion of gasoline vapors. A board of inquiry eventually determined that the disaster most probably started when a 4.5-inch mortar shell exploded—possibly due to a defective fuse—while being loaded onto the truck by the Army working party on LST 353. However, the board could not entirely rule out an explosion from gasoline vapors, and there was a widespread feeling later that a careless cigarette smoker had inadvertently ignited gasoline fumes from the hundreds of barrels stored above deck. No one would ever know for sure. None of the loading party in the immediate vicinity survived to testify.[41]

Admiral King placed much of the blame on the LST crews, but Admiral Nimitz was more forgiving. He refused to assign fault or charge negligence to any naval personnel. The exigencies of the situation—lack of cargo space, a shortage of ammunition ships—demanded that normal safety practices be pushed to the limit. "It is considered impossible to avoid nesting combat loaded vessels between the final rehearsal and departure," he wrote. "During this period repairs, waterproofing of equipment, and final preparation of personnel and material for assault necessitates proximity to facilities which are not available at atolls and other anchorages. It is a calculated risk that must be accepted."[42]

Nimitz could afford some magnanimity. In the end the West Loch disaster did not significantly delay the *Forager* timetable. The six LSTs were replaced, as were the dead and injured men, albeit with troops from the Replacement Center who were not as fully trained or integrated into the units. Prior to the West Loch disaster, the LSTs had been scheduled to sail on the morning of May 24. The scramble for replacement LSTs and men took four days. The LSTs sailed only twenty-four hours behind schedule and were able to make up the lost day en route.[43]

Like a great unwinding steel coil, the invasion force began to emerge from its island lair for the journey westward. Moving the 71,034 Marine and

Army troops required a total of 110 transports. These included thirty-seven troop transports of various types, eleven cargo ships, five LSDs [Landing Ship, Dock], forty-seven LSTs, and ten converted destroyers. A number of Navy-manned Liberty ships were pressed into service to transport elements of the 27th Infantry Division.[44]

The slow-moving LST groups carrying assault troops, amphibian tractors, and artillery left Pearl Harbor on May 25. Attack Group One, with its faster transports carrying the remainder of the 4th Marine Division and Headquarters, Expeditionary Group, sailed on May 29. Attack Group Two, with the 2nd Marine Division and Headquarters, Northern Troops and Landing Force (NTLF), sailed from Pearl on May 30.

Among those wishing them goodbye was Tokyo Rose, the Japanese radio propagandist who was quite popular among the Marines who felt the selections of American music she played more than compensated for her predictions of doom for Allied forces in general and the U.S. Marines in particular. "She told us when we first left that we were going to hit Saipan, and that none would come back alive," recalled Navy chaplain Charles W. Goe. "She also informed us that they were definitely waiting for us and that the reception would be a rough one. She would play some sweet music and then say, 'Now, what are you boys doing out there fighting us? Wouldn't you like to be home with your wife—dining, dancing and having a good time? Why don't you just quit this and go on home?'"[45]

Undeterred by the sweet-talking Rose, Richard W. Mason and his buddies in the 2nd Armored Amphibian Battalion were champing at the bit to get underway. "One day Major [Ralph C.] Bevans told us we would be leaving for combat in eleven days," recalled Mason. "As crazy as we were, we thought this was great." Never having been in battle before, they dismissed Bevans's obvious concern. "Most of us did not know that we did not know as much as we thought we knew," admitted Mason.[46]

Chapter IV

On to the Westward

As the elements of the Northern Troops and Landing Force plowed westward through the vast expanse of the Pacific Ocean in the early morning hours of May 29, aircrews from the 98th and 431st Bombardment Squadrons were boarding their B-24 Liberators at Eniwetok for the thirteen-hour flight to Saipan. With the Marianas beyond the reach of U.S. land-based fighters, the heavily armed long-range bombers had been assigned to ride shotgun on a last-minute photo reconnaissance mission by seven PB4YP-1P Navy aircraft from Fleet Air Photographic Reconnaissance Squadron VD-4.[1]

Standard operating procedure called for two B-24s—each carrying a ten-man crew, ten .50-caliber machine guns, and two .30-caliber machine guns—to accompany each photo aircraft. The twenty-one aircraft swept across Saipan at 20,000 feet, with the nine photo planes slightly forward of the bomber escort, just close enough to each other to provide vertical overlapping coverage of the assigned target area. Navy lieutenant commander Charles H. Clark noticed black blossoms of antiaircraft fire reaching up for them, but most of the air bursts were low and behind. While encouraging, that did not mean the aircrews were home free. Clark knew that Japanese fighter pilots customarily waited until the B-24s flew clear of the antiaircraft fire before launching their attacks.[2]

The first trouble came not from enemy fighters but from a malfunctioning engine. B-24 pilot Lt. Robert Rushing was flying the No. 3 position off Clark's left wing when he lost his No. 2 engine and had to feather the prop. Pilots had been told during their briefing that the formation would slow down if one of the navy photo planes ran into trouble, but any army aircraft that fell behind was on its own. As Rushing began to drop back, Capt. Loren Stoddard, flying the No. 2 position in the B-24 "Cloudy Joe," ignored that directive and pulled over to ride herd on the cripple.

A devout Mormon, the twenty-five-year-old Stoddard had been awarded the Silver Star for bravery during the Japanese attack on Hickam Field on December 7, 1941, climbing into a transport plane, starting the engines, and taxiing away from another burning aircraft while under enemy attack. He and his crew had flown thirteen missions since March, including raids on Truk, and they knew what they were doing, but their luck was about to take a turn for the worse. "At first Captain Stoddard flew in a tight formation off the right wing of Lt. Rushing," reported Lt. John Gartland, watching from one of the accompanying bombers, "but in letting down from 20,000 to 12,000 feet, fell back approximately 300–400 feet. When at about 12,000 feet, one Zeke made a one o'clock overhead pass out of the sun directly at the two-plane formation and hit Captain Stoddard's airplane in the left wing behind #2 engine."

Clark thought the Japanese fighter had actually been gunning for Rushing's crippled B-24. Whatever the case, Cloudy Joe now had big trouble. Flames poured from the left wing and engine nacelle and pieces of the aircraft's skin were peeling off. Auxiliary fuel tanks in the bomb bay were also aflame. Stoddard called out over the interphone that he was going to "let down." Two Japanese fighters made several more passes at the crippled B-24, but Stoddard persevered, finally leveling out at about 1,000 feet in preparation for a water landing. The escorts saw two men bail out as the plane descended. To their horror, one of the Japanese pilots turned his attention to the parachutes. "One of the enemy aircraft spotted these two men who had jumped," reported S/Sgt. James R. Schneider; "[it] started to circle around their chutes and went approximately 300 yards out and started strafing the two men. One of the chutes collapsed because it was pretty well shot up, besides the man that was shot. The second man went limp as soon as the first shots were fired at him. He sort of stiffened up. They were more than likely to be dead when they hit the water because when the chutes hit the water there didn't seem to be any resistance to get free from the chutes."[3]

At the controls of Cloudy Joe, Stoddard had no idea that two of his crew had bailed out. The fire in the bomb bay had cut off communication with the men in the rear of the aircraft. He alerted the men in the forward section to brace for a water landing and started his glide. "He lit on his tail very smooth, but as soon as he dropped the nose of the ship the left wing broke off on the inboard side of No. 2 engine and burst into flames," reported Schneider. "As soon as the plane landed, these two Jap planes (Zeros) started strafing the ship and there was no sign of life coming from the ship. The air-plane stayed afloat for about 32 seconds. Zeros then went back and strafed the water where the ship had landed."[4]

The plane came down about 50 miles east of Saipan. The formation broke radio silence to report the crash site to the rescue submarine that was supposedly in the area, but the crew was not recovered. "Photographs of the plane going down crashing and burning make it almost certain that none survived," observed the aircraft action report. A member of the squadron subsequently wrote to Stoddard's brother, "Officially he is listed as missing but from the information that I have been able to collect the general feeling is that there isn't much hope, if any."[5] Lieutenant Rushing, the pilot Stoddard had gone to help, was more fortunate, limping back to Eniwetok on three engines.

Miraculously, four members of Cloudy Joe's ten-man crew had managed to cheat death. As the plane came down, Stoddard's last sensation was that a hose had been turned on his face. He came to his senses to find himself under water. He had been thrown from the aircraft still strapped to his seat and was now descending into darkness. Realizing he was drowning, he released his seatbelt, shed his heavy flak vest, and struggled to the surface, fortuitously bumping into a life raft that had deployed during the landing. His co-pilot, 2nd Lt. Peter Hryskanich, and the bombardier, 1st Lt. Ernest F. Peschau Jr., had also been thrown from the plane when it hit the water. The radio operator, T/Sgt. Lincoln S. Manierre, was still inside, but managed to fight his way out the bomb bay of the sinking aircraft. The four men clambered into the life raft. Aside from cuts and bruises, all but Peschau had escaped serious injury. The bombardier had suffered internal injuries and was unable to use his legs.[6]

Driven by the prevailing easterly winds, their raft came ashore at Saipan the morning of June 2 and the four airmen were taken prisoner. Sixteen-year-old Saipanese native Manuel T. Sablan heard police talking about some Americans in a rubber boat who had been picked up on the east coast and brought to the Garapan jail. Curious, he got on his bicycle and pedaled down to the jail house. "So sure enough, I went to the jail and a truck pulled up," he recalled. "There were four Americans. They were blindfolded and their hands were tied behind their backs. They were white and extraordinarily big. Their hair was gold. At first I didn't even know they were Americans."[7] Stripped of their clothing, the prisoners were given pajama-like Japanese uniforms and confined in separate cells.

The airmen were questioned for four days. "After being on display in the local village, the Japs separated us and blindfolded us and questioned each one of us," recalled Hryskanich. Their interrogator claimed to have graduated from UCLA before the war and spoke excellent English. The interrogators began with big smiles and expressions of sympathy—assuring the prisoners they had only a few simple questions—but their attitude soon hardened. "At first we gave them all the Geneva Convention required; name, rank, and serial number. They assured us that this was not adequate and they applied greater pressure over time," said Hryskanich. Threatened with beheading and beaten with a length of heavy rope until they lost consciousness, the airmen abandoned the "name, rank, and serial number" obstinacy, but were careful to provide information that seemed of little value. In some cases, they simply lied. "They asked us if we had done something to confuse the Japanese radar as we approached Saipan," said Hryskanich. The flyers denied it, though in fact they had dropped chaff—aluminum strips—on their approach.[8]

Oddly enough, their interrogators made evasion easier by failing to ask what would seem to be the most obvious questions: the purpose of their mission, details about their units, and information on U.S. plans. In what would seem to be an egregious breach of security, the most valuable information the airmen possessed—the timing of the Saipan landings—had been part of their pre-mission briefing. The topic apparently never even came up during their questioning.[9] American intelligence later obtained a page from the log of an unidentified Japanese air unit indicating that the prisoners provided no information of value and gave only their name, rank, and serial number. "Their spirit (BUSHIDO) was reported very high by the Japs," observed the intelligence report.[10]

On the morning of June 6, the four airmen were blindfolded and taken by truck to the Japanese naval air base up the coast where they were hustled onto an Emily flying boat. The passenger compartment was fitted with wooden benches equipped with seatbelts. The plane lumbered into the air and later that afternoon set down in what the Americans learned was Tokyo Bay. Shortly thereafter they were transferred to the Ofuna Naval Interrogation Center about 7 miles southwest of Yokohama. Still unable to use his legs, Lieutenant Peschau survived the plane ride to Japan, but succumbed to his injuries on June 8 after being denied medical attention. Stoddard, Hryskanich, and Manierre were more fortunate. All three survived to be liberated from prison camp fifteen months later.[11]

The May 29 photo mission over Saipan revealed a significant increase in the number of gun installations since February. "All available intelligence indicated the enemy was continuing his feverish defensive preparations," observed NTLF.[12] Photo interpreters noted an increase of thirty medium antiaircraft guns, seventy-one light antiaircraft cannon or machine guns, sixteen pillboxes, a dozen heavy antiaircraft guns, and other miscellaneous weapons.[13] Despite the buildup, U.S. intelligence did not believe the Japanese anticipated an immediate threat to the Marianas. That appraisal appeared vindicated when large numbers of naval air service personnel (there were no army air units at Saipan) and about half of the 420 aircraft on Saipan, Tinian, and Guam were pulled out during May and early June to counter U.S. landings on Biak island northwest of New Guinea.[14]

Unfortunately, U.S. intelligence was seriously wrong in another assessment: planners had grossly underestimated the number of Japanese troops on Saipan. As of March, intelligence estimates put Japanese troop strength in the Saipan-Tinian area at between 5,500 and 6,500 men. That estimate was revised upward in early May to 9,000 to 10,000 combat troops on Saipan when considerable shipping in Tanapag Harbor suggested an influx of reinforcements. An intelligence summary toward the end of the month warned that if the enemy "continues his present rate of enforcement, it seems logical to estimate that by D-day combat troops will number 15,000 to 18,000."[15] As it turned out, even that higher figure was woefully short of the actual Japanese troop strength on Saipan. The total was somewhere around 30,000 or 31,000 men, including about 25,000 army troops and over 6,000 naval personnel, nearly double the lower estimate proffered by U.S. intelligence.[16]

The main units were General Saito's *43rd Division* and the *47th Independent Mixed Brigade*, commanded by Col. Yoshira Oka. Numbering 2,500 men, Oka's brigade consisted of the *316th, 317th,* and *318th Independent Infantry Battalions*, along with three artillery battalions and an engineer company. A menagerie of other forces was also available, some the result of the Japanese penchant to form oddball specialized units and others stranded on Saipan by ship sinkings. Among them were 1,500 men of the *9th Expeditionary Unit*, which was originally bound for Yap; the *15th Infantry Regiment*, originally destined for the Palaus; the *150th Infantry Regiment*; the *1st Battalion* of the *18th Infantry Regiment*; and about 120 survivors of the *3rd* and *4th Independent Tank Companies* who also arrived in disarray, courtesy of the American submarine service.[17]

Principal Japanese naval units included the *55th Naval Guard Force*, *5th Special Base Force*, and the *1st Yokosuka Special Naval Landing Force*, which was made up of paratroopers. The *55th Naval Guard Force* manned coastal defense guns. The *1st Yokosuka Naval Special Landing Force*, numbering 800 men, manned the Flores Point naval base where Admiral Nagumo had established his headquarters. They were joined by the 400-man *41st Naval Guard Force*, which had originally been bound for Truk. There were also various naval construction, supply, communications, transportation, and administrative units present for a total of about 6,200 personnel.

While lacking building materials, the Japanese had plenty of artillery, including a number of large-caliber coastal guns. Units included the *3rd Independent Mountain Artillery Regiment* with six batteries of 75mm guns; the *3rd Battalion, 10th Field Artillery Regiment*, with one battery of eight 75mm guns and two batteries with fourteen howitzers; and the *9th Field Heavy Regiment* with twelve 150mm howitzers and thirty 75mm mountain guns. All told there were about sixty-five artillery pieces preregistered on potential landing beaches.[18]

For the first time in the war, U.S. troops would also face Japanese tanks in substantial—and unanticipated—numbers. Though two tanks had been spotted in aerial photographs, U.S. intelligence did not believe there were significant armored forces on the island.[19] Intelligence was wrong. Post-battle estimates would put the overall number of Japanese tanks at about a hundred, though the actual number was probably closer to eighty and possibly even less.[20] The largest single organization was the *9th Tank Regiment*, commanded by Col. Takashi Goto, which had arrived in the Marianas in April. Three and a half companies were assigned to Saipan with thirty-six Type 97 medium tanks and twelve Type 95 light tanks. Naval Special Landing Force troops on Saipan also had some tanks, including a handful of Type 2 Ka-Mi amphibious tanks featuring detachable pontoons.

General Obata recognized that any amphibious assault would likely come either at Magicienne Bay on the eastern side of Saipan or over the narrow beaches on the southwestern coast. He was especially concerned with Magicienne Bay and assigned high priority to defense of this area. Defense works included trenches, a blockhouse, and artillery and machine-gun emplacements along the beach and burrowed into the hills just behind. However, he also paid close attention to the southwestern beaches where the Marines actually intended to land. The coast from Flores Point south to Agingan Point bristled with artillery, machine-gun positions, pillboxes, and entrenchments. Agingan Point concealed a battery of two 6-inch Whitworth-Armstrong, Model 18 guns set in casements. Each of these big guns could hurl a 100-pound shell 5½ miles. Farther up the coast, Afetna Point, jutting out on what would be the right flank of the 2nd Marine Division during the landing, had been transformed into a mini fortress with 37mm guns in pillboxes, 20mm guns, machine guns, and even howitzers set to place plunging fire on boats attempting to cross the reef. Every man was expected to do his utmost to stop the Americans at the shoreline. "We must use our bodies to construct a bulwark in the Pacific," General Obata exhorted his troops.[21]

The flaw in the Japanese plan was its reliance on a beach defense in an effort to repel the enemy at the water's edge. This tactic had been unavoidable on the small open atolls in the Marshalls and Gilberts, but Saipan's larger land mass and rugged interior provided the opportunity for a defense in depth—a defense much more likely to survive the heavy U.S. naval bombardment certain to pulverize the beach areas during an amphibious landing. The defense plan for the *1st Expeditionary Unit* (later *47th Independent Mixed Brigade*) dated May 10, 1944, reflected a failure to adapt tactics to that battlefield reality:

> It is expected that the enemy will be destroyed on the beaches through a policy of tactical command based on aggressiveness, determination, and initiative.
>
> When the enemy elements are attempting to land: The main firepower will be directed at the enemy landing forces prior to their arrival on the beach. Taking advantage of the confusion, the enemy will be rapidly destroyed by counter-attacks, mounted from all sectors wherever the opportunity presents itself.
>
> Should the enemy succeed in getting a foothold on the beach, intense fire will be concentrated and determined counter-attacks launched with the aid of reserves and tanks. Although the advantages of surprise will be lost, the enemy landing forces can be dealt with by further attacks after nightfall.[22]

Further lines of defense would be constructed behind the outer shell "if time allows," noted *31st Army*, "strongly built and also completely equipped for counter-attack." The overall "position in depth" would convert the island "into an invulnerable fortress."[23] The problem was time. Arriving with the

43rd Division, Maj. Takashi Hirakushi estimated it would take at least six months before the defense would be fully in place. Japanese planners initially thought they would have until November to prepare. It was a fatal miscalculation. The American landing would catch the Japanese with more guns in storage or yet to be fully installed than were operational. Concrete gun emplacements stood empty or unfinished; mines that would have impeded access to the beaches remained in storage or rested on the seabed in the holds of sunken ships, along with the barbed wire needed to block attacking infantry.

A Japanese POW later said that if the American assault had come three months later, "the island would have been impregnable."[24] But time was a luxury the Japanese did not enjoy. "We had a concept of what the plan should be, but before we could put it into effect, the attack came," said Major Hirakushi.[25]

Under the brilliant blue bowl of the Pacific sky, the various elements of the invasion fleet carrying over 70,000 officers and men of Holland Smith's Northern Troops and Landing Force plodded westward toward their staging area at Eniwetok 2,370 nautical miles from Hawaii. "Our platoon was on LST 484 and in a very large convoy of ships, as far as the eye could see in all directions," recalled Robert W. Wollin, a member of the 2nd Armored Amphibian Battalion. The fast transports were crowded, but nowhere near as cramped or uncomfortable as the slow-moving LSTs, unaffectionately referred to as "floating bathtubs," "Large Slow Targets," or "sea-going coffins" and now crammed with men and equipment and reeking of gasoline. "It seemed that every square foot had a Marine in it or as part of it," remarked Wollin.[26]

"They had bunking facilities, but there was only room for about a third of the guys down there," observed Pvt. Albert G. Sutcliffe. "And anyway . . . it was so damn hot. So we all slept on the deck. You couldn't walk across the deck at night as guys were sleeping on that hard iron deck all night long."[27] It was only marginally better aboard the transports. "Down in the troop compartments, the bunks were white canvas stretched tightly and lashed onto metal tubes," remembered PFC Rick Spooner. "The men slept six high on bunks that were only two feet above one another."[28]

Mike Masters recalled, "We did everything standing up: waiting in chow lines, eating at the narrow tables, and waiting to stand at the troughs of the heads."[29] There were cold saltwater showers with poorly lathering soap. Cool fresh water was available from the scuttlebutts—a convenience that would soon be remembered "with great yearning and desire," observed PFC Rick Spooner.[30] Haircuts were popular. "Quite a few of the fellows had all their head shaved," recalled Chaplain Goe of the 4th Marine Division troops. "Others left a two-inch strip of hair from the front to the back of their heads and had the rest of it shaved off. We called them Mohawks. Some had an initial in their hair, with the rest shaved; and plenty of freakish-looking heads were observed."[31]

Army sergeant John Domanowski spent a lot of time at the rail watching dolphins. "They were with us for days. I thought a lot about my family, and hoped they wouldn't worry too much," he remembered. Morale in his infantry company was high—it went even higher when their captain told them their destination "had a half mile of Geisha houses."[32]

Once at sea, the men were told of their destination and the briefings began. Three-dimensional rubber mock-ups of the island were pulled out to better demonstrate general terrain features. "Every day we were briefed on what to expect," recalled PFC S. G. Silcox. "We went over and over the maps and listened to lectures of how many Japanese troops were there, how many Chamorros civilians there were and even about their religion."[33]

The landing area covered a 6,000-yard front extending from about a mile south of Garapan down through Charan Kanoa, marked by the tall smokestack over the sugar refinery, to Agingan Point. The 2nd and 4th Marine Divisions would land abreast—the 2nd on the left and the 4th on the right. "At the shoreline is a sandy beach in rear of which is comparatively level ground rising to a ridge about 200 feet high about 1500 yards inland which overlooks the beach," observed the NTLF operations report.[34]

The ridge was designated as the first objective line or O-1. Until it was taken, the Japanese would be looking down the landing force's throat. D-day was June 15. H-hour was set for 0830.[35] A contingency plan was also in place: If it turned out that the designated beaches were too strongly defended to permit landings, the 2nd Marine Division would land on Black Beach north of Garapan, followed three hours later by the 4th Marine Division, which would land on Scarlet Beaches in Tanapag Harbor.[36]

Key to getting ashore were the ungainly, boxlike amphibious tractors—the LVTs—that would carry the Marines over the wide fringing reef which ranged from 800 to 1,200 yards off the beaches. Just over 700 amtracs had been allotted to NTLF. Powered by seven-cylinder radial aircraft engines, the tractors were 26 feet long and nearly 11 feet wide. They were capable of speeds of about 20 mph on land and 7.5 mph on water and could carry between eighteen and twenty-four combat-loaded men. Grousers on the tracks propelled the vehicle through the water, while the tracks themselves enabled the tractor to climb up and over the reef or proceed on dry ground. If the Japanese hoped Saipan's reef would protect them, they were in for an unpleasant surprise.

Of the 719 amphibious vehicles participating in the operation, 367 would be furnished and crewed by the Army. The 2nd Marine Division was allotted the 2nd, 5th, and 715th Amphibian Tractor Battalions, the latter being a U.S. Army unit. The 4th Division was assigned the 534th and 773rd Amphibian Tractor Battalions (both Army) and the 10th Amphibian Tractor Battalion (less Company A) and Company C of the 11th Amphibian Tractor Battalion.[37]

The first wave of troop-carrying amtracs would be preceded by armored amphibian tractors—LVT(A)s or "amtanks"—each armed with machine guns and either a 37mm gun or a snub-nosed 75mm gun in a forward turret. Weighing about 16 tons, the LVT(A)s carried a crew of six. Though only lightly armored, the amtanks would provide immediate gun support as the Marines came ashore. The 2nd Armored Amphibian Battalion would lead the way for the 2nd Marine Division, while the Army's 708th Amphibian Tank Battalion would precede the 4th Marine Division LVTs. In an effort to capitalize on the effects of shock and mass, the waves of LVTs were to swarm ashore in rapid succession. "An interval of two minutes between waves 1 and 2, and intervals of five minutes between succeeding waves of assault troops should produce the desired effect," observed the operation plan.[38]

Holland Smith's chief of staff, Brig. Gen. Graves B. "Bobby" Erskine, who was recognized throughout the Marine Corps as an expert in operational and tactical planning, hoped to exploit the impact of shock and mass even further. He proposed that the first two waves of troop-carrying LVT waves—preceded by the armored amtracs—surge forward with their passengers all the way to the O-1 line roughly three-quarters of a mile inland. By punching deep instead of stopping to unload at the beach, this amphibious blitzkrieg would disorganize the enemy defense and quickly establish a larger and more secure beachhead. "I wanted to go ashore and run as far as possible in the amtracs," Erskine explained later. "You saved a hell of a lot of time, and if you could get beyond their machine gun defenses, it should be easier to continue."[39] If the maneuver succeeded, the 4th Marine Division could potentially launch still another LVT-mounted assault on Aslito Airfield later in the day.

The 4th Marine Division incorporated Erskine's mechanized charge into its landing plan, but 2nd Marine Division commander Tommy Watson balked. Despite Erskine's forbidding reputation—the chief of staff was described as "a relentless, brooding, brilliant officer with . . . an abrupt manner that cowed the timid and irritated the strong"[40]—Watson had serious doubts about the tactical soundness of riding the lumbering amtracs so far inland, and he was not afraid to voice those concerns to Gen. Holland Smith. Watson saw three significant problems with Erskine's plan: First, he felt the terrain in his landing area offered too many obstacles to a mechanized thrust inland; second, leaving the troops isolated aboard the LVTs any longer than necessary would prolong a lack of unit control; and third, the troop-filled tractors were too vulnerable a target, particularly with their high profile once they emerged from the water. A hit through the thin sides of the LVTs would wreak havoc on the men packed inside.

Watson persuaded Smith to let him modify the plan for his division. Instead of pushing all the way to the O-1 line as Erskine proposed, the armored LVTs would proceed inland 300 yards to the Tractor Control Line, marked by the sugar cane railway running parallel to the shore, where they would provide covering fire for the landing. The first wave of troop-carrying LVTs would follow them and discharge troops beyond the beach area. All succeeding waves would debark on the beaches. It was well short of Erskine's amphibious blitzkrieg, but subsequent events would prove Watson's concerns to be well founded.[41]

The Marines had been at sea for a week when the outside world intervened. "[A] surprise bulletin came over the ship's PA system," recalled Mike Masters. "*The Allies have landed at Normandy . . . Heavy fighting.* There was a short cheer throughout the ship, then dead silence. It was strange . . . We were pleased to hear that the Allies were on the move in Europe, but then we had second thoughts. We still had the Japs to take care of in the Pacific."[42] Recalled PFC Joseph G. Clifford, "The radio said the invasion of Europe had started at Normandy, please everyone pray for them. . . ." Presumably echoing the sentiments of more than a few Marines, Clifford remarked, "If I'm going to pray for anyone, it will be us."[43]

G. Milton Shirley, a member of the 2nd Armored Amphibian Battalion, didn't fully understand that prayer might be in order until he wandered into a room where an officer was briefing his men on the coming invasion. "He had a model of Saipan Island on a table," recalled Shirley. As Shirley looked on, the officer remarked, "Now this operation is going to be spearheaded by the 2nd Armored Amphibian Battalion. God help them poor devils."[44]

A man in Harry Pearce's rifle outfit decided not to trust to luck or God. A division boxer who was much admired by the other men, this individual began worrying about the coming battle, recalled Pearce. One night he managed to accidentally "throw himself" down a metal ladder. The fall dislocated his shoulder and broke his arm, taking him out of combat, observed Pearce, who was convinced there was nothing accidental about the incident.[45]

Sgt. Maj. Howard O. Culpepper in the 2nd Marine Division's Headquarters Battalion found himself with the opposite situation. A day or so after their ship sailed from Hawaii, twenty-one-year-old Sgt. Pete Grennan—a "very Irish" kid from Brooklyn, New York—emerged from the hold, "sheepish but grinning," having gone AWOL from the naval hospital where he had been confined with some undetermined malady. Determined not to be left out of the division's next battle, he had sneaked out of the hospital and stowed away aboard ship. The battalion CO was ready to throw the book at Grennan—no one knew what sort of illness he was suffering from or if it might be contagious, and it was impossible to break radio silence to contact Hawaii and find out.

The CO decided to put the youngster ashore at Eniwetok for transfer back to Hawaii for court-martial. Grennan protested vigorously. The war was passing him by and he had to get into it. "I can't go back home and say I was a Marine who never got into the war," he declared indignantly. Culpepper finally prevailed on the CO to relent and found Grennan a berth with the 1st Battalion, 8th Marines, though that outfit's sergeant major was openly skeptical of the mental capacity of a man who would voluntarily trade the safety of a naval hospital for the uncertainties of combat. Nevertheless, he took the youngster and Grennan spent the rest of the voyage profusely thanking Culpepper for his intervention and letting him "get into the war."[46]

Among the thousands of Marines heading for battle were several hundred men—members of the 1st Battalion, 2nd Marines—who had already escaped almost certain death.

Forager planners had given the battalion what in retrospect can only be considered as a suicide mission. They were directed to "land on the night of D minus one-D day, on selected beaches of Magicienne Bay, move rapidly inland, seize Mt. Tapotchau before daylight and defend same until relieved."[47] If successful, this bold gambit to seize the highest ground on Saipan would deprive the enemy of a key observation point overlooking the beaches, or so the creators of the scheme postulated.

Arriving off the east coast on six fast destroyer transports (APDs), the battalion, accompanied by Company A from the VAC Amphibious Reconnaissance Battalion, would board rubber boats on D minus 1. The rubber boats would be towed by landing craft to within about 50 yards of the beach at Magicienne Bay and the Marines would then paddle ashore. The amphibious reconnaissance company would precede the battalion by one hour to mark and locate the beach and secure a shallow beachhead until the follow-up force landed. The combined group would then head for the summit of Mount Tapotchau over 3 miles to the northwest. Since speed was critical, the Marines would bring no weapons heavier than 60mm mortars. Once the men were in place on Mount Tapotchau, their heavier equipment and supplies would be parachuted to them from torpedo planes.

Like the plan to push troop-carrying tractors through enemy defenses on D-day, the Mount Tapotchau scheme originated with Graves Erskine. Years later, Erskine would claim the proposal was merely a cunning song and dance to pry shipping out of the Navy for an additional battalion; there was no intention of carrying through.[48] However, if it was a charade, no one else seemed to be aware of it.

Battalion commander Lt. Col. Wood B. Kyle conceded that the assignment "came as somewhat of a shock."[49] Corp. Gene Adkins, a member of the amphibious reconnaissance company, recalled being advised by their executive officer that his platoon, which would bring up the rear of the climb up Mount Tapotchau, would probably have to fight off "the enraged hordes of Japanese" in pursuit. "I actually believed we could do it," remarked Adkins.[50] PFC Carl Conover was less sanguine. "It sounded like pure suicide to me," he admitted. Nevertheless, he added, "I would have gone over the side just like the rest of them if necessary."[51]

The scheme, which reflected a gross underestimation of Saipan's rugged central terrain and the strength of Japanese defenses at Magicienne Bay, was hotly debated at higher levels. Predicting disaster, the 2nd Marine Division staff recommended that the plan be cancelled. Lt. Col. Thomas J. Colley, the 2nd Division intelligence officer, flew to Pearl Harbor to make his case to the powers that be. Colley pointed out that aerial photographs, though "somewhat fuzzy," indicated that the Japanese had constructed strong defensive positions facing Magicienne Bay. Trying to paddle ashore in their rubber boats, Kyle's men would likely be slaughtered long before they got anywhere near Mount Tapotchau.

The Expeditionary Troops Operations Section shared Colley's skepticism. According to the section's Col. John C. McQueen, "The section firmly believed that Kyle's battalion would completely fail in its mission and also believed that those of the battalion who might successfully be landed would be wiped out before getting very far toward their objective ... To us the idea of this battalion successfully reaching the summit of Mt. Tapotchau before daylight, even from the viewpoint of terrain alone, seemed incredible."[52]

The reprieve, when it arrived, came from Holland Smith. On May 7 an order came down putting the Mount Tapotchau plan on hold. Kyle's battalion would remain under NTLF control as a ready reserve, to be committed if and when circumstances demanded. In a nod to the original plan, the battalion was directed to "be prepared after How-hour to land on order on selected beaches of Magicienne Bay, or on other beaches to be designated later."[53]

"We were greatly relieved when we learned . . . that the mission had been cancelled by General Smith," McQueen observed.[54] Those sentiments were echoed by Colonel Kyle, who later admitted, "We were quite happy that the thing was cancelled . . . If we'd gotten ashore at all, we probably would have gotten a ways in, but probably not very far."[55] As the author of the official Marine Corps monograph on Saipan was to conclude, war is full of risk, but "the exact point where gamble becomes foolhardy venture is sometimes difficult to determine."[56]

Over a period of days the invasion armada filtered into the vast lagoon at Eniwetok, gathering for the final 1,000-mile leg of the voyage to Saipan. The carriers and big guns of Task Force 58 left Majuro for the Marianas on June 6 in advance of the troopships. The assemblage of warships took almost five hours to clear the lagoon. A Japanese pilot snooping around the day before missed the sortie by a matter of hours.

TF 58 was commanded by fifty-seven-year-old Vice Adm. Marc A. "Pete" Mitscher—codenamed *Bald Eagle*—a pint-sized Oklahoman with outsized ability and a face so seamed by wind and sun that he looked like some sort of wizened seagoing elf— a man who spoke so softly his officers sometimes had to strain to hear him. Shaded by his trademark long-billed ball cap, he typically turned his swivel chair to face aft on the flag bridge because, it was said, he didn't like the wind in his face. He had a soft spot for his aviators and complete faith both in them and in the capabilities of the airpower at his command.

In the pyramid of command, Mitscher answered to Fifth Fleet commander Ray Spruance, but the task force answered to him. TF 58 was made up of four task groups, which allowed flexibility in assigning multiple missions. Each task group consisted of new battleships, cruisers, and destroyers built around a core of two to four carriers. Each Essex class carrier fielded an air group averaging ninety planes, consisting of a fighter squadron, a dive-bomber squadron, and a torpedo bomber squadron. Task Group 58.1 commanded by Rear Adm. J. J. "Jocko" Clark consisted of the carriers *Hornet*, *Yorktown*, *Belleau Wood*, and *Bataan* with four air groups totaling 267 planes. Rear Adm. Alfred E. Montgomery's TG 58.2 consisted of the carriers *Bunker Hill*, *Wasp*, *Monterey*, and *Cabot* with a total of 263 aircraft. TG 58.3 was led by John W. "Black Jack" Reeves Jr. and consisted of *Enterprise* (the legendary "Big E"), *Lexington*, *San Jacinto*, and *Princeton* with 228 planes. The smallest task group was TG 58.4, commanded by William H. "Keen" Harrill, with *Essex*, *Langley*, and *Cowpens* carrying a total of 163 planes. As perhaps the most lethal seagoing force in history, the task force had a dual mission: destroy the enemy and protect the invasion force. Admiral Mitscher would subsequently find that settling on which task should have priority could be a matter of disagreement.

CHAPTER V

Opening Moves

SUNDAY, JUNE 11, STARTED QUIETLY ON SAIPAN. THIRTEEN-YEAR-OLD
Pedro Arriola Tenorio was helping his grandfather with some chores. It was
about noontime. "There wasn't any breeze," he remembered. The calm was
suddenly interrupted by the distant shriek of sirens. Looking skyward, he
saw planes winging toward Aslito Field. Then he heard an explosion. The
planes were bombing the airfield.[1]

The arrival of U.S. planes over Saipan that afternoon marked a slight, but
eventful change of plan. Original plans called for the softening-up process
to begin at dawn on June 12. The dawn schedule was standard procedure,
but Admiral Mitscher suggested a last-minute change. He recommended
a fighter sweep over Saipan on the afternoon of the 11th, hoping it would
catch Japanese air defenses off guard.[2] Spruance concurred. At 0930 on June
11, Mitscher ordered the fighters to take off at 1300. "Cut their damned
throats," he messaged his Hellcat squadrons. "Wish I could be with you."[3]

Though a Japanese language expert aboard *Lexington* intercepted radio
traffic indicating the task force had been spotted, Mitscher went ahead and
launched 208 Hellcat fighters and eight torpedo bombers from about 225
miles off Saipan for the hour-long flight to the target.[4] Primary targets
included the airfields on Guam, Rota, Tinian, and Saipan. Task Groups
58.3 and 58.4 hit Saipan. The sixty fighters of TG 58.3 concentrated on
Aslito Field. *Enterprise*'s "Grim Reapers" harvested six Zekes (Mitsubishi
A6M2 fighters), a Betty (Mitsubishi G4M twin-engined bomber) and a
luckless Kawanishi four-engine flying boat that happened to venture onto
the scene and was sent down in flames. Watching from *43rd Division* Headquarters at Charan Kanoa, Japanese staff officers clapped excitedly at the
sight of flaming planes plummeting toward the earth. "We thought they
were U.S.," said Maj. Takashi Hirakushi. Their error became painfully clear
as a Hellcat winged over to strafe the headquarters area, shooting up part

of a communications unit and knocking out contact with Garapan.[5] The Japanese hastened to light smoke pots on the eastern shore and the prevailing breeze soon pushed the smoke across the island, obscuring Tanapag. U.S. pilots also reported radio interference as the enemy broke in on their frequencies with music, a woman's voice, and other chatter.[6]

Eighteen-year-old Shizuko Miura, an office worker with the Nanko Suisan fish cannery operation in Garapan, had just finished lunch when the air raid sirens began to wail. As antiaircraft guns banged away and her coworkers fled to the air raid shelter, Shizuko ran to a second-floor window and gazed skyward. Passing overhead were what seemed to be hundreds, even thousands, of planes. The building shook, windows rattling as bombs began to explode in the near distance. Flames and plumes of black smoke rose skyward in the area of the Navy Headquarters building. Antiaircraft fire seemed ineffectual as the enemy planes went about their deadly work.[7]

While it might not have been apparent to Shizuko, at least a few Japanese antiaircraft gunners demonstrated a lethal competence. Flying off *Lexington*, Hellcat pilot Lt. (j.g.) William E. Burckhalter, a former Colgate University wrestler and football player with six enemy planes to his credit, took a hit in the engine during a strafing run over Aslito Field. He made a smooth water landing about 6 miles off shore, but as he left the cockpit his parachute somehow deployed. Circling overhead, fellow pilots saw Burckhalter standing halfway out on the port wing with the parachute shrouds extending back into the cockpit as the Hellcat sank under the surface, dragging him to his death.[8] *Enterprise* lost two planes, but both pilots were picked up—one by a destroyer and the other by a float plane from USS *Indianapolis*.

Task Group 58.4, working over Tanapag Harbor and Marpi Point with thirty-nine fighters and two divebombers, suffered more heavily. Lt. (j.g.) Leo T. Kenney from the *Essex* was hit during his dive and never pulled out. Two planes from *Langley* were downed during the same strike. One pilot ditched and was picked up by a destroyer, the other was killed. Also lost was Ens. Paul A. Parker of Fighting 25. Flying off *Cowpens*, he disappeared after an encounter with some Zekes.

The afternoon strikes on Guam, Tinian, Saipan, and Rota cost the task force eleven Hellcats downed in combat. Six pilots were killed or unaccounted for. The fighter pilots claimed eighty-six enemy aircraft destroyed in the air, thirty-three destroyed on the ground, twenty-six probables, and seventy damaged. Ten of the kills had been chalked up by the Combat Air

Patrol over the Task Force.[9] While those numbers were almost certainly overblown, Mitscher's gambit had paid big dividends. Vice Adm. Kakuji Kakuta's land-based First Air Fleet had been badly hurt.

In an apparent effort to save face, Kakuta brazenly downplayed his losses. The Japanese claimed to have lost only thirty-six planes, while shooting down sixty-five U.S. aircraft. That pipe dream could not change the reality. And Japanese losses would only get worse as the softening-up process continued in succeeding days. Capt. Mitsuo Fuchida, air staff officer to the commander in chief *Combined Fleet*, later conceded, "On 11th, 12th and 13th [June], practically all of [our aircraft] were wiped out."[10]

In Garapan, Shizuko Miura, who had received rudimentary first-aid training as a member of the Young Women's Association, spent the afternoon assisting the injured brought to the air-raid shelter at her office building. Some buildings were on fire and the streets were full of smoke. The sun seemed a light brown behind the haze. As night fell, unable to sleep, Shizuko stepped outside to find the street full of soldiers. Some carried ammunition boxes on their shoulders; others pulled what appeared to be gun carriages. They passed silently by her, heading toward the shore.[11]

U.S. air attacks continued the next day, pounding away at enemy installations on Guam, Rota, Tinian, Pagan, and Saipan and shipping in the harbors and surrounding waters. Among the victims was a Japanese tanker caught by *Enterprise* Avengers 15 miles northwest of Saipan. Struck by two 500-pound bombs, the ship rolled over to port and quickly sank as white-clad Japanese sailors scrambled down the exposed sides and into the sea. A convoy fleeing 160 miles north-northwest of Saipan suffered a similar fate: Ten merchant ships were sunk, along with an Ootori class torpedo boat, three subchasers, and a handful of fishing boats.[12]

An Avenger crew from Torpedo Squadron 10 (VT-10) flying off the *Enterprise* had a scare when their so-called "flying pig" took two antiaircraft hits over Saipan—one smashed the flaps on the starboard wing, while the other blew off the portside horizontal stabilizer and elevator. Thinking they were going down, pilot Ernie Lawton radioed his two crewmen to bail out. He rescinded that order seconds later as he regained control, but radioman Jim Geyton had unplugged his headset in the scramble and was already going out the hatch. Turret gunner George Hamilton reached for Geyton at the last second. "I grabbed him and pulled him back in, damn near went out with him," said Hamilton. Lawton got the badly damaged aircraft back to

Enterprise, "relying more on ballistics than aeronautics," recalled Hamilton. "Ernie got the Distinguished Flying Cross for that—Jimmy and I got a change of shorts."[13]

Also from VT-10, thirty-four-year-old squadron commander William I. Martin could see gunfire winking at him as his TBF Avenger nosed into a dive by the radio towers off the northern end of the Charan Kanoa airstrip. At 3,500 feet, Martin pressed the electric bomb release and was pulling the backup manual release when something slammed into the plane with "a teeth-shattering jolt." As the aircraft tumbled, he found himself on his back. "I knew we were crashing," he said. "I felt a heat wave go past me and thought the plane was in flames."

Flying off Martin's wing, Avenger pilot Gibby Blake watched in horror as his skipper's aircraft came apart. "His plane did a tumbling act with his whole tail section blown off," reported Blake. Martin groped for the microphone to tell Aviation Radioman 1st Class Jerry T. Williams and Aviation Ordnanceman 2nd Class Wesley R. Hargrove to jump, but couldn't find it as the plane plunged toward the lagoon. It probably didn't matter. A 5-inch shell had hit behind the cockpit, cutting the aircraft in half. On a count of one, Martin released his safety belt; on two, he pulled the rip cord on his parachute; on three, he felt the chute take up the slack on his harness. Before he could count four, he slammed into the water.

Martin had bailed out at about 3,000 feet. His parachute had opened, but ripped under the strain, so instead of floating gently down, he plummeted toward the lagoon. The damaged parachute and low altitude probably saved his life, as Japanese gunners on shore lost the opportunity to riddle him at leisure as he hung in the air. He plunged into only 4 feet of water, hitting bottom with a stunning impact. Opening his eyes, he found himself sitting in soft sand, still miraculously alive despite a badly bruised hip. "I was about 300 yards off the beach in a reef encircled lagoon near the airstrip," he recalled. Japanese soldiers were clearly visible on the beach, cheering the destruction of his plane. What was left of the Avenger had crashed into the water nearby and was burning with an intense heat. Parts of the tail were still splashing into the lagoon. No other parachutes were in sight. Neither Williams nor Hargrove had managed to get out.

As rifle fire from shore peppered the water around him, Martin ducked below the surface and began working his way toward the reef about a thousand yards away, towing his seat-pack with his emergency raft and clutching his soggy parachute under one arm, popping up only when his lungs ached for air. As two boats headed toward him, he redoubled his efforts to get out to the reef, but when he looked again, the boats had disappeared, apparently discouraged by U.S. planes.

Nearing exhaustion, he finally reached the reef and paused to rest in the foot and a half of water washing over the coral. He saw that he was opposite the 2nd Marine Division landing beaches north of Charan Kanoa and tried to pick out enemy positions and memorize details to report to intelligence in the event he managed to escape his predicament. "It was hard to keep from thinking of Williams and Hargrove," he admitted. "They had been flying with me since the summer of 1942. They were just like brothers to me."

When a couple of 20mm bursts from the shore came uncomfortably close, Martin got moving again, picking up his raft and chute and stumbling across the reef toward the breakers on the outer edge. He plunged into the breakers and inflated his life jacket. An American airstrike momentarily distracted his tormentors on shore, so he inflated his yellow raft and clambered in. "[It] took some time to get into it," he remembered; "I swallowed much sea water so I was nauseated (it acts as a laxative too). I was throwing up and also had diarrhea suddenly, and cramps."

Drifting seaward as shells from U.S. battleships chugged overhead like lethal freight trains, he rigged up his parachute as a sail and cruised out toward the fire support area. His voyage ended at about 1130 when a little Curtiss SOC Seagull floatplane from the cruiser *Indianapolis* splashed down nearby and taxied up to the raft. "Come on, Commander!" exclaimed the anxious Seagull pilot as Martin started to pull his gear aboard. "We've got to go!" Martin shortly found himself face to face with Admiral Spruance reporting what he had seen along the shoreline, including enemy positions, the depth of the water, lack of underwater obstacles, length of reef, and the height of the surf. Martin's observations were sent out by dispatch, including his report that the reef was dotted with "white or red pennants" at roughly 300-yard intervals.[14]

While Martin survived, *Lexington* lost one of her squadron commanders over Aslito Airfield that afternoon. A handful of Avengers in *Lexington's* Air Group 16 had been experimentally armed with rockets with the idea that pilots could knock out enemy positions with more accuracy. The flyers were skeptical; the Avengers were not especially fast or agile and the rocket fittings did not improve the plane's flying characteristics. Nevertheless, during the afternoon thirty-four-year-old Lt. Cmdr. Robert H. Isely led the rocket-carrying Avengers into the air. "Most of us really wanted to get off as lightly as possible, but the Skipper always wanted the heaviest assignments," observed fellow pilot Fred Gwynn.[15]

The pilots made their runs on the airfield in shallow glides. Isely's plane was leading with two others behind when his Avenger was hit by antiaircraft fire at about 4,000 feet. The aircraft burst into flames and exploded at the southern end of the airfield. Neither Isely nor his two crewmen—Lt. (j.g.) Paul Dana and Airman 1st Class J. E. Carey—had time to get out. Another Avenger took a hit in the bomb bay but managed to limp back to *Lexington*.[16]

Also lost from Isely's VT-16 that morning was Lt. Frank M. Delgado and his crew. Delgado dropped his bomb on the aircraft shop area north of Aslito Field, but was hit by antiaircraft fire during the pullout. All three men bailed out as the ship burst into flames, rolled over on its back, and plunged into the water just offshore. All parachutes opened. The first crewman went down on land south of the airfield; the second landed in shallow water about a hundred yards off the beach. Delgado was descending over the water just to the south when Japanese machine gunners on shore opened up on him. His parachute collapsed and he plunged some 400 feet into the sea. Neither he nor his two crewmen were ever found.[17]

Despite the inevitable losses, the campaign was getting off to a strong start. Mitscher fired off an enthusiastic dispatch to the approaching invasion force. "Keep coming, Marines," he messaged; "they're going to run away."[18] If anyone wondered where thousands of armed Japanese—who, incidentally, had never shown any inclination to flee a fight in the past—were going to run to on an island in the middle of the ocean, he kept it to himself.

The Japanese high command had been aware for nearly two weeks that the Americans were on the move—they just were not sure of the destination. Based at Tinian, Lt. Cmdr. Takehiko Chihaya of the *121st Naval Air Group* had led a reconnaissance mission to Majuro, 1,800 miles to the southeast, on June 4. Flying single-engine Nakajima C6N1 Saiun "Myrt" long-range reconnaissance planes, with a cruising speed of 210 knots and a range of 1,663 nautical miles, the mission refueled at Truk and Nauru, timing their arrival over the lagoon for the morning of June 5. Chihaya was stunned at the array below, reporting six Essex or Enterprise class carriers, eight converted carriers, six battleships, eight or more cruisers, sixteen or more destroyers, ten tankers, and a multitude of other vessels.[19]

"The exploits of these scout planes ascertained where the enemy was, but we could not guess where he would go," wrote Japanese *Combined Fleet* chief of staff Ryonosuke Kusaka. "To Saipan or Palau, it still remained uncertain."[20] The uncertainty intensified on June 9 when a follow-up reconnaissance flight found the Majuro anchorage virtually empty; only one transport ship and three destroyers were spotted.

Such was the confusion that when American planes appeared over Saipan on June 11, *31st Army* commander Hideyoshi Obata was absent on a tour of the Palau defenses. Gen. Yoshitsugu Saito, who had command in Obata's absence, initially saw no cause for panic. Such was his sangfroid that later that afternoon *43rd Division* Headquarters ordered construction of a new road between Aslito Airfield and the new field being built at Marpi Point. The general felt the main coastal roadway would be too exposed in the event of an attack. The new road would be located farther inland where it would be better protected.[21]

But as the air attacks continued the next day, General Saito's interest in road building waned. The magnitude of the air attacks and commencement of naval shelling persuaded him that an invasion was imminent. As thousands of air-dropped propaganda leaflets showered down on Garapan with instructions on how to surrender and warning civilians to stay off the roads, he became sure of it. General Obata boarded a plane in an effort to return to *31st Army* Headquarters, but could get no farther than Guam due to American air interdiction.

In Tokyo, *Combined Fleet* commander Adm. Soemu Toyoda learned of the U.S. strikes the morning of June 11. Having inherited the Z Plan following Admiral Koga's disappearance, Toyoda had tweaked some of the details—the revised document was now known as the A Operation or A-Go plan—but he remained fully committed to the concept of a decisive battle. However, as late as May 3 when the *Combined Fleet* issued *Secret Fleet Operations Order No. 76* there was little expectation that the battle would be joined in the Marianas. "It designated waters off the Palaus as one area for the decisive battle, the seas off the western Carolines as a second," recalled junior staff officer Minoru Nomura. "Under this plan, the enemy was expected to invade the islands of the western Carolines. As for the Marianas, only carrier-based air attacks were anticipated; no invasion was foreseen."[22] At least that was the desired scenario—what a Japanese naval officer described somewhat bitterly in hindsight as "wishful thinking."[23]

There was a hard reality behind this wishful thinking: lack of fuel. The Japanese navy simply didn't have enough processed fuel—or the tankers to carry it—to readily accept battle in the Marianas. This awkward topic came up during high-level meetings held on Saipan between May 8 and 13: What if, despite expectations, the Americans attacked the Marianas?[24] The answer was to rely on unprocessed fuel oil from the Borneo fields at Tarakan and Balipapan. Pure enough to be pumped directly into ships' bunkers, the unprocessed oil was volatile and contained impurities that could foul boilers, but Admiral Toyoda decided it was worth the risk. Using Tarakan oil would at least partially solve the navy's fuel shortage problem and allow his ships to fight in the Marianas should that be necessary.

The Japanese briefly thought the overall picture was coming into better focus when U.S. Army forces invaded Biak island, northwest of New Guinea, on May 27. Deciding that this was the anticipated attack, on June 3 Admiral Toyoda launched Operation *Kon* to recapture Biak and hopefully draw U.S. naval forces into the long-awaited decisive confrontation. In what proved to be a serious miscalculation, the Japanese pulled large numbers of aircraft from the Marianas to participate in the anticipated showdown.

The *Kon* operation was still getting underway in fits and starts when reports arrived on June 11 that Saipan was under heavy bombardment. Toyoda initially suspected the attacks were a diversion.[25] But as further reports arrived, the admiral grew increasingly concerned. At 1830 on June 12, following a report that U.S. transports were approaching Saipan, he ordered the *Mobile Fleet* to prepare to execute the A-Go plan.

Back on Saipan, the garrison was preparing for invasion. Major Hirakushi made his way to Garapan to give a situation report to *31st Army* chief of staff Gen. Keiji Igeta. Fires burned in Garapan as he made his way to the concrete bunker housing *31st Army* Headquarters. General Igeta, whom Hirakushi considered more competent than Saito, his own division commander, said the U.S. landing could be expected soon and he depended on General Saito's forces to defend the south. On his return to Charan Kanoa, Hirakushi paused to chat with members of the *136th Infantry Regiment* dug in along the southwestern beaches. He was pleased at the state of their morale. "I detected no signs of defeatism," he recalled. He too was optimistic, despite the ferocity of the preparatory bombardment, that they would be able to throw any landing back into the sea.[26]

As Admiral Toyoda contemplated American intentions, the *First Mobile Fleet* left its anchorage at Tawi-Tawi the morning of June 13 and headed into the Sulu Sea. Commanded by Adm. Jisaburo Ozawa, the fleet was to be the cutting edge of A-Go. It included Ozawa's newly commissioned flagship, the massive carrier *Taiho*; fleet carriers *Shokaku* and *Zuikaku*, both veterans of the Pearl Harbor attack; medium carriers *Hiyo* and *Junyo*, veterans of the Aleutians campaign; and light carriers *Zuiho*, *Ryjo*, *Chitose*, and *Chiyoda*. The carriers would be joined east of the Philippines by Adm. Matome Ugaki's battleship force, which included the super battleships *Yamato* and *Musashi* with their massive 18.1-inch guns capable of firing a 3,000-pound shell 26 miles. These behemoths would be accompanied by three more conventional battleships, ten cruisers, and about fourteen destroyers.

The admiral in charge of this potent assemblage, fifty-seven-year-old Jisaburo Ozawa, stood 2 meters tall, quite large for a Japanese, and was said to be one of the homeliest admirals in the navy—his nickname was "The Gargoyle." More importantly, he was also acknowledged to possess one of the sharpest intellects. Following graduation from the Naval Academy in 1909, he had commanded everything from destroyers to battleships and served as Combined Chief of Staff from 1937 to 1938. A torpedo expert, he was also knowledgeable about naval aviation and had been among the farsighted officers who supported the then-innovative idea of building a striking force around carriers.

After the Japanese defeat at Midway, Ozawa had replaced Adm. Chuichi Nagumo as commander of the *Third Fleet*, which included most of the navy's carriers. He promptly integrated his battleships and cruisers into his carrier groups, imitating the American model. In March he was named to lead the newly organized *First Mobile Fleet*. "Ozawa was probably one of the most courageous officers in the Imperial Navy," observed one of his carrier commanders. "He . . . interpreted Horatio Nelson in terms of the Samurai code and lived accordingly."[27] Now, the hopes of a nation rode on his shoulders. As *Combined Fleet* chief of staff Kusaka observed, all fervently believed in A-Go and "a triumph of the battle would without fail reverse dramatically our situation."[28]

Unfortunately for Ozawa, A-Go got off to a less than auspicious start. It had been hoped to leave Tawi-Tawi in secret, but the *Mobile Fleet*'s departure did not go unnoticed. Lurking nearby, the submarine USS *Redfin*, skippered by Lt. Cmdr. Marshall H. Austin, observed two heavy cruisers, four destroyers, and a torpedo boat at 0616, followed an hour and a half later by more ships. As the main body steamed past the sub at 0900, Austin counted six carriers, four battleships, five heavy cruisers, one light cruiser, and two destroyers. "All carriers had about one-half of their flight deck filled with planes," he reported later. Unable to get into position for an attack, though a battleship passed within about 4,500 yards, *Redfin* finally lost contact at 1055. Nine hours later, under cover of darkness, the sub surfaced and transmitted a contact report to home base.[29]

Redfin's report found its way to Admiral Spruance aboard the cruiser *Indianapolis* that same night. Cerebral, cautious, and remote, Spruance had won a great victory at Midway two years before. Now, the fifty-seven-year-old admiral—he was three months older than his Japanese counterpart—was about to face another great challenge . . . and opportunity. Judging from the reported heading, it appeared the Japanese fleet was bound for Saipan. In the planning for *Forager* it had been anticipated—even hoped—that the Japanese might commit their fleet to battle, though some high-ranking naval officers had been skeptical. The Japanese had not sought a major fleet action for over a year and a half, and it was felt in some quarters that Toyoda would husband his strength to fight on better terms closer to home.[30] In fact, not only were the Japanese coming out to fight, they hoped to catch the Americans fully committed to the landing so there would "be no retreat for the enemy."[31]

Spruance, who liked to believe he had a superior grasp of the Japanese mindset, had a reasonably good picture of enemy intentions, courtesy of Col. James Cushing and his Filipino guerillas. Admiral Koga's Z Plan had arrived on the desk of Capt. Edwin T. Layton, Admiral Nimitz's fleet intelligence officer, at the beginning of June. Layton had mimeographed copies of the documents rushed by flying boat to every flag officer associated with *Forager*. Spruance had received his copy on June 8.[32]

Now, as Spruance prepared for the Saipan landings, an intelligence bulletin from Admiral Nimitz arrived. Based on sub sightings, radio traffic, and a "meager amount of cryptoanalysis," the bulletin opined that the Japanese were gathering to contest *Forager*. The evidence indicated that the Z Plan was "in general effect with slight modifications." U.S. intelligence estimated that the enemy force consisted of six battleships and nine carriers, with attendant cruisers and destroyers. Based on speed and refueling, it appeared Admiral Ozawa could not be in position to threaten U.S. naval forces off Saipan before D plus 2 at the earliest. The bulletin warned of the possibility of "surprise from flank," adding, "In estimating enemy capabilities it may be well to consider possibility his launching [aircraft] at extreme range to land in Marianas after attack.[33]

With at least a four-day window before Ozawa's arrival, Spruance arranged for increased reconnaissance and moved forward with the more immediate task at hand: putting over 40,000 Marines on a hostile shore.

Cowering in a trench behind Oleai Beach where the 2nd Marine Division was scheduled to land in less than four days, Sgt. Takeo Yamauchi survived the June 11 carrier raid but was greatly shaken. When the planes finally broke off the attack that afternoon, large parts of the surrounding hillsides had been burned black and the island was thick with smoke. A dozen or so naval defense planes took to the air to meet the Americans, but were quickly shot down. "I actually saw them falling," Yamauchi recalled. "After that, no Japanese planes flew over Saipan."[34]

The American planes returned the following morning, strafing ammunition dumps and anything else that caught their attention. Choking clouds of smoke rose over the island as planes dropped incendiaries on the cane fields behind the beaches on the southwest shore to deprive the defenders of concealment. "We tried to shoot at American planes with our rifles," remembered Yamauchi. "Not many Japanese antiaircraft guns remained. I saw a few American planes explode in midair, but there was no effective fire from the ground anymore."[35] Tokuzo Matsuya, a member of the *9th Tank Regiment*, lamented in his diary: "The enemy holds us in utter contempt. If only we had a hundred planes or so."[36]

Worse was to come. Surface ships of TF 58 began to work over Saipan on June 13. Sergeant Yamauchi would remember that day the rest of his life. "I was eating a large rice ball," he recalled, "when I heard someone call out, 'The American battle fleet is here!' I looked up and the sea was completely black with them. What looked like a large city had suddenly appeared offshore. When I first saw that, I didn't even have the strength to stand up."[37]

The task force boasted seven new (fast) battleships: *Alabama, South Dakota, Indiana, New Jersey, Iowa, Washington*, and *North Carolina*. They pounded away with their big guns for seven hours, leveling above-ground installations and rearranging the landscape. "The area I was in was pitted like the craters of the moon," recalled Yamauchi. "We just clung to the earth in our shallow trenches. We were half buried. Soil filled my mouth many times. Blinded me. The fumes and flying dirt almost choked you."[38] By late in the day, thousands of shells had been directed at the island. The USS *Washington* alone fired 360 rounds of high-capacity 16-inch and 2,164 5-inch shells. "We in the Supply Office figured that every time a 16-inch shell was fired it was just about the price of a good new car," observed Storekeeper Gerard Thibodeau.[39] Aboard the light cruiser *Montpelier*, bluejacket James J. Fahey noted in his diary, "Thick smoke miles high was all over the island. I never saw anything like it before, it was like the great Chicago fire."[40]

As naval gunfire descended on Charan Kanoa, General Saito decided it would be expedient to vacate his headquarters, located in a wooden schoolhouse on the south side of town. It was also becoming apparent that the Americans intended to land over the island's southwestern beaches, which was likely to put him directly in harm's way. Gathering his staff the night of June 13, the general climbed into a dark green Ford sedan captured from the Americans in the Philippines and moved inland to a cave located northwest of Hill 500.[41]

While terrifying, the initial naval bombardment had its limitations. The seven fast battleships conducting the softening-up were required to remain well off shore due to concerns about counter fire from Japanese shore batteries and the threat of mines in the unswept shoal area extending about 6 miles to the leeward of Saipan. Fires were delivered from ranges in excess of 10,000 yards, well beyond what was generally considered effective in shore bombardment. This handicap was compounded by novice air spotters who lacked the training and experience to pick out hidden positions. The highly visible sugar mill at Charan Kanoa was riddled with shot and shell though it was not serving any military purpose. Meanwhile, well-camouflaged gun emplacements, such as a 140mm battery on Nafutan Point and reinforced concrete blockhouses on the southern beaches and at Magicienne Bay, went unnoticed and untouched.[42]

The effectiveness of the naval bombardment improved on June 14 with the arrival of the fire support ships of the Northern and Southern Attack Forces under command of Rear Adm. Jesse B. Oldendorf. These crews had been specifically trained in the patient adjustment required to destroy land fortifications, and they packed a powerful punch. The battleships included *Maryland* and *Colorado*, each with eight 16-inch guns, and *Pennsylvania*, *Tennessee*, *California*, *New Mexico*, *Mississippi*, and *Idaho* with twelve 14-inch guns each. Also available were six heavy cruisers with nine 8-inch guns each; five light cruisers with twelve or fifteen 6-inch guns; and about twenty-six destroyers with 5-inch guns.

Huddled in an air raid shelter in Garapan, the earth trembling under the bombardment, Shizuko Miura prepared herself for death. There were thirty-four people crammed into the shelter, including twenty wounded.

The occupants included two dead soldiers, one shot through the back and the other in the head by a strafing plane the day before. Shizuko, who was sitting near the two corpses, noticed they had begun to stink. She found a blanket and covered the bodies, but to no avail. The naval bombardment continued, even more violently. She resolved that the time to die had come. She was somewhat surprised to find that she was not afraid.[43]

A Japanese soldier wrote in his diary, "I have at last come to the place where I will die. I am pleased to think that I will die calmly in true samurai style. Naval gunfire supported this attack which was too terrible for words. Towards evening the firing died down but at night naval gunfire continued as before."[44] A Japanese officer confessed to his diary that he resorted to the bottle to calm his nerves. "I quietly opened the quart I brought along," he wrote, "and took my first 'shot' from it. There is something indescribable about a shot of liquor during a bombardment."[45] A twenty-four-year-old Japanese corporal named Takayoshi Igata was less sanguine. He was so scared during the bombardment that his "testicles shrunk," he confessed.[46]

Japanese shore battery gunners took what vengeance they could as the opportunity arose. The U.S. support group shelling nearby Tinian was taken under fire by enemy shore batteries. The gunners hit the battleship *California* (one dead, nine wounded) and the destroyer *Blaine* (three killed, fifteen wounded). The next day another battery on Tinian hit a 5-inch gun mount on *Tennessee*, killing eight men and wounding twenty-six. At Saipan, the battleship *Pennsylvania* spent approximately eight hours shelling the Nafutan Point and vicinity. Almost as soon as the ship ceased fire, an enemy shore battery opened up on the cruiser *Montpelier*. The *Montpelier* escaped unscathed, but the incident served as a sobering reminder that even the most methodical approach to shore bombardment offered no guarantees.[47]

Lt. Cmdr. Draper Kauffman's first look at Saipan came from the deck of the destroyer transport *Gilmore* in the early morning hours of June 14. The island loomed lush and green in the distance, the hillsides dotted with the red blossoms of indigenous flame trees. A tall stack marked the location of the now shell-gutted sugar refinery at Charan Kanoa.

Commanding the Underwater Demolition Teams (UDTs) assigned to the operation, the forty-two-year-old Kauffman had a colorful history. A 1933 graduate of the Naval Academy, he had been denied a commission due to poor eyesight. Even his status as the son of an admiral could not salvage his chosen career. He went to work for a steamship line; after war broke out in Europe, he served in the American Volunteer Ambulance Corps and was taken prisoner by the Germans; then, upon his release, joined the British navy and ended up in a bomb disposal unit. Shortly before Pearl Harbor, the U.S. Navy belatedly decided it could use the services of an expert—albeit nearsighted—bomb disposal officer and Kauffman finally found himself in the uniform of his own country, tasked with organizing the Navy's Bomb Disposal School. In the convoluted logic of the military, "bomb disposal" somehow morphed into an assignment in mid-1943 to organize an underwater demolitions instruction course to train swimmers to destroy beach obstacles before amphibious landings. Wrangling ceaselessly for action, the nearsighted warrior finally found himself in command of the three UDT teams assigned to reconnoiter and clear the beaches at Saipan.

While he had been eager for combat, his chances of surviving the upcoming operation did not appear promising. In April, shortly after being named senior UDT officer for the operation, Kauffman was summoned to Pearl Harbor for a briefing with Adm. Kelly Turner, the hard-drinking, rough-tongued, but brilliant amphibious assault commander. Turner drew a rough outline of Saipan, indicating the reef and lagoon off the western beaches. "Now, the first and most important thing is reconnaissance to determine the depth of water," advised Turner. "I'm thinking of having you go in and reconnoiter around eight."

"Well Admiral," replied Kauffman, "it depends on the phase of the moon."

"Moon?" retorted Turner. "What in the hell has that got to do with it? Obviously by eight o'clock I mean 0800."

Kauffman was dubious. The teams had trained extensively for night operations, expecting to use darkness as concealment. It was Kauffman's considered opinion that Turner's insistence on a daytime reconnaissance would cost his UDTs 50 percent casualties. "I just don't see how you can do it in broad daylight," he objected.

"The main reason is you can see in the daytime and you can't see at night," replied Turner, ending the conversation.[48]

Three UDT teams—each numbering fourteen officers and eighty-six men—were designated for the Saipan operation. Minesweepers had swept the shelf off the western beaches and found nothing. Close-in inspection would fall to the frogmen the day before the landing. UDT 5 would examine the beaches to the north of Afetna Point where the 2nd Marine Division was to land. UDT 7 would survey the area to the south where the 4th

Marine Division was to come ashore. The third team, UDT 6, would be held in reserve.

The reconnaissance was scheduled for 0900. A 2-foot surf was washing across the reef as the two teams embarked in eight landing craft. Huddled in the boats, the swimmers looked like visitors from another planet. Each man was camouflaged blue and painted from chin to toe and down each arm with black horizontal stripes, each a foot apart with shorter lines between. This was an innovation by Kauffman, who wanted more precision than a report that the water was "just knee deep." The stripes transformed the swimmers into human yardsticks. All they had to do to measure depth in shallow water was to stand up and look at the stripes on their bodies while hoping not to get shot. Also aboard was another of Kauffman's innovations—8-foot-long air mattresses fitted with battery-powered propellers. Dubbed "flying mattresses," these two-man contraptions were intended to give officers more mobility and help them keep better control of the reconnaissance effort.

Personally leading UDT 5, Kauffman's fears about daylight reconnaissance appeared well founded as the mission got underway. Apparently thinking the invasion had begun, the Japanese gunners responded in earnest—one boat was trailed by twenty-six misses as it made its way toward the reef where the swimming pairs flopped into rubber boats lashed alongside and then into the water. Entering the lagoon, the swimmers came under small arms fire. "Mostly it was machine guns that were firing at us," recalled Robert Marshall. "The bullets would only zip into the water a couple of feet and then just sink to the bottom. A number of them dropped past my face as I was swimming underwater."[49] Kauffman's "flying mattresses" received particular attention and were quickly abandoned, but not before twenty-two-year-old Shipfitter First Class Bob Christensen was shot dead.

Some assistance was scheduled for 1000 when carrier planes were supposed to strafe the beach to allow the swimmers to reconnoiter closer to shore. Precisely at 1000 the ships redirected their covering fire 500 yards inland in anticipation of the airstrike. But there were no planes. As the naval gunfire lifted, Japanese soldiers stood up in their trenches just yards beyond the waterline and fired point blank at the swimmers. "Not one plane appeared," Kauffman later wrote to his father. "I got to about 100 yards from the beach, and even with my bad eyes I could see Japs moving around, manning their bloody machine guns."[50]

Swimming in near Afetna Point, one swimmer defiantly hung his face mask on a Japanese marker only 30 yards from the shore and somehow made it back without being killed, but it was time to get out.[51] Making their way back to the reef, the exhausted teams were retrieved by landing craft under Japanese mortar fire. Despite Kauffman's prediction of as much as 50 percent casualties, UDT 5 lost only Christensen killed. Another swimmer had been blown completely out of the water by a mortar round, but survived. Two swimmers thought to be missing were subsequently picked up when they were spotted clinging to a buoy off the reef.

To the south of Afetna Point, UDT 7 ran into its own share of trouble off the 4th Marine Division beaches. The Japanese had hidden mortars and light machine guns on a cluster of barges tied up in the lagoon by Charan Kanoa. A mortar round exploded on one of the UDT boats, killing the coxswain. The coxswain aboard another boat was hit in the spine and a crewman took a round through the stomach. Two swimmers were wounded. At 0956 the swimmers withdrew under cover of smoke put down by the destroyer *Wadleigh*.[52]

The teams had generally good news for the landing force. There were no obstacles that needed to be blown to clear the way for the tractors. No mines had been detected along the beach or in the lagoon. The water in the lagoon was a little deeper than expected, but not prohibitive. Beach defenses appeared to consist of scattered pillboxes and numerous trenches. Some mobile artillery had been observed shifting into position. Curiously, neither UDT team mentioned the "white and red pennants" Commander Martin had observed on the reef the morning before.[53]

One discovery did necessitate a significant change of plan. The 2nd Marine Division had intended to land tanks across the reef at Red Beach 2 to provide immediate armored support to the infantry. Team 5's survey determined that the water along the selected route—chosen on the basis of air intelligence—was 2 feet deeper than estimated and would drown out the tanks. Based on the soundings, Kauffman had charted an alternative route farther south.

This was no small change at this late hour, and it was not enthusiastically received by General "Terrible Tommy" Watson. Kauffman had briefed Adm. Harry Hill on his findings when the volatile division commander burst in. "What is this I hear about your changing the route for my tanks?" he snapped. When Kauffman started to explain, Watson cut him off. "I know, I know, all this has been explained to me, but I want them to go in across Red 2," he insisted.

"General, they'll never, ever get through there," said Kauffman.

"Well, all right," conceded Watson.

"Just tell your tank commander to follow Demolition Plan Baker," Kauffman advised the general.

Terrible Tommy's temper flared again. "Who the hell's tanks do you think these are?" he inquired irately. Kauffman apologized, but Watson was going to get his pound of flesh. "Young man," he told Kauffman, "you're going to lead that first tank in and you'd better be damned sure that every one of them gets in safely, without drowning out."[54]

Aboard the LSTs and transports now closing on Saipan, the Marines were getting ready. Weapons were oiled, Ka-Bar fighting knives were given a final edge, last letters were dashed off to the folks at home. Though the Marines slated to hit the beach didn't know it, the estimate of enemy troop numbers was again being revised upward. As of June 15, the estimate was 19,200–22,200 combat troops (including construction units) and 3,000 Home Guard Units for a total of 22,200–25,200,[55] which was still well short of the actual number.

In addition to military personnel, for the first time in the war, U.S. forces would encounter large numbers of Japanese civilians. On Hawaii, troops had been taught some elementary Japanese phrases—the instruction taking place before movie screenings on the theory the students would be more attentive. Troops were also issued cards with a pronunciation guide to Japanese phrases. *Tay-oh-ah-gat-tay-sah-tay-koy* meant "Put your hands up"; *Boo-Kee-oh-oh-toe-say* meant "Throw your rifle away"; others translated to "Come out," "Raise your hands," and even "Shut up."[56] A pamphlet handed out to 2nd Marine Division units advised them that non-Japanese civilians "may be friendly to us if given the chance." Japanese civilian reaction was less certain.

The intelligence pamphlet and briefings also warned that untreated water could carry organisms causing dysentery, typhoid, and paratyphoid fevers. The widespread use of feces (night soil) for fertilizer in farm fields could result in illness if uncooked vegetables were consumed. Some kinds of fish were poisonous—the natives presumably knew the difference, but could not be relied upon to be truthful. Flies carried a variety of diseases. Yaws, which included festering body sores, was probably present among the natives. While there were no malarial mosquitoes, there were other mosquito-borne diseases such as dengue (breakbone) fever, as well as mites that could transmit scrub typhus. Native women could be expected to harbor an assortment of horrific venereal diseases.

A widely repeated story told of a group of Marines who listened attentively to the seemingly endless litany of natural and unnatural hazards. Concluding his lecture, the briefing officer asked if there were any questions. "Sir," replied a Marine, raising his hand soberly. "Why don't we just let them keep the damned place?"[57]

Aboard the attack transport USS *Feland*, twenty-one-year-old PFC Jack Eardley of Grand Rapids, Michigan, attended evening services on the deck. A warm breeze tugged at jackets as the chaplain led the men in prayer for the Lord's protection and mercy: "Men, dear friends, some of you will not be among the living at this time tomorrow. Let us invoke the Lord's mercy in this invasion, our hour of destiny, to protect us and keep us from harm, but if we should fall, may we dwell in His House forever and ever, Amen."[58] Eighteen-year-old PFC Paul Paulson also attended services. "Although I had no religious training, my mother often had told me about God," he remembered. "So I went, too. However, I did wonder why many of those who went to pray that night didn't attend church on other occasions."[59]

A lot of questions went unasked, conceded John Lane, a rifleman with the 25th Marines; questions such as: "Can we do this? Am I going to live through it? Suppose I get my balls shot off? Am I going to piss in my pants going over the side? Do I look as scared as I feel? What about the other guys? Are they as scared as I am? They don't look it."[60]

Baby-faced Pvt. Frank "Chick" Borta, at age seventeen probably one of the youngest Marines in the assault force, found himself with a bad case of the jitters. He was only sixteen when he persuaded his mother to attest that he was old enough to enlist in the Marines. The ploy worked, somewhat to the surprise of Borta's tough Polish-American father, who blurted, "Jesus Christ. I knew we were losing the war, but not bad enough to take you." Borta was a tough kid, but now, on the verge of the unknown, his youthful sense of immortality seemed to be slipping away. He confided his fears to Corp. Richard Carney, a self-assured, former Golden Gloves boxer from the Bronx who had demonstrated great coolness at Tarawa. "Stick with me, Chick," Carney reassured him. "There isn't a Jap mother who has a son that can kill Mrs. Carney's boy."[61]

Slated to go in with the 6th Marines, PFC Jeremiah Hanafin didn't feel overly apprehensive about being in the first assault wave until he was approached by PFC Robert Overby. Hanafin had talked with Overby from time to time and considered him a "nice guy," but he wasn't prepared for what Overby said now. "Do you want me to write home to your family?" he asked Hanafin. "I have a feeling you're going to get killed." Hanafin was stunned. He assumed Overby's intentions were good; still, the prediction of his own death wasn't something he needed to hear just before going into combat. "Don't worry about me," he replied; "just take care of yourself." As it turned out, Overby had less than three days to live.[62]

A battalion commander in the 8th Marines issued a written statement to his scattered troops, wherein he went on at some length about duty and being the best fighting men in the world. A gunnery sergeant in PFC Ronald E. "Gene" Adkins's company offered a somewhat less nuanced pep talk. "Every living thing in front of you not wearing Marine green is going to try to kill you," warned the gunny. "Every Jap has one mission—to kill you—so you goddamn better kill him first. That is your sole purpose for being here!"[63] PFC Bob Everett's veteran sergeant simply told his men to grab a Navy spoon from the ship before they left—Marine issue spoons tended to rust—and to put something like an overseas cap inside their helmet to soften concussion.[64]

Carl W. Matthews was packing up his sea bag when Wendal Nightingale, a nineteen-year-old farm kid from Skowhegan, Maine, pulled him aside. Nightingale had begun smoking cigarettes since joining the Marines—a habit his family would frown upon if they knew. "His seabag was fully packed except for a carton of cigarettes he had purchased when we had PX rights," recalled Matthews. "He looked at that carton, looked at me, and asked if I would pack them in my sea bag. He explained that, should something happen to him, and if the Marine Corps sent his sea bag home, he did not want his mother to open the sea bag and see the cigarettes." At that point, a carton of cigarettes would presumably be the least of her concerns, but Matthews shoved the smokes in his bag.[65]

Robert Sherrod, who had been present for the Tarawa landing seven months before, thought the overall mood was less tense as final preparations were made to hit Saipan. There seemed to be an air of quiet confidence among the veterans. Commanding the 6th Marines, Col. James P. Riseley was in an upbeat mood as he approached Sherrod shortly before midnight. "I've just got a hunch this is going to be the easiest one of all," he told the combat correspondent.[66]

Sherrod, unable to shake off memories of the carnage he had witnessed at Tarawa, was less confident. Earlier he had informally polled some of the high-ranking officers on what they anticipated at Saipan. Nobody was predicting a cakewalk. General Merritt "Red Mike" Edson, a Medal of Honor recipient for his actions on Bloody Ridge at Guadalcanal nearly two years earlier, now serving as assistant division commander with the 2nd Marine Division, voiced the dark expectations of a veteran infantryman. "This one is not going to be easy," he told Sherrod. "Maybe I'm wrong, and I hope I am, but you know I've got a reputation as a pessimist."

But it was Gen. Holland Smith who, for all of his personal shortcomings, seemed to understand enemy capabilities better than anyone else in Sherrod's opinion. The temperamental general offered up the most thoughtful—and perhaps the darkest—appraisal of what awaited them at Saipan. "We are through with the flat atolls now," he told Sherrod. "We learned how to pulverize atolls, but now we are up against mountains and caves where the Japs can dig in." Fighting on a "limited land mass" would be tough and it would be expensive. "A week from today there will be a lot of dead Marines," he concluded soberly.[67]

Waiting at *31st Army* Headquarters in Garapan, General Igeta fired off a message to Tokyo: "[T]he units are prepared for the enemy landing, morale is high and we are in complete readiness."[68] Admiral Nagumo weighed in on that same day with an exhortation to the island's defenders: "The opportunity to repay the benefits received this many years from our country is now. Every man will mobilize his full powers to annihilate the enemy on the beach, to destroy his plan and to hold our country's ramparts."[69]

The hours before the landing were also the last on earth for two captured American aviators who had been held in the local jail in Garapan by the civilian Japanese police. Manuel T. Sablan, who worked as a messenger boy for the police, heard the prisoners had been brought to Saipan from Truk Lagoon. "We sneaked in and we saw the two Americans in two different cells," he recalled. "One was sitting in the corner holding his stomach as if he were in pain. The other one was just walking around the cell, smiling and talking. Of course, we didn't know what he was saying. He got shot in the arm; he showed us the wound."[70]

A Palauan named Neratus encountered the Americans about two weeks before the landings when he was arrested for theft and placed in an adjacent cell. He recalled that one flyer was tall, the other slightly shorter and had been wounded in the left arm. The wounded flyer was treated by a doctor, but both Americans were suffering from diarrhea. When they asked for soup or soft cooked rice, the chief of police told them, "You eat what we give or else you don't eat at all," recalled Neratus. "The Chief of Police was very angry at the request and did not feed the flyers anymore."

Neratus sneaked hardtack and sugar to the two prisoners until June 13 when the American air raids became so intense, the jailers fled to the hills. They took Neratus, but left the two flyers behind. When the jailers returned the night of June 14 for food, the Americans were still there, but the "short one" was dead, apparently killed in a strafing attack by U.S. planes. "The small flyer had blood on his chest and his body was stiff," recalled Neratus.

The tall flyer was removed from his cell and seated on the ground with his hands tied behind his back as four Japanese police officials gathered around. The chief of police, a man by the name of Nitta, drew his saber. Neratus turned away, unable to watch. "I heard a thud, turned around and saw blood on the flyer's neck," he reported later. The head jailer than drew his sword and hacked at the flyer's arms and back.

Nitta ordered Neratus to burn the two bodies. The tall flyer was still alive, but clearly dying. Neratus carried him a few yards away. "The flyer was breathing hard so I waited until he died before stacking wood on his body and setting it afire," he testified later. "While waiting for the flyer to die, I took his cross and chain from around his neck and made a wooden cross, placed the chain and cross on it, and placed it at the head of the flyer. I waited forty minutes before lighting the wood and starting the fire."

He watched for about ten minutes until the fire was burning briskly, then turned and fled into the hills.[71]

CHAPTER VI

Across the Reef

CRAMMED TO THE BULKHEADS WITH MARINES AND EQUIPMENT, THE blacked-out ships carrying the landing force steamed around the northern tip of Saipan and down along the western shore the night of June 14. Flashes from naval gunfire flickered like heat lightning in the distance.

Reveille was at 0200. Sacked out on the bow of his LVT(A) in the bowels of LST 450, Corp. Marshall E. Harris, a crewman with the 2nd Armored Amphibian Battalion, heard a disembodied voice on the public address speaker boom out *"Reveille!"* followed by *"Chow down at 0430!"* Harris got rid of the mattress he had "borrowed" from the Navy to make his nights on the tank deck more comfortable, and headed for the mess hall. Breakfast consisted of sizzling steaks, fried potatoes, eggs, bacon, ham, fresh milk, toast, butter, and juice of all kinds.[1] "The steaks were small, tough and rather well done and the eggs were powdered but they seemed delicious . . ." remarked PFC Rick Spooner.[2] The steak and eggs menu was a 2nd Marine Division invasion day staple from its days in New Zealand. "Not good for punctured guts," remarked a regimental surgeon, "but excellent psychologically."[3]

The psychological benefit was lost on PFC Charles B. Orloski, whose amtank would be among the first on the beach—assuming it survived the run in to shore. "I tried to eat, but I could not," he remembered. "I shoved an orange into my pocket. We were all excited."[4] Out in the darkness loomed an island most of them had never known existed only a few weeks earlier. "Nobody had ever heard of Saipan," recalled eighteen-year-old PFC Edgar T. Spurlock. He was more excited about the opportunity to take a fresh shower, though he knew the real purpose was to reduce the chance of infection should he be wounded.[5] Aboard the USS *Warhawk*, Rick Spooner, who had joined the 8th Marines as a replacement in April, was trying to maintain a calm exterior. "I was scared to death, but I hoped no one around me knew it," he admitted.[6]

Robert Sherrod ate breakfast amid a litter of helmets, packs, and weapons in the wardroom of the troopship *Bolivar*. The mood was one of "alert tenseness," he recalled. By 0530 Sherrod was topside, joining the men lining the rails as the sun came up golden off Marpi Point. Saipan emerged against the horizon like "a low-lying prehistoric monster" under rose-tinged clouds.[7] The temperature was already 83 degrees at daybreak. The sea was covered with ships from horizon to horizon—aircraft carriers with planes lumbering into the air, massive battleships shelling beaches, the concussion of the big guns rolling across the water to slam into spectators on ships thousands of yards away.

It all reminded 2nd Lt. Robert Wollin, watching from the rail of his LST, of an outsized Fourth of July display. "Now and then a Japanese oil storage tank or ammunition dump would be hit," he remarked. "This created large explosions and fires so that the whole shoreline would be illuminated. With daylight, Navy fighters and bombers started their runs along the shoreline adding to the fire from all the ships of the line . . . Many of us thought nothing could stand up to that pounding and that this was going to be easy."[8]

What Wollin didn't know was that the naval gunfire was limited to a band within 1,000 yards of the shoreline. Targets farther inland were to be attacked only by aircraft until H-hour. Intended to simplify the coordination of air bombardment and naval gunfire, the restriction allowed much of the Japanese artillery, set well back from the beaches, to escape the barrage. Daylight revealed further cause for worry as the fringing reef became visible. Though Commander Martin of VT-10 had reported "white and red pennants" on the reef after being shot down on June 13th, the UDT reconnaissance the day before had made no mention of any markers. But now, as the sun came up, numerous red and white artillery registration flags were clearly visible dotting the reef and lagoon. Whether they had been overlooked, or more had been set out overnight by Japanese swimmers was not clear; but if ever there was an indication that the enemy was ready and waiting, this was it.

Be that as it may, there was no turning back now. At 0542 Admiral Turner ordered, "Land the Landing Force." Aboard Rick Spooner's transport 10 miles off shore, the shrill whistle of a boatswain's pipe was followed by a loudspeaker announcement: "Now hear this! Now hear this! Prepare to land the landing force! That is, prepare to land the landing force! Men assigned to Boat Groups 1, 3, 5 and 7 who are in the first and second waves lay up to your debarkation stations!"[9]

The LST Flotilla began to maneuver into position 1,250 yards behind the line of departure, an imaginary line 4,000 yards off shore. The assault elements of the 2nd and 4th Marine Divisions would launch their amtracs from the bowels of thirty-four LSTs. Once the troops were debarked, the LSTs—with the exception of three designated as temporary hospital ships—would retire seaward.

Over the loudspeaker on Bob Sherrod's ship, a chaplain asked God to protect the assault troops, observing "most of you will return, but some of you will meet the God who made you. . . ." An officer standing next to Sherrod murmured, "Perish-the-thought department."[10] Getting ready to go in with the 3rd Battalion, 6th Marines, twenty-year-old Corp. Benet Praught and his buddies were given a last send off by one of their officers. "Good luck. You will never die any younger," the officer told them. This observation was apparently supposed to be encouraging.[11]

In a War Department pamphlet issued in 1944, the military attempted to reassure soldiers that fear before going into battle was normal. "If you say you're not scared, you'll be a cocky fool," advised the authors. "Don't let anyone tell you that you are a coward if you admit being scared." A study, based on the experience of 2,095 combat veterans, reduced the symptoms of fear about going into combat to percentages: Violent pounding of heart (84 percent), Sinking stomach feeling (69 percent), Shaking and trembling (61 percent), Sick stomach (55 percent), Cold sweat (56 percent), Feeling faint or weak (49 percent), Feeling of stiffness (45 percent), Vomiting (27 percent), Losing control of bowels (21 percent), Urinating in pants (10 percent).[12]

Saddling up with his communications unit, Pvt. Jack Eardley found himself moving like an automaton, such was his fear. "I was dimly aware of the troop movements, the undercurrent of tension and uncertainty," he wrote later, "and more directly conscious of the pack straps cutting into my armpits and the salty sweat on my lips that I licked continually. My movements were automatic. I was forcing my body to obey the conditioned responses gained through months of training. A broken record in my brain kept repeating, *Keep moving. Keep moving.*" Eardley had taken some comfort in the church service the evening before and the idea that God would watch over him. Now he got a reality check as the communications personnel waiting at the rail were admonished: "Men, if you get hit, remember, try to save your radio. They're in short supply and hard to replace, but you're expendable and can be replaced easily. Now move out!"[13]

Sherrod watched as Marines crawled like flies down cargo nets into landing boats waiting below. They would circle and wait, nauseous and scared, until it was time to go in. The thud of the battleship guns was jarring. Airstrikes began at 0700 and within a few moments the area behind the beaches was obscured by columns of dust and smoke. It all looked very impressive, but Sherrod had too much experience to be beguiled. He jotted in his notebook, "I fear all this smoke and noise does not mean many Japs have been killed."[14]

The landing beaches stretching for 6,000 yards along Saipan's western coast had been subdivided into sectors and coded by color. In an effort to reduce confusion, LVT crews had painted colored stripes on each side and on the front and rear of their amtracs, conforming to their assigned beach. With the exception of Red 1 and Green 3 in the 2nd Division area

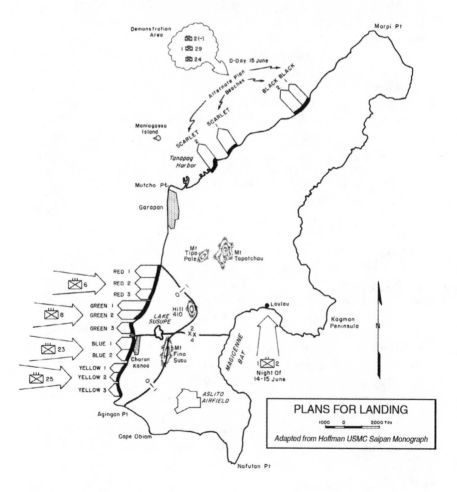

PLANS FOR LANDING

Adapted from Hoffman USMC Saipan Monograph

and Yellow 3 in the 4th Division area, each beach would be assaulted by a single battalion. From north to south, the 2nd and 3rd Battalions of the 6th Marines would land on Red Beaches 2 and 3; the 3rd and 2nd Battalions of the 8th Marines would come in at Green Beaches 1 and 2. In the 4th Division zone, from left to right, the 3rd and 2nd Battalions, 23rd Marines were to come ashore at Blue Beaches 1 and 2; the 2nd and 1st Battalions of the 25th Marines were to land at Yellow Beaches 1 and 2. There would be no landings on Red 1, Green 3, or Yellow 3.

PFC Orvel Johnson's company filed down to the LST's tractor deck to board their amtracs. The interior of the ship was like a "huge garage," recalled Johnson. The tank deck was 288 feet long and 29.5 feet wide and could accommodate seventeen LVTs or eleven of the amphibious trucks known as DUKWs. Rows of amtracs were parked side by side facing the off-ramp at the bow of the ship. The cavernous hold was a hive of activity as drivers and ship's crew hustled to free the tractors from their moorings and get ready for departure. Johnson's platoon had to scramble across the tops of other tractors to get to their assigned craft, LVT 1-7. They climbed down inside, shoulder to shoulder in the confined passenger compartment.

"The engines were being started and the diesel fumes that filled the tractor deck were the worst I had ever been in contact with," recalled Johnson. "While huge exhaust fans attempted to move the fumes out of the garage compartment, they were not adequate for the job by a long shot. It's a miracle we survived from carbon monoxide poisoning before we were free of the LST and in open water away from the ship."[15] Corp. Joseph Fiore's LVT was at the back of the line waiting for the huge clamshell doors in the bow to open. "The fumes were out of this world," recalled Fiore. "Talk about guys being sick. And just before that we had our breakfast at 4 A.M. It was steak and eggs, as many steaks as you wanted."[16]

Waiting off the 4th Division beaches on LST 129, PFC John E. Lane and his mates choked breakfast down into knotted stomachs as ventilators roared in a largely futile effort to cool the overheated galleys. There were many trips to the head. Finally the order came. "Get your gear on! Down to the tank deck!" The 230 men of George Company, 2nd Battalion, 25th Marines, filed down to the waiting LVTs. Each amtrac, or "alligator" as some called them, would carry nineteen men, with the twentieth "boat space" left for extra gear or supplies to be dumped on the beach as soon as they landed. The tank deck reverberated with the din of engines as the LVTs were started up and the air quickly turned blue with a reeking fog of diesel exhaust. Corp.

Frank Rzeszutek noticed blue exhaust flames reaching toward the drums of aviation gas, mortar shells, and small arms ammunition stacked along the bulkheads. "I thought we'd blow up right there," he remarked.[17]

Eyes watering from the clouds of exhaust, the Marines watched the "traffic lights" in the tank compartment. The lights went from red to amber and finally green. With the green light, the LST's clamshell bow doors swung open and the ramp went down. For men at the back, the open doors looked like the light at the end of a long dim tunnel. Tracks screeching on the steel deck plates, the amtracs lurched toward the ramp. From there it was "over and down, your belly pushed up into your lungs," recalled Lane, as the tractors plunged off the ramp into the water, then bobbed back up like giant corks. As each LVT emerged, it moved off to join the other tractors circling as they waited for the control boats to signal them to form up at the line of departure for the run to the beach.[18]

Waiting on the main deck of LST 31, PFC Roy W. Roush watched as the huge front doors on a nearby LST swung open to disgorge its amtracs. As each amtrac lumbered to the end of the ramp, the driver would pause, trying to time his entry to coincide with the crest of an oncoming wave pushing up below the ramp. The idea was to gun the LVT off the ramp into the water as the wave came in. "Even when it was done properly, it was rather dangerous," observed Roush. "The amtracs would sink low and some would take on some water." Loaded with troops and equipment, there was not much freeboard.

Roush watched as the first three or four amtracs churned safely off the ramp and into the water. Then the driver of an armored amtrac—distinguished by its turret and 75mm howitzer—misjudged the crest of the wave. The LVT(A) plunged off the ramp after the crest passed. Horrified, Roush saw the LVT(A) plunge about 20 feet into the trough of a wave. "It plummeted below the surface like a brick and never came up again—taking the driver and crew down with it."[19]

The accident set Roush on edge, not only because he had just watched six men die, but because he knew he would soon be launching in the same manner. Loaded down with weapons, ammunition belts, and heavy backpacks, escape from an amtrac that failed to survive the plunge was highly unlikely. Fortunately, he didn't have long to brood about it. His platoon was ordered below and he was soon lurching toward the open bow doors. Roush held his breath as the amtrac moved out onto the ramp. "It was like being at the very end of a huge diving board before you jump into the water," he observed. Suddenly the engine roared and the amtrac plunged off the ramp and into the water. "It was more thrilling than any carnival ride. The timing was right and although it was rough and a lot of water splashed over us, we stayed afloat."

The LVT cleared the area and joined the other amtracs circling nearby like so many steel water bugs.[20]

A total of 393 amphibious tractors (LVTs) and 140 amphibious tanks (LVT(A))s formed the assault waves of the two Marine divisions. Of these, Army units furnished 200 tractors and sixty-eight tanks, most of them assigned to the 4th Marine Division. Leading the way onto the 2nd Marine Division's beaches would be seventy LVT(A)s of the Marine 2nd Armored Amphibian Battalion. As the tip of the spear, the armored amphibian crews knew they ran great risks. Just before PFC Harlan T. Rosvold's LVT(A) took to the water, Corp. Alvin Caldwell took him aside. The nineteen-year-old asked Rosvold to send his religious medal and wristwatch back to his family in Oregon if anything happened to him. Rosvold agreed, shrugging off Caldwell's fears. Most of the men assumed it would be some other poor guy that got killed, he recalled. "We expected to be lucky," he observed, adding in retrospect, "Things didn't quite work out that way, at least not for Alvin."[21]

Despite their fears, morale was high among the tank crewmen. One of the LVT(A)s in Pvt. Charles G. Fultz's unit refused to start. A crewmember from the balky vehicle came over to Fultz's tank and asked to take his place for the run to the beach. Fultz refused. "We argued back and forth as neither of us wanted to miss it," recalled Fultz. The other crew finally got their tank started, rendering the argument moot. "An hour later I would have traded with him," observed Fultz with the benefit of hindsight.[22]

Harlan Rosvold's tank crew could see and feel the bombardment underway as they moved into position off the reef. Nerves, engine exhaust, and 4- to 6-foot swells cost some of the tankers their steak and eggs breakfast. The afflicted tried to vomit into the cardboard tubes used to package shells for the amphibious tank's 75mm gun. The tubes were about 2 feet long and maybe 4 inches in diameter, making them a difficult target for a sick Marine on a rocking amtrac in 6-foot waves, but it was more genteel than simply puking on the deck.[23]

Peering out from his amtrac, Sgt. Mike Masters caught a glimpse of the island silhouetted in the morning light, Mount Tapotchau prominent in the center. Red flashes and billowing smoke were visible from one end of the island to the other. Most of the Marines packed into his amtrac remained hunched down below the gunnels, looking at nothing in particular. The usual chatter was noticeably absent. Veterans tried to pass along words of encouragement to visibly nervous new men. Now and again someone would pipe up to joke nervously, "Now hear this! There will be no movies tonight!" or "Is this trip necessary?" Masters thought most of the men looked tense, but determined.[24]

Pvt. James Milar, a BAR man with the 2nd Division, had joined the Marines in hopes of seeing some action. Saipan was his first landing and if he'd been anticipating glory, he was learning a harder reality. "After what seemed like hours of floating around in our amtrac, most of us got so seasick that we didn't give a damn about anything but getting to shore," he admitted.[25]

Milar would have to wait a bit longer to set foot on dry land. At 0753 Admiral Turner delayed H-hour from 0830 to 0840 to allow the boat waves more time to get organized. Shortly after 0800, the central control vessel hoisted its signal for the twenty-four rocket-firing LCI(G)s to head for shore. The gunboats would precede the first landing waves as far as the reef to pound the shoreline with waves of 4.5-inch rockets and fire from their 20mm and 40mm guns. At H minus 30 minutes the naval fire support groups increased their fire on the landing beaches. The battleship *Tennessee* sent a hundred 14-inch shells into the Blue and Yellow Beaches; *California* fired another hundred into the Red and Green beaches. Special attention was paid to Afetna Point, which jutted out between the two Marine divisions. The cruisers *Birmingham* and *Indianapolis* put 450 high-capacity 8-inch shells into the rocky outcropping.

At 0812, the waiting ended for the men in the circling amtracs. Fluttering in the breeze, the flags were hauled down, signaling the first wave of amphibian tractors to head for the beach. Estimated time to landfall on the enemy shore: twenty-seven long minutes.[26]

Standing along the line of departure off the 2nd Marine Division beaches, sixty-eight LVT(A)s of the 2nd Armored Amphibian Battalion started the 4,000-yard dash to shore. Companies A and B were to assault the Red Beaches, Companies C and D the Green Beaches, each of which was about 600 yards long. Each company had seventeen amtanks expected to clear the way for the more vulnerable troop-carrying LVTs lining up behind them.

Heading in toward Green Beach 2, Lt. Robert E. Wollin noticed no Japanese reaction during the dash to the coral reef. Naval gunfire boomed overhead. Just outside the reef, LCI gunboats blasted away at the beach. As tracks gripped coral and the line of armored LVTs clambered up onto the reef, the naval gunfire shifted inland. Wollin peered over the side and noticed a scattering of small red flags sticking up out of the shallow water. He had scarcely processed the fact that they were Japanese aiming stakes than the water erupted under a rain of enemy mortar and artillery fire. Near misses sent seawater cascading into the open turret of his LVT(A). "I looked back for a second to see how the LVTs behind us were doing and it looked like the reef was one gigantic waterfall of explosions and water," he recalled.[27]

Earlier, waiting for the signal to go in to the beach, eighteen-year-old PFC Willard "Wayne" Terwilliger had been feeling "excited, proud, cocky, with a sense of wonder at what lay ahead, but very little fear" as he surveyed the procession of amtanks forming up at the line of departure. Now, as small arms fire rattled off the thinly armored tank, he exchanged an "Oh boy, now we're in for it" look with the driver seated to his left. Seconds later, something smashed into Terwilliger's periscope. He recoiled and belatedly realized he had pissed himself. "I could feel it, warm and running down my leg."[28]

Corp. Marshall E. Harris was in radio contact with PFC Robert B. Lewis, the radioman in an adjacent LVT(A), when the transmission abruptly went dead. Lewis's tank had been hit. It was burning and starting to sink. "Fire and smoke were coming out of all of their hatches," recalled Harris. Nineteen-year-old Lewis, who a year earlier had been playing high school baseball in Bellingham, Washington, didn't make it out and was subsequently listed as missing in action. His remains were never recovered.[29]

The periscope bubble on driver James D. Mackey's tank was torn off by a close miss before he reached the reef fronting Green Beach 1. Mackey opened the front hatch and guided on the sugar mill stack to his right front. The amtank on his right suddenly exploded as it reared up to get onto the reef. Mackey's tank made it across the reef and plunged back into the lagoon on the other side as tracers floated out toward the LVTs from a dozen different points on the beach.[30] Submerged coral heads and holes in the sea bottom made for a rough ride as the armored amtracs bounced up and down and were jolted sideways. English-speaking Japanese tried to add to the confusion, breaking in on radio channels to order, "Turn right," or "Turn left," "Stop" and "Go" in an effort to disorient the drivers.[31]

As PFC Marshall "Neil" Mumford reached shore on the far left of the division landing zone, he saw that the amphibious tank next to them had lurched to a halt and was on fire. The side hatch was rattling up and down. Mumford thought someone was trying to get out through the hatch, then realized the movement was caused by the intensity of the fire consuming the tank. About that time the tank's ammunition began to cook off, putting rest to any thoughts about helping the doomed crew.[32]

Nearing Red Beach 2, Sgt. Winton W. Carter noticed the cloying smell of wood smoke, bringing unbidden memories of burning twigs and leaves back home in Florida. On the shore, two men suddenly scrambled to their feet and ran inland toward the hills. They were wearing short-sleeved shirts and steel helmets. Carter watched for one paralyzed instant as it dawned on him that these were the Japanese he had come so far to kill. He opened up with his machine gun, but the last glimpse he had of the pair they were still on their feet and headed into the hills.

Moments later, as his amtank crawled up onto the narrow beach, he was rocked as a shell slammed into the driver's compartment, killing the driver and another crewman. The survivors scrambled out as the tractor started to burn. Carter felt a sharp sting as a piece of shell fragment sliced into his right thigh, but found he could still walk. A Marine lying in the shallow water beckoned to him. "Part of my leg is gone," he said calmly. Carter helped get him onto the beach.[33]

Corp. Roscoe J. Lee had volunteered to serve as a runner in Lt. James Prickett's tank. His job was to provide liaison between Prickett and the company commander if the tank's radio went out. Coming ashore off course on Red 1, their LVT(A) seemed to be a target for every Japanese weapon north of the landing area. Unable to get past the thick undergrowth and a deep trench paralleling the shoreline, the driver backed out into the shallow water. A Japanese shell slammed into the turret. Lee looked behind him. Smoke was filling the turret and the three occupants—including Prickett, a onetime biology major at Florida Southern College—were obviously dead.

As the smoke thickened, Lee moved to the front compartment and told S/Sgt. James H. Webb what had happened. "Let's get the hell out of here before she blows up!" exclaimed Webb. The five survivors bailed out and started wading toward the beach. Lee saw Pvt. Gus Evans holding his rifle up over his shoulders to keep it dry just as he had been taught in training. He yelled at Evans to get lower as small arms fire snapped at them. Just as

Lee shouted his warning, Evans was shot in the face. Not realizing Evans was already dead, Lee reached out for him and was himself hit twice. The first bullet glanced off his helmet, but the second one penetrated the steel and hit him in the head.

Lee fell into the shallow water. In his mind he heard his four-year-old son urging him to get up and keep going. Somehow he made it to the beach where he collapsed. A corpsman came by and Lee heard him say, "This guy is dead." He knew he wasn't dead, but he couldn't seem to move or say anything to the contrary. A second corpsman stopped and gave him a shot of something and Lee managed to stagger over to the company commander and report the obvious—that their left flank was wide open. The next thing he remembered he was being lifted over the side of a landing craft and heading back out to sea. He later learned he was the sole survivor of the crew.[34]

Waiting in a shallow trench south of Garapan with elements of the *136th Infantry Regiment*, Sgt. Takeo Yamauchi assumed the naval gunfire in the early morning hours was just a continuation of the bombardment that had been working them over for the past two days. His first intimation that the landing was underway was a shout, "The American Army is coming!" He lifted his head and peered out to sea. "They advanced like a swarm of grasshoppers," he said later. "The American soldiers were all soaked. Their camouflage helmets looked black. They were so tiny wading ashore. I saw flames shooting up from American tanks, hit by Japanese fire."[35]

Vice Adm. Chuichi Nagumo, the onetime hero of the Pearl Harbor attack, viewed the landing from a 30-foot observation tower perched on the hillside behind Garapan. He stared as if mesmerized at the armada of ships off the beaches. Finally he turned to Yeoman Mitsuharu Noda and observed that at least four of the battleships he had sunk at Pearl Harbor two and a half years earlier were now back in action shelling Saipan's defenses. His tone was almost admiring, thought Noda.[36]

Aboard the attack transport USS *Callaway*, chaplain Charles W. Goe listened to a wardroom speaker as a disembodied voice radioed instructions to the amphibious tractors: "Quit bunching up! . . . Get on in there! . . . Quit trying to get ahead of each other! . . . Get out and get into the beach!" An amtank radioman broke in. The staccato of machine-gun fire came over the speaker, then a voice said, "We must have been way behind, weren't we?" Then another voice: "Come on up here, what is wrong with you people? Let's go forward!"[37]

Wave officer Lt. (j.g.) M. H. Goldman was guiding six troop-carrying LVTs on the right flank of the second wave headed for Green Beach 2. "I saw one direct hit on an LVT. Two others were burning on the reef. Others were continuing through to the beach. A couple seemed to turn over as a result of nearby explosions." Of his six LVTs, only three returned twenty minutes later.[38]

Robert Sherrod followed the landing from a subchaser 3,000 yards off shore. A captain read reports aloud as they came over one of the subchaser's radios. "The first waves are 2,000 yards from Beaches Blue and Yellow [4th Division] and 1,000 yards from Red and Green [2nd Division] . . . There is enemy machine gun fire on boats going into Red Beaches. . . ." The smoke and dust along the shoreline was now so thick that Sherrod could not make out Mount Tapotchau. Suddenly the captain shouted, "They're on the beaches, both Red and Green! Anti-boat fire does not seem to be effective." The words were no sooner out of his mouth than a shell sent up a geyser of water 150 yards away from the subchaser. "Landing seems to be successful," added the captain, undeterred.[39]

It was 0845.

Meanwhile, the Demonstration Group was in action off Tanapag Harbor in an effort to confuse the enemy. While Fire Support Unit 4 provided an element of realism with naval gunfire on the Tanapag shore, landing craft occupied only by the intelligence section of the 2nd Marines headed toward the beaches. Coxswains motored to within 5,000 yards of shore, circled for a few minutes, then headed back to their ships. By 0920 the boats were being hoisted back aboard the transports. The Japanese, it was later learned, were not fooled. Nevertheless, the *135th Infantry Regiment* and naval troops in the Tanapag area stayed in place as the landing developed just to the south.[40]

Despite the enemy fire raining down on the reef, the 2nd Armored Amphibian Battalion lost only three of its tanks before hitting the beach. Moving inland from Green 1, Corp. James D. Mackey's LVT(A), nicknamed "8 Ball," spotted flashes coming from a clump of cedar trees. The driver accelerated, crashing into the trees. Some Japanese infantry got up and ran as 8 Ball rolled over their gun, a small artillery piece about the size of a 37mm.[41]

Corp. Richard Mason's tank lumbered over the airstrip to the sugar company railroad track where the crew found themselves all alone. They were taking stock when Mason and the radio operator noticed a bunch of "little Marines" scurrying around out beyond the railroad embankment. A closer look told them the "little Marines" were actually Japanese troops. A Japanese tank clanked into view. The Marine crew got off a shot from their 75mm, but the shell hit a tree and when they tried to fire again, the gun failed to cooperate. They contented themselves by directing machine-gun fire at the enemy tank until it rattled off into the trees.[42]

PFC Robert W. Urbatsch's LVT(A) emerged from the water onto Green 1 and crashed into a big tree right at the beach. The tree won. Urbatsch, who was driving, backed off and went around. He had just gotten to the other side of the airstrip when a small-caliber artillery round slammed into the tank. Corp. Alvin Caldwell, manning the machine gun just to Urbatsch's right, was killed. The crew bailed out and set up a machine gun in a ditch. Uniformed figures moved around among the trees to their front. "We couldn't figure out how all that infantry got into the woods ahead of us," recalled Urbatsch. "We were first to land and that tree on the beach didn't hold us up for more than a few seconds." It suddenly dawned on them that the men in the trees were Japanese soldiers.

One beach defender fell victim to PFC Simon Miller. His tractor had made its way about 20 yards inland when Miller, riding in the turret, glanced behind to see a Japanese soldier climbing out of a hole with a rifle in his hand. Miller grabbed a carbine he had stashed in the turret and shot him dead.[43] Another tanker, heading back to the beach on foot, was attacked by a Japanese with a bayonet. The tanker yanked the bayonet away, slicing his hand open in the struggle, and drove it into the Japanese, killing him.[44]

PFC Glenville D. Barringer's tank made it across the railroad track before getting stuck trying to pass over a trench. "We could hear Japs crawling around under the tank," recalled Barringer. "We didn't know what they were doing." Two more LVT(A)s came up. One of them also got stuck. The commander climbed out and started to hook up a tow cable to the LVT behind him. A sniper shot him dead. Barringer's platoon leader, 2nd Lt. Philo Pease, told the crew to stay in the tank and went out to complete the hookup. The sniper killed him, too. Then a Japanese antitank gun put a round through the third LVT(A), killing the driver.[45]

Stalled at the berm beyond Red Beach 2, Marshall Harris's LVT(A) came under small arms fire from a bunker located just inland. Harris and two other crewmen worked their way up to either side of the firing slot. A tanker killed one of the occupants with a burst from his Thompson submachine gun. Harris put two rounds through the helmet of another. "As if in slow motion, he rolled over, alive but dying."[46] They could still hear someone moving around in the bunker, so Harris readied a hand grenade. "I pulled the pin, let the spoon fly off, counted a fast two and tossed the grenade in. The grenade did its job and just for good measure, we tossed a couple more and then got the hell out of there."[47]

Corp. John F. Sullivan encountered another bunker just to the south. Hoping to find shelter from the mortar fire falling on the beaches, he left his disabled amtank and ducked into "a huge pillbox." Instead of sanctuary, he interrupted three Japanese firing an anti-boat gun toward the incoming amtracs. He shot them down, but failed to see other occupants in the dark recesses. "Then they opened fire on me. As the bullets chipped concrete near me, I felt the sprays on my face and body." Sullivan shot one man lying prone on a table and another who started toward him. He reloaded and pumped a few more rounds at the shadowy figures before ducking back out the entrance. Outside, he found twenty-one-year-old PFC Donald Speck standing by a stack of Japanese teakettle landmines. Tears were running down Speck's cheeks. "They just killed Kilgore," he managed to tell Sullivan.

Sullivan knew that Speck and PFC John R. Kilgore were best friends, but at the moment he was more concerned with what was going on in the pillbox. After a pause, he ducked back inside with Speck on his heels. With a grunt, a waiting Japanese swung a bayonet at him as he passed through the doorway. "Speck saved my life as he grabbed the enemy's hands and squeezed them together as one would squeeze a lemon, and letting the bayonet drop at my feet," remembered Sullivan. They subdued the enemy soldier, then examined the inside of the pillbox. There were nine dead Japanese lying around, all killed in the chaotic shootout with Sullivan. "As we moved our prisoner out into the glaring sun my main thought was, how lucky I was to still be living," admitted Sullivan.[48]

Following behind the amtanks, PFC Roy Roush's troop-carrying amtrac had been circling for an hour or more before the vehicles jockeyed into line for the run in to the beach. Engines revved to a deafening roar as the coxswains throttled up to full speed. Twin rooster tails of water sprayed up in their wake as the grousers on the spinning treads dug in.

Roush's company was supposed to land at the northern edge of Red Beach 2 on the far left flank of the 2nd Marine Division. Now, glancing over the side of the amtrac, he could see a mile or more of amphibious tractors extending to his right, but—somewhat to his discomfiture—nothing at all to his left. The twenty or so Marines in the amtrac huddled shoulder to shoulder, grim-faced, weapons at their sides. Roush hoped his luck would hold or that God would watch out for him. He had always been a religious youngster and even now was carrying a small Bible in the shirt pocket over his heart.[49]

Corp. Gene Adkins heard some of the ships playing the Marine Corps hymn over their loudspeakers as the landing craft passed by. He could see sailors on deck shouting encouragement. He recalled: "The order comes, lock and load your weapons, fun's over . . . Lock and load your weapons. The adrenaline begins to flow. Off to the left Japanese mortars and artillery begin to take their toll on other amtracs. . . . glad it's them, not us. We remain indifferent to the plight of those in the amtracs as long as it isn't us . . . A tremendous explosion at the pier serving the Japanese sugar mill. Jesus, what the fuck?

"The amtrac grinds . . . plunging over the reef with gut wrenching sounds and motion throwing us about. . . . we approach the beach. The operator states the second we pull up on the beach, get the hell out . . . With all of my equipment, in addition to which I have ten anti-tank grenades, two bandoleers of ammo, a cartridge belt of 80 rounds, two canteens of water and some assault rations which were carried in a gas mask container, the gas mask having been discarded as useless. These amtracs were of the old variety. We had to climb up and over the sides with an eight-foot drop to the beach, which being covered with sand, prevented us from getting the hell off the fuckin' beach as quickly as we wanted to!

"Off to my left a Marine had knelt beside a disabled amtrac to fire his rifle. A small purple hole appeared between his eyes. Shit, they said the Japs couldn't shoot, what the fuck is this? Off to our right, Marines are cut down by artillery fire. . . . Shit, these men are dead. What the hell have I got myself into? . . . This is no goddamn movie or book; this is for fuckin' real."[50]

As the line of troop-carrying tractors approached the Red Beaches, the formation began to spread out. An unanticipated current pushed the two assault battalions some 400 yards north of their designated beaches. The 2nd Battalion, 6th Marines, under Lt. Col. Raymond L. Murray, landed on Red 1 instead of Red 2 and the 3rd Battalion arrived on Red 2 instead of Red 3. Shells sent up geysers of water, showering the Marines in Roy Roush's tractor with seawater. An amtrac very close by was hit and stopped dead in the water. Roush's amtrac lurched up and over the reef and into the lagoon, entering a haze of dust and smoke. Though the naval shelling was supposed to shift inland, he could see that the area directly ahead was still being heavily shelled. "We could hear the shells as they approached," he recalled. "They sounded like fast freight trains." The noise and concussion were terrific.[51]

The Marines kept their heads down as the amtrac churned up onto the narrow beach. Roush went over the left side and hit the sand on his stomach. He found they had come ashore well to the left of their designated landing area on Red Beach 2, another victim of the strong current. Roush dashed to cover behind a 4-foot embankment just inland. Marines around him were fixing bayonets. Trotting forward at a crouch, they approached the dirt coastal road that linked Garapan with Charan Kanoa, then took cover in an abandoned Japanese trench as mortar fire began to descend. Peering out over the barrel of his BAR in the direction of the enemy, Roush noticed his weapon seemed to be vibrating. It took him a moment to realize that his legs were lying across those of the Marine next to him and the other man was trembling so violently it was transferring through him to his BAR.[52]

Lugging a BAR, PFC Stan Miller ran up the sand to the vegetation line. Two nearby amtracs had taken direct hits. One had stopped and was on fire, but the other was plowing around erratically, its driver apparently dead or badly injured. Miller did not recognize anyone from his squad, but direction was not long in coming. A Marine captain got up out of the sand and shouted, "Get these men the hell off this beach!" Miller later remarked that it was one of the most forceful commands he had ever heard. "I ran forward about thirty yards, shooting two magazines of ammo into holes and trenches." After another 30 or 40 yards, whatever rear guard infantry the Japanese had left behind seemed to have vanished and the Marines set up a line in the abandoned trench.[53]

Twenty-year-old PFC Benet Praught, one of the L Company men who had been wished good luck and reminded that he wouldn't die any younger, landed in bedlam. They were hardly on the beach when PFC Leroy L. Look, a father of four from Pekin, Illinois, was shot in the head and killed. A sergeant Praught didn't recognize shouted, "Let's move in!" As Praught followed after him, a Japanese soldier stepped out of the bushes and rammed a bayonet into the sergeant. Praught killed the Japanese, then helped the sergeant the 50 feet back to the beach, telling him how lucky he was to be getting out of there with only a flesh wound. The sergeant didn't reply. A corpsman came along with some plasma. He took a look at the wounded sergeant. "Save the blood," he said, moving on to the other wounded. "The sergeant looked at me with a strange stare and then fell forward in the sand," recalled Praught. "He was dead."[54]

Pvt. Harry Johnson saw his first dead man that morning before he even got out of his amtrac. As they neared Red Beach 2, a warrant officer stood and peered out through the gap between the gun shields up front. "As he looked, he was hit right between the eyes and flopped back in the amtrac," recalled Johnson. The platoon sergeant started to go over the side, was hit in the arm, and fell back inside. Johnson climbed out after a couple of other Marines, dropping several feet into knee-deep water. Crouching low, he waded a short distance to the beach and threw himself down in the sand. An officer yelled for the men to move inland. Johnson looked up and saw a cement pillbox just in front of him. He sidled over and was about to hose it down with his BAR when he realized there was no one inside, just a few wooden boxes with Japanese writing on them. Continuing forward at a crawl, he saw a Japanese helmet lying on the ground. He picked it up to find the top of a head inside. "From here we had to cross a small road that had a few shacks on either side," said Johnson. "As we crossed the road I saw movement through the cracks in the boards of a shack. I asked [Corporal] P.C. Hill if I should fire on the shack. He said, 'Go ahead.' I let a blast go from the hip just like John Wayne. We then rushed the building and found a goat inside. Good thing it wasn't a Jap because I hadn't hit it."[55]

Coming into Red 2 with the third wave, PFC Lloyd Streubel, a twenty-year-old mortar man, followed Lt. Donald A. Larson and Sgt. James "Curly" Moore to the top of the beach embankment. They lay there for a while as they regrouped and took stock. Finally Moore, a twenty-seven-year-old prewar Marine from Fort Worth, Texas, yelled, "Let's go!" As he and the lieutenant rose up, both were instantly cut down by a Japanese machine gun. Streubel saw a bullet exit out the back of Moore's ammo belt as he fell. Moments later, Streubel felt a sting on his left hand and looked down to see a sliver of metal sticking out near his thumb. He yanked it out and put some sulfa powder in the small hole as he tried to figure out what to do next.[56]

2nd Lt. Bryon Bird never got off the beach. A former star Oklahoma A&M football player described by his coach as "the greatest blocking back he ever laid eyes on," Bird had left college in early '42 to join the Marines. Assigned to the 6th Marines, he had earned a Silver Star at Tarawa. He had hardly arrived on the beach at Saipan when an artillery shell knocked him sprawling. He regained his senses to find one foot dangling; the bone had been shattered above the ankle, the foot hung by tattered flesh. "No one could assist me when that shell hit," he said later. "I was losing a lot of blood and, because of the dirt and insects, I was afraid of gangrene." Gritting his teeth, Bird took out his combat knife and amputated his dangling foot. "It was the only thing left to do," he said later. The young lieutenant was finally evacuated seven hours later. He left his football career with his foot on the beach at Saipan, but he survived.[57]

Shortly before 0900, Robert Sherrod witnessed death from afar as a Navy Hellcat fighter strafing ahead of the landing force was hit by antiaircraft fire at an altitude of about 700 feet. The plane flared and plunged into the water, just missing a guide boat. Boat operators coming in later could see the aircraft just below in the shallow water, the pilot's parachute caught in the wreckage, the pilot still in the harness floating about 5 feet beneath the surface.[58] In the distance Sherrod could see fires burning in the foothills of Mount Tapotchau. The second, third, and fourth waves were reported ashore. "Third battalion, 6th, is 100 yards inland and 2/6 is all ashore, but don't know how far," he wrote in his notebook.[59]

Not far from Sherrod, PFC Stanford Slama's tractor was returning from a run in to the Red Beaches, having managed to get in and out without damage, thanks in part to the protection of a sandbank just inland. About 300 feet off shore, they started past an immobilized LVT. Slama, a twenty-two-year-old farmboy from North Dakota, noticed a hand sticking up over the side. The fingers were moving. "Swing this around," he told the driver. As they came alongside, Slama jumped for the other tractor, but slipped on the rail and landed on his face in the passenger compartment amid a bloody mess of dead Marines and shattered body parts. There was a hole in the side about 3 or 4 inches in diameter where a shell had penetrated the tractor's thin skin before exploding among the Marines inside. "They were all blown to pieces, but there were two still alive," recalled Slama. With the help of one of his crewmen, he lifted the two survivors into his amtrac. Back out past the reef, they hailed an LVT to take the badly wounded men to a ship for medical attention. "One was so bad that I'm sure he never lived," observed Slama.[60]

Sgt. Mike Masters's reconnaissance team, which had been detailed to check out Red Beach 2 for supply dump sites, faced a bit of a conundrum as they came ashore. Their equipment included a 4-foot-by-10-foot canvas sign painted with a half-moon symbol to indicate the site of a food dump. The Marines jokingly referred to this contraption as their "Outhouse Sign." Now, as they approached the shore, their mission seemed highly premature. Dead and wounded Marines littered the sand among burning amtracs. Exploding ammunition in the burning amtracs added to the hazard of enemy shell and small arms fire. As the amtrac lurched to a stop and they went over the side onto dry land, one of the men asked Masters, "Hey, Sarge, what should we do with this outhouse sign?"

"Throw the damn thing over the side and take cover!" retorted Masters. "We sure don't have to advertise with a billboard that we are here!"

Trying to get his bearings, Masters realized they had missed their assigned area and come in somewhere well to the left. Before he could consider what to do next, an artillery shell exploded nearby and someone's entrails flopped wetly down next to him. He glanced over his shoulder and saw body parts strewn around a big hole in the sand. An instant later he was rocked by the concussion and hot flash of a second blast and a shell fragment tore into his left buttock grazing his spine and neatly removing a sizeable chunk of flesh as well as his wallet with forty dollars tucked inside. One of his men stood over him in a daze. As Masters yelled at him to get down, he heard someone shout, "Corpsman!"

In what seemed like seconds, a Navy corpsman appeared beside him. He stuck Masters with a morphine syrette, sprinkled some sulfa powder in the gaping wound, and bandaged him up. For Mike Masters, active participation in the battle of Saipan had lasted mere minutes.[61]

To the south of where Mike Masters lay bleeding near his "outhouse" sign, battalion commander Lt. Col. Henry P. "Jim" Crowe found himself on the wrong beach in a chaotic tangle of mixed up units. The amphibious assault on Green Beaches 1 and 2 had begun to go wrong almost as soon as the first wave crossed the line of departure and the guide boat on the right flank started to crowd to the left. At least one Japanese tried to compound the confusion by breaking in on G Company's radio frequency, calling, "Georgie, Georgie 6, come in" and issuing confusing instructions.[62]

Bigger problems were caused by the unexpected northern current in the lagoon. The strong current, combined with anti-boat fire from Afetna Point—which remained unsubdued despite the working over by cruisers *Birmingham* and *Indianapolis* earlier that morning—pushed the LVTs even farther out of position. Tractor commanders tried to wave the guide boat farther to the right, but were unable to make anyone in the boat understand. Embarked in the third wave, Crowe worked up behind the first wave and also tried to redirect the guide boat, but to no avail. By now, some tractors had veered so far left that they were ahead of the amtanks, forcing the armored amphibs to hold their fire. As a result of the confusion, Crowe's 2nd Battalion, 8th Marines came in on Green Beach 1, well to the north of its designated Green Beach 2 and hundreds of yards from the regiment's right boundary.[63]

Nineteen-year-old PFC Warren Jack O'Brien came in on one of the first wave amtracs with G Company, which had been assigned to reduce Afetna Point. "Just before we hit the reef which surrounded Saipan, we passed through a line of boats called Landing Craft Infantry (LCI) which had been fitted with rack after rack of anti-personnel rockets," he recalled. "These were fired as we passed. The impact on the beach was awesome. It was obliterated in dust and smoke. I thought that nothing could survive that bombardment." O'Brien was wrong. As his amtrac hit the beach, the platoon clambered over the side into a trench full of enemy soldiers, "very much alive and angry." Luckily for O'Brien, the BAR man ahead of him kept his cool. The man bailed out shooting and killed the Japanese in their immediate vicinity.[64]

O'Brien's company commander, Capt. Carl W. Hoffman, had barely exited his LVT when a bullet smashed into his carbine, breaking it in half and sending a chunk of metal up into his chin under his tongue. A Marine close to him was hit and went down and Hoffman, spitting blood, dropped his now useless carbine and snatched up the man's weapon, a 12-gauge shotgun.[65]

Twenty-two-year-old 1st Lt. Russ Hofvendahl came ashore in charge of a small artillery liaison party. What had seemed to the recent San Jose College graduate like a fairly routine mission—finding Colonel Crowe's command post and preparing for the arrival of the artillery—became considerably less routine as he found himself virtually alone on what was probably Green 2. "I could hear the rapid chatter of the Japanese light machine guns beyond the crest of the beach, the heavier crack of our M1s, the reports of grenades, all continuously punctuated by the deafening explosions of the enemy artillery rounds hitting the beach," observed Hofvendahl. "Other than my Marines, I couldn't see anyone alive in either direction ashore." The only landmark he could make out—and then only occasionally through the heavy smoke—was the tall stack of the Charan Kanoa sugar mill about a mile to the south.

Hofvendahl was still taking stock when a lone Marine came charging over the inland crest, grenades hanging from his belt, a .45 pistol in his hand. Hofvendahl assumed from the pistol he was an officer and he could see the man's eyes light up as he saw a group of able-bodied Marines, his for the asking. "Come on!" he yelled, gesturing northward with the .45. "There's a Nip tank just over the crest there."

"Are you the commanding officer of this sector?" asked Hofvendahl.

"Hell, no," came the reply, "I'm just a buck private, but I really need some help to get that Nip tank!"

"I'm sorry, son, these are artillery people," said Hofvendahl. "I've got just one mission—to get them to the 8th Marines command post."

Eyes full of contempt, the anonymous buck private retorted, "Suit your-self, sir!" Then he was gone. Hofvendahl would never forget that look, but he knew he had made the right decision.[66]

Crowe stalked along the beach trying to forge some order from the chaos. Standing 6-feet-6-inches tall and weighing in at 200 pounds, the forty-five-year-old Kentuckian was a Marine Corps legend, a tough-talking former enlisted man who broadcast his don't-give-a-damn aggressiveness with a flamboyant red handlebar moustache twisted into defiant points. It was not mere show: He had received a Silver Star for his actions on Guadal-canal and a Navy Cross for heroism at Tarawa. Now he sent Carl Hoffman's G Company south toward Green Beach 2 and Afetna Point, while the rest of the battalion moved inland.

Having landed over a half-mile out of position—and another three-quarters of a mile from the 4th Marine Division's left flank—G Company set out through the dunes toward the point. In an effort to prevent "overs" from hitting the adjacent 4th Marine Division, Regiment had allocated its entire supply of shotguns to G Company, providing one shotgun for every two Marines, who also carried their regular weapons. "We were glad we were armed with shotguns because the entire beach that we were moving along was a honeycomb of World War I–type open trenches," observed Hoffman. "The Japanese were in these open trenches and had survived the bombard-ment from naval gunfire. And they were ready to fight. So we had a lot of hand-to-hand fighting, and there's nothing more effective in hand-to-hand fighting than shotguns . . . Many of the Japanese were ready to do battle with bayonets or even sabers. We had some of our Marines wounded with both sabers and bayonets." In addition to the trenches, there were mutually sup-porting pillboxes and strongpoints containing 37mm or 47mm guns—nine of them all together—which continued to fire on the landing craft as Hoff-man's Marines approached.[67]

Carrying carbines, Crowe and his runner, twenty-year-old Corp. Frank W. "Dinie" DiNatale, headed about 35 yards inland to scout out the ground. In what Crowe described as a sort of deadly "quail hunt" through the scrub, they flushed several Japanese and shot them down. Then it was Crowe's turn. "I was standing up waving my arms like a damn fool when I got hit," he remembered. The slug probably would have killed him except the .45 pistol he carried in a shoulder holster had shifted forward over his chest. The bullet tore both grips off the pistol, but was deflected slightly downward, smashing a rib and punching through his left lung below the heart. DiNatale was also shot, hit in the side near his left kidney.

Crowe thought he was probably dying, but as he continued to breathe, albeit laboriously, he decided "maybe I'd better take a little interest in things." The Japanese, located in an emplacement about 30 yards away, kept picking away at them but couldn't get an effective angle without jumping up, which they didn't seem willing to do.

He got ahold of his carbine and put his fist over the hole in his chest. He noticed DiNatale, lying nearby, raise his arm to look at his wristwatch. "Why are you looking at your watch, Bill?" gasped Crowe.

"Sir," said DiNatale. "I want to see what time I die."

They lay there for about forty-five minutes, getting weaker and weaker, when one of Crowe's sergeants appeared over a hummock of sand. By now too weak to speak above a whisper, Crowe managed to lift his head a little and twirl the end of his legendary red moustache. The gesture was as effective as waving a sign. Crowe and DiNatale soon found themselves in the dubious sanctuary of the battalion aid station located at the bottom of a 7-foot-deep tank trap just off the beach. Five dead Japanese lay sprawled nearby alongside a dismantled machine gun they had apparently been trying to carry inland when they were hit.

Deadly mortar fire walked up and down the beach. A Navy corpsman kneeling next to Crowe was eviscerated "and everything in him flew against me," said the colonel. A battalion surgeon was also hit and Crowe got some metal in his leg.[68] Corp. Bernard Riggs stumbled onto the scene while helping two wounded Marines back to the beach. "We witnessed several dead, then one officer appeared to still be alive," he recalled; "however, shrapnel had removed his skull as skillfully as a professional surgeon might have done and his brain was exposed to the sun and sand."[69]

Lying helplessly on his back, Crowe covered his stomach with a pack, arranged his folded poncho over his chest, and buried his face under his helmet. The poncho didn't help much. A shell hit a tree above his head and drove fragments into his chest, right shoulder, and right hand. Despite those injuries, what hurt most was a sharp sliver of steel that hit him in the other hand and peeled back part of his left thumbnail.

Hours later the colonel was lying on a table in the wardroom of a transport offshore. As a doctor started to cut off his blood-encrusted dungarees, Crowe stopped him. "Before you do anything else, cut off that hanging thumbnail, Doc," he said with as much strength as he could muster.

The doctor tried to placate the colonel, telling him to be quiet; he was very sick man.

"Sick man, hell," rasped Crowe. "Cut off that thumbnail. It's damned annoying."[70]

Word spread throughout the division that Crowe had died aboard ship and been buried at sea. The scuttlebutt was widely believed by all but the old-timers who insisted that if you didn't kill Jim Crowe outright, he'd find a way to pull through. They were right. Crowe had a long recovery, but he lived to add a second Purple Heart to his chestful of decorations. DiNatale also survived to return to his native Boston where he would eventually become a police detective.

CHAPTER VII

Failed *Blitzkrieg*

OPPOSITE THE 4TH MARINE DIVISION'S BEACHES, AMPHIBIAN VEHICLES— amtanks and troop-carrying tractors—began launching from LSTs at about 0700. As PFC Robert Graf's tractor passed one of the sleek fast destroyers, a disembodied voice on the ship's public address system called out over the water, "God bless you all."[1] The big naval guns were firing directly overhead, the slam of the concussion followed by fire-tinged eruptions of dust and debris on Saipan's hillsides. A young-looking major in Sgt. David Dempsey's LVT passed out sticks of chewing gum and warned the men to make sure their cartridge belts were unfastened in case they ended up in the water. "The minutes spent in the rendezvous seemed like hours," remembered PFC Carl Matthews. Some of the men became seasick, adding the rank smell of vomit to the cloying engine exhaust.[2]

Matthews was about as ready as he would ever be. His platoon leader had prepared a checklist to ensure each man was wearing or carrying every item required: clean dungarees, leggings, rifle, cartridge belt, filled canteen, first-aid pack, steel helmet, bayonet, folding shovel, Ka-Bar combat knife, gas mask. In addition to the cartridge belt, many men slung one or two cloth ammo bandoliers—each holding six extra clips of .30-caliber ammo—over a shoulder. In his backpack Matthews had stowed one set of skivvies (dyed green), three pairs of socks, K-rations, and his poncho. Veterans tucked toilet paper and treasured photos in their helmet liners where they would hopefully stay dry barring a personal disaster.

The run into the 4th Division beaches would be spearheaded by sixty-eight armored amphibians of the Army's 708th Tank Battalion. At 0756, as the amtanks waited to cross the line of departure, a radio message alerted crews to the Japanese artillery markers scattered along the reef. Amtank crews were warned to steer clear of the small flags if possible.[3] The Marine assault battalions from left to right were: 3rd Battalion, 23rd Marines (Lt.

Col. John J. Cosgrove) and 2nd Battalion, 23rd Marines (Col. Edward J. Dillon) on Blue Beaches 1 and 2; and 2nd Battalion, 25th Marines (Lt. Col. Lewis C. Hudson) and 1st Battalion, 25th Marines (Lt. Col. Hollis U. Mustain) on Yellow Beaches 1 and 2.

At 0812 word finally came over the radios: "The flag is down. Move out!"

The Army amtanks churned forward, followed three minutes later by the first wave of troop-carrying LVTs. Above the din of the engines, Robert Graf's platoon leader shouted, "Lock and load your pieces! Fix bayonets!" There was a clatter of metal on metal as bolts snapped forward on eight-round clips and bayonets snicked into place.[4]

Peering curiously over the edge of his tractor, Carl Matthews picked out some of the landmarks mentioned in intelligence briefings. A tall smokestack loomed over the wrecked sugar mill to their left, just where it was supposed to be. The concrete sugar dock extending from Charan Kanoa lay straight ahead. The Japanese had yet to react as the tractors neared the reef. "Down on the beach there was nothing," observed G/Sgt. Keith Renstrom, approaching Yellow 1. "And then we came within mortar range."[5]

The relative calm ended in an instant as the reef erupted under a cascade of shells. "Sweet Jesus," exclaimed a Marine in Bob Graf's amtrac.[6] Seconds later, their tractor was rocked by an explosion. "We began to see huge geysers in the water ahead of us, made by exploding shells from Japanese guns," remembered Matthews. A shell made a direct hit on a nearby amtrac. The tractor disintegrated. "It was at that moment that I decided to do less looking and do some serious praying," admitted Matthews. "I glanced behind me and here were several men—mean and ugly Marines—already on their knees, some with rosary beads in their hands and all with their heads bowed." Matthews's hand strayed to the New Testament he had wrapped securely in heavy plastic and stowed in his breast pocket. "The fact that it was there gave me comfort," he confessed.[7]

Standing in the stern of one of the control boats keeping order among the first wave, twenty-five-year-old Lt. (j.g.) Joseph B. McDevitt—most recently a law student at the University of Illinois—could clearly see an active Japanese pillbox on the right of Blue 2 as he approached the reef. "Heavy fire was concentrated on the town of Charan Kanoa, and a dense pall covered the island both to the north and to the south of our beach which itself remained clear and sunny," he reported. Three enemy barges appeared to be underway beyond the reef; two of them were being shot up by LCI(G) gunboats, but McDevitt could not tell if they were returning fire. Mortar fire was falling as far as a hundred yards to the seaward side of the reef as the assault waves approached.

McDevitt didn't have opportunity for further inspection. His boat was still 50 to 70 yards off the reef when it was rocked in rapid succession by three near misses. The third explosion blew him into the water and riddled his back, upper arms, and buttocks with metal fragments. One of the assistant boat commanders pulled him back into the boat. It was 0845 and the first wave had yet to make landfall.[8]

Heading in toward Yellow 1 with Fox Company, the LVT carrying PFC Albert "Greg" Sutcliffe lurched up onto the reef. The amtrac suddenly went from showing about 2½ feet of freeboard to enemy gunners to now exposing about twice that area as it lumbered across the reef. "They laid into us with machine guns," remembered Sutcliffe. "They picked my tractor up with a machine gun and they never let go . . . You could hear it rattling off the side . . . There were tractors going down on either side of us."[9]

Over the past couple of days, some of the 708th's amtank officers had tuned to radio traffic from airplane spotters directing naval gunfire on the island. They had found reassurance in the oft-repeated declaration, "Target destroyed," as each fire mission concluded. Now, as water cascaded down on them from near misses, those assurances rang especially hollow.[10] Peering through the driver's compartment slit in a troop-carrying LVT following the amtanks toward Blue Beach 2, Corp. Richard Hicks saw the tractor on his left take a direct hit. Then the tractor on his right was hit. Over the din of the engine the hyped-up crew chanted "*Go! Go! Go!*"—half cheer, half prayer—as they concentrated on getting ashore.[11] As they neared landfall, Robert Graf's platoon leader shouted, "Unlock your pieces! Good luck! Keep low, get inland as fast as you can and get off the beach as they are zeroing in on it!"[12]

Amtracs had begun to nose ashore all along the beaches. As Carl Matthews's amtrac lumbered onto the narrow beach, his lieutenant shouted to the packed Marines, "Get out and move fast!" Matthews clambered over the side. "Get off the beach, boys!" shouted the lieutenant. "Get off the beach!"[13] Matthews followed the others up a small rise, through a cluster of soft-needled ironwoods and into a clearing with a few scattered coconut trees. An exploding shell sent him diving for the sand. Finding himself still alive, he lifted his head to see three less fortunate Marines sprawled lifelessly nearby. He recognized one of the dead men as an avid gambler who had won several hundred dollars on the LST on the way to Saipan. Seconds later he heard a shot. "Witte!" someone yelled. "They got him. Head shot. He's dead!"[14]

Despite heavy enemy fire on the reef, all but three of the sixty-eight amtanks made it to shore.[15] Arguably the worst spot that morning—in a multitude of "bad spots"—was Yellow Beach 2 on the division right. The beach had been assigned to the 1st Battalion, 25th Marines, which rode its LVTs straight into a kill zone covered by enemy guns to the front as well as enfilade fire from Agingan Point just to their south. Particular attention had been paid to the point in the naval gunfire plan, but it had not been enough.

Preparatory fires had also failed to neutralize enemy mortars and artillery located along the inland ridge overlooking the 4th Marine Division beaches. "On the forward and reverse slopes of the edge of the saucer which followed our O-1 line the enemy had placed batteries of 75mm and 105mm field pieces," reported the division intelligence officer, Lt. Col. Gooderham L. McCormick. "They were all well placed, with excellent fields of fire and artful concealment. Crew's quarters and ammunition were all below ground . . . Entrances were invariably well back on the reverse slope . . . Wall diagrams in observation posts marked registration points on the reefs, the channels, the beach lines, roads and intersections adjacent to the beach."[16]

Churning through the shallow water at Yellow 2, the LVT(A)(1) commanded by twenty-two-year-old Sgt. Harold Gabriel of Mitchell, South Dakota, took a point-blank hit from an antitank weapon firing from a range of about 25 yards. The driver and scarf machine gunner were killed outright. The assistant driver, PFC Henry C. Zymbroski, scarf gunner, and ammunition passer were all injured but managed to bail out of the stricken vehicle in a scene so confused and chaotic that Zymbroski could not remember later just how he found himself outside the doomed tank.

Turret gunner John J. Dombrowski, a twenty-two-year-old former metal worker from Erie, Pennsylvania, was literally hurled from the turret by the blast. Though wounded in the face, neck, and both legs, Dombrowski crawled to the rear scarf gun position of the burning tank, only to find the crewman there had been killed. He returned to the turret where he found Sergeant Gabriel, who appeared to be dying. As he struggled to pull the stricken sergeant from the turret, a second shell slammed into the tank, blowing Dombrowski into the water and inflicting more wounds. Climbing painfully back aboard, he checked the forward hatches for survivors. Again the tank was hit and again Dombrowski found himself in the water. Trying and failing to climb back up onto the amphibian tank—now an inferno of exploding ammunition, gasoline, and burning oil—he waded toward deeper water where crewmen from another tractor pulled him to safety.[17]

By now the troop-carrying LVTs were beginning to nose ashore. Sgt. James McLean's tractor halted just behind Gabriel's burning amtank and almost immediately took three direct hits from what survivors believed was a Japanese mortar. Thirteen of the two dozen men aboard were killed, leaving the troop compartment an abattoir of blood and body parts; only the driver escaped without injury. An amtrac machine gunner spotted the gun that had knocked out Gabriel's tank and hosed down the crew, putting it out of action. Another tractor was knocked out by small arms fire, but the sergeant in command fought back with the tractor's machine gun until the grips were shot out of his hands.[18]

The mood was somber in twenty-three-year-old PFC Robert T. Webster's LVT as they approached Yellow 2. "We were all very quiet and praying," he remembered. As they closed on the beach, Webster opened up with the machine gun mounted on the LVT. Then they were ashore. "We were all carrying full combat gear and it wasn't easy to move very quickly, but when we hit the beach, the first thing I saw was one of our sergeants crawling on the beach with one leg dragging behind him and bloody all over," he remembered.

Only a couple dozen feet of sand separated the water's edge from the vegetation line. The brush beyond concealed a web of antitank ditches and fire trenches. Leaving the tractor, Webster saw a Japanese officer charge out of the undergrowth holding a long sword above his head with both hands. "He was running toward Corporal [Robert L.] Herbold, and Herbold fired about ten rounds from his carbine rifle into the Jap," said Webster. "The Jap was still able to bring the sword down as Herbold threw his rifle up to ward off the blow. The force of the blow broke the rifle stock and the sword hit Herbold's neck." Both men fell, dying together in the sand.

Lugging a machine-gun tripod, Webster followed 1st Lt. George J. Burns inland. "It was so thick with jungle and bushes and so forth that you couldn't see anything," he recalled. They hadn't progressed more than 15 yards when Burns swore and recoiled in surprise. They had nearly stumbled into a trench occupied by a half-dozen Japanese. "Give me a grenade, quick," he hissed. Webster handed him a grenade. Burns lobbed it toward the trench, but it hit a branch and dropped back in front of them. They hit the deck as the grenade exploded. "As I looked up from where I had fallen, I saw a Marine with a BAR step to the edge of that trench and spray the ditch with his BAR," remembered Webster. "As I looked up at him, he was hit in the face with enemy fire and his face was red with blood, as he fell forward into the trench." A Japanese emerged from a spider hole and threw a grenade. He was quickly shot down, but when Webster went to pick up his machine-gun tripod he found he couldn't move his right arm. His sleeve was red with blood where he'd been hit by the grenade fragments. Unable to continue, he left the tripod and headed back toward the water.[19]

The Marines were ashore on Yellow 2, but just barely, clinging to a mere 12 yards of beach in a predicament one officer described as "differing little from Tarawa."[20] Among the casualties was a supposedly well-laid plan to neutralize Agingan Point immediately upon landing. While the first three waves rode their tractors straight through to the O-1 line, B Company, arriving in the fourth wave, was supposed to unload on the beach, pivot to the right, and attack south to clean out the point. The company would be supported by a platoon of amtanks from the 708th Battalion.

During the briefing aboard ship, 1st Battalion commander Lt. Col. Hollis U. Mustain had exhorted B Company's Capt. Edward L. Asbill Jr. to take possession of the point within fifteen minutes after they hit the beach, "regardless of losses." While that may have looked reasonable on paper, an amtank liaison officer explained to Asbill, a twenty-seven-year-old reserve officer from South Carolina, that the armored amphibs could not cover the approximately 1,000 yards to the objective in fifteen minutes. This was faster than the tanks could travel on good terrain, he said, never mind what they were likely to run into upon arrival on shore.[21]

Asbill was not deterred. He insisted he could get his men to the point within fifteen minutes after hitting the beach. If that meant moving out ahead of the assigned amtank platoon, he told the liaison officer, then so be it. But now, as the liaison officer had feared, the reality on the beach turned Asbill's fifteen-minute timetable on its head. B Company came ashore on Yellow 2 to find themselves caught up in a tangle of pinned-down Marines and burning amtracs that had never made it off the beach.

"We knew we were in for it when Jap shells started bursting around us on the beach," Asbill recalled. "We soon ran into nests of machine guns which held us up until we could get them with grenades or pick off the crews with rifle fire. The Japs along the beach were most stubborn. They held on until it was necessary to call for flame throwers. A few of the enemy waited until we were practically upon them, then rushed at us with knives. Two fanatics came out of holes waving grenades. They apparently expected to be in our midst before the grenades exploded, but we shot them first and their grenades went off after they were killed. I never will know why they didn't just hurl the grenades. Most of our own casualties were caused by shrapnel. The Japs had us pinned down under mortar fire in an open field for quite a while and for them it was a field day."[22]

PFC Herbert Kiser, a twenty-one-year-old former A&P grocery store worker from Beckley, West Virginia, was making his way back to A Company after delivering a message to an adjacent unit when the sudden snap of bullets passing close by his head sent him diving for the deck. Peering cautiously around, he spotted two Japanese riflemen maneuvering toward him. Kiser, who had fired expert on the rifle range at Parris Island, shouldered his M1 and firing from the prone killed them both. Climbing to his feet, he was loping toward the company command post (CP) when he heard a shell coming in much too close. The explosion caught him in midair as he dove for cover, shattering his left elbow, breaking his jaw, and riddling the left side of his face and body. Somehow he managed to make his way back to the command post, where he learned that his company commander had been evacuated with severe wounds. Kiser soon followed.[23]

Among the early casualties that morning was a nineteen-year-old private from Columbus, Ohio, named Kenneth J. Tibbs, who came ashore in the fourth wave at Yellow 2 with the 20th Depot Company. Depot company personnel were supposed to unload supplies, but there was no unloading to be done in those first minutes on Yellow 2. Company commander Capt. William C. Adams recalled, "All hell was breaking when we came in. It was still touch and go when we hit shore, and it took some time to establish a foothold." Tibbs, who was Adams's orderly, had worked variously before joining the Marines as a porter, a car mechanic, and a laborer in a manufacturing plant. One of seven children, he faithfully sent home sixty dollars of his pay each month to his mother and was considered an outstanding Marine, receiving high marks on aptitude tests and conduct reports. Only minutes after landing on Yellow 2, he was fatally wounded by a bullet that struck him in the side of the head, the first African-American Marine to be killed in action during World War II.[24]

Hunkered down in a shell hole with two buddies, PFC Donald Boots felt the mortar and artillery fire intensify—though it didn't seem possible it could get any worse. The Japanese guns were paying particular attention to the amtanks. "I looked out and the tanks were moving in," said Boots. "[The Japanese] were trying to knock out our tanks and [the fire was] right in the

middle of the tanks . . . Some of our guys were up ahead and I heard screaming from some of them."[25]

Commanding the amtank platoon assigned to assist Asbill's company
in the push to the point, twenty-four-year-old Lt. Dean Coulter was down
to four tanks following the destruction of Sergeant Gabriel's LVT(A).
Now he also lacked infantry support. Nevertheless, Coulter pushed inland
and turned south toward the point according to the original plan. On his
second try, he managed to get three tanks up by the point at about 0945.
Three intact pillboxes were visible, but did not seem to be contributing to
the mayhem on the beach—Coulter wasn't even sure they were occupied.
Most of the heavy mortar fire appeared to be coming from positions farther
inland. As he waited hopefully for infantry support, naval gunfire began
falling nearby. Coulter radioed his liaison officer to have it stopped and was
told that Colonel Mustain had called for the fire to break up a counterattack reportedly forming by the point. This was news to Coulter. He sent one
of his tanks inland to have a look around. The reconnaissance revealed no
sign of an impending counterattack, but as the naval gunfire continued, now
accompanied by strafing from Navy aircraft and with no infantry support
in sight, Coulter pulled his tanks out, leaving the point to the Japanese.[26]

While the predicament on Yellow 2 was dire, the situation was only marginally better on the other 4th Marine Division beaches. PFC Robert Baker's
LVT made it across the reef and waddled ashore on Yellow 1. The gently sloping beach was dotted with palms and mangroves. Thirty-five yards
inland was a road and about 700 yards beyond that, the sugar mill railroad
track ran roughly parallel to the beach. "Our orders were to stay with the
amtrac and ride in it for 1,300 yards, then attack the Jap airfield if there
wasn't too much resistance," he recalled. It didn't happen. "With the help
of God and the 23rd Psalm, we made thirty feet on the beach."[27] One of
the first casualties in his company was Sgt. Robert R. Mitchell of Saluda,
South Carolina. A former Marine Raider with nearly twelve years of service,
Mitchell was hit just as his LVT reached shore. "[He] just put his hands on
his head and died," said a witness. "He never made it out of the amtrac."[28]

G/Sgt. Keith Renstrom's men had been a little nervous to learn they
would be brought ashore by Army personnel, but in Renstrom's opinion the
Army amphib crew gave no cause for criticism. "They did more," he recalled.
"They even came in further with the amtracs than they were supposed to
come. . . ." Leading his men inland on Yellow 1, Renstrom saw Warrant

Officer Anthony J. Vroblesky, a fourteen-year veteran, go down with a bullet through his hip. Beyond Vroblesky a Marine lay out in the open firing a light machine gun.

Vroblesky shouted to Renstrom, calling his attention to another Marine huddled in the sand beyond them. "Gunny, I don't know whether he's hit or not, but he's not moving." Renstrom made his way over to find the youngster was alive, but petrified with fear, lying face down in the sand and shaking uncontrollably. "Gunny, I'm too scared to move," he choked. "I'm too scared to move!" Renstrom tried to reassure him, but finally had to move on when the youngster could not force his body to respond.[29]

PFC William A. Griffin's squad was pinned down by shattering automatic and small arms fire from a network of trenches just inland from Blue 2. Griffin, a twenty-one-year-old BAR man from Brooklyn, New York, got up out of the sand and pressed forward over open ground toward the nearest trench, firing bursts from his automatic rifle. Reaching the edge, he jumped in among the Japanese. In the melee that followed, Griffin was mortally wounded, but managed to kill every Japanese in his immediate vicinity— about fifteen in all—allowing his squad to break free.[30]

Eighteen-year-old Pvt. Darius W. "Bill" Latch also ran into the web of entrenchments at Blue 2. "I was approaching this trench and saw a Japanese soldier and we pointed our rifles at each other at the same time," he remembered. "I pulled the trigger and my rifle clicked. He got a big smile on his face and charged me. I turned my rifle around to use as a club, and when I hit him in the head, my rifle shattered into pieces. I jumped on him and began banging his head on the ground." Other Japanese in the trench grabbed him and Latch blanked out. "When reality returned to me, I was downstream with two Japanese soldiers sitting on me and one standing over me with his rifle and bayonet pointed at me." Arriving Marines saved Latch, bayoneting one Japanese and shooting a second. "They left the third one for me to dispose of," observed Latch, who not many months before had been sitting in a high school classroom in Heber Springs, Arkansas.[31]

The LVT carrying Roberson Hughes stuck with the original plan and headed inland from Yellow 1 toward the O-1 line. Hughes, carrying his company's spare SCR 300 radio on his back, perched up on the engine housing with a BAR at the ready, scanning the undergrowth for Japanese. The LVT made it about 40 yards off the beach before a Japanese gun put a shell through the engine compartment behind Hughes. The spray of metal fragments raked the troop compartment and killed or wounded most of the men aboard. Hughes was struck in the back and right arm. Another fragment hit him just over the left eye, stunning him and ripping open his forehead. He came to his senses to find himself lying on another Marine in the bottom of the tractor. He rolled out over the side into a burned-out cane field with the other Marine right behind him. A Japanese machine gunner shot the radio off Hughes's back as he desperately pressed himself into a shallow furrow. Survival was a matter of inches: The machine gunner could not depress the muzzle enough to hit him, and Hughes eventually made his way out of the field and back to the beach.[32]

PFC Thomas Salina's amtrac—LVT 2-10—got farther, jolting about 200 yards inland on Yellow 1 before the occupants piled out. As he went over the side, Salina felt a blow to his back as if someone had kicked him. When he reached around to feel his back, his hand came away covered in blood. A sergeant took a look and informed Salina he had been shot in the chest—it was a through and through—the blood on his back was from the exit wound. Salina climbed back into the amtrac to find another Marine hemorrhaging from a wound to his throat. Salina stuck his finger in the hole, staunching the flow of blood on the ride back to the beach and then aboard an LVT to a ship off shore.[33]

Landing on Blue 1 at Charan Kanoa, PFC Jack Claven's squad started over a low sea wall under very heavy artillery and machine-gun fire. "Upon thrusting my BAR over the parapet, I came face to face with an enemy rifleman approximately 25 yards away," recalled Claven. "We looked at each other in complete surprise for what seemed like minutes, but must have been only a few seconds, when I squeezed the trigger and separated his head from his shoulders."[34]

The landing was still in its infancy when one hard reality became evident: General Erskine's plan to ride the amtracs inland 1,200–1,800 yards to the high ground marking the O-1 line along Fina Susa Ridge—a brainstorm an infantry captain later characterized as "an untried pipe dream of some stateside idiot"—was simply not feasible.[35]

While 2nd Marine Division commander Tommy Watson had been allowed to amend the order for his division, the 4th Marine Division had gone along with Erskine's idea to use the LVTs as tactical ground assault vehicles. It was a bold and imaginative plan, but one with a number of serious flaws: it overestimated the capabilities of the amtracs—both mechanical and their resistance to enemy fire—and it underestimated the difficulties of terrain and the large amount of Japanese artillery that would survive the preparatory barrage.[36] Interviews with members of the 708th Amphibian Tractor Battalion after the campaign indicated that thirty-three amtanks—less than half of the total in the assault landing—reached the O-1 line that morning. A subsequent Marine monograph suggests the number may have been even less. According to that study, of the tractors assigned to Yellow 1 alone, only five amtanks (of seventeen) and three troop-carrying LVTs managed to get to the O-1.[37] The rest fell victim to terrain, mechanical difficulties, enemy fire, and general disorganization.

The experience of the 708th's A Company on Blue 2 was typical of the obstacles encountered in the effort to push to the O-1 line. Having lost one tank that burned in the water off the beach, the other crews encountered a steep embankment just inland. Those drivers able to get past the embankment ran into a network of entrenchments just beyond. The company lost seven tanks bogged down in the maze or hung up on obstacles within 200 yards of the beach where they were subjected to small arms fire from Japanese infantry still holding out in the trenches. Six hundred yards inland, three more tanks were completely demolished by artillery fire. The six surviving tanks lumbered on to the O-1 line, reaching the foot of the ridge by 1010.[38]

Capt. John B. Straub, commanding the B Company amtanks on Blue 1, had one of the more bizarre experiences of the day. Straub lost one of his seventeen tanks on the reef during the landing and two more on the beach. He expected worse when he hit the wrecked town of Charan Kanoa, but B Company caught a lucky break. One of his platoon commanders located a route through town by turning left toward the sugar mill and then right onto a roadway. The amtanks rolled through, harassed only by a few snipers hiding in drainage ditches along the road.

By 0915, thirteen of Straub's tanks had made their way to the O-1 line at Fina Susa Ridge, but due to the mess on the beaches, none of the troop-carrying LVTs had been able to follow. Straub turned south along the base of the ridge to have a look around. He had gone about 400 yards when he came across about thirty Japanese infantrymen standing around in the open. The Japanese were armed, but made no effort to engage the amtank and did not seem particularly alarmed by its appearance in their midst. Mystified, Straub watched them approach, rifles in right hand, left hands upraised. Some carried what seemed to be pieces of white cloth. Their intent was not clear—possibly they thought Straub's amtank, being so far forward, was one of their own armored vehicles.

Straub ordered his crew to fire and the scarf machine gunners mowed them down. As he turned to head back, a second group of enemy soldiers approached in the same manner. The amtank machine gunners killed them, too. Throughout the afternoon, Straub encountered smaller groups of enemy that demonstrated the same odd behavior. It never did become clear to him what the Japanese were thinking.[39]

Many of the tractors that managed to get off the beaches ended up stalled at the railroad embankment running parallel to the shore a few hundred yards inland. About half the troop-carrying LVTs in the two initial waves at Yellow 1 succeeded in reaching the embankment—a high success rate in comparison to the other beaches. Japanese riflemen firing from positions along the embankment withdrew, but the tractors, unable to climb the steep 10-foot slope, were forced to stop 600 to 700 yards short of the O-1 line and it was obvious they weren't going any farther.

Dead and wounded Marines began to accumulate along the embankment, recalled Sgt. Shirley Gilbert. "The air was full of steel of all types. Sergeant Jim Little had been decapitated. I could tell it was him by a ring on his finger with a large red stone."[40] The heat—83 degrees combined with 78 percent relative humidity—drained the living of energy. "The hot tropical climate was almost a physical force, melting us down," observed John Eardley.[41]

"By God, it was hot, 105 degrees," recalled PFC Gene Adkins. "We had emptied our canteens within the first hour of hitting the beach. Working parties had unloaded cans of drinking water at the surf's edge. We quickly discovered, to our disgust, that the water in the G.I. cans tasted of gasoline or diesel oil. There was better water available in the canteens of the dead Marines."[42]

Gunny Sergeant Renstrom's group arrived at the railway embankment on foot. Intent on getting forward, Renstrom was startled to find himself literally face to face with a Japanese officer. He had no idea where the man came from; "all of a sudden he was in front of me, pointing a pistol at my head. He pulled the trigger and I heard this click." An alert Marine killed the officer before he could pull the trigger again. Renstrom picked up the pistol and ejected the cartridge that had misfired. It had a dent in the primer from the firing pin, but for some reason had failed to go off.[43]

Nineteen-year-old PFC Greg Sutcliffe, a bazooka man with F Company, also made it to the railway embankment. Jumping out of his LVT at the tree line under heavy machine-gun fire, he hit the ground to find himself looking right at a Japanese soldier. Sutcliffe shot him. The beach was total confusion. Officers and NCOs were shouting, "Get off the beach! Get off the beach!" Sutcliffe headed inland. He was sweating so profusely his jacket eventually turned white with salt. "It was so damned hot. I've never been so hot or so thirsty in my life," he remembered. "I drank all the water I had, I just couldn't get enough."

Approaching the railway embankment, he noticed a little pathway that led about 10 feet up to the tracks. "I ran down there and went over the embankment and track and was going down the other side with a guy behind me when there was a tremendous blast right behind us," he recalled. "They dropped an artillery shell right in behind us." The blast knocked Sutcliffe into a barbed-wire fence running along the slope. "In retrospect I realize I was unconscious for a while," he said. "The kid behind me was blown up and lying right on top of me. And when I was finally able to turn my head around, his arm was detached and the stump of his arm was rubbing in my mouth and blood all over me and he was moaning and his face was the color of chalk. My ears were just destroyed. I couldn't hear a damn thing."

Sutcliffe finally managed to squirm out from under the other Marine. He got up on his knees and took his belt off. "I was putting it around the stump of his arm," he remembered. "He wasn't making any noise. I realized I had to do something for this kid so I jumped up and I ran back to the beach and got a medical corpsman." The corpsman bent over the grievously injured Marine and blurted, "Charlie Bass!" He knew the man, a private first class from E Company. "We went to pick the boy up and his insides were laying underneath him," said Sutcliffe, "and the corpsman said, 'He's gone.'" Minus his belt and bazooka, which had disappeared in all the chaos, Sutcliffe turned away from the broken remains of PFC Charles J. Bass of Elizabeth, New Jersey, and headed down the path toward the O-1 line.[44]

Still aboard ship, Sgt. Bob Cary's squad watched from topside as the lines of amtracs continued to churn ashore. Their artillery unit, Fox Battery, 2nd Battalion, 10th Marines, was not scheduled to land until later in the day. A few of the tractors lay motionless on the reef, indicating that Japanese fire was taking some toll. Sobered by the sight, Cary turned to Corp. Larry Zinck. "You know what today is?" inquired Cary.

"Yeah, June 15," replied Zinck.

"You know what June 15 is back in Illinois?"

Zinck responded with a blank look. "What is it, Sarge?"

"June 15 is the opening day of bass fishing season and I wish I was fishing on the Fox River back home."

Zinck eyed the destruction on the reef. "I wish we were both fishing on the Fox River," he said soberly.[45]

CHAPTER VIII

Into the Maelstrom

DESPITE THE HEAVY ENEMY FIRE AND DISORGANIZATION OF UNITS ALONG the landing area, the Marines were ashore. Within twenty minutes, 700 LVTs had put 8,000 men from two divisions on Saipan's narrow beaches and more were on the way.

With some units landing out of position and others trying to deal with open flanks, regimental commanders committed their reserve battalions fairly early. The 1st Battalion, 6th Marines, led by Lt. Col. Bill Jones—affectionately known to his men as "Willie K" and at age twenty-seven one of the youngest battalion commanders in the Marine Corps—headed ashore at 1015 to assist in the fight on the Red beaches where the 2nd and 3rd Battalions were struggling to expand a shallow 75- to 100-yard beachhead. The 1st Battalion, 23rd Marines, was committed an hour and twenty minutes after H-hour in an effort to anchor the 4th Marine Division's left flank near Charan Kanoa where a wide gap remained between the two divisions. At 1100 the 2nd Division's so-called Orphan Battalion, the 1st Battalion, 29th Marines, commanded by Lt. Col. Guy Tannyhill, was ordered to land on Green Beach 1 north of Charan Kanoa to help the 8th Marines secure that flank.

While the 2nd Division assault had reached the far side of the coastal road, there were significant gaps, as Col. James P. Riseley, commanding the 6th Marines, found out the hard way when he came ashore near the center of Red Beach 2 at about 1000. "It was pandemonium on the beach," he recalled: "corpsmen running everywhere, doctors busy."[1] Riseley scarcely had time to get his bearings when fifteen to twenty Japanese charged down the beach into the command post and congested rear of the 2nd Battalion. The Marines rallied, established a firing line, and shot them down.

Mortar fire on the 2nd Division beaches continued to take a heavy toll. "The guys were pinned down and couldn't move," recalled Pvt. Malcolm

Garner. A shell exploded very close by—whether it was a mortar or artillery, Garner was never sure. The shell probably would have killed him except that PFC Charlie Moore of Perryville, Missouri, who was huddled alongside him, caught most of the blast. Moore was instantly killed, his flesh and viscera spattering all over Garner's dungarees. Ironically, Moore shouldn't even have been on the island. He had suffered serious burns to his legs in an accident back in Hawaii, but he refused to be left behind. "He could have been evacuated, but he didn't go," recalled Garner.[2]

Heading in with the reserve battalion, faces tense behind streaks of brown and green camouflage paint, the men in PFC Jack Powell's tractor quickly shed any illusions about how well the battle was going. "[F]rom 1,000 yards out I knew, and we all knew, that we were in for a lot of trouble," recalled Powell. "At 500 yards, we began to hear and see artillery and automatic weapons directed at us, and I remember seeing the amphibious tractor on my left with half of our 48-man platoon inside, stall on a coral reef and begin taking enemy fire. We were only 30 yards away, agonizing over their plight as they fought to exit the amtrac. . . ."[3]

Adding to the mayhem, a supposedly knocked-out Japanese tank by the water's edge suddenly came to life and opened fire on the approaching LVTs with devastating results. The gunner, whoever he was, knew his business. Watching from off shore, Robert Sherrod noted, "Three hundred yards away LVTs were getting direct hits; big plates of steel flew into the air; men could be seen swimming." One lieutenant was badly wounded by a bone from another Marine's body when a shell slammed into his amtrac, blowing several men to pieces.[4]

About 200 yards from shore, Bill Jones's operations officer, twenty-five-year-old Capt. Charles H. Triplett of Pine Bluff, Arkansas, rose up to get a look at the beach. Jones was aware of a sudden flash overhead and Triplett's head exploded. Jones noticed a hole through the side of the tractor just above him. His hand was covered in blood though he felt no pain. The gore was from Triplett and another Marine who remained propped in the press of men, blood still pumping from their decapitated bodies.[5]

The approach was going smoothly in PFC Edward F. "Ted" Bailey's amtrac until the driver down-shifted to clamber up onto the reef. "We could hear the treadle clunking on the coral when it happened," he recalled. "WHAM! The amtrac shuddered and vibrated. The engine went dead and the amtrac slid back down the reef into the water on the seaward side of the reef." The coxswain at the rear of the tractor frantically yelled for the drivers to restart the engine and get moving. When there was no response, he scrambled over the packed Marines and disappeared into the driver's compartment. To their relief, the engine suddenly kicked in and the amtrac surged forward over the reef and made it to the beach. Bailey paused to unload ammo. Before he rolled over the side, the door to the driver's compartment opened to reveal the ashen-faced coxswain. Both the original drivers were dead, victims of a Japanese shell that struck the LVT just 6 inches in front of the troop compartment. Bailey tried not to think about what might have happened had the shell exploded a mere 6 inches farther aft among the massed troops.[6]

Heading into the chaos of the Red 2 beachhead, Staff Sgt. Jack Pepper, a combat correspondent with the 18th Marines, knew he was in trouble when he saw men floundering in the water. "They had been hit in their tractors and without weapons or protection, could only swim out toward other boats, hoping to get another try at landing." As they neared the beach, he heard the rattle of machine-gun fire against the side of the LVT. The small arms fire was followed by two anti-boat shells that hit the LVT head on and slightly to the port side, wreaking havoc in the troop compartment. Pepper's carbine was torn from his hands in the blast. Four men, including their lieutenant, were instantly killed and many others were wounded. "There was blood over all of us," recalled Pepper. "My shirt was a red splotch from the blood of the men who had been killed and wounded next to me. I was pinned down by bodies and tried to get up to a crouching position." The wounded men looked at him with an expression that was both pleading and bewildered, he remembered later.

Rising above the shock and confusion, thirty-three-year-old Lt. Coyle H. Whitworth of Athens, Georgia, took charge. As machine-gun fire continued to rattle against the tractor, Whitworth, an artillery forward observer, told the coxswain to head down the shoreline to the right. Pepper expected a broadside from enemy guns to blow in the exposed side of the LVT at any moment, but Whitworth managed to guide them in to Red 2, circling in behind a knocked-out amtrac that offered some protection from enemy fire.

Pepper grabbed the dead lieutenant's carbine and bailed out of the tractor, leaving his typewriter, notebook, and pencils behind. Several survivors from the amtrac were hit by Japanese fire as they dashed inland. Pepper crawled up to a hole occupied by a couple of Marines. He realized he was shaking uncontrollably. One of the Marines lit a cigarette and stuck it between Pepper's lips. "Relax," he said.[7]

The beached Japanese tank was knocked out in a flurry of antitank grenades, but not before inflicting terrible damage. Jones estimated that his battalion suffered over a hundred casualties before even reaching the beach. Many survivors of the stricken LVTs lost their equipment when they took to the water, but were able to replace the basics from dead Marines littering the beach. Meanwhile, Colonel Riseley attempted to sort out the confusion on the Red beaches. By about 1100, the 2nd Battalion was reported to be 400 yards inland, but the 3rd Battalion's attack on the right was losing momentum. Battalion commander Lt. Col. John Easley remained in command despite a leg wound, but had lost several of his key subordinates. In an effort to get things moving, Riseley ordered Bill Jones to take the newly arrived 1st Battalion through Easley's lines and continue the attack toward the high ground marking the O-1 line. Somehow Jones was able to get his people moving within about twenty minutes, with some scattered platoons reorganized and led off the beach by sergeants and even corporals. "This will always be incredible to me," admitted Jones, "because I'm damned if I know how they did it."[8]

Among them was Ted Bailey's machine-gun crew, who found themselves in a dried-up rice field. "We were crawling along an irrigation ditch trying to keep a low profile," he remembered. "The small arms fire was heavy. I heard a loud 'POP!' and [PFC Stanley] Cooper, a fellow machine gunner [from Geneva, Wisconsin], fell back into me with a crimson hole in his head. DEAD! This was the first time I had witnessed someone die. I remember thinking, *Where is Cooper? He was here a minute ago. But where is he now?*" Lying there in the dirt beside Cooper's body, the nineteen-year-old Bailey was suddenly deeply impressed with the fragility of the veil between life and death.[9]

Unbeknownst to Colonel Riseley, a new threat was developing out beyond his tenuous beachhead: Japanese tanks from the *4th Company* of Col. Takashi Goto's *9th Tank Regiment* were on the move. The company's fourteen tanks—eleven mediums and three lights—had originally taken up position on the beaches before the landings, with the rather optimistic plan to bring the landing craft under direct fire as they approached the shore. U.S. naval gunfire quickly persuaded them of their error, immobilizing at least one of the tanks and driving the rest inland.

That setback did not dissuade the tankers. Toward noontime, two Marine amtank crews that had pulled up in a banana grove out past the railroad embankment were startled to see four Japanese medium tanks heading in a column toward the beach. "Apparently they had not seen us and were intent on reaching our infantry and having a field day," observed PFC Milton Shirley. The amtanks opened fire. The Japanese turned, guns blazing. A dud 37mm round hit Sgt. Benjamin Livesey's LVT(A) in the engine compartment, but did no serious damage. "We fired everything we had at them," said Livesey. His gunner knocked out two of the enemy mediums; the other crew got another. The fourth disappeared in the confusion. "We probably fired no more than six rounds each and the Japs were immobilized with their tanks burning," observed Shirley. "Hardly any of their crew got out."[10]

Two other enemy tanks showed up on the coastal road from the direction of Garapan, clattering and clanking toward Company F on the division's left flank. Prior to the landing, platoon leader Lt. James R. Ray had repeatedly cautioned his men to be prepared: The Japanese were likely to throw everything they had at them—including "the kitchen sink." When the odd-looking—to Marine eyes—Japanese tanks appeared, one irrepressible PFC raised his head out of the dirt and shouted, "Pass the word to Mr. Ray that the Japs have arrived from Garapan with the kitchen sink!"[11]

The tanks were spotted by the pilot of a Grumman Avenger, who roared over and dropped his bomb-load with a tremendous crash much too close to the forward line. The Marines were badly shaken and huge clouds of dust billowed into the air. The bombs missed, but the commotion persuaded the enemy crews to pause for a look around. As the lead tank commander unbuttoned his turret hatch, the Marines opened up with bazookas and antitank grenades.[12] One tank was knocked out. The other rattled forward, firing its machine guns and cannon. Tucked into a shell hole, Corp. Jack Keiningham took aim with a rifle grenade and smashed one of its tracks. The tank lurched to a halt. Keiningham rose up and fired a second grenade, hitting the bottom of the turret. As the tank began to burn, the driver gunned the engine, but the vehicle only spun helplessly around on its one good track. Keiningham clambered up onto the deck and shoved a grenade through the hatch. When two crewmen tried to crawl out, the nineteen-year-old Texan shot them both.[13]

PFC Bill Hoover had a nightmarish encounter with yet another pair of tanks after his LVT(A) burned out its clutch near the airstrip. "By this time, the Japanese had recovered from the Navy bombardment and were all over the place," observed Hoover. The immobilized amtank took a couple of hits and the commander ordered the crew to bail out and get back to the beach as best they could. "While running towards the beach, I knew there was no chance of making it across open ground through the mortar fire, so I dove into a crater, made by either a bomb or a large shell from a battleship," recalled Hoover. Inside he found four other Marines. The five of them decided to wait out the mortar fire before moving.

Further discussion was interrupted by the clanking and squealing of tank tracks. They peered over the rim of the crater to see two Japanese light tanks heading directly for them. "Everyone started to climb up the side to get out," recalled Hoover, "and one guy got his head inside the sling of my rifle. I wasn't about to let him pull it away from me so I jerked him back down the side, and the two of us ended on our backs on the bottom of the crater. The next thing I knew, he went back up the side and I heard machine gun fire and then the tanks were right at the edge of the crater. I never knew if he made it to the beach or was hit right after he left the crater."

Provided with a worm's-eye view of the tanks' main gun muzzles, Hoover desperately hoped neither of them was equipped with a flamethrower. One of the tanks, a Type 95 Ha-go with a three-man crew, slowly lowered its gun toward the shell hole and Hoover figured he was about to die. "It pissed me off that no one would ever know what even happened to me, and I would probably be listed as missing in action. This actually went through my mind."

Luckily for Hoover, the tank could not depress its main gun enough to fire directly into the bottom of the crater. "When they fired, the shell went over my head and into the sandy bank before exploding. I was blown around the bottom, and covered with coral sand but not hit. They fired three or four times, I'm not really sure, then the hatch opened and a Jap soldier looked down into the crater. I first thought about shooting him and trying for the beach, but decided to play dead and hope for the best. He stared at me for what seemed like an hour, then closed the hatch and both tanks backed off and pulled away." As soon as the clatter of tracks faded away, Hoover crawled out of the crater that had nearly been his grave and ran back toward the beach.[14]

The assault was scarcely a half an hour old when *31st Army* Headquarters radioed higher command that the American landing strength consisted of "two divisions." Less than three hours later, the Japanese added that the landings were in the Oreai and Charan Kanoa sectors and "there is no indication that there will be landings on other fronts." Personnel losses up to that time were believed "slight."[15]

Waiting in his shallow trench overlooking the 2nd Marine Division's beaches, Squad Leader Takeo Yamauchi saw all of the men in the more forward positions wiped out during the course of the day. American Marines advanced to within 80 meters of his position. The Japanese fired at them from trenches located behind some rocks at the top of a slight slope and managed to hold them off.

A couple of hours after noon, a lieutenant from battalion headquarters showed up and ordered the soldiers to get out of the trench and attack. No one moved. The lieutenant stood directly behind Yamauchi and demanded, "Why don't you charge?"

Yamauchi replied he hadn't received orders from his platoon commander.

"Everyone else has charged!" shouted the lieutenant. "I order you to charge!"

Yamauchi didn't notice any of the other squads heading forward, but the lieutenant was insistent. The officer drew his sword and struck a violent pose. Again he shouted, "Charge!"

Fully expecting to be killed, Yamauchi burst out of the trench into a hail of fire and slid to cover behind some small boulders. A soldier named Goto and a machine gunner, Private First Class Tsukahara, huddled alongside him. There appeared to be no one else. Yamauchi was terrified. Bullets ricocheted off the rocks. He fired at an American who seemed to be practically on top of him. He felt something burn along the side of his neck and realized he had been grazed by a bullet. He was too frightened to move.

"We'll try to get back to our trenches," he called out to Goto. There was no response and Yamauchi realized Goto was dead. He had seen Tsukahara firing his machine gun, but now he too failed to answer. Yamauchi gathered his courage and dashed back to the trench. The bloodthirsty lieutenant was nowhere to be seen, but Tsukahara was there. He had been wounded in the right eye and his face was covered with blood. His machine gun had been hit and disabled.

The rest of the men in the trench had failed to charge. "I asked the others why they hadn't obeyed my order," recalled Yamauchi. "They just apologized."[16]

Nineteen-year-old Hospital Apprentice 1st Class William R. Keyser, a corpsman with the 4th Medical Battalion, landed on the 4th Division beaches in the early afternoon. His Higgins boat was still circling off shore when a derelict landing craft drifted past. Keyser could see it had taken a direct hit. "I couldn't even make out any individual bodies of men who had been killed," he recalled. "They were all just lumped together. This was my first image of war, and I knew then I was in the real thing."[17]

Sgt. David Dempsey pitched in to help at the medical aid station on Blue 2, digging shallow foxholes for the wounded and helping load casualties on tractors going back to the ships. "One man was brought in with his leg almost blown off between the hip and the knee," he remembered; "the doctor amputated without removing him from the stretcher. The shellshock cases began to come in, too—boys who had 'cracked up' under very heavy fire at the front and had to be led or carried in. They hid behind trees and cowered at each shell burst. Some could not remember their names."[18]

Under the medical evacuation plan, hospital ships were not scheduled to arrive until D plus 3. In the interim, three specially designated "hospital" LSTs—one for each division and a third in reserve, each flying a red X on white background "Victor" flag—were to receive casualties boated out from the beach. Upon receiving one hundred casualties, the LST would bring them out to troop transports for more comprehensive medical care. Use of the hospital LSTs would be discontinued when it was safe enough for the transports to approach the beaches and receive casualties directly.[19]

The first casualties were received on board the designated LSTs at about 1040. They were the earliest in an ever-increasing stream that far exceeded expectations. By 1300, an estimated 35 percent of Colonel Riseley's 6th Marines alone had been wounded or killed.[20] The inadequate medical system quickly broke down. In less than two hours, two of the hospital LSTs had taken over 200 wounded on board and the third was filled to capacity soon after.[21] Boat crews trying to evacuate the wounded had difficulty finding the inadequately marked hospital LSTs and were turned away when they approached other vessels. The 23rd Marines reported that "several loads of casualties were refused by ships and LSTs. These casualties had to be returned to the beach, and several of them died in transit."[22] The problems were compounded off the 2nd Division beaches when LVTs returning with wounded discovered that LST 218, one of the designated hospital ships, was not available. Due to some misunderstanding, the LST had withdrawn all the way out to the transport area and had to be brought back.

Wounded soon after landing on Beach Red 1, Sgt. Mike Masters endured a harrowing journey back to the ships off shore. As one of the early casualties, he was the only passenger in an amtrac leaving the beach. They never made it out to the reef. Bullets slammed into the sides of the tractor, then a shell punched through the body. It didn't explode, but water poured in through the holes and the tractor settled in about 8 feet of water with the leading edge about a foot above the surface. Masters inflated his life belt and hung on until another amtrac came along and brought him back to the beach. As he was being helped ashore, a Marine ran up and asked if he needed a priest. "Hell no!" retorted Masters.

Eventually, he and a few other wounded were loaded onto an amphibious tank lighter and taken out to the troop transport USS *Bolivar*. Sailors strapped him into a wire mesh basket and hauled him aboard with a deck crane. Stripped of any weapons and grenades, the men with life-threatening wounds were rushed into surgery. Those not in immediate peril, including Masters, were set down on the deck and tended to by corpsmen and sailors. "They were kind and sympathetic while giving us glasses of orange juice," he recalled.[23]

The *Bolivar* took aboard 229 casualties, both from LST 218 and from small boats. A subsequent report from *Bolivar* criticized the process, observing that "on D-day, men who had been injured at 0845 were still being handled aboard from the LST 218 at 1630, while men who had been injured as late as 1400 were being received aboard from small boats at 1600. Badly injured men were left to suffer, and some to die, aboard the LST before they could be transferred to transports and receive proper medical attention." The ship's beach party medical officer observed that amphibious tractors and many boats were not equipped to handle stretcher cases, adding, "There were many drownings in this operation."[24]

Twenty-year-old Carl Carlson, an amtank driver with the 708th Armored Amphibian Tractor Battalion, spent hours floating off shore after his tank took a hit that killed most of the crew. Finally plucked from the water, he was appalled by the scene aboard ship. "That hospital ship was worse than a butcher shop," he recalled. "They had to wash the deck down with a hose all the time from the blood and stuff."[25]

One of the wounded evacuated that morning was twenty-year-old Pvt. John C. Bruns. Somewhat bizarrely, Bruns had been predicting for months that he would lose a limb in battle but would survive. He had even written to his mother in Baltimore, Maryland, that he would lose an arm, but she shouldn't worry. His prophecy came true while moving off Red Beach 2 with the 3rd Battalion, 6th Marines. "I knew I'd get hit, but I didn't know when," he said later. "As I was making my way up the beach around 11 o'clock in the morning, I found a foxhole and jumped into it, holding my helmet on with my right hand. That's when a Japanese mortar hit me in the right arm and took it clean off at the elbow. Thank goodness the shell didn't go off. I picked up my arm and ran to the aid station and was back in the States before I knew it."

Bruns spent about nine months in naval hospitals, where doctors amputated his arm at the shoulder. Bruns had to learn to write with his left hand, "but just like I promised my mother, I made out fine," he declared.[26]

Marine tank battalions began landing on both beachheads during the early afternoon. The first tank was guided ashore at Green Beach 1 at 0900 by Lt. Cmdr. Draper Kauffman of the UDTs in compliance with Terrible Tommy Watson's disgruntled invitation of the day before. The Sherman made it safely ashore, only to be disabled by antitank guns burrowed into Afetna Point, but the route had been marked. At 1300 the rest of the 2nd Tank Battalion started crossing the reef in groups of two and three under heavy mortar and artillery fire.[27]

Arriving on Green 1 and heading inland, Sgt. Charles Frederick's Sherman ran into trouble almost immediately when "a bunch of Japs came out of the brush" and swarmed up on his tank. The tank behind Frederick hosed them off with its machine gun but "all of a sudden there was a big explosion, and inside that tank, why all our ears and heads just went to hell," remembered Frederick. "It's like [being] inside a 50-gallon drum or something that was hit with a sledge hammer."

As it turned out, the gunner on the tank behind them had spotted a Japanese trying to place a magnetic mine on Frederick's Sherman. In his excitement he hit the trigger for the main gun. The 75mm shell hit the Japanese about 10 feet from Frederick's tank, obliterating him and sending his helmet pinwheeling into the air. An instant later, the trailing tank was hit three times in succession by a Japanese antitank gun located somewhere to their rear. The battering shook up the crew and knocked out their lights, but the projectiles failed to penetrate the Sherman's armor. An alert Marine halftrack crew knocked out the enemy gun before it could do any more damage.[28]

To the south, the 4th Marine Division brought its tanks in over the reef in what was a last-minute change of plan. The tank battalion had originally intended to boat the Shermans through the channel leading to the long concrete pier near the Charan Kanoa sugar mill. Commanding C Company,

Capt. Bob Neiman had been skeptical about that route from the start. "We figured the Japanese would certainly have the whole channel, and especially that ramp, zeroed in with their heavy weapons," he observed. "Sure enough, the first vehicles that tried it were amphibious tanks, and they got blasted." Neiman landed his company over the reef, the tanks preceded by a crewman who temporarily marked potholes with strips from a roll of toilet paper, and they all got ashore.[29]

The rest of the battalion did not fare as well. A Company lost three tanks trying to land on Blue 1. Only four of B Company's fourteen Shermans got ashore on Blue 2. Six of the others were mistakenly diverted to the 2nd Marine Division's area in what was a stupendous display of poor judgement by some individual in Navy Control managing offshore traffic. Five drowned out in deep water. Of the eighteen flame-throwing tanks in D Company, eight failed to make it ashore.[30]

As enemy guns continued to pound the Marine beachhead, efforts also began to get Marine artillery ashore. The amount of enemy artillery fire brought to bear on the landing area and out along the reef shocked officers and men. It was later learned that sixteen 105mm howitzers and thirty 75mm field pieces had been massed on the high ground and reverse slopes 3,000 yards southeast of the Green and Blue Beaches. A 150mm howitzer battery consisting of four guns was located 3,000 yards directly east of Green 3. "These weapons were particularly well sited and undoubtedly were responsible for much of the prolonged fire on the landing beaches," observed a subsequent study of the Japanese defense. Evidence indicated that one battery alone fired more than 1,000 rounds.[31]

Air spotters had a difficult time targeting enemy artillery positions. "The guns were heavily camouflaged and could only be spotted when they fired," recalled Airman Chuck Shinneman, a crewman aboard an Avenger assigned to spot and suppress the enemy artillery. "The muzzle blast would flatten the jungle growth making them momentarily visible from the air."[32] It could have been even worse. The two 6-inch British Whitworth Armstrong guns located on Agingan Point—one of them housed in a completed concrete casement and the other in an unfinished casement—had been damaged by naval gunfire or aerial bombardment and were unable to contribute to the carnage.

Perched on the gunnel of an amtrac, Lt. Paul Harper had no idea of what he was getting into as his artillery control section headed toward the 4th Division beachhead shortly after 1300. Harper, who by his own admission had avoided math at Yale and was mechanically illiterate, felt no fear but admitted in retrospect "this was ignorance, not bravery." When a shell sent up a geyser of water 30 feet from the amtrac, a major ordered him off the gunnel, acidly suggesting that he could do his sightseeing some other time. The major's caution proved timely as a deluge of mortar fire descended. Harper's bravado melted away as he huddled in the troop compartment listening to shell fragments ping off the thin steel sides and squeezing the stock of his carbine until his knuckles turned blue. Nobody moved. No one spoke. Finally the major managed to observe weakly, "I don't think they want us here."[33]

The amtrac ground ashore at Blue Beach 2. The artillerymen jumped out and flattened themselves on the sand as the tractor spun hastily around and churned back out to sea. Two amtracs lay in flames at the water's edge. Dead Marines bobbed in the waves alongside. Corpsmen were tending to wounded men on the sand, as more amtracs ground ashore, disgorging men on the beach. A beachmaster was shouting instructions in an effort to bring order to the chaos. Barges carrying 105mm howitzers nudged up on the beach. Gun crews began wrestling the artillery ashore, dropping to the sand when they heard incoming shells.

Planners had expected the beachhead to be substantial enough by early afternoon to accommodate the big guns. The artillery team now saw that there was little room beyond the beach. The regimental command group settled in among a grove of trees crisscrossed by abandoned Japanese trenches about 300 yards from the water. Within minutes, Japanese observers began to zero in on the newly arrived guns. Harper's sergeant was struck in the head and killed. By the time Harper finished his survey, five of the battery's twelve 155mm guns had been knocked out. The battery commander had been killed and casualties were mounting among the gun crews. A lieutenant had lost so many men he was loading and firing one of the guns by himself. "The accuracy of the Japanese fire was uncanny," observed Harper.[34]

Harper's 155s went after an enemy gun firing from the high ground about 1,500 yards inland. The seven-man fire direction control group set up shop in a shell crater just uphill from the beach, making calculations with their oversized slide rules and passing on target information to the howitzer crews. Harper had just left the hole to consult with his operations officer when he heard the shriek of an incoming shell. As he threw himself to the ground, there was a tremendous explosion behind him. "I ran back to the crater," he recalled. "It had been a direct hit. All seven of my men were dead or dying. Some had been dismembered, others were writhing in agony." Harper helped lug the corpses—and pieces of corpses—out of the gore-drenched hole, then he and the major in command moved back in and did their best to keep the guns firing, computing the orders themselves.[35]

General Watson came ashore at about 1800 to set up his division headquarters. Shelled out of its first location on the southern edge of Beach Red 2, he moved inland to a clump of eucalyptus trees bordering the beach road. By then it was already dark; "the distant night was alive with fires, and shelling from enemy artillery and mortars was unremitting," recalled Watson. The command group was gratified to find trenches and shelters already awaiting them, courtesy of their former Japanese occupants, a number of whom had to be dragged aside to make room for the new tenants.[36]

To the south, the 4th Marine Division advance command post was established at 1630 among the shattered trees and stumps of a former palm grove about 50 yards from the shoreline on Yellow 2. General Schmidt arrived at about 1930. Digging was easy, but a nearby stockpile of partially buried gasoline drums provided a source of worry. Japanese counterbattery fire continued unabated through the night. Generally imperturbable, Schmidt admitted later, "It was the hottest spot I was in during the war not even excepting Iwo Jima."[37]

The two division commanders were ashore in force, but otherwise they did not have a lot to celebrate as shells continued to crash down on the crowded beachheads. Among the operational casualties was the tentative plan to use the LVTs in a mechanized infantry assault on Aslito Airfield. The 4th Marine Division had planned for two options, both using the reserve 24th Marines once the O-1 had been captured—hopefully by early afternoon. By late afternoon, it was clear that any effort to continue to Aslito was out of the question. The 24th Marines came ashore between 1630 and 1800 and were ordered to an assembly area approximately 800 yards inland where they settled in for the night. "All around us was the chaotic debris of bitter combat," observed Lt. John C. Chapin. "Jap and Marine bodies lying in mangled and grotesque positions; blasted and burned-out pillboxes; the burning wrecks of LVTs that had been knocked out by Jap high velocity fire; the acrid smell of high explosives; the shattered trees; and the churned up sand littered with abandoned equipment."[38]

The regiment's reserve 3rd Battalion was particularly unlucky as it landed on Yellow Beach 1 at 1730. The battalion suffered numerous casualties on the way in when two of its LVTs overturned in heavy surf, which had picked up to as much as 15 feet. Lt. Col. Alexander A. Vandegrift Jr. moved his battalion inland to the railroad tracks. The newcomers had scarcely started to dig in when they were engulfed by a well-directed Japanese artillery barrage. By day's end, the battalion had lost twenty-five killed, seventy-two wounded, and thirty-nine missing (most of the latter from the overturned LVTs), though it had yet to enter the front lines.

At the battalion aid station in the tank trap on Green 1, Bob Sherrod found a dozen wounded awaiting evacuation as casualties continued to trickle in. A puddle of water at the bottom of the ditch had turned dark brown with blood. As he began to scrape out a foxhole for the night, Sherrod estimated he had seen about a hundred dead Marines and less than two dozen dead Japanese during his survey of the beach. It seemed that his shipboard skepticism that Saipan would be "the easiest one of all" had been all too well founded.[39]

In fact, the situation by day's end was more serious than anyone had anticipated, but not cataclysmic: the two Marine divisions had managed to carve out a toehold ranging from a few hundred yards to 1,500 yards deep along a 10,000-yard front. This was about half the size of what planners had projected and the Japanese still held the dominating ridgeline, leaving the two Marine divisions in a sack dominated by enemy artillery. The plan to burst through Japanese defenses aboard the amtracs had been a failure. The two divisions also remained separated by an 800-yard gap at Charan Kanoa. The 8th Marines had finally secured the northern side of Afetna Point, overrunning all but two of the anti-boat gun positions there, but the southern half remained in Japanese hands. To the right of the 4th Marine Division, the situation had improved as the 25th Marines fought its way inland and expanded south to take most of Agingan Point.[40]

The gains, limited as they were, had not come cheap. While records were sketchy due to the confusion of the landing, the total number of Marine casualties that first day at Saipan were officially estimated at over 2,000—far more than had been anticipated. In fact, the 2,000 was just a guess and the total was probably much higher. The 4th Marine Division did not compile casualty figures for D-day, but the 2nd Marine Division subsequently estimated its losses at 1,575—238 killed, 1,022 wounded, and 315 missing in action.[41] The greater proportion of these losses had been inflicted by enemy artillery and mortar fire. Many Marines died in the beachhead area without ever seeing a live Japanese, falling victim to enemy guns firing from defilade hundreds of yards away.

Some indication of the lethality of the Saipan beachhead could be seen in the casualty rate among higher-ranking officers. June 15, 1944, turned out to be the roughest day in Marine Corps history for majors and lieutenant colonels. All four commanders of the 2nd Marine Division's initial assault battalions were wounded on D-day, including the commander of the 3rd Battalion, 8th Marines, Col. John C. Miller, who was wounded by shell fragments while still in his amtrac and then again on the beach when a Japanese grenade exploded between his feet and stripped much of the flesh from his legs. In ten hours, the 2nd Battalion, 6th Marines alone went through four commanders.

Now, with darkness looming, efforts began to organize scattered units, tie in flanks, and prepare for anticipated counterattacks. Japanese infantry typically counterattacked after dark and the Marines intended to be ready. A particular concern was the gap separating the two divisions, which, as one officer put it, "could easily become a direct, nonstop chute to the beach for the Japanese."[42] The 2nd Division anchored both flanks on the beach with the left dug in near a coral excavation pit about a mile south of Garapan and the right near the middle of Afetna Point. The 4th Division tied its right flank into the beach just south of Agingan Point. On the northern flank, Col. Louis R. Jones, commanding the 23rd Marines, harbored deep concerns about the few of his men that had actually reached the O-1 line on Fina Susa Ridge. Fearing they would be overrun, he pulled them back after dark, establishing a defense line about 800 yards short of the ridge for the night. It was almost certainly the right decision: one 81mm mortar platoon, under severe shell fire, actually had to abandon its mortars in its haste to withdraw. They would not see those mortars again for several days.[43]

About 40 miles to the west, TF 58 air groups were recovering aircraft at twilight when radar picked up a bogie at 1800 hours. Fighters from *San Jacinto* investigated and shot down what they believed was an enemy "Nick" fighter. Six other intruders were downed over the next half-hour. This incursion was followed by a more substantial air attack, launched from Yap, 561 nautical miles away, that arrived over Saipan at about dusk. *Enterprise's* radar picked up the planes about 22 miles out. The carrier had launched two F4U-2N Corsair night fighters at 1845, about ten minutes before sunset. Twenty minutes later they were vectored toward the bogies, now only 5 miles away. The intruders proved to be a tight formation of eight twin-engine Frances bombers approaching at about 800 feet with a fighter escort. A smaller formation of three or four planes preceded the main group.

With a range of some 3,000 miles, the Fran had a three-man crew, two 20mm guns for defense, and could carry either one torpedo or a 2,200-pound bomb-load. Piloting one of the Corsairs, Lt. Cmdr. Richard E. "Chick" Harmer made a starboard pass on the formation, with no discernible result beyond attracting return fire from every Japanese 20mm that could get a clear shot at him. His problems were compounded as a fighter latched onto his tail and sent a stream of tracers past his wings. As Harmer tried to evade, a 20mm shell from one of the bombers hit the trailing edge of his right wing and his formation lights blinked on. Lit up like a Christmas tree, Harmer couldn't shut the lights off and the enemy fighter, which he identified as a Tojo (it was probably a Zeke), was still on him. His wingman, Lt. (j.g.) R. F. Holden, came to the rescue. "Holden made high side on my opponent and apparently damaged him or killed the pilot as he broke off with a split-S and continued in a vertical corkscrew dive," reported Harmer later. "He was below 1500 feet at this point." Pursued by yet another fighter, Harmer wisely took his well-illuminated Corsair into a cloud.[44]

Dropping a variety of flares and float lights, the Frans made their move on the task force at about 1900 hours. Battleships *North Carolina* and *Washington* opened up without noticeable effect. Seven minutes later, *Princeton's* lookouts spotted seven aircraft coming in low at about 100 feet. Taking evasive maneuvers, the ships sent a barrage of 40mm and 5-inch shells at the Frans, which singled out *Lexington* for attention. All five were knocked out of the air by a wall of antiaircraft fire. One of the flaming bombers nearly hit the carrier's bridge before falling into the sea to the starboard. Another mortally wounded Fran "streaked like a fireball close aboard to port," so close that crewmembers manning the antiaircraft guns could feel the heat on their faces.[45] The Japanese pilot appeared to be trying to crash his stricken aircraft into the planes parked on *Lexington's* deck and might have succeeded except his right engine suddenly failed and the Fran splashed into the water just off the carrier's stern. *Enterprise's* 20mm and 40mm gun crews also splashed two Frans. In three minutes, *Enterprise* gunners ran through 3,507 rounds of 20mm ammunition and 608 rounds of 40mm directed at bombers that came in as low as 50 feet and as close as 200 yards.

Despite the wall of fire, the doomed Japanese pilots managed to get torpedoes in the water—one directed at *Enterprise* was dropped only 600 yards out—and these gave the American carriers another scare as they took evasive action. Two torpedoes missed *Enterprise* by less than 50 yards and *Lexington* had a similarly close call. There were no hits and by 2230 the radar screens were clear. Of the twenty-two aircraft that mounted the attack, *Lexington* claimed five, *Enterprise* gunners claimed two and an "assist," and *Princeton* claimed one. All U.S. casualties were self-inflicted: three sailors were killed and fifty-eight wounded by misdirected antiaircraft fire from other ships attempting to stop the Japanese torpedo planes.

On shore, the Marines were digging in. As darkness fell over the 2nd Marine Division beaches, PFC Henry Murowsky's fire team found themselves with a small problem. "We had picked up a farmer," observed Murowsky; "he said he wasn't a soldier, he was a farmer and he didn't want to get involved in any of this." With no place to send him, they handed the man a shovel and motioned for him to dig himself a hole. The prisoner promptly threw the shovel aside. A Marine handed it back to him and he tossed it away again. It finally dawned on the Marines that the frightened man thought they were ordering him to dig his own grave.[46]

Inland from Green Beach 2, PFC Bob Everett's outfit was getting organized for the night under sporadic shell fire when a Japanese soldier suddenly materialized and shot their gunnery sergeant in the left arm and leg at point-blank range. The gunny went down, but hung on to his rifle. Rolling away, he shot and killed his attacker.[47]

Not far to the north, Robert Sherrod was digging in near the edge of the Charan Kanoa airfield, when someone shouted, "There's a Jap in that hole!" The "hole" turned out to be a sand-covered log emplacement close to where Sherrod had started to dig his foxhole.

Realizing he had been discovered, the Japanese fired a wild shot, then dropped his rifle and broke for the open. A Marine tossed a grenade after him. The blast knocked the man down, but failed to kill him. He was a pitiful specimen, no more than 5 feet tall and scrawny, observed Sherrod. Now armed only with a bayonet, the Japanese pointed the blade at his own stomach.

If he intended suicide, he never got the chance: One of the Marines raised his carbine and shot him four times. "The last shot peeled off an inch of black-covered scalp and the Jap kicked, trembling in his death throes," Sherrod observed with the cold detachment of a veteran who had witnessed much violence since the war began.

The Marines went back to digging their foxholes.[48]

CHAPTER IX

Under the Gun

DESPITE THE UNNERVING PANORAMA OF AMERICAN NAVAL MIGHT CROWD-
ing the waters off Saipan's coast, General Saito remained optimistic as the
day drew to a close. His artillery remained intact; his forces held the high
ground; and the American beachhead was still vulnerable. With darkness,
he fully intended to sweep the invaders into the sea. He radioed Tokyo:

> *After dark this division will launch a night attack in force and expect to
> annihilate the enemy at one swoop.*[1]

Waiting in an assembly area about 3 miles from the invasion beaches,
noncommissioned officer Tokuzo Matsuya of the *9th Tank Regiment* took
the opportunity to note in his diary: "one enemy division landed . . . but
was surrounded by our troops. Our plan would seem to be to annihilate the
enemy by morning."[2]

As night fell just south of Garapan, Sgt. Takeo Yamauchi ordered Private First Class Nakajima to stand watch in their shallow trench. Nakajima
had been recently married; apparently something of a dandy, he sported a
beard modeled after the famous American actor Ronald Colman. Enemy
fire was falling. As Yamauchi moved down the trench, Nakajima suddenly
called out, "Honorable Squad Leader!" followed by a cry of pain. Yamauchi
returned to find Nakajima slumped down in the trench. There was a hole in
his arm where a projectile had passed clean through. Yamauchi assured him
he would be all right, but the private continued to cry out. Looking again,
Yamauchi discovered a horrendous wound to Nakajima's back, where the
flesh had been carved out to the bone. There was nothing he could do and
the dapper young private soon died.

Word arrived that the *136th Regiment* would launch an attack on the
American beachhead. Yamauchi's platoon was directed to remain behind

in the trenches. They could hear men shuffling in the dark, trying to keep the noise to a minimum as they moved up for the assault. When American flares lighted the area, the men stopped until the light flickered out, then resumed their cautious shuffle forward.[3]

Waiting with the 6th Marines on the division flank south of Garapan, Roy Roush dreaded seeing the sun go down. The nineteen-year-old BAR man, a veteran of Tarawa, well knew the Japanese predilection for mass night attacks. Just before dusk, large numbers of Japanese began streaming down from the hills onto the coastal flats north of Roush's battalion. Observers called for artillery and naval gunfire, but to no avail: The artillery battalion assigned to the 6th Marines was firing another mission and both the naval gunfire spotters had become casualties. The battleship *California* belatedly fired several salvos, but by then the enemy movement from the hills was largely complete.

The Marines heard truck engines from the direction of Garapan. It sounded to Roush as if vehicles were dropping soldiers off out in the darkness. "They were so close that we could hear the sounds of their personal gear, like canteens and rifles, as they unloaded from the trucks."[4] Word passed down the scattered foxholes, "The Japs are out there getting ready for an attack soon. Be ready."[5]

Dug in with the 2nd Marines, PFC Warren Smith was trying to get a grip on his nerves. At boot camp, the gung ho teenager had naively asked his drill sergeant if he could volunteer to go into combat. "Don't worry about it," the sergeant assured him, "we'll get you there soon enough." Now that he had his wish, Smith was feeling considerably less bloodthirsty. "I looked at that water," he remembered, "and I said to myself, 'If I could swim home, I'd be home by now.'"[6]

Night brought a new dimension of uncertainty and terror to the separate Marine beachheads. Crouched in shallow foxholes, trigger-happy sentries fired at anything that moved—and a lot that only seemed to move. The password for the night, if challenged, was any month of the year. The challenger would then reply with another month. Among the victims was a piece of Saipan livestock that wandered into the Marine lines. With remarkable forbearance, a guard challenged the intruder three times before opening fire. "The next morning, about thirty feet in front of our gun was a huge ox lying on his back with all four feet sticking up in the air," recalled PFC Paul E. Cooper.[7]

The incident would be funny only later. Up toward the 4th Marine Division's forward line, Greg Sutcliffe peered sleeplessly into the gloom. He had been bleeding from the ears all day, the result of the shell concussion he had suffered at the rail bed earlier that morning. "My bell had really been rung and I was groggy all day long," he recalled, but he couldn't relax. "The Japs were going through us all night, making their way up from the beach and getting back to their own lines. At one point I was on watch sitting in this hole and this guy went by me . . . it was a little guy and I thought it was a buddy of mine named King and I'm talking to him and he's going right by me." Only later did Sutcliffe realize he had been talking to a Japanese. Luckily, the enemy soldier was only intent on escaping.[8]

While darkness finally blinded enemy observers on the heights, shell fire on the constricted beachheads continued to take its toll. Bob Cary was dug in with his artillery unit when a treeburst sent fragments slamming into the foxhole occupied by the battery joker, Corp. Norman A. Wolff. Wolff was a little guy, recalled Cary, Jewish, and "funnier than the dickens." Even under fire, he generally had something amusing to say. A corpsman crawled over in response to Wolff's screams, but he couldn't do much for him. Wolff's screams got louder and then, after what seemed an interminable time, finally began to weaken. "Eventually, all we could hear was the little guy sobbing, 'Mom! Mom!'" remembered Cary. "It was a god-awful night." By daylight Wolff was dead.[9]

The Marines were in a sack and the Japanese gunners were taking full advantage. Even areas that should have been shielded from enemy observers in the hills were being pinpointed. It was later found that Japanese spotters had taken up position in the Charan Kanoa sugar mill smokestack, giving them a bird's-eye view of the entire beachhead. "We were in a hell of a barrage and they were knocking the hell out of us," PFC Lee Marvin wrote to his brother. "The hole I was in was about 4 feet deep and 12 across. There were four of us in it." Marvin was looking over the edge when a shell nearly landed on them. "Man, it sounded like it was in the hole with us. It hit about three feet from my head and blew off my pack, gas mask and canteen, killed one of the boys and wounded the next. But what I can't figure out is why it didn't blow my head off; that it didn't even scratch me yet it hit all the rest. Damn, I saw red for the next ten minutes and it sounded like Big Ben in my head."[10]

Twenty-two-year-old PFC Tibor Torok, a Hungarian-born former machinist who had become a naturalized citizen less than two years before, had come ashore as a member of an artillery fire observation team. He had nearly been killed earlier in the morning when an exploding mortar round shredded his radio. Armed only with a .45-caliber pistol, he took an M1 rifle and two bandoleers of ammunition from a dead Marine, but left the blood-soaked cartridge belt. Now, lying in a hole with the dead man's rifle, he heard someone nearby crying out in agony, "Mama! Oh, Mama! My leg, oh, my leg!" Torok took his life in his hands and crept over to see what he could do. He felt for the man's leg. There was nothing there. "He bled to death before I could take his belt off for a tourniquet," said Torok.[11]

Lt. Ben Toland was caught in a mortar blast when he rose up on his knees to start digging a foxhole for the night. "[T]the next thing I knew I was lying on my side with my ears ringing and my head buzzing, trying to open my eyes." His left leg "felt funny" and when he summoned up the courage to look, he found a hole oozing blood through his legging. There was another small hole in his wrist that didn't seem to be bleeding as much. He scraped a hole in the sand and tried to control his fear. "Shells were whistling back and forth over our heads all night long, and every fifteen minutes or so rifle and machine gun fire would start up 300 yards away. . . ." Among the casualties in Toland's company were two buddies from Brooklyn. "They were always arguing about ball teams; one liked the Giants and one liked the Dodgers," remembered PFC Thomas Smith. During the night, a shell landed in their foxhole. "There was nothing left."[12]

A Marine near Toland's hole was also badly hit. The man kept crying for more morphine. Another Marine told Toland he thought the youngster was hoping an overdose would finish him off, but Toland passed over his own syrette anyway. "I knew that after three quarters of an hour a second shot wouldn't kill him unless he was going to die anyway, so I gave it."[13]

The waiting for Roy Roush and the Marines on the 2nd Division flank ended at around 2200 as the enemy buildup out in the darkness finally came to a head. A bugle blared, followed by screams of *Banzai! Banzai!* as a Japanese company—180 men at full strength—charged down the coast road from the direction of Garapan. A flare popped overhead revealing a mass of running figures in odd mushroom-shaped helmets. "We could see a wall of Japs charging right at us, screaming and shrieking like madmen," said PFC Jeremiah "Josh" Hanafin, manning an I Company machine gun.[14]

The charge faltered and faded away under a deluge of Marine rifle and machine-gun fire. "I was feeding [the machine gun] belts of ammo, firing my .45, throwing grenades," remembered Hanafin.[15] The Japanese launched a series of probing attacks over the next few hours followed at 0300 by a more serious effort. Once again a bugle blared from the darkness and masses of enemy infantry—later estimated to be about a battalion—charged the Marine line. Standing offshore, the destroyers *Halsey Powell, Coghlan,* and *Monssen* lofted flares over the battlefield, casting the running figures in a sickly green light. The battleship *California* joined with salvos in front of the lines.

"Wave after wave came at us, stopped, came again, hour after hour," recalled Hanafin. "At times they got as close as ten yards, their dead and dying bodies stacked up in front of our gun. I was just fighting on instinct, doing my job as best I knew how. It was my only hope of survival."[16]

The constant call for more star shells outstripped the supplies allotted to the destroyers. "The first counterattack below Garapan found the Marines asking for star shells rather steadily, and it was depressing to hear them begging for more stars when there were none available," admitted Capt. Harry B. Jarrett, commander of the task force unit charged with supplying the illumination.[17]

The attack peaked at about 0545 as three enemy tanks, accompanied by infantry, clanked down the coastal road past a litter of their own dead. Nineteen-year-old Corp. Jack Keiningham, who had already knocked out one marauding Japanese tank earlier in the afternoon, realized that the 37mm gun posted along the roadway had fallen silent, the crew killed or wounded. Keiningham raced over to the gun and managed to get off eight rounds of canister at the approaching infantry before a Japanese heavy machine gun stitched a line of holes through the gun shield, knocking him to the ground.[18] Salvation arrived as five medium tanks from Company B, 2nd Tank Battalion rolled up to direct concentrated cannon and machine-gun fire at the exposed Japanese. The enemy attack fell apart. Leaving some 700 dead on the field, the survivors fell back.

The Japanese, who prided themselves on their night fighting skills, were stunned by the landing force's lavish use of illumination, which deprived them of the cover of darkness and exposed them to massed American weaponry. A report from *31st Army* Headquarters later noted, "The enemy is under cover of warships nearby the coast; as soon as the night attack units go forward, the enemy points out targets by using the large star shells which practically turn night into day. Thus the maneuvering is extremely difficult."[19]

Dozing in his trench south of Garapan, Sgt. Takeo Yamauchi had been awakened by the tremendous outbreak of gunfire as the Japanese attack hit the Marine line. He could pick out the distinctive "duh-rah-rah" of American machine guns in the near distance. Tracers cut through the night sky. Yamauchi thought they were beautiful.

After a time, Japanese soldiers began to filter back through the lines. Yamauchi could tell the attack had failed. "What should we do, Squad Leader?" asked one of his men. "Shouldn't we fall back?" A soldier Yamauchi didn't recognize shouted for him to move out of the way. Yamauchi suddenly realized that survivors of the attack were trying to flee down the trench and he was blocking their exit. Dropping his ammunition box and his rifle, he crawled after them on all fours, scraping his elbows, knees, and hands raw on the rough coral.[20]

In the hills above Garapan, hundreds of Japanese wounded from the failed infantry assault waited for medical attention near a large cave serving as a field hospital. Shuzuko Miura, who had escaped from Garapan before the U.S. landing, watched as a captain from the Navy parachute force was carried in on a stretcher. Severely wounded in the leg and covered with blood, the officer kept repeating, "It's a pity that I only did not die." The stretcher-bearers put him aside to await treatment. Sometime later Shizuko heard a cry, "Long live the Emperor!" followed by a muffled shot. Someone shouted, "Captain! Captain!" Medical personnel ran toward the cries and found the parachute captain, a pistol still in his hand, lying on his stretcher with blood pouring from his head. He had killed himself. They stared a moment, then went back to treating the long line of waiting wounded.[21]

At the other end of the American beachhead, the 4th Marine Division fended off two counterattacks during the early morning hours, both directed against the center of the 25th Marines toehold just beyond the Yellow Beaches. During the second attack at 0430, the Japanese approached behind a large group of civilians—including women and children. The Marines held their fire until the last minute and quickly found themselves in deep trouble. A halftrack went up in flames, silhouetting them to Japanese observers who brought artillery fire down on the area. In danger of being overrun, C Company scrambled back about 200 yards. Twenty-two-year-old PFC Harry S. Bowman, a former hosiery factory worker from Wilmington, Delaware, stayed in his foxhole to provide cover as his buddies got out. Bowman fired steadily at the approaching Japanese until he ran out of ammunition and was killed. The line was stabilized with the help of halftracks from the regimental Weapons Company, but it had been a near thing.[22]

Over on the division left, the 23rd Marines spent a sleepless night fending off persistent infiltration attempts. Exploiting the gap between the two divisions at Charan Kanoa, small enemy groups probed at the left flank into the early morning hours, some of them filtering down along the railroad track leading to the sugar mill and hiding among the dozens of railroad cars still piled high with sugar cane. Others were summarily dealt with by Beach and Shore Party personnel. The Marines gave much credit to "the colored Army units forming part of the Shore Party."[23] These labor troops pitched in again shortly before sunrise when about 200 Japanese—probably former defenders of Afetna Point along with strays who had taken refuge in the Lake Susupe swamp—struck toward the pier, setting it on fire. The 3rd Battalion, 23rd Marines eradicated the bulk of the force with an assist from the 311th and 539th Port Companies.

Just to the north of the Charan Kanoa gap, Frank Borta and half a dozen other Marines spent the night in a ditch nervously watching tracers float overhead. "My mother had sent me a cross that she had blessed. I tied it to the end of one of my dog tags with telephone wire," he recalled. During the night he reached up to touch the cross and it was gone. "I thought for sure I was a dead man."

As dawn approached, Borta's sergeant passed the order, "Fix bayonets." The Japanese usually attacked before dawn and they'd better be ready. The men nervously fixed bayonets, but the Japanese did not come. They finally picked up and headed back along the beach past dead men and pieces of dead men, all victims of enemy artillery fire during the night. Some of them were from Borta's platoon. "Our executive officer had lost an arm . . . The other scout/runner in our platoon, William L. Larson from Wisconsin, was cut in half," he observed. Borta asked about his friend, Corp. Richard T. Carney, the self-assured Golden Gloves boxer. "He had his head blown off," came the reply. Carney's boast that no Jap mother's son could kill him had been terribly wrong.[24]

1st Lt. John C. Chapin and his runner spent the night in a shallow trench. Chapin took the first watch. The hours crawled by, but finally it was time and he shook his runner awake. He rolled over and was asleep in an instant. In no time, it seemed, someone was shaking him and insisting, "Wake up!" Chapin jerked upright. A glance at his watch showed it was almost dawn. His runner was lying against him, fast asleep. "Let's go!" said

Chapin. "Pass the word to the squad leaders to get set." The runner didn't move. Chapin shook him. He still didn't move and Chapin realized he was dead. He rolled him over, pulled out the man's canteen and poured the precious water into his own canteen. "Then I left him lying there."[25]

Lt. Ben Toland survived the night. The badly wounded Marine who had been begging for morphine did not. Also among the dead was a member of the 23rd Marines found in the morning with a knife in his back, apparently the victim of an enemy infiltrator. Toland was loaded onto a DUKW which took him back down to the beach and out to an LST where his wounds were cleaned and dressed and he was given cold pineapple juice, coffee, and donuts. X-rays revealed the shell fragment had torn through his flesh without touching the bone. He was out of the battle, but not out of the war.[26]

About a mile south of Garapan, Josh Hanafin and his buddies emerged from their holes to a landscape littered with corpses, rifles, pistols, machine guns, swords, and personal equipment from the failed counterattack. Among the prized souvenirs was a bullet-riddled bugle. Some of the Marines prowled around, kicking the bodies to make sure they were all dead. An occasional shot bore testament to their caution.

Among the corpses was former naval paratrooper and diarist Lance Corp. Genkichi Ichikawa, lying face down in the dirt with his knapsack still on his back. A Marine PFC searching for souvenirs slashed open the knapsack with his Ka-Bar, rifled through the contents, and pocketed Ichikawa's diary. The last entry, made days before, observed that the troops were practicing for a ground battle and complained about the hot sun.[27]

Hanafin was enjoying a well-deserved cigarette when someone told him his good friend, twenty-year-old PFC Lawrence Knop of Union Grove, Wisconsin, had bled to death during the night from a gunshot wound. Killed alongside Knop was PFC Robert Overby, the Marine who had injudiciously predicted Hanafin's imminent death in a conversation aboard the LST before the landing. Hanafin walked over to their machine-gun position and lifted the poncho covering Knop. He was relieved to see that his friend's face was undamaged. No more than 6 feet in front of Knop's machine gun was a Japanese soldier who had died on his knees. "He faced forward, rifle in his hands, the bayonet pointed straight at the machine gun," recalled Hanafin. "You would have sworn he was alive. Knop or Overby must have killed him just before he made his final lunge."[28]

Roy Roush found his group leader, Corp. Jack Keiningham, among a cluster of dead Marines and expended shell casings surrounding the 37mm gun guarding the coastal road. "He was lying on his back. He was pale and looked very dead," recalled Roush. "I could see where he had been shot through the left side of his head, his neck area and once or twice on the left side near the heart. Blood was all around him. It had stained his jacket and had poured out onto the sand around him."

Roush knelt down, touched Keiningham's shoulder and spoke his name, then almost jumped out of his skin when Keiningham suddenly opened his eyes and stared at him. Dumbly, Roush asked if he was okay. Keiningham asked for water. When Roush pulled out his canteen, Keiningham grabbed it and almost drained the contents. Roush and a couple of Marines loaded Keiningham onto a door they tore off a nearby shack and lugged him to the battalion aid station a couple hundred yards down the beach. He hoped they had acted quickly enough, though he didn't really think Keiningham had a chance to pull through.[29]

The *31st Army* chief of staff transmitted a message to higher headquarters the morning of June 16 conceding that "the counterattack which has been carried out since the afternoon of the 15th has failed because of the enemy tanks and firepower." However, he added, "We are reorganizing and will attack again."[30]

Help was on the way. At 0855 on June 15, as Marines were storming ashore on Saipan, Admiral Toyoda formally activated A-Go, setting the stage for the long-awaited decisive fleet confrontation. The *Kon* operation directed at Biak was suspended. "The Combined Fleet will attack the enemy task force which has come to the Marianas area, then annihilate its invasion force . . . Decisive battle Operation A will begin," he ordered.[31] Minutes later, in an effort to impress all hands with the importance of the coming engagement, Toyoda followed the A-Go directive with Adm. Heichachiro Togo's famous exhortation before Japan's stunning victory over the Russian fleet at the Battle of Tsushima Strait in 1905, messaging:

The rise and fall of Imperial Japan depends on this one battle. Every man shall do his duty.[32]

The Japanese would seek decisive battle, not in the Palaus or Western Carolines as had been hoped, but in the Marianas area. The ships would steam into battle with volatile Tarakan oil in their bunkers.

That same evening the U.S. submarine *Flying Fish* reported that a powerful Japanese naval force, consisting of "definitely identified 1 Nagato BB [battleship] and estimate 2 more BBs plus 3 carriers plus several cruisers and DDs [destroyers]," had debouched from the San Bernardino Strait into the Philippine Sea that morning and was steaming eastward at high speed. It was estimated this force could reach Saipan within three days. Based on that timetable, the Japanese would be in position to launch airstrikes on American shipping as early as the morning of June 18.[33] The message from *Flying Fish* was followed by a report from USS *Seahorse* that another enemy task force (Ugaki's battleship group, as it turned out) was steaming on a northerly course about 200 miles northeast of Mindanao, only two days from Saipan.

Recognizing that the Japanese would attempt to stage planes south through Iwo Jima to Guam, Yap, and Rota, Spruance ordered two of his four task groups to work over airfields in the Bonin and Volcano Islands on June 16. They were then to return without delay so they would be within range of Saipan by June 17 and able to rejoin Task Force 58 by June 18.[34] In view of the submarine reports and unexpectedly stiff resistance on Saipan, Spruance also canceled the Guam landings which had been scheduled for June 18. Meeting with Kelly Turner and Holland Smith aboard *Rocky Mount*, Spruance told them bluntly, "The Japs are coming after us."[35] He asked Turner if the transports could be moved to the east, out of the immediate area. Turner was reluctant. The ground battle was turning out to be tougher than expected, he said. The transports contained food and ammunition that would be desperately needed by the troops ashore.

"Well," replied Spruance, "get everything that you don't absolutely need out of here to the eastward and I will join up with Mitscher and Task Force 58 and try to keep the Japs off your neck." Unloading would continue through June 17. As many transports as possible would be retired the night of the 17th. Only those with urgently needed supplies would return to the transport area on the morning of the 18th.[36] Meanwhile, patrol planes based in the Marshalls were to begin night searches as far as 600 miles to the west of Saipan.

Col. Justice Chambers began the morning of June 16 pinned down in a sweet potato field by a Japanese machine gun that shot the spare battery off his radioman's pack. Shell fire continued to fall on the 4th Division beachhead—among the early morning casualties was Col. Maynard C. Schultz, the highly regarded commander of the 1st Battalion, 24th Marines, who was killed by a shell fragment that struck him in the head during a conference at the regimental command post.

Chambers spent the rest of the morning mopping up enemy groups to his rear. The term "mopping up" tended to understate the situation as Chambers found when he ventured up a low rise. "As we neared the top of the rise, we heard voices chattering all over the place," he recalled. "They were Japanese." Peering over the top, they saw a mob of enemy troops. "There must have been hundreds of them," said Chambers. "They were, among other things, rolling a number of what I call mountain guns along the road. They were moving down the road straight for us." The Marines had about five grenades between them. They threw them over the rise and then "we all jumped up and ran like hell down the road," said Chambers.[37] By late morning his battalion had knocked out five machine guns, two mountain guns, and killed approximately sixty enemy soldiers.

With the immediate situation somewhat improved, the 4th Marine Division mounted a major push shortly after noon in an effort to break out and seize the dominating high ground from the *47th Independent Mixed Brigade*. Capt. Robert Neiman's tank company's role in this effort was to spearhead an attack straight up the Aslito Road. Neiman did not like the looks of the place. "The entire area from the beach to the ridge line was wide open," he recalled. "There was no cover. It had been sugarcane fields that had been harvested and there was absolutely nothing. The Marine infantry had to cross two thousand yards of wide-open space." Followed by a column of troop-carrying amtracs, halftracks, and amtanks, his tanks were supposed to attack up the road over the ridge and continue on for about another a mile to Aslito Airfield.[38]

Neiman's four-tank spearhead made it to the narrow road cut through the top of the ridge to find the Japanese waiting for them. Driver Charles B. "C. B." Ash looked out the port side of the tank to see a Japanese soldier staring back from some brush at the side of the road. Neiman spotted another Japanese setting up some kind of tripod-mounted weapon by the side of the cut. His gunner was blasting away at enemy infantry on the port side of the tank, but Neiman finally got his attention with a kick in the ribs.

The gunner turned his machine gun on the Japanese laboring over the tripod of what Neiman now saw was a heavy machine gun. The Japanese seemed to be having trouble with the weapon; he would fire a few rounds, then the gun would jam. Nevertheless, he stuck to his gun even when the tank gunner took him under fire. "I could see tracers going into him, but hell, he was still shooting," recalled Neiman. Finally the exasperated tank gunner fired the 75mm main gun at the man and vaporized him.[39]

While Neiman threaded the road cut, other Shermans from the 4th Tank Battalion clambered up the forward slope. The Sherman commanded by G/Sgt. Robert McCard, a soft-spoken twenty-five-year-old from Syracuse, New York, topped the crest of the ridge and started down the other side, directly into the kill zone of four Japanese Type 88 field guns. "We was told it was a machine gun nest," recalled McCard's driver, nineteen-year-old PFC Garland Dankworth. "We went up on the nose and got up and found out it was German howitzers up there."[40]

Commanding an adjacent tank, Lt. Ed Bollard was stunned. "As we nosed over the crest, they opened up at us with point blank fire, not more than fifty feet away," he reported. McCard's tank was hit, losing a track. "We saw we were in a hot spot and I gave the order to withdraw," said Bollard. "The tank McCard was in had been hit, however, and was out of commission."[41] Immobilized in the open, the crew briefly tried to fight it out with their 75mm main gun and the tank's co-axial machine gun, but without the ability to maneuver, it was obvious the Sherman would eventually be shot to pieces by Japanese artillery or fall victim to enemy infantry now swarming over the slope. With no outside help in sight, McCard ordered his crew to bail out and run for their lives.

The loader, gunner, and driver squeezed out through the hatches and ran back toward the crest. The bow gunner was shot and killed as he crawled out the bottom escape hatch. Dankworth squirmed out the bottom hatch and crawled out from under the tank to find another crewman who had been hit in the legs. He grabbed the wounded man and they stumbled toward the rear. "It seemed like from here to forever," recalled Dankworth. "I was hit too, but I didn't know it. I got shot through the leg, but it was the fleshy part of the leg, but I never did know it."[42]

McCard made no effort to follow his crew. As Japanese infantry closed on the disabled Sherman, he remained in the open turret, lobbing fragmentation and smoke grenades, buying time for his people to get clear. His body was later found slumped in the turret. Sixteen dead Japanese lay around the derelict tank.[43]

Meanwhile, Neiman radioed back from his tank "Ill Wind" to see how the rest of the column was doing. "There's nobody back there," came the reply. The thin-skinned amtracs and other vehicles had backed off in the face of the heavy fire from along the ridge.

Some of the heaviest fighting of the day fell to the 25th Marines, which tried all afternoon to secure the O-1 line along the high ground back of the

Yellow beaches. Justice Chambers nearly joined the parade of dead colonels during the morning when his men went after four antiaircraft guns that had been lowered to fire on ground troops. Peering cautiously over the crest of a slope, the colonel found himself staring directly into the muzzle of a Type 88 75mm antiaircraft/antitank gun no more than 25 to 30 yards away. "They had swung the damn thing around and it was pointing right up the hill," he remembered. "I dropped down as hard as I could and then the damn gun went off." The shell tore through some heaped-up dirt, took the head off a nearby Marine, and exploded 20 to 30 yards behind him.[44]

"We headed out toward the railroad track, hit the flat (cane fields) and all hell broke loose," recalled Pvt. Edward J. Early. A bullet glanced off Early's canteen cap; another hit the blasting caps he had stowed in his gas mask bag. The explosion shredded his gas mask, ruined his harmonica, and peppered his flesh with bits of metal. He settled in with about thirteen other wounded men behind the railway embankment. Apparently unimpressed with the extent of Early's injuries, a sergeant sent him and another man over to a native house to check for Japanese and see if there was any water. There were no Japanese, but they did find a cistern with some water in the bottom. "We figured it was safe to drink as the frogs swimming around in it were alive," Early remarked.[45]

PFC David I. Getman's fire team, moving forward with the 24th Marines, was also looking for water. The Marines had been warned about drinking water out of streams, but by afternoon their canteens were empty and they weren't about to be fussy. They came across a rivulet that looked clean enough. The men looked at Getman. "Go ahead," he said, "we could all be killed by nightfall." They filled their canteens and had a good long drink before someone glanced upstream and spotted two dead Japanese lying in the water. "We all looked at each other and laughed," recalled Getman.

The remainder of the afternoon was not so funny. As the platoon crossed a cane field, a mortar shell killed his BAR man, drove a piece of metal into Getman's hip, and wounded two other Marines. Sgt. Shirley B. Gilbert was trudging through some farmer's yam patch when he was hit in the right leg just over the knee. As he hobbled on, he was hit again, this time in the left knee and right forearm. PFC Robert A. Verna was hit in the chest by some kind of projectile that broke up and left several holes as it exited his back. PFC Walter Zakowski was hit by a shell fragment that tore his left breast away. Corp. Robert L. Baker went to his aid and was himself wounded in the head by an air burst.[46]

PFC John Pope was pushing up the slope of Fina Susa Ridge under mortar fire with his friend PFC Aldo Passante, a New Jersey kid who had just celebrated his twenty-third birthday two days before. A near miss knocked Pope to the ground. As his head cleared, he looked over at Passante and saw that his friend's right foot was gone. Pope rolled him over, grabbed the stump just below the knee, and squeezed as hard as he could to stop the flow of blood. Passante was lucky; a corpsman responded quickly. The doc tied off the stump with a tourniquet and stuck him with a morphine syrette before moving on. Dopey from morphine, Passante demanded a cigarette. Pope reminded him that he didn't smoke. Passante irrationally persisted until Pope placed a lighted cigarette in his mouth. Passante inhaled, gagged, and promptly spit it out. Soon after, a stretcher arrived and Pope headed up the slope as his friend was lugged back toward the rear and out of the war.

Japanese infantry lurked on the wooded slope, picking off exposed Marines. Pope's lieutenant, James R. Donovan, made the mistake of spreading out his map in an effort to orient himself. A sniper promptly shot him. Keeping low, Pope leaned over the lieutenant and asked him where he was hit. "I don't know," replied Donovan, "but I can't feel my legs." Pope pulled up Donovan's utility jacket and saw a hole just under his rib cage with a bit of intestine protruding. Donovan survived evacuation to the USS *Pierce*, but died two days later and was buried at sea. He left a wife in Peoria, Illinois.[47]

The 4th Division failed to break through, but by 1730 had managed to get onto the ridge roughly along the O-1 line. The two divisions had also finally closed the gap at Charan Kanoa. Most of the Japanese defenders of Afetna Point had either pulled out or been eliminated in counterattacks against the left flank of the 23rd Marines the previous night. Supported by tanks, the 2nd Battalion, 8th Marines mopped up remaining diehards on the point and pushed inland toward Lake Susupe and the surrounding marsh. By late morning the battalion had made contact with the 23rd Marines at Charan Kanoa pier, and by early afternoon the 8th Marines had secured its area as far inland as Lake Susupe. The operation was still far behind schedule, but the situation was starting to shake out a bit. "Things are looking up now," the 2nd Marine Division intelligence officer told correspondent Bob Sherrod.[48]

Navy chaplain William C. Goe came ashore in the 4th Marine Division area at about 1600 on June 16. Many of the dead still floated in the water or lay in untidy heaps on the beach and inland among the palms and the soft-needled ironwoods that had been planted as windbreaks beyond the high-tide line. Most of the dead Marines on shore had been covered with ponchos. Hibiscus and bougainvillea were in bloom alongside the brilliant red of the island's flame trees. It was a beauty hard to appreciate. "The odor of dead flesh began to penetrate most of the air we breathed," recalled Goe. Most of the dead were Marines, he observed. "We saw very few dead Japs."[49]

Medical personnel struggled to keep up with the continuing stream of wounded. Located on the Blue Beaches, the medical team for USS *Knox* alone evacuated 480 casualties to ships over a period of seventy-two hours. They included 149 shrapnel wounds, 142 cases of combat fatigue, 111 bullet wounds, 36 blast concussion, 16 heat exhaustion, 8 psychoneurosis (hysterical type) and a miscellany of others including one "bayonet wound of side."[50] Hospital Apprentice First Class Eli Silverman recalled a Marine sergeant with a handlebar moustache, yelling, "My feet hurt! My feet hurt!" Both the noncom's legs had been blown off about 3 inches above the knee. When Silverman went to help him, the surgeon called him away, observing, "Silverman, come with me; he's not going to make it." Years later, Silverman could still picture the stricken sergeant's face.[51]

P/Sgt. Arthur W. Wells spent much of the day transporting wounded men out to the ships aboard his amphibious truck, more familiarly known as a DUKW (pronounced "Duck"). In less violent times, Wells and his 2nd Amphibian Truck Company mates were subjected to derisive "quacks" from self-styled comedians as they rolled by, but no one was quacking now. On one of his trips, the load of casualties included a Marine with a severe head wound. It appeared that the entire back of his skull was shattered. "He lay on his stomach, moaning and attempting to move at times," remembered Wells.

Greatly disturbed, Wells kept a hand on the man's shoulder in an effort to comfort him, and as they neared an LST equipped to accept casualties, Wells hailed the vessel. An officer standing by the gangplank responded that the LST had all the wounded men it could handle. Wells pointed out the critical condition of the man with the head wound, but the officer refused to make an exception. "The only empty bunks on the ship are in officers' quarters," he informed Wells.

Wells exploded. He proceeded to dress the gaping officer down with every foul appellation that came to mind, concluding with, "Sir! You can take those bunks in officers' quarters and stick them up your ass!" In his fury, he contemplated shooting the by-the-book prig of an officer. Instead, the DUKW got back underway and finally found a transport ship to take the wounded aboard. The Marine with the head injury was still alive when they arrived; whether he survived or not, Wells never knew.[52]

Wells's experience was not unique. Aboard the staff and command ship USS *Fremont*, Navy lieutenant Emile L. Bonnot bore witness to the "heart-rending" chaos as small boats and amtracs loaded with seriously wounded Marines sought medical help from the ships. The *Fremont*'s sick bay was soon filled to capacity and ship's crew began to wave off all boats. "The men in the boats pleaded with the men on deck, saying the casualties aboard were dying but they were sorrowfully forced to order them to shove off. . . ." Recalled Bonnot, "There was no liaison between the ships and the shore and the boats kept coming out into the rolling swells of the ocean with men who were dying en route as the coxswain hunted to find some ships that could take them . . . Seeing the horribly wounded and dying men with intravenous bottles swaying above them and hearing the groans as the boat rolled in the swells of the ocean left a lasting impression on the officers and men of the *Fremont* who were unable to help."[53]

PFC David Getman, one of the twenty-eight men his company lost in the 4th Division's push toward the O-1 line during the day, was evacuated to the troopship USS *Storm King*. Casualties were lifted aboard with an overhead crane. Medical personnel cut all the clothes off the wounded men and they were prepped for surgery. While waiting his turn, Getman saw Marines having their legs amputated. "I got sick to my stomach and the doctors held a sheet in front of the legs, but you could still see it," he recalled. "It was bad."[54] By late afternoon of June 16, Transport Group A reported it had taken 1,082 casualties aboard ship, plus nineteen dead not previously reported. Ships were ordered to bury any dead at sea rather than return them to Graves Registration on shore.

Recovering aboard one of the offshore transports was PFC Herb Kiser, who had been wounded by mortar shell fragments in the carnage at Yellow Beach 2 on D-day. Kiser's older brother Virgil was a rifleman with the 24th Marines, which had come ashore under heavy shell fire late on the afternoon of the landing. Months earlier, Virgil had told Herb he had a bad feeling about their next operation. When they parted, Virgil dispensed with their usual handshake and reached out and hugged his brother. The morning of D+1 a wounded man from Virgil's outfit recognized Herb aboard ship and told him his brother had been killed the night before.[55]

On the afternoon of June 16, the USS *Monrovia* committed the remains of twenty-three Marines and one GI to the deep. All had been killed or fatally wounded during the landing the previous d? were already dead when they arrived at the *Monrovia.* Th.. cumbed to their wounds aboard ship. All but three had been evacuated .... the 2nd Marine Division beaches.

A clerk entered data about the deceased and the cause of death, misspelling an occasional name. The first name on the list was PFC Glen M. Adler.

NAME: ADLER, Glen M. PFC USMC, 370899
TYPE OF CASUALTY: Killed in Action (Battle Casualty)
DATE AND PLACE OF CASUALTY: June 15, 1944 at Saipan.
DIAGNOSIS: CRUSH, Left side of Chest and abdomen.
PROGNOSIS: Fatal
SOURCE OF ADMISSION: From Beach (Dead on Arrival)

PFC Adler was followed in careful alphabetical order by twenty-three other names, each accompanied by a terse summary of the cause of death. The impersonal record did not reveal that twenty-year-old PFC Glen Milton Adler had left Murray High School in St. Paul, Minnesota, to join the Marines in 1942 or that Sgt. Verner Carl Clemmensen (gunshot wound, head) was the son of Danish immigrants—his father was a milkman and his brother Henry was serving with the 1st Marine Division.

Sgt. Delbert R. Cornelius (lacerated head, shrapnel), a crewman with the 773rd Amphibious Tank Battalion, died just a week before his twenty-second birthday; nineteen-year-old PFC Santo Doccolo (lacerated skull, shrapnel), known to his friends as "Sandy," had played guard on the Wadsworth (Ohio) High School Grizzlies football team; 1st Lt. Loyd S. Harvick (gunshot, chest and head) of Superior, Wisconsin, was the son of Norwegian immigrants and had been wounded at Tarawa. A friend recalled later that he liked to go fishing. Corp. Loren G. Ikenberry (lacerated head, shrapnel) listed his occupation as pin-setter at a bowling alley when he joined the Marines. English-born Warrant Officer Stephen F. MacNeill (gunshot, right lumbar) had attended Eton and Trinity College and later earned a master's degree in history at the Sorbonne in Paris. He served as an officer in the British army during World War I. He came from a well-known family of actors and had gained some renown as a New York stage and radio actor between the wars. Entering the Marines, he had refused a commission for fear it would keep him out of combat. He left his actress wife and a young son in Milwaukee, Wisconsin.

2nd Lt. Lawrence Paul Jordan (lacerated, head and face, shrapnel) had been ROTC captain at Schurz High School in Chicago, Illinois, as well as a member of the football and fencing teams. A 1940 graduate of the University of Illinois, he had married fellow graduate Virginia Maurer in 1942, and they had an eight-month-old son, Lawrence Paul Jr. Sadly, Mrs. Jordan was about to endure even further heartbreak: Three days after her husband's death at Saipan, her brother, Lt. Frank Maurer, died of wounds suffered while serving with the 29th Infantry Division at Normandy following D-Day.

And so the list continued: twenty-two-year-old Pvt. Cody Hubert Johnson (fracture, compound, left femur and tibia) one of seven kids from Oklahoma where his father was a "cash rent farmer"; Corp. Robert Leonard Marshall (lacerated, left upper thigh and right elbow) a former paperboy from Tacoma, Washington; Italian-born PFC Concetto Pavone (punctured right chest and liver), who had come to the United States in 1927 when he was three years old; PFC Richard James Roos (crush, chest), the son of a traveling salesman for a rubber company from Denver, Colorado; PFC Theodore Nicklos Schleicher (crush, chest) a thirty-four-year-old volunteer who had written his father a month earlier, "A Marine never backs up ... he always keeps on the march"; Corp. Kenneth Spiess (lacerated chest, shrapnel), one of five sons of a grain company salesman from Minnesota; Pvt. Ramiro G. Telles Jr. (gunshot, multiple, head and face), whose father worked as a capper/bottler in a soft drink factory in Los Angeles; Sgt. Leon Henry Tujague of Louisiana (lacerated head, shrapnel) who had worked with his shoemaker father before joining the Marines in 1940....

The twenty-four dead, just a handful of the more than 2,000 Americans lost on D-day, were buried together at sea an hour before sunset on June 16, location 15 degrees 18'N. Latitude and 145 degrees 38'E. Longitude. There would be no remains to send home to their families; only their names would be recorded on the memorial wall at the National Cemetery of the Pacific in Hawaii.[56]

CHAPTER X

Tanks!

UP ON THE WOODED SLOPES OF THE O-1 LINE WHERE PFC JOHN POPE's
company had dug in the night of June 16, the early morning hours brought
the babble of agitated voices approaching from the darkness. Some of them
sounded like women. Word passed along the line to hold fire.

It was the wrong decision. Japanese soldiers had mixed in with the terrified civilians, using them as a screen to get in among the Marines. The
night erupted in a hand-to-hand melee among the foxholes. Pope caught
a glimpse of Corp. Felix Nawodczynski, a big twenty-three-year-old from
Jersey City, New Jersey. What looked like an undersized teenager jumped on
Nawodczynski's back. Nawodczynski, who weighed in at over 200 pounds,
was trying to reach over his back and throw the man off when his assailant
detonated a grenade, killing them both.

The Japanese finally melted back over the crest of the slope leaving a litter of dead comrades, dead civilians, and wounded and dead Marines. Pope,
who hadn't fired a shot in the confusion, heard another Marine weeping in
a nearby foxhole. He asked him if he was all right. "I just killed Murphy,"
the man replied, sobbing. He had unintentionally shot his foxhole buddy in
the chaos. Murphy joined the eight killed and twenty wounded recorded by
Baker Company, 1st Battalion, 24th Marines for the day. The survivors took
their lesson to heart, promising themselves they would never again make the
mistake of allowing civilians into their lines after dark.[1]

On the line in the 23rd Marines sector, Carl Matthews and his buddies were exhausted, but their efforts to get some sleep were disrupted by a
wounded Japanese lying somewhere out beyond their holes. Hit during an
earlier probe, he moaned and screamed throughout the night. "Will someone please shoot that son of a bitch so I can get some sleep?" shouted one of
the Marines in exasperation. The moaning and screaming subsided sometime before dawn as the Japanese finally succumbed to his injuries.[2]

Elsewhere, the Japanese were on the move. Pvt. Frank Borta's platoon spent the night huddled in cold swampy foxholes near Lake Susupe just northeast of Charan Kanoa. Taking his two-hour early morning watch, Borta heard revving engines accompanied by a loud clanking and rattling from out beyond the marshes. "Tanks," someone said. They waited apprehensively, painfully aware they had no bazookas or supporting arms to deal with enemy armor. To their relief, the sound of engines gradually faded as the tanks continued off to the north.[3]

Though stunned by the number of troops the Americans had been able to put ashore in such a short timeframe, General Saito continued to believe he could push the invaders back into the sea if he struck before the bridgehead could be consolidated. Unable to coordinate an overwhelming assault the night of the landing, he now intended to launch a massive tank/infantry assault on the 2nd Marine Division—the American hinge pin—at the northern end of the beachhead. Guiding on an easily recognizable landmark—the inter-island radio station just east of the northern end of the Charan Kanoa airstrip, now about 400 yards behind the lines of the 6th Marines and 500 to 600 yards inland from the lagoon—the attack would punch through the U.S. perimeter, then fan out with tanks and infantry, destroying supply dumps and artillery.

The bulk of the infantry—about 1,000 men—would be drawn from Col. Yukimatsu Ogawa's *136th Infantry Regiment.* The steel fist of the attack would be provided by Col. Takashi Goto's *9th Tank Regiment* headquartered in the Chacha Village schoolhouse 4½ miles from the beachhead. After his losses on D-day, Goto was still able to muster forty or more tanks for the counterattack, most of them later Type 97 Chi-Ha mediums with 47mm guns and two 7.7mm machine guns, along with some older Type 97s mounting lower-velocity 57mm guns. The regiment also had a number of light Type 95 (Ha-Go) models with 37mm main guns.

Goto's tankers were well trained, but their equipment was no match for tank-on-tank confrontations with the American Shermans. The Type 97 medium was fitted with armor plate from 8mm to 25mm thick. The light tanks, with armor only 6mm to 12 mm thick, were even more vulnerable. By contrast, the American M4(A)2 Sherman boasted a 75mm main gun and armor up to 75mm thick.[4]

General Saito hoped to hit the Marines in late afternoon before they were fully dug in for the night and while there would still be enough light to maintain direction and organization. This timetable fell apart almost immediately. The tankers were late getting out of their assembly area in the woods near Chacha Village, then found slower than expected going on the route to the invasion beaches. It was 0315 before they arrived in position. Now committed to an unintended night attack, Major Goto and General Saito's chief of staff, Col. Takuji Suzuki, argued about how to proceed. Suzuki wanted to launch a combined tank/infantry attack with the tanks in the lead. Goto didn't want to be held back by the slower pace of the infantry; he insisted he be allowed to use his tanks independently. Suzuki finally prevailed, but circumstances would give Goto his wish. The argument settled, the force divided into seven sections and started toward the Marine lines.[5]

Down on the flats, the 1st Battalion, 6th Marines had dug in facing the higher ground, utilizing abandoned enemy trenches and the shallow irrigation ditches that meandered across the reddish-brown plain. A few farm buildings and scattered banana and bread fruit trees were visible to their front. Artillery had been dueling back and forth for most of the night, with the Marine guns getting the worst of it. The 4th Battalion alone lost five 105mm howitzers and the 2nd Battalion lost three of its twelve 75mm guns.[6]

At about 0330 the Marines began to hear the growl of tank engines and squeal of tracks. Their appearance was not completely unexpected: Aerial surveillance had spotted tanks on the move behind Japanese lines before nightfall. Commanding B Company, thirty-two-year-old Capt. Claude G. Rollen rang up battalion headquarters. An attack appeared imminent—tanks and troops could be heard approaching from the hills and along a ravine to his direct front, he reported. "[We] could actually hear them talking and shouting over the noise of their tanks," remembered Jack Powell, waiting sleeplessly with Rollen's riflemen.[7]

Mortars coughed and flares popped overhead, casting the fields in a garish green light. "We hunkered down and looked straight ahead to keep from being blinded by the light," said Powell. "All of a sudden, the world stopped. An area about two miles square seemed to be lighted, and all we could see was tanks and infantry, some as close as fifty yards and all the way back to Mount Tapotchau. I remember that instant seemed to last forever."[8]

Somewhere between twenty-four and thirty-two tanks from the *3rd* and *5th Companies* of the *9th Tank Regiment* surged across the open plain. "Riding on the outside of each tank were a few riflemen, usually four," noted a subsequent special action report. "Each of these groups carried at least one light machine gun. Some of the guns were strapped to the backs of the men who carried them."[9]

Marine machine gun crews opened up, bouncing orange tracers off the sides of the enemy armor. Infantry readied rifle grenades and crouched low in their foxholes. Probably confused by darkness and lack of inter-tank communication, the armored assault seemed to lack cohesion. Some tanks cruised around aimlessly; a couple bogged down in the wet ground out front; some stopped to let riding infantry leap off; others raced directly into the Marine lines, leaving the supporting infantry behind. "[A] lot happened at once," observed Powell. "Japanese officers waved sabers, buglers sounded their charges. Our machine guns, 37mm antitank guns, bazookas and mortars were all firing at once . . . We were literally overrun by the enemy. . . ."[10]

Capt. William A. McIntyre listened to the developing battle from the Marine artillery positions on the constricted beachhead. "Our special weapons battalion had just been issued new bazookas," he observed. "We had no idea if the rocket launchers could stop a massed Nip tank assault . . . We were all tensed up about this. We were only yards from the surf, and if we couldn't stop light armor, we would be pushed into the water and shot like ducks . . . We could hear this haroop, haroop, haroop as the bazookas fired. . . ."[11]

As a tank rolled up to the B Company command post, Captain Rollen jumped from his foxhole, took aim, and loosed a rifle grenade at point-blank range. The explosion burst his eardrums, but the tank was on fire as it clanked away. "By that time the whole company position had been penetrated by the tanks and the battle evolved into a madhouse of noise, tracers and flashing lights," recalled 1st Battalion executive officer Maj. James A. Donovan Jr. "Many of the tanks were unbuttoned, the crew chief directing from the top of his open turret. Some were led by a crew member afoot. They seemed to come in two waves, carrying foot troops on the long engine compartment or clustered around the turret, holding on to the hand rail. Some even had machine guns or grenade throwers set up on the tank."[12]

The bulk of the infantry followed on foot, but lost formation as they came under fire from four heavy machine guns B Company had placed in the front line. "Those following afoot were badly cut up," noted Donovan.[13] The tanks pushed on regardless and rampaged through the battalion area. Two 60mm mortar positions were overrun, the crews flattening themselves in their holes as the tanks rolled over them, one of the engines leaking oil so badly it saturated the dungarees of the Marines crouching below.[14]

PFC Tom Biondi, a round-faced, smiling twenty-three-year-old from Middlesex, New Jersey, shot an enemy crewman as he clambered down from a stalled tank. Two other tanks rolled over the shallow ditch sheltering Biondi's squad. At Biondi's side, Corp. Richard A. "R.A.F." Fanning managed to duck down between the treads, but a shell from yet another tank blew off Biondi's right arm. "It wasn't more than six feet from me," said Biondi. "I knew I was hit, but all I felt was a gush of warm blood. Then I heard R.A.F. ask me if I was hurt. He came over and got out my first aid kit and fixed it up some."[15]

Dug in back by the beach, PFC Segal Silcox heard the roar of tank engines and the din of gunfire, though he could not see the enemy armor. A Seabee heading toward the rear paused long enough to announce, "They are coming through." As the Seabee moved on, the veteran corporal sharing Silcox's foxhole turned to him and said, "We don't move. This is where you and I are going to die." Silcox knew he meant every word.[16]

Fortunately for Silcox, the attack never got that far. As tanks penetrated the front line, bazooka-wielding Marines maneuvered to hit them from all angles. Unable to use the sights in the darkness, the gunners resorted to "Kentucky windage" at ranges of 80 yards or less. The newly issued bazookas proved deadly. PFC Herb Hodges's team hit seven tanks with seven rounds. Another team got three hits out of four.

Sgt. Dean T. Squires of Taloga, Oklahoma, blew off the head of a Japanese tank commander who rose out of his turret for a look around, then ran when the tank came at him. "Still the tank kept coming after me," he recalled. "I glanced down and saw a full demolition kit in a foxhole. I grabbed it, stuck a fuse in the pack and then ducked to the side and let the tank go by. As it did, I jumped up and threw the pack on the back end of the tank." The explosion demolished the rear of the tank.[17]

Hit in the hull with a rocket, one Japanese tank churned on for another 20 yards before bursting into flame. A rifleman jammed another tank's track with a piece of timber, then dropped a grenade into the turret when the crew chief unbuttoned the hatch to investigate. "The Jap tanks, blind even under favorable conditions, appeared confused," observed Donovan. "As their guides and crew chiefs were hit by Marine rifle and machine gun fire, what little control they had was lost. They ambled on in the general direction of the beach, getting hit again and again until each burst into flames or turned in aimless circles only to stop dead, stalled in its own ruts or the marshes in the low ground."[18] One of the poorly armored light tanks had its turret knocked completely off by an antitank grenade.[19]

As tanks were hit and set on fire, they silhouetted other tanks. Crews manning 37mm guns fired on approaching tanks and then turned their guns around to fire on the rear of those that overran their positions. "[The] 37mm guns did not penetrate the turret of the tank but were effective against the bogie wheels and tank tracks, stopping the tanks and enabling our troops to destroy them with other weapons," noted an after-action report. "Bazookas and anti-tank grenades were especially effective."[20] As the melee raged, the field phone at Colonel Riseley's regimental headquarters rang. It was General Watson at division headquarters only about 500 yards distant from the fighting seeking an update on the situation. "Well," observed Riseley laconically, "we've got a five-cigar counterattack going on."[21]

At 1st Battalion headquarters, Bill Jones ordered Headquarters Company commander Capt. Norman K. Thomas to go forward and help Rollen. Thomas, who had won a Silver Star for heroism at Tarawa, loaded up with extra bazooka rockets and headed out with a platoon. In the confusion, they walked into the Japanese. Sgt. Lewis J. Michelony saw them first—three enemy soldiers sitting behind a machine gun at point-blank range. Yelling "Hit the deck!" he and his gunnery sergeant dove for the ground as the gun opened fire, but Thomas was a step too late. "I hit the deck," recalled Michelony, "and as I hit it . . . we were touching elbows, the three of us, and he caught it first in the stomach and then in the head. I mean, I could see daylight through him. By that time, the tanks started to follow us. The Japanese were chasing us with tanks, and their officers were chasing us with sabers."[22]

Some of the Japanese tanks spilled into the lines of the 2nd Battalion, 2nd Marines, which had been attached to the 6th Marines after coming ashore the previous morning. As one of them overran PFC Frederick W. Cramer's machine-gun position, the twenty-year-old Sequin, Washington, native pulled out his .45 pistol and ran alongside shooting at the tank commander standing in the open turret. The duel came to an end when Cramer finally managed to get a grenade into the open hatch, but was then himself killed.

On B Company's other flank, nineteen-year-old PFC William L. Jefferies of A Company took his bazooka team toward the tank breakthrough. As they ran across an open field, Jefferies shot and killed a Japanese soldier. Seconds later, a Japanese officer charged them, swinging a sword over his head. "Get him, Jeff!" yelled his gunner, who had his hands full with the rocket tube. Jefferies pulled the trigger on his carbine, but the weapon jammed. Jumping protectively in front of his gunner, he threw his carbine up to block the sword, then knocked the Japanese down, landing on top of him as they both fell. "I pounded him with my carbine and then jumped up, cleared my carbine and killed him," he recounted.

Jefferies's bazooka team killed four Japanese tanks before running out of rockets. It was getting towards daybreak when they saw yet another tank approaching. Jefferies told his team to stay low and ran back across the open field to obtain more rockets. "[I] spotted something move to my right and I could make it out as a Jap—a Jap on his stomach like he was going to throw a hand grenade at me, so I shot him on the run." Obtaining the rockets, he returned to find the enemy tank "exploding like the 4th of July." His team told him that when the tank came up to them, the Japanese commander raised the turret hatch. One of the Marines climbed up on the deck, dropped a grenade inside, and slammed the hatch cover back down.[23]

Over in C Company, PFCs Frank Howard and Robert E. Nolan found themselves in a close-quarter bayonet fight as the Japanese infantry overran their foxhole. "The one I was fighting with cut me on both arms," recalled Howard. "I side-stepped to the left when he rushed at me and cut through my dungarees on my right side of my waist and I ran my bayonet through his chest. My bayonet got stuck, between his ribs and when I was trying to pull it out, a Jap came from behind and got me three times: once in the ribs and twice near my spine." Howard's legs buckled and he collapsed in the foxhole. His attacker was about to finish him off when Nolan intervened, bashing the Japanese in the head with his rifle stock and then killing him with his bayonet. "When he hit the Jap, he broke the stock so he got my rifle and I used a captured Jap luger to protect ourselves as [Japanese] were running all over the place," said Howard.[24]

Halftracks from the Regimental Weapons Company and U.S. Shermans from the 2nd Tank Battalion arrived at dawn. Stationed near regimental headquarters, the halftracks had been alerted at 0415 but had difficulty getting forward over the soft ground and meandering irrigation ditches. Their 75mm guns finished off a number of disabled enemy tanks that continued to fire on Marines despite being unable to maneuver.[25] "Tanks were burning everywhere," recalled Jack Powell.[26]

"By 0700 the field was quiet except for the small arms fire of a few Nip snipers and the answers of the Marines who mopped them up," observed

Major Donovan. "The last Jap tank was spotted as it climbed the winding road to Hill 790. Its turret could be seen among a small group of buildings on top of the hill. The naval gunfire officer quickly adjusted and fired twenty salvos on this target. The tank sent up an oily smoke and burned the rest of the day."[27]

Lieutenant Colonel Jones's 1st Battalion suffered seventy-eight casualties. Fox Company, 2nd Battalion, 2nd Marines, to the 1st Battalion's immediate right, lost nineteen killed and wounded.[28] Corpsman Leslie E. Gutzman spotted a Marine who had been shot just forward of the ear. "When I saw the blood, I told him to sit down; he had been wounded. He denied this and then I noticed there was a wound on the opposite side also. He died within a few minutes."[29]

Lying in his foxhole with his buddy Nolan, Frank Howard was still alive as the sun came up. When he was bayoneted, it had felt like the shock from an electrical wire, he recalled. Despite the severity of his injuries and the loss of blood, he was still conscious when a corpsman came for him at about 0600. He was evacuated to the transport *John Land* and eventually to Pearl Harbor and out of the war.[30]

Major Hirakushi, who had watched the tank/infantry assault get off, started back to division headquarters before dawn after hearing a report that General Saito might have been killed. An officer told Hirakushi that Saito had disappeared on the way to the front. Narrowly escaping incineration in a burning cane field, Hirakushi made his way to Saito's headquarters cave to find the general dozing, chin on chest. He patted Saito's shoulder. "Division commander, are you all right?"

Saito opened his eyes. "I won't die," he replied.[31]

But many of his soldiers had died in his stead. Instead of wreaking havoc on the Marine beachhead, General Saito's counterattack resulted in the destruction of the *9th Tank Regiment* and severe losses to the *136th Infantry Regiment*. Enemy tank losses were hard to determine given the destruction inflicted on the armor. Some estimates placed enemy tank losses at as high as thirty-one. The number of tanks involved came as a surprise to U.S. forces. A summary by Headquarters, Expeditionary Troops, Task Force 56 noted, "the enemy threw into action more tanks than were thought to be on the island. The total number involved was not ascertained, but 29 were destroyed."[32] The Japanese left about 300 infantrymen and tank crewmen on the field. Major Goto never returned and was presumed to have been killed.

Wandering among the still smoking enemy tanks, PFC Jack Eardley came across the bodies of two immaculately dressed Japanese officers. One of them, presumably a tank commander, sported a waxed moustache, black gloves, highly polished boots, and a sword. The other officer, whose brains had been blown out, was notable mostly for "an oozing mass of pinkish gray matter dangling from his nose."[33] Eardley stepped on something soft and looked down to see a severed human hand. Japanese corpses lay around like so much garbage, covered with buzzing flies and already bloating and bursting their uniforms.

Also looking over the carnage, Capt. William A. McIntyre detected the aroma of fried bacon. "I stopped into a clearing and discovered it was not bacon I smelled," he remembered. "The commander of a smoldering Japanese tank was sprawled across the blackened turret and was being thoroughly burned."[34]

At regimental headquarters that morning, a weary but victorious Colonel Riseley found himself the beneficiary of five cigars, sent personally by General Watson in honor of the enemy's failed "five cigar" counterattack.[35] "I don't think we have to fear Jap tanks any more on Saipan," said "Terrible Tommy" following the debacle. "We've got their number."[36]

With his Marines still trying to slug their way off the beachhead—and keenly aware that the Japanese fleet was steaming toward Saipan—Gen. Holland Smith decided to bring the reserve 27th Infantry Division ashore. As a matter of general policy Smith believed it was "always better to get [forces] on the beach rather than have them sitting out at sea on ships" where they were not only ineffective, but vulnerable in large numbers. One other reality was also becoming clear: Despite his low opinion of the Army division, he was going to need the additional manpower.[37]

The commander of the 27th Division, fifty-year-old Maj. Gen. Ralph C. Smith, received the warning order shortly after noon. A veteran of some of the bitterest fighting of World War I—he had been wounded in action during the bloodbath in the Meuse-Argonne—Smith had spent the years between the wars in a variety of staff and teaching positions. Fluent in French and a graduate of the prestigious l'Ecole de Guerre, he was one of the few genuine European experts in the U.S. Army, and yet, in the inexplicable wisdom of the military, in November 1942 he was assigned to lead the 27th Division, which would spend the war in the Pacific.[38] Smith himself may have been somewhat perplexed by his assignment. Prior to the campaign, he confessed to Graves Erskine, whom he knew well from their days at Command and Staff School at Fort Leavenworth, "I don't think I'm really a combat commander. I've been highly trained for staff work, particularly in the intelligence field, and that's where I feel my abilities could best be used."[39]

Unlike the loud and overbearing Holland Smith, Ralph Smith was soft-spoken and courteous to a fault. One of his staff officers, Col. Henry Ross, recalled that he had never seen the general become angry or curse. Similarly, then-colonel S. L. A. Marshall, who considered Holland Smith a boor, thought highly of Ralph Smith, describing him as "a generous Christian gentleman." If he had a fault, observed Marshall, it was that he was too considerate of others.[40]

Originally organized from New York National Guard units, Smith's division had been federalized in late 1940, but had undergone significant changes since then. Many of the unfit had been weeded out during the rigors of training, but the division had also periodically suffered from a hemorrhage of key noncoms and junior officers skimmed off to fill other organizations. A battalion commander later observed of the division that both the training and the quality of the men was very good. "I do think there was one thing that hurt us," he added, that being the nearly two years the 27th spent in the Hawaiian islands awaiting combat. "We spent one hell of a long time on the beach in defensive positions . . . I think this probably took the edge off."[41]

The uncertainty of division's role in the *Forager* operation also put strains on Ralph Smith's staff. Though designated as the reserve for Saipan, plans called for its employment at either Guam or Tinian should it not be required there. The multitude of possibilities resulted in a mountain of staff work. As of mid-May, with a month to go before the landing on Saipan, sixteen different plans had been developed: twelve for Saipan, two for Tinian, and two for Guam. By the time *Forager* actually got underway, a total of twenty-two plans had been drawn up for possible operations on any of the three islands, including one that would land two regiments over Purple Beaches 1 and 2 in Saipan's Magicienne Bay. Fortunately for the GIs, that particular plan never came to pass.[42]

As of noon on June 16, two of the division's three infantry regiments—the 165th and 105th—were afloat about 30 miles off Saipan. Summoned to a conference with Brig. Gen. Graves Erskine aboard the *Cambria*, Smith was directed to land his artillery battalions as soon as possible. The 165th

Infantry Regiment was to land immediately and move into position on the 4th Marine Division's right flank to join in the next day's attack toward Aslito Field. The 105th Infantry was to follow as rapidly as practicable. The 106th Infantry Regiment would remain afloat in Joint Expeditionary Troops Reserve.[43]

Despite considerable confusion, two battalions of the 165th Infantry got ashore in the early morning hours, having been landed willy-nilly in the dark with no regard for organizational integrity. Assistant division commander Brig. Gen. Ogden J. Ross got in touch with 4th Marine Division headquarters and was directed to enter the line and be prepared to jump off in an attack on Aslito Airfield at 0730. With less than four hours to get in place, the GIs started walking.[44]

Aboard the carrier *Lexington*, Mitscher's air operations officer, Cmdr. William J. "Gus" Widhelm, had been a man on a mission since the Saipan landings got underway. A hustler of almost mythical proportions, Widhelm haunted the pilot ready rooms, offering all takers a chance to bet against his thousand-dollar wager that there would be a fleet engagement before June 20. Though the airmen should have been wary given Widhelm's inside track, the offer sold out. The final $125 was taken by Lt. (j.g.) Alex Vraciu, a fighter pilot with *Lexington*'s "Pistol Packin' Airedales."[45]

Vraciu had made a bad bet. More evidence that the Japanese *Mobile Fleet* was on the move toward Saipan arrived the morning of June 17, courtesy of the submarine *Cavalla*. On her maiden patrol, *Cavalla* was heading west to relieve *Flying Fish* at San Bernardino Strait when contacted by ComSubPac. Admiral Lockwood had digested the previous report from *Flying Fish* and now ordered *Cavalla*, skippered by thirty-two-year-old Cmdr. Herman J. Kossler, to scout across the estimated track of the Japanese carrier force. At 2300 on June 16, *Cavalla*'s radar picked up two tankers and three destroyers heading east at high speed. Kossler had maneuvered into position to attack by 0402, when one of the Japanese destroyers began to get too nosy. Kossler had to pull the plug and was at only 75 feet when the destroyer passed directly over him. Surfacing an hour and a half later, *Cavalla* sent a contact report and resumed course for the Philippines.

It was not to be. Lockwood saw the tanker convoy as a key piece in the developing situation at Saipan. If the tankers could be sunk, the Japanese main forces would be deprived of critical fuel, which would limit their capabilities. ComSubPac radioed Cavalla:

DESTRUCTION THOSE TANKERS OF GREAT IMPORTANCE . . . TRAIL . . . ATTACK . . . REPORT[46]

Kossler changed course and headed after the convoy at high speed. But by morning, it was clear *Cavalla* would not be able to catch up and was consuming fuel at too high a rate. Orders arrived to follow the convoy's track at normal cruising speed. The oilers had been steaming at 16 knots, but they were certain to pause at some point as they neared the U.S. forces. Deducing from *Cavalla's* report that the Japanese fleet intended to refuel somewhere in the vicinity of 13 N., 137 E., less than 500 nautical miles southwest of Saipan, Lockwood ordered four subs—*Finback, Bang, Stingray,* and *Albacore*—to relocate 100 miles south, and *Seawolf* 150 miles south. If his deduction was correct, this arrangement would place his subs directly in the path of the Japanese fleet.[47]

Meanwhile, Adm. Joseph J. "Jocko" Clark was doing his part. Clark's Hellcats had spent June 16 cleaning out Japanese air forces in the Bonins, tangling with thirty to forty Japanese planes in the air and catching another one hundred on the ground, pretty much eliminating any imminent threat from that quarter.[48] U.S. losses totaled eleven fighters. Heading back toward TF 58 the following day, Clark received orders from Mitscher to send searches out to the southwest. The position of the enemy fleet was roughly known; it might be possible to hit the Japanese from two sides if Clark's aircraft could pin down the location. Clark sent twelve search planes 350 miles to the southwest then steamed after them, both to recover his aircraft and to close distance with the enemy. The planes did not sight the enemy fleet, which was still 700 miles away.

That night Clark found himself contemplating what might be the opportunity of a lifetime. He later wrote, "Had I steamed to the southwestward all night, by the next morning I could place myself between the Japanese fleet and its homeland, thereby blocking off its retreat and boxing in the enemy between our four task groups." He ran the suggestion by TF 58.4 commander Rear Adm. William K. Harrill, who had reluctantly accompanied Clark's task force into the Bonins. Perhaps predictably, Harrill, who was developing a reputation for timidity, would have nothing to do with the idea. He promptly changed course and headed off to the south, leaving Clark's TG 58.1 alone.[49]

Clark and his staff considered their options. With Harrill, the two task groups could have put up 300 fighters and 200 attack planes, which Clark considered more than a match for the entire enemy carrier force. Harrill's hasty departure had deprived the force of some ninety fighters and seventy bombers. Clark was not confident that what he had left would be sufficient. "I did not wish to find myself on a windy corner with so many Japanese airplanes that I could not shoot them all down," he conceded.[50]

Clark did not dare break radio silence to check with Mitscher. Though he thought Mitscher would approve of his plan, he doubted the more cautious Spruance would show similar enthusiasm. "If Mitscher had been in command of the Fifth Fleet, I would have continued to the southwest," Clark said later. But Mitscher was subordinate to Spruance. "I admired both men, but it was obvious to me that Spruance did not understand the full capabilities of the fast carriers," Clark admitted later.[51] After debating the pros and cons, Clark decided against striking off on his own and turned TG 58.1 to follow Harrell back toward Saipan. Much later, Mitscher told Clark he should have continued to the southwest in an effort to box in Ozawa's fleet. "I almost ordered you to do it," he confessed. But by the time of that conversation, the moment had long passed.[52]

CHAPTER XI

Toward the Airfield

JUNE 17 WAS A SATURDAY, NOT THAT IT MATTERED MUCH TO THE SWEATing Marines and GIs on the line. A new day only meant a renewed effort to break out of the beachhead. Attacking with the 23rd Marines, Orvel Johnson's platoon lost its first man when his fire team leader, twenty-five-year-old Corp. Merrill Quick, decided to take a look through his binoculars at the reverse slope on the Fina Susu Ridge. Crawling up to an overhanging bush, Quick raised his head and was immediately picked off by a sniper. It was shortly after 0900 and the assault hadn't even begun.

The plan of attack called for tanks to join in from the south while the 1st Battalion charged over the top of the ridge and down the enemy-held reverse slope toward the next ridge. What the Marines didn't realize—and Corporal Quick didn't live long enough to find out—was that the Japanese had pulled back about 200 yards and were waiting for them. At the command to move out, the first line of Marines crossed the military crest on the run. "Every one of us who came over the top was a sitting duck waiting to be shot," recalled Corp. Rowland Lewis. "We were sent over in waves of 20 (+ or −) men about two minutes apart, until about three-fourths of the company were over."

The waiting Japanese hit them with a wall of fire. Running down the grass-covered hillside, Johnson spotted a Japanese mortar crew. He opened up with his BAR and knocked down a bicyclist—possibly a messenger—who chose that ill-advised moment to pedal away from the gun pit. Another Marine abruptly shoved him aside and killed a Japanese emerging with a bayoneted rifle from a spider hole directly in front of him. Johnson felt a piercing pain on his right hip and realized his ammo belt was on fire. As he struggled to drop the belt, he heard shouts, "Fall back! Withdraw!" He turned and ran back up the slope, his ammo belt dangling. The entire failed assault took longer to describe than to experience, he observed later. He returned to find he was the sole survivor of his fire team. Among the dead was PFC Moses Iadanza. When word came to pull back over the ridge, the Italian-born twenty-three-year-old paid no attention and continued to loose bursts from his BAR at the Japanese. His buddies yelled at him to get back.

"Fuck 'em!" retorted Iadanza.

His body was found there the next day. He had expended all his ammunition before being killed.[1]

Noon found G/Sgt. Frank Routh's company on the edge of a large cane field facing a palm grove near the juncture with the adjacent 2nd Marine Division. Routh heard something crashing through the brush in his direction. "About this time, out of the corner of my eye, I saw this Jap stop and throw up his rifle," he recalled. Before the man could pull the trigger, Routh shot him three times, rapid fire, with his M1. "I just plain beat him to the draw."

The Marines started through the cane field toward the palm grove. "As the cane had ripened, but had not been harvested, it was a tangled mess," recalled Routh. "It was like a thousand hands were holding me back." A halftrack rattled up to the edge of the grove and fired its 75mm gun. Routh saw the crew pointing from the open back. One of them grabbed a machine gun mounted on the rail and hosed down the treetops. Two Japanese tumbled from a platform hidden in the branches. As Routh continued forward with his bayoneted rifle at the ready, someone to his right yelled, "Look out, Gunny! The tree!"

Routh wheeled to find a Japanese practically on top of him. He took a half step back and thrust at the enemy soldier with his bayonet. "My bayonet entered into his neck and on into his chest," he recalled. "As a result of our collision, we fell sideways to my right. The long cold steel paralyzed him and as I watched the blood run up my rifle stock and all over me, I noticed that as he relaxed, a little black Jap grenade rolled out of each hand."

Recovering, Routh noticed a row of air vents protruding from the ground and realized he was standing by the roof of a bombproof shelter. He threw a grenade into the entrance. Before he could throw another, two Japanese soldiers emerged from the far end of the shelter. "I let the spoon fly and just upped my throw as far as I could and although one of the Japs was going down, it looked like my grenade went off right between them. It really flattened them."

In the confusion, a mob of Chamorros poured out of the ground from what looked to Routh like "a regular old storm house" like those used in

Texas to shelter against tornadoes. The frightened civilians ran toward the Marines holding out crucifixes and crying, "Francisco, Francisco, Francisco." Routh got one of them to shout to the occupants of the bunker to come out. "About this time a Jap soldier, fully dressed, helmet and all swung out the entrance toward me and threw a grenade. I immediately shot him in the gut as the grenade spewed a little past my left side. I started moving to my right and pin-wheeled the Jap's helmet with my next shot. About this time the grenade went off and as my right leg was back, a large fragment entered on the inside of my thigh. It was as if a hot poker had been stuck in my thigh. Some fine pieces of the grenade caught in my left shoulder and arm. All this time the Chamorro women were still pleading with us with the crucifixes of Christ and repeating 'Francisco, Francisco, Francisco.' We finished off the bomb shelter with flame throwers." By now, the remaining Japanese were fleeing down out the back side of the palm grove. Routh handed his dispatch case and message book to a lieutenant and began hobbling in the other direction, to the rear.[2]

Corp. Edwin Donley, a twenty-three-year-old forward observer from Cincinnati, Ohio, spent the morning calling in artillery support for the assault. As he and his two-man team completed a fire mission they heard a voice pleading, "Will somebody please help me?!"

"That sounds like Mac," said Corp. Charles A. ("Red") Jones.

The three Marines ran down the slope toward the sound of the cries. As Jones had suspected, it was twenty-two-year-old PFC Louis McGowan. He had been hit and was lying in a patch of sugar cane about 30 or 40 yards away. "Cover me," Donley told Jones. "I'll go get him."

"The Japs were on the other side of the hill; as soon as I got out in the open they started firing and I had to crawl all the way to him," recalled Donley. He arrived to find McGowan, a former high school football star from Silver Creek, New York, was in dire straits. "His arm was just hanging; he had a hole in his side about the size of a grapefruit and one of his legs was nearly torn off," observed Donley. "I told him, 'Mac, hang on, I'll go get some morphine.'" Retracing his route, Donley found a corpsman and obtained a morphine syrette, then once again crawled out into the field. "And I did give it to him, but I don't think it helped," he remembered.

He lay in the cane trying to figure out how he was going to get McGowan out of there. "I couldn't carry him; he was too big and heavy, so I said, well I'll lay him out on a poncho and I'll pull him across. And it was a job getting him on that poncho. I tried to move him and he tried to help and it weren't doing no good. Finally I got what I thought was enough of him on the poncho to give it a try. So I laid down prone all the way down and tried to pull him and it didn't work so I had to get up on my knees and that worked a little better."

As soon as he emerged from the clump of cane, the Japanese opened fire from the far side of the field. Fortunately, Red Jones had picked up four or five more riflemen and they kept the Japanese occupied while Donley labored along, pulling McGowan on the poncho. "And we finally got close enough for two guys to run out and help me get him back," he said. "And I laid him down. His eyes were open. And I said, 'Hang in there, Mac; they'll take you over to the aid station.' And he closed his eyes . . . He died right there when he closed his eyes."[3]

For Corp. Daniel W. Smith, a gunner on a 4th Tank Battalion Sherman, the day began with orders to destroy enemy gun positions just past the O-1 ridgeline. "The first thing we saw was the blue flame of a gun firing at us," recalled Smith. "We thought, 'Holy mackerel! What have we walked into?'" The tank commander tapped him on the shoulder and said, "Smitty, did you see that?" Smith said he had. The tank commander exclaimed, "Well, do something about it." Smith put a 75mm shell into the enemy gun and "blew it all to hell."

As other enemy guns took the exposed tank under fire, the driver dodged back and forth, pausing to allow Smith to get off an occasional shot in return. "So we jig-jagged to the left and jig-jagged to the right and kept going one way or another," recalled Smith. "I was scared to hell." The noise was deafening. "We ran over a few emplacements. We ran into some. We were running over people . . . I didn't honestly think we were ever going to get out of there." Every so often the tank would shudder under the impact of a hit. The shells didn't penetrate, but finally, one of them hit the Sherman in the track and stopped them dead. Something was burning. "Let's get the hell out of here, boys!" shouted the tank commander.

Smith was outside before he realized he had broken his right arm. He couldn't pull his .45-caliber pistol from his shoulder holster. A crewmember took it out, chambered a round, and put the gun in Smith's left hand. "Then, thank goodness we heard the roar of another tank, and another one steaming up the same path we had followed," recalled Smith. They all got out, making their way slowly 500 yards back to the ground troops back of the crest. Their Sherman and another had knocked out three enemy 77mm dual-purpose guns. Smith's tank was retrieved later in the day. It had sustained seven hits. A total of eighty-nine dead Japanese were counted in the vicinity.[4]

Less than an hour after finishing off the early morning Japanese tank/infantry assault, the 2nd Marine Division was also on the move, advancing through the litter of enemy corpses and smoldering armored vehicles. Colonel Riseley's 6th Marines and the attached 2nd Battalion, 2nd Marines seized the remainder of the O-1 line and proceeded northeast to the O-2 line into the foothills of Mount Tipo Pale fronting the looming hump of Mount Tapotchau. On the division right, the 8th Marines finally reached the O-1 line, but the 1st Battalion, 29th Marines, which was attached to the regiment, bogged down in the swamp extending north from Lake Susupe. Men carrying machine guns, mortars, and ammo sank waist deep into the muck. The swamp was far larger than indicated on Marine maps and it was infested with snipers. "The water was up to our chest in places and snipers were shooting at us," recalled Corp. Frank Borta. "We couldn't move very fast and some of the guys got hit."[5]

"We moved up and were almost there when we were hit by mortar fire," said PFC Bob Everett. "We ran forward, hitting the deck as we went. I stopped behind a tree about four-feet wide. A mortar shell landed on the other side. I heard someone moaning on the other side and went around to check. There were two dead Marines in a hole about 4x4. One was Billy Trimmier, my 'bunkie' earlier aboard ship. His head was severed about eye level. I knew it was him because his name was printed on the back of his jacket."[6]

The attack ground to a halt under fire from a tree-covered hill that dominated the front. Battalion commander Lt. Col. Guy Tannyhill was hit in the hand and evacuated. Marines finally gained the hill. The Japanese counterattacked. Fighting was hand-to-hand. Three Japanese went after Corp. Richard J. Lynes, a twenty-four-year-old from Morris, Illinois. Though wounded in the exchange, Lynes shot two of them and grappled with the third, who was armed with a saber. Lynes threw the man to the ground, wrenched the saber from his hands, and killed him with his own blade.[7] Aided by tanks, the Marines finally prevailed.

Frank Borta felt little sense of victory. Among the eighty casualties suffered by his battalion was his veteran sergeant, John Rachitsky, fatally shot after taking over the platoon when the lieutenant was wounded. Borta found

Rachitsky's poncho-covered body lying on a stretcher. Determined not to cry, he recited the Lord's Prayer over him, then took Rachitsky's wristwatch. The sergeant didn't need it anymore and, as a runner, it was important for Borta to know the time.[8]

In the air over Garapan that afternoon, Ens. Jesse Boyce Holleman, flying a TBF off the light carrier *Gambier Bay*, was on call with two other Avengers to attack possible ground targets. Holleman, who had been working his way through his freshman year at Ole Miss washing dishes in the cafeteria before the war, had joined the Navy in 1942, but Saipan was his first experience with combat. The past two days had been spent strafing enemy trenches and gun positions and June 17 proposed to be more of the same.

Their first target that afternoon was a wooded area thought to conceal enemy troops. The three TBFs pushed over from 5,000 feet and hit the woods with wing guns and rockets. Spotting some trucks along the roadway, they went back for another run. "About the time I released the bombs, one lucky shot, something about a twenty millimeter size, hit in the right side of the cockpit, right in the floor board," recalled Holleman. "It went right by the right leg, and set it on fire, and it just flamed up and hit me right in the face." Burning alive in the flame-filled cockpit, Holleman started to bail out over Garapan, but had second thoughts as he remembered stories of the Japanese beheading prisoners.

He forced himself to sit back down in the flames. "I really thought it was going to hit right in the middle of the town," he remembered of the stricken aircraft. "Then all of a sudden, I just, I was blind; I was burning pretty bad." Hoping the plane might land itself, he grabbed the stick and leveled it out. By some miracle, the TBF came down off shore on the water-covered reef and skidded to a stop. Holleman clambered from the burning cockpit and tried to get his raft out. "I had no hands to get it out by that time because all the flesh had burned off," he recalled. He noticed his two air crewmen—nineteen-year-old Aviation Machinist's Mate Second Class Jack Bacon of Albany, Oregon, and twenty-three-year-old Aviation Radioman Second Class Howard M. "Red" Rivers of Northfield Center, Ohio—were gone; they had bailed out. "I understand later one chute opened and one didn't," observed Holleman. "They wouldn't have been burned if they had stayed in, but they didn't know that."

As the plane lay on the reef and showed no sign of sinking, Holleman got back up on the wing. He was only a couple of hundred yards from shore and as he pondered what to do, he saw some Japanese readying a boat. Fortunately for Holleman, a U.S. plane put in an appearance, persuading the Japanese to shut off the engine and disappear. In agony from his burns, he sat on the wing and waited for dark and rescue. "I knew they'd come in," he said. Hours later he heard a boat engine approaching from the seaward. A voice came out of the darkness, "Just stay there, Mac, and we'll get you." A group of sailors in a Higgins boat nudged up by the downed plane. They got Holleman into the boat and headed back out to sea.

A day later, Holleman was aboard the USS *Solace* being treated for burns to his face and over a third of his body. He would spend fourteen months in various hospitals and undergo thirty-six operations to repair the damage, but he would survive. No trace was ever found of his two missing crewmen.[9]

About noon on June 17, correspondent Robert Sherrod commandeered a small boat and headed over to the command ship *Rocky Mount* to get a look at the big picture. Gen. Holland Smith's wall chart was incomplete, but told some of the story. Casualties in the 2nd Marine Division assault battalions were as high as 40 percent. The 3rd Battalion, 6th Marines alone had lost 197 men and seven officers, according to the chart. Over in the 4th Marine Division, casualties in the 23rd and 24th Marines were "very heavy, especially in the 23rd."[10]

It was also becoming apparent that estimates of enemy troop strength had been wide of the mark, though efforts to compile an enemy order of battle were greatly complicated by the large number of straggler units on Saipan. A 4th Marine Division intelligence report noted that the original estimate of 12,000 to 15,000 troops "was far short of the real total," and now put the actual number at "around 24,000 Army and 4,000 Naval personnel."[11]

Despite those unwelcome surprises, the situation ashore was showing signs of improvement. Aslito Field had yet to be seized, but GIs from the 165th Infantry had made it to the outskirts during the day, despite the confusion of their arrival the night before. Though held up on the right by enemy pillboxes along a low ridge, the GIs on the left found easier going. Seizing that end of the ridge, they sent patrols poking cautiously through installations along the near edge of the airfield. They found the field undefended except for some 20mm guns located on the far side of the runway. Regimental commander Col. Gerard W. Kelley, a forty-one-year-old West

Pointer, felt he could have gone ahead and seized the airfield, but decided it would be more prudent to wait until morning. By day's end, his 2nd Battalion was firmly dug in just 200 yards from the airfield—all at a cost of only six killed and thirty-two wounded.[12]

Attacking to the left of Kelley's GIs, the 25th Marines had also finally broken through the crust of enemy defenses. Jumping off from positions along the O-1 line the morning of June 17, elements of the regiment advanced approximately 1,500 yards, passing the northern end of the airfield to secure the higher terrain along the O-2 line only 1,000 yards from Magicienne Bay. Finding no one home among the warren of abandoned Japanese installations just north of the airfield, a platoon commander checked in with the GIs busily digging in on the approaches to the field just behind and to the south of the Marine high water mark. The platoon leader told the Army battalion commander, a lieutenant colonel, that the airfield was undefended and suggested that the GIs simply move up and tie in with the Marine flank. When it became clear the colonel had no such intention, the 25th Marines positioned the 3rd Battalion on the north side of the airfield and faced it south. Though a relatively small annoyance on its face since the Japanese had chosen not to defend the airfield, the incident was a harbinger of much larger disagreements to come.[13]

In the early afternoon, Gen. Holland Smith debarked from USS *Rocky Mount* and came ashore to establish his headquarters in Charan Kanoa, a once-tidy arrangement of houses built of plaster, wooden slats, and concrete with corrugated metal roofs. Curious Marines found the walls of one row of bungalows adorned with numerous photos of semi-nude Asian women, which were quickly pocketed as souvenirs. "Most of the houses were destroyed," observed Seabee David Moore, prowling around with a couple of sailors. "Tables, pots and other household items were scattered about the streets . . . On the far side of the village was a baseball diamond . . . At home plate were sand bags, a machine gun and three dead Japanese soldiers."[14]

General Smith set up camp in one of the abandoned houses amid the stench of a rotting carabao carcass in the back yard. His aide saw to it that the beast was properly interred, which improved the air quality immeasurably.[15] An intelligence team exploring General Saito's hastily evacuated headquarters in the Charan Kanoa schoolhouse found a treasure trove of documents. Translated under flashlight that same night, the documents included the location of tank units on the island and the original Japanese defense plan.[16]

Another windfall discovered early in the operation was a Japanese 1:25,000 scale terrain map, which was far more accurate and detailed than the U.S. pre-invasion map derived from vertical and oblique photographs. The captured map was reproduced, blown up to a scale of 1:20,000, and overprinted with a grid to conform as nearly as possible to the grid on the U.S. Special Air and Gunnery Target Area Map, providing some relief to units struggling with the multitude of errors on the original.[17]

By now some order was beginning to take shape on the beaches. Black troops from stevedore and port units were busily unloading supplies. The labor pool even included numbers of Chamorros. "They were all very young, some perhaps only 12 or 14 years old," observed PFC Segal Silcox. "They were trying to do everything they could to impress us. They laughed and smiled a lot." Whenever the Marines said anything to them, they got only one answer, "Okay." The youngsters held on to the "k," making it sound as if they were singing it, recalled Silcox. Soon everyone was saying "okay" and trying to make it sound like the Chamorros.[18]

Work had also begun on the 4th Marine Division cemetery. "It was of necessity about 100 feet or perhaps a little more from the shore, and of course it was very dusty and sandy in that area," recalled Lieutenant Goe.[19] Several hundred bodies awaited burial, many horribly blackened and bloated from the heat. "The only way to distinguish Jap from American was by the helmets, leggings (Jap, wrap-around; American, canvas), or belts (black leather or khaki web)," observed Robert Sherrod.[20]

A stockade on the beach south of Charan Kanoa was slowly filling with civilians—mostly Chamorros—who trickled in through the lines. Women and children were placed in one barbed-wire enclosure; the men were segregated under guard in another. The handful of captured military personnel were confined in a stockade erected in the town baseball park. A few Marines gathered curiously by the wire at the civilian stockade and passed the prisoners candy and chewing gum and cigarettes from their rations. The occupants seemed pleased, but also at a loss as to what was going on, observed Goe. Many of the women seemed to be suffering from malnutrition; some were pregnant and others carried children that couldn't have been more than a day or two old.

Before the landing, the men had been given a little book about the Marianas and the supposed dialect of the native Chamorros, which appeared to be a mixture of Spanish and some other tongue. Goe pulled out his copy of the pamphlet and tried a couple of phrases on the detainees. "*Ha fa ga*," he declared. According to the booklet, this meant "Hello, pal." The natives just returned a "frightened, strange look." He tried, "*Ha fa cheluho*," which the booklet claimed translated to "Hello, sister." Again, the only response was perplexed looks.[21]

While it may not have been apparent to the average Marine or GI, the deterioration of the Japanese situation on the third day of battle was all too clear to Shizuko Miura. Shizuko had escaped into the hills as Garapan burned and made her way inland to the field hospital at Mount Donnay. "Field hospital" was an optimistic description of what she found there. Wounded men lay on the ground in a large natural bowl—a sort of geological amphitheater. The stench was overwhelming. An Army captain tried to shoo Shizuko away when she asked to help, but she persisted until the captain finally relented. "All right," he said. "From now on you are a nurse."

Shizuko found herself holding a flashlight for medics as they worked their way down a long line of wounded. A shell fragment protruded from one man's back. A medic yanked at it without success. The injured soldier groaned and fainted. "It's easier when they pass out," the medic remarked to Shizuko. He tried again to pull out the chunk of metal and again he failed. A surgeon finally cut away the flesh and the shell fragment, a chunk of metal the size of her fist, came free. The surgeon gave the patient an injection. The medic took a mouthful of water and sprayed it in the victim's face.

Another soldier was wounded in the foot. Handed a pair of scissors, Shizuko cut off his trousers to expose a blood-encrusted bandage. As the patient gritted his teeth, the surgeon tore the bandage away from the wound revealing shattered white bones as new blood welled up. Determining the soldier had no feeling in the foot, the doctor told Shizuko to snip away the torn flesh with the scissors. The soldier trembled and broke into a greasy sweat, but managed not to cry out as Shizuko cut away, exposing the bone. The surgeon asked how many anesthetic injections were left and was told there were only three boxes. He decided to amputate later and told Shizuko to replace the old bandage on the wound.

The man was still alive hours later when the surgeon returned to amputate. His stretcher was placed on two boxes and a medic brought out a tray of instruments. He was injected in the back and as soon as the painkiller took effect, the surgeon began cutting the flesh away from the bone with a scalpel. The medic took out a small saw and began cutting through the bone. The patient groaned. "Cheer up! It'll be over in a minute," a medic encouraged him. It seemed like hours to Shizuko, but the bone was finally severed and the surgeon began trimming the dangling flesh. Blood spurted from a severed artery. When the doctor had trouble gripping the blood vessel, Shizuko asked him for the forceps and managed to secure the spurting artery and clamp it. The doctor tied it off, finished trimming the stump, then covered it with gauze.

"Thank you very much," whispered the patient.[22]

Flying the legendary Z flag—the flag flown by Adm. Heihachiro Togo when he won his great victory over the Russians thirty-nine years before and later by Japanese forces during the attack on Pearl Harbor at the start of the present war—the *Mobile Fleet* steamed toward Saipan. Adm. Matome Ugaki's battleships rendezvoused with Ozawa and the force refueled until early afternoon on the 17th. By this time the fleet had closed to within approximately 750 miles of Saipan. From naval headquarters on Saipan, Admiral Nagumo radioed Ozawa, urging him not to delay and possibly "miss the chance."[23]

Intercepts of American radio traffic led Ozawa to conclude the enemy knew he was coming. "After five or six hours after we left San Bernardino Straits, I thought we were found by an American submarine or shore watchers," he said later.[24] After the war, a Japanese officer revealed that Ozawa was also aware of the composition and organization of the U.S. fleet and the identity of its commanders thanks to the capture of an American pilot shot down over Saipan on June 11. According to the Japanese source, the pilot had violated security and was carrying a list of secret call signs on his aircraft. Whether that was truly the case or whether the information was tortured out of the unfortunate airman, the Japanese obtained the intelligence and Admiral Nagumo sent it out to the proper commands that same night. The pilot, presumably, was disposed of once his usefulness ended.[25]

Knowing his nine carriers were outnumbered, Ozawa dispatched a Yokosuka D4Y1 Judy divebomber to Peleliu shortly before noon to secure the assistance of that base's aircraft in the coming battle. In a message to the *Combined Fleet*, he reported that he expected to engage the American fleet west of Saipan on June 19. The Gargoyle was in no hurry. He and his staff continued to believe that as many as 500 land-based aircraft under the command of Admiral Kakuta on Tinian had begun to savage the Americans, evening the odds for the subsequent naval action. Still more aircraft were expected from Japan, staging through Iwo Jima before continuing on to Saipan to attack the American carriers.

The *Mobile Fleet* would go into battle with 473 aircraft—222 fighters, 113 divebombers, 95 torpedo bombers, and a number of floatplanes—roughly half of U.S. carrier air strength.[26] Their main fighter was still the highly maneuverable Mitsubishi A6M5 Zero. The primary torpedo bombers included a handful of the older B5N Kates that had wreaked such havoc at Pearl Harbor and eighty or so of the newer B6N Jills with three-man crews and a range of about 1,000 nautical miles. The first-line divebomber was the speedy Judy. Operated by a two-man crew—a pilot and a navigator/radio-operator/gunner—it typically carried a 1,100-pound bomb and had a range of 910 miles. Ozawa also had a number of the older Aichi D3A1 Val divebombers, crewed by a pilot and gunner. This model had seen service at Pearl Harbor and was now approaching obsolescence.

While lacking parity in carriers, Admiral Ozawa was not without certain advantages in the coming confrontation. Lacking armor, his planes had longer legs than the heavier American aircraft. His search aircraft could range 350–560 miles farther to pinpoint the enemy fleet while his own ships remained unseen. His attack aircraft could search out to 500 miles and attack at 300, while U.S. aircraft could search out to about 350 miles and were unable to attack much beyond 250.[27] Adding to his advantage, the prevailing wind from the east would allow Japanese carriers to launch and recover aircraft while heading toward the enemy. That same prevailing wind would force the American carriers to turn away to launch and recover aircraft, limiting their ability to close quickly.

Finally, Ozawa was counting on the personality of his opposite number to help him prevail. Interrogation of captured U.S. airmen had identified the presence of the Fifth Fleet under Spruance. Japanese intelligence assessments of Spruance's character and "known caution" led Ozawa to conclude that the American admiral lacked aggressive fire.[28] Ozawa anticipated that the conservative Spruance, concerned with protecting the landing force, would not venture more than 100 miles west of Saipan; he would avoid risks and take action only if he had little or no choice. If Ozawa was right and Spruance reacted in character, the Japanese would have the benefit of the initiative, able to strike boldly to savage a moribund enemy.[29]

He would need that advantage and any others. While Japanese morale was high—Ozawa said "all personnel burned with desire to destroy the enemy and place the Imperial Country on safe ground"—his carrier pilots lacked experience.[30] The consummate professionals who had flown into Pearl Harbor in 1941 were largely gone, decimated at Midway and the air battles around Guadalcanal. By mid-1944 the average carrier pilot in the Japanese *Third Carrier Division* had about three months training, compared to American pilots who had between eighteen months and two years of training before seeing combat. While American aviators had up to 400 hours flying time, some Japanese pilots had logged as little as twenty.[31]

American capabilities—both in tactics and weaponry—had also grown by leaps and bounds: The nimble Japanese fighters were still dangerous, but could not compare to the well-armored Hellcats flying off the U.S. carriers. Hard lessons learned earlier in the war—including the caution, "Don't dogfight a Zero"—had resulted in new tactics where U.S. fighters teamed up on their more maneuverable opponents. Unlike the Japanese, the Americans also made widespread use of radar to locate enemies invisible to the naked eye. Communications between ships and planes had been refined to a deadly art, with shipboard fire detection officers (FDO) vectoring fighters toward intruders while the enemy was still miles away from the fleet. Battleships and cruisers had been converted into formidable antiaircraft platforms to protect the new queen of the seas— the carrier—from molestation from the sky. They were capable of throwing up astonishing amounts of fire, made all the more lethal by the newly developed proximity fuse which exploded the shell as soon as it came anywhere near the enemy aircraft.[32]

Two other developments were also to have an impact on the upcoming battle. One was the elimination of Japanese submarines as a significant threat to Spruance's Fifth Fleet. At least twenty-five Japanese submarines were dispatched for supply or scouting missions in connection with A-Go. Seventeen were sunk, most of them during May and early June. I-176 was put down on May 17 by U.S. destroyers while on a supply mission to Bougainville; RO-42 was sunk by a hedgehog salvo from destroyer escort *Bangust* on June 10 near Eniwetok; RO-111 was surprised on the surface north of the Admiralties on June 11 by USS *Taylor*, hit by gunfire and finally finished off with depth charges; RO-44 was caught by destroyer escort *Burden R. Hastings* on June 16 near Eniwetok and depth charged to oblivion; I-5 disappeared somewhere off Saipan; RO-36 was sunk by destroyer *Melvin* on June 13 near Saipan. Perhaps the most astonishing performance was turned in by the destroyer *England*, which in late May, rolled up a Japanese scouting line, sinking six submarines in only thirteen days. This massacre by U.S. hunter-killer teams virtually ensured that Japanese subs would not be on hand to assist in Admiral Ozawa's decisive battle.[33]

The Japanese admiral would also suffer from a shortage of destroyers to screen his valuable carriers. Prowling off Tarakan, USS *Harder* sank *Minatzuki* with a down-the-throat shot on June 6. *Harder* repeated the performance the next day, sinking the destroyer *Hayanami*. That same day USS *Hake* sank destroyer *Kazegumo*, while an American air attack put *Harusame* on the bottom. On June 9 *Harder* was back on the warpath, sinking destroyer *Tanikaze*. As if U.S. subs weren't enough, Ozawa lost yet another destroyer in the early hours of June 15 when *Shiratsuya* sank after a collision with a fleet oiler while steaming east toward Saipan (ironically, the collision occurred as she hastily maneuvered to avoid an attack by a nonexistent submarine). The ship went down before her depth charges could be put on safe and the resulting explosions killed many of her crew in the water.[34] The shortage of destroyers was to cost the Gargoyle dearly.

Early in the afternoon of June 17, Admiral Nimitz radioed Spruance: "On the eve of a possible fleet action, you and the officers and men under your command have the confidence of the naval services and the country. We count on you to make the victory decisive."[35] At 1415 Spruance issued his battle plans. Considering his cautious nature, they were surprisingly bold. "Our air will first knock out enemy carriers as operating carriers, then will attack enemy battleships and cruisers to slow or disable them," he observed. "Task Group 58.7 [the battleships] will destroy the enemy fleet either by fleet action if enemy elects to fight or by sinking slowed or crippled ships if enemy retreats. Action against the retreating enemy must be pushed vigorously by all hands to insure complete destruction of his fleet."[36]

Hours later, at 1757, the submarine *Cavalla*, still chasing after the Japanese tanker convoy, found Ozawa. An intermittent radar contact turned into "seven good-sized pips" indicating a carrier flanked on the port quarter by two columns of ships, probably battleships or cruisers. "It was fairly dark, but I could make out one of the ships as a carrier," observed Kossler. "It looked like the Empire State Building."[37] The range to the carrier, which was the closest ship, was 15,000 yards, and it wasn't alone. Sound picked up the screws of at least fifteen different ships. "By now it was apparent that we were on the track of a large, fast task force, heading someplace in a pretty big hurry," reported Kossler.[38]

Under orders to report first and attack second, Kossler resisted the urge to send a spread of fish into the flattop and laid low as the enemy carrier division rushed past. At 2245 he surfaced to radio a contact report that he had seen at least fifteen ships at 12 degrees 23'N and 132 degrees 26'E heading due east at 19 knots. He then began pursuit. "Chasing task force at four-engine speed," noted the last entry in the log for the day. "Hoping for a second chance."[39]

A rainy night fell over the Marine beachhead as shipping retired out of harm's way. Over in the 4th Division area, Col. Justice Chambers was heading back by jeep for a conference at regimental headquarters. It was dark and the jeep was blacked out. "Somewhere along the way, we started running over dead bodies," he recalled. "As we rolled across them, they would burst. All of us were vomiting, and we had maybe 300 yards of bodies to go across. By the time we got back to the CP [Command Post], no one there would let us, or our jeep, anywhere near them."[40]

Up on the slopes of Fina Susu less than a mile and a half east of Charan Kanoa, PFC Bob Tierney's outfit had caught a lucky break that afternoon. "We were moving out and there was a large ridge, and there was like a cliff, a two hundred foot cliff," he recalled. "And there were caves and stuff in it, and we thought for sure we were going to have a real battle getting up that cliff." Instead they found an unguarded path and made it to the top without a fight. They dug in for the night with their backs to the cliff. It was a precarious position. Tierney's captain told the men, "Whatever you do, don't fire your rifle at any single or small group. We don't want to give our position away."

Around about midnight or shortly after, Tierney spotted a figure silhouetted against the sky to his right front. It was a Japanese soldier. He was only about 20 yards away. Tierney had a BAR and could have killed him easily, but he remembered the captain's warning and resisted the temptation to open fire. As he watched, the infiltrator struck a grenade on his helmet to arm it and tossed it in the general direction of the Marine foxholes. It exploded and the Japanese disappeared into the darkness. Tierney figured all was well, but he was wrong. Suddenly there were cries for a corpsman. As ill fortune would have it, the grenade had landed in a foxhole occupied by twenty-year-old PFC Bobby Vail of Worcester, Massachusetts. "One of my very best friends," recalled Tierney. "Blew his leg off. The corpsmen worked on that. They put ponchos over it so the light wouldn't show. And the corpsman worked on him all night but he died in the morning."

Tierney would survive Saipan, but his failure to shoot that Japanese infiltrator would haunt him for the rest of his life.[41]

Adm. Ernest J. King (U.S. NAVY)

Adm. Richmond Kelly Turner
(U.S. NAVY)

Adm. Raymond A. Spruance
(U.S. NAVY)

Lt. Gen. Holland M. Smith
(U.S. NAVY)

Lt. Gen. Robert C. Richardson Jr.
(U.S. ARMY)

Maj. Gen. Ralph C. Smith
(U.S. ARMY)

Adm. Marc Mitscher
(U.S. NAVY)

Adm. Jisaburo Ozawa

Gen. Yoshitsugu Saito

Gen. Graves B. Erskine
(USMC)

Maj. Gen. Harry Schmidt (USMC)

Maj. Gen. Thomas Watson
(USMC)

Adm. Chester Nimitz
(U.S. NAVY)

Vice Adm. Chuichi Nagumo

An LST sets sail, crammed with fuel and equipment for an invasion. Similar loading contributed to the West Loch disaster as LSTs assembled for the Saipan landings. (U.S. ARMY)

An LST burns in Pearl Harbor's West Loch. Questions remain about the cause of the disaster, which was kept secret from the public for decades. (U.S. NAVY)

The largest settlement on Saipan, Garapan was the seat of Japanese holdings in the Marianas.

An Avenger lifts off from a carrier deck for an early morning raid on Saipan. (U.S. NAVY)

Cmdr. Bill Martin (center) with his radio-man, Jerry Thomas Williams (left), and turret gunner Wesley Ray Hargrove (right), both of whom were killed when their aircraft was shot down on June 13. (U.S. NAVY)

Marines board a landing craft off the coast of Saipan. (USMC)

Mount Tapotchau looms in the distance as amphibious tractors head toward the landing beaches. (U.S. NAVY)

An LCVP heads toward the reef where the passengers will transfer to the tractors for the final leg to shore. (U.S. COAST GUARD)

Marines stay low as their LVTs head toward Saipan's fringing reef. (USMC)

Marines move inland off the beaches. (USMC)

Marines coming ashore on the Blue Beaches in the 4th Marine Division area pause before climbing the berm and heading inland. (USMC)

Three Marines lie where they were cut down on the beach during the initial landing. (USMC)

Two Marines keep low as enemy fire sweeps the narrow beach. Just beyond them, an amtank stands in the shallows. (USMC)

Marines await the word to move inland. Enemy artillery fire wreaked havoc on the crowded beachheads during the first day of the assault. (USMC)

Two Marines take cover in a shell hole after hitting the beach. (USMC)

Two amphibious tractors lie abandoned on the beach, while an amtank appears to have been knocked out on the reef in the background. (USMC)

Corpsmen treat the wounded amid the clutter of the landing beaches on D-day. (USMC)

Nowhere to go but forward. Marines gather themselves to move inland. (USMC)

An amtank from the 2nd Armored Amphibian Tractor Battalion knocked out on the Charan Kanoa airstrip on D-day. (USMC)

Knocked-out amphibian tractors and amtanks clutter the narrow invasion beach on D-day. (USMC)

LVTs and amtanks head inland in an effort to reach the O-1 line on D-day. Their high profile once out of the water made them easy targets for enemy guns. (USMC)

Graves Registration personnel go through the grim task of identifying dead Marines collected on the beach. (USMC)

Nonchalantly perched on a dud naval shell, a young Marine empties sand from his boondocker. (USMC)

A Japanese ammunition bunker. Lack of concrete and building materials hampered efforts to build defense works in the months before the U.S. landing. (U.S. ARMY)

A dead Japanese infantryman lies in front of a knocked-out tank following the attack on the 6th Marines the night of June 16. (USMC)

Surrounded by dead Japanese and knocked-out tanks, three Marines survey the battlefield the morning after the failed tank/infantry assault on the 6th Marines. (USMC)

"We've got their number." Gen. Thomas "Terrible Tommy" Watson examines a knocked-out Japanese tank after the June 16–17 counterattack. (USMC)

Weapons at the ready, Marines advance warily through a shattered coconut tree grove. (USMC)

Enemy tank bogged down in the futile Japanese counterattack on the Marine beachhead the night of June 16. (USMC)

Marines look over a medium tank knocked out during the futile Japanese counterattack on the Marine beachhead the night of June 16. (USMC)

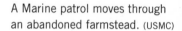

A Marine patrol moves through an abandoned farmstead. (USMC)

Marines prowl along the rail tracks in Charan Kanoa. The sugar mill with its landmark tower is visible in the background. (USMC)

Marines aboard a U.S. Army amphibious tractor, facetiously named Poop Deck Pappy. Tractor losses due to enemy fire and mechanical trouble were high at Saipan. (USMC)

Covered with a poncho shroud, his helmet and rifle marking the location for Graves Registration, a fallen Marine lies almost within arm's length of his dead enemy in the adjacent trench. (USMC)

Burials at sea were a common sight as seriously wounded men evacuated to offshore ships for medical treatment succumbed to their injuries. (USMC)

Sailors aboard the light cruiser USS *Birmingham* view the contrails in the sky over Task Force 58 as the air battle unfolds on June 19. (U.S. NAVY)

A Hellcat returns to the carrier *Lexington*. (U.S. NAVY)

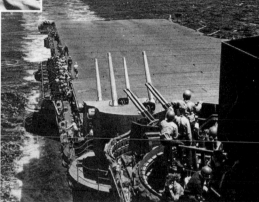

A Japanese aircraft plummets toward the sea after being shot down during an attack on the escort carrier *Kitkun Bay*. (U.S. NAVY)

The Japanese carrier *Zuikaku* and two destroyers maneuver frantically while under attack by U.S. divebombers. (U.S. NAVY)

A grinning Lt. (j.g.) Alex Vraciu celebrates his score after returning from aerial combat on June 19. (U.S. NAVY)

Lt. Ronald P. "Rip" Gift relaxes with other pilots in a ready room on board USS *Monterey* after landing on her at night following strikes on the Japanese fleet, June 20, 1944. Note the admonition "Get the Carriers" on the chalkboard in the background. (U.S. NAVY)

Task Force 58 in the waters off Saipan prior to the engagement with the Japanese Mobile Fleet on June 19–20, 1944. (U.S. NAVY)

Douglas SBD Dauntless dive-bomber in the air over Task Force 58 on June 15, 1944. (U.S. NAVY)

CHAPTER XII

A Gathering of Eagles

THE MARINES AWOKE THE MORNING OF JUNE 18 TO EMPTY SEAS. THE MAS-
sive fleet that had brought them to Saipan had vanished overnight. "It got
bright the next morning, we looked out and there was nothing in the harbor," recalled PFC Albert J. Harris. The ground troops were stunned. "My
God," Harris recalled thinking, "are we doing that bad, they left us here? I
knew we weren't doing very good but . . . They'd all pulled out. I didn't want
anybody to leave me there."[1]

Aboard the *Indianapolis*, Admiral Spruance was preparing for battle.
However, as Admiral Ozawa had anticipated, his earlier aggressiveness had
started to ebb as his natural caution reasserted itself. By the evening of June
17 Spruance had already begun worrying that the Japanese might divide
their force in an effort to slip past his guard. The Japanese were inordinately
fond of decoys—indeed, as Spruance was aware, the Z Plan captured in the
Philippines called for a possible feint at the center followed by a flanking
attack. Koga's plan had also suggested that, given the circumstances, the
landing force could become a primary target.[2] Now Spruance worried that
if he allowed himself to be drawn away to confront Ozawa, the vulnerable
amphibious forces at the beachhead would be left open to an attack from
around his flank. That was a risk he was not willing to take. "The task of Task
Force 58 was to cover our amphibious forces and to prevent such an enemy
attack," he observed.[3]

Cavalla's contact report reached Spruance at 0321 on the 18th.
Mitscher received the news less than half an hour later. Their reactions were
a study in contrasts. The more aggressive Mitscher saw *Cavalla*'s report as an
opportunity. If the enemy kept the current pace, he would be 650 miles from
Saipan by dawn. By heading directly toward the Japanese, TF 58 might be
able to get in an airstrike in late afternoon. This could well lead to a night
surface action involving TF 58's battleships. Mitscher radioed Vice Adm.

Willis A. "Ching" Lee, who commanded TG 58.7's seven fast battleships: "Do you desire night engagement? It may be we can make air contact late this afternoon and attack tonight. Otherwise we should retire to the eastward for tonight."[4]

Ching Lee was no mouse—one dark night off Guadalcanal in 1942 he had taken two battleships and four destroyers into the equivalent of a naval knife fight and sank a Japanese battleship and destroyer—but he was also no fool. He responded that he did not think a night engagement was advisable. The advantage of radar notwithstanding, he was concerned about communications and—unlike the Japanese—his crews had not been specifically trained in night actions. Spruance concurred. The timing of the various sightings and the number of ships reported by *Cavalla* sharpened his concerns that Ozawa might have split up his forces, again raising the specter of a Japanese end run. What Spruance could not know, of course, was that Admiral Ozawa's ability to maneuver was severely limited by his lack of fuel reserves. The Japanese commander planned to come straight at him.[5]

The four U.S. task groups rendezvoused at noon with TGs 58.1, 58.3, and 58.2 stationed 12 miles apart on a north-south line. Fifteen miles west of *Lexington* was Ching Lee's battleship force with its tremendous antiaircraft capability. Twelve miles north and slightly east of Lee was TG 58.4. By now, Spruance had made up his mind that he would assume a defensive posture. He informed Mitscher and Lee he expected the main Japanese attack to come from the westward, though it might shift to come from the southwest. "Consider that we can best cover Saipan by advancing to westward during daylight and retiring to eastward at night so as to reduce possibility of enemy passing us during darkness," he observed. With that decision, Spruance did exactly as Ozawa had anticipated.[6]

For his part, submarine force commander Admiral Lockwood was eager to unleash his wolves. Upon receipt of *Cavalla's* report, he sent out a message to his submarine skippers directing that henceforth they were to shoot first and report later. "Indication at this end that the big show may be taking place at the present time," he radioed *Finback*, *Bang*, *Stingray*, and *Albacore*. The exact time and location was still unknown, but events were moving forward. "Do not miss any opportunity to get in a shot at the enemy," he urged. "This may be the chance of a lifetime."[7]

As U.S. supply and support ships withdrew to the east in anticipation of the naval engagement, a welcome sight hove to off Saipan's western shore: the hospital ships *Bountiful* and *Solace*. Painted a brilliant white, each with a red cross superimposed on a broad green stripe around the hull, they were two of four hospital ships assigned to the invasion—the others being *Relief* and *Samaritan*.

It had become clear early on that pre-invasion estimates of casualties had been far off the mark. By evening of D plus 2, the troop transports had already received 3,600 wounded. "All the hospital ships in the area could not have handled this number," observed the subsequent Medical Report for *Forager*.[8] The ramifications were reflected in a report from the attack transport USS *Sheridan*, which received its first casualties from Saipan at 0800 on June 16. Most of the 160 wounded taken aboard were brought out by LST 450, though the ship also took on casualties from small boats that came alongside. "The men who were received on board had been wounded twenty-four hours to thirty-six hours before being treated," observed the *Sheridan's* action report. "These men still had the original battle dressing which had been acquired on the beach . . . Due to the length of time which had elapsed from the time these men were wounded and seen by us, thirteen cases of gas bacillus infection developed. Two cases necessitated the amputation of arms and one required the amputation of the leg below the knee."[9]

Solace took aboard 584 patients to the point that "all beds were filled to capacity and that patients were overflowing to crew's spaces." For some, it was too late. The ship reported several deaths, including Corp. Howard Reid (gunshot wound, abdomen), PFC Joseph Thomas Bejgrowicz (gunshot wound, right thigh), PFC Vincent Clark (gunshot wound, chest), and Pharmacist's Mate 1st Class Maurice Tedford Hunt (amputation, traumatic, left arm) among others. Still others would die in the days ahead. Wounds to the abdomen proved especially lethal.[10]

Within six hours of arrival, *Bountiful* had loaded over 500 patients— only 150 of whom were ambulatory. Nurse Lt. Ethel Himes recalled, "The patients we received were the severest kind of casualties one could ever imagine. Many were in shock and hemorrhaging. Some had been shot through the head and would probably be blind the rest of their lives. Some were shot through the chest, already a hemothorax had developed and possibly a pneumothorax along with it. Some had badly mangled legs that had caught mortar fire, and it was a question whether the legs could be saved or not. Some had an arm or a leg cut off, or perhaps an arm just hanging which had to be amputated immediately after admission to the ship. Some had blast injuries that had done quite a bit of internal damage. These fellows were covered from head to foot with Saipan red sand and mud. In many instances, clothing had to be cut off. . . ."[11] Gas gangrene continued to be a persistent problem, aggravated by the Saipanese farm practice of using human feces to fertilize the fields. Affected limbs were packed in ice for six hours, then amputated. The ice reduced the amount of pain, blood, and the terrible odor of rotting flesh. Despite the trauma, the patients did not demand much, recalled a nurse. Most were happy to just have a bath.

Meanwhile, back on Saipan, Sgt. Maj. Howard Culpepper was looking over the casualty sheets for the 2nd Marine Division when he came across a familiar name: Sgt. Pete Grennan. The Irish stowaway from Brooklyn who had been so desperate to get into the war that he went AWOL from the hospital had been killed in action on June 17.[12]

The Japanese soldier was nothing if not persevering, but the failure of the tank/infantry attack the night of June 16–17 shook the Saipan garrison's confidence. Maj. Takashi Hirakushi sensed a developing "sense of confusion and fear" among the troops. His own optimism had also suffered a blow. Up until now he had thought a counterattack immediately after the enemy landing had a good chance of success. Now, as the Americans began to break out of their beachhead, he feared it would be necessary to concede the southern end of the island to the invaders and withdraw to the north.[13]

They were not about to go quietly. In the early morning hours of June 18, heavily laden Japanese soldiers from the *1st Battalion, 18th Infantry Regiment* clambered aboard landing barges at the Flores Point naval base roughly 4 miles up the coast from the Marine-held beaches. The battalion—designated a month earlier by *31st Army* as an amphibious attack force should the enemy establish a beachhead on Saipan or Tinian—had been ordered to land behind the American lines and raise havoc in the rear areas.

The 49-foot "gondola type" wooden barges, each capable of carrying seventy fully equipped soldiers and a seven-man crew, set off down along the coast at about 0430. The flotilla, consisting of between twenty-five and thirty-five landing barges, motored as far as Garapan when it ran into seven LCI(G) gunboats standing watch over the U.S. beachhead. The gunboats opened fire with their 20mm and 40mm guns. "This ship clearly distinguished registering numerous hits on three barges, one of which caught fire and later exploded," reported LCI(G) 458.[14] LCI(G) Flotilla Three subsequently reported "13 or 14 enemy barges laden with troops were sunk and others probably damaged." The rest fled.[15]

By now the Japanese knew at least one of the Marine divisions facing them. A dog tag taken from a dead Marine included the personal inscription "4th Marines." More detailed data was provided by a 1:20,000 map retrieved from the body of a dead 4th Marine Division officer. The map included a symbol at Charan Kanoa that apparently indicated some type of headquarters, but the Japanese were unsure whether it was battalion, regimental, or division. The right side of the map featured a drawn-in number "4," substantiating the information gained from the dog tag.[16]

In view of the deteriorating situation, Maj. Gen. Keiji Igeta had already moved *31st Army* headquarters into the mountains east of Garapan. Despite a previous agreement to work together, *31st Army* and *43rd Division* headquarters were often out of touch with each other. The lack of contact caused Igeta to radio Tokyo on the morning of June 18 that General Saito had apparently been killed. "Homare Unit (*43rd Division*) Headquarters underwent an enemy attack this a.m. and the division CO died along with his staff officers," he reported. The enemy was gradually completing seizure of the southern part of the island, assisted by fierce naval gunfire, bombing, and strafing, he observed.[17]

While wrong about General Saito, he was right about developments on the ground. To the south, the U.S. 165th Infantry Regiment swept forward virtually unopposed onto Aslito Airfield the morning of June 18. Enemy troops could be seen withdrawing toward Nafutan Point, a warren of rocky crevices and caves south of the airfield. The airfield was reported in hand at 1000. About thirty minutes later, as the 165th Infantry set up its command post at the field, a lone Japanese—a wounded Navy weatherman—was found hiding between the double doors of the control tower and taken prisoner.[18]

The coral-concrete runway was in relatively good condition, though littered with "2- to 4-inch rock chunks" and dud 16-inch naval shells.[19] The airfield had no turning circles, but the wide runways provided ample room for that function. The main service apron—900 feet long and 600 feet wide—gave access to the three main hangars. A smaller service apron provided access to two smaller hangars. An oxygen plant, a power plant, a million-gallon reservoir, and a sprawl of shelters and warehouses with steel-reinforced concrete walls were still intact and soon put to American use. The Japanese had abandoned numbers of airplanes and stores of aircraft parts as well as maintenance logs and other intelligence material. The Air Crash Intelligence Team from JICOPA subsequently crated up twenty-three

Zeros and one Kate torpedo bomber, either intact or only slightly damaged, plus engines and parts, and shipped them back to Hawaii for evaluation. The capture of the Kate was noteworthy in that it was equipped with radar, believed to be the first such aircraft to fall into American hands.[20]

As it turned out, the first plane to land on the newly captured runway was a Japanese Zero damaged in a dogfight between Navy planes and two or three intruders late that afternoon. "The plane, which was engulfed in flames, rolled a few hundred feet and finally tipped on its nose, and the pilot jumped out . . ." remarked a watching GI.[21] The lucky airman, Petty Officer Hari Tsubu of the *261st Air Group* based on Guam, was promptly apprehended. Suffering from burns on his hands and legs, he told interrogators he had been advised on Guam that the airfield was still in Japanese hands.[22]

Pleased by the 165th's conquest of the airfield, Gen. Ralph Smith waxed poetic about the "perfect teamwork that has existed between the Navy, Marines and the Army." He expressed annoyance with stories about dissension between the services. "Nothing could be farther from the truth out here in the field," he remarked. "One of the 165th's officers remarked to me this morning that Saipan has sealed the brotherhood between the services." Unfortunately, his remarks would prove to be premature, but for the moment, the spirit of cooperation prevailed.[23]

By day's end on June 18, Holland Smith's divisions held approximately three-quarters of southern Saipan. The main prize—Aslito Field—was in U.S. hands. The 24th and 25th Marines had reached part of the O-3 line—which essentially followed the eastern coastline overlooking Magicienne Bay—cutting the island in half. The 23rd Marines on the 4th Division's left continued to encounter significant resistance and were still about 400 yards from the O-2 line.

The day brought one momentary scare when a halftrack fired into a cave containing a picric acid plant. Cries of "gas" went up as a noxious yellow cloud spewed from the entrance. As most men had long since discarded their gas masks, the alarm created temporary pandemonium. One shaken lieutenant unceremoniously burst into General Schmidt's dugout in search of a spare gas mask. The panic eventually subsided as it became clear that no gas attack was underway, leaving a lot of relieved Marines and at least one chastened lieutenant.[24]

In the face of the unrelenting pressure, the Japanese conceded defeat in the south and began withdrawing to the north. The new so-called "line of security"—which roughly paralleled the American O-4 objective line—extended from just below Garapan on the west coast, across the southern slopes of Mount Tapotchau to a point on Magicienne Bay near the village of Laulau. "The Army is consolidating its battle lines and has decided to prepare for a showdown fight," General Igeta radioed his superiors in Tokyo.[25]

In reply, Imperial General Headquarters ordered General Igeta to hang on to the beaches still in his possession so that reinforcements could be landed. He was also directed to "hinder the establishment of enemy airfields." Igeta replied that he would neutralize American operations on Aslito Airfield by infiltration raids "because our artillery is destroyed." The Marpi Point Airfield, the last in Japanese hands, would be repaired and defended to the end. "We vow that we will live up to expectations," he promised.[26]

In the unlikely event that Generals Igeta and Saito failed to understand the gravity of the situation, the emperor himself weighed in, messaging, "Although the front line officers are fighting splendidly, if Saipan is lost, air raids on Tokyo will take place often, therefore you absolutely must hold Saipan."[27] Tojo, who months earlier had expressed complacency about the defense of Saipan, now radioed the beleaguered defenders, urging them to hold on and to "destroy the enemy gallantly and persistently" and "thus alleviate the anxiety of our emperor."[28]

From General Saito's cave headquarters on a hill just northwest of Hill 500, *43rd Division* chief of staff Col. Takuji Suzuki radioed back, assuring the prime minister that Saipan's defenders were prepared to sacrifice all on behalf of the empire. "By becoming the bulwark of the Pacific with 10,000 deaths we hope to requite the Imperial favor," he concluded.[29]

The defenders of Saipan would man their new defense line while awaiting reinforcement. But while resolved to do his best, General Igeta was obviously not oblivious to the reality of his situation, radioing later that night that "the secret documents in custody of the *31st Army* headquarters . . . were completely burned at 1830 of 18 June."[30] Spirited martial rhetoric might stiffen morale, but it would not stop an American tank.

The morning of June 18, an unidentified noncommissioned officer on nearby Tinian noted in his diary that the enemy continued to land on Saipan. "Where is the fleet?" he lamented.[31]

Ray Spruance was asking the same question. On the afternoon of the 17th, six PBM3Ds patrol bombers, which had a range of 1,947 nautical miles, lumbered into the air from Eniwetok in response to a request by

Spruance who wanted to give longer legs to his search patterns. The big, two-engine seaplanes from VBP-16 made a rough landing in open water off the west coast of Saipan and had just motored over to gas up at the tender *Ballard* when a Japanese divebomber broke through the overcast and headed directly for the ship. *Ballard*'s antiaircraft guns knocked a chunk off the plane's wing and the pilot dropped his bomb wide. There was no damage, but it was an unsettling welcome and the crews were not reassured by the intermittent explosions and gunfire emanating from the island itself during the afternoon and into the night.[32]

Spruance summoned VBP-16's Lt. Cmdr. William "Scrappy" Scarpino and told him to begin an immediate search for the Japanese fleet to the northwest of Saipan. Scarpino explained that getting his planes airborne in the present rough seas was out of the question. He thought he had made his case, but Spruance was back in touch a couple of hours later to insist that Scarpino commence the search. He told the skipper he was willing to sacrifice four planes in order to get at least one in the air to search for the enemy fleet. Scarpino had little choice but to comply.

Conditions had not improved that night as the patrol bombers readied for takeoff. The seas were rough, it was pitch black, and the area was under occasional fire from guns on Saipan. The porpoising on takeoff was so bad that one seaman suffered a broken leg. Two pilots were injured when they smashed their heads into the windshield as they jolted along. Nevertheless, by some miracle and great flying skill, the PBMs lumbered into the air, though some pilots had to make two or three attempts. They flew a pattern 700 miles north and northeast, took a left dogleg for 100 miles, then returned. There was no sign of the enemy fleet.[33]

Mitscher's scouts were up early that morning, ranging out some 325 miles to the west. Assigned to Sector 235-245, Avenger pilot Lt. (j.g.) Charles E. "Hotshot Charlie" Henderson from *Enterprise* was approaching the end of his cross leg at 0804 when he spotted a Japanese floatplane 6 or 8 miles ahead at an altitude of about 1,000 feet. The enemy was heading north-northeast, "fat, dumb and happy," he reported. "I had my shoes off, feet up on top of the instrument panel, smoking a cigar. I still don't know what happened to the cigar."[34]

Using the clouds as cover, Henderson and his wingman, Lt. (j.g.) Clifton R. Largess, climbed rapidly toward the floatplane, which now changed course to the east, apparently at the end of his own search leg. Reaching a point abeam at about 3,500 feet, Henderson peeled off and dived through a cloud after the bogie—now clearly identifiable as a twin-float Aichi E13 Jake. Making a flat run on the tail, he squeezed off a seventeen-round burst of .50 caliber. Taken completely by surprise, the Jake spiraled down in a ball of fire and crashed.[35]

The unlucky floatplane was probably among the fourteen Kates and two or more Jakes that set out at 0515 to locate the American fleet, snooping along 425-mile-long legs, well beyond the U.S. search envelope. Like Henderson's doomed Jake, several of them had the misfortune to run into U.S. carrier aircraft embarked on the same mission. The victims apparently included eight Kates from Rear Adm. Sueo Obayashi's *Carrier Division 3* led by the division's senior torpedo officer, Lt. Cmdr. Masayuki Yamagami. The eight aircraft disappeared over the horizon in the early morning launch, never to return.[36]

Lt. (j.g.) Raymond L. Turner, piloting a Helldiver from the *Essex*, came across what was presumably one of Ozawa's Kates at 0755. He and his Hellcat escort gave chase, taking the Kate unawares. The Hellcat made a pass, starting a fire in the Kate's left wing root. Turner contributed about 100 rounds of 20mm, knocking off a large piece of the left wing that nearly smashed into his Helldiver. He saw the gunner hanging limply out of the cockpit and the pilot frantically trying to bail out as flames swept through the aircraft, setting their clothes on fire. An instant later, the Kate spun into the ocean.[37]

The Japanese search failed to locate the U.S. fleet, but did report multiple sightings of American carrier planes, Ozawa launched another effort at noon, sending out thirteen Judys and two Jakes. Again reports began coming back of U.S. carrier planes. Finally, as the pilot of Plane No. 15 turned on the dogleg at the limit of his 425-mile search pattern, he spotted carriers. At 1515, he keyed his radio and reported, "Enemy task force, including carriers" and the location. Further reports soon followed as Plane No. 13 radioed a sighting of enemy carriers heading west. Minutes later Plane No. 17 reported a group of two carriers and ten to fifteen destroyers; a second group, also with two carriers and about ten other vessels; and a third group of the same size, all heading west.[38]

The report by Plane No. 15 was delivered to Admiral Ozawa at 1530. Ten minutes later he ordered a course change that would allow him to maintain his distance from the American fleet. Rear Adm. Sueo Obayashi, leading *Carrier Division 3* from the *Chitose*, was more impetuous. Without waiting for authorization from Ozawa, he began launching planes at 1637, only to be summarily reined in by Ozawa's Operation Order 16. The order directed the *Mobile Fleet* to steam southwest during the night. The battle would be joined the next morning. Admiral Obayashi hastily recalled his disappointed pilots. "Let's do it properly tomorrow," he reassured his staff. Privately, however, he feared Ozawa was letting a golden opportunity slip away.[39]

But Ozawa was determined to get his chess pieces in order before engaging Spruance. At 2020, in an effort to coordinate with land-based air forces, he broke radio silence to inform Vice Adm. Kakuji Kakuta on Tinian that he intended to attack the American fleet the next day. Ozawa believed he could rely on as many as 500 or more planes from Kakuta's *First Air Fleet* in the Marianas and other bases within range.[40]

In reality, Kakuta's force was a shadow of what was called for by the A-Go plan. Large numbers of aircraft had been stripped away earlier in the month to support the ill-conceived *Kon* operation aimed at the U.S. landings on Biak. The remainder had been badly shot up in unrelenting U.S. fighter sweeps, while the airfields Ozawa expected his pilots to use on Guam, Tinian, and Rota to refuel and rearm were under almost continuous attack.

Typical was the fate of *Naval Air Group 263*. Thirty of the group's Zeros flew into Guam on May 30. Four were destroyed in air combat over the island on June 11. From June 15 to 18, losses amounted to more than twenty aircraft. By the time of Ozawa's alert to Admiral Kakuta, *Air Group 263* had virtually ceased to exist.[41] As of June 11, Kakuta could field roughly 435 aircraft—which was still well short of the *First Air Fleet*'s authorized complement of 1,750 planes. According to reports received by the Naval General Staff, by June 18, only 156 planes remained.[42]

This was a serious development. According to A-Go, Admiral Kakuta's air arm was expected to destroy at least one-third of the enemy task force carrier units prior to the fleet confrontation.[43] As far as Ozawa knew, that process was already well underway. On June 17, a mixed force of bombers and fighters from Yap reported hitting a U.S. carrier task force 30 miles east of Tinian. The Japanese crews claimed to have sunk two or three carriers and left another ship burning. In fact, the only damage inflicted was to the carrier *Fanshaw Bay*, which took a hit on her aft elevator.[44] Other reports were similarly overblown and Kakuta, who was said to suffer from alcoholism, did not attempt to correct the misconception. Unaware that this critical element of A-Go had already failed, at 0300 Ozawa ordered the *Mobile Fleet* to increase speed and go into battle formation following behind the protective shield of Kurita's C Force battleships. He would begin launching his scouts before daybreak.

Ozawa's radio message to Admiral Kakuta had not gone unnoticed. A U.S. Navy "Huff-Duff" high-frequency direction-finding shore station picked up the transmission and fixed the *Mobile Fleet's* position at 13N, 136E (correct to within 100 miles), only about 300 miles from TF 58. The information was promptly passed on to Spruance, whose searchers had yet to catch a glimpse of the *Mobile Fleet*.[45]

Mitscher got the report at 2245. Though Spruance felt Ozawa's radio transmission could be a Japanese trick, Mitscher thought it was legitimate. His staff calculated that if the fix was accurate, Ozawa's ships were only 355 miles away. That was too far for a strike now, but if the U.S. carriers reversed course they could be within range by 0500. At 2325, Mitscher radioed Spruance recommending that they steam west toward the presumed location of the enemy fleet.[46]

But Spruance was soon chewing over yet another hard-to-digest morsel of intelligence, this being a garbled message from the submarine *Stingray* on patrol about 435 miles from Saipan and about 175 east-southeast of the Huff Duff fix. Still wary of a multi-pronged attack, Spruance inexplicably deduced that *Stingray* had spotted another part of Ozawa's fleet and the enemy had jammed the sub's transmission. "It showed that there may have been two Japanese forces operating," noted Spruance's chief of staff, Capt. Carl J. Moore. Still another message—this one from the sub USS *Finback* reporting that searchlights had been seen in the sky at yet a third position—did nothing to embolden Spruance.[47]

In conversation with two of his officers, Spruance observed, "If I were the Japanese admiral in this situation, I would split my forces and hope that the ships remaining to the west were sighted in order to decoy the main forces of the American fleet away from Saipan. Then I would slip behind with my separated strike force in order to get into Saipan and if possible destroy the transports."[48]

Back on *Lexington's* bridge, Mitscher and his staff waited for Spruance's decision as minute after minute ticked away. At midnight there had still been no response from "Blue Jacket," regarding Mitscher's suggestion. The flag plot was so quiet, the humming of the communications equipment was clearly audible. At 0038 on the 19th, the TBS [Talk Between Ships] speaker on *Lexington* came to life. "Bald Eagle—Bald Eagle this is Blue Jacket," announced the speaker. "Change proposed does not appear advisable. Believe indications given by *Stingray* more accurate than that determined by direction finder. If that is so, continuation as at present seems preferable. End run by other carrier groups remains possibility and must not be overlooked."[49]

Mitscher and his staff were stunned. In their view—a view most likely shared by virtually every naval aviator in the fleet—Spruance was throwing away an opportunity of historic proportions to put an end to the Japanese navy right then and there. Instead, he was going to give the Japanese the first shot. "We knew we were going to have hell slugged out of us in the morning and we were making sure we were ready for it," recalled Mitscher's chief of staff, Capt. Arleigh Burke. "We knew we couldn't reach them. We knew they could reach us."[50] *Enterprise* captain Matt Gardner was so incensed, he threw his hat on the deck and stomped on it.[51] The outrage among some fleet officers verged on the mutinous, but in the end they would do as they were ordered. Spruance was wrong, but he was in charge. The battle would begin on Japanese terms.

In the early morning hours of June 19, Scrappy Scarpino's flying boats and their nine-man crews were up again, droning through the darkness to the west of the U.S. carriers. Lt. Herman Arle's plane had been in the air for two hours when at 0115 the radar scope suddenly lit up like the Fourth of July. The operator reported forty blips in two separate groups on the glowing green scope. Though the flying boat crew had no way to know, the blips marked Admiral Kurita's *C Force*, only 75 miles from the H/D fix Spruance had dismissed as a possible Japanese trick less than an hour before. "As we got to within twelve miles, one of the ships, an aircraft carrier, turned on its deck lights," reported co-pilot Bob Caldwell. "They must have thought we were a search plane returning."[52]

Arle, a thirty-one-year-old former forestry student from Minnesota, told his radio operator, CPO James G. Tibbets, to send out a coded message, then waited in frustration as Tibbets struggled to make radio contact with the task force. Despite repeated attempts, there was no reply. The problem appeared to be something known as "skip distance" bouncing the message off the ionosphere. The message was picked up by other receivers in scattered places, but not by the intended recipient. None of the unintended recipients, including a nearby plane and the seaplane tender *Casco* at

Eniwetok, acted to forward the coded message to the proper address. Out of desperation, Arle directed Tibbets to send the message in the clear. Still there was no response. Arle turned back to the east. By the time he returned to Saipan at 0900, the information that might have dramatically affected the course of the battle was useless.[53]

Japanese planes were also up in the darkness. At 0100, a scout that may have been flying out of Guam dropped a series of flares near TG 58.1. A destroyer fired on the plane and a night fighter scoured the area, but the enemy pilot gave them the slip. The flares remained, burning brightly on the water, a beacon for all to see. A destroyer tried to extinguish them with depth charges but without success. On the carriers, crewmen were busy fueling planes, loading bombs and machine-gun ammunition, and making certain engines were in order. At 0218, *Enterprise* sent fifteen Avengers aloft to range westward in search of the Japanese fleet. The torpedo bombers searched out for about 325 miles in patterns from 240 to 270 degrees. They missed Kurita's *C Force* by about 45 miles.[54]

Admiral Ozawa began launching reconnaissance aircraft at 0430. By 0600, he had forty-three planes in the air looking for his quarry. The effort paid off at 0730 when a Jake spotted two carriers, four battleships, and ten other ships 160 miles west of Saipan. Minutes later another scout plane corroborated that sighting, reporting fourteen ships, including four battleships. The Jake pilot then reported another four U.S. carriers. Ozawa calculated that the *Mobile Fleet* was only 380 miles from the American fleet.[55] His forward-ranging *C Force* under Admiral Kurita was about 80 miles closer.

Deprived of his opportunity the day before, Admiral Obayashi, commanding *Carrier Division 3*, could no longer contain himself. He began launching planes at 0825: sixteen Zeke fighters; forty-five Zeke fighter-bombers, each with a 550-pound bomb; and eight Jills with torpedoes from *Chitose, Chiyoda,* and *Zuiho.*[56]

Ozawa, who had merely been awaiting more confirmation reports, began launching planes a half an hour later. The first Zeke lifted off from *Taiho* at 0856, followed by aircraft from Lt. Cmdr. Akira Tarui's *601st Air Group* flying off of *Shokaku* and *Zuikaku.* Representing Ozawa's main blow, the force consisted of twenty-seven torpedo-laden Nakajima B6N Jills; fifty-three Yokosuka D4Y Susei Judy divebombers, each lumbering into the air with a 1,000-pound bomb; and forty-eight Zekes to keep U.S. fighters at bay. They were preceded by two Jills acting as pathfinders. A third Jill carried packages of foil "window" to be dropped in an effort to confound American radar.[57]

Japanese morale in the *Mobile Fleet* was stratospheric, with some officers expecting to take the Americans completely by surprise. Commanding the *Hiyo*, Capt. Toshiyuki Yokoi had entertained doubts about the operation, which he called "the frantic poker player's last bet, our whole pile against our opponent's." But now, as the planes launched, he found himself caught up in the general euphoria. "We were completely undetected, we were sure of it; sure also we would sight the American fleet before it sighted us, and destroy it," he recalled. "Morale was at a fever pitch, from the supreme commander right down to the lowest mess hand."[58]

Patrolling west of the U.S. fleet, the USS *Albacore*, one of four subs Admiral Lockwood had repositioned scarcely twenty-four hours before, spotted an enemy plane—believed to be a Betty—a little after 0700. Cmdr. James W. Blanchard assumed the presence of a carrier attack bomber in the vicinity had some significance and he was soon proved right. Less than forty-five minutes later, the *Mobile Fleet* steamed into view.

Blanchard submerged and eyed the parade through his periscope. He identified a carrier, a cruiser, and the superstructures of several other ships in the distance. Range was about 7 miles. Blanchard had started an approach on the carrier, when he picked up a second carrier group. This bunch consisted of a carrier, a cruiser, and several destroyers. Angle on the bow of the carrier, which was flying a large eight-rayed flag, was only 10 degrees to the starboard, putting *Albacore* in an excellent attack position. Though Blanchard didn't know it, the carrier was Admiral Ozawa's flagship, the 34,000-ton *Taiho*. The largest carrier in the Japanese fleet, the "Great Phoenix" had been commissioned only three months before. The heavily armored behemoth was designed to survive almost any conceivable damage—one Japanese officer remarked that the carrier "reminded us of a huge armored insect."[59]

Blanchard brought *Albacore* around and closed to 9,000 yards. The angle on the bow of the carrier was 15 degrees starboard. Distance to the "track"— the spot where his torpedoes would intercept the carrier if it continued on course—was 2,300 yards. A moment later, however, *Albacore*'s perfect setup was ruined when a Japanese destroyer shifted course and blocked the shot. Blanchard had little choice but to amend his course and allow the destroyer to pass through his line of fire. It appeared he would be able to salvage the lost opportunity. At 0804 *Albacore* was 5,300 yards from *Taiho* and 1,950 yards from the target's track. Speed of the carrier was plotted at 27 knots. As the data was fed into the sub's Torpedo Data Computer (T.D.C.), Blanchard raised the periscope at 0806 for a last visual check of the target. Two minutes later, he was ready to shoot. The T.D.C. chose that moment to malfunction. The light indicating a correct solution to the firing problem refused to illuminate.

With *Taiho* rapidly drawing away, Blanchard knew he had no chance of keeping up. Raising the periscope again, he hoped the data entered into the T.D.C. would work—solution light or no solution light—and fired a six-torpedo spread by eye at 0909. He had no time to observe results. Less than thirty seconds after the torpedoes were away, three destroyers charged toward *Albacore*. Blanchard pulled the plug and took the sub down deep. As they descended, the crew heard a muffled explosion. Timing indicated it was a hit by torpedo number 6.

Warrant Officer Sakio Komatsu had just lifted his Jill off *Taiho* when he spotted the wake of a torpedo heading for the carrier. Komatsu immediately dove his plane into the path of the torpedo. There was a huge explosion. Whether it was from the Jill and its bomb exploding or the torpedo, or both, the "fish" did not hit *Taiho*. But Komatsu's sacrifice proved futile. Two minutes after leaving *Albacore*'s tubes, a second torpedo—Blanchard's number 6—slammed into *Taiho*'s starboard side near the forward gasoline tanks. "[A] water column rose high on the starboard side forward of the bridge," observed Chusa Shioyama Sakuichi. "Some of the bridge personnel got wet and the ship reeled under [the] shock."[60]

The explosion jammed the 100-ton forward elevator and ruptured the holding tanks along with gas and oil lines, but any fires were doused by the in-rush of seawater. Damage appeared minimal. Staff officer Capt. Toshikazu Ohmae observed that Admiral Ozawa appeared unperturbed and continued to "radiate confidence and satisfaction."[61] Slowed by only one knot, the carrier steamed on. Within half an hour the damaged elevator—with an A6M5 fighter still stuck on the inoperable lift—had been planked over using benches and tables from the mess room and *Taiho* resumed launching planes.

Less than two minutes after loosing her torpedo spread, *Albacore* was under depth charge attack. The first pass was the worst. Six depth charges exploded around the sub, the fourth and fifth close enough to knock cork from the conning tower bulkheads. Japanese destroyers hunted *Albacore* for nearly an hour, dropping a total of forty-eight depth charges. Fortunately for the sub, the effort seemed to grow increasingly random and inefficient after the initial attack. The destroyers finally steamed off after the carrier group, leaving Blanchard to ponder the vagaries of fortune that would place the target of a lifetime smack in his sights and then allow his T.D.C. to break down. Though he was reasonably sure he had scored a hit, he did not believe one torpedo would have much of an effect on a carrier. Sick with disgust and disappointment, he did not even bother to transmit a radio report of the attack, leaving it for his patrol report.[62]

While *Albacore* hid in the depths, a Hellcat piloted by twenty-three-year-old Lt. John R. Strane from the *Essex*'s VF-15, familiarly known as "Satan's Playmates," was droning along thousands of feet above the ocean. Strane had been awakened at about 0330 and ordered to fly escort for a Curtis SB2C Helldiver on a four-hour search pattern. "The outbound and inbound legs were about 300 miles, plus a cross leg of perhaps 60 or 70 miles," he recalled. "The searches were to be conducted under radio silence; only when the enemy task force was located were messages to be sent in code by the radioman-gunner who occupied the rear seat of the Helldiver."[63]

Strane had been assigned to Satan's Playmates less than a year before and, like many of the squadron's pilots, had yet to see a Japanese plane. That changed about fifteen minutes before reaching the end of his outbound leg when he suddenly caught sight of a single-engine Aichi E13 Jake floatplane. Heart pumping wildly, he maneuvered into position about 800 feet behind the other aircraft and gave it a short burst from his .50s. Small pieces of metal flew off the Jake; then it burst into flames and dove almost straight down into the water from an altitude of about 500 feet. What appeared to be a pontoon remained floating on the surface, but there were no survivors. It was 0725 and Strane had just claimed what may have been the first Japanese victim of the battle of the Philippine Sea.

Ten minutes later, now on the return track, Strane spotted a Nakajima B6N Jill torpedo bomber approaching from the right and slightly above. The enemy pilot headed for nearby cloud cover with Strane in pursuit. Strane got in a couple of bursts, then positioned himself behind the Jill, which was carrying a torpedo slung under its belly. The aft cockpit canopy was open and the rear-seat gunner was firing his machine gun. Strane followed the torpedo bomber down through the clouds and fired again. "I am positive that the rear-seat gunner was dead by then," he observed. "He was hanging over the canopy rail. I have no idea if the pilot was dead at the control." The Jill continued in a tight downward spiral from 3,000 feet and smashed into the water. It was 0741.

Some two hours later, nearing the U.S. fleet, Strane radioed *Essex* and asked for landing instructions. "Stand by," came the reply. "We are under attack. We will get back to you as soon as possible."[64]

CHAPTER XIII

Showdown

AT 0957 RADAR OPERATORS ABOARD THE BATTLESHIP *ALABAMA* PICKED UP Adm. Sueo Obayashi's *653rd Air Group* 140 miles out. A few minutes later *Lexington* fixed the bogies at a bearing of 260 degrees. The Japanese were approaching in two groups between 121 and 124 miles out at an altitude of 20,000 feet. Warning horns blared as ships not already on full alert went to general quarters. Shipboard guns swung toward the west and antiaircraft crews peered skyward from their tubs.

At 1005, Mitscher moved to gather all outlying fighters, radioing, "Hey, Rube!"—the old circus call to assemble. Divebombers and torpedo planes were launched from carrier decks and sent east where they would be out of the way. At 1010, the order went out to prepare to launch all available fighters, followed nine minutes later by the command, "Execute." Within fifteen minutes about 140 Hellcats clawed their way skyward, while eighty-two others already in the air headed west.[1]

Ens. Al Slack was in the officers mess aboard *Essex* when general quarters sounded. As the public address speaker blared "Pilots, man your planes," Slack raced up to the hangar deck and climbed into the cockpit of his Hellcat. He could hear planes taking off on the deck overhead as he waited for handlers to pull his plane onto the elevator. Moments later he was in the air, pushing hard to catch up with the rest of his group.[2] An unusual atmospheric condition created long white contrails from the scores of aircraft. Radio channels crackled with excited chatter as the fighters rushed to intercept the enemy air attack. Meanwhile, the Japanese airmen had made a rookie error by stopping to assemble and reorganize 74 miles from the task force. Obayashi had sent out eight torpedo planes, sixteen fighters, and forty-five fighter-bombers. The fifteen-minute pause as the attacking aircraft milled around at 18,000 feet only gave U.S. pilots more time to respond.

First in were eight Hellcats from *Essex*, slashing into the milling Japanese from 24,000 feet. Cmdr. Charles W. Brewer went after the formation leader, giving him a burst of .50s from 800 feet. The enemy aircraft exploded "practically in my face."[3] Flying through the debris of his victim, Brewer pulled up on another Zero and blew half its wing off, sending the now flaming plane tumbling toward the water. Brewer knocked down another Zeke with a no-deflection shot from a distance of about 400 feet, then got involved in a one-on-one with yet another fighter that roared up on his tail. Brewer came around abruptly and fastened on the tail of the Zero, which was now frantically maneuvering through a series of half-rolls, barrel rolls, and wingover in an effort to escape, but all for naught. Brewer sent him flaming into the sea.[4]

As another Zero latched onto Brewer's tail, his wingman, Ens. Ralph E. Fowler Jr., made a diving turn, centered the enemy in his sight, and gave him a series of short bursts. The Zero started to smoke, then fell off to the right, executed a barrel roll, and spiraled into the ocean. Fowler went after two other Zekes at 10,000 feet, but got into trouble when he overran them and missed with his .50s. The two quickly maneuvered onto his tail. Fowler tried to dive away, but the Zekes stayed with him. Salvation came in the form of another Hellcat, which went after the Zeros, giving Fowler an opening to turn out and get in a burst at one of his two tormentors. The stream of .50s took off about 10 feet of the Zero's port wing. The pilot got out as the plane spun in, but his parachute failed to open. Undaunted by his close call, Fowler went after yet another Zero. As he opened fire, the Zeke skidded violently from left to right and Fowler noticed that the plane's vertical tail section had been shot off. He continued to fire until flames burst from the cowling. The fire quickly spread and the Zero plummeted like a torch into the sea. Fowler then opened up on a Zero that popped out of a cloud where it had been chased by two other Hellcats. All but one of his guns cut out, but one was enough as slugs slammed into the fuselage and cockpit. The Zero went down trailing smoke.[5]

Lt. (j.g.) George R. Carr, a veteran of the Royal Canadian Air Force, got his first score of the war when he set a Jill on fire, flying through a hail of debris as the torpedo bomber exploded. Climbing, Carr flamed another Jill, sending it into a graveyard spiral from which it never recovered. A Zeke got on Carr's tail, but the young Floridian dove away at full throttle and lost him. Pulling out, he looked through his fogged windscreen to see another Zeke coming at him head on. Closing at 600 miles an hour, both fired. A 7.7mm slug spidered the glass on Carr's windscreen, but his own six .50-calibers were lethal: Hit in the engine and wing roots, the Japanese exploded.

Spotting two more Zeros, Carr got behind one and fired. Something flew out of the plane as it started down—it may have been the pilot—but Carr didn't pause to see. Sliding behind the second Zero, he pressed the trigger. The Zero started to smoke and fell off on one wing. Carr maneuvered to stay behind it and was about to give the coup de grace when the Zero exploded.[6]

Al Slack spotted a Judy divebomber at about 24,000 feet with some Zeros farther behind and above. Ignoring the Zeros, Slack turned on the Judy and opened fire. Smoke and flames erupted from the divebomber, but it continued on course. Slack was having trouble with a weak engine, but he persisted, continuing to fire on the bomber. There was a sudden explosion behind his head and he saw the metal on the Hellcat's left wing stub pull through the rivets. He flipped the fighter to the right and went into a dive, looking for the Zero that had hit him. He saw nothing. He also lost track of the Judy he had set on fire and was unable to claim it as a kill.[7]

About forty Japanese planes survived the initial onslaught and broke through, only to run into more waves of Hellcat pilots eager to send them into the hereafter. Lt. (j.g.) Don McKinley, a fighter pilot with VF-25, was scrambled shortly after 1000 from *Cowpens*. The pilots were told to forgo the delay of organizing by division and just head west. McKinley's was the third plane off the deck. Once in the air another F6F took up position on his left wing. McKinley recognized the pilot as one of his roommates, Lt. (j.g.) Fred Stieglitz, as they headed for the expanding web of vapor trails marking the site of the air battle.

That battle was well underway as they arrived about 50 miles southwest of TG 58.4. The sky seemed to be full of planes. Some spiraled toward the sea trailing flames. McKinley was at about 7,500 feet when he spotted three Jill torpedo planes about 1,000 feet below heading in the direction of the American fleet. The Jills were painted a brownish gray with big red meatballs on the wings and fuselage. Each carried a torpedo slung below the belly. There was so much chatter on the air, McKinley couldn't raise Stieglitz on the radio. He managed to get the other pilot's attention visually and motioned toward the Jills. Stieglitz nodded and they turned. The enemy crews spotted them and split up, one plane breaking off to the left and the other two diving off to the right. McKinley kept after the two on the right, while Stieglitz stayed with the single.

Closing to within 100 yards, McKinley targeted the lead Jill. After three or four bursts, the plane began to smoke. The pilot appeared inexperienced; he took little evasive action. Flames erupted and the Jill tumbled toward the ocean. McKinley turned to the second Jill, closing the gap rapidly. The Japanese pilot had taken the torpedo plane down to about 250 feet; he now dropped to within 50 feet of the waves in a desperate effort to throw off pursuit. The rear gunner was firing at McKinley, but without effect. McKinley also noticed splashes in the water but, intent on his quarry, did not give them much heed. He squeezed off a burst and apparently hit the pilot. The Jill smoked, nosed over, and slammed into the water. Only then did McKinley see that he was approaching an Essex-class carrier about a mile away. The splashes he had seen in the water were from friendly antiaircraft fire directed at the torpedo plane. Well aware that antiaircraft fire—friendly or not—didn't discriminate, McKinley pulled up and turned away.[8]

Their formations slashed to ribbons, only a handful of Japanese pilots made it as far as the task force. *Indiana*'s gunners knocked the wing off one attacker, sending the plane plummeting into the water 200 yards ahead of the battleship. A Judy managed to put a bomb into *South Dakota*, the only real Japanese success of the morning. The explosion killed twenty-three men and wounded another twenty-seven, but did not affect operations. Two other fighter-bombers came in from astern on the *Minneapolis*. One dropped a 500-pound bomb close off the starboard side, injuring three crewmen and causing a small fire and some minor damage. One of the Japanese was shot down, the other escaped.

By 1057, the attack, later dubbed "Raid I," was over as the few Japanese survivors limped back toward the *Mobile Fleet*. Though American claims of one hundred kills were exaggerated, the actual score—forty-two—was devastating enough. Not a single plane had penetrated to the carriers, and the Japanese had been blown out of the skies miles from the flattops or uselessly expended themselves on the antiaircraft protective line. Of the force that had set out so eagerly, only eight fighters, thirteen fighter-bombers, and six Jills made it home. Eight of the nine squadron leaders in *Air Group 653* had been killed. Among the dead, joining thirty-one of his men, was senior fighter-bomber leader Keishiro Ito.[9]

American losses were four pilots missing in action, including the commander of *Princeton*'s air group, Lt. Cmdr. Ernest W. Wood, who went down when his horizontal stabilizers failed as he attempted to pull out of a dive. Also missing was Don McKinley's roommate, Fred Stieglitz, who disappeared somewhere in the melee. At one point he had radioed, "Scratch one fish," indicating he had downed a torpedo plane.[10] Another pilot reported seeing Stieglitz giving hand signals indicating two kills, but the former

Washington University student who had first joined the Royal Canadian
Air Force in 1941 in order to get into the war failed to make it back to the
Cowpens and was never seen again.[11]

Al Slack was one of the lucky ones. As he set down on *Essex*, he saw
sailors on the catwalk staring at his plane in disbelief. Parking the fighter
and climbing down from the cockpit, he saw why. A 2- to 3-foot hole had
been torn out of the metal fuselage directly behind his seat. The gaping hole
was surrounded by twelve smaller perforations.

Mrs. Slack's second son was very fortunate to be alive.[12]

Division leader Lt. (j.g.) Alexander Vraciu, who was on the verge of losing
his $125 bet with Gus Widhelm on the imminence of a fleet engagement,
seemed doomed to spending a frustrated morning orbiting over his home
carrier *Lexington*. Vraciu had taken off at 1030 with thirteen other Hellcats
to join the air battle, but almost immediately had trouble with his engine
leaking oil on the windshield. Then his supercharger failed. Finally, much
to his disgust, he was told to take his group back over the task force. The
twenty-five-year-old son of Romanian immigrants—his father was a Chicago police officer—Vraciu was no stranger to aerial combat. Six months
before Pearl Harbor, shortly after graduating from DePauw University, he
had enlisted in the Navy flight-training program. By the time the Marianas
show rolled around he already had a dozen victories to his credit—he had
shot down number twelve, a Betty bomber, north of Saipan on June 14—
and he was eager to add more.

He was about to get his chance. As he cut circles over the flattop, his
engine settled down and the gauges were reading normal. At 1107, *Lexington's* radar picked up aircraft approaching from 160 miles out. It was the
main attack—Raid II—following in the wake of Obayashi's now decimated
early strike. *Lexington's* fighter direction officer broke in on the radio: "Vec-
tor 265!" Vraciu could tell by the FDO's tone that something big was in the
works. He charged his guns and set off on the designated heading.

Led by Lieutenant Commander Tarui, the *601st Air Group* experienced
an inauspicious start. Passing over Admiral Kurita's C Force, the planes were
taken under fire by trigger-happy antiaircraft crews who apparently couldn't
tell west from east, or were too enthusiastic to care. Two of Tarui's planes
were shot down and eight were so badly damaged they had to return to
the carriers—this in addition to eight that had already turned back due to
mechanical problems. The rest droned on and by 1100 were drawing close

to the U.S. task force when Commander Tarui made the same mistake as his predecessor—he paused to organize his inexperienced aircrews. Down on *Lexington*, a Japanese language expert, Lt. (j.g.) Charles A. Sims, monitored Tarui's radioed briefing, passing the details on to the fighter direction officer as TF 58's Hellcats closed in.

First on the scene at 1130 were ten *Essex* Hellcats led by Cmdr. David McCampbell. By now the Japanese formation was only about 45 miles from the task force. McCampbell singled out a Judy that promptly blew up in his face, then nailed another one that tumbled away trailing smoke. Moving toward the head of the enemy formation, he sent another Judy down trailing smoke, then made a run on the leading plane. His first pass had no noticeable effect. He came around and went after the leader's left wingman from seven o'clock high. The bomber exploded.

Returning attention to the leader, McCampbell gave it a lengthy burst from his .50s until the bomber finally burst into flames and spiraled down out of control. Experiencing gun stoppages, McCampbell broke off to recharge the .50s, then returned to the enemy formation still stubbornly forging ahead. He opened up on one of the Judys, but only his starboard guns fired, which threw the Hellcat into a skid. The Judy tried to dive away, but McCampbell kept after it, firing short bursts with what guns he had working. Finally the Judy pulled up, then nosed down, smashing into the water.[13]

Ten minutes and about 35 miles after leaving *Lexington*, Vraciu spotted three specks about 10 miles ahead. "Tally ho!" he announced over the radio. He continued to scan the sky in that direction and soon made out "a large, rambling mass of at least fifty enemy planes, 2,000 feet below, portside and closing."[14] He picked up his mike again. "Tally ho, eleven o'clock low!"

Within minutes the specks resolved themselves into a mob of Japanese aircraft: bombers, torpedo planes, and fighters. Vraciu noted they seemed to be painted a light color instead of the typical dirty greenish-brown. The Hellcats tore into them. Vraciu set after a Judy, but veered off as another Hellcat cut in. He spotted another Judy and closed quickly to within 200 feet. "It was doing some wild maneuvering, and the rear gunner was squirting away as I came down from the stern," he recalled. "I worked in close and gave him a burst."[15] The bomber caught fire and headed down to the sea, trailing a long plume of smoke. "Splash one Judy!" shouted Vraciu, adding to the excited chatter on the radio.

Some of the enemy bombers and torpedo planes had dropped lower, preparing to make their runs on the American task force. Vraciu spotted two Judys flying side by side and thought he'd try for both with one pass. He shoved the throttle forward and came up behind the bomber to the right. The rear seat gunner was firing at him, but had little hope against the Hellcat's .50-calibers. Vraciu hit the gun button; the Judy staggered, started to smoke, and fell off on the right wing. The Japanese rear gunner was still firing as the plane plunged into the water. "For a split-second, I almost felt sorry for the little bastard," remarked Vraciu.[16] Slipping left, he got behind the second Judy and fired a short burst. The bomber caught fire and fell out of the sky.

Vraciu closed on another Judy that had become separated from the enemy formation. Apparently unobserved by either the pilot or gunner, he worked in close and put a burst into the wing root. The plane immediately burst into flames and fell off to the right, twisting crazily out of control. Spotting three more of the divebombers beginning their attack on the ships below, Vraciu got to the last in line as the first arrived over a U.S. destroyer. As antiaircraft fire blossomed in the sky around him, he opened up on the tail-end bomber. Pieces of the engine tore away and the plane disintegrated in midair. Still at full throttle, he went after the second bomber as it winged over in a dive on the destroyer below. Almost vertical, the big Hellcat screamed downward after the Judy. Intense antiaircraft fire exploded all around both planes. As the bomber filled his sight ring, Vraciu fired. The Judy continued its dive. Vraciu was wondering just how long he could stay with it when there was a sudden flash and the bomber disappeared.

Vraciu yanked back on the stick and pulled out of his dive. Below and in the near distance, he saw the first of the three Judys still flying, apparently headed for one of Ching Lee's battleships. The ships had thrown up a curtain of antiaircraft fire. Suddenly the Judy exploded. Craning his neck, Vraciu looked for more enemies, but the Japanese were gone. He had destroyed six enemy aircraft in eight minutes. Armorers later told him he had expended only 360 rounds—world-class shooting by any standard.[17]

Like Vraciu, twenty-two-year-old Lt. (j.g.) Dan Rehm was flying air cover over the fleet at 20,000 feet when *Bataan*'s FDO alerted him to the bogeys coming in from the west. A short time later, the former Loyola University student spotted a large formation of enemy planes—he thought about ninety-five, though it turned out to be more—at about 18,000 feet. Rehm didn't see any separate fighter protection; the fighters seemed to be mixed in with the bombers and torpedo bombers. He began a high-side turning dive on a Zero to the left of the enemy formation. His guns were bore-sighted to converge at 800 feet. He placed the sighting pip just ahead of the enemy fighter and squeezed the trigger. The Hellcat seemed to slow as the guns pounded away, but Rehm knew this was an illusion. His tracers streamed into the Zero; debris began to fly off, then the left wing folded and tore away. Smoking, the plane spun down toward the water.

Rehm pulled out of his dive at about 1,000 feet so abruptly he almost grayed out. Checking for his wingman, he rolled over into a high-side dive on another Zero. By now the formation seemed to be breaking up as more Navy fighters arrived and tore into the gaggle of planes. Rehm's chosen victim saw him coming and attempted to evade. Rehm put the pip just ahead of him and let loose with his six .50s as the other pilot rolled left to dive. The Zero abruptly blew up.

Looking around, Rehm saw that the sky seemed to be full of burning aircraft spiraling down toward the sea. "I observed several parachutes deployed, each with an enemy pilot, either dead or alive," he remembered. "The whole area looked like a large Christmas tree with its lights turned on." Spotting a Zero heading toward the fleet at very high speed, he gave chase. The Zero attempted a variety of evasive maneuvers, turning, rolling, then diving for the water. Rehm stuck to him and as the other plane rolled over and they were both inverted, he let go with his .50s. Tracers poured into the Zeke and it exploded in flames.[18]

Yorktown fighters were also in on the brawl. A paraphrase of the after-action report conveys the chaos of the action. Led by Cmdr. B. M. "Smoke" Strean, a ten-plane combat air patrol hit a Japanese group coming in at 20,000 feet. Strean made an aft no-deflection run on what he thought was a "Tony" [what *Yorktown* pilots consistently described as Kawasaki-built army Ki-61 Tonys were probably Judys as there were no army fighters present] in a starboard turn; he observed hits in the cockpit and wing roots. The "Tony's" engine seemed to stop, he lost speed rapidly, nosed over, and went straight down. Strean then made a no-deflection run on a Zeke at 17,000 feet, chopping up the engine, cockpit, and wing roots. The Zeke smoked and burned and fell over in a dive.[19] Lt. (j.g.) Roy A. Bechtol fired on a "Tony" coming head-on, hitting the engine, cockpit, and wing roots. The aircraft burst into flames. His next kill was a diving no-deflection shot on a Zeke at 4,000 feet. The Zeke "did a starboard flipper turn, nosed down and dove into the water."[20]

Lt. (j.g.) Jack Hankins got his first Zeke at 18,000 feet. Two or three Zekes turned into him and he made a full-deflection shot from the starboard on the nearest plane. The aircraft smoked badly, but appeared to recover, so he made a second pass. The Zeke started jinking but to no avail. Hankins hit the engine, wing roots, and the starboard wing and his victim went up like a torch. Later in the melee the twenty-three-year-old Virginian climbed to 18,000 feet where he engaged a "Tony," making a no-deflection tail shot and scoring hits in the cockpit. The "Tony" smoked, caught fire, and went straight down. Hankins followed with a no-deflection shot on a lone Zeke attempting an overhead run on an F6F. The Zeke burst into flames, but pulled away, smoking as the flames subsided. Hankins made a second attack, a no-deflection run on the tail. The Zeke blew up, leaving a cloud of debris in front of Hankins's Hellcat.[21]

Lt. (j.g.) M. M. Tomme Jr. of Troup, Texas, made a port high-side full-deflection shot on a passing Zeke, hitting the engine, cockpit, and probably the gas tanks as the Zeke completely disintegrated. Pieces of the tail hurtled past Tomme's Hellcat. The twenty-two-year-old former Texas farmboy then proceeded to flame a "Tony" at 10,000 feet, again torching the vulnerable gas tanks.

Ens. Jim Duffy of VF-15 had a close call when a Zero got behind him and stayed there despite Duffy's best efforts to shake him off. "I was raked by machine gun fire, which sounded like someone banging on the plane with a sledge hammer." Duffy's wingman, Lt. John Strane, finally shot the Zero off his tail. Later, back aboard the *Essex*, he congratulated Duffy on his invention of the "Duffy Weave." From now on, he said, Duffy would act as bait and he would shoot down any takers. "It took me awhile to find the humor in that," admitted Duffy.[22]

Lt. Richard T. Eastmond led the second division of Commander Strean's flight. As he drew near, he noticed bogies dropping belly tanks at 17,000 feet. On his first attack he dove for an aft no-deflection shot on a Zeke. Hit in both wing roots and the cockpit, the plane burst into flames and plummeted toward the water, trailing debris as it fell. Recovering altitude, Eastmond looked around, counting seventeen burning aircraft in the air. He picked up a Zeke that tried to evade by zigzagging, but Eastmond got on his tail and put in a burst that apparently killed the pilot. The Zeke nearly spun into him, but then fell away burning and crashed into the water.[23]

By now the dogfight extended all over the sky. Parachutes and burning planes seemed to be everywhere. Eastmond saw a Zeke closing on the tail of an F6F and started over to help the American pilot, but the F6F went down before he could get there. Spotting a Zeke to the starboard and slightly below at about 7,000 feet, he made a semi-deflection shot from the tail end and exploded the starboard wing root with a long burst. The Zeke rolled over, dove straight down, and crashed. Climbing to 11,000 feet, Eastmond joined up with four other F6Fs, then dove on a "Tony" from directly behind. He fired about 250 rounds before his victim blew up, the pieces rattling off his Hellcat.

Lt. (j.g.) Charles Ambellan started one Zeke smoking, before losing sight of it. Another Zeke made a head-on run at him. Ambellan pulled up shooting and the Zeke exploded. He followed with a 45-degree deflection shot on the starboard side of a passing Zeke. It smoked but appeared to recover, so he came back with a no-deflection tail shot. The Zeke burst into flames and dove into the water. By now the air battle had become more dispersed. Ambellan gave chase to a Zero that promptly went down to the water, weaving back and forth in an effort to throw him off. Each time Ambellan started a good burst, the other pilot would pull up sharply and elude him. Finally Ambellan had just one gun left firing. By kicking his hydraulic chargers he got all three guns on his starboard side to operate and the Zeke burst into flames. "It was just one big orange puff when it hit the water," he reported.[24]

Lt. (j.g.) Robert A. Frink, a twenty-two-year-old former University of Iowa student, engaged his first enemy fighter (another purported Tony) at about 18,000 feet. The rear man of a Japanese formation, the "Tony" attempted to evade with slow rolls, but Frink put a burst into the wing root and the plane fell off in a dive, intermittent flames spreading until it was burning furiously. Spotting a Zeke at 17,000 feet, Frink climbed and got a long burst into the starboard wing root. This Zeke went into a dive and never recovered, splashing into the water. Another Zeke got on Frink's tail. As he dove to escape, the Zeke was knocked off by another F6F. At 12,000 feet Frink encountered a lone Zeke in the middle of a loop. He caught it with a full-deflection shot just as it hit the top of the loop, registering hits in the fuselage and on the wings. The Zeke dove smoking into the water. His final victim was a "Tony" on the tail of another Hellcat at 8,000 feet. Frink made a high turn approach and fired a long burst. The "Tony" rolled over emitting flames and smoke, but Frink didn't see it go in.[25]

Ens. Rudolph "Rudy" Matz accounted for two kills and two probables. The first was a "Tony" that approached him head-on at 14,000 feet. Matz pulled up and gave him a burst, hitting the engine and wing roots. The enemy aircraft burst into a solid sheet of flame before Matz's eyes. As his Hellcat passed almost through the flames, he could feel the heat through his canopy, which was slightly open. Continuing on, he saw three Zekes, two of them being chased by another F6F. He dove on the third one with a 30-degree deflection shot from the port and hit the gas tanks. The Zeke burst into flames and went down in the water. He ended the day by smoking another "Tony" and a Zeke. He did not see either of them crash, though the Zeke was in flames when last seen.[26]

Despite the massacre in the sky, some of the Japanese planes leaked through. Out in front of TG 58.7, the destroyer *Stockham* found itself an unwelcome center of attention for about twenty minutes as enemy aircraft appeared from various directions. The ship shot down three and escaped damage. The task group's battleships also came under attack between 1150 and 1215 by divebombers and torpedo planes. A torpedo directed at *Indiana* fortuitously exploded prematurely 50 yards away from the battleship. *Indiana* antiaircraft gunners shot down five of the attackers. A Jill going down in flames hit the ship at the waterline but caused only minor damage. Another Jill launched a torpedo at *Iowa*, but missed. Two bombs aimed at *Alabama* also went wide. Among the injured, probably by friendly fire, the automatic weapons officer aboard the cruiser *San Francisco* orated his way into naval history as he held up his bleeding finger and shouted, "The bastards have drawn blood, shoot them down!"[27]

At about noon, a Judy and three Jills penetrated to Rear Adm. John W. Reeves's TG 58.3 and went after *Enterprise* and *Princeton*. All were shot down. Two bogies that got through to Rear Adm. Alfred E. Montgomery's TG 58.2 were mistakenly dismissed as friendlies. They turned out to be a pair of Judys. One dropped a bomb off *Wasp*'s port beam, killing one sailor and wounding others. Both aircraft were promptly shot down. Two other Judys went after *Bunker Hill* at 1203. One turned away and was blown in half by a direct hit; the pilot was catapulted from the plane with his parachute streaming behind. The other kept after the carrier and got its bomb away before crashing. Both bomb and plane exploded close off the port side, spraying the hangar deck with shrapnel, knocking out the port elevator, and starting several fires, but not seriously impairing the ship's capabilities. A Marine lieutenant and a seaman second class were killed; twenty-two sailors were wounded seriously enough to be admitted to sick bay, and sixty-two more were slightly wounded.[28]

By 1215 the radar scopes were clear and TF 58's fighters were coming home to roost. Back on *Lexington*'s flight deck, Alex Vraciu, taxiing toward the parking area with his canopy shoved back, saw Admiral Mitscher looking down from the bridge. Grinning, Vraciu held up six fingers. Moments later, as Vraciu shared his story with pilots and deck crew, Mitscher himself appeared in the crowd. A photographer was taking shots of the exuberant group. The diminutive admiral shook Vraciu's hand, then asked a photographer to take their picture together. "Not for publication," he added. "To keep for myself."[29]

Mitscher had more reason to celebrate than Admiral Ozawa. Of the 128 Japanese planes launched for Raid II, only thirty-one—sixteen Zekes, eleven Judys, and four Jills—returned to the carriers or made it to Guam. Only four of the twenty-seven Jills launched that morning survived; forty-two of the fifty-three Judys failed to return, along with thirty-two of the forty-eight Zeros. Mitscher had lost just three Hellcat pilots—one each from VF-1, VF-14, and VF-15. Compiling the after-action report on *Yorktown* later, an officer spoke for the entire fleet when he concluded, "The action of all pilots involved leaves little to be desired."[30]

In Yokosuko Harbor in the southwest corner of Tokyo Bay, officers aboard the *Combined Fleet* flagship, the light cruiser *Oyodo*, were almost giddy that morning with optimism about Admiral Ozawa's prospects. The staff gave their admiral a four out of five chance of victory over the American fleet. Chief of staff Adm. Ryunosuke Kusaka was less certain. As one of the prime architects of A-Go, he firmly believed in bringing the U.S. Navy to decisive battle. However, he had been shaken earlier in the year by the lack of defenses at Saipan, to the point that he nagged army officials until Tojo himself responded in writing, "I personally guarantee with a large seal the defense of Saipan!" This assurance was delivered by an army colonel who further advised Kusaka that the army *hoped* the Americans would attempt to invade Saipan as they would be promptly annihilated.[31]

Of course, if Japan lost the present naval engagement, army bravado would count for little and Kusaka had some reservations about Ozawa's plan to stand off and pummel the Americans from long range. Still, the upbeat mood of his staff was infectious. "We so firmly believed in our victory that we nearly drank in celebration," he recalled.[32] He briefly considered summoning his steward to prepare celebratory cups of sake, but decided to wait. His caution seemed well advised as two hours passed without any word, and optimism began to give way to apprehension. Finally a message arrived and it was not good news. *Taiho* had been "somewhat damaged."[33] The mood aboard *Oyodo* suddenly grew sober.

The mood in the *First Mobile Fleet* had also darkened. Following the morning launch of Raid I, staff officers waited expectantly in *Hiyo*'s intelligence center for word of contact with the American fleet. Finally, they heard the staccato clicking of Morse Code: "Attacked ... [static] ... enemy carriers ... battleships ..." followed by silence. A radio contact with subsequent launches indicated many pilots had failed to find the Americans. Some were returning to the carriers, others were proceeding to Guam to refuel. Noon arrived and still there was no definitive word. "Lunch was a nervous torture," remembered Capt. Toshiyu Yokoi. "The rice was cold and I almost gagged on it."[34]

While Captain Yokoi agonized over the lack of news from his carrier planes, sailors aboard the Great Phoenix were busily coping with the damage caused by *Albacore*'s torpedo. Even as *Taiho* continued to launch planes, efforts were underway to repair ruptured gas and oil lines and to empty damaged fuel tanks by pumping the contents overboard. In the process, considerable gas was spilled on the hangar deck. As fumes from the avgas and highly volatile unprocessed Tarakan fuel oil grew increasingly oppressive, damage control parties knocked out glass portholes with hammers to try to clear the air, but to no avail. In desperation, an inexperienced damage control officer ordered the ventilating ducts to be opened. Instead of clearing the fumes, the ventilating system only spread them throughout the ship. It was a disaster in the making.

While damage control parties worked on *Taiho*, more immediate trouble lurked beneath the waves. Capt. Herman Kossler's *Cavalla* had been doggedly following the *Mobile Fleet* since the night of June 17, hoping for a second chance at one of Ozawa's carriers. At 1152, about 60 miles away and three hours after *Albacore*'s attack, Kossler raised periscope to see a forest of masts heading his way. "When I raised my periscope this time, the picture was too good to be true," he recalled. "I could see four ships, a large carrier with two cruisers ahead on the port bow and a destroyer about 1,000 yards on the starboard beam!" The flattop was *Shokaku* (Flying Crane), one of two surviving carriers that had participated in the December 7 attack on Pearl Harbor, now part of Ozawa's *Carrier Division 1*. The ship was a hive of activity, busily recovering and refueling aircraft. "When first sighted, three planes were circling for a landing and the flight deck had almost a complete load," Kossler reported. He estimated there were as many as thirty aircraft on the deck. Kossler was initially not sure the carrier was hostile, though the large "bedspring type radar mast" on the foremast practically shouted "Japanese." He risked three periscope sightings as he approached, trying to get a clear view of the ship's flag. "I took a last look and—God damn!—there was the rising sun as big as hell."[35]

Riding herd on the carrier, the destroyer *Urakaze* failed to detect *Cavalla*'s approach. "I put the periscope up," recalled Kossler. "We were at 1,000 yards. I got ready to fire six torpedoes in such a way that if our dope was good at least four would hit." Kossler fired four torpedoes set for a depth of 15 feet with the destroyer "still on my neck." He fired the fifth torpedo before pulling the plug, sending off the sixth fish as *Cavalla* started to go deep. It was now 1220. Range was 1,200 yards.[36]

Shokaku's watch, preoccupied with scanning the skies for enemy aircraft, neglected to devote equal attention to the surrounding waters. By the time a lookout spotted the torpedoes approaching off the starboard bow, it was too late. Capt. Hiroshi Matsubara ordered evasive action, but at least three torpedoes slammed into *Shokaku*.[37]

Kossler heard a solid hit at fifty seconds, followed by two more at eight-second intervals as he headed for the depths and rigged for silent running. Then he had other concerns as the Japanese destroyers were on him. Two sets of four depth charges exploded close to the sub, but that was only the beginning. Over the next three hours, *Cavalla* was pummeled by over a hundred depth charges—at least fifty-six of them very close. The pounding wrecked the sonar gear and air induction pipelines, but the sub survived.[38]

Though Kossler heard only three detonations, as many as four of *Cavalla*'s six torpedoes may have slammed into *Shokaku* on the starboard side forward and amidships. One of the fish struck below and just forward of the carrier's island. The explosion ruptured an aviation gasoline main and the resulting fireball engulfed the front of the bridge. Several aviators taking a break by the island were immolated in the spray of burning gasoline. Aircraft being fueled in the hangar exploded and the blast lifted the elevators nearly 3 feet. As the wrecked platforms plummeted back down into the wells, sailors who had been standing on the forward lift were pitched into the conflagration below.[39]

As a veteran ship, *Shokaku* had an experienced damage control party. Twice already during the war she had survived nearly fatal damage, once at Coral Sea and once in the Eastern Solomons. But now, as gas poured from damaged aircraft and ignited and ammunition started to cook off, all power failed. Circuits went out, fire suppression equipment failed, and no one could reach the hangar's mains through the inferno. Burning gasoline sprayed from ruptured pipes "like burning rain on their heads." Portable fire extinguishers and bucket brigades had no effect on the conflagration. Crewmembers trying to bring the fires under control were cut down by exploding bombs and gas tanks, strewing the deck with dismembered bodies.[40]

As seawater poured through the huge holes ripped in *Shokaku*'s side, the ship began to list to the starboard. In an effort to correct the list, spaces were counter-flooded on the port side, but damage control parties overcompensated and the carrier canted over to port. Wracked by fire and explosions fed by gasoline and volatile fumes from the unrefined Tarakan fuel oil, *Shokaku* slowed, became unnavigable, and finally stopped dead in the water. The carrier began to settle and water poured in through the forward elevator.

Capt. Hiroshi Matsubara realized his ship was doomed. The order was passed at 1330 for all hands to assemble and abandon ship. Sailors called out to alert comrades, officers checked smoke-filled compartments, and several hundred men gathered aft on the flight deck for a roll call. Water had begun to swallow the bow of the ship and was rising nearly to the level of the forward flight deck. As the deck started to slant downwards at the bow, wreckage, munitions, and burning planes slid forward. Some crew sections threw rafts and anything that would float overboard and abandoned ship, but others, incredibly, continued to conduct roll call amid the fire and explosions.[41]

It was a fatal delay. At 1508 an aerial bomb went off—whether cooked off by fires or by impact as it tumbled forward, no one would ever know—but the result was devastating. The blast ignited the volatile fumes that had accumulated below. There was a grumbling from deep within the ship, followed by four explosions that tore the heart out of the carrier. As the bow dipped and water poured into the number one elevator, the ship abruptly upended. Screaming and clutching in vain at any handhold, hundreds of sailors assembled for roll call slid in a white-uniformed mass down the deck into the inferno that had been the number 3 elevator as survivors in the water watched in horror. The stern rose nearly vertical, then *Shokaku* slid bow-first beneath the waves with what survivors described as a "groaning roar."

With her went 1,263 officers and men—887 crewmembers and 376 personnel of *Air Group 601*—out of a ship's complement of about 2,000. Among the dead was *Shokaku*'s veteran air officer Mitsue Matsuda, who had led the bombing raids on Wake Island at the outbreak of the war. Destroyers *Yahagi* and *Urakaze* rushed in to pull men from the water, but the suddenness of the catastrophe—a mere two minutes from the bomb explosion to

Shokaku's disappearance beneath the waves—left few survivors. Arriving on the scene in *Hiyo*, Captain Yokoi saw "nothing but floating wreckage and thick floating oil." Not far beyond, wounded *Taiho* lay at a 50-degree list under a mounting canopy of black smoke.[42]

Meanwhile, *Cavalla* continued to lay low. By 1420, only one destroyer remained overhead. Ten minutes later the depth charging moved off and the sub's sound gear "began to report loud water noises in the direction of the attack." Kossler thought to himself, "That thing is sinking." Between 1508 and 1511, the sub's crew heard explosions from the direction of the attack followed by a prolonged rumbling. "I've been bombed and depth charged, but I never heard noises like that before," reported Kossler.[43] Planing up to periscope depth, Kossler took a look around but could see nothing through rain squalls that had descended on the scene.

Kossler radioed ComSubPac at 2125, "Hit Shokaku class carrier with three out of six torpedoes at zero two one five . . . accompanied by two Atago-class cruisers three destroyers possibly more. Received 105 depth charges during three-hour period . . . hull induction flooded . . . no other serious trouble . . . sure we can handle it . . . heard four terrific explosions in direction of target two-and-one-half hours after attack . . . believe that baby sank."

Admiral Lockwood radioed back, "Beautiful work, *Cavalla*. One carrier down, eight more to go."[44]

Only minutes after Herman Kossler loosed his torpedoes at *Shokaku*, radar operators from Rear Admiral Harrill's TG 58.4 picked up bogies at 110 miles. They watched, mystified, for an hour as the distant planes wandered about uncertainly, pausing occasionally as if trying to figure out what to do. These lost souls were elements of the third raid of the day, fifteen Zeke fighters, twenty-five Zeke fighter-bombers, and seven Jills from the *652nd Naval Air Group* that Ozawa had been holding back. Launched at 1000 from Rear Adm. Takaji Joshima's *Carrier Division 2*, this puny force would go down in U.S. annals as Raid III.

Sent out with an erroneous target location after a scout plane pilot neglected to compensate for compass deviation, the Raid III aircraft had been redirected after they were in the air, but only about half the planes got the word and headed for the proper interception point. The others continued to the original destination, only to find empty seas. They milled around for a while looking for something or someone to attack, then returned to their carriers. The rest of the launch attracted the attention of Jocko Clark's TG 58.1. Eight F6Fs were sent out, four from *Hornet* and four from *Yorktown*, to have a look. They found fifteen bandits at 16,000 feet 50 miles northwest of TG 58.4 and immediately tore into them, claiming nine. A Zero fighter-bomber from the Raid III launch found Harrill's TG 58.4 at 1320 and managed to drop a bomb 600 yards wide of *Essex*. The Japanese pilot made a run for it, but was shot down in flames by a fighter from USS *Langley*. U.S. pilots claimed fifteen kills, but actual Japanese losses were only seven.[45]

As stragglers from Raid II were being gunned into the sea and Raid III fell apart, Ozawa's final punch was in the air. Consisting of eighty-four planes—twenty-seven Aichi D3A Val divebombers, nine Judys, ten Zero fighter-bombers, thirty-two fighters, and six Jills—this group, later known as Raid IV, had taken off at 1100 to excited cheers. Reaching the contact point 60 miles southwest of Guam to find an empty expanse of sea, they searched for a while, then broke up as fuel dwindled. Some headed for the airfield at Rota; about twenty headed home to the carriers; and the largest group—twenty-seven Vals, two Jills, and twenty Zekes—made for Guam.

The group headed for Rota, including all the Judys, accidentally hit the jackpot when they ran across Montgomery's TG 58.2. Leading the bomber division, Lt. Zenji Abe's radio came to life as one of his pilots exclaimed, "Sir! Big enemy formation, left forward!" Abe looked down to see a ring of ships, including carriers. Expecting a swarm of Hellcats at any instant, Abe ordered all aircraft to attack and gunned his Judy toward the vessels below.[46]

For once, American vigilance lapsed. Unsure of the identity of the approaching aircraft and then experiencing communications issues, TG 58.2 allowed the sixteen intruders to get within 50 miles before realizing they were bandits. Three were knocked down by patrolling fighters in the scramble that followed, but the surviving Judys pushed through at about 6,000 feet and six of them began attack glides on the *Wasp*.

As *Wasp* went into a hard right evasive turn, her aft gunners set the leading plane on fire at about 8,000 yards. The gun crews quickly shifted to the second plane and hit it at about 5,000 yards, then shifted to a third plane, which turned away smoking. One of the stricken bombers went into the drink with its bomb about 200 feet off the port bow; the resultant explosion sprayed the side of the carrier with metal fragments, including one big chunk that knocked down four men crewing a 20mm gun who got back up and kept shooting. Two near misses off the starboard quarter wounded one sailor. An incendiary exploded about 300 feet overhead, showering the deck with tendrils of phosphorus but did little damage. Another Judy dropped three bombs near *Bunker Hill*, again without causing any damage, before crashing into the water. *Cabot* blew the tail off yet another.

Disconcerted by the hail of antiaircraft fire, Lieutenant Abe missed with his bomb. Under attack by four Hellcats he somehow managed to get clear, eventually landing his shot-up bomber at Rota, one of the few survivors of the ill-fated attack.[47]

As Lt. Zenji Abe's Judys spent themselves on USS *Wasp* and company, Ens. Wilbur B. "Spider" Webb of *Hornet*'s V-2 "Rippers" was turning his Hellcat toward home after flying cover for a strike at Agana Field on Guam. Passing over Orote Point, the twenty-four-year-old native of Ardmore, Oklahoma, spotted a pilot in a life raft a couple of hundred yards off shore. A Kingfisher floatplane had landed nearby and was picking up a second downed pilot. Webb lowered his landing gear to slow his speed, dropped down to within about 100 feet of the water, and circled over the raft while his wingman flew cover for the Kingfisher. Tossing out a couple of extra dye packets to the downed pilot, Webb caught sight of a line of aircraft flying along the mountainous spine of the island, apparently headed toward Orote Airfield. The procession stretched as far as he could see. He estimated there were at least thirty or forty planes and maybe more. They were low and many of them had their landing gear down. "What in the dickens are our planes doing that low over the island with their landing gear down?" he wondered to himself.[48]

The answer became clear as the aircraft drew within a hundred yards of him. They were Japanese Vals, identifiable by their fixed landing gear, flying in divisions of three with Zeros overhead. As they began to assemble in a landing pattern for Orote Field, they banked away from Webb, displaying the big red meatballs painted on the fuselages. Webb, who had enlisted in the Navy in 1938, talked his way into pilot training, and been commissioned from the ranks, could hardly believe his eyes—it was a fighter pilot's dream. "I just thought, 'Boy this is it. Make it good and get as many as you can before they know you're here,'" he recalled.[49]

Webb picked up his mike, told his wingman he was going in, then retracted his landing gear, closed his canopy, flipped on his camera and gun switches, and hit the gun chargers for the six .50s in the wings. Realizing he had not been spotted, he decided to just slide into the enemy's traffic pattern like a wolf in a herd of sheep. As he started in, he picked up his microphone

one last time and sent out a general broadcast that would make him a Navy legend: "Any American fighter, I have forty Jap planes surrounded at Orote Airfield. I need some help!"

By the time Webb dropped the mike, he was less than 20 yards behind the first group of Vals. He had to drop his landing gear and flaps to avoid overrunning the slow-moving divebombers. Focusing on the Val to the left, he squeezed his gun trigger. The Val promptly exploded. Webb shifted to the center plane and fired again. "The top of the Val's vertical stabilizer disintegrated, and several bullets hit the rear seat gunner in the chest," he recalled. "Then the starboard wing of the aircraft came off and the plane exploded."

Webb slid in behind the third Val. His speed had started to build up and he was in danger of overrunning his intended victim. The Japanese rear seat gunner opened up at him with his machine gun. Webb held down the trigger on his .50s, but the Val stubbornly refused to go down. "Burn you bastard, burn you bastard," he chanted as he poured slugs into the Japanese. Finally the divebomber exploded, the debris knocking several holes in Webb's Hellcat.

Webb pulled around and slipped behind another trio of divebombers, again starting with the Val on the left. The backseat gunner was firing from less than 30 yards away—so close that Webb could make out the color of his flight suit, helmet, and skin. Suddenly, the enemy gunner seemed to just give up, or perhaps he saw death coming for him. He put his hands up in front of his face an instant before several of Webb's .50-caliber slugs tore into him. The Val caught fire and the pilot bailed out. They were only 200 feet off the ground; Webb doubted the pilot's parachute had time to open. The middle Val in the group eluded him, but Webb got behind the plane on the right and started him smoking. "Then his tail disintegrated and he just fell," Webb noted.[50]

Tracers floated past his Hellcat as ground gunners sought revenge. Though Webb did not realize it, he had been taking hits. But by now he had help. A swarm of American fighters had descended on Orote. It seemed that everywhere he looked there was a parachute or a burning plane falling from the sky. "By this time the Vals were gaining altitude and the Zekes came in above them," reported Webb. "I made a head-on run on one from below at 1500 feet. I fired and saw pieces fly from the plane. It returned fire. A few seconds later a parachute was in the air and the plane crashed." As he came around the point he saw another Val coming in 20 feet off the water. "I got on it from above at 7 o'clock. I fired at it and it started to smoke." As he pulled up, the Val went into the water. Circling out to check his guns, Webb saw two more Vals making passes at the field. A Hellcat sent one slamming into the runway. The second fled out over the harbor. "I went back and killed the rear seat man. The plane was smoking when I left and I pulled up quickly to clear the hill and didn't see it again."[51]

All in all, forty-one U.S. fighters converged on Guam, claiming sixty kills and racking up at least thirty. Another nineteen enemy aircraft were damaged so badly by gunfire or rough landings on the cratered field as to be unserviceable. Victims during the afternoon included *Air Group 652*'s fugitives from Raid IV as well as some Zeros from *Air Group 253* that arrived from Truk, low on fuel, to find themselves caught up in an aerial gunfight. Guam, the safe haven, had proved to be anything but.

It was not completely one-sided, however. On a sweep over Orote at 1825, VF-15 commander Charles W. Brewer and his wingman, Ens. Thomas Tarr, descended after some enemy planes landing on the field. Brewer knocked one down for his fifth kill of the day, but it cost him his life. Zeros pounced on the pair from higher altitude and shot down both Brewer and Tarr. Fellow *Essex* pilots claimed eight kills, but considered it a lousy trade. Also lost over Orote was twenty-three-year-old Ens. Thomas E. Hallowell from the *San Jacinto*, gunned down by two high-flying Zekes from *Air Group 652*.[52]

Spider Webb called it a day when his guns finally quit for good. He turned out to sea, back to *Hornet*. Only then did he notice that his canopy was shot up, there were holes in his wings, his radio was out, and the cowling and windshield were covered with oil. He later learned there were over one hundred holes in the Hellcat. Back at the carrier, Webb's gun camera film confirmed four victories. The camera had jammed after number 4. The Navy gave him credit for six kills and two probables. His Grumman was so badly shot up, deck crews shoved it over the side.[53]

Taiho was doomed.

Admiral Ozawa had not been overly concerned by the single torpedo hit inflicted by *Albacore* earlier in the day. There had been no fires, speed was scarcely affected, and damage control was underway. *Taiho* was state-of-the-art, considered the most formidable aircraft carrier ever put into service by the Japanese navy, designed to be virtually unsinkable. Unlike U.S. and other Japanese carriers with their traditional wooden decks, *Taiho*'s armored flight deck was designed to survive multiple hits from 1,100-pound armor-piercing bombs to ensure she could continue to launch planes—both her own fifty-three aircraft, and any others that needed to be taken aboard if their own carriers were put out of action. The smaller complement of aircraft allowed *Taiho* to carry a much larger inventory of bombs and gasoline with the idea that she could supply them to planes from other carriers as they ran low on fuel or munitions. There was one weakness: While the bomb and torpedo magazines were well protected, the fuel tanks were only partially armored.[54]

By afternoon, Ozawa and many of his crew had become keenly aware of the latter oversight. Efforts to ventilate volatile fumes from gasoline and the unprocessed Tarakan petroleum had only managed to spread them deeper into the ship. Survivors of the first strike starting to return to their carriers at about 1350 found *Shokaku* in flames, her bow awash. *Taiho* looked intact, but the building threat posed by gas vapor forced many of the returning planes to land on *Zuikaku* instead. Thanks to U.S. Hellcat pilots, there was plenty of room.

At 1532, six and a half hours after *Albacore's* torpedo slammed into her, a monstrous explosion wracked *Taiho* as the accumulated vapor in the forward part of the ship ignited. On the bridge, staff officer Capt. Toshikazu Ohmae saw the armored flight deck suddenly "blossom up like Mount Fuji." A mile away, aboard 30,000-ton *Hiyo*, Captain Yokoi was thrown violently against the bulkhead by the force of the explosion. The sides of *Taiho's* hangar deck blew out. The shock of the blast ruptured the hull below the waterline and killed everyone in the engine spaces. All power failed. Fires broke out and the massive ship went dead in the water.

Damage control parties initially contained the fires to the forward part of the ship, but within thirty minutes a series of explosions shook the stricken carrier and the ship was soon ablaze from the island forward. Realizing *Taiho* was probably doomed, officers urged Admiral Ozawa to leave. He refused, determined to go down with his ship. Finally, Captain Ohmae, who had served with Ozawa for years, crafted an approach that allowed his commander to save face. "The battle is still going on and you should remain in command for the final victory," Ohmae told him.[55] Taking the emperor's portrait for safekeeping, Ozawa transferred his flag to the cruiser *Haguro*. Soon after he left, *Taiho* was rocked by yet another massive explosion. Burning furiously, the ship began to list slightly to port, then settled slowly by the head. Fuel leaking from her tanks spread on the sea around her and caught fire. Reluctantly conceding that *Taiho* could not be saved, Capt. Tomozo Kikkuchi ordered survivors to abandon ship.[56]

At 1728, *Taiho*, still settling upright, disappeared below the waves on a semi-even keel. Japanese sources indicate that destroyers *Isokaze*, *Wakatsuki*, and *Hatsuzuki* rescued over 1,000 officers and men, including Captain Kikkuchi. If accurate, that would put the loss of life at twenty-eight officers and 632 enlisted—a third of her crew. Other sources put losses at 1,650 officers and men out of a complement of 2,150.[57] Whatever the true figure, the Great Phoenix had gone to the depths of the Philippine Sea—15,000 feet to the bottom—never to rise from her own ashes.[58]

By dark, the greatest carrier battle in history had been decided. Twelve hours of almost continuous air combat had ended with the evisceration of Japanese naval airpower in the Pacific. Admiral Ozawa had sent 374 of his 473 planes against Spruance. Only 130 made it back to their ships. Another eighteen planes went down with *Taiho* and nine with *Shokaku*. Also lost were fifty or so land-based aircraft—part of Admiral Kakuta's meager contribution to A-Go. Total Japanese plane losses on June 19 were slightly over 300.[59]

The outpouring of Japanese blood bought little. None of the U.S. carriers was hit during the melee. U.S. aircraft losses totaled thirty-one, including six lost operationally. Twenty pilots and seven air crewmen were killed. Ship crew losses during the air attacks numbered four officers and twenty-seven sailors.[60]

U.S. pilots returning to their carriers excitedly exchanged stories of multiple air victories. Aboard *Lexington*, Lt. Cmdr. Paul D. Buie, commanding VF-16's "Fighting Airedales," heard Lt. (j.g.) Zeigel "Ziggy" Neff, a twenty-eight-year-old former college student from Salisbury, Missouri, who had knocked down four bandits during the day, exclaim exuberantly, "Why hell. It was just like an old time turkey shoot!" Ziggy Neff would never shoot down another Japanese, but thanks to his widely repeated off-the-cuff remark, the battle of the Philippine Sea would go down in history as "the Great Marianas Turkey Shoot."[61]

Over 1,200 miles away at *Combined Fleet* Headquarters aboard the *Oyodo*, there was no exuberance. Certainly no one was now offering four out of five odds on a Japanese victory. Cooped up with staff in the Operations Room of the Naval General Staff in Tokyo, Lt. (j.g.) Minoru Nomura became increasingly uneasy as the day wore on. First indication that things were seriously amiss came with the alert, "Planes of the First Carrier Division, land on the *Zuikaku*." What had happened to *Taiho* and *Shokaku*? This was followed by a transmission from Ozawa: "As of 1600 will exercise command from *Haguro*." It was now clear that something had happened to *Taiho*. Late in the day, Ozawa ordered the *Mobile Fleet* to a new position. Nomura checked the grid chart and was stunned to see that the position was far to the west of the Marianas.[62]

It was not until the middle of the night that anxious staff officers learned what had happened to *Taiho* and *Shokaku*. A messenger from the Navy Ministry's Telecommunications Section arrived with a sealed telegram bearing the bad news. "The atmosphere in the Operations Room, which up to then had been a mixture of uncertainty and anxiety, began to change to genuine despair," recalled Nomura.[63]

Aboard *Lexington*, as day waned and bogies vanished from U.S. radar scopes, Mitscher's Japanese linguist, Lt. (j.g.) Charles A. Sims, monitored a last message from the enemy strike coordinator droning around off in the distance. Sims had been eavesdropping on radio traffic from various enemy air coordinators all day long, picking up important information about Japanese plans and dispositions. Now, as the present strike coordinator radioed that he was returning to base, some on *Lexington*'s bridge suggested sending out a few Hellcats to gun him down. Mitscher's chief of staff, Arleigh Burke, reportedly demurred, observing wryly that the enemy coordinator had made too important a contribution to the American victory, "So let him go home. . . ."[64]

The enemy plane disappeared to the west, unmolested.

CHAPTER XIV

Mission into Darkness

Where were they?

As darkness fell over the Philippine Sea on June 19, not a single American pilot had yet laid eyes on one of Admiral Ozawa's carriers since the sighting by Lt. Herman Arle's patrol bomber in the early morning hours. Having won a defensive victory, Admiral Spruance was now ready to take the fight directly to the enemy fleet, presuming he could locate it. Unfortunately, time and fuel were not in his favor. The day's air battle had drawn TF 58 easterly, away from Ozawa, as carriers were compelled to turn into the wind to launch and recover planes. By 1500, *Lexington* was only 20 miles off the northwest tip of Guam.

With his aviators champing at the bit to get at the Japanese fleet, Spruance agreed to a plan that would continue to protect the Saipan beachhead while at the same time giving his fliers their chance. TG 58.4 under William "Keen" Harrill, who had not impressed anyone as a fighter over the past days, would remain behind to watch over the landing force. The rest of TF 58 would head out in pursuit of Ozawa. Spruance signaled Mitscher at 1630: "Desire to attack enemy tomorrow if we know his position with sufficient accuracy." The fleet would turn westward as soon as practicable. Mitscher's carriers were still recovering aircraft, but by 2000—five hours after Spruance's directive—the three task groups had reversed course in hopes of catching up to the *Mobile Fleet*.[1]

As day closed, Admiral Ozawa had changed course to the northwest, opening the distance between the two fleets. Like Spruance, the Japanese admiral was hampered by a lack of information. Still aboard *Haguro* and without adequate communications—never believing *Taiho* could be sunk, the Japanese had not provided backup arrangements for a substitute flagship—he remained unaware of the extent of his air losses. His optimism was bolstered by misleading feedback from Admiral Kakuta on Tinian as

235

well as wildly exaggerated reports about the damage supposedly inflicted on the U.S. fleet by Japanese aircrews. Reports suggested that four of Spruance's carriers had been sent to the bottom, six damaged, and scores of aircraft destroyed. In the pipe dream of all pipe dreams, Tokyo announced that eleven U.S. carriers had been sunk. At 1820, Ozawa ordered, "All forces will proceed north." He intended to fuel on June 20 and resume the battle the next day in coordination with the planes he wrongly thought had found safe haven on Guam and Tinian.[2]

Back in Tokyo, Admiral Toyoda also failed to fathom the extent of the disaster that had befallen the *Mobile Fleet*. In the early morning hours he directed Ozawa to reorganize his forces and "according to the situation, you shall advance and direct your attack against the enemy task force, cooperating with the land-based air units. After this has been done, you shall dispatch your air units to land bases. . . . After the 22nd, according to the conditions, you shall manage most of your craft in mopping up operations around Saipan."[3]

Out on the dark expanse of the Pacific, Lt. (j.g.) Cox Birkholm, late of the USS *Lexington*, huddled in his cramped life raft. Earlier that morning, the twenty-three-year-old former University of Southern California rugby player had taken off with VT-16 to intercept Raid II. At 15,000 feet, only fifteen minutes out from the flattop, the prop governor on his Hellcat—Fox 36—gave out, and he was forced to turn back. As his oil pressure plummeted, Birkholm removed his oxygen gear, dropped the belly tank, and opened and locked his canopy to prepare for a water landing. The Hellcat's prop lurched to a halt as the engine froze only 25 miles from the task force. Descending in a long glide, flaps up, harness tight, tail dragging, he slammed into the water. He momentarily blacked out, but quickly recovered, unbuckled his harness, and climbed out of the cockpit. Fox 36 floated only four or five seconds before settling beneath the waves.

Clinging to the floating seat cushion, Birkholm struggled out of his parachute harness. "The weight of my Marine shoes was pulling me under so I inflated my life jacket which just kept my head above water." Within a few minutes he had inflated his life raft and clambered in, "taking life easy," as he put it. The air battle was well underway in the skies overhead and he saw an occasional "flamer" plunge earthward as he bobbed around on the waves. Opening one of his three emergency green dye markers, he emptied it over the side and let it spread out around the raft. About twenty minutes later a team of Hellcats spotted his marker and circled twice before continuing on their way. About this time Birkholm belatedly noticed he was bleeding from a cut on his head, but the wound soon clotted. He felt exhausted, drained of energy. At 1300 three Japanese Judys passed low overhead at about 180 knots. As Birkholm watched, one of them suddenly exploded for no apparent reason. "The rest of the afternoon I rested and just sat and thought what a hell of a place to be . . . I was sick due to shock, but toward evening regained energy and felt good."

The hours passed and darkness fell. At about 0100, the young veteran— he had three and a half aerial victories to his credit, the first gunned down in the Marshalls the previous November—felt a vibration and heard engines. He pulled out his waterproof flashlight. It was a new model made by Delta Electric Company, issued after pilots found that the old type of flashlight had proven "absolutely useless in every case in which one of our pilots went into the drink," observed Birkholm's squadron. The new Delta light worked just fine and Birkholm flashed an SOS in the direction of the engine noise. "A hundred and fifty yards away I saw a ship going by very fast." He continued his SOS and the ship—it turned out to be the destroyer USS *Boyd*— pulled alongside and took him aboard. Five minutes later Birkholm "was drinking coffee and telling sea stories." He had been in his life raft fourteen hours when he was picked up.[4]

Both Mitscher and Ozawa began launching searches as soon as light permitted. At that time—about 0530—the opposing fleets were between 330 and 350 miles apart, with Ozawa still steaming to the northwest. "We flew search quadrants like you cut a piece of pie," observed Aviation Ordnanceman 3rd Class Bennie Roland, a crewmember on one of *Enterprise*'s eight search planes.[5] Neither side spotted the other's ships, though there were a number of encounters between aircraft. At 0905 an *Enterprise* Hellcat from the Grim Reapers downed a Jake. About forty minutes later another *Enterprise* search team spotted a Jill about 3 miles ahead, coming straight in and low about 200 feet off the water. Cmdr. William R. "Killer" Kane— still sporting a pair of shiners he sustained during a water landing on the 15th—made a pass from the five o'clock. The belly tank of the Jill caught fire, the flames spreading quickly to the tail and engulfing the entire plane. The burning aircraft nosed up to 700 feet, then dove toward the water. The pilot jumped clear at 200 feet, too low for his parachute to open. "Plane and pilot hit with a splash," noted the after-action report. "The Jap's body could be seen underwater with a pool of blood forming above."[6]

As the hours passed with no sign of the Japanese fleet, frustration gripped Mitscher's staff waiting anxiously by the radios aboard *Lexington*. Chief of staff Arleigh Burke reflected the general mood, muttering, "Damn! Damn!" as he gnawed on the stem of his unlit pipe.[7] It seemed increasingly likely that Ozawa had managed to slip away. In fact, the search teams, ranging out to the usual 325-mile limit, barely missed the Japanese. Ozawa was only 50 to 75 miles beyond the search pattern.[8]

Twelve fighter-bombers manned by volunteers took off at noon for a long-range search out to 475 miles, but the pattern was too far north. Japanese scouts had no better luck, though a group of Kates did spot two U.S. carrier planes at 0713. Concerned by this report, Admiral Kurita suggested that the *Mobile Fleet* continue to retire west, but Ozawa demurred. He intended to refuel and ready his force to resume the battle the next day. Even after transferring to *Zuikaku* at 1300 and getting a better picture of his losses—he had only about a hundred planes immediately available—he continued to believe he could rejoin the battle with the assistance of land-based air assets. This assumption was encouraged by Admiral Kakuta, who advised that a number of planes had taken refuge on Rota and Guam. The air base admiral failed to add that most of the refugee aircraft were no longer operational. Ozawa also mistakenly assumed that Kakuta's forces had been augmented with substantial reinforcements from Iwo Jima, Yap, and Truk. In fact there had been no such influx.[9]

Finally, as the afternoon crept by, the Americans caught a break. At 1500, piloting an Avenger launched from *Enterprise*, Lt. Robert S. ("Stu") Nelson sighted a Japanese single-engine Kate about 5 miles off. Thirty-eight minutes later, flying at 700 feet and nearing the end of his outbound leg, he noticed sort of "a ripple" off to his left about 30 miles ahead. He asked his radarman for a check, but the target was too far off. Contacting his two wingmen—Lt. James S. Moore in a second Avenger and Lt. (j.g.) William E. Velte Jr. in a Hellcat—Nelson led the search team into the concealment of a rain squall and closed to within 10 miles of the mysterious ripple.

Moments later the airmen realized they'd hit the jackpot. Down below, spread out over miles of ocean, was the *Mobile Fleet*. A northern group consisted of a carrier, three cruisers, and eight destroyers. A southern group, which was heading away and was less visible, seemed to consist of two or three carriers, two oilers, two cruisers, and six destroyers. One of the oilers appeared to be fueling a destroyer. Nelson got on the radio:

Enemy fleet sighted, time 1540, Long. 135-25 E, Lat. 15-00 N, course 270 (degrees) and speed 20 knots. Two groups, one heading west and one heading east. Ten ships in northern group and twelve in southern. They seem to be fueling. Large CV in Northern Group. "[10]

Soon after, Moore radioed Nelson to say he had checked the original position and found it in error by about 60 miles. Nelson replotted it in less haste and found a 1-degree error in longitude. He sent out the corrected information at 1606.[11] In *Lexington*'s flag plot, the pervading gloom changed to jubilation. At 1548 Mitscher signaled his carriers: "Prepare to launch deckload strike." He advised Spruance, "Expect to launch everything we have. Probably have to recover at night." In the ready rooms aboard the carriers, pilots and aircrews abandoned card games, letter writing, magazines, and bull sessions and began to buckle on the accoutrements of their trade: shoulder holsters, goggles, canteens, life vests, backpacks, knives, and good luck charms. Ready room chalkboards were emblazoned with the exhortation, "Get the Carriers!"[12]

Meanwhile Mitscher's staff hurriedly measured distances and made calculations. Finally the navigator jotted down a figure. According to Nelson's original plot, the enemy fleet lay over 275 miles away. TF 58's air operations officer and gambler extraordinaire Cmdr. Gus Widhelm greeted the calculation with a somber whistle. Mitscher asked, "Well, can we make it?"

There was a moment of silence. "We can make it," said Widhelm, "but it's going to be tight."

"Launch 'em!" ordered Mitscher.[13]

In Fighting 16's ready room on *Lexington*, Lt. James Alvin "Sy" Sybert plotted the course data he had been provided and stared at the result in disbelief. The position fell outside the perimeter of his navigating circle. "I've got to fly out to here?" he exclaimed.[14] The intercom squawked, "Pilots man your planes!" Ready rooms emptied as the flyers picked up their helmets and chart boards and trooped up to the flight deck. Well aware of the distance involved and that the return would be in darkness, the mood was somber, observed Lt. Cmdr. J. Bryan III aboard *Lexington*. There was none of the usual banter. Signal flags fluttered and the ships completed the turn into the east wind at 1621. Aircraft engines coughed and roared. The Fox flag—white with a red diamond—fluttered up the yardarm. Launching officers unfurled their checkered signal flags.

Lt. Arthur Abramson found the three members of his deck crew waiting by his Hellcat. Like most pilots and deck crews, they had a casual relationship devoid of the usual military formality between officer and enlisted man. But today was different. They got him into the plane, then stood back, came to attention and gave him a precise salute. Abramson felt tears well up behind his goggles at the gesture. They knew it was most likely a one-way mission and they were telling him good-bye.[15]

Aboard *Lexington*, a Hellcat piloted by twenty-six-year-old Lt. Henry Kosciukos was first off the deck climbing into the air at 1624. Roaring down *Lexington*'s flight deck in the backseat of a divebomber, Harry Kelly noticed sailors lining the catwalks cheering and giving the thumbs up as each plane took off. Kelly was not impressed. "Thumbs up, hell!" he thought darkly. "What they mean is, *So long, sucker.*"[16]

Climbing somewhat reluctantly aboard his Avenger on *Enterprise*, radioman Jim Geyton had similar sentiments as a young officer called out, "Go get them, son. We need the protection!"

Geyton responded, "Shit, sir, I need the protection!"[17]

Within ten minutes the carriers had launched their deck loads and by 1636 had turned back on a northwest heading. A total of 240 planes launched from eleven carriers, but aborts due to mechanical problems reduced the number to 226: ninety-five Hellcats, some carrying 500-pound bombs; fifty-four Avengers, some with torpedoes, but most carrying four 500-pound bombs; and seventy-seven divebombers consisting of fifty-one Helldivers and twenty-six of the older Dauntless divebombers.[18]

The first strike had already been in the air thirty minutes when the aircrews belatedly received Nelson's revised contact point—a correction that put the enemy 60 miles farther west than thought. Mitscher immediately cancelled the second strike. "Have launched deckload strike," he informed Spruance at 1644. "Expect retain second deckload for tomorrow morning."[19]

The added distance only heightened the worries of first-strike pilots who felt they were already cutting things too close. "Prior to launch we were given the Japanese position as about 270 miles to the west: beyond our range, but it didn't seem to be a problem," recalled Lt. Cmdr. James "Jig Dog" Ramage, commanding officer of *Enterprise*'s Bombing Squadron Ten. "It did become of great interest when, after launching, we found out that the fleet was one degree (60 miles) farther out; definitely out of range. Upon receiving this information, I felt certain that all the SBDs [divebombers] would take a bath. I was not worried about the TBFs [torpedo planes] and F6Fs [Hellcats]."[20]

Pearl Harbor survivor Cmdr. Jackson D. Arnold, leading *Hornet*'s air group, was prepared to accept a one-way mission if he could only get a crack at the enemy fleet. After hitting Ozawa, he would regroup with as many of his planes as possible and head eastward, back toward TF 58, until their fuel ran out, he decided. After sending out Morse code messages pinpointing their location, they would conduct a mass ditching, which would make them easier to find and allow them to assist one another.[21]

Ducking in and out of the clouds around the *Mobile Fleet*, Nelson's search team kept visual contact until 1610. "Then my gunner reported a biplane float plane and a Zeke heading our way so we took departure pronto," he said.[22] Their exit was given added impetus when *Zuikaku* let loose with a starboard battery in their direction. The last view Nelson had of *Zuikaku*, she was turning north. He noticed there didn't seem to be any planes on her deck. Forty-five minutes from home, he began to pick up chatter from the U.S. strike groups streaming west. He radioed what he had observed before landing at 1730 to be greeted as the man of the hour.

Ozawa knew they were coming. Cruiser *Atago* had intercepted Nelson's revised position report and the admiral had to assume the Americans would follow with an attack. Nevertheless, he waited another half an hour before ordering all fueling stopped.[23] He then directed the fleet to change course from west to northwest and increase speed to 24 knots. Perhaps he could outrun Spruance's divebombers. Ironically, as he prepared to evade, one of the Kates sent out earlier in the afternoon to search for the Americans finally spotted two carriers and two battleships. It was too late. The Americans were already on the way.

As the *Mobile Fleet* got underway, A Force (*Zuikaku* accompanied by cruisers *Myoko*, *Haguro*, and *Yahagi* and seven destroyers) was farthest north, on a heading of 320 degrees at 24 knots. Approximately 18 miles to the southwest was B Force (carriers *Junyo* and *Hiyo*, light carrier *Ryuho*, battleship *Nagato*, cruiser *Mogami*, and eight destroyers). Eight miles farther south was C Force with Sueo Obayashi's *Carrier Division 3*, each light carrier surrounded by a protective screen of heavy ships. To the north of the group was light carrier *Chitose* with battleship *Musashi* and cruisers *Takao* and *Atagi*; then light carrier *Zuiho* with battleship *Yamato* and cruisers *Chikuma*, *Kumano*, *Suzuya*, and *Tone*. Light carrier *Chiyoda* steamed on the southern flank with battleships *Kongo* and *Haruna* and cruisers *Chokai* and *Maya*.

C Force also included seven destroyers and light cruiser *Noshira*. Finally, bringing up the rear about 40 miles to the south and slightly east were the slow-moving oilers, escorted by destroyers.

At 1800 *C Force* reported a radar sighting, which turned out to be a false reading. But twenty-five minutes later, as the sun began to settle low on the horizon, a scout plane spotted U.S. aircraft approaching. Manning their antiaircraft weapons, Japanese gunners waited, peering eastward.[24]

Among the first to arrive over the *Mobile Fleet* were four torpedo-laden Avengers from *Belleau Wood* led by Lt. (j.g.) George P. Brown, a hard-nosed thirty-three-year-old from Rochester, New York. Before setting out, "Brownie" had stated he intended to get a carrier "or else."[25] Now, arriving over the *Mobile Fleet* with a 2,200-pound Mark 13 torpedo nestled in his bomb bay, he found his chance. As other planes focused on *Zuikako*, Brown saw *Hiyo* steaming along unmolested in the light of the fast-sinking sun.

Descending from 12,000 feet, Brown led his four-plane division in a 180-degree turn to put the setting sun at their backs. Breaking through scattered clouds at 2,000 feet, the Avenger pilots found themselves with 5,000 yards to go before they would be close enough to launch torpedoes. They separated for a standard "anvil" attack on the carrier. Brown came in off *Hiyo*'s port bow. Lt. (j.g.) Benjamin C. Tate bored in from the starboard bow while Lt. (j.g.) Warren R. Omark approached from the starboard quarter. The fourth Avenger in the division, flown by Ens. W. D. Lutton, had become separated from the rest and went after another carrier.[26]

The Japanese saw them coming. Intense antiaircraft fire blossomed in the sky around the Avengers. Pilots from USS *Bunker Hill* noted that the first burst seen as the planes approached appeared over the center of the enemy force at about 14,000 feet and was a deep red color. "Whether or not this was a signal to all ships is not known but immediately thereafter, all ships opened fire," reported Cmdr. R. L. Shifley, leading Air Group 8. "Bursts were of various colors, including black, red and white. Black was predominant. The white bursts gave off a fountain-like effect of white streamers in all directions." Accuracy was very good: of the nine *Bunker Hill* divebombers that eventually made it back, six suffered damage over the target area.[27]

Brown's plane was hit several times as it descended. "I looked out and saw the left wing hanging off," recalled Brown's gunner, Airman 2nd Class George Platz. Flames broke out in the stern. Platz tried to get Brown on the intercom, but there was no response, so he crawled into the fuselage and found Air Radioman 2nd Class Ellis C. Babcock with one leg hanging out the escape hatch. "The latch was jammed and there were flames in the fuselage. So I shoved Babcock out and followed him," said Platz. Dangling from their chutes, they drifted down from about 1,000 feet over the middle of the Japanese fleet. Still at the controls of the Avenger, Brown kept the damaged torpedo plane on course toward *Hiyo*. The fire in the fuselage had gone out and he pressed in doggedly, finally dropping his torpedo as *Hiyo* made a sharp turn to port. Fellow pilots believed he scored a hit. Brown then flew the length of the carrier in an effort to draw off fire from the other two Avengers boring in for their own drops. Tate's torpedo apparently missed, but Omark's fish smashed into *Hiyo*'s side about a quarter of the way back from the bow.[28]

Manning a machine gun on *Hiyo*'s stern, CPO Mitsukuani Oshita heard someone shout, "Torpedo coming!" He began to count, relaxing when he hit twelve. The torpedo had missed. The deck suddenly shuddered under his feet. In his excitement, Oshita had counted too fast. The engine room flooded and *Hiyo* lost headway.[29]

Arriving over the enemy warships, Ens. Marcellus H. Barr, piloting a Hellcat from *Belleau Wood*'s VF-24, heard a call over his radio that Japanese planes were in the air. The warning was punctuated by a stream of tracers passing by his canopy and he saw he had a Zero on his tail. Most of the Zeros were painted a brownish olive drab color and sported large red discs on the wings and fuselage. The one on Barr's tail pulled up and away, but Barr spotted two more that had fastened themselves on another Hellcat.

"I pulled over to assist him," reported Barr, the twenty-two-year-old son of a West Virginia doctor. "He pulled up and the Zekes after him. They flew into range and I opened fire so that they both flew through my fire. The first one exploded and the second one smoked, rolled over and went into a steep dive and out of sight." Tracers floated by Barr's Hellcat and he saw that another Zero had gotten behind him. "He overshot and slow rolled in front of me and into my line of fire. Pieces flew off the plane around the cockpit and starboard wing. He smoked and went down, apparently out of control."

Seeing yet another Zero pursuing the Hellcat piloted by Lt. (j.g.) Rodney C. Tabler, Barr was maneuvering into position to shoot when "all hell broke loose." Part of his instrument panel exploded and fire broke out in the cockpit. Barr glimpsed another aircraft behind him. In the confusion, he was unable to determine the nationality, but later realized he had been shot up by another Hellcat. "I went into a dive at once, then leveled out and prepared to go over the side, though I was right over the Jap force," he recalled. "I pulled out the radio cord, opened the cockpit hatch, loosened the straps and put one leg over the side." Before he could jump, the fire went out, so he climbed back in and decided to try to get farther away from the enemy fleet before ditching.

It was questionable how long he could remain in the air. The wings and fuselage had been torn up by heavy machine-gun fire. "Two or three inches of gasoline were sloshing about in the cockpit," he recalled. "All the instruments on the right side of the cockpit were blown out and the engine was missing fire. The hydraulic system was out and I saw the dump bottle had been shot out . . . Sparks began to fly from under the port wing, but I could see no fire."

As he lost altitude, the engine began to struggle. The wing fairing plates began to buckle and peel off and Barr saw a fire raging inside the wing. Descending toward the ocean, he got the tail down and managed what he described as "an easy water landing, despite the fact that the left wing kept 'falling off' and looked like it would crumble." As water poured into the cockpit, he climbed out and tried to swim away, but was too loaded down with gear. He finally managed to get his raft inflated and clambered in, pulling his backpack in behind him.[30]

Leading Bombing 16 from *Lexington*, Lt. Cmdr. Ralph Weymouth spotted the tankers at about 1835 but bypassed them in hopes of getting a crack at the main force. Ten minutes later, an awed voice came over the radio: "Looks like we found the whole goddamn Jap Navy!"[31]

Spread out below in three groups was the *Mobile Fleet*. The main group, 10 miles ahead, consisted of two carriers, one light carrier, two Kongo-class battleships, and a number of cruisers and destroyers. Twelve miles to the north was another carrier, and three or four cruisers and destroyers. The third group was 30 miles west, too far for Weymouth to make out details. The northern group was already under attack. The bombing crews could see torpedo planes boring in under impossibly heavy antiaircraft fire.

As Weymouth led his divebombers toward the main group, they were bounced by eight Zeros. Bombing 16 gunners fired back and claimed three, but a TBM piloted by Lt. (j.g.) Warren E. McLellan was hit. Riding as gunner in Lt. Kent Cushman's TBM, radioman Frank Frede saw that McLellan's aircraft was doomed. He radioed Cushman, "Mr. McLellan's plane is on fire, sir, they're bailing out." Cushman wrote them off as dead. He forced the thought out of his mind and turned back to the enemy ships below. Lt.

(j.g.) Harry "Buzzie" Thomas, flying abreast of McLellan's plane, saw three men scramble out, but only one chute opened. He had to fight the urge to vomit.[32]

Arriving with Bombing Squadron 10 from *Enterprise*, Lt. (j.g.) Don "Hound Dog" Lewis took his SBD after *Junyo*. "There were great black puffs all over now and small white ones, looking for all the world like small balls of cotton," he recalled of the antiaircraft fire. At 10,000 feet he pushed over into his dive. "[I] saw a plane smoking horribly away on my port [and] wondered if it was one of ours. I heard Japs talking on our radio frequency. They were counting, then more talk. They were excited. Who wasn't?" His dive seemed to be taking an eternity. "The carrier below looked big, tremendous, almost make-believe." Having often dreamed of such a sight, he felt a surge of pure joy, then decided he must be crazy.

Descending through 3,000 feet, Lewis yanked his bomb release and began his pull-up. His altimeter read 1,500 feet. Looking back he could see some smoke and flame, but it wasn't nearly the conflagration he had hoped for. Then he remembered that his section carried semi-armor-piercing bombs that would pierce the flight deck and explode deep inside the ship. He realized that his ears hurt. He had the SBD flat out at 280 knots, but still couldn't seem to go fast enough. "There were ships all about," he observed. "They were all shooting far above the carrier, which was dark with smoke and its own AA. I saw a plane burst into flames and then slowly float downward. I saw a small carrier off my other wing with the flight deck a mass of planes. A torpedo plane flying at only a few thousand feet left a vicious path of black smoke and dark flames before it plunged into the sea. I wondered if I would get out of this yet."[33]

Jig Dog Ramage led his six Dauntless divebombers against the 13,360-ton *Ryuho*. Adding to the heavy antiaircraft fire, six Zekes appeared on the scene; one of them passed within a few feet of Ramage as he pushed over into a steep dive over the enemy carrier. Concentrating on the frantically twisting flattop below, Ramage opened fire with his two .50-caliber machine guns at 8,000 feet. He watched the tracers stream directly into the ship's forward elevator before finally releasing his 1,000-pound bomb at 1,800 feet. He was just a little late; the bomb scored a near miss off the *Ryuho*'s stern. The next three Dauntless pilots also missed the target, putting their bombs in the carrier's wake; the fifth could not get his bomb to release, but the sixth, Lt. (j.g.) Albert "Ack Ack" Schaal, scored a hit on the after port quarter of the flight deck, the bomb apparently passing through the deck overhang before exploding alongside.[34] As Ramage pulled out, his backseat gunner, J. Cawley, yelled into his mike, "Skipper, look back. She's burning from asshole to appetite!"[35]

Ramage's effort was followed by a glide bombing attack by five Avengers from *Enterprise*'s Torpedo 10. Third to dive was Lt. (j.g.) Ernie Lawton. The carrier deck was "rimmed with flashing lights—bright red from the heavy batteries, and orange pin-points from the small guns along the side," he recalled. "I sensed, rather than saw the heavy crossfire from the screening cruisers and destroyers . . . On the way down, my cockpit glass blew out, with a loud report and I thought we'd been hit. Vaguely, I even imagined I felt blood on my neck."[36] At 5,500 feet, Lawton had built up over 350 knots. At 5,000 feet he released his four bombs. Three missed; the fourth, which would have hit the carrier squarely on the deck, hung up. VT-10 later claimed eight hits on the carrier and reported a tremendous explosion with flames shooting 200 feet high, but in truth, the *Ryuho* had not been seriously damaged.

The sky above the Japanese fleet was full of divebombers and torpedo planes running a gauntlet of antiaircraft fire as pilots, having expended their ordnance, started for home. Some of the enemy ships fired their main batteries into the sea, sending up cascades of water 200 to 300 feet high in an effort to knock down the aircraft. Skimming the waves 1,000 yards to the port of a huge Japanese battleship, Ens. Eugene Conklin was taken under fire by one of the ship's secondary batteries. His backseat gunner, twenty-three-year-old Air Ordnanceman 3rd Class John Sample, swung his twin .30-caliber machine guns around and sent three short bursts in the battleship's direction, more as a show of defiance than anything else. The ship swung a main turret around and fired, sending up a pair of waterspouts, one of them only 20 yards from the wing. Conklin pushed the throttle forward and hustled the divebomber out of there.

Once the bombers cleared the belt of antiaircraft fire, they found themselves again contending with enemy fighters. Lawton saw a Zero knock down an SBD low on the water, only to be destroyed in turn by a Hellcat. His turret gunner drove off another Zero with a burst that appeared to go into the fighter's starboard wing as it closed to within about a thousand feet of the Avenger. "Ahead I saw a Zeke after Lieutenant [Van] Eason, but lost track of him," noted Lawton.[37]

Another Zeke put a burst into the SBD flown by Lt. (j.g.) James A. Shields Jr. Flying nearby, Lt. Tom Sedell, who had been Shields's roommate for the past two and a half years, saw Shields go suddenly rigid in the cockpit. His goggles flew off and he appeared to be screaming. Then he fell forward over the stick and the SBD headed for the water. In the backseat of the stricken plane, twenty-three-year-old Aviation Radioman 2nd Class Leo LeMay continued to fire his machine gun until the plane plunged into the sea.[38]

Flying an SBD with *Enterprise*'s Bombing Squadron Ten, Lieutenant Don "Flash" Gordon got some measure of revenge. "As we departed at very low altitude, heading for home, I saw a Zero heading in the opposite direction about 500 feet above us," he recalled. "I pulled up with my wingman for an upside down overhead. It worked. My wingman fired when I did at about 200 feet from the Zero's belly. The Zero blew apart, and we completed our loop, through the debris, to rejoin the formation for a long ride home."[39]

As the survivors of the attack converged on the rendezvous point, Hellcats flamed one Zeke and sent a second plunging into the water. The remaining Japanese seemed to hesitate and then disappeared. Weymouth saw that the surviving U.S. planes represented a variety of air groups. Some showed obvious damage. One irrepressible pilot grinned and waggled a finger through a hole in his canopy, presumably happy to be alive. Weymouth didn't wait for the groups to sort themselves out. His pilots didn't have fuel to waste. He set the SBD on a course of 100 degrees and started for home. It was 1918. It had been only fourteen minutes since he had arrived over the carriers.[40]

Coming into the fight with fourteen bomb-laden Hellcats and an assortment of divebombers and torpedo planes from *Hornet*, Cmdr. Jackson D. Arnold sent his bombers and "torpeckers" after *Zuikaku*, then making 24 knots to the northwest. One of the pilots was Lt. Harold L. Buell, a former Iowa farm boy leading a six-plane division of SB2C divebombers from VB-2. A veteran of the Coral Sea and the Eastern Solomons fighting, Buell had dropped bombs on a number of enemy warships over the past two years, but this was the first time he'd had a crack at a Japanese carrier. Finding himself in an ideal position to attack, he radioed Arnold, "This is Ripper Hal. I request permission to dive now."

Arnold's voice sounded in his earphones. "Go ahead, Hal. Show them how it's done."

Followed by his five Helldivers, Buell began a high-speed approach on the carrier. He was stunned by the amount of antiaircraft fire thrown up by the circle of enemy ships below—most of it seemingly aimed directly at him. "In addition to tracer ammunition, the enemy ships were using shells that exploded in a variety of bright colors," he recalled. "Some threw out long tentacles of flaming white phosphorus, unlike anything I had ever seen before." As Buell pushed over into his final dive at about 12,000 feet, the return fire intensified to the point that he saw no hope of ever getting through. "My dive brakes were already open and I was well into a good dive, but because of the potent defensive fire, I felt like I was moving in slow motion in quicksand," he said. "I would never make it."

The veteran pilot now did something he had never done before—he closed his dive brakes. Relieved of the braking action, the Helldiver plummeted like a stone. The heavy antiaircraft fire was left behind, but now Buell was going so fast he feared he would never be able to pull out of his dive. Shouting a prayer to his guardian angel as he reached 6,000 feet, he turned the dive brakes selector back into the open position. Somewhat to his surprise—and probably contrary to any manufacturer's representations—the wing brakes opened. "When I pulled to reopen the dive brake, it was like somebody grabbed me by the tail," he remarked. The enemy carrier was dead in his sight, turning into his flight path along its lengthwise axis. "I fired point blank at 1,800 feet." The 1,000-pound semi-armor-piercing bomb penetrated the middle of the deck and exploded. "When it did, it lifted a section of that *Zuikaku* flight deck. Blew it right off."

Buell started his pullout, closing his wing flaps and bending forward to activate the bomb bay door lever. That routine action at just that particular moment saved his life. As he leaned forward, a Japanese antiaircraft shell smashed into his starboard wing about 8 feet from the fuselage, passed through, and exploded 2 or 3 feet above the upper wing surface. A shell fragment punched into the cockpit and sliced diagonally across his back from right to left, from just below his lower rib area to his upper left shoulder, ripping open his flight suit. "The force of the blow from this shell fragment, as it tore through my protruding parachute backpack, was like being clubbed from behind with a baseball bat," he remembered. At the same instant, he felt a stabbing pain as a piece of shell about the size of a .45-caliber pistol slug punched into his back.

"Oh God, I've been hit bad," thought Buell, but he stayed in control of the divebomber, leveling out at 50 to 100 feet over the water and racing between the ships of the Japanese destroyer screen as he fled. Looking to the right, he saw a hole about a foot in diameter in his starboard wing. The hole was on fire: he could see it growing larger as the edges burned away with a white glow. Already he was having trouble holding the wing up as the hole increased in size.

Leaving the destroyer screen behind, Buell joined up with his wingman and two other aircraft. He slowed his air speed in an effort to avoid fanning the flames in his wing, but to his dismay, the hole continued to grow. Finally, at 125 knots airspeed, the fire abruptly went out. It was none too soon. By now the hole was nearly a yard across and Buell had to hold the stick far to the left just to maintain level flight. In the fading light, he could see the wing section beyond the hole flexing slightly. He offered up a prayer that the wing would hold together and turned for home.[41]

The air attack on the *Mobile Fleet* lasted no more than twenty or thirty minutes. As the American planes headed east for the long dark trip home, they could see *Zuikaku* on fire behind them. A solid bomb hit aft of the bridge and six near misses had left the carrier seriously damaged. A navy commander standing next to Admiral Ozawa on the bridge was struck by a machine-gun bullet fragment from a strafing plane. "The three or four strafing planes were very brave and came in low," observed Capt. Toshikaza Ohmae.[42] Fires raged through the hangar deck. Water mains failed, leaving damage control parties trying to beat down fires with handheld extinguishers. The "Abandon ship" order was given at one point, only to be rescinded minutes later as damage control began to make some progress.

The main blow fell on Rear Adm. Takaji Joshima's *B Force*. American pilots had been instructed to focus on the Japanese flattops. *B Force*, with large carriers *Junyo* and *Hiyo* and light carrier *Ryuho*, was hard to resist. *Hiyo*, which a year earlier had survived two torpedo hits from the U.S. submarine *Trigger*, was hit the worst, mortally wounded by *Belleau Wood*'s torpedo planes.

The disaster began with a bomb, probably dropped either by *Enterprise*'s Air Group 10 or *Lexington*'s Air Group 16. Standing on the bridge, Capt. Toshiyuki Yokoi could see it coming. "It was a certain miss, but a close one, the way it was arced," he recalled. Yokoi was wrong. Angling in, the bomb grazed the foremast and exploded above the bridge. The blast destroyed Captain Yokoi's left eye and killed nearly all the bridge personnel. Another bomb apparently exploded on the flight deck. "When the smoke cleared, the navigating officer lay dead at my feet, but I could barely make out the body through the curtain of blood that covered my eyes," remembered Yokoi. "I wiped the blood away; my left eye was gone. I could feel the shrapnel all over me."[43] Then he heard a voice cry out, "Torpedo planes off to port!"

Peering through a mask of blood, Yokio saw a white streak slashing through the water toward his carrier. "At this range it was too late to evade," he said later. One fish struck the starboard engine room, with a possible second hit to the port quarter that disabled the steering. "There was a tremor to port somewhere near the engine room. White steam poured from the funnel. All motion stopped," recalled Yokio.[44]

Attacks on *Junyo* inflicted two bomb hits near the smokestack and six near misses. Pilots from VT-10 saw one bomb blow several aircraft overboard. When last seen, the carrier was burning heavily, listing to starboard and down at the stern. With her stack "utterly crushed" and her mast destroyed, *Junyo* was forced to cancel flight operations but remained underway. Bomb-carrying Hellcats from *Hornet* claimed a hit on *Ryuho*, though Japanese records indicate only minor damage from near misses over the course of the action. To the south, the light carrier *Chiyoda* absorbed a hit on the flight deck that destroyed two fighters and caused moderate damage. Battleship *Haruna* was hit by two bombs aft and near misses that warped her hull. A bomb exploding close to cruiser *Maya* started some fires but caused only minor damage.[45]

The slow-moving oilers bringing up the rear of the *Mobile Fleet* were less fortunate. Passed over by earlier air groups intent on the Japanese carriers, the oilers finally came under attack by *Wasp's* Air Group 14, much to the disgust of other pilots who—considering that enemy carriers were present—felt that going after the oilers was a lot like kissing your sister. Hit by several bombs, *Seiyo Maru* was set on fire and had to be abandoned. She was subsequently torpedoed by one of her escort destroyers. Her engines flooded by near misses, *Genyo Maru* was sunk by gunfire from another destroyer after her crew was taken off. A third oiler, *Hayasui*, took one bomb hit and two near misses, but was able to continue. In exchange, a *Wasp* Helldiver was shot down by Zeros. Also lost was VF-14 lieutenant Kenneth E. Cotton, who disappeared in a flash of light when a Zero collided head-on with his Hellcat.[46]

Despite the fears of his friends in Torpedo 16 who had seen his TBM go down in flames, twenty-two-year-old Lt. Warren McLellan was still alive—though for how long remained to be seen.

He never saw the Zeke that shot him down as he approached the enemy carriers. The first inkling McLellan had of trouble was a stream of tracers floating past his canopy. Before he could evade, flames poured into the cockpit. He reached for the microphone to tell his radioman Selbie Greenhalgh and gunner John Hutchinson to bail out, but recoiled as fire erupted around his wrist. When he looked for the microphone a second time, it was gone. By now fire had spread into center cockpit behind him and he assumed his two crewmen would have sense enough to get out. They'd all been shot down once before at Palau and they could take care of themselves.

McLellan unbuckled his safety belt, stuck his head over the side of the cockpit in an effort to get a breath of air away from the smoke and fire, then stood up in his seat, forced himself out of the plane against a wall of air resistance, and tumbled past the tail. He could see other planes in the air below him. Through some trick of perspective, they seemed to be flying upside down. He puzzled over the illusion as he fell.

Despite McLellan's assumption that his crew had bailed out, Greenhalgh and Hutchinson were still aboard the stricken TBM. They had felt the plane lurch, then saw that the whole forward area was on fire. Nevertheless, they were taking their time about jumping when they suddenly saw McLellan go tumbling by outside. "Let's get out of here!" Hutchinson yelled. "This thing is going to blow!" The escape hatch stuck, but Hutchinson kicked it free and they went out. Greenhalgh pulled his ripcord right away. Hanging in the air, he watched as the plane continued to fly level, flames licking from the fuselage. Finally, it pulled up a bit, engine screaming, then nosed down and disappeared like a flaming comet.

McLellan and Hutchinson waited before opening their chutes, hoping to get below the antiaircraft fire and avoid the unwanted attentions of enemy fighter pilots. McLellan tried to stuff the ripcord handle into his pocket for a souvenir, but had so much trouble he finally let it fall. Below him, a Zero was strafing something in the water. He wondered if it was what was left of his TBM. Then the ocean rushed up at him. He unfastened the chest buckle and left hip buckle of his chute and pulled the short lanyard to inflate the left side of his life vest. As he plunged into the water, he unfastened the right hip buckle and shed the parachute harness.

McLellan's backpack with his survival gear was strapped over his shoulders; his raft pack was attached to his parachute. As he tried to free his backpack, the parachute sank, taking the raft pack with it and nearly dragging him down too when he tried to hang on to it. He inflated the other side of his life jacket and floated there in the water feeling really frightened for the first time since he'd jumped.

Hutchinson and Greenhalgh also landed safely, but their rafts tore loose when their parachutes opened because they had neglected to fasten the safety clasps. Greenhalgh watched divebombers pressing the attack as he floated down. He saw a carrier take a bomb hit just forward of the island and then a near miss. Flames erupted from another carrier. Greenhalgh was waiting for it to explode when he plunged into the water. Tangled in the parachute shrouds, he choked down quantities of saltwater before he could cut himself loose and inflate his life jacket. He vomited, then looked around for McLellan and Hutchinson. A Japanese cruiser steamed by, almost running him down. To his horror, he saw that one of his dye-markers had burst and a bright green stain was spreading in the water around him. Despite his fears, the cruiser passed him by.

McLellan also saw the cruiser steam by. He could discern men on deck in the gathering darkness and was surprised to see they seemed to be dressed in khaki. If they saw him floating in the water, none paid any particular attention. He assumed the attack was continuing as he could feel concussions through the water. A carrier came into view. Fire and smoke poured from the ship. There was a massive explosion. Fire flared and then settled into a steady glow out in the darkness. After about half an hour, the glow disappeared.

Floating there alone in the darkness, McLellan shouted briefly for Hutchinson and Greenhalgh, but there was no answer and he soon gave up.[47]

CHAPTER XV

Winners and Losers

Lᴛ. Bᴇɴ Tᴀᴛᴇ ᴀɴᴅ ʜɪs ᴄʀᴇᴡ ᴡᴇʀᴇ ᴠᴇʀʏ ʟᴜᴄᴋʏ ᴛᴏ ʙᴇ ᴀʟɪᴠᴇ. Aꜰᴛᴇʀ ᴛʜᴇ attack on *Hiyo* with George Brown and Warren Omark, their Avenger was set upon by Zeros. The big torpedo plane had already taken multiple hits from antiaircraft fire during the attack run, including one that blew the top off Tate's control stick so he couldn't operate his wing guns. The turret gun had also stopped working.

A pair of Zeros started to work them over, but Tate managed to survive by turning into each attack and forcing them to break off momentarily. He finally found refuge in a cloud and his tormentors disappeared. Emerging into the clear, he saw another Avenger flying low over the water. It was George Brown. His torpedo plane was a wreck. Part of one wing was hanging loose, there were holes all through the fuselage, the tail was damaged and the hook gone; the bomb bay doors were open and much of the fuselage had been scorched. Brown himself was obviously badly hurt. He was flying with his cockpit open and at one point he held up his right arm which appeared to be drenched with blood. Tate tried to guide him along, but Brown could not seem to hold to a straight course and Tate eventually lost him in the gathering gloom.

Omark also managed to shake off a Zero and a couple of aggressive Vals. As he headed east, he too came across Brown struggling toward home. Omark led his squadron mate toward the task force, but Brown's flying became increasingly erratic. Omark turned on his wing lights, hoping it would help, but Brown did not respond and dropped closer and closer to the water. Finally, at 2045 Omark's gunner reported, "We've lost him." Omark made a few S-turns, but Brown was gone, never to be seen again.[1]

Alex Vraciu was in a despondent mood as he turned his Hellcat for home. In the air battle over the *Mobile Fleet* he had lost his wingman, Ens. Homer W. Brockmeyer, when they were jumped by eight Zekes—part of the same group that sent McLellan into the drink. One of the Zekes got on Brockmeyer's tail; when Vraciu signaled to him to go into a scissors maneuver, Brockmeyer turned too flat. "[He] must have been hit because he didn't turn back like he should have on the weave," he recalled. Vraciu managed to nail the Zeke, but the kill came too late for Brockmeyer. "I'm hit!" he radioed as his Hellcat spiraled down into the water. There was no parachute.

Vraciu joined up on the wing of a lone Avenger flying east. The torpedo plane had a hole in the port side of the fuselage, the bomb bay doors were open, the wing lights were flickering, and Vraciu could tell the engine was running rough. There was a small "3" painted on the tail, but it was not a marking Vraciu recognized. After a while the other pilot signaled to him, "How's your gas?" Vraciu gave him a thumbs up, then asked, "How's yours?" The TBM pilot spread his hands and shrugged.[2]

After flying for some time in the gathering darkness, the torpedo plane slowed and dropped lower until it was just over the waves. Vraciu thought the pilot was going to make a water landing, but the plane continued on. Then he saw seven planes circling, possibly preparing to ditch. The TBM moved into the circle. Vraciu flew on to the east.[3]

Zuikaku, which had appeared to be burning from stem to stern when last seen by American pilots, managed to knock down the fires after the attack and the "Happy Crane" was now limping along to the westward with the *Mobile Fleet*. The other damaged vessels were also still underway, with the exception of hard-hit *Hiyo*, now dead in the water. Though immobilized, the carrier did not seem to be in imminent danger of sinking. Damage control teams were hard at work and the cruiser *Nagato* was ordered to reverse course and return for a possible tow.

But at 1826 *Hiyo* was rocked by a tremendous explosion. The Japanese believed the ship had been struck by a torpedo from a U.S. submarine, but there were no subs in the area. The most likely culprit was, once again, avgas fumes and volatile Tarakan fuel. The main switchboard panel was damaged, cutting off all power. Fires broke out, fed by leaking gas, and soon engulfed the entire rear of the ship. The destroyer *Michishio* approached to assist, but the conflagration spread. "Gasoline flowed out through cracked seams and ignited," reported Captain Yoshio. "Heavy firefighting equipment failed; hand pumps were useless. Flaming oil flowed toward the magazines."[4] The carrier began to settle at the stern, then returned to an even keel, listing to port. With the captain dazed from his wounds, executive officer Shigaki

Kenkichi gave the order to abandon ship. Destroyer *Akishimo* came along the starboard bow, the flag was struck, the Imperial portrait was retrieved, and crewmembers began to abandon ship.[5]

At *Hiyo*'s stern, CPO Mitsukuani Oshita and his gun crew failed to get the word. They waited nervously as fires raged and the ship settled. Finally, as water surged up around their machine gun, they conceded the obvious and headed for the rail, only to be confronted by an ensign who had apparently become unhinged. "Wait!" ordered the officer, drawing his sword. "Sing *Umi-Yukaba*!"

They rushed through the patriotic song ("If I Go Away to the Sea"), considered Japan's second national anthem, but the sword-wielding ensign was not mollified. "Now sing 'The Naval March,'" he ordered them. The men began to sing, but as the water reached their knees they finally broke away and went over the rail. Oshita looked back at the doomed carrier. The crazed ensign remained on deck, still singing, clinging to the rail, sword in hand. Oshita lost sight of him as the bow reared up. "The ship is going down!" someone cried. Oshita swam frantically for fear he would be dragged under by the suction. When he turned again, *Hiyo* was nearly vertical. A moment later, at 2032, the "Flying Falcon" plunged beneath the waves.[6]

Considering the rapidity of the sinking, loss of life was comparatively light: thirty-five officers and 212 men. Sixty-nine officers and 1,331 men were picked up by escorting destroyers. The survivors included Captain Yokoi and the ship's executive officer.[7] Yokoi's survival was a virtual miracle; he had intended to go down with the ship. When the last officer left the deck, the captain saluted, sat down on an empty shell box, and lit a cigarette. His wounded eye socket throbbed painfully. The bow of the carrier suddenly reared skyward, paused, and then the ship plunged beneath the waters. "I vividly remember the rushing water, the debris swirling past, the strange world of dancing corpses, boxes, pirouetting wreckage . . . ," he said later, then a jolt, a sharp pain in his side, and a cascade of bubbles. When he opened his eyes again, he saw stars above. He was on the surface. Rescuers from the destroyer *Michishio* pulled him from the water. "To an old-fashioned sea captain like myself, it was my duty to go down with my ship," he observed later. "But what was I to do when it sent me back up?"[8]

To the east, the U.S. pilots straggled homeward, keeping a close eye on fuel gauges edging toward empty. Some planes had been damaged; others had consumed large quantities of fuel over target. With the carriers between

240 and 300 miles away—some two and a half hours of flying time—they weren't all going to make it.

It appeared one of the unlucky ones was going to be twenty-two-year-old Lt. (j.g.) Harwood Sharp of *Bunker Hill*'s VB-8. Five of the *Bunker Hill* Helldivers were jumped by Zeros after their divebombing attack on the *Chiyoda*. Two Helldivers were shot down—one in flames with no parachutes. Sharp put a 20mm shell in one Zero aft of the cockpit, but another Zeke came in from the other side and hit his Helldiver in the prop and engine. Acrid fumes filled the cockpit to the point Sharp had to don his oxygen mask for a while, but the plane stayed in the air. Now and then his engine would cut out, but he was able to make it catch again by nosing over and pumping in all the fuel he could. The thing ran, but vibrated so violently that his compass and most of his radio and electrical gear went out. With 130 gallons of gas in his tanks when he was hit, he was not optimistic about making it back to the "Holiday Express," as his carrier was fondly known.[9]

Nursing his divebomber back to *Lexington*, Lt. Cmdr. Ralph Weymouth began to hear an increasing number of voices—some frantic, some calm, some defiant—come over the radio as pilots ran low on gas or lost their way.[10]

"I've got ten minutes of gas left, Joe. Think I'll put her down in the water while I've still got power. So long, Joe!"

"This is Forty-six Inkwell. Where am I, please? Somebody tell me where I am!"

"Can't make it, fellows! I'm going in. Look for me tomorrow if you get the chance, will you?"

"I'm running low and I'm not picking up the beacon. Where's home, somebody? I'm lost."

Weymouth shut down his radio, unable to listen any more.[11] Mitscher, heading west in an effort to close as much distance as possible, ordered his task groups to open up to 15-mile intervals to expedite the recovery of returning aircraft. Jocko Clark's TG 58.1 carriers, which were farthest west, began retrieving the first planes at about 2015. The radio chatter indicated that others were having difficulty locating the task force. *Enterprise* launched a night fighter to gather in a bunch of aircraft milling around 80 miles away. As others began arriving overhead at about 2030, the task force turned east and increased speed to 22 knots. Because night landings weren't emphasized in training or part of routine operations, many pilots had trouble picking out the colored deck light identifying their home carrier. With gas tanks nearing empty, they didn't have time to learn now.

But the pilots were about to get an assist. Earlier in the day, knowing the strike aircraft would be returning after dark, Mitscher and Arleigh Burke had arranged to have the ships turn on their lights if necessary.[12] The display would light up the fleet for any submarine or enemy within miles, but Mitscher thought his flyboys were worth the risk. Now, as desperate pilots jammed radio frequencies, Jocko Clark threw out "the book" and ordered his ships to turn on their lights. A few minutes later Mitscher passed the same order to the entire task force and the ocean came ablaze. All vessels turned on their red truck lights and red and green running lights. Carrier flight deck lights were turned up. A spotlight on each group's flagship was directed skyward as a beacon. Star shells from cruisers and destroyers added to the display.[13]

Lexington landed her first plane at 2050. It was a TBM. "Whose plane is that?" asked Mitscher.

"The *Hornet*'s, sir," came the reply.

"*Hornet*? She's not even in our Task Group," said Mitscher. "If the boys are having that much trouble finding their ships, we might as well tell them to land wherever they can. Just so we can get them down tonight, we can unscramble them tomorrow morning."

Word went over the air at 2052. "All planes, from Commander Task Force 58. Land on any base you see."[14]

Hal Buell's damaged Dauntless was still holding together as he made his way back to TF 58 in the darkness. Earlier, when there was still enough light to see, he had raised up in his seat for a moment. As he did, his severed parachute backpack and harness fell away. His wingman, Dave Stear, thinking he was preparing to bail out, radioed urgently, "Ripper Hal from Ripper Dave. Don't bail out, Hal, you're too low. Your plane is okay—stay with it—don't bail out!" Bailing out without a working parachute was the furthest thing from Buell's mind, but he appreciated the show of concern. He felt little pain from his wound, but had a moment of panic when he reached behind to check his back and his hand came away wet with blood. He comforted himself with the thought that the wound probably wasn't fatal or it would hurt more.

As the hours passed and his fuel gauge needle slowly descended, he listened as more and more pilots radioed they were out of gas and landing in the water. Buell could no longer see the damaged wing and the flexing action, but he could feel the effects in the controls and it scared him. He kept the stick to the far left to maintain level flight, switching hands as one arm tired. "We flew along in a sort of grim, quiet silence, almost as if in a time warp, the glow from our engine exhausts giving us hope," he observed. Manning the rear cockpit, gunner Red Lakey had tuned on the homer. Finally a faint signal began coming through Buell's earphones. They were dead on course.[15]

Jig Dog Ramage figured he was about 30 miles out from TG 58.3. He could see a carnival of lights dead ahead. Ironically, the lights intended to help also had their drawbacks. "The panic was getting worse in the air," he recalled. "No small blame for the panic must go to the excessive number of lights on the ships. And some cruiser was firing star shells into the air—just what you need with a couple hundred planes in the area. Our problem wasn't finding the force, that was a piece of cake. With everything, including destroyers, lighting up, it became a real mess!"[16]

The rush to the carriers became the equivalent of an aerial cattle stampede as pilots low on fuel and unaccustomed to night landings cut each other off in approaches. Lt. (j.g.) E. J. Lawton Jr.'s Avenger had almost reached the task force when he saw the ships' lights come on. Unable to land on home carrier *Enterprise*, he circled for a few minutes watching the lights of planes below as they fanned out to form landing circles. That bit of order melted away as landing circles became overcrowded, intervals were lost, and deck crashes interrupted landings. Many pilots could wait no longer—they announced their gas was gone and they were going into the water. "Seen from above it was a weird kaleidoscope of fast moving lights forming intricate trails in the darkness—punctuated now and then by tracers shooting through the night as someone landed with his gun switches on, and again by suddenly brilliant exhaust flames as each plane took a cut, or someone's turtleback light getting lower and lower until blacked out by the waves closing over it," recalled Lawton.[17]

Lawton finally made a pass at *Lexington*, but was cut out of the circle; then he tried for *Enterprise* just as her deck became fouled again. Climbing to 500 feet, he picked out a light carrier close by the *Enterprise* and landed. It was the *Princeton*. Lawton's Avenger was the last plane she had room for. He landed at 2205 with 12 gallons of gas left in his tanks. "Small as that deck had looked, I was awfully glad to see it," he admitted.[18]

Lt. (j.g.) Harold Buxton from *Bunker Hill* put his Avenger down in the water next to a destroyer. His gunner got out, but his radioman, twenty-year-old Joseph R. Roberge of Burlington, Vermont, did not. Buxton desperately tore at the hatch to Roberge's compartment, but the plane sank beneath him, taking the young radioman with it. The *Lexington*'s log gave testimony to the unfolding chaos:

> *2124. Plane ditched on port beam.*
> *2134. From a destroyer: One in the water off our starboard quarter. Do you see him?*
> *2136. Plane ditched on port beam.*
> *2144. From a destroyer: We are going to pick up plane that crashed on our starboard beam.*
> *2146. TBF in water on port beam.*
> *2154. From a battleship: We hear a cry for help on our port quarter.*
> *2157. Plane in water on starboard beam.*
> *2158. From a carrier: A plane just went in the water about 500 yards astern of us.*
> *2159. From a destroyer: I am in a line to pick up that man.*
> *2214. From a cruiser to a destroyer: Pick up a man on my port.*

Twenty-two-year-old Ens. George Wendorff had started his turn in the flight circle when a plane with no lights came at him. Wendorff avoided a collision, but not a crash. His left wheel hit the water, then his left wingtip. The Hellcat cartwheeled through the water. Wendorff woke up as cold water cascaded through the broken canopy. The Hellcat was on its back and he was hanging upside down in his seat. He unbuckled himself and pried his canopy open, forcing his way out through the rushing water. The canopy slammed shut, catching his parachute pack. The plane was sinking and taking him down with it. His lungs burning, Wendorff finally broke free and pushed for the surface. Exhausted, he managed to inflate his life jacket, but it took him an hour to inflate his raft and then he was too weak to climb aboard.

Wendorff finally got into his raft and began bailing it out with his one remaining shoe—the other had apparently gone to the bottom with his Hellcat. He spotted what appeared to be a piece of wreckage by the raft. He started to reach for it, then recoiled. It was a shark. There was another and another. Wendorff went berserk, screaming and cursing, pounding the water with his shoe. He threw the shoe at the gliding fins, then pulled out his pistol and fired at them. He fell back, overcome with nausea and when he looked again, the sharks were gone.[19]

Hal Buell picked out a large carrier and swung around to get into the landing pattern. He told Lakey in the backseat to get ready for a water landing, just in case the engine quit. Lakey pleaded for Buell to get the Dauntless down on the deck; he was a poor swimmer and didn't think he would survive a water landing at night. Buell lowered his landing hook and brought his flaps down as he made his approach. He would only get one chance. The engine at full power was just barely keeping him above a stall. He was fully committed when the landing officer on the deck below attempted to wave him off at the last moment.

Buell felt he had no choice. He put the Dauntless down on the deck. The big plane came down among the arresting cables, but the hook bounced and failed to catch. The Helldiver cleared the first two barriers, then came down on the third, tore loose, and slid along the deck, smashing into a Helldiver that had landed only moments before. The backseat gunner in the Helldiver was cut in half by Buell's prop. A sailor on the ship's port catwalk was also killed in the crash. Deck personnel smothered the planes with foam. There was no fire and Buell and Lakey were soon extricated from their wrecked aircraft. As the two ruined planes were pushed over the side, Buell noticed two stretchers with covered bodies near the carrier's island. He asked someone about them. "Those are the two men you killed with your aircraft," came the cold reply.

Soon afterward, Buell learned he had landed aboard *Lexington*.[20]

Lt. (j.g.) Warren R. Omark, whose torpedo helped put *Hiyo* on the bottom, also got down on the *Lexington*. He landed with 1 gallon of gas left in his tanks. Lt. (j.g.) V. Y. Irwin cut it still closer. Flying overhead for forty-five minutes waiting for an open deck, he finally got down on *Yorktown*. As he taxied past the island, his engine coughed and quit, out of gas. An Avenger pilot that landed on *Cabot* got out of the cockpit, fell to his knees, and kissed the deck.

Deck crews did a tremendous job as air discipline broke down. *Yorktown* began landing planes at 2043 and took her last aircraft—an SBD—aboard at 2205. *Bunker Hill* began landing planes at 2033. A crash at 2056 involving two planes that ignored a wave-off and red warning flares killed the ship's air officer and four crewmen. One of the dead crewmen was so entangled in the wreckage he had to be pushed overboard with the plane in the frantic effort to clear the deck. *Bunker Hill* began landing planes again at 2144, had another landing accident at 2236, and landed her last plane at 2305. *Wasp* began taking planes aboard at 2046 and dealt with one crash, a Hellcat that flipped over on its back. The pilot survived, the deck was cleared, and *Wasp* took her last plane aboard at 2245. *Enterprise* took her first plane at 2055 and the last at 2210. She too had her share of close calls, including one Helldiver pilot whose 20mm guns went off just as he touched down.

One of the more bizarre incidents happened to USS *San Jacinto*. As planes milled around, a Japanese aircraft, identified as a Val, made two landing approaches. Upon being waved off, the Japanese pilot flew down the flight deck without opening fire and veered off to port. The same pilot then apparently tried to land on *Enterprise* before heading off into the night. He was tracked on the radar screen to a distance of 50 miles before he disappeared.[21]

By 2250, the frantic scene in the air over TF 58 was over. There were no more planes coming. All were down—either on carrier decks or somewhere in the water. At 2351, destroyers were dispatched to search for survivors. Exhausted airmen trickling into *Lexington's* ready room tended to be pensive and a bit shaken. A medicinal cocktail of brandy and pineapple juice was available to sooth tattered nerves. Some men talked too much; some didn't talk at all. One crewman who had lost his best friend over the *Mobile Fleet* paced around the ready room silently shaking his head as if he were sick.[22]

Aboard *Enterprise*, some of the *Lexington* flyers came across Air Radioman 2nd Class Theodore Lemieux. A backseat gunner in one of *Lexington's* SBDs, "Pop" Lemieux was the oldest man in the squadron—ancient to most of the youngsters flying. They liked to tease him about his age, asking him after every mission if he was still young enough to fly. Now somebody asked him the usual question. Pop paused and replied slowly, "No. I'm forty-three ... I guess I'm too old to fly."[23]

Jig Dog Ramage put his SBD down on *Yorktown*. He did not feel the damage to the Japanese had been as great as pilots were claiming. After a cursory debriefing by an exuberant officer whose questions indicated he had never been shot at, Ramage was assigned a bunk in an empty room. The previous residents had not made it back. Sleep was impossible. "I went through the sequence of the day's operation and could see no place where I had gone wrong," he recalled years later. "I was still unhappy. We should have done better."[24]

Admiral Ozawa was nothing if not a warrior. At 1900 he ordered cruisers *Haguro* and *Myoko* and most of his destroyer force to join *C Group*, proceed east, find the Americans, and initiate a night engagement. Ironically, at 1912—only twelve minutes later—Pete Mitscher proposed to Spruance that TF 58.7 with Ching Lee's battleships be released to go after the *Mobile Fleet*.

What might have shaped up into a surface battle was not to be. Spruance turned Mitscher down. He did not give the battleships much chance of catching Ozawa. Better to wait and reach out again in the morning with airstrikes if the *Mobile Fleet* was still within range. Admiral Ozawa also found himself reined in by more cautious superiors. Admiral Toyoda and his staff had been following developments with increasing concern. At 2046, fourteen minutes after *Hiyo* plunged beneath the waves, Ozawa received orders to retire. Ozawa recalled Admiral Kurita at 2205 and the fleet resumed its retreat to the westward.

Of the 226 U.S. planes that had reached the *Mobile Fleet*, ninety-nine had been lost, most on the long return flight.[25] Nearly 200 Task Force 58 pilots and aircrew failed to make it back to the carriers. Some were dead, either killed by enemy fire or drowned in crash landings or the aftermath. Others bobbed hopefully in rafts and life jackets, praying for rescue.[26]

Among the latter was Ens. George Wendorff, who had nearly gone down with his Hellcat and then had a close encounter with sharks. Once the sharks left, Wendorff settled down for the night in his rocking raft. He threw up once, but then his stomach seemed to recover. Shortly before dawn, a light carrier appeared out of the gloom. Wendorff opened his mouth to call for help, but couldn't think of what to say. Finally he shouted, "Ahoy! Ahoy, you!"

An officer on the deck heard the shout and spotted Wendorff bobbing in his raft. "A pilot on the port side!" he shouted. "Drop a smoke light over!" He assured Wendorff a destroyer would be along in about fifteen minutes to pick him up. His prediction was a bit off: it was more like five minutes. USS *C.K. Bronson* pulled up, threw Wendorff a line, and brought his raft alongside. It was 0415.[27]

Also pulled from the water was Cmdr. William "Killer" Kane, who lost his second plane in less than a week, picking up thirteen stitches in his head to complement the pair of black eyes he had acquired in the previous crash. "Everyone was running out of gas, but I ran out of altitude," he joked later.[28]

Nearly 300 miles to the west, Warren McLellan had spent the long night bobbing around in his life jacket and contemplating an uncertain future. He retrieved his Verey pistol from his backpack and fired a red flare, followed by shots from his .38 revolver, but there was no response. He waved his flashlight, blew on his whistle, and shouted. He might as well have been alone in a dark room. At one point he considered putting the pistol to his head and just getting it over with, but put the thought from his mind and began instead to sing to himself on the open ocean. He sang his favorite song, "No Love, No Nuthin'" over and over until the saltwater swelled his lips and tongue to the point that the words became a hopeless mumble.

Only a few hundred yards away, John Hutchinson was also floating in the water. He never heard McLellan's shots or saw the flare. He too was singing to himself, a tune called, "I'm an Old Cowhand." He sang it over and over and the more he sang it the better he liked it. He dozed from time to time through the night. A fatalist, he felt that what would happen would happen. His only regret was that his mother back in Burbank, California, would not know what had happened to him and would go on hoping for his return after he was long gone.

Miraculously, Selbie Greenhalgh too was alive. Unlike Hutchinson, the twenty-two-year-old airman did see McLellan's flare. He fired three shots in response and struck out in McLellan's direction, but could not locate him. In the process he lost his canteen. He hung on to his pistol, two knives, a flashlight, and the New Testament his father had carried in the last war. The shoes he was wearing belonged to another man in the squadron, Ike Davidson, and Davidson had loaned them only after making it clear that if Greenhalgh lost them, Davidson would murder him. The threat seemed a bit ludicrous at the moment. Greenhalgh kicked them off.

Around midnight, McLellan fired off another flare and saw lights flashing. Greenhalgh also saw the lights and waved his flashlight, but got no response. McLellan realized the lights were from a Japanese destroyer, which may have been signaling a plane looking for survivors. His tongue swollen in his mouth, McLellan took a swallow from his canteen and promptly vomited.[29]

In the wee hours of the morning, as exhausted sailors slept wherever they could find space aboard the carriers, Lt. Bob Nelson sat in the cockpit of his Avenger on *Enterprise*'s catapult. The man who had found the Japanese fleet less than twelve hours before was being asked to do it again.

The original plan had been for Nelson and Lt. (j.g.) Jim Moore to launch at 2200 with belly tanks to shadow the retreating Japanese fleet and guide in a night bombing attack by VT-10. The chaos of retrieving aircraft from the late-afternoon strike forced a postponement. Word finally came to man planes about 0030. "Just as the catapult officer was about to wave us off, we were told to cut engines," recalled Nelson. "In a few moments we were told to return to ready room." The night strike for VT-10 was cancelled. By 0230, they were back in their Avengers, now charged with locating the enemy fleet and any cripples that might remain within range. This time there was no cancellation. They roared off the carrier deck and headed west.

Thanks to a PBM snooper that had reported Ozawa's position shortly before midnight, they had a general bearing. "We were flying blacked out, no moon, no horizon, hazy, sky . . . covered by scuddy clouds getting worse toward the target, forcing us to stay below 1500 feet," recalled Nelson. At about 0330 he attempted to raise the PBM, but there was no response from the other pilot, who had been scheduled to stay on station until 0250. Expecting to intercept at about 0440, the Avengers began climbing slowly at 0435. At 0512, Moore's radarman picked up blips on his scope. They lost and regained the contacts several times, then, as the sky lightened, they picked up an oil wake. Ten minutes later, the radars lit up again. As visibility improved, the airmen spotted six destroyers. A group of enemy cruisers steamed just ahead and about 10 miles beyond that was the Japanese carrier group. "After a few minutes of contemplating this awesome sight, I looked to the left (south) about ten miles and beheld the [battleship] group . . . It was about 0605 by this time," reported Nelson.

The ships were in a ragged diamond formation with the carriers in the lead, battleships on their port and cruisers on the starboard, the six destroyers forming the fourth point at the rear, but lagging badly as if they were having trouble keeping up. "One of the carriers had apparently been hit as it was trailing oil which had left the slick which we were following," he added. "We did not see any planes on the decks of any of the carriers."

They shadowed the carrier force until 0655. A destroyer, apparently thinking the planes were about to attack, began to lay down smoke, but soon stopped. As they ventured closer, one of the battleships opened fire on them. When a carrier finally turned into the wind as if about to launch planes, Nelson and Moore decided to stretch their luck no further and turned for home. When last seen, the enemy carriers were heading into a heavy rain squall. "It's a beautiful day," Nelson hopefully radioed the U.S. task force, "I hope you sink them all."[30]

TF 58 aircraft were already in the air. Based on the information from Nelson and Moore, *Enterprise* launched twelve SBD divebombers from VB-10 and nine bomb-laden Hellcats from VF-10. *San Jacinto* contributed four TBFs from VT-51. The pilots were instructed to go after any cripples first. Other vessels in the vicinity should be secondary targets. But, as Nelson and Moore had belatedly deduced, it was too late. Their plot put the Japanese 360 miles west of the U.S. carriers. "Our striking planes would not be able to reach those sitting duck targets," observed Nelson gloomily.[31] The U.S. planes flew out to the end of their 250-mile tether, spotting large, trailing oil slicks, but no ships. Though Spruance and Mitscher persisted until later in the day, it became clear early on there would be no catching the Japanese. Ozawa was gone.[32]

Daylight found Warren McLellan and his two crewmen still bobbing in the vast Pacific at the scene of the previous day's attack on *Hiyo*. A rain squall swept through shortly before dawn, followed by brightening skies and a flock of twittering birds. Watching the clouds drift by, McLellan considered striking out for Saipan, 500 miles to the east. He had just started paddling in that general direction when he heard engines. He looked at his watch. It was 0730. He saw planes, but they were too high. He knew there would be more. Half an hour later, his optimism was vindicated as eight Hellcats swept by only 500 feet over the water. McLellan pulled open one of his dye packets and the green coloring spread out in the water around him.

Moments later the eight fighters were circling overhead. Two dropped rafts, but McLellan couldn't reach them. Then TBMs appeared above him and rafts rained down on McLellan and his two crewmen floating not far away. They each managed to grab one and climb aboard. McLellan promptly vomited, pulled the sail over himself, and went to sleep. Hours later, three OS2U Kingfisher floatplanes settled down on the water to pick up the three survivors. As the Kingfisher taxied over to McLellan, the pilot leaned out and grinned, "How about it? Want a lift?"

"You're the best sight I've seen since I've been living," croaked McLellan. By 2005 he was back aboard the *Lexington*, 15 pounds lighter, but alive.[33]

Also picked up in the morning were George Brown's crew, Ellis Babcock and George Platz. When he hit the water after bailing out, Platz found that half his Mae West life jacket had been holed by shrapnel and wouldn't inflate. He lay back in the water and watched the planes overhead. One went down in flames; he could not tell if it was Japanese or American. As the attack ended, he was nearly run down by a Japanese warship—possibly the same one seen by McLellan—which passed close enough that he was tossed around by the wake. Platz whistled and treaded water until Babcock answered him and they joined up. *Hiyo* was burning, lighting up the night, but after a couple of hours she reared up against the sky and disappeared. A Japanese destroyer swept the water with a searchlight, then steamed off. Platz and Babcock locked arms and treaded water until daylight.

The next morning at 0900 they saw a formation of planes flying high and identified three or four Grumman Hellcats. Babcock opened a dye marker and they thrashed the water to spread it around. A few minutes later torpedo bombers arrived overhead and dropped life rafts. They climbed on, lashed two rafts together, and gulped down the fresh emergency water stowed aboard. As they drifted, they spotted a head in the water. It appeared to be a Japanese airman. "He mumbled something we couldn't understand as he swam toward us," recalled Babcock. "Then he pulled a gun on us and we just paddled away from there. It was the last we saw of him." The two were finally picked up later in the day.[34]

Ens. Marcellus Barr also survived. Rain fell overnight and he tried to collect some in his sail cloth, but it wouldn't hold water. He did manage to catch some water in his cupped hands and then dug out some soggy chewing gum that seemed to ease his thirst. "I could not sleep," he recalled. "I was freezing because of the rain and water coming in over the side." As the sun came up, he saw a flight of planes pass overhead. He spread out his dye marker as two Hellcats flew over at between 500 and 1,500 feet, but they did not see him. Finally, a couple of hours after noon, he heard a Hellcat engine and put out more dye marker. The pilot saw him and circled the raft until a floatplane arrived and plucked Barr out of the ocean.[35]

Three reluctant Japanese were also pulled from the water on June 22 after their rubber raft was spotted by the destroyer USS *Eaton* a few thousand yards west of Tinian. The three gave up only after being laced with machine-gun fire that wounded one man in the arm and another in the chest. The latter subsequently died, but not before he revealed they were aviators from the defeated enemy carrier force. The prisoners stated that *Shokaku*, *Zuikaku*, *Hitaka*, *Ryuko*, and *Zuiko* had been among the enemy carriers.[36]

While it would never be known for sure, of the 226 U.S. planes that reached the *Mobile Fleet* on June 20, six Hellcats, five divebombers, and six Avengers were believed to have gone down in the actual attack on the

Japanese carriers. Another seventeen fighters, forty-two divebombers, and twenty-three torpedo planes were lost in crashes and water landings on the way back from the strike. On June 21, fifty-one pilots and fifty crewmen were pulled from the water; over the next few days another thirty-three pilots and twenty-six crewmen were rescued, including Lt. Harwood Sharp and his radio-gunner, who had finally ditched when their balky engine quit for good. They were spotted by the destroyer *Miller* that morning. Sixteen pilots and thirty-three crewmen were never found.[37]

Spruance had his victory, though there were many disgruntled naval officers who felt it was but a shadow of what might have been. Among them was Mitscher, who was deeply disappointed by the outcome. "The enemy had escaped," he stated bluntly in his battle report. "He had been badly hurt by one aggressive carrier air strike, at the one time he was within range. His fleet was not sunk."[38] Jocko Clark was even more candid, observing, "A chance of the century was missed. Had we sunk the entire Japanese fleet, as I am sure we could have done, the war in the Pacific might have ended in a matter of days, rather than some fifteen months later."[39]

Most of Admiral Ozawa's carriers had gotten away and had it not been for the U.S. submarine service, his losses would have been lighter still. Of the three Japanese carriers sent to the bottom during the battle, only one—the *Hiyo*—had been sunk by TF 58 aircraft. Spruance's critics believed that his excess caution on June 18–19 had cost him the chance to destroy the better part of the Japanese navy. Back in Pearl Harbor there were rumblings that Spruance should be fired.

Though Admiral Nimitz defended Spruance, evidence of his disgruntlement crept into the CinPac summary for June 1944: "There may be disappointment to some in the fact that in addition to the successful accomplishment of our purpose—the occupation of the Southern Marianas—there was not also a decisive 'fleet action,' in which we naturally hope to have been victorious, and to thereby shorten the war materially," he noted. The summary went on to observe that it "may be argued" the Japanese never intended any kind of an end run, as Spruance had feared, or the U.S. carriers could have proceeded safely westward to seek out a decisive action. However, Nimitz concluded, the "basic fact cannot be ignored or minimized" that Spruance's mission was to protect the landing force.[40] Spruance himself later conceded that as a matter of tactics "going after the Japanese fleet would have been much better and more satisfactory than waiting for them to attack us," but he again emphasized that he was unwilling to risk the success of the amphibious landing on Saipan.[41] Nevertheless, his biographer, Thomas B. Buell, maintained that Spruance's "failure to meet the enemy fleet in decisive action would forever haunt him. . . ."[42]

On the other hand, Mitscher's pilots had scored a stupendous victory over their Japanese counterparts. The enemy had lost 426 planes and 445 aviators. Japanese naval airpower would never recover. The planes and pilots lost on June 19 could not be replaced. Aircraft carriers had survived, but carriers without planes might as well be floating docks, or, as *Combined Fleet* chief of staff Ryonosuke Kusaka observed darkly, "The task force without planes was, as it were, a living corpse."[43] Just as importantly, the American beachhead at Saipan remained secure. The Japanese garrison was doomed. There would be no succor. In coming weeks, Imperial soldiers on Saipan would fight on amid diminishing hopes for a naval armada that would never arrive.[44]

At home in Japan, an anonymous sign posted in at least one navy office observed grimly, "Our Imperial Combined Fleet is now powerless. Prepare at once to re-form the cabinet so we can make peace."[45]

CHAPTER XVI

Dead Men, Flies, and Thirst

UNAWARE OF THE DEBACLE UNFOLDING AT SEA, JAPANESE TROOPS ON Saipan continued their fierce resistance as Marines and GIs tightened their grip on the southern part of the island. "You never knew what they were going to do," recalled Lt. Fraser P. Donlan. "They were nuts. They'd kill themselves to kill you."[1] Marines and GIs learned to take no chances and began shooting or bayoneting any corpses that didn't appear thoroughly dead. "Our instructions were that if it didn't stink, stick it," observed Justice Chambers.[2]

The Marines were now joined by the bulk of the 27th Infantry Division, brought ashore in the scramble to unload the transports before the Japanese fleet could intervene. In addition to the 165th and 105th Infantry, Holland Smith put in a request for the 106th Infantry, the previously designated reserve for the Guam landings. Adm. Kelly Turner was reluctant to let the regiment go as it would force the indefinite postponement of the Guam operation. Smith responded that he had an urgent need for the GIs "in order to maintain the continuity of the offensive"—an acknowledgement of the unanticipated difficulties that had thrown the operation off schedule.[3] Turner released the GIs to Smith. They came ashore on June 21. Four days later, the ships carrying the rest of the Guam assault force—the 3rd Marine Division and First Provisional Marine Brigade—headed back to Eniwetok to await developments.

The newcomers came ashore to a sobering reality as they passed boat crews fishing dead Marines out of the lagoon with grappling hooks. "They were in a boat and would bring on board a dead American," observed Sgt. John Domanowski, who landed with the 105th Infantry. "If it was a Japanese, they would push it aside."[4] PFC Sam Dinova, an eighth-grade dropout from Troy, New York, paused at the sight of three dead Marines lying unburied where they fell. One of them still had a flamethrower strapped to his back.[5] "The odor was terrible—so bad that it was absorbed into the C rations we ate that evening, leaving a bad taste in the mouth," remembered Lt. Luke Hammond.[6]

Domanowski's company took its first casualties the day after landing as the GIs moved up around Aslito Field. They were victims of an artillery shell apparently fired from Tinian. "It sounded awfully loud as it came over our heads and landed about fifty yards in front of me," noted Domanowski. Four men were killed, including 1st Lt. Norman C. Arnold, a popular twenty-five-year-old from Liberty, Iowa. "His head was sliced in half as if an ax fell on it," said Domanowski.[7]

The 105th Infantry spent the first couple of days working around the lower end of the airfield toward the Japanese holdouts at Nafutan Point. Sam Dinova's unit came across a crashed American torpedo plane at the southern end of the field. "The tail was up in the air and the motor was in the ground and they had a parachute all unloosed and on top of the tail of the airplane," recalled Dinova. The charred remains of an airman lay half buried by the cockpit. The dog tag identified the dead man as Paul Dana, USNR. The wreck was Bob Isely's Avenger, downed June 13 during the rocket attack on Aslito Field. Twenty-two-year-old Lieutenant (j.g.) Dana had been Isely's radioman/gunner. The GIs buried what remained of the young officer, fashioned a rudimentary cross from some scraps of wood, and attached Dana's dog tag to await Graves Registration.[8]

With Aslito Field in hand, the 165th Infantry attacked east on June 19 and speedily swept over the rolling landscape to Magicienne Bay—universally corrupted to "Magazine Bay" by linguistically challenged GIs and Marines. Meanwhile, the 105th Infantry advanced toward Nafutan Point, a jumble of sheer cliffs, tumbled boulders, and tangled brush jutting out from the shore southeast of the airfield. The 27th Division believed Nafutan was defended by perhaps 200 to 300 Japanese. That turned out to be a gross underestimate. Intelligence subsequently identified a hodgepodge of enemy units, including survivors of the *317th Independent Infantry Battalion*, men from the *25th Antiaircraft Regiment* from Aslito Airfield, numbers of service troops, including naval personnel assigned to the coast defense guns, and a miscellany of civilians and military stragglers. The polyglot force—totaling as many as 1,250 men—was commanded by a Captain Sasaki from the *317th Infantry Battalion*.[9]

Holland Smith's headquarters assumed the 27th Division would clean out these motley remnants in short order, but the first attack on the point was not encouraging. Tackling Ridge 300, which barred direct access to the point, the 1st Battalion, 105th Infantry got two companies onto the crest before stalling under fire from a series of well-sited pillboxes on the flats just beyond. The intensity of enemy fire forced both companies off the ridge. Late in the afternoon, the battalion tried twice more to seize the high ground without success. Shortly after 1800 the GIs retired to their original line of departure for the night.[10]

At the same time, the 4th Marine Division's "swinging door" was pivoting to the north, sweeping diehard enemy holdouts before it. The enemy retreat was accomplished in good order, though the Japanese had to abandon much of their artillery due to a lack of prime movers. Casings littering the ground at one battery position indicated at least 1,000 rounds had been fired by those guns alone. Combat correspondent Gilbert Bailey reported of the Japanese, "They fell back and they have kept falling back, gradually by night ... When the Marines go after them, some of them stay in their holes and fight it out. Most of them keep moving back ... burying their dead as they go and dragging their mobile equipment with them."[11]

The Marines followed through the cane fields, past ramshackle farmhouses dotting the plain. "Behind the building would be the inevitable crude privy," observed Lt. John C. Chapin. "Inside the houses were always the pathetic, battered, scattered remains of the owner's belongings. Strewn around in chaotic confusion: empty sake bottles, cheap Japanese picture prints, dilapidated furniture, with loose papers helter-skelter all over the floor."[12]

Despite efforts to remove their dead, enemy losses appeared heavy. On June 17, the 2nd Marine Division reported 2,650 enemy dead in its area; a day later, the 4th Marine Division reported 2,700 dead in its sector. A captured journal of the "553rd Unit," commanded by a Lieutenant Marakami, revealed that as of June 19 the unit's strength had been reduced from 218 men to only 31.[13]

Lt. Paul Harper's forward artillery team came across a covered mortar emplacement containing half a dozen Japanese dead. Each man had held a grenade to his stomach and blown himself wide open. "There were guts and blood everywhere," observed Harper. "The flies were already swarming." The sole survivor was an emaciated woman clad in a blood-spattered kimono who lay in a stupor on a pallet in the dark interior. She appeared to have been beaten and raped. The Marines gave her some water and later turned her over to a passing corpsman for medical assistance.[14]

Progress did not come without cost. Among the casualties was twenty-five-year-old Lt. John L. Lockwood. A former teacher from Cortland, New York, Lockwood was investigating a pillbox along Magicienne Bay when a sword-swinging Japanese officer darted out and cut him "right under the rib clear up into his lung," recalled Sgt. Keith Renstrom. The enemy officer was shot down as he ran off waving his bloody sword, but it was too late for Lockwood. "[H]e was coughing and saying, 'Stop the blood, stop the blood.' Well there was nothing you could do, so he just got weaker and weaker until he died," observed Renstrom.[15]

Also killed as the 4th Division door swung across the island was PFC Wendal M. Nightingale, the kid from Skowhegan, Maine, who had been afraid his mother might find the cigarettes in his sea bag, should something happen to him. Shot as his platoon withdrew across an open field under heavy fire, he struggled to get to his feet. Twenty-one-year-old Pvt. Richard V. Freeby of Quanah, Texas, threw down his rifle and ran back after him. As bullets kicked up dirt around him, Freeby grabbed Nightingale and started to drag him back to safety. For a moment, it seemed that they might make it. Then Nightingale was hit again. Realizing his friend was dead, Freeby finally let go and ran back across the open field to the platoon, where he put his face in his hands and broke down in tears. His pack had been shot full of holes; by all rights he should be lying out there dead with Nightingale, and he felt he had failed his buddy.[16]

A key 4th Division objective for June 20th was Hill 500, a cave-pocked hump overlooking the southern plain roughly three-quarters of a mile from the shores of Magicienne Bay. General Saito had established his headquarters northwest of the hill after vacating Charan Kanoa before the landings, but on the morning of June 18, he moved again, this time to a cave above Chacha Village on the neck of the Kagman Peninsula. Col. Yoshira Oka, commander of the *47th Mixed Brigade*, had operated his brigade headquarters on Hill 500 for a time, but by June 20 he too had vacated the premises, leaving a holding force in place.[17] The Japanese continued to obsess about a possible American amphibious landing at Magicienne Bay. As late as the afternoon of June 19, General Saito ordered the *118th Infantry Regiment* to hold its sector just north of Hill 500 and "particularly it will prevent the enemy's plans of landing on Magicienne Bay."[18]

Seizure of the hill fell to Lt. Col. Jumpin' Joe Chambers's 3rd Battalion, 25th Marines. Described as "tougher than a fifty-cent steak," Chambers had been ducking Japanese artillery fire and plugging various hot spots for the past four days and he wanted some revenge. The colonel gathered up his officers and senior noncoms and they trudged up to the crest of a nearby ridge where they looked over the objective, drank some beer, and planned the attack. A key to the plan was to blind the defenders with a smoke screen. Knowing from past experience that the commanding officer of the 14th Marines was not enthusiastic about the use of smoke, Chambers approached the exec of the artillery regiment's 1st Battalion. "He had come up on the evening of D+4 when we were planning this thing," recalled Chambers. "I asked him to get ahold of all the smoke he could get his hands on and lay it by his guns for when we came through. He said not to worry, it would be there."[19]

The attack jumped off at 1000 with I and L companies abreast and K following to the left rear. The artillery exec was as good as his word. "The 14th smoked the living hell out of Hill 500 and the area to our immediate front," said Chambers.[20] Division artillery pounded the objective. The 1st Provisional Rocket Detachment's truck-mounted launchers chimed in with a rippling barrage, punctuated by 37mm fire from Regimental Weapons Company and the 3rd Battalion's own 81mm mortars. The battalion reached Laulau Road in front of the hill, reorganized, and jumped off again as smoke blossomed on the slopes ahead.

"When the word was given to move out, we all started running toward this hill, a half-mile away, yelling at the top of our lungs," recalled PFC Albert J. Ouellette. "It was like a charge in a Wild West movie. I guess we figured the Japs would get scared seeing 900 men strong coming at them and run for cover." As he charged forward with his BAR, Ouellette's cartridge belt came unhooked and started banging into him. He kept running.[21]

Following along behind, Chambers saw a squad trying to talk a couple of bypassed Japanese into surrendering. "I suspect these were home guard types, and they were not armed with anything other than pitchforks," he observed. "When I came upon them, I figured these Marines had already wasted ten or fifteen minutes trying to capture these two guys. I can remember thinking that this was a good way to get a lot of people killed. So I hollered, 'Shoot the bastards!' And they did."[22]

The Marines hit the base of the hill, paused to reorganize, and started up the slope. "We had to sling our weapons and start climbing hand-over-hand straight up while the Japs threw grenades and rocks at us," said Ouellette. As he made it to the top and tried to catch his breath amid the noise and confusion, a Japanese officer emerged from an opening in the hillside, pistol in hand. Ouellette fired his BAR from the hip, joined by another BAR man and a Marine with a pistol. "Anyway, we put twenty-eight rounds in this poor guy," remarked Ouellette. They found five more Japanese in a nearby bunker, which turned out to be some sort of artillery observation and communications center. Climbing on top, they dropped grenades down the air vent, killing everyone inside.[23]

By noon the hill was under Marine control at a cost of forty-nine casualties, including nine killed, which Chambers considered "a pretty cheap price to pay for this type of objective."[24] Unfortunately, in what was an all-too-common occurrence on Saipan, the battalion then took twenty-three more casualties when "friendly" artillery fire directed at Japanese retreating to the north fell short. The Marines counted forty-four dead Japanese on the hill. Mop-up parties added a few more, including an enemy soldier clad only in a loincloth who charged out of a cave with a sword as some engineers were getting ready to seal the entrance. A BAR man shot him down.

A safe in the abandoned brigade headquarters yielded two sacks of Japanese currency. A considerable amount of classified material was also discovered. Uncovered in another cave were two U.S. Signal Corps trunks, which had apparently been captured earlier in the war. The trunks were crammed with documents from the *3rd Independent Mountain Artillery Regiment*, including operations maps, casualty reports, journals, decorations, and field orders pertaining to the unit's operations on Bataan during the fall of the Philippines.[25]

Among paperwork found in General Saito's abandoned headquarters near Hill 500 was a poem, purportedly penned by the general himself. Subsequently translated by an intelligence officer and passed around, the general's poem addressed the Shinto gods and asked that following his death his spirit be permitted to continue fighting the enemies of the emperor. He requested that he and his soldiers be reincarnated as waves in the ocean so they could batter the enemy's ships trying to steam toward Japan. "Apart from the literary quality," recalled Lt. Paul Harper, "we took the poem as an encouraging sign that Saito knew the jig was up."[26]

As the battle expanded from the beachhead, the plight of the civilians on Saipan was spiraling into a multitude of individual tragedies. Eleven-year-old Victoria Akiyama's family fled Garapan the night before the landings and made their way to the Aslito area where they took refuge under her uncle's house. As the din of gunfire drew near, Akiyama heard her cousin exclaim, "Oh, look! They are fighting!" She stuck her thumbs in her ears and covered her eyes with her fingers. The next thing she knew, the house was coming down around them and catching fire. Her sister Teruko simply disappeared. Her baby brother lay nearby. "His head was cracked open and his brains were hanging out," she recalled. "I am sure he was dead, but his lips were still moving as if sucking on his mother's breast." Her aunt was also dead. Her brother had a small hole in his chest, but when she rolled him over, she saw that his back had been blown out.

One of Akiyama's cousins was praying as blood leaked from her multiple wounds. Complaining she was hot, she took her clothes off, making a vain attempt to wring the blood out, but soon died. Another cousin lay on the ground trying to push her intestines back into her abdomen with her dirty hands. A sudden blast of fire from a flamethrower scorched Akiyama's back. She screamed. When she came to her senses, Americans were treating her injuries.[27]

Language teams and individual soldiers and Marines attempted to coax civilians from hiding, but with mixed results. The Chamorros were most likely to respond. Devoutly Catholic, they often emerged with hands up, or carrying religious objects such as crucifixes, crying, "Pas Chamorro!" [Peace! I am Chamorro!] Japanese civilians, long indoctrinated that they would be tortured, raped, and killed, were less inclined to trust their enemy. In a sadly typical incident, a U.S. Army patrol encountered a man and woman and three children on a road by Nafutan Point. When the GIs approached, the man killed the woman, then himself. The bewildered children were taken into custody.[28]

Civilians who did emerge to seek help were often on their last legs. "They were in terrible shape," remembered Tibor Torok. "Some were carrying dead babies. The dead babies were covered with black, stinking flies. We had to bury the dead babies, but the women fiercely resisted this. They fought us, but we finally managed to bury them." The plight of the children moved even hardened troops. "We were all suckers for kids, because nobody wanted to kill a kid," observed Corp. Hawley Waldron.[29]

One of those children, ten-year-old Shinsho Miyagi, had fled into the hills with his mother and father and twelve-year-old brother. Miyagi's father was badly wounded by a shell fragment from U.S. artillery fire. No longer able to walk, he insisted that the others leave him. As they ran across an open area with other civilians, Miyagi was wounded in the right hand. His mother was shot through the abdomen. She died in front of the two boys.

The two brothers wandered aimlessly about for days. A Chamorro boy shared his water with them. A Japanese soldier took time to bandage Miyagi's wounded hand. The brothers were finally captured while hiding with other civilians in a large cave. Ordered to sit along the road, Miyagi was certain they were about to be run over by tanks and killed, as Japanese propaganda had promised. Instead, an American gave him water and expressed concern about his now gangrenous hand. "You're the ones who did this," Miyagi's brother snapped at their benefactor. Miyagi was rushed to the hospital where surgeons were forced to amputate his right hand, but he, like Victoria Akiyama, would survive. He never saw his father again.[30]

With the breakout from the beachhead, the logistical situation was rapidly improving. American shore parties were hard at work to improve beach approaches and egress. UDT teams blasted a channel through the reef off the Red Beaches. Seabees floated pontoon sections into place to form a causeway off Charan Kanoa. Engineers blasted two channels through the reef just north of Agingan Point to allow small boats easier access to Yellow 3. The 1341st Engineer Battalion removed mines from White Beach I below Agingan Point and carved out access roads leading inland.

Work was also underway to put Aslito Airfield back into operational shape. Marines were still firing mortars at pockets of diehards north of the runway as Seabees arrived to work their legendary magic. Between clearing debris and filling in holes ranging from small ruts to gaping bomb craters, the always ingenious Seabees found time to transform a Japanese windmill into a washing machine to launder their clothes. Within a few days, the narrow-gauge rail line would also be back in operation, the undersized locomotives hauling cars loaded with gasoline and bombs instead of sugar cane.

The airfield also underwent its second name change in a matter of days. Upon securing the field, the 27th Division had promptly nailed up a large sign naming their conquest Conroy Field, in honor of one of their colonels who had been killed at Makin the preceding November. Colonel Conroy's recognition would prove to be fleeting. This was a U.S. Navy show and the Navy named captured airfields after its own. The paint on the Army sign had scarcely dried when, by order of Admiral Nimitz, the field was formally renamed Isely Field in honor of the *Lexington* air commander who had died there in the rocket attack on June 13. The Conroy placard came down and a sign honoring Commander Isely went up. The moment was somewhat diminished by the fact that the sign-maker misspelled the dead commander's name, putting it down as "Isley." The error was never corrected and the facility remained "Isley Field" throughout its operational lifetime.

As the airfield cleanup continued, a persistent rumor circulated that Amelia Earhart's plane had been discovered hidden in one of the hangars and that the long-missing aviatrix and her navigator Fred Noonan had not been lost at sea in 1937: They had been taken prisoner by the Japanese and held on Saipan. According to stories related by some of the island's civilians, Earhart had died of disease, whereupon the Japanese executed Noonan. Military intelligence looked into the stories and even dug some holes in search of remains, but no definitive proof was found—or at least never made public—that Earhart had ever been on Saipan.[31]

On June 22, twenty-five P-47 "Thunderbolts" from the 318th Air Group's 19th Squadron were catapulted off the escort carrier USS *Natoma Bay* 60 miles off shore and landed at their new home at Aslito. Others flew in over the next two days, bringing the total to seventy-three P-47s. They immediately went into action in support of the ground troops. The P-47D carried six 5-inch rockets, had eight .50-caliber machine guns, and could handle two 1,000-pound bombs. The squadron's ground support missions— some of the shortest of the war in the first few days—were "down and dirty," flown low level at point-blank range.

From June 22 through July 17, the P-47s flew 2,500 sorties and dropped 260 tons of bombs, and fired 500 rockets and 530,000 rounds of .50-caliber ammunition. Among the air group's first casualties were lieutenants Wayne F. Kobler and Richard B. Witzig, who were killed during a mission against Tinian on June 27 when the Japanese set off a buried 500-pound bomb that caught their two Thunderbolts full blast during a low-level strafing attack. The Japanese buried Kobler; his grave was found weeks later when Marines secured Tinian. Witzig simply vanished.[32]

While staff officers charted progress with careful marks on situation maps, the day-to-day—sometimes minute-to-minute—existence of the front-line rifleman edging through the cane fields with his heart in his throat was far removed from any such clinical pursuits. Debilitating heat, clouds of mosquitoes at night, swarming bloated flies by day, and sudden, random death—that was his Saipan. Lt. John C. Chapin remembered the "countless fields—one after another. And it was the same old story: in every field the company would lose a man or two. It was wonderfully quieting to the nerves to start into a growth of head-high cane and wonder who would not be coming out on the other side! The Jap snipers who were doing the damage were dug in so deeply, and camouflaged so well, that it was impossible to locate them before they fired. And then it was too late: you were right on top of them and they had nailed another one of your men—or maybe you!"[33]

"Saipan was very tough," observed PFC Albert J. Harris. "It was physically demanding . . . [T]he only thing we had left was what we carried. I just had my ammunition on my belt and my carbine and water. That was it . . . No pack . . . It was hot. And the place was full of bodies. And bodies cause maggots and maggots cause flies. During the day you couldn't even put any food up to your mouth because the flies would cover the spoon. You couldn't go to the bathroom because they'd be after that. You'd have to wait til night to have a bowel movement. You'd walk along, the flies would get on every little scratch you had, five or six of them trying to get to the blood. And that went on for most of the time."[34] A disgusted news correspondent wrote, "All the flies in Asia are on Saipan. You don't shoo them from your food. You pick them from your teeth."[35]

Temperatures during the day averaged in the mid-80s, with relative humidity as high as 78 percent. With the cloying heat, water became almost an obsession. "Water, water, water or the lack of it nearly drove most of us crazy on Saipan," recalled PFC Alva Perry. "Here we are fighting in temperatures of over 100 degrees and we couldn't get any water for days on end."[36] Initial plans called for bringing ashore enough water to provide each man with 2 gallons a day for five days. Water distillation units were operating within three days of the landing but struggled to keep up with demand. Water came up in 5-gallon GI cans, some of which had originally held gasoline, and was tainted to the point that it was barely drinkable. Nevertheless, when the water cans arrived, everyone crowded thirstily around. "The water was lukewarm, rusty and oily as it came out of the cans, but it still tasted like nectar!" observed Chapin.[37]

Clouds of choking dust rose from the burned-over cane fields as the men trudged through. "With water so scarce, one of our chief sources of liquid sustenance was sugar cane juice," said Chapin. "We'd whack off a segment of cane with our combat knives, then chew and suck on it till only the dry fibers were left. In these burnt-out fields we weren't even able to do this, as the cane was spoiled and tasted lousy."[38]

The Marines weren't the only ones suffering. Using a captured enemy map showing all water supply sources on Saipan, U.S. artillery zeroed in on water points in enemy territory with dire consequences for Japanese troops and civilians. A U.S. intelligence report dated June 19 noted that "POWs came in crying for water, saying that rain was practically the sole source of drinking water."[39]

For some, it was worth dying for. Alva Perry shot a Japanese who broke from some bushes. "I walked up to see if he had any water," he recalled. "The shot had hit him in the back of the head. I removed his raincoat and found he had canteens tied around his waist on a rope. He had obviously been out hunting for water for his own people; these canteens must have been taken off dead Marines. I started to drink from one of the canteens and looked down at the face of the dead man, he was just a young kid maybe 15 or 16 years of age." Perry passed the rest of the water around to his parched buddies. Years later, he observed, "Every time I drink cold water I think of Saipan and Tinian, oh how good it tastes and how much I appreciate water."[40]

Flies, heat, no water . . . as bad as it got, it could almost always be worse. Twenty-one-year-old Sgt. Mike Mervosh was beating his gums one day about their living conditions to their forty-year-old gunnery sergeant, "Pop Brengle." Brengle replied, "Mike, if you live to be my age, you'll be doing great."

Mervosh retorted, "Gunny, if I live to my next birthday I'll be doing great!"[41]

Out in the boondocks, the push continued. Corp. Orvel Johnson's unit pulled up for the day by a road running along a cane field. The Marines cut fire lanes through the cane and laid the stalks across the furrows so they would hear anyone trying to pass through. "As holes were completed, gear was stowed, smoking lamp was out and the troops settled in alongside their weapons," recalled Johnson. "Gradually talking between foxholes ended and one man in each hole took the first watch for the evening. No star shells illuminated the night sky and the sounds of crickets, frogs and other varmints seemed to become louder as darkness settled in."

In the early morning, they heard low voices drawing near along the dirt road. Cheek pressed against the stock of his BAR, Johnson nudged his foxhole companion, only to find he was already awake. A Marine called out a challenge. The talking cut short and something sailed through the air toward the Marine sentry. There was a tremendous explosion by the line of foxholes. Johnson cut loose with his BAR at two figures bolting down the road. Both pitched forward. "There was great commotion and shouting off to my left and calling for corpsman," he recalled. A sergeant yelled for everyone to stay put.

Quiet gradually returned. The two huddled figures by the road remained motionless. Then one called out faintly, "Mercy, Maleen!" Three or four times during the next hour came the call, "Mercy, Maleen!" No one responded and finally the voice went still. Morning revealed two dead Japanese, an enlisted man and an officer. The explosion Johnson had heard had been some sort of demolition charge they had hurled into a Marine foxhole. One of the occupants had rolled out of the hole in time, but his buddy had been a step too slow. The dead man lay nearby, his entire midsection blown away. Pieces of his body and uniform hung from the branches in the trees behind the row of foxholes.[42]

"At night there were three different types of Japs," observed Pvt. Frank Borta. "There were the ones who were behind our lines and trying to get back to theirs. Then there were the ones trying to get through our lines to hit our patrols bringing up ammunition and food. The third type were the ones trying to get us in our foxholes . . . We had two men to a foxhole . . . One night a Jap jumped into my foxhole. I saw that he had a knife in his hand and I was able to get my knife and stick him in the guts. Then I dumped his body out of the hole. I don't remember who my foxhole buddy was, but he slept through it all. On another night we had a Jap slide into our foxhole from the side, and both of us stuck him at the same time. My foxhole buddy stuck him in the throat and I stuck him in the stomach."[43]

PFC James D. Bacon woke one night to an exploding grenade. He reached for his rifle but found he couldn't pick it up—the grenade blast had blown off two fingers of his left hand and cut up his right. A Japanese materialized over him and in quick succession bayoneted him in the right thigh and neck and then slammed him in the jaw with his rifle butt, knocking him unconscious. When Bacon awoke, the Japanese was gone, but he was choking on his own blood. He stood up and found he could breathe if he held his head down. After he was evacuated he learned there had been four Japanese all together—two officers and two enlisted men. All had been killed by other Marines.[44]

There was no respite. A sergeant in Bob Everett's outfit got up one morning and started to dig a small hole preparatory to moving his bowels. As he was digging, a Japanese officer suddenly appeared out of nowhere brandishing a sword. Someone shouted a warning and the sergeant ducked under the swinging blade. "This sergeant was short and stocky and quick like a cat," recalled Everett. "He caught the Jap officer up the side of the head with his shovel and beat the bastard to death with it."[45]

Other infiltrators would cut communications wires at night, then tie the severed ends head-high in a tree so a troubleshooting linesman would be forced to reach up to retrieve the wire. The Japanese would hide, wait for a signalman to come along to fix the break, and then shoot him. Wiremen countered by going out in teams of three—one man to check the line and two to ride shotgun. The system worked: In one instance four Japanese were killed by wiremen who suspected a trap and investigated before trying to repair the break in the line.

Despite precautions, intruders inevitably got through—in at least one case with catastrophic results. About an hour before midnight on June 21, infiltrators succeeded in blowing up the 2nd Marine Division ammunition dump. Survivors later reported hearing a sentry issue a challenge, followed by a shot and then an explosion. A fire broke out and ammo began to cook off. The battalion supply officer raced through Bob Cary's area, shouting, "Everybody out! Everybody out! Grab your shovels and follow me! We gotta put this fire out!" Pvt. Frank Cirricione, a recent replacement, started to climb out of their hole. Cary grabbed his shirt and pulled him back.

Suddenly the whole place exploded. "The crash must have been heard in downtown Tokyo," recalled Cary. "The dump became a thundering inferno with shells exploding and belts of 50-caliber machine gun ammo going off like strings of huge firecrackers." He and Cirricione hugged the ground and prayed as shells and munitions of all sizes exploded and whizzed through the air.[46] The concussion from tons of ammunition going up at once shook sailors aboard ships off shore. "I was resting on a cot in the office when an explosion shook me out of my sack," recalled Storekeeper First Class Vincent R. Perrone aboard the USS *Fremont*. "It seemed to have hit right outside of the office but no damage was done."[47]

The dump burned all night, the column of smoke rising hundreds of feet over the island. As daylight arrived, Cary emerged from his foxhole. "Outside of a few piles of burning junk, the dump was gone," he observed. "Scattered about like bundles of charred rags were the bodies of a dozen of our people on the edge of where the dump once stood."[48] Among them, he learned later, was Corp. Joe Henger, a former grocery clerk from Milwaukee who was one of his best friends.

The Japanese units scrambling to block the American advance north had yet to learn of the defeat of Admiral Ozawa's *Mobile Fleet* at the hands of

Task Force 58. The Japanese Imperial Navy had sought a decisive battle and it had gotten one—but not with the anticipated outcome. In fact, the defeat was even more lopsided than the Japanese realized. While aware of their own losses, they greatly overestimated the damage they had inflicted on Spruance. Japanese after-action reports claimed "1 carrier, and 1 battleship or cruiser set on fire for certain in attack by 3d Carrier Division . . . In attack by the 1st Carrier Division, fires were started on 4 American carriers . . . In all, it is certain that 4 or 5 aircraft carriers and 1 battleship or large cruiser were sunk or damaged, and it is not possible to assert that others did not blow up and sink."[49]

But even this fantasy could not transform defeat into victory. Having withdrawn beyond the reach of the American fleet, a dejected Admiral Ozawa composed a letter to Admiral Toyoda tendering his resignation. Toyoda refused to accept it. "I am more responsible for this defeat than Admiral Ozawa," he declared, "and I will not accept his resignation."[50]

For the moment, details of the disaster remained confined to the highest levels. During dinner with several naval officers from General Headquarters the evening of June 21, Toshikazu Kase, a high-ranking diplomat with the Foreign Ministry, was assured that Japan had won a great victory. "They were profuse in assuring me that our fleet had emerged victorious from the engagement," he recalled. "They even drank hilariously to the spectacular victory." Only after the party broke up did a highly placed officer reveal to Kase that what he had just heard was the "official" version of the battle: In fact, the fleet had suffered a devastating defeat. Kase was not entirely surprised. "It was customary for GHQ to make false announcements of victory in utter disregard of facts, and for the elated and complacent public to believe in them," he observed.[51]

Still, Tokyo had not written off the defenders of Saipan—at least not yet. Stunned staff officers at naval headquarters scrambled to devise a way to snatch victory from disaster. Spurred by the Japanese tendency to take the offense no matter what the practical circumstances, the view began to form that the navy should commit all its resources to another attack. The goal this time would not be to destroy the American carriers as Ozawa had originally intended, but to pour troops into Saipan and recapture the island itself. A potent covering force could be formed by combining Ozawa's remaining ships with Vice Adm. Kiyohide Shima's *Fifth Fleet* and the escort carriers *Kaiyo*, *Shinyo*, and *Taiyo*. The decimated naval air arm would be replaced by naval air training groups and army fighter units.

As part of the plan, troop reinforcements would be loaded aboard the old battleship *Yamashiro* and sent to Saipan to carry out a counter landing. Upon arrival, the obsolete ship would beach itself to serve as a shore battery against the invading Americans while 3,000 troops from the *145th Infantry, 46th Division,* poured ashore. *Combined Fleet* chief of staff Rear Adm. Ryunosuke Kusaka himself wanted to participate, eager to test his swordsmanship on the American invaders. As enthusiasm grew, so did the plans as more and more ships were added to the daring foray, codenamed Y-Go. According to the proposed timetable, the *Yamashiro* would sail on June 25 and run itself ashore at Saipan on July 8.[52]

Most of the impetus for Y-Go, observed Kase, came from "the younger officers of the Navy [who] were clamoring for an all-out attack to recapture the island and were growing critical of the Army for not sharing their enthusiasm." Kase, who believed the loss of Saipan "would make further war efforts altogether futile," was informed by a former minister of the navy that "although he was perfectly certain such an attack would only end in disaster, he thought it advisable to let the 'young fellows' have their own way once in order to reconcile them ultimately to their inevitable fate—defeat."[53] Though based on wishful thinking and an unrealistic assessment of the situation, enthusiasm mounted and on June 21 the Naval General Staff drew up a proposal for the recapture of Saipan calling for the departure of an army division on July 1, followed by carrier forces with pilots from naval air training groups and army air units.

It was a reckless scheme born of desperation. Even the Naval General Staff entertained serious misgivings. If the Americans spotted the approaching force early on, it could be neutralized before it even drew close to Saipan. Could control of the air really be seized from U.S. dominance and if so, how long could it be retained? Would Japanese army fighter pilots even be able to take off from carriers? Would the contemplated ground force be sufficient to defeat the American divisions already on Saipan? There was so much that could go wrong. Nevertheless, on June 22 Admiral Toyoda ordered Admiral Ozawa, who had just arrived at Nakagusuko Bay, to prepare for the Saipan recapture operation.[54]

Among those anxiously awaiting rescue were the isolated defenders of Nafutan Point. "I am still alive," an unidentified sailor observed to his diary on June 20. "I wish I can fulfill my duty today." A day later he wrote, "No reinforcements came. No food or water. It's quite a hardship . . . Everyone is saying that there are no reinforcing planes. Also, no naval reinforcements to aid us. We feel it more than the others because we are Navy men. . . ."[55]

The point and the band of brush and upheaved coral along Magicienne Bay provided refuge for large numbers of stragglers. Leading a patrol from the 165th Infantry, PFC James Cowley was working cautiously along a rough trail when he suddenly found himself face to face with three Japanese soldiers. After a startled instant, all four scrambled to raise their rifles. Cowley's rifle misfired. The lead Japanese got off a shot that hit Cowley in the arm and knocked him down. As he raised his bayonet to finish off Cowley, another GI leveled his tommy gun and killed all three Japanese with a long burst.

The commotion attracted PFC Walter T. Simmons, who came up lugging his BAR. As he paused to speak to his squad leader, he spotted two Japanese soldiers walking toward him down the trail and shot them both. To his astonishment, Japanese soldiers began to pour out of a hole in the cliff face just beyond, scrambling in all directions, actually tripping over one another in their haste to get away. Simmons began firing. He was quickly joined by two other BAR men. In a matter of minutes, the three Americans killed over forty Japanese.[56]

What was supposed to be a coordinated assault on Nafutan Point itself went less well. The 1st and 2nd Battalions of the 105th Infantry were scheduled to attack on June 20 at 1000, but Gen. Ralph Smith was forced to push the time back to 1115 and then to noon as the units seemed unable to position themselves. The attack finally got off after a fifteen-minute barrage from division artillery, followed by a smoke screen delivered by a company from the 88th Chemical Battalion. All the noise and fury was for naught. Coming under machine-gun fire from the left, punctuated by shells from a heavy, flat trajectory weapon on the right flank, the assault stopped in its tracks.[57]

To the left, the 3rd Battalion, 165th Infantry had also run amok. K and L Companies gained about 1,000 yards, but I Company was pinned down in the open fields. Support from the 766th Tank Battalion only added to the confusion. The light tanks were operating buttoned up, radios failed, and the GIs could not communicate with the crews. The tanks roved around firing at random, some of the shells landing among the assault companies. This unhappy incident ended when the Japanese brought dual-purpose guns and mortars to bear on the American armor. The tanks promptly retreated to the battalion CP. A highly irate major ordered them back to the front, but by 1730 the advance on Nafutan had ended for the day.[58] The 105th Infantry suffered a grand total of one man killed and five wounded; the 165th reported six killed, twenty-one wounded, and one missing.

The circus continued the next morning as junior officers repeatedly failed to advance in the face of enemy fire or remained immobile while they contacted superior officers for guidance. One company waited two hours to burn off a cane field for fear the Japanese were using it for cover. Losing three men wounded when the GIs finally advanced at 1255, the company commander ordered his men back into the foxholes they had occupied the night before and radioed for tank support. By day's end the division's assault on the point had made no progress on either flank and only a slight advance in the center. Casualties for the day's fighting on Nafutan came to seven killed and 57 wounded. An Army observer subsequently criticized the 105th Regiment for its unimpressive performance, saying it manifested "a certain amount of inertia" and "lack of offensive spirit." By the end of the campaign, there would be many who felt this observation applied to the entire 27th Division.[59]

In the division's defense, by now the GIs had begun to realize that Nafutan Point was more heavily defended than anyone had suspected. After two days of fighting, the division had revised the estimate of enemy troops up to at least 500. The division also learned from POWs that caves on the point were so deep they were impervious to artillery fire. There was even a report of a field piece firing from a cave protected by moveable steel doors.[60] Other armament included numerous dual-purpose guns and at least one 8-inch mortar capable of firing a 30-pound projectile.

Unfortunately, Gen. Ralph Smith was not going to have the luxury of time—or forces—to deal with the unexpected resistance at Nafutan, which Gen. Holland Smith viewed as a sideshow. Having started his Marines on the drive north, Howlin' Mad now wanted to add 27th Infantry Division muscle to the push. The division learned of Smith's intentions at 1215, while still involved in the disorganized assault on Nafutan. NTLF Operation Order 9-44 directed the division to prepare to join the main attack, leaving one battalion and one light tank platoon to "mop up remaining enemy detachments" in the Nafutan area.[61]

In light of recent developments, 27th Division staff did not believe one battalion would be sufficient to reduce Nafutan. Ralph Smith visited NTLF headquarters that afternoon to consult personally with Holland M. Smith.

The latter expressed concern about the slow pace of the effort to clear Nafutan Point. He told Ralph Smith that "he did not wish to be unreasonable,
but that Colonel [Leonard A.] Bishop [Commanding Officer, 105th Infan-
try] must not be permitted to delay. If he couldn't do it, send somebody who
could." Ralph Smith "pointed out difficult terrain and Jap positions in caves
and said rapid advance was impracticable if undue losses were to be avoided
and if Japs were to be really cleaned out." He said that continuing pressure
would be applied and he thought the point could be cleaned "in a couple of
days more."[62]

Holland Smith remained skeptical of Army claims of heavy resistance.
In what was either a display of frustration or his lack of tact—or perhaps
both—he told combat correspondent Robert Sherrod of a conversation he
claimed to have had with the 27th Division commander. According to Holland Smith, he asked the Army general how many Japanese were down on
the point. Ralph Smith replied there were probably somewhere between
300 and 500. According to Sherrod, Holland Smith retorted scornfully,
"You know damn well there are not two hundred."[63]

That the bellicose Marine commander remained unimpressed with
the Army general's argument became abundantly clear following the meeting. Checking in with Holland Smith's chief of staff, Gen. Graves Erskine,
Ralph Smith was told that the 27th Division would go into the line alongside the Marines the following day. The GIs would be inserted between the
two Marine divisions in the center of the drive north. One battalion would
be left to deal with the point.

While given no choice, Ralph Smith remained concerned about the
ability of a single battalion to contain and eliminate Japanese forces on
Nafutan Point. The next day he wrote to Holland Smith to request that
the garrison in the Aslito Field area be advised that infiltrators from Nafutan could pose a threat. Seabees and other personnel should be warned to
provide security against this possibility. The warning was issued on June 23.
Headquarters may or may not have given much weight to the advisory, but
Ralph Smith's concerns would prove prescient.[64]

As the Americans consolidated their hold on the south of the island, General Saito's surviving troops fell back to a new "line of security" athwart
central Saipan's high ground. U.S. intelligence gleaned some details from
a map found on the body of a Japanese captain from the *2nd Battalion,
136th Infantry*, killed the morning of June 23. The map indicated the enemy

defensive line was being formed across the island from below Garapan and extending to the east. Ironically, the position roughly paralleled Holland Smith's O-5 line objective.

Japanese units had been hard hit. A message from the voluble General Igeta to his assistant chief of staff on June 22 summarized the fate of some of Saipan's unit commanders: "Colonel Oka (CO *Mixed Brigade*) is believed to have died in breakthrough at Charan Kanoa, dawn of the 18th. Colonel Arima (CO *9th Expeditionary Unit*) wounded in battle, hospitalized. Colonel Goto (CO *9th Tank Regiment*), whereabouts unknown since night of 16th. Believed to have died in battle. Colonel Koganezawa (CO *7th Engineers*) missing since morning of 19th, believed to have died in battle. Lieutenant Colonel Nakajima (CO *3d Independent Mountain Artillery*) wounded, hospitalized."[65]

Personnel losses in line units were reported to be as high as 50 percent. Estimated strength of the *43rd Division* and attached units was about 9,000 men. Another 6,000 men were available from straggler units, but "their fighting ability is reduced by lack of weapons," observed Igeta's headquarters.[66] Remaining heavy weaponry was listed as twelve field pieces, twenty-seven tanks, six antiaircraft guns, nine machine cannons, and nine Type 95 field guns. Nevertheless, there was no thought of quitting. A junior officer in the tank regiment observed, "Even if there are no tanks, we will fight hand to hand . . . I have resolved that, if I see the enemy, I will take out my sword and slash, slash, slash at him as long as I last, thus ending my life of twenty-four years."[67]

The determined young Japanese officer was nearing his day of reckoning. With southern Saipan—excepting only Nafutan Point—in hand by nightfall on June 21, Holland Smith was ready to begin the much-delayed drive to secure the remainder of the island.

Combat efficiency in the Northern Troops and Landing Force as of the evening of June 21 was reported as "very satisfactory," despite higher than anticipated casualties. Losses since June 15 totaled just over 6,000. The 2nd Marine Division had suffered 2,514 killed and wounded; 4th Marine Division losses totaled 3,628; and the 27th Infantry Division had lost 320 officers and men to date.[68] Nevertheless, the mood in Lt. Fred Stott's 1st Battalion, 24th Marines, was upbeat. The battalion had not run into any significant resistance for the past four days. One officer joked half-seriously that he thought he could hop in a jeep and safely circle the northern end of the island to meet up with the 2nd Division.[69]

Holland Smith wasn't going to ask quite that much, but the division's next objective—pushing north to the O-5 line—running west from Laulau Village, was "an optimistic bite to be sure," observed the subsequent Marine Corps monograph on the battle.[70] The 4th Marine Division jumped off with the 24th Marines and 25th Marines abreast at 0600 after a ten-minute barrage delivered by eighteen artillery battalions. A haze of smoke rose into the air as the lower slopes of the hills ahead erupted in a hail of shells. By 0841, elements of Stott's battalion reported they were only a few yards from the day's objective. Division quickly assigned a secondary objective, which was reached by 1025. After a brief rest, the sweating Marines shouldered their gear and headed still farther north, toward an elevation marked on the maps as Hill 600.

Adjacent to the 24th Marines, Justice Chambers's 3rd Battalion was also making good progress. "The attack went very fast," remarked Chambers. "We killed a lot of Japs as we moved north."[71] However, as Chambers paused to reorganize, the Japanese counterattacked Company K on the battalion left. In close fighting, ninety Japanese were killed and an enemy tank was knocked out, but Marines also took serious casualties. The dead included K Company commander "Big Jim" Goforth, a 6-foot-tall, 200-pound former University of Kentucky basketball star. "He and his company command group had bypassed a Japanese machine gun," recalled Chambers. "The Jap gunner let them go by and opened up on them from the rear. When the gun began to fire, Goforth turned and started walking straight toward it, firing as he went. This duel didn't last very long. After a few moments, you could see Jim just sag and slump down to the earth. There must have been eighty slugs in him."[72]

The push slowed as the battalion ran into defenses built around a series of low ridges that ran down to the coast. "This was mostly machine guns protected by riflemen," observed Chambers. "It got rougher and rougher as we went along." Among the casualties was a Marine Corps legend, forty-eight-year-old Col. Evans F. Carlson, now serving as division operations officer. A former Raider Battalion commander, Carlson had spent months as an observer with Chinese Communists fighting the Japanese in the 1930s and had introduced the term *gung ho* to the Marine Corps. There were those who thought Carlson himself was a Communist, but no one doubted his courage. Seeing Chambers's radioman cut down by machine-gun fire, Carlson started to drag him to safety and was himself hit by a burst in the right arm and left thigh. Both he and the radioman survived, but Carlson's long war was over.[73]

The adjacent 24th Marines were also headed for trouble. The lead platoon of the 1st Battalion's Company A made its way to the top of Hill 600 to find the Japanese positions there had been abandoned. The heat was stifling. "We got to the top of the hill and we were exhausted," recalled PFC Howard Kerr. "We were dragging a lot of equipment, machine guns, mortars, and a couple straps of MG belts around our neck. We settled down in what looked like a real nice spot. Just all zonked out."[74]

Their lack of caution proved deadly. Twenty-year-old PFC David Brunjes was good-naturedly joking around when he suddenly slumped over. It took an instant for the others to realize he had been shot dead. As they scattered, Corp. Norman Reber spotted several Japanese maneuvering around the company's open flank. He hustled over to warn company commander Capt. Irving Schechter, but the enemy was already infesting the hill. As Reber started back to his squad, he was cut down by a Japanese machine gun.

Whatever reason the Japanese originally had for leaving the hilltop position unguarded, it was clear they intended to get it back. Artillery and mortar fire descended on the Marines, already pinned down by snipers and machine guns. PFC George Smith's machine gun jammed after two rounds. He was shot in the wrist as he went to clear the jam. The Marine next to him let out a scream as a bullet shattered the bone in his upper arm, leaving the limb hanging by a piece of skin. A platoon from Charlie Company pushed up the hill to help. Under the direction of twenty-six-year-old 1st Lt. Thomas Schultz, the Marines killed an estimated forty enemy soldiers in scattered positions around the hill, but the Japanese kept coming. Schultz was overseeing the evacuation of his many wounded when he was killed by an artillery shell.

George Smith made his way off the hill with a handful of other wounded, including one Marine with a sucking chest wound and another who had been blinded and was weeping from pain and fear. Smith tried to keep his good hand over the Marine's chest wound, but the air continued to make a whistling sound as the man gasped for breath. Smith suddenly realized they were unarmed except for his Ka-Bar. "A Japanese boy scout could have taken all of us," he said later. They made it to the battalion aid station, which was flooded with wounded. Two of Smith's buddies passed him a couple of bottles of rice wine. He drank them both before a corpsman finally came along and stuck him with a morphine syrette. By that time he wasn't feeling any pain at all.

Unable to hold, Company A pulled off Hill 600. A squad led by Sgt. Jack W. Aeby tried to keep the Japanese off as the Marines withdrew. As the covering squad finally pulled out, Aeby, who at age thirty was the old man of his platoon, was shot and killed.[75] Also among the dead, found the next day when the hill was finally secured, was a radio operator who had managed to destroy his SCR 300 radio before he died.

CHAPTER XVII

Holland Smith vs. the Army

THE MORNING OF JUNE 23 THE GIs DOWN BY NAFUTAN POINT ATE A COLD breakfast in the dark before starting for the Marine lines, 3 miles away. Day was just breaking. With slung rifles and light combat packs, they filed along both sides of the roads through fields heavy with the stench of dead men and rotting livestock. The heat rose with the sun and the GIs were soon drenched with sweat as they slogged northward to relieve the 25th Marines on the 4th Division's left. They arrived to find the Marines glad to be out of there following the previous day's action. "It's the toughest friggin' place we've ever been in, Captain," a battalion commander told one of the Army officers.[1]

Capt. Charles H. Hallden's L Company (2nd Battalion, 106th) relieved two Marine companies from Lt. Col. Justice Chambers's battalion. The Marines had suffered heavily. The two companies undergoing relief had a combined strength of only 185 men after a week of combat. An account executive with the stock exchange in civilian life, Hallden was a heavy-set, open-faced Swede who had joined the National Guard in 1931 as a private. Events would prove the thirty-four-year-old New Yorker to be a natural soldier.

Chambers told Hallden there were "plenty of Japs" in the area. "He pointed to the activity on the side of Mount Tapotchau where Japs could be seen running along the side of the mountain into caves," recalled Hallden. Hallden asked Chambers about his line of departure and why it was so far behind the map location. Chambers told him the Marines had been pushed back approximately 400 yards by counterattacks the preceding afternoon and night.[2]

The fighting overnight had been intense. One of Jumpin' Joe's non-coms, twenty-eight-year old Sgt. Maj. Gilbert L. "Irish" Morton, a longtime reservist from New Orleans, had taken over a platoon after their lieutenant was killed. Tucked into the rocky heights near the juncture with the 2nd Marine Division, the platoon, running low on ammunition, had nearly been overrun in hand-to-hand fighting. Four Japanese jumped into Morton's foxhole. "He had a Thompson submachine gun he had stolen from some-place," said Chambers. "Fearing the Thompson would hit his own people, [he] killed all four Japanese by beating them to death. It must have been one hell of a fight. I had never seen a human body so beaten up in my life as was Morton's when I saw him the next day."[3]

The Marines said the terrain up ahead was the strongest defensive posi-tion they had seen since landing.[4] The ground facing Ralph Smith's GIs—a place that was about to go down in evil fame as "Death Valley"—was essen-tially a long sunken corridor. About a thousand yards wide, the corridor was bounded on the left by the heights of Mount Tapotchau and on the right by a line of low, tree- and brush-covered hills—soon to be dubbed Purple Heart Ridge—which extended roughly northeast for about a mile. The opposite wall of the corridor consisted of a series of sharp drops from Mount Tapotchau, forming sheer cliff faces riddled with caves and crevices that allowed occupants to dominate the ground below. The corridor floor was mostly open fields, some covered with knee-high grass, others with burned-over sugar cane. A narrow road—described as "little more than a cow path"—ran up the center of the valley. From a military standpoint, the corridor was essentially one big trap.[5]

Holland Smith's headquarters, which seems to have made a habit of underestimating enemy strength, believed the 27th Division faced no more than a few hundred artillery and engineer troops—mostly rear-echelon per-sonnel pushed back into the hills by the Marine advance. It was a woeful underestimate: After-action reports and POW interrogations later revealed the actual numbers may have been as high as 4,000 men, including elements of the *118th* and *136th Infantry* regiments, supported by tanks and moun-tain howitzers.[6] They had been badly mauled, but were far from broken. Among the survivors waiting for the Americans was Matsuya Tokuzo of the *9th Tank Regiment*, who wrote in his diary: "The fierce attacks of the enemy only increase our hostility. Every man is waiting for the assault with all weapons for close quarters fighting in readiness. We are waiting with 'Molotov cocktails' and hand grenades ready for the word to rush forward recklessly into the enemy ranks with our swords in hands. The only thing that worries me is what will happen to Japan after we die."[7]

Tanker Matsuya Tokuzo and his comrades found little necessity to dash forward recklessly into the 27th Division ranks with swords or anything else the morning of June 23. The American attack, scheduled to begin at 1000, got off to a piecemeal start. Troops on the left attacked on schedule, but in the center the commander of 2nd Battalion, 165th Infantry sat on his hands for another hour because the company supposed to be on his left had been caught in traffic on the way up.

The overall assault developed tentatively. Companies from the 106th Infantry on the left came under mortar fire and became disorganized. In the center, the late-starting 2nd Battalion, 165th, advanced to a tree line at the mouth of Death Valley, a process that took twenty minutes though opposed only by some long-range rifle fire from the cliffs to their left. Battalion commander Lt. Col. John F. McDonough then pulled up and waited for the units on his left to take care of what should have been viewed as a minor nuisance. Despite repeated calls from division requesting the location of his front lines and disposition of forces, McDonough didn't move. Finally, shortly after noon, a presumably exasperated Ralph Smith directed the 165th to "push your advance rapidly regardless of advance of 106th Infantry. Employ reserve if necessary."[8]

McDonough got his battalion going an hour later following a fifteen-minute artillery preparation along Purple Heart Ridge. The first man to emerge into the open took two steps before he was shot. One platoon made it to the cover of a shallow ditch 75 yards away where the GIs came under small arms fire from cliffs along the left side of the valley. The bewildered platoon leader decided to run back to the company for instructions, an exercise that took him three hours. Meanwhile, the platoon on the right stalled under fire from Purple Heart Ridge. McDonough finally pulled everyone back under cover of a smoke screen.[9]

Attacking toward the end of Purple Heart Ridge on the right, GIs from the 1st Battalion, 165th, ran into heavy fire almost as soon as they passed heavily wooded Love Hill. Separated from the main mass of Purple Heart Ridge by about 100 yards of cane field, Love was not defended, but when the GIs started into the cane field they came under what was described as a "storm" of fire from Charlie Hill, the next elevation in the ragged ridge.

Commanding a platoon of Stuart tanks, twenty-five-year-old 1st Lt. Louis W. Fleck, later described as "a man brave to the point of indiscretion," took his light tank north up the Chacha Road at 1430, hoping to get at the Japanese positions from the side or rear.[10] His audacity was to have fatal consequences. Reaching a sharp turn about 400 yards ahead, his lone tank came up short as dozens of flaming Molotov cocktails rained down from ambush. The engine died as the driver tried to turn around. Scores of Japanese descended on the burning tank. Gunner Isadore Goldberg scrambled out of the turret and rolled into a ditch alongside the road. Fleck emerged next. He had armed himself with a Thompson submachine gun, but as dozens of Japanese soldiers approached, he dropped the weapon and raised his hands. A shot rang out. Hit in the back, Fleck dropped to his hands and knees. From the ditch, Goldberg saw several Japanese rush up and bayonet the fallen tank commander. The driver, Technician Fourth Class Emmanuel Duhon, was also stabbed to death as he vainly tried to surrender. Bow gunner Pvt. Henry Kilbridge was riddled with bullets as he emerged from the hatch of the burning tank.

Petrified with fear, Goldberg lay motionless in the ditch, feigning death. For over an hour Japanese walked around him and even stepped on his hands, but by some miracle neglected to look more closely. After dark, Goldberg crept away toward what he hoped were friendly lines. Severely traumatized by his ordeal, his hands swollen from being trampled by Japanese soldiers, his left foot punctured by shrapnel, he eventually stumbled into a Marine unit and was evacuated to a field hospital.[11]

Back at his bungalow headquarters in Charan Kanoa, Holland Smith was becoming increasingly frustrated with the performance of the 27th Division. It seemed that almost any level of opposition from the Japanese was enough to stop the GIs, first at Nafutan Point and now in Death Valley. Graves Erskine, who knew and liked Ralph Smith, admitted later, "I didn't really think he was pushing the way he should."[12]

The Nafutan Point situation was compounded by administrative confusion. Holland Smith considered the Nafutan battalion to be under NTLF command following his directive sending the remainder of the 27th Division north. He was therefore annoyed to learn that Ralph Smith had issued what he (Holland Smith) considered an unauthorized directive to the battalion. He warned General Ralph Smith: "2d Battalion, 105th by my operations order 10-44 not under your tactical control and should not be included in your tactical orders. Please take steps to rectify."[13] Holland Smith's more troubling dilemma, however, was evolving to the north where the progress of both Marine divisions was endangered by the sluggish effort of the 27th Division in the center.

Howlin' Mad had held an unflattering opinion of the 27th Division from the start; now, what he viewed as the division's lack of aggressiveness and poor leadership down through battalion level threatened to hold up the whole advance. Smith's disdain was shared by his operations officer, Col. Robert E. Hogaboom. Investigating the situation at Nafutan Point, Hogaboom was stunned to find the battalion headquarters some 1,000 yards behind the lines. "I finally got up to a company that was actually involved in the attack and met the company commander and he was practically in tears, saying he had been ordered to withdraw for the night. He had taken a hill and here he was ordered to drop back to some other position for the night. The troops were not being personally led ... the division was not functioning well," he observed.[14]

During the afternoon of June 23, as the advance into Death Valley stalled, Holland Smith summoned Army major general Sanderford Jarman for a sensitive discussion. Familiarly known as "Sandy," Jarman was supposed to take over as the Saipan Garrison Force commander once the island was secured. An artillery expert and 1908 graduate of West Point, Jarman was a huge man, standing 6-feet-5-inches tall and weighing in at 250 pounds, described by a classmate as "big of stature and big of heart." He was a highly capable administrator with a true gift for organization, but no experience handling large numbers of troops in combat.[15]

Smith told Jarman he was dismayed by the 27th Division's failure to advance. "He indicated that this division had suffered scarcely no casualties and in his opinion he didn't think they would fight," recalled Jarman. Smith asked Jarman for "advice." Presumably sensing where the discussion was headed, Jarman demurred, observing that any decision should be Smith's alone. Smith was candid. He declared that if the 27th were a Marine division he would immediately relieve the commander. However, he recognized the interservice implications of taking such action over an Army unit, telling Jarman "there would be a great cry set up more or less of a political nature." Smith finally got around to the point and asked Jarman to confer with Gen. Ralph Smith to find a way to get the GIs moving.[16]

Jarman immediately went to 27th Division Headquarters, only to find Ralph Smith absent. When the general returned late in the afternoon, Jarman learned he had been up at the front lines and was aware of the lack of progress. Jarman explained the situation as he understood it. He added that it appeared the division was not carrying its full share. Ralph Smith did not dispute that assessment. Jarman recalled, "He immediately reported that such was true; that he was in no way satisfied with what his regimental commanders had done during the day and that he had been with them and had pointed out to them the situation. He further indicated to me that he was going to be present tomorrow, 24 June with this division when it made its jump-off and he would personally see to it that the division went forward. He added that if he didn't take his division forward on the 24th, he should be relieved."[17]

Hours later Ralph Smith received a dispatch from Holland Smith complaining that the 27th Division had failed to launch its attack at the designated hour on June 23. The NTLF commander added that the division had shown a "lack of offensive spirit" in its failure to advance to the O-5 line "when opposed only by small arms and mortar fire." This failure forced the 4th and 2nd Marine Divisions to halt their attacks on the flanks of the 27th Division in order to prevent exposure of their interior flanks, adding, "It is directed that immediate steps be taken to cause the 27th Division to advance and seize objectives as ordered."[18]

Though their stronghold in Death Valley held fast against initial attacks, the Japanese situation in general was rapidly deteriorating. During the night of June 23, three Japanese were killed in the 25th Marines command post area. "They had come down from caves, apparently seeking water," reported the regiment. Another fifteen enemy, also seeking water, were killed in the 1st Battalion command post area. "They were either unarmed or had only hand grenades and bayonets," reported regiment. "All Bn's. reported enemy dead had little or no water in canteens."[19] GIs uncovered about a hundred enemy "old dead" hidden in dugouts. "A rear area in the zone of [the 25th Marines] gave evidence (probably olfactory) of freshly-buried enemy dead," observed an intelligence summary.[20]

With the 4th Marine Division closing in on Kagman Peninsula, General Saito evacuated his most recent command post north of Chacha Village—his second since D-day—and relocated to an elaborate cave dug into the sheer cliffs northeast of Mount Tapotchau's rugged spine. Army chief of staff Gen. Keiji Igeta summarized the overall situation as of the evening of June 23 from the sketchy information available to him. Units of the Homare [*43rd Division*] were in action "with the firm decision to hold out until the last the hill line [and] expects to smash the enemy," he declared. However, the enemy attack was progressing under cover of shelling and bombing, he admitted.[21]

Somewhat later, as more information arrived at *31st Army* Headquarters, the general's mood plummeted further. The enemy had broken through around Chacha in the eastern area, he observed. The fighting strength of the *43rd Division* was now less than two infantry battalions. Nothing the defenders did seemed to make any difference in the face of the enemy's overwhelming firepower. "Though our forces have called on all kinds of methods to hinder the enemy advance, we are regrettably reduced to the condition where we cannot carry out this plan with our present fighting strength," he admitted.[22] Days before he had suggested using "small boat amphibious units" to bring in more troops from Rota, Tinian, and Guam, slipping them through the American naval blockade after dark. Now he reiterated that request. What was needed "with all haste," pleaded Igeta, was immediate reinforcement.[23]

His pleas were destined to go unfulfilled. Back in Tokyo, plans to recapture Saipan had foundered as the Army General Staff refused to participate. The chance of success was too slim, declared the army (truthfully), and it was unable to spare any aircraft (perhaps less truthfully). In any case, without cooperation from the army, the plan was doomed.[24]

Emperor Hirohito was informed on June 24 that the loss of Saipan appeared inevitable. An entry in the Imperial General Headquarters Army Section Confidential Diary conceded defeat and called for a fight to the last man [*gyokusai*], demonstrating to the Americans that the nation's one hundred million people were prepared to die as one. "The Saipan Defense Force should carry out *gyokusai*," observed the entry. "It is not possible to conduct the hoped-for direction of the battle. The only thing left is to wait for the enemy to abandon their will to fight because of the '*Gyokusai of the One Hundred Million*.'"[25]

The emperor was dismayed. Reluctant to give up on Saipan, he asked War Minister Tojo to call a meeting of the Supreme Military Council, but any hopes for a reversal were quickly dashed. On June 25, a conference of fleet admirals and field marshals at the Imperial Palace formally agreed to abandon the Saipan recapture effort. Shocked, the emperor retreated to his garden. "Today the emperor was again gazing at the fireflies in the garden of the palace," one of his chamberlains confided to his diary. "Under the circumstances, there is nothing better for him than to divert himself and to recuperate."[26]

If the GIs digging in at the entrance to Death Valley at day's end on June 23 thought they were getting a respite, they were mistaken. At 1940, just as darkness fell, the Japanese launched a tank attack down the road through the valley. Six tanks were involved, striking the seam between the 3rd Battalion, 106th Infantry and 2nd Battalion, 165th Infantry along the roadway.

For some reason—presumably lack of vigilance—no one apparently noticed the approaching tanks. "The attack was not discovered until the leading vehicle was almost at our lines," reported L Company's Captain Hallden. "Due to the proximity of this leading vehicle, fire could not be placed upon it and therefore it came through the lines along the road." As the GIs recovered, the trailing tanks were taken under fire with everything from bazookas and antitank guns to rifle grenades. All five were knocked out, but the lead tank continued along the road "spraying everything as it went with fire from its turret gun and from machine guns," recalled Hallden. Either by intent or lucky accident, a shell from the tank's turret gun set off an abandoned Japanese munitions dump in the 3rd Battalion's area. "The dump began exploding, slowly at first, then in a mounting crescendo," recalled an officer.[27] Within minutes, ammunition was exploding in every direction.

Apparently satisfied, the tank rattled off to the east where it was finally knocked out by a bazooka team from the 23rd Marines, but the exploding ammo dump provided a beacon for Japanese on Mount Tapotchau who saturated the area with mortar and machine-gun fire. In the next twenty minutes, Hallden's company lost twelve men wounded, two of them fatally. The battalion withdrew 100 yards to get away from the inferno, thereby erasing the small gain it had achieved during the day.[28]

The 3rd Battalion's mission the next morning, June 24th, was to take care of Japanese positions in the cliffs on the western side of Death Valley. Twenty-one-year-old PFC Thomas A. Menafee jumped off on schedule with L Company at 0800, advancing about 60 yards through a clump of woods without receiving so much as a shot. Walking point, Menafee emerged from the woods to find the way barred by a towering pile of rocks. He scrambled over, only to land alongside five Japanese manning a machine gun. All six men recoiled in shock, but Menafee recovered first. He shot two of the enemy and rammed his bayonet into a third. Dropping a grenade in the lap of a fourth Japanese, he scrambled away.[29]

PFC Bob T. Brown edged around another of the rock piles and spotted five more Japanese approaching. They were lugging a light machine gun and were obviously unaware of his presence. Brown sat down, shouldered his rifle, and carefully squeezed off five shots, killing the entire enemy crew. Meanwhile, the platoon on the left had spotted two 40mm gun positions on the cliff. They opened up with rifles, but only succeeded in stirring up the entire cliff face. A tank platoon clanked up and knocked out one gun, but return fire damaged two of the tanks, one of which took a direct hit on its 75mm gun tube.

As the duel continued, 27th Division Headquarters received a call from Holland Smith's headquarters that the failure of the GIs to advance on the left was holding up the 2nd Marine Division on top of the cliffs. At 0949, Gen. Ralph Smith radioed 106th Infantry commander Col. Russell G. Ayers: "Your failure to maintain contact with unit on your left is most embarrassing. Advance on your left at once." If the general's displeasure wasn't sufficiently clear, this exhortation was followed two minutes later with: "Adv of 50 yards in one and one half hours is most unsatisfactory. Start moving at once."[30]

Ralph Smith's ultimatum came down the pipe to Lt. Col. Harold I. "Hi" Mizony, commanding the 3rd Battalion, 106th Infantry. Capt. William Heminway's K Company had been waiting while L Company pushed through the woods. Now Mizony showed Heminway the message ordering an immediate advance. "Bill, I hate to do it, but I've got to send you out there," he said.[31] Faced with the prospect of moving into the open under enemy guns in the cliffs, Heminway, a thirty-one-year old former National Guardsman from Watervliet, New York, remained philosophical. "Don't apologize, Hi," he replied. "I know how it is." He turned to go, then paused and gave the colonel a little wave, "So long, Hi. It's been damned nice knowing you."[32]

Supported by a platoon of medium tanks from the 762nd Tank Battalion, Heminway pushed out into the valley with two platoons abreast. He had picked out a small ditch about 100 yards down the slope as a natural line to pause and reorganize. Forming a long skirmish line, Heminway's platoons advanced into the open valley while the tanks and supporting arms worked over the high ground on their left. They made 50 yards before the entire cliff face opened up on them. Five men went down. The others ran for the scanty cover of the ditch, which turned out to be only about a foot deep. The fire was murderous. Six more GIs were killed and ten wounded. Heminway tried to reorganize his platoons, but as he rose to wave them forward again, he was shot in the head and killed.[33]

Three of the Sherman tanks moved farther out into the valley and opened fire on the cliff face. They were immediately taken under heavy return fire from antitank guns, mortars, and machine guns. One Sherman pulled out with a load of wounded GIs clinging to the deck. Another was hit in the rear by a high-velocity shell that destroyed the engine. The third tank, hit multiple times by antitank guns, burst into flames. The crew bailed out and ran for K Company. It was only 30 yards, but three of the tankers were wounded along the way.

Mizony called for smoke, but only one platoon got the word to withdraw. As it was, the platoon that got out lost another seven men wounded. The remaining GIs were finally extracted late that morning with the help of two tanks. Those wounded unable to walk were pulled up into the tanks through the bottom escape hatches. An eight-man patrol of volunteers helped the others, half-carrying, half-dragging some of them back to the trees at the foot of the valley using the tanks as a shield from enemy fire.

Meanwhile, Mizony's I Company also found itself in deep trouble. Sent up shortly after 1000 to fill a gap between L and K companies, Item Company walked into a hail of fire from mortars, small arms, and machine guns. By now, the whole valley was a cloud of dust. Platoon leader Lt. John P. Kolling was mortally wounded. As he lay dying, he called for P/Sgt. Benjamin Morra to take over. Morra was wounded by a mortar blast as he moved up, but managed to drag himself forward and assume command. There wasn't much he could do. Caught on an open slope, unable to lift their heads to fire back or withdraw to the tree line, the GIs were trapped. Their nightmare only worsened when three Japanese tanks charged into them down the road from the north. Lying by the body of Lieutenant Kolling, Sergeant Morra was killed by fire from one of the tanks. Thirteen other GIs were wounded, before the enemy armor was knocked out by battalion antitank platoons.[34]

By now, Mizony had every available man—including those from battalion headquarters—pouring fire into the cliff face in the effort to spring the I Company GIs from the trap. A few men from the 2nd Battalion who clambered up onto the cliff spotted a Japanese field piece on a shelf about 500 yards away. The gun was firing on GIs in the valley below. The crew would run it in and out of a cave to fire. Dozens of other Japanese were visible nearby, all blasting away at the valley floor with small arms. The GIs called in a concentration of mortar fire, which caught the Japanese gun in the act of firing, knocking it out and killing approximately thirty enemy, but the carnage on the valley floor continued.

The noise was deafening. Japanese began infiltrating into the woods toward the GIs. Several were killed by I Company's reserve platoon. Mizony finally managed to get the last of his battalion back to the shelter of the tree line at 1400. Since jumping off at 0800 the battalion had lost fourteen killed and 109 wounded. The survivors were deeply shaken. The battalion was finished for the day. Regiment sent up the 1st Battalion to relieve Mizony's men and the division dug in. The 106th had gotten nowhere. "We were thrown right back on to the original line of departure," admitted Colonel Ayers.[35]

General Ralph Smith was walking along the Chacha Road toward Love Hill south of Purple Heart Ridge at about 1500 when a jeep pulled up beside him. Holland Smith's aide climbed out, handed an envelope to the Army general, and "turned around and got the hell out before he read it."[36] Smith tore it open, read the message inside, refolded the paper, and placed it in his pocket as the jeep disappeared back down the road. Though the general did not share the contents with fellow officers at the scene, the message informed him that he was being relieved of his command. He was to turn his division over to Major General Jarman and report immediately for transportation to Pearl Harbor.[37]

The decision to relieve Ralph Smith had been made earlier in the day. During the morning Admiral Spruance's flagship *Indianapolis* dropped anchor in the transport area off Saipan so that Spruance—having sent Admiral Ozawa fleeing homeward—could confer with Adm. Kelly Turner and Holland Smith about the situation ashore. Smith and Turner brought discomfiting news. The 27th Division was not performing, said Holland Smith. The failure of the GIs to advance the previous day had left the flanks of both Marine divisions open and forced cessation of the attack. "Ralph Smith has shown that he lacks aggressive spirit," declared Howlin' Mad, "and his division is slowing our advance. He should be relieved." Smith added that he had discussed the problem with Jarman and Jarman had stated he could make the 27th Division fight if he were given command.[38]

Spruance was not oblivious to the ramifications of such an action. It was not unheard of for flag and general officers to be relieved for failure to perform, but such reliefs were typically conducted by the officer's own service and handled discreetly. In this instance, Spruance, a Navy man, would be authorizing the relief of a U.S. Army officer on the recommendation of a Marine. Such action could not help but impact interservice relations.

Smith, Turner, and Kelly searched for a tactful way to get rid of Gen. Ralph Smith without creating an uproar. The discussion, recalled Spruance's chief of staff, Carl Moore, "bid fair to be rather endless."[39] As they went round and round, Moore put together a bare bones dispatch for Spruance to sign. All three officers read the draft and approved the wording. Spruance signed the orders relieving Ralph Smith and placing General Jarman in command of the 27th Division.[40]

After reading the message along the Chacha Road, Ralph Smith returned to the 165th's command post where he conferred with his two regimental commanders. He had spent all day at the front, attempting to get his division under control. "He showed a tremendous amount of bravery—took charge in organizing things, talking to company and battalion commanders, and getting the front organized, primarily for the next day's attack," recalled Maj. Jacob Herzog, the division's assistant G-2.[41] The general said nothing about being relieved of command. The discussion focused instead on a plan he had formulated to deal with the Death Valley defenses. Smith then left for his division command post. He arrived at about 1700 to find General Jarman waiting for him.[42]

Despite Holland Smith's claim that Jarman had said he could get the GIs moving, the Army general had resisted taking command of the division, telling Graves Erskine he didn't want the job. Smith and Erskine gave it to him anyway, with the admonishment from Erskine, "If you want any briefing or anything here, say what you want and I'll give it to you, but that outfit's got to get going or you'll get the sack."[43]

Now, as Ralph Smith and General Jarman conferred, it became clear that Jarman had no idea as to what was going on in the front lines. Smith contacted NTLF headquarters and was granted permission to remain with Jarman until the following morning in order to orient him on the situation. This orientation included the plan Smith had formulated for the next day's attack on Death Valley.

Smith had come to the conclusion that a direct assault into the valley was impracticable due to the defenses along the cliff wall. He proposed to bypass the center of resistance. According to this plan, Colonel Ayers would take two battalions of his 106th Regiment out of the line before daylight and march them about a mile up the eastern side of Purple Heart Ridge before turning west into the valley. This maneuver would put them beyond Hill Able at the far end of Purple Heart Ridge. As they secured their hold on the end of the valley, the 165th Infantry would follow and tie in with the 106th's right flank. Once a new division front had been consolidated, the advance to the north would resume. The lone battalion of the 106th at the southern end of the valley would clear out the bypassed Japanese with help from the division reserve if necessary.[44]

Jarman agreed with the plan—no wonder, as Ralph Smith later observed, "that was about the only plan going"[45]—and the regimental commanders were briefed accordingly. At 2230 NTLF headquarters contacted 27th Division and ordered General Smith to report to Blue Beach before 0330 where he would be provided with air transportation back to Hawaii. Smith and Jarman ended their discussion. Smith packed his belongings and left for Blue Beach shortly before midnight. At 0500 he boarded a Mariner PBM seaplane for the ten-hour flight to Eniwetok.[46]

The Army commander was gone, but Holland Smith would soon find he had not solved his issues with the 27th Division. Worse still, he had lighted the fuse to an interservice powder keg.

CHAPTER XVIII

Into the Valley

0200: June 25, 1944

OBLIVIOUS TO THE RUMINATIONS OF GENERALS AND ADMIRALS, THREE enlisted Marines from C Company, 1st Battalion, 6th Marines, crouched behind their Browning light machine gun in the rugged hills north of Mount Tipo Pale, hoping they'd live to see the sunrise. Two of the three— PFC Malcolm "Mac" Jonah and PFC Harold Epperson—had survived the carnage of Tarawa the preceding November. The third, nineteen-year-old PFC Edward "Ted" Bailey of Yakima, Washington, was new to the outfit.

On this night they had set up to the left of a 37mm gun overlooking an open area about 50 yards wide. Considering the heavy undergrowth they had been moving through the past couple of days, it was a good spot. "The terrain towards the Japs was fairly open with some thick bushes about three to five feet high," recalled Jonah. "[At] 0200 Epp took over the watch on the machine gun and I was relieved." Epperson, familiarly known as "Egghead," was "a gung ho sort of kid," recalled Jonah. "He came from a big football area and had that football kind of attitude.... He was a go-getter type."

Jonah had scarcely turned over the gun when a small counterattack developed. "We were all awake then...." There were maybe fifteen or twenty Japanese total, Jonah guessed, and they came not in a mad rush but in spurts, using what cover was available. The 37mm gun to Jonah's right blew one of the infiltrators to pieces, but others kept coming. "When they were right in front of us, they threw grenades and attacked," recalled Jonah.

The first grenade missed their foxhole, but was followed by an earsplitting explosion as some sort of demolition charge landed by the adjacent 37mm gun. "Jap bayonets flashed in the moonlight and came directly for us—about six of them," recalled Bailey. "We tried to knock them down with our carbines. Two of them ran right by us and jumped into the 37 pit. We could hear the sound of clubbing and knifing going on. When they thought the two Nips were dead, they threw their bodies out of their gun pit a few yards in front of our gun."

Then the grenade came arcing down. "We saw the sputtering light of a grenade come into the foxhole," recalled Jonah. Epperson pushed away from the gun and went for the grenade, shielding the others. Bailey tried to roll away while the grenade was still in the air. "Before I could move very far, the blast went off. I felt the shrapnel skim over my body." Shielded by Epperson's body, he and Jonah survived the blast. Epperson was also still alive, though grievously hurt—the explosion had torn away much of his left arm and shoulder.

Dazed, Bailey heard the machine gun start up. His first thought was that the Japanese had taken over the gun, but when he looked up he saw Jonah was sweeping the ground to his front. Jonah later testified he had taken over from Epperson who, despite his terrible injury, had pulled himself back up behind the machine gun after the grenade blast. "After he took the whack, he got back up and fired the gun for a while with half of his shoulder gone," said Jonah. Epperson soon slid away from the gun and collapsed. Jonah took over the machine gun and sprayed the field in front as Epperson sprawled at the bottom of the pit with his lifeblood hemorrhaging out of him. There was little Jonah and Bailey could do for him, even when the immediate Japanese threat had passed. "We had no way of getting him out of there to get medical attention," said Jonah of their impossible situation.

A corpsman eventually materialized. He stuck Epperson with a morphine syrette, but couldn't do much about the bleeding. They waited in the hole with their friend until finally, at first light of dawn, they heard a jeep chugging up the hill. Epperson was still alive, but clearly near death. "We loaded Egghead onto a stretcher on the jeep," recalled Bailey. "He was turning gray from the massive loss of blood."[1] The jeep jolted off, but it was a useless effort. Epperson died soon after. With cool bureaucratic detachment, NTLF subsequently logged a report from the 6th Marines that "they killed eight members of a Jap demolitions team which unsuccessfully attempted to destroy a 37mm gun."[2]

As morning arrived, hot and steamy over Death Valley, General Jarman prepared to implement Ralph Smith's plan to bypass the core of enemy resistance and bring the GIs abreast of the 2nd and 4th Marine Divisions to the north. The entrance to Death Valley remained littered with unburied corpses from the previous two days of fighting. "There were probably about a dozen dead enemy soldiers lying within about seventy-five feet of us, and the sun made them ripen quickly," recalled 1st Lt. Leigh M. Trowbridge, who had come up with a forward observation party from the 104th Field Artillery. The body of Capt. Bill Heminway still lay about 100 yards away on the valley floor. Trowbridge had played bridge with Heminway—"a real nice guy"—aboard ship before the division came ashore. Now the affable captain was just another bloated corpse adding to the describable stench in the air. A sober Trowbridge observed, "There is one thing the best of war movies cannot duplicate: smell."[3]

The 27th Division's plan for June 25 involved pulling two battalions of the 106th Infantry from the mouth of Death Valley and slipping them around to the right of Purple Heart Ridge. Consisting of a succession of hills labeled Queen, Love, George-How, Xray-Yoke, Oboe, and King, the ridge terminated in Hill Able, which was where the GIs planned to cut back into the valley, leaving the main enemy defenses behind. The 1st Battalion, commanded by forty-four-year-old Lt. Col. Winslow Cornett, a square-jawed former enlisted man who had earned two Silver Stars and a Purple Heart in heavy combat with the First Infantry Division in World War I, would spearhead the effort.

As was becoming typical with the 27th Division, the movement got off to an inauspicious start. The 0600 jump-off was delayed for an hour and a half while the 2nd Battalion, 106th extended its lines to seal off the southern end of the valley. Cornett finally got his battalion moving up the Chacha Road to Lt. Louis Fleck's burned-out tank where the dead crew still lay among shards of glass from Japanese Molotov cocktails. Here the road looped well out to the east into the 4th Marine Division's zone of operations. Ralph Smith's plan called for the battalion to leave the road and continue cross country along the base of the ridge. Cornett, riding in a jeep at the head of the column, considered the descent too steep for his vehicles so he radioed regiment and received permission to stay on the roadway. That decision had two potentially serious ramifications: The amended route took him farther away from the ridgeline, and it encroached on the zone of the 4th Marine Division.[4]

Nevertheless, Cornett's battalion reached a road junction near Hill Able at about 1030. There the road climbed gradually upward, proceeding northwest through grassy open terrain toward Purple Heart Ridge.

Approximately 200 yards from the ridge, the road passed between two knobby hills and crossed some open ground before entering Death Valley just north of Hill Able. Cornett sent two companies to seize the knobs. Supported by howitzers, antitank guns, and all the battalion machine guns, Company A seized the northernmost knob within twenty minutes at a cost of four men killed and seventeen wounded, including the company commander. They then waited for two long hours for B Company to come up and take the southernmost hill. B Company finally arrived at 1410, having lost one man killed and four wounded during a 400-yard advance.

The battalion was now within 200 yards of Purple Heart Ridge and Hill Able. What the GIs didn't know was that they were knocking on the door of General Saito's recently evacuated command post. Much later, when this ground was finally captured, it would give up twenty radios and the message files of General Saito's communications with Tokyo. Of more immediate concern, the area was defended by an estimated battalion of infantry armed with as many as twenty-five machine guns and supported by three tanks that had been dug into revetments. Four artillery pieces and several 37mm guns added to enemy firepower. Pillboxes blocked access to the ridge from the two newly seized knolls.[5]

The GIs had been hoping for an end run around Death Valley. Instead, by sheer bad luck, they had walked straight into one of the most heavily defended positions on the island. All efforts to push beyond the knolls were thrown back. The 3rd Battalion remained at the junction on the Chacha Road waiting to join the advance—an opportunity that never arrived. Meanwhile, the road, which was in the Marine division's sector, became seriously congested. The Japanese took notice and registered artillery on the traffic, creating havoc. When the Marines complained, 106th Infantry commander Col. Russell G. Ayers insisted that his battalions were well within the 27th Division zone. When it became obvious that he was mistaken, Ayers ordered the 3rd Battalion back to the mouth of Death Valley.

Just before darkness, Cornett conceded defeat and pulled his men back to the road. The next morning they straggled back to Death Valley. Few of the GIs had so much as seen a Japanese soldier during the day. The now-absent Ralph Smith's hopes of extricating his GIs from a knife fight by use of maneuver had come to naught.[6]

Eleven days after the landing, Lt. John Chapin's men found some much-appreciated water in a cistern on the side of a ridge. Chapin took a bath of sorts with the water in his helmet. "Then, in the filthy black water that remained, I washed my only pair of socks. They hadn't been off my feet for twelve solid days. . . ." A couple of men came up with razors, which were passed around. "It was really great to be alive," observed Chapin—a gratification that was brought home to him as he looked at the remnants of his platoon. Out of the original platoon strength of fifty men who had come ashore on D-day, only twenty were left.[7]

Chapin's platoon was far from alone in its losses. With casualties mounting beyond expectations and no immediate end in sight, NTLF was compelled to abandon a now unworkable scheme to replace combat losses. Anticipating a quick campaign, NTLF had planned to replace losses in the 2nd Division with personnel from the 4th Marine Division as the latter departed the area. But the 4th Division had been hit hard. One battalion— the 3rd Battalion, 23rd Marines—had taken so many casualties it had to be reorganized into just two companies. With both divisions engaged in heavy combat beyond the anticipated timetable, a replacement draft was hastily organized at the Transient Center in Hawaii and 1,693 officers and men were dispatched to the battlefront; 848 subsequently went to the 2nd Division and 845 to the 4th Division.[8]

The setbacks only intensified Holland Smith's determination to expedite the push to the north, seize the high ground looking down on his forces, and get things moving. The main objectives for the two Marine divisions on June 25 were Mount Tapotchau to the west of Death Valley and Kagman Peninsula on the east coast. The groundwork for the assault on Tapotchau had been laid on June 22 when the 6th Marines clambered to the top of 1,100-foot Tipo Pale about 1,200 yards to the southwest. Possession of Tipo Pale was essential to any movement up the western slope of Tapotchau, which was the bigger prize.

The push up Tapotchau began the morning of June 25 with a two-pronged advance through terrain the division historian described as the geological equivalent of "a handful of rusty razor blades jumbled in a box."[9] Col. Rathvon Tompkins's "Orphan Battalion," the 1st Battalion, 29th Marines, attacked up a valley to the front, while the 2nd Battalion, 8th Marines attempted to negotiate a ridgeline on the right flank. The valley turned out to be infested with enemy, but the 2nd Battalion had better luck. Perhaps because Japanese attention was focused on the lower slopes, the battalion managed to climb several hundred yards and by mid-morning reached the foot of a sheer, 50-foot cliff at the base of the actual peak. Maj. William C.

Chamberlin, who had taken over the 2nd Battalion after Colonel Crowe was wounded on D-day, sent an E Company platoon commanded by Lt. Walt Rimmer scrambling up the rocky cliff. To their good fortune, they found no one waiting for them as they came over the edge. Rimmer sent a patrol to explore farther up the mountainside to a small plateau. It, too, was deserted.

Seizing the opportunity, Colonel Tompkins sent 1st Lt. Marion M. Drake's twenty-three-man Reconnaissance Company platoon up to the crest. "For some reason or another the Japs had leveled the very tip of the mountain and there was a flat area about thirty feet in diameter right at the tip of the highest point," observed Drake. There was also a large enemy dugout—about 12 feet square and deep enough to stand upright in—nearby, but no defenders. "When we arrived there was a Jap apparently asleep in the [dugout] and he ran off before we could get our sights on him," noted Drake.[10]

The recon Marines established a hasty perimeter while Tompkins went back for more men. "Tommy told me he would return and get the battalion and come hell or high water would get back there by dark that evening," said Drake. "He asked me if we could hold the mountain and I told him I thought we could sure try."

Gazing out over the expanse to the north and east, Marine observers could see enemy troops and vehicles heading north in the far distance. It didn't take long for the Japanese to realize they'd been hoodwinked. "They started coming at us about an hour later and my guys had something of a turkey shoot," recalled Drake. To get to the recon Marines, the Japanese had to cross a cleared area, which made them easy targets. Drake's men killed about twenty-five of them. "It was one of the rather sickening sights to watch because when the guys shot them they all seemed to have a grenade that they pulled the pin on and blew themselves up," observed Drake.[11]

Drake pulled his men up to the very top, positioning them in a circle with their feet inboard. As the afternoon wore on and light faded with no sign of Tompkins and the promised battalion, some of the Marines began getting a little nervous. "Just as we could barely see at all, I heard the battalion coming up the back side of the mountain . . ." said Drake. It was Tompkins with Companies A and C of the Orphan Battalion. By now there were only about forty men in each company, well below the normal complement of about 215. Pvt. Frank Borta's A Company settled in on the narrow plateau. The mountaintop was mostly rock and digging in was a challenge. The Marines compensated by piling up makeshift rock barricades and settled down to wait. They could hear Japanese talking below them and someone seemed to be waving a flashlight around.

The Japanese hit them after dark. "The attack started when two Marines were scraping out a foxhole when a flare lit up the sky," recalled Borta. "One of the Marines was silhouetted against the sky. A Jap stabbed him in the back with a bayonet tied to a long pole. He screamed and fell over the cliff. His friend looked down for him and was shot in the head." Again and again the Japanese tried to sweep the Marines off the mountaintop. "All night long they would holler, 'Maline you die!' or 'Corpsman!'" recalled Borta. "We would drop hand grenades down on them."

After venturing out in search of more grenades, Borta returned to find Pvt. Wallace "Chief" Querta, a nineteen-year-old from the Walapai Indian Reservation in Arizona, huddled in his shallow foxhole. Groaning in pain, Querta gasped that his foxhole had been overrun and he had been bayoneted. His companion had been killed. Borta couldn't see very well in the dark, but he felt around for the wound and his hand came away wet with blood. He gave Querta some water from his canteen, then crawled off to the company command post in the slim hope he could locate a corpsman. His captain promised to send a corpsman to help Querta and told Borta to join a replacement BAR man on the flank. He was drifting in and out of sleep during the early morning hours when the new man suddenly opened up with his BAR. Jolted awake, Borta looked out over the edge of the hole. "I heard something," the new man whispered. Borta was disgusted. For all he knew, the rookie had gunned down some luckless Marine trying to take a crap. He told the man to stand down while he took over. As the sun came up, Borta found that his annoyance with the rookie BAR man had been misplaced. Four dead Japanese lay just beyond their foxhole, cut down by a single burst from the BAR. The greenhorn had saved his life.[12]

Another Marine was less fortunate. As morning arrived, a mortar shell landed in his foxhole. The explosion "blew out his guts, ripped off his hand . . ." observed Borta. "He was still living but just groaning. We covered him with a poncho to keep the flies off, and fifteen minutes later buried him there."[13]

The arrival of the 27th Division GIs had taken some of the pressure off the 4th Marine Division. The push by the 24th Marines up the coast the day before had met little resistance, but it did demonstrate the wisdom of cancelling the harebrained D minus 1 landing of a battalion over the Purple

Beaches to capture Mount Tapotchau. The beaches were backed by an extensive trench system, barbed wire, artificial obstacles, blockhouses, well-sited 120mm guns, and two 200mm mortars. While taken without difficulty by the assault from the flank and rear, the area would have been a killing ground for Marines attempting to come in by sea.

Once in possession of the Purple Beaches, the 23rd and 24th Marines jumped off the morning of June 25 to sweep the Kagman Peninsula. Chaplain W. Charles Goe watched through binoculars as tanks moved out into the peninsula's open cane fields. "They didn't seem to have much trouble, and our infantry followed on with apparently light resistance. We soon learned that most of the Japanese had evacuated the area. . . ."[14]

As had been the case with the Purple Beaches, the Marines found the Brown Beaches on the northwestern part of the peninsula well fortified against an amphibious landing—including an extensive trench system extending the width of the beaches and to a depth of 150 yards inland. Bunkers and firing apertures faced out to sea. One 20mm gun position boasted concrete walls 5 feet thick with another 8 feet of concrete overhead.

Lt. John Chapin came across a large gun emplacement sited to fire down the beach line, but the guns had never been installed. They lay nearby on wooden skids, "huge, 5-inch, dual purpose naval guns thickly covered with grease and wrapped in burlap."[15] Phony coastal defense guns constructed from logs had been set out to draw enemy fire. There was even a mock watchtower, complete with a scarecrow observer. "He was holding binoculars and looking toward Magicienne Bay," recalled Tibor Torok. "We fired a few rounds at him, but he didn't move. And we found out why. It was a dummy. A very lifelike dummy, just to draw our fire."[16]

PFC John Pope encountered one of the few stragglers when a Japanese officer emerged from a bunker with a pistol in hand. "It was one of those surreal moments for me," remembered Pope. "I did not hear anything. I just stood and stared down that man's arm as he pointed that gun at me. The muzzle of the pistol was a dark hole with fire coming out, then another black hole [and] more fire when he pulled the trigger again. As I looked down his arm behind the pistol I could see in great detail [that] his tunic was covered with loose dirt and dust from crawling out of the hole."

As if in a fog, Pope was shooting back. "I could see what appeared to be little puffs of dust as if someone was thumping his chest the way you would thump a watermelon. As I watched, it began to look as though the pistol was suddenly too heavy for him to hold up. He tried to bring it back up using both hands but his arm continued to sag, lowering the pistol in spite of his best effort. His knees gave way and he fell and died about ten feet from where I was standing."[17]

By 1145, all of Kagman Peninsula was in American hands. The 23rd Marines had also made good gains, despite harassment from a single Japanese field piece or antitank gun located on Purple Heart Ridge in the Army's area of operations. Some of the men took the opportunity to venture out into surf along the Kagman ledges to wash off the accumulated filth from a week and a half of combat. "We had gone all of this time without a change of clothing, without shaving and without a bath," observed Sgt. Harry Pearce. "My dungaree trousers had rotted off at the knees. I no longer had any leggings. All that I carried was a poncho and a cartridge belt, my helmet and a pack I had retrieved from a dead Marine."[18]

Now in reserve up on Hill 500, Justice Chambers was also tending to his hygiene. "It was a hot, sultry day," he said. "I took off my shoes for the first time since landing on the island. I was pulling chunks of meat from between my toes, when I heard this soft voice coming from down the hill, 'Well, I'll be a goddamned son of a bitch!'"

Chambers glanced up to see Sgt. Lewis E. Robinson of the Scout Sniper Platoon holding out a baggy pair of issue dungaree trousers. Robinson, who was about 6-foot-3 and "skinny as a rail," saw Chambers looking at him. "Colonel," he said, holding up the trousers. "Isn't that the damnedest thing!" A bullet had gone through both legs by the upper thighs without touching Robinson, who had been wearing them at the time. "There was no way this could happen, but it did," said Chambers.

Robinson grinned at Chambers, and remarked, "I bet I know just when this happened, Colonel, and if I hadn't been thinking of my wife's sister, I'd be a ruined man today!"

Still chuckling years later, Chambers observed, "I loved these guys."[19]

On the other side of the island, anchoring the 2nd Division flank just south of Garapan, the 2nd Marine Regiment sent patrols prowling through the outskirts of town the morning of June 25. Garapan's once neat streets were choked with piles of rubble, riddled tin roofing that rattled noisily underfoot, chunks of concrete, and charred timbers. Some of the streets had been mined with converted aerial bombs and there was an occasional sniper. Of particular interest were a couple of red framed buildings the Marines figured to be "geisha houses." The hallways were littered with brightly colored kimonos along with thousands of condoms and numerous bottles of cheap perfume, which the conquering Marines happily poured on each other's stinking dungarees. A dead cow lay in the backyard.

The aroma was not improved by the remnants of a Japanese tank/infantry counterattack from the night before. A half-dozen Japanese tanks had been knocked out. One was still smoldering when Bob Sherrod dropped by that morning. Eighty-three Japanese were killed, including a navy commander from the *55th Naval Guard Force*. Their corpses, now buzzing with thousands of flies, lay in contorted heaps around the vanquished armor. "One tankman's crisp, upraised hands stuck out of his turret, as if in supplication to a power beyond his reach," wrote Sherrod. The dead enlisted men wore the usual wrap leggings and split-toed shoes; the officers sported black rubber boots. Sleeve patches embroidered with an anchor identified them as navy troops.[20]

Scouting through the ruined town, PFC Guy Gabaldon and Corp. Clifford Jolly came upon a substantial-looking concrete building just as two Japanese soldiers emerged. Gabaldon, who had learned rudimentary Japanese from Nisei friends while growing up in East Los Angeles, yelled at them, "*Te o agete, haiyaku, koroshitakunai da*" (Raise your hands and I won't kill you). They spun toward him, one of them drawing his sword. "I fired off fifteen rounds, point blank," said Gabaldon. "They were so close that it wasn't necessary to aim. I emptied the clip right from the hip. They both fell, one down the steps onto the grass, the other on the concrete deck."

Gabaldon shoved a fresh magazine into his carbine. One of the Japanese lay dead in the grass, but the one with the sword was still squirming. His left arm had been nearly shot off and he was bleeding from bullet wounds to his torso. As Gabaldon approached him, the wounded Japanese tried to lash out with his sword. Gabaldon shot him in the head.[21]

In the center, the gathering darkness on June 25 brought terror to dozens of GIs from the 2nd Battalion, 106th Infantry, who had ventured into the maw of Death Valley during the afternoon. Hoping to get something going, General Jarman ordered battalion commander Maj. Almerin O'Hara to slip two companies north along the base of the cliff looming over the western side of the corridor. The objective was a line of trees that crossed the valley about 600 yards from the line of departure. Once there, they would deploy and quickly advance to a second line of trees 200 yards farther away.

Spotted from the heights, the two companies—E and G—came under a hail of fire, pinning down GIs that survived the scramble to the second tree line. Commanding a platoon from E Company, twenty-two-year-old Lt. Elwin F. Cassady of Lyndonville, Vermont, found himself out of contact with the rest of the company. He hung on for a while, but with darkness gathering and believing he was alone, Cassady decided to pull his men back to the first line of trees. Taking note of a small lane that ran from his tree line back through the tall grass on the floor of the valley, he started to send the platoon back one man at a time. But the Japanese were already in motion. The first GI had no sooner moved out than Cassady discovered that large numbers of Japanese had infiltrated into the tall grass and were closing on the platoon's position. What he had intended as an orderly withdrawal quickly degenerated into a gut-wrenching exercise in pure terror.

The division historian reported, "Americans would rise to run a few steps and enemy soldiers would pop up out of the grass on all sides to intercept them. Cassady instructed his riflemen to watch closely where the enemy were, then to train rifles on the spot and shoot every time a Japanese showed himself. As the movement progressed farther to the rear, the platoon broke up into small groups to cover one another. The enemy soon adopted the same tactics and the field between the two tree lines became a madhouse of men jumping up and down to take a shot at one another."

Still in the second tree line, G Company was also under heavy pressure. Among the casualties was the company medic, Joseph Lusardi, who suffered a compound fracture of the leg. Despite his injury, Lusardi dragged a wounded sergeant to cover, then crawled around helping casualties where he could. Company commander Capt. David B. Tarrant, a former newspaper circulation manager and Guardsman with the old 7th New York Regiment, ordered his men to prepare defensive positions for the night, but soon began to have second thoughts as large numbers of Japanese filtered down onto the valley floor and began probing his position.

PFC Allen R. Kennedy volunteered to take a radio and head back in an effort to locate E Company. As he made his way through the tall grass, he stumbled upon an E Company lieutenant and seven wounded GIs hiding in a ditch. The lieutenant directed Kennedy to E Company captain David Waterson, who contacted Tarrant on Kennedy's radio. By now Tarrant realized that his position was perilous. He and Waterson agreed that they should withdraw while they still could.

The decision came none too soon. As Tarrant's men moved out they bumped into a band of Japanese, sparking a point-blank shootout in the tall grass. Tarrant maintained control and the GIs made their way back to the ditch where the wounded E Company men were holed up. G Company was already lugging its own wounded, including their medic, Lusardi, who had become delirious and had to be carried on a rifle litter. Now they picked up the others. The whole valley seemed to be infested with Japanese. An E Company survivor later said some groups as large as a company had passed by as he hid in the ditch.

By 2230 the survivors of the two companies had made it back to the first tree line. Unable to contact Major O'Hara at battalion, Tarrant and Waterson talked over their situation. They were out of water and low on ammunition. There were Japanese everywhere. Once daylight came, they could expect to attract murderous attention from the Tapotchau cliffs. At about midnight, they tried once again to contact O'Hara for instructions, once more without success. Left on their own, they agreed they should withdraw back to the mouth of the valley.

Incredibly, the two officers decided to leave their wounded—many of them in great pain and unable to walk on their own—for fear they would give the others away. The casualties would remain behind under the protection of a volunteer guard. Once the others had reached safety, a tank could be sent to bring them out. E Company had already moved out in a long column, and G was preparing to follow when an E Company sergeant stopped Captain Tarrant. The sergeant told Tarrant he didn't think many of the wounded would survive to see the promised tank and asked permission to bring them out with G Company. Tarrant relented and detailed a platoon to help, quite possibly averting a massacre.

For the next two hours the American column zigzagged across the valley floor, freezing in its tracks as flares popped overhead. At one point the light of a descending flare revealed foxholes filled with enemy troops. Perhaps mistaking the column for fellow Japanese, the occupants didn't fire. At the rear of the American column, the walking wounded dragged themselves painfully along. Those unable to walk were borne on makeshift litters. Some of them died, relieving their weary bearers of their burden. Among the fatalities was G Company's heroic medic, Joseph Lusardi, who bled to death.

About three hours after midnight, the column finally stumbled into outposts manned by the 165th Infantry. Too exhausted to dig foxholes, the GIs dropped to the ground and went to sleep. The wounded were passed on back to the battalion aid station. But not everyone was accounted for. Though Captain Tarrant didn't realize it, ten of his men under the command of sergeants Carl P. Swineford and Herman Salisbury had missed the withdrawal order. Hearing whispers of "Come on, come on," they feared it was Japanese trying to pinpoint their location so they didn't respond.

As the night progressed and the Japanese seemed to have moved off, Swineford, in charge of a three-man outpost, decided to check in with Captain Tarrant. Creeping back through the grass, he discovered the company was gone. Swineford alerted his three companions, then tried to find Salisbury who had settled in with a five-man outpost just to the north. Unable to locate Salisbury, Swineford's group headed south. In the early morning hours, after repeatedly hiding from groups of wandering Japanese, they stumbled into the lines of the 165th Infantry. No one knew the fate of the six GIs left behind.[22]

The attempted envelopment of Purple Heart Ridge had failed, the victim of poor coordination, a failure to press the attack, and a certain amount of plain bad luck. General Jarman was not pleased with the performance of the 106th Infantry or its commander on June 25. The fifty-one-year-old Ayers, who was apparently something of a showboat—a fellow officer recalled he "walked around with a swagger stick and changed his uniform three or four times a day"—had arrived on Saipan with a reputation for overcaution and inefficiency, and nothing he had done since had contradicted that impression.[23]

Jarman asked Ayers to explain the failed attack. He seemed "muddled," reported Jarman. "He had no excuse and could offer no explanation of anything he did during the day. He stated he felt sure he could get his regiment in hand and forward the next morning (June 26). I told him he had one more chance and if he did not handle his regiment, I would relieve him."[24]

Jarman did not have long to wait. When the 106th Infantry assault again bogged down the following day, he sent his artillery commander, Brig. Gen. Redmond Kernan, and his operations chief, Lt. Col. Fredric Sheldon, forward to see if artillery might be employed to help punch the way through the valley. The two staff officers returned with unsettling news about the 106th's performance. "They both came back and stated that the battalions were standing still and there was no reason why they should not move forward . . . ," recalled Jarman. "They indicated that the regiment was somewhat demoralized and they didn't know whether it would ever move."[25]

Jarman's patience, already worn thin, now snapped. He immediately dispatched division chief of staff Col. Albert K. Stebbins to relieve Ayers of his command. The executive officer was also relieved. Ayers returned to

Jarman's headquarters shortly before noon and was sent packing to Pearl Harbor. General Jarman followed this house cleaning with a message of encouragement to all 27th Division units:

> *This division is advancing against a determined enemy that must be destroyed. Upon capturing a position, never give it up; hold and send reinforcements. I know I can depend on every member of the 27th to get into this fight with everything he has. Good hunting to every man.*[26]

Martial rhetoric notwithstanding, Stebbins was compelled to spend the rest of the afternoon attempting to reorganize the dispirited battalions. "He stated that they seemed to lack the will to go forward," reported Jarman; "he had to personally get the units in hand and show them where to go and push the battalions out." Jarman observed it was "apparent that upon the first firings of any kind by snipers the battalions immediately asked to be allowed to retire."[27] In a subsequent report to General Richardson, Jarman observed, "a lack of offensive spirit among the division in general. A battalion will run into one machine gun and be held up for several hours. When they get any kind of minor resistance they immediately open up with everything they have that can fire in the general direction from which they are being fired upon."[28]

After the campaign, Colonel Ayers was asked what he thought the result would have been had he pressed the attack and charged into the open ground to his front. Ayers replied, "My candid opinion is that the regiment would have disappeared."[29] Stebbins would later concede that the GIs were up against a tough nut. And while the GIs seemed to lack élan, he agreed with his predecessor that a headlong assault was not the answer. "Rush and die tactics would never have succeeded," he observed later.[30]

The number of tanks lost in the fighting reflected the level of enemy resistance in Death Valley. On June 24 alone, the 27th Division reported that four medium tanks had been knocked out and ten others required repairs. All damage was due to heavy antitank gun fire.[31] The 762nd Tank Battalion had arrived on Saipan with seventy-two vehicles. As of June 27th, only ten medium and eighteen light tanks remained in operating condition. Almost all of the damaged or destroyed armor had been hit in the Death Valley area since June 23.[32]

The fate of Tank #54 in the 766th Tank Battalion's Company D the morning of June 27 demonstrated the lethality of the constricted valley. The tank was shelling the cliffs when the driver made the mistake of exposing its side to an enemy gun. A high-velocity shell pierced the armor, sending slivers of steel ricocheting around the crew compartment. Three of the crew, two of them wounded, bailed out just as two more shells hit the tank in rapid succession. The bow gunner, twenty-three-year-old Pvt. Martin L. Petosa, didn't make it. His badly burned body was found several days later, still inside the tank.[33]

If anyone had cause to be discouraged by developments in Death Valley, it was Sgt. Herman Salisbury and his five-man outpost, who had spent the last day and a half trying to avoid Japanese notice on the floor of that killing ground. As the sun edged into view over Purple Heart Ridge the morning of June 26, the six GIs had no idea they had been abandoned. But daylight brought trouble as a Japanese machine gunner on the cliff picked them out on the valley floor. A burst of fire caught PFC Glen E. Fultz in the legs. Sgt. Patrick F. Massineo crawled over to Fultz—a twenty-two-year-old former bakery worker who had been in the Army scarcely a year—and tried to bind up his shattered legs with the contents of his personal aid kit. Only when Massineo called for a company aid man did the GIs discover they were on their own. There was no medic. There was no company, just them.

They were debating what to do when a second machine gun opened up on them, followed by a third. Japanese riflemen joined in. Massineo and Salisbury grabbed Fultz by the arms and dragged him into a little ditch to get him out of the line of fire. The five uninjured GIs decided their only chance was to leave Fultz and bug out for friendly lines, but they were reluctant to expose themselves to the guns on the cliffs. In the end, they took shelter in foxholes where they stayed pinned down for the rest of the day without food or water. Fultz remained in the shallow ditch where they had left him. Every attempt to reach him only attracted a deluge of fire from the cliffs.

By late afternoon Fultz had become delirious. He finally quieted, apparently losing consciousness as darkness fell. Night also brought Japanese patrols down from the cliffs. The GIs had hoped to make a break for their own lines under cover of darkness, but there were too many enemy patrols prowling the valley floor. Several times Japanese passed within a few feet of them. With morning, the Japanese disappeared and the Americans settled in for another day. Fultz had regained consciousness and seemed somewhat better, but remained in considerable pain.[34]

While the bulk of the 27th Division struggled to make headway in Death Valley, the 2nd Battalion, 105th Infantry continued its efforts to eradicate

Captain Saito's holdouts on Nafutan Point. As Gen. Ralph Smith had fore-seen, lack of numbers and the expanded frontage severely restricted the battalion's effectiveness. Nevertheless, the GIs had begun to see some successes thanks to the assistance of light Stuart tanks from the 766th Tank Battalion.

On June 23, three tanks led by Lt. Willis K. Dorey spotted a column of Japanese troops moving through a sugar cane field down in Nafutan Valley. The tankers charged after them, firing into "brush, caves, houses and dugouts." They set several small ammunition dumps ablaze and destroyed a 75mm and one 47mm gun. Three Japanese clambered on top of a tank and tried to knock it out with hand grenades. Two were swept off the vehicle by machine-gun fire from the other Stuarts; the third escaped. One tank driver reported the slopes had been "swarming" with Japanese. The tankers estimated they had killed as many as 200 enemy—a claim greeted with some skepticism.

The next day, supported by self-propelled howitzers (SPs), the GIs overran a rock wall barricade on Ridge 300, knocking out four machine guns. Sweeping along the extended nose of Mount Nafutan, they found no live Japanese, but counted approximately 150 dead, apparently killed by Dorey's tanks the day before. Dorey's tanks chalked up another victory on June 24, slipping "through an opening between two huge boulders barely wide enough to let the tanks pass," to make an end run on two enemy dual-purpose guns. Coming from behind, the tanks took the guns under point-blank fire, destroying both and killing dozens of Japanese.[35]

On the afternoon of June 25, supported by tanks and machine guns, the GIs rushed the Japanese defensive line on Ridge 300. It was over within minutes. The GIs found six machine guns, seventeen mortars, two wrecked dual-purpose guns, and large quantities of abandoned grenades and ammunition. Over a hundred dead Japanese lay sprawled about. The carnage came as a pleasant surprise to one platoon commander who noted he hadn't seen more than three live Japanese over the past several days.[36]

Captured documents later revealed that by nightfall on June 25 Captain Sasaki's force had no more heavy automatic weapons. Ammunition was in short supply and food and water were running out. Japanese mortar fire, so deadly in previous days, seemed to have tapered off, indicating the enemy might be running short of ammunition. A Japanese sailor chronicled the deteriorating situation in his diary:

June 21: No food or water It's quite a hardship . . . In everyone's mind he is thinking that before he dies he would like to have a belly full of water, but there is none to be had.

June 22: Oh! I wish our fleet and air force would come to help us! . . . The naval shelling is terrible.

June 25: To die instantly is simple but to fight on and on is hard. No way to treat the wounded; I feel very sorry for them. The enemy planes are taking off from Aslito Airfield, flying freely in the air; it's maddening to see them flying.

June 26 [last entry]: The shelling began before dawn; the mortar and naval shelling increased today. The shrapnel is flying everywhere and it is getting very dangerous. Between the shelling, I can hear the enemy machine gun and rifle fire nearing us. Why don't our reinforcements come? I wonder if they don't need Saipan any more.[37]

Sgt. Angelo D. Nicoletti saw indications of a pending collapse when he led a patrol into one of the side ravines that ran up into Nafutan's interior. A week earlier, the twenty-four-year-old from Brooklyn, New York, had skipped out of sick bay when his unit went ashore, despite still suffering from drainage from removal of a gangrenous appendix.[38] Now, making his way up the ravine, Nicoletti spotted considerable activity around the entrance of a large cave. Japanese soldiers were coming and going, while other groups gathered outside as if waiting for orders. Nicoletti promptly got on the radio and called in air burst fire from the 751st Antiaircraft Artillery Battalion. The first salvo landed dead on. Later in the afternoon, the GIs saw enemy personnel burning papers outside the cave. Eventually the Japanese made off into the hills.[39]

What no one realized was that the Nafutan Point defenders had had enough. Under constant artillery and naval gunfire, short on food and water and on the verge of being overrun, Captain Sasaki decided to lead a breakout. He hoped to link up with friendly forces at the *47th Independent Mixed Brigade* headquarters at Hill 500, not realizing this strongpoint was now in American hands. On June 26, the captain issued what was presumably his final battalion order, stating in part:

> *"The Battalion will carry out an attack at midnight tonight. After caus-*
> *ing confusion at the airfield, we will advance to Brigade Headquarters*
> *in the Field . . . Casualties will remain in their present positions and*
> *defend Nafutan Mount. Those who cannot participate in combat must*
> *commit suicide . . . We will carry the maximum of weapons and supplies*
> *. . . The password for tonight will be "Shichi Sei Hokoku" (Seven lives*
> *for one's country)."*[40]

Roughly 500 Japanese moved undetected through the thinly manned lines of the 2nd Battalion, 105th Infantry in the early morning hours and headed for Aslito Airfield less than 2 miles to the northwest. The first indication anything was amiss came at about 0200 when "an extremely large group" of Japanese stumbled into the 2nd Battalion command post some 1,500 yards behind the front lines. A firefight broke out and the infiltrators melted away, leaving twenty-seven dead. The GIs suffered twenty-four casualties, including four dead.[41]

About thirty minutes later Captain Sasaki's first group surged onto Aslito Airfield. Marauding Japanese set fire to a P-47 named "Hed up 'N Locked" in the parking area on the south side of the strip. A couple of other planes suffered minor damage; one P-47's gas tank was punched full of holes with a bayonet in a futile effort to set it on fire.[42] Seabees and engineers rallied and somewhat indiscriminately cleared the field of intruders. "They were shooting anything and everything that moved, including a half dozen of our own planes," remarked Justice Chambers.[43]

A second arm of the assault headed toward Hill 500, 3½ miles away, where they expected to find Colonel Oka's *47th Independent Mixed Brigade* headquarters. Instead, at about 0520, they encountered the 25th Marines. There is some question as to who was the most surprised. "They marched up the road in a column of twos and threes unchallenged," admitted the 25th Marines Special Action Report. "They reached the 3d Bn area at 0520 and marched so boldly that they were in the CP itself before they were recognized as enemy."[44]

"At just about daybreak . . . all hell broke loose in the battalion CP," recalled Chambers. "I sat bolt upright, there were bullets, grenades and curses flying in every direction. I remember distinctly trying to get my boots on, pull on my helmet, work the slide of my .45 and call for help on the radio, all at the same time! About twenty feet from me was a Japanese machine gun just chattering away like mad! My jeep, which was sitting on the side of the hill, was completely chopped to pieces by this gun."[45]

PFC James Ferguson and his buddy had covered their foxhole with a sheet of tin. As the melee began, Ferguson knocked the cover aside with the muzzle of his tommy gun to find a Japanese staring down at him. Ferguson pulled the trigger while still pushing at the tin and dropped the man. PFC James Davis went down under a blow from a Japanese swinging a shovel. Another Japanese bayoneted PFC Robert Postal, who had just returned to the outfit the day before after being wounded on the beach eleven days earlier. Postal shot and killed his assailant as the Japanese withdrew the bayonet for a second thrust.[46]

PFC Albert J. Ouellette remembered, "My platoon sergeant was sleeping in my foxhole when a Jap officer with a sword opened his head like a cantaloupe. This was also when Bob Bergson sat on a Jap grenade to protect Limey and had his legs blown off . . . Limey sat up and had his arm shot off by machine gun fire."[47]

The 14th Marines, encamped with their guns between Hill 500 and the airfield, were attacked at about the same time. According to one account, the 2nd Battalion held its fire to the last moment, mistaking the Japanese column for a U.S. Army patrol. Justice Chambers heard a less flattering version. According to that account, the Japanese marched smartly down the road until they ran into the artillery battalion. "There was some knuckleheaded kid, hunched down in his poncho, with an unlit cigarette and no match," related Chambers. "Down the road came these figures, and this Marine stood up and asked for a light! If the Jap had given him a match, that idiot Marine would probably have let them pass. Instead, the Jap shot at him. It really hit the fan then."[48]

Chambers estimated the brawl around his command post lasted about fifteen minutes. His battalion lost eleven men killed and thirty wounded. Thirty-nine dead Japanese were found in the CP area alone. "We found seven Jap heavy machine guns and two light machine guns right there in the CP!" observed Chambers.[49] Some of the corpses wore U.S. uniforms and had carried M1 rifles. Among the dead found in the 25th Marines area was the disconsolate sailor who had wondered in his diary if Saipan had been forsaken. If Captain Sasaki's body was identified, that information did not find its way into the record.

At daybreak on June 27, the GIs from Sergeant Salisbury's abandoned outpost tried yet again to retrieve PFC Fultz from his shallow ditch. They no sooner moved out of the tree line than they were taken under close-range fire and had to dash back to cover without Fultz. It appeared the Japanese on the cliffs had spotted the wounded man and were using him as bait. By now Fultz's condition had deteriorated badly. He was obviously in great pain and the others could hear him crying out.

Fultz's agony finally ended later that morning when U.S. artillery fire began falling on Purple Heart Ridge. A number of short rounds exploded around the cowering GIs. One of them killed Fultz. Sgt. Patrick Messineo was also killed and PFCs Scarcella and Bara were seriously wounded. When the barrage finally lifted, Salisbury and O'Dell tried to tend to the two wounded men, but their injuries clearly required more medical attention than they could provide. Salisbury decided their only hope was to leave them and make a dash for friendly lines to try to obtain help.

He and O'Dell started crawling along the line of trees toward Purple Heart Ridge. Finally reaching the slope, they ducked into the heavy foliage. They were climbing toward the top in an effort to get their bearings when they bumped into five Japanese sitting on a rock. Salisbury opened fire without even aiming and killed all five at a range of only a few feet. The two sergeants continued across the ridge and finally ran into some GIs from the 165th Infantry. They gulped down their first water in many hours, then reported to their own battalion. Scarcella and Bara were retrieved later in the afternoon. Both survived their ordeal.[50]

Glen Fultz's body was recovered and the standard telegram went out to his parents in tiny Belleville, Pennsylvania, population about 1,100. Sadly, his parents were soon to endure another heartbreak. Three months later, Glen's older brother Ralph—their only other son—was killed in action serving with an infantry unit in Italy. The two were buried together in St. John's Lutheran Cemetery in Belleville in a twin service on December 5, 1948.[51]

CHAPTER XIX

Every Soldier Must Stand His Ground

THE GREAT PREPONDERANCE OF PRISONERS TAKEN BY U.S. FORCES OVER the first couple of weeks were civilians who were initially confined in barbed-wire enclosures at the landing beaches, and later at a more permanent stockade located by Lake Susupe in the 2nd Marine Division area. The stockade formed the basis of what would become "Internment Camp Number One"—more familiarly known simply as Camp Susupe—sprawling out like some cartoon Dogpatch come to life on about 50 acres of sandy plain between the coast and the Susupe marshes.

Unfortunately, the effort to manage the civilian population fell short from the beginning. Planners had not anticipated that the island's infrastructure—both physical and social—would be so completely shattered by the invasion. Instead of remaining in place, the civilian population had fled into the interior as individuals and small groups, hiding where they could in caves and holes, often mixing in with Japanese military personnel. It was sheer chaos. As one report subsequently observed, "The problem on Saipan was not one of superimposing a control organization on an existing government structure, but of coping with situations arising from complete disintegration of a society."[1]

Large numbers of prisoners began arriving before the camp was even marginally operable. The 4th Marine Division began encountering civilians—primarily Chamorros—almost immediately upon landing; the 2nd Marine Division recorded its first civilian prisoners, 250 of them, on June 17. It was the first of a flood that would eventually total some 18,000. The civilians were often in bad shape, dehydrated and starving. Some had suffered wounds. Many were in shock or hysterical from their ordeal. A report observed "many captured civilians are dying in collecting areas; some had no food for 7 days before our forces arrived and is presenting problems."[2] Harris Martin, a member of the Civil Affairs team, saw one woman still trying to nurse her dead baby.

Lacking experience and undermanned, the small Civil Affairs contingent was overwhelmed. To avoid friction, it was found necessary to separate the Chamorros and Carolinians in one area, Koreans in another, and Japanese civilians in yet another. Food and water were in short supply. The internees slept huddled together in makeshift lean-tos or under captured Japanese tarpaulins, discarded Marine Corps ponchos, and whatever else came to hand. A scattering of trees—pines, palms, papaya, and banana—provided some shade.

"In Camp Susupe we were always hungry," remembered Chamorro internee Vicky Vaughan. "I think that is where most of us tasted Spam for the first time. Sometimes American soldiers would call us over to the barbed wire fence and give us chocolate. We were provided with no shelter. We had to make our own with whatever materials we could salvage. Pieces of rice sacking might be all we had for a door. We were all covered with lice. We must have looked like monkeys at times, all sitting in a line picking bugs out of the hair of the person in front of us. We had to be on guard at night because sometimes American soldiers would come into camp looking for young women."[3]

Eleven days after the landings, a unit of the Army's 31st Field Hospital set up a thirty-bed tent facility to care for the estimated 1,200 civilians requiring hospitalization. On D plus 15 army carpenters began construction of 150 20-by-40-foot covered shelters, the size determined by the lumber lengths available. "They were pretty flimsy buildings they put up," recalled Martin. "They had corrugated tin roofs and were open at the sides."[4] Each barracks-type building could accommodate 200 people—families lived together—with 4 square feet of space per person. The captives were fed captured rice and other stores, but food remained scarce. Large breadfruit leaves served as plates; discarded GI ration cans were put to use as cups and bowls for tea and soup. A *Philadelphia Inquirer* correspondent called it "the most amazing shanty town ever administered by the U.S. Navy."[5] In fact, the term "shanty town" was generous; it would be months before the refugee situation was brought under control with adequate food and shelter.

In the mountainous area to the west of the 27th Division, most of the heavy lifting had fallen on the 2nd Marine Division's right where the 8th Marines were struggling through a nightmarish jumble of steep dropoffs and tangled vegetation crowned by Mount Tapotchau. Getting water and ammunition up and casualties down was a backbreaking ordeal. Ironically, a wounded Marine created more trouble in some ways than a dead one. A dead man didn't require four other Marines to lug him down off the mountainside: He deprived his unit of only one rifle instead of five. In some cases it took as many as eight bearers to manhandle a stretcher out of the rugged highlands.

The toll of dead staff officers continued. This time it was Lt. Col. Kenneth F. McLeod, executive officer of the 6th Marines. A survivor of the bloodbath at Tarawa, McLeod, oddly enough, held the Japanese in great disdain and usually refused to even wear a helmet, recalled an acquaintance. He was picked off by a sniper on Tipo Pale on June 25. Pvt. Harry Johnson recalled, "A Marine colonel came up in a jeep behind the hill. He had a clean, pressed khaki shirt on and walked up to a high point on the hill. He took out a pair of field glasses to look things over. A sniper fired and he was taken back to our lines and to the jeep feet first. I don't know how dumb you can be."[6]

Up on Mount Tapotchau, Frank Borta got a new captain. He didn't know what happened to the previous captain and didn't much care—he'd never liked the man. The new company CO was twenty-four-year-old Capt. Patrick G. Leonard, another veteran of Tarawa. Obviously just up from the beach, he wore a nice clean uniform with the sleeves neatly rolled up, in sharp contrast to the rest of the company with their filthy ragged dungarees. The captain wanted to get the lay of the land and Borta was told to give him the tour. The two picked their way among the rocks and thickets for about half an hour as Borta showed Leonard—who seemed like a decent fellow— around the ridge. Finally they took a break. Borta sat down against a rock and took out his canteen. Leonard kneeled down next to him, removed his helmet, and wiped the sweat off his face. Borta had just taken a sip from his canteen when a sniper, probably spotting the new uniform, shot Leonard through the throat. "I looked up," recalled Borta; "his eyes were half open and blood was shooting out a couple of feet. His heart was still pumping. Some blood got on me." There was nothing Borta could do and the captain bled out within a couple of minutes.[7]

Borta went back to the company and reported that the captain had been killed. A corporal radioed regimental headquarters. "Goddammit," said a voice over the radio before the corporal could give his message. "Isn't the captain there yet?"

"Yes sir," replied the corporal. "But he's dead."

Borta returned to where he'd left the captain and found the body had been stripped down to the skivvies. He wasn't shocked. Walking around in rags, the living Marines needed serviceable clothing more than the dead officer did. It was a simple matter of practicality. Borta would have taken the captain's pants himself, but they were the wrong size.[8]

Such attitudes would have shocked civilians at home, but for combat Marines and GIs, the brutality of war had become a familiar companion. "One morning one of the sergeants and I were sitting on a log eating our rations while we waited for the word to move out," recalled PFC John Pope. "A Jap killed himself with a grenade out in front of us. A piece of his blown off hand landed right at the Sarge's feet. The guy's fingernails were shining in the morning sun. They were strangely white. Sarge was eating with his big knife and noticed two green flies land on the hand. He swore at the green flies, reached down with his knife, stuck the hand and flipped it over his shoulder. We kept on eating."[9]

Up on the shoulders of Mount Tapotchau, everything smelled of death, but Sgt. Bob Cary thought his foxhole reeked more than the average. He found out why when he noticed several human fingers protruding from the side of the hole. A little excavation revealed an entire hand. Cary gave it a tug and found it was apparently attached to a body. He piled some clay over the hand, which seemed to diminish the aroma, and settled in for a night of swatting mosquitoes.

Toward morning, it began to rain and Cary became aware that the stench in his foxhole had returned to the point of being overpowering. At first light, he discovered the reason: The hand had reappeared along with the shoulder and part of the head of a Japanese soldier. Still unwilling to admit defeat, he piled more dirt and clay around the cadaver. He was assisted in this task by the interested commentary of his buddies, one of whom opined that Cary's foxhole companion smelled better than he did. The next night passed quietly, but by daybreak, the Japanese corpse had reemerged from its muddy crypt and a cursing Cary finally conceded defeat. Gathering his gear he moved to a spot 30 yards away and started to dig a new hole, accompanied by jibes from his squad mates, who caustically observed it was the first time they had ever seen a Marine driven from the field of battle by a dead enemy.[10]

Lt. Leigh Trowbridge remembered a bloated Japanese corpse near his position. "A private, probably from down south judging by his accent, was roaming through the area, cheerful and profane, apparently without a care in the world," recalled Trowbridge. "He had a really foul mouth. He approached the repulsive dead enemy soldier who was on his hands and knees. He took one look and said, 'Boy, this SOB looks ready! I'm gonna fuck this one!' We all snickered...."[11]

While desensitization was to be expected in the face of so much death, some men lost their moral compass. A man in Paul Harper's unit was nicknamed "Dietz the Dentist," for his macabre collection of gold teeth extracted from enemy corpses. As he accumulated the teeth, he would add them to a necklace he was stringing together for his girlfriend back home.[12] PFC David Getman recalled a machine gunner who cut the finger off a dead Japanese woman to get her ring, but even his cold-bloodedness paled in comparison to a man in Corp. Richard Hicks's amtrac company who seemed surrounded by a horrible stench. "The fellows finally made him open his seabag and he had a Japanese head in there he was going to bring home," recalled Hicks.[13]

Most men limited their souvenir hunting to stripping enemy dead of flags, thousand-stitch good luck belts, swords, and pistols. One man in Carl Matthews's outfit lugged around a heavy microscope he had come across somewhere. There were also occasional reminders that the Japanese might actually be human. Stripping a corpse for souvenirs, Tibor Torok came across what appeared to be a wedding photo depicting a handsome man standing next to a young woman who was holding a bouquet of flowers. Another photo showed the same young couple posing with two pretty little girls. Torok, who had no reason to love the Japanese, felt a momentary pang of compassion for the dead man.[14]

By now it had become clear that the key to conquering Death Valley lay in an advance along Purple Heart Ridge, as Ralph Smith had originally contemplated. But this remained no simple matter. On June 26, GIs had occupied Hill Oboe without opposition, but when a platoon descended into the saddle to ascend King—the next hill in the line—they were met with a blast of fire from at least two machine guns and any number of rifles. The assault lasted for only ten minutes, observed the division historian. "It did not die out. It simply melted away."[15]

Six men were killed, seventeen wounded. Company commander Charles Hallden recalled, "[PFC Thomas G.] Hill was killed as he dived for a hole to get out of the line of fire of the machine gun. He got to the hole all right, but a sniper was waiting for him in a tree just above the hole and killed him as he hit the prone position. [PFC John] Miner found a hole without being hit, but when he got to it he found Private First Class Stephen Witkowski in it, badly wounded. He tried to give Witkowski aid, but in doing so exposed a shoulder and was hit. He then tried to get back to the jump off point to an aid man, but in doing so was hit three or four more times and finally killed. [PFC Robert C.] Peters was hit as he advanced and fell into a hole with Lieutenant Sedmak. He watched his chance to get back out of the hole and finally managed to scamper back a few yards to a rock where he thought there was some protection. While hiding behind the rock he was hit again and killed. [Private First Class Donald M.] Ratcliff, the company commander's radio operator, was killed instantly while advancing. [Private Martin B.] Otten was killed in much the same fashion as Peters, being hit a second time." The survivors finally got out when the platoon commander, who had been hit in the arm and leg, called for smoke grenades to screen them from enemy fire.[16]

General Jarman's hopes for a breakout on June 27 were pinned on a variation of Ralph Smith's original maneuver to sidestep enemy positions in the Tapotchau cliffs. Jarman's plan called for the 2nd Battalion, 165th Infantry to attack north up the outside edge of Purple Heart Ridge, while Lieutenant Colonel Mizony's 3rd Battalion, 106th Infantry advanced along the top of the ridge to Hill King. Upon reaching King, Mizony's battalion would turn left onto the valley floor, effectively cutting off Japanese defenders to the south.

Artillery might have assisted the assault on Hill King, but division refused requests for support for fear it would endanger adjacent units that had pushed ahead as the advance into the valley lagged behind. The lieutenant commanding Item Company protested the decision so vehemently that Mizony sacked him on the spot, replacing him with his battalion intelligence officer.[17] The attack went forward without artillery support and without the lieutenant, whose fears turned out to be well founded. When the assault platoons reached the bottom of the saddle between Hills King and Oboe—the scene of Captain Hallden's platoon-sized debacle the day before—they were met with a withering fire that killed one man, wounded eight, and pinned down the remainder. Faced with the possibility of another failure, Jarman relented and authorized the artillery support.

At 1045, Hills King and Able erupted under a deluge of shells. When the GIs jumped off thirty minutes later, hardly a tree remained standing and the thick foliage had been obliterated. L and I Companies were already climbing the forward slope of Hill King as the last shells exploded. Reaching the crest, I Company passed through a litter of dead Japanese without encountering a single live defender. But the enemy wasn't gone. As the GIs continued onto the reverse slope, they found numerous Japanese hunkered down in the grass and rocks, waiting in defilade for the barrage to end. The Japanese mistook the Americans for friendly troops and gestured frantically for them to take cover. The GIs hesitated as the two sides looked at each other, then grenades began flying as all realized the truth.

At least one GI and several Japanese were killed in a five-minute fire-fight before Lt. Robert J. Bonner pulled his platoon back and called for mortar fire on the reverse slope. Ten minutes later, Bonner and his men got up and walked down the reverse slope without resistance. "This whole area showed many Japs dead, four machine guns bent and twisted, small arms along the trail and cartridges scattered about," observed Captain Hallden. The GIs now saw why they'd had so much trouble with King: the Japanese had constructed a spider-type defensive position on the hill consisting of a series of trenches connected to a central position, which allowed them to move quickly from one spot to another.[18]

Mizony's battalion now implemented phase two of the plan and turned west across the valley toward the Tapotchau cliffs 1,000 yards away. The immediate objective was a low ridge that ran across the valley between Hill Able and the cliffs. Machine-gun and mortar fire from Hill Able, from the Tapotchau cliffs, and from a tree line to the south raked the GIs as soon as they descended from King. By 1530, the battalion was scattered across the valley floor. Lieutenant Bonner reached the objective with fourteen men from I Company, but had no contact with the rest of the company. Nevertheless, Bonner kept his head and stayed put.

With the whole maneuver in jeopardy, Captain Hallden suddenly appeared, stalking upright across the valley floor. Paying no apparent heed to the hail of bullets, he went from man to man as they lay prone on the ground, cajoling and coaxing them to get up and continue forward. Within ten minutes Hallden had all three companies moving again. By 1600, what remained of the battalion had reached the objective line, where Bonner's handful of men had been stubbornly hanging on for over an hour. They were resupplied with ammunition and enough water for about half a cup per man, but real help did not arrive until that evening when the 2nd Battalion came forward. The weary GIs settled in for the night, getting what rest they could before jumping off the next morning toward the head of the valley.[19]

As the Tapotchau defense line showed signs of cracking, General Saito moved his headquarters yet again—this time to a cave in an overgrown ravine about a mile and a half north of Mount Tapotchau where he appears to have joined up with General Igeta. According to Major Hirakushi, Admiral Nagumo was also present, though the onetime naval hero offered little input to discussions on how to stem the American advance. Just who was actually in overall charge—General Igeta or General Saito—remained unclear to Hirakushi, but he suspected it was Igeta, who, in his opinion, demonstrated more vitality and efficiency than the older Saito.

Witnessing the proceedings, Hirakushi sensed a loss of spirit. "Igeta conducted the meeting," he said. "Saito just listened, so did the others . . . Nagumo listened silently."

Igeta advocated establishing a final line of resistance. The new line—the third effort to hold back the Americans after the failure of the shore defense on D-day—was to extend across the island from Tanapag on the west coast, through Hill 221 and Tarahoho, to the east coast. Asked for their views at the conclusion of Igeta's presentation, a senior navy officer replied only, "Leave it to the Army." Nagumo said nothing.[20]

Despite his show of determination, General Igeta was losing hope. "Please apologize deeply to the Emperor that we cannot do better than we are doing," he messaged the chief of staff in Tokyo.[21] According to his calculations, the *118th Infantry Regiment* now numbered about 300 men, the *135th Infantry Regiment* about 350, the *136th Regiment* about 300, and the *47th Independent Mixed Brigade* a mere 100. The *9th Tank Regiment* had three tanks left. The *47th Mixed Brigade* was now under command of a first lieutenant. The *7th Engineers* was commanded by a mere sergeant. Reserve units, hospital units, equipment, maintenance, and supply units "are either completely wiped out or reduced to the point where no fighting strength can be expected from them."[22] In desperation, an effort was made to train some 400 men, the remnants of non-combat units, in hand-to-hand fighting.[23]

If nothing else, it was becoming increasingly clear that Japanese fighting spirit was no match for American firepower. "[W]e are menaced by brazenly low-flying planes, and the enemy blasts at us from all sides with fierce naval and artillery cross-fire," reported *31st Army* headquarters. "As a result, even if we remove units from the front lines and send them to the rear their fighting strength is cut down every day."[24] Naval gunfire was particularly devastating. "If there just were no naval gunfire, we feel that we could fight it out with the enemy in a decisive battle," wrote General Saito.[25] General Igeta reported, "In our front line units, the troops have been three days without drinking water but are hanging on by chewing leaves of trees and eating snails."[26] A directive from the "Chief of Operations" called for economizing ammunition, while also moving weapons frequently in an effort to "decrease the heavy losses inflicted by the enemy...."[27] At the same time, a General Order directed that "positions are to be held until the bitter end, and unless he has other orders every soldier must stand his ground."[28]

General Igeta also continued his pleas for reinforcements from Tinian, Guam, Rota, or Yap, inquiring about the availability of "large motor launches" and "collapsible boats" that could slip through the U.S. naval blockade.[29] Those pleas did not go completely unanswered. After darkness the night of June 25, eleven troop-laden barges set out from Sunharon Harbor on Tinian's west coast. Spotted by destroyer *Bancroft* and destroyer escort *Elden*, the flotilla was taken under fire. One barge was sunk and the rest scurried back to Tinian. The commander at Truk, ordered by Imperial Headquarters to send two battalions to Saipan, replied that there was no transportation available, but Guam dispatched two infantry companies and some artillery in thirteen large landing barges. The barges made it as far as Rota, but no farther.[30]

Such was their desperation that Japanese staff officers on Saipan contemplated a plan to bring in reinforcements through Iwo Jima where they would board submarines for the trip to Saipan.[31] Though hopes were fading, work also continued on Marpi Airfield at the northern end of the island. "There is no hope for victory in places where we do not have control of the air and we are still hoping here for aerial reinforcements," radioed Igeta. "Praying for the good health of the Emperor, we all cry, 'Banzai!'"[32]

Among the Japanese still doggedly standing their ground were the defenders of Hill Able—the sheer-faced, 50-foot-tall chunk of rock at the northern end of Purple Heart Ridge that had been giving the 27th Division fits for nearly a week. Taking over Hill King as Hallden's men entered the valley below, the 2nd Battalion, 165th Infantry had been preparing to take a crack at Able during the afternoon in an effort to finally secure the whole of Purple Heart Ridge. The Japanese struck first. Filtering down a wooded corridor between the two hills, the attackers got in among G Company. Thirty-five Japanese were killed, but a fifteen-minute mortar barrage on King wounded twenty-four G Company men; five subsequently died. F Company lost ten men. Maj. Gregory Brousseau, who had taken over the battalion after Col. John F. McDonough was wounded on June 25, was also hit. The major refused to be evacuated until the other casualties were taken care of. He later died of his wound aboard a hospital ship. It was all largely for nothing.

The 2nd Battalion abandoned King and pulled all the way back to Hill Xray-Yoke where it had started earlier in the day. The Japanese promptly reoccupied King.[33]

General Jarman could not have been pleased. Only the day before, once again hoping to put a stop to his division's tendency to relinquish hard-won ground, he had ordered, "No withdrawal will be made for the night for the purpose of consolidation."[34] His concerns about giving up ground were justified in the worst way when the assault resumed the next morning. The 2nd Battalion jumped off from Xray-Yoke at 0630, advanced rapidly over Hill Oboe, and promptly stalled in the face of fire from enemy troops that had reoccupied Hill King. By 1330, G Company, which had the lead, had taken twenty casualties. The company tried to reorganize, only to dissolve in utter confusion under an enemy mortar barrage.[35]

The mess on Purple Heart Ridge had serious ramifications for the two battalions waiting out on the valley floor the night of June 27. Daybreak was just after 0500. By 0530—an hour before the scheduled jump-off toward the next ridgeline about 400 yards away—it was light enough for the Japanese on Mount Tapotchau and Hill Able to start picking away at targets on the valley floor. Artillery support had been promised, but when Captain Hallden called for fire on the cliff area to his left front, the mission was denied for fear it would threaten Marines up on Mount Tapotchau. Carefully studying the slopes through his binoculars, Hallden could see no sign of any Marines. Summoning his forward artillery observer (FO), he pointed out the target area. He wanted artillery fire put down there, he said, and he didn't care how the observer got it done.

The FO proceeded to draw up coordinates far to the right of the spot Hallden had indicated. He then called division artillery and had the mission approved. Ten minutes before the preparation began, the FO rang up the firing batteries and told them there had been a mistake in the original calculations. He gave them the "corrected" coordinates for the target area Hallden had pointed out. A few minutes later the artillery barrage slammed in right where Hallden wanted it. "Japs came running from the cliff in all directions and most of them were killed," the captain observed with satisfaction. The dust was still settling ten minutes later when division called Hallden to say the mission on the revised coordinates could not be fired.[36] The infantry attack jumped off on time and reached the first ridgeline at 0930.

They had little time to relish their success as they came under intense mortar fire from Hill Able, now to their right rear. Seven men were killed and twenty-two wounded in a matter of minutes. The fatalities included Lt. Robert J. Bonner—I Company's fourth commander in three days. As the barrage continued, I and K Companies broke, many of the GIs fleeing into a thick grove of trees on a spur about 50 yards to the north.[37]

As casualties mounted, Hallden called Colonel Mizony on the field telephone. Unless he was allowed to advance at once and get the remnants of the battalion off the fire-swept ridge, he could no longer be responsible for the conduct of the men, he said. The place was a killing field. Mizony gave him the okay. Hallden was getting the men ready to go when Japanese fire from Hill Able abruptly ceased, but the low crest—soon to be dubbed "Bloody Ridge"—was a frightful sight. "Dead men and wounded were strewn along the ridge and equipment was scattered all along the crest," reported the division historian.[38] Hallden scrubbed the attack and ordered his men to deepen the shallow foxholes they had scraped out under the impression the halt would be temporary. The wounded were carried into the grove of trees.

Hallden's situation seemed to improve further as Company F, which had been operating along the edge of the cliffs for the past few days, came abreast of Bloody Ridge and started down from the heights. Emerging onto a wide shelf by a farmhouse, the GIs surprised a few dozen Japanese busily shooting up the beleaguered companies below. They killed fourteen Japanese in about ten minutes. The rest scrambled away and disappeared into the landscape. As F Company continued down the escarpment toward Bloody Ridge, all enemy fire from the cliffs had ceased.

Fox Company joined Easy in the wooded grove. Ten minutes later, 2nd Battalion commander Almerin O'Hara arrived and settled in among the trees with his CP group. He was followed at 1255 by Colonel Mizony and his command group. As the division historian subsequently reported, "By 1315 . . . one little group of trees on Bloody Ridge, not more than a hundred yards square, optimistically speaking, contained two full rifle companies, E and F, 2nd Battalion headquarters and Headquarters Company, 3rd Battalion headquarters and Headquarters Company, approximately forty badly wounded men, and various messengers, weapons, battle-fatigue cases and stragglers from I, K, H, L, and M companies." As one GI observed, "there wasn't enough room to sit down."[39]

Realizing they had to get the battalions moving, Mizony and O'Hara gathered their company commanders and headed to the northern edge of the woods to examine the terrain ahead. The staff conference had scarcely gotten underway when two Japanese tanks poked their armored snouts over the crest of the far ridge only 200 yards away. Uncomprehending GIs watched them maneuver into position side by side. "I saw them," remarked one GI. "I looked at them. Everyone did. It was just as though they were part of the scenery."[40] After what seemed like an eternity, but was probably only seconds, the tanks opened fire. The first directed its turret gun and machine guns on the crowded copse of trees. The other swept the rest of the ridge. After raking the woods, the first tank also deliberately traversed its guns along the ridgeline before both slowly withdrew back over the crest and out of sight. Not a shot had been fired in return, so complete was the surprise.

In those few minutes, twelve men were killed and sixty-one wounded. Among the dead was Colonel Mizony, Captain Tarrant of G Company, and Lt. John McGregor of M Company. Panicked GIs scrambling back to the reverse slope to get away from the tanks were promptly taken under fire by Japanese on Hill Able. Officers got the men under control and back on the line by 1330, but any thoughts of a further advance were abandoned.[41]

By June 28, a week of fighting had transformed Death Valley into a reeking testament to the costs of war. "From the line held by the 106th Infantry back to the south gate, the floor was littered with dead who could not be picked up for another three days," observed a division officer. "Burned and broken tanks could be seen wherever one looked and the once peaceful little farming valley was now a litter of broken buildings, blasted bridges, leafless trees and gaping shell holes."[42]

General Jarman was finally making progress up the deadly corridor, but he was not to preside over the finish. At 1030 on June 28 command of the 27th Division passed to forty-eight-year-old Maj. Gen. George W. Griner Jr., the former commander of the 98th Infantry Division in Hawaii. The change was no reflection on Jarman, who had filled in as division commander on an interim basis; Griner had received his orders almost as soon as news of Gen. Ralph Smith's relief reached General Richardson in Hawaii.

The son of a Methodist preacher, Griner had seen combat in France during the First World War and was no prima donna. However, he found himself in a somewhat awkward position as he arrived on Saipan. He knew little of the circumstances of Ralph Smith's relief or the trials of his new division beyond what he was now told in a lengthy briefing by Holland Smith. Griner recalled that Smith went on for about an hour about "all the deficiencies" of the 27th Division. He said "that the division would not fight and that General Ralph Smith would not make them fight," observed Griner. The 27th had performed dismally at Nafutan Point, added Smith, and presently was holding up the two Marine divisions on its flanks in the advance to the north.

Griner wasted no time taking charge. Preparing for the advance on June 29, he relieved the 3rd Battalion, 106th which, in addition to losing Colonel Mizony, had been virtually decimated since arriving at the mouth of Death Valley a week before. They were replaced by the 1st Battalion, which was sent in with the admonishment, "It is of utmost importance that you gain contact with the 8th Marines today before dark."[43] The 3rd Battalion, 105th Infantry was put in on the right of the advance, with the 2nd Battalion, 106th Infantry remaining in the center.

Considering the carnage of the previous day, the morning assault got off well as the GIs descended from newly named Bloody Ridge and headed for the transverse ridge where the Japanese tanks had unexpectedly materialized with such deadly consequences the day before. As the GIs started up the slope, a Japanese soldier suddenly stood up from behind a concrete pillbox and threw a grenade, wounding two advance scouts. PFC Robert M. Stevens pushed over the crest and nearly ran into a camouflaged Japanese tank. Stevens shouted a warning, but it was too late. The tank turret gun and two machine guns opened fire. Three GIs were killed instantly. As the tank continued to rake the slope, four more men were killed and fourteen wounded. A GI sprinting up the hillside was shot and killed by fire from the concrete pillbox. A sergeant shouldered a bazooka to take a shot at the tank, but was seriously wounded before he could squeeze off the rocket. A rifle grenadier was hit in another effort to knock out the tank. A medic and another GI were gunned down when they went to the aid of the wounded bazooka man. The platoon commander was shot as he tried to drag the fatally wounded rifle grenadier out of the line of fire.

Taken under fire, the tank finally backed away. A sergeant summoned a U.S. light tank operating nearby and guided the driver up the slope, pointing out the Japanese tank, now retreating northward up the optimistically named Aslito-Tanapag highway. Tank commander Sgt. John R. Reidy fired two rounds. The first missed, but the second scored a direct hit. As Reidy started to follow up, he was taken under fire from what appeared to be a stack of straw. He replied with a round from his turret gun. The blast revealed a second Japanese tank concealed in the stack and set it on fire.

The crust of Japanese resistance gave way and by early afternoon the three battalions in the assault had advanced between 900 and 1,000 yards. It was a huge leap considering that past progress had been measured practically in inches. By 1530, the GIs had visual contact with Marines on the northern slopes of Mount Tapotchau to their left.[44] Progress was also being made to the east where E Company of the 2nd Battalion, 165th Infantry cleared Hill King for the last time, finding most of the Japanese hiding in foxholes in the wake of a preparatory artillery barrage. Over 125 enemy dead were counted, all freshly killed; the blackened bodies lying around from previous assaults were not included in the tally.

Finishing with King, E Company tackled Able. A platoon started up the sheer face, which was broken by a series of little ledges. In the lead, PFC Michael N. Deperri and Pvt. James W. Hyland had reached the fourth ledge about 30 feet up when Deperri, pulling himself up to the next level, found himself staring into the eyes of a Japanese soldier only inches away. The Japanese reached out and dropped a grenade down Deperri's back.

Deperri and Hyland lost their grip and fell 30 feet to the base of the cliff. Luckily for Deperri, the grenade also fell free and exploded harmlessly, but the hillside erupted in a flurry of explosions as Japanese all along the edge began dropping grenades on the GIs below. Others stood to fire down with rifles. Clinging to the side of the hill, PFC Jack B. Staus was killed instantly by rifle fire. PFC Aubrey D. Varney fell over backward when a grenade exploded almost in his face. He lay unconscious for a time in the top of a small tree while Japanese continued to drop grenades on him. Finally regaining consciousness, he crawled out of the tree and made his way to an aid station where he later died. Five other men were seriously wounded and the platoon lost its hold on the cliff and backed away. Able would have to wait another day.[45]

Despite Able's continued obstinance, overall progress for the day was encouraging. For once, even Howlin' Mad had something to be pleased about. Watching the advance from the western heights, he "expressly complimented" the performance of the Army division.[46] In fact, there was evidence the Japanese were withdrawing. The night of June 29 large numbers of enemy soldiers were spotted along the road leading north out of Death Valley. Down toward the southern end of the valley, thirty Japanese pulling a field piece up the road bumped into an Army unit shortly before midnight. The GIs cut them down when they stopped to rest not 20 feet from the outposts. The next morning the field piece—and the dedicated artillerymen who refused to abandon it—remained in the roadway where the gunners had paused to catch what turned out to be their last breath.[47]

The end came that same morning. Pounded all night by U.S. mortars, Hill Able fell with more of a whimper than a bang. The bulk of the defenders had pulled out overnight, leaving a scattering of dead. By 0940 the hill was reported secure at the cost of one GI killed. In the hills to the north, a Japanese officer with a unit of the *136th Infantry* sent a dispatch to his regimental commander, Colonel Ogawa, on the morning of June 30. He reported that his unit, consisting of approximately 280 men, had retreated from "previous positions" the night of June 29, regrouping 1,200 meters north of Mount Tapotchau. The unit had been under heavy artillery and naval gunfire, but had managed to throw back a tank/infantry attack. "By utilizing the terrain we have prevented the approach of the tanks," wrote the unidentified officer, "but although we drove back the soldiers who left at least 16 dead, they are now enveloping us on both flanks . . . depletion of munitions is extremely rapid in the present fighting . . . I have food enough for one and a half days [and] would like to be supplied during the night. . . ." The officer reported the unit had three heavy machine guns, twenty light machine guns, and twenty grenade launchers, adding, "morale is generally excellent."[48]

At the Japanese field hospital near Donnay, the approach of U.S. forces along the eastern coast brought another in a litany of horrors. Hundreds of severely wounded men lay in the open air, many of them beyond human assistance. Former vocational school student Saburo Arakaki was a witness to the open-air charnel house. Caught up in the fighting near Garapan, he had originally been accompanied by two friends, but one had disappeared somewhere in the confusion; the other had been shot through the head by a strafing American fighter plane. Saburo spent three days helping a wounded Japanese sergeant named Aoki over Tapotchau's foothills to Donnay, subsisting on sweet potatoes from abandoned garden plots and assuaging his thirst with sugar cane.

They arrived to find hundreds of wounded men lying on the grass and rocks by a grove of South Sea pines. Most had received only rudimentary treatment. Many were nearly insane with thirst, pleading incessantly for water. The surrounding jungle teemed with civilian refugees who had no place to go. Babies died as malnourished mothers could no longer supply breast milk. Women roamed mindlessly through the undergrowth, their kimonos hanging open.[49]

For a time Saburo and the others continued to believe the Imperial Navy would come to their rescue. But now, as enemy artillery fire began to fall nearby, medical personnel handed out grenades—one grenade for every eight men. The chief medical officer climbed onto a low hummock and announced that the "hospital" was being relocated to the north. "All ambulatory patients will accompany me," he announced. "But to my great sorrow, I must abandon you comrades who cannot walk. Men, die an honorable death as Japanese soldiers."[50]

As Saburo and Sergeant Aoki prepared to leave, nurse Shizuko Miura took final goodbyes from her many patients. Over the past days, Shizuko had descended into a nightmare abyss of maggot-filled wounds and rotting corpses, the groans and cries of men in agony, endless pleas for water and continuous attacks from U.S. planes and artillery. She helped amputate arms and legs of men who had to be held down as there was no more anesthesia. They screamed and struggled under the surgeon's saw until they mercifully passed out. The nonstop cries of "Nurse! Nurse! Nurse!" from multitudes of suffering men degenerated into a continuous buzz, reminding her—somewhat bizarrely—of the drone of cicadas in the summer mountains. The dead became corrupt and collapsed. At night the corpses gave off a faint phosphorescence.

Many of the patients now crowded around Shizuko, some able only to crawl. All wanted only to give some message or words for her to relay someday to families at home. Unable to speak, a soldier whose jaw had been shot away scrawled his name and home prefecture in the dirt. A badly wounded lieutenant asked her if she knew the verses to *Kudanzaka*." Shizuko began to sing the melancholy song about a mother who brings her dead son's medal to the Yasukani Shrine in Kudanzaka. As she finished, there was silence, broken by an occasional sob.

"We too will go to the Yasukani Shrine!" exclaimed the wounded officer. Others cried out in agreement.

As Shizuko accompanied the ambulatory wounded toward the north, those left behind called out, "Thank you, nurse!" and "Good-bye, nurse!" The column, consisting of two or three hundred men, many of them hobbling along with the aid of sticks, had reached the end of the field when Shizuko heard someone cry out, "Good-bye, mother!" followed by the explosion of a grenade. More explosions followed as she continued north in the moonlight.[51]

CHAPTER XX

Beyond the Valley

By day's end on June 30 it was clear the Death Valley position had been broken. During the early evening Marine and Army observers spotted columns of enemy infantry withdrawing along the road to the north. Moving lights were visible in the distance after dark. Spotters called in artillery and mortar fire with undetermined results.[1]

Late in the evening a sailor from the *55th Keibitai* (Naval Guard Force) walked into the lines of the 27th Division. He said he had been stationed in the Garapan area when he was wounded on June 28. After being treated at the dressing station, he found his unit had gone north. "The prisoner states that he became disgusted and due to the pain of his wound, decided that the best way to end it all would be to walk toward our lines, believing he would be killed by us," according to an interrogation summary. "He states that in moving south, he met many soldiers moving north, all of whom told him he was going the wrong way. This movement north is substantiated by the statement made by a civilian woman taken just northeast of Mount Tapotchau, who said that the Japanese in that area had withdrawn in the early evening of June 30, taking with them 20–30 wounded."[2]

Ryoko Okuyama and her family joined the procession heading away from the Americans. She and her parents, sister, and two brothers had been scheduled to board a ship for evacuation to Japan in early June, but the American invasion had intervened. Now they trudged past the weak and injured who had collapsed alongside the narrow trail. Fourteen-year-old Ryoko, most recently a second-year student at the Girls School of Saipan, heard their pleas as she passed: "I cannot stand the pain. Kill me. Please give me water." Some had no arms, others had lost legs, still others had been sliced open so that their bones were visible. She kept walking north.[3]

The Japanese exodus marked the end of the battle for central Saipan. In the center of the U.S. line, it had taken the 27th Division eight days to advance 3,000 yards. In the same timeframe, the 2nd Marine Division had advanced 2,600 yards through the Mount Tapotchau heights and 1,500 yards along the coastal area, where it marked time waiting for the rest of the advance to come abreast. Progress had been better on the right where the 4th Marine Division pushed about 4,400 yards east to the tip of Kagman Peninsula before surging another 5,000 yards northwest past the villages of Donnay and Hashiguru. Those gains would have been greater had the division not been held up by the delays in the Army zone.

The struggle for Saipan had now dragged on for over two weeks. Slower than expected progress had come with greater than anticipated losses. As of June 27, the 2nd Marine Division reported 607 killed in action, 2,872 wounded, and 393 missing; the 4th Marine Division officially listed 589 killed, 3,009 wounded, and 398 missing; while the 27th Division reported 158 killed, 878 wounded, and 46 missing. NTLF recorded a total of 4,043 enemy dead buried as of the afternoon of June 27, but many more lay rotting in the open air.[4]

"The men are getting pretty worn," chaplain W. Charles Goe, serving with the 23rd Marines, confided to his diary. "It's beginning to tell in many ways. We are having more and more combat fatigue cases. Many of the men have used all available energy and just can't go any farther, so they drop down in a field or road to be picked up and carried back."[5] By the end of the Saipan operation, the 4th Marine Division medical companies would log 414 cases of combat fatigue and 169 cases of psychoneurosis.[6]

PFC George Smith found himself crying after a near miss by an exploding artillery shell. He wasn't hurt, but he could not seem to control his emotions. "What are you crying for?" asked the corpsman. Smith replied, "I don't know; this shell went off." The corpsman gave him some medicinal brandy and Smith pulled himself together.[7] Others could not. Corpsman William R. Keyser recalled leading one distraught Marine across an open field. The man was weeping uncontrollably, as if he had just lost his best friend—and perhaps he had. "He would do anything I asked, but he just had no direction of his own," said Keyser. "I didn't see too many men in this condition, and I never saw a man criticize another Marine who was in this condition because but for the grace of God, we all weren't very far from it ourselves."[8]

After a while, the mind had a tendency to retreat. "[I]t's very stressful of course," explained former lieutenant Dean Ladd of the unrelenting grind of combat, "but after a while . . . you're getting steeled to it too. Then you're . . . almost to the point where you don't care. . . ."[9] Justice Chambers found he developed a sort of numbness to what was going on around him. "You are moving, almost subconsciously, through another world," he observed. "Things are happening all around you. You see them, are aware of them, but they don't hit you in a sharp manner. They are just the things happening around you. You concentrated only on getting the job done."[10]

But all too many sights and experiences, hastily shoved aside in the moment, were not gone or even diminished—they were only waiting deep in a man's memory for an opportunity to reappear. Some memories would haunt men for the rest of their lives. For Pvt. Harry Johnson, it was Corp. Lowell Burton, "as nice a man as you could meet." Unlike so many others, the twenty-four-year-old from Kansas City, Missouri, had resisted the fleshpots of Hilo. "When he got to Saipan, he was still a virgin," observed Johnson. Two weeks into the campaign on Saipan, Burton was fatally wounded. "When he was hit, he screamed, the only person I ever heard do that," recalled Johnson. "As someone helped me carry him back to our lines, snot ran out of one nostril. It's a shame I have that final picture of such a fine man in my mind. . . ."[11]

For Leigh Trowbridge, it was the sight of a GI lying alongside the road near Death Valley. "As we walked along this road on our way out, I came as close to vomiting as I had at any time," he remembered. "An American soldier, still wearing his helmet, had been killed beside the road. I'm guessing that probably at night and without lights, a vehicle, probably a tank, had run over his helmet with his head still in it. I thought I had seen the worst, but this was the grossest sight I had ever seen."[12]

Pvt. John M. Eardley found one of his buddies lying in the mud one morning. "A deadly crossfire had ripped open his groin and severed an artery in his leg," remembered Eardley. "He had lain in the mud all night and had bled to death before we found him. His dirty torn dungaree pants were soaked from the spurting blood that left him limp and lifeless." One of the next to die was Eardley's sergeant. Every morning before an advance the veteran noncom would say, "If you survive this, you can tell it to your grandkids." One steamy morning a Japanese machine gun put a burst into his chest, leaving it a mass of bloody pulp.[13] The seemingly indestructible "Sarge" would be telling no stories to grandchildren.

There was no logic to the dying, observed PFC Gene Sawulski, a mortar man with the 6th Marines. "The first day we were moving into some woods and they zeroed in on us with mortars," he recalled. "There was one short, one long, then the next one dropped right in our pit. Everybody in that pit but me got killed. It blew me off the ground, and I got a little hunk of steel in my jaw. . . . I remember this Greek kid from Idaho . . . this sniper came out of a hole and shot him right through the heart. Seventeen years old."[14] PFC Robert Tierney was returning with two other men through a cane field after a scouting mission when they were ambushed by a Japanese machine gunner. The first burst killed the men on either side of him. Tierney wasn't touched.[15]

"Every three or four days, we would get about eight or ten replace-ments to fill in for our losses," recalled Roy Roush. "They were always fresh out of boot camp and in combat for the first time. Then I began to notice something unusual. Many of them didn't last long before getting hit and sometimes on the very next day. But, if they could survive for ten days or two weeks, their chances of survival greatly improved. Most of the veterans had developed something like a sixth sense to warn them of danger, and the more we were in combat the stronger it became, often without becom-ing aware of it ourselves."[16] Corp. Robert A. Cunningham recalled a group of replacements that joined his outfit later in the campaign. Two of them became casualties within a couple of hours; one was hit in the leg, but the other was killed. "He stood up when he shouldn't have and got it right in the head," observed Cunningham matter-of-factly.[17]

Combat experience helped, but veterans also died; the smart were killed alongside the stupid. 1st Lt. Bob Stewart's platoon sergeant, Aurellio M. Finco, was killed in an artillery barrage. "He'd been hit by some kind of phosphorus shell," remembered Stewart. "I'm sure he never knew what hit him—the poor guy was burned to a crisp. He was a perfect example of our helplessness. He was not only a great guy, but one hell of a Marine. If knowing what to do would have made any difference—and plenty of times it did—he probably would have made it. But in a situation like the one we were in, all the training and knowledge in the world didn't mean a thing. It was just plain luck, good or bad."[18]

A steady trickle of casualties sapped unit strength. The 2nd Marine Division lost twenty-six killed and ninety-two wounded on June 23; thirty-one killed and 105 wounded on June 24; thirty-six killed and 150 wounded on June 25; twenty-two killed and 119 wounded on June 26; twenty-four killed and 123 wounded on June 27; fifty-four killed and 130 wounded on June 28.[19] It happened bit by bit, recalled John Lane, a rifleman with the 25th Marines, of the casualties on Saipan: "Send a squad down to check out that draw. See if there's any Japs. Send a few guys over to check out those caves. Take three men and dig out that sniper. Check those farm buildings. Blow that pillbox. All accompanied by a slow but steady trickle of casualties. You turn around and realize there aren't that many of you left."[20]

"Mount Tapotchau was rough, damn rough," observed PFC William Bilchak. "You had Japanese shooting and throwing grenades down on you while you're climbing ropes. . . . Our guys knocked out 30–32 caves. They said there were 300 or 400 of them. We'd go in groups of four—one BAR, one M1 (rifle), one flamethrower and me. You'd put the flamethrower on one side, and the BAR on the other. When the smoke and flame got to them, they'd start coming out. They didn't have a chance . . . You sent out four [Marines] and if they got killed, you sent out another four. You all got your turn to live. You all got your turn to die. You don't blame anybody. That's just the way it was."[21]

Corp. Ernest "Ray" McElveen's turn came on the afternoon of June 27 about halfway to the top of Mount Tapotchau when his platoon came onto an open area. "About 200 feet in front was a cornfield with stalks about three to four feet tall," he recalled. "There was no cover at all between our platoon and the cornfield." McElveen had a very bad feeling. "I had never looked at an area before where I could not pick out some form of cover," he observed. "For the first time in my life I felt I was making a decision to forfeit my life. I felt the odds of my making it were totally nil."

The platoon was about halfway to the cornfield, when the lieutenant apparently saw something he didn't like. He ordered a halt, followed a moment later by the order to pull back. The Japanese, who had been waiting in the corn, immediately opened up with a hail of fire. McElveen had dropped to one knee and was returning fire when a bullet hit him in the upper left shoulder and plowed through his body, exiting by his spine. "The impact of the bullet knocked me to the ground, and I lost consciousness," he recalled. "When I came to, I was lying with my face on the ground, blowing bloody foam, and coughing up blood when I breathed. The upper part of my body was paralyzed, but I could move my legs. I could not see our lines, but I could see enemy troops lying in the corn ahead. I seemed to have lost all my hearing; and when I yelled at the top of my voice, I could hardly hear myself. I began to call for someone to help me, but I felt it would do no good because I was coughing up blood and trying to face the fact that nothing could save me even if I could be pulled out of the area."

A familiar face suddenly looked down on him. It was PFC Eddie Grant, a twenty-one-year-old Irish kid from West Orange, New Jersey. Grant dragged him to his feet, yelling, "Run, Mac! Run!" He supported McElveen for a short distance and then ducked for cover as the fire directed toward them intensified. McElveen tried to run, but his upper body wouldn't cooperate and he fell down. He could hear Grant encouraging him, but he could not move. The Japanese had stopped firing, patiently waiting.

Grant dashed out again. As the Japanese opened up, he was hit, but he got a grip on McElveen and dragged and pulled until they were finally out of the line of fire. McElveen spent five days and nights in a field hospital before being evacuated to the hospital ship *Bountiful*. A doctor told him the bullet had missed his spinal cord by less than one-eighth of an inch. Eddie Grant was also evacuated, but his wound was not serious and he returned to the platoon. He survived Saipan, only to be killed a few weeks later on Tinian.[22]

Many a Marine that survived Saipan owed his life to a corpsman or the front-line medical care administered by a Navy surgeon. Their dedication was beyond reproach. Frank Borta came across a dead Marine still lying on a stretcher out in the bush. A corpsman was sprawled alongside, half his head blown away by a bullet that had caught him as he knelt to give aid. His open medical pack still stood beside him.[23] A member of the 25th Marines whose right leg was nearly torn off by a Japanese grenade during a night attack was more fortunate. Two corpsmen managed to retrieve him under heavy fire, then held a flashlight while the battalion surgeon, still under fire, amputated the leg and stopped the bleeding, using a pair of scissors, two hemostats, and a tourniquet.[24] The Marine survived.

"Often, the wounded men would be hollering or crying from the pain or fear while I tended to their wounds, but you would be amazed at how often the wounded men would become at ease when their fellow Marines held their hand and told them everything would be all right," remembered Hospital Apprentice 1st Class William R. Keyser. Some men, shot and knocked down, would get up and run 50 yards to cover, only to be completely paralyzed by the time Keyser reached them. Some fell to the ground screaming; others just dropped.[25]

PFC Stanley Wilson was shot attempting to cross an open field. He had taken cover behind a rock; when he got up to continue the advance, a bullet slammed into his chest: "Hit me like a sledge hammer," he observed. Wilson went into shock and lost consciousness. At some point he awoke and tried to cut his pack off his injured shoulder. "I tried to lift my rifle and couldn't," he recalled. "I tried to call out to a corpsman, and all that came out of my throat was a gurgle. 'I am dying,' I thought. 'I am dying.' I prayed for my mother. I began to pass out again. I tried to stay awake. I tried not to die." He lost consciousness again. "Then I woke up and I was alive. I was surprised." He felt stronger and managed to crawl back about 50 yards. Snipers were picking away at the Marines, but a buddy helped him out of the line of fire. He passed out again.

Wilson was taken aboard the USS *Solace* where he was given eight transfusions and put into an oxygen tank. Surgeons and 12,500 units of penicillin given intravenously saved his life and his lung. Such is the resilience of youth that Wilson's biggest relief after learning he would live was the assurance from surgeons that he would still be able to play basketball.[26]

Corp. Joseph Fiore earned his second Purple Heart on July 2 in the foothills of Mount Tapotchau. The twenty-one-year-old son of Italian immigrants from Glens Falls, New York, Fiore had been wounded by mortar fragments during the Marshall Islands campaign. As casualties mounted on Saipan, his unit, the 18th Marines, had been organized into an infantry battalion to stiffen the 2nd Marine Division's depleted line companies. Fiore was working his way along a steep ledge when a chunk of shrapnel smashed into his upper right leg. He tumbled over the edge, losing his rifle. His best friend, PFC Warren R. "Bob" Ackerman, and another Marine came after him. "They got my hands and pulled me up on the ledge and they had a stretcher there . . ." said Fiore. Four litter-bearers lugged him back to the battalion CP where he was lashed into a jeep for the ride down the mountain. It took about an hour to negotiate the steep track down. Fiore was a bit surprised they made it without tipping over.

His next stop was the 2nd Division field hospital, set up in the roofless ruin of the former Japanese radio station at the end of the Charan Kanoa airstrip. There were nineteen surgical tables on the lower floor of the burned-out building and in big blackout tents. Fiore was one of about 180 cases coming in each day. A doctor probed his leg wound and asked him if he could feel anything. "I said no, I'm pretty numb," recalled Fiore. "So he had this long scissors, you know. So he goes right in where the bullet came out or the shrapnel and he hit something solid and he took it out and he said, 'You're going to be okay now.'"[27]

Also landing at the radio station hospital that night was PFC Jack Gresham. Earlier in the day he had been bayoneted high up in the back during house-to-house fighting in Garapan, but a corpsman took care of the injury and he stayed with his unit. His reprieve was brief. That night a

Japanese mortar round fluttered in and wounded a number of men, including Gresham. He didn't seem to be seriously hurt, but when he went to help the others, he found his legs wouldn't work. An ambulance took him and a wounded corpsman to the 2nd Division hospital. Gresham felt embarrassed as they sat on the edge of a surgical table waiting for attention. His wounds seemed minor, even though he couldn't move his feet. The corpsman, meanwhile, had been hit through the chest. He was smoking a cigarette and every time he took a drag, smoke drifted out through the hole in his back.[28]

In the morning the wounded were lugged down to the beach and left on stretchers to await evacuation. "It had to be 95 in the shade," recalled Fiore. "It was terrible. And this big black sailor came over. I never saw a man so big in my life. And he says, 'Hey, Marine. Want a cold drink?' I gave him a few choice words. He came back and he had a can of Dole pineapple juice and he said, 'C'mon,' and he knelt down and lifted my head and he gave me a drink. And I said, 'Where in the hell did you get this?' And he said, 'The Seabees right over there.' They had a refrigeration system right on the beach." Not long after, Fiore was boated out to the USS *Solace*.[29]

One of four hospital ships evacuating the wounded off Saipan—the others were *Relief, Samaritan,* and *Bountiful*—*Solace* had already made one trip back to Guadalcanal with a full load of 583 casualties. Known in peacetime as the *Iroquois,* the converted vessel had been part of the Clyde Line, which carried tourists between New York and Miami. She had beds for 480 and could accommodate another hundred or more in a pinch, such as the opening days at Saipan. There were six double-bunked wards, a convalescent ward, five operating tables, an X-ray room, a pharmacy, and the various accoutrements of a well-equipped hospital. *Solace* carried seventeen doctors, thirteen nurses, and 175 medical corpsmen. Medical personnel dressed in white; ordinary crewmembers wore the usual blue dungarees.[30]

Arriving at the end of a specially wide gangway, the filthy, bloody casualties were taken by stretcher up to the deck where a doctor examined their red-bordered casualty tags and checked wounds as he sorted them out for the various wards. The patients' clothes were cut off and tossed overboard. Sixty-five percent of the wounds were from shell or mortar fire, while a surprising 6.6 percent were the result of knives or bayonets—a reflection of the number of hand-to-hand encounters on Saipan. The remainder were caused by small arms fire.[31]

Hit by a shell fragment the first day, Sgt. Mike Masters was already on his way back to Hawaii aboard the USS *Bolivar.* The unanticipated flood of casualties was clearly straining the system. "We were tiered in bunks three high and were assisted by ambulatory patients, because of the shortage of medics," he recalled. "A Marine across from me and another above my bunk died during the first night. Others succumbed en route to Hawaii. I don't know if they would have made it with closer attention, or maybe their time was up." Noticing his wound's putrid smell and fearful of gangrene, Masters asked the lone doctor if his bandage should be changed, but was told it was better left alone until they got to Hawaii. The bandage stayed and so did the stink.[32]

Back on Saipan, Graves Registration personnel did their best to keep up with the parade of dead. Within days of the landing, each division had laid out its own cemetery. "The dead were removed from the stretchers and gently placed in the back of trucks that had been driven as close as possible to the front lines," remembered PFC John Eardley. "It was a gruesome business as some of the bodies had broken bones that protruded through torn dungarees at crazy angles . . . Arms, legs, heads, torsos and bits of bodies were thrown on the truck . . . and a tarpaulin spread over the remains."

Transported back to the appropriate division cemetery, the bureaucratic process began. "A bulldozer scooped out a pit fifty feet by ten and six feet deep and the dead were taken off the trucks and laid onto stretchers alongside the pit and searched for identification," observed Eardley, a witness to the procedure at the 2nd Marine Division cemetery located on the flats near the former Japanese radio station. "They were then placed in the pit and covered over with sand . . . The smell was overpowering and nauseating, and this along with the sweltering heat caused me to throw up."[33]

At the 27th Infantry Division cemetery, established near Yellow Beach 3 on D plus 4, all dead were wrapped in blankets and buried in trenches scraped out by a bulldozer. When a shortage of GI blankets developed, Graves Registration used new white wool Japanese navy blankets found stockpiled in a captured warehouse.[34] Less easily resolved, the division discovered the crosses and Stars of David issued to the Graves Registration platoon on Oahu had been poorly painted and were so unsightly they could not be used until repainted, a job that was not undertaken until the end of the campaign.[35]

Japanese remains were treated with considerably less ceremony, dumped into holes and covered over, generally more out of sanitation concerns than compassion. Burials of individual enemy soldiers tended to be perfunctory. No one exerted any more energy than necessary; if the hole wasn't quite large enough, so be it. "The Marines had a habit of burying Japanese and letting their feet stick out," remarked Sgt. Roland Fronheiser, who came ashore with an Army artillery outfit. "There was one buried right there where our guns were mounted for a long time with its legs sticking out, just from the knees up. One day our captain walked by and saw those feet sticking out and said we should be ashamed of ourselves. Eventually we had to cover it up."[36]

The direness of the Japanese situation was revealed in appalling fashion on June 28 when GIs from the 105th Infantry stumbled into the recently abandoned field hospital near Donnay. Horribly wounded and dying Japanese soldiers lay intermingled with more than 400 of their dead comrades. Though incapacitated and unable to walk, the surviving patients refused to surrender and began blowing themselves up with grenades. A few of the GIs started shooting the wounded, but were quickly reined in. Virtually all of the abandoned patients eventually died, either by their own hand or from wounds and exposure.[37]

Despite impending collapse, units and fragments of Japanese units fought on. "As we moved up the eastern side of the island, we lost men daily—many to snipers, some to small battles while taking a gun position," said PFC Bob Tierney. "The Japanese were extremely fanatical. They had had the idea that it was an honor to die for the Emperor instilled in them. There were a number of instances where ten to twenty men were firing from a trench. We would call up a flame-throwing tank and before we used it, we would hear numerous explosions and shots. The Japanese would commit suicide. Most wore shoes with the big toe of the shoe split like a glove. They would put the toe on the rifle trigger and shoot themselves in the head."[38]

"We used hand grenades and flamethrowers to get them," observed Charles Toth. "When the flamethrower goes up, you hear the screaming and yelling in the caves, people burning to death. When they come out, you kill them."[39] It was terrible, but necessary. "I always felt bad when the Japanese would run out of their holes . . . almost naked, but with fuel and fire from the flamethrowers covering their bodies, screaming and dying," observed PFC Carl Matthews. "But if we gave them half a chance we would have been the ones dying."[40]

Others had lost any vestige of compassion. As PFC Harvey Hunt's squad walked by an unseen cave a Japanese shot one of the Marines in the chest, fatally wounding him. The squad went after the cave with a flamethrower. "The flamethrower [bearer] stepped up and cut loose with the flamethrower and it didn't ignite," remembered Hunt. "All that came out of it was napalm. And this gook knew what it was. And he came out. He was just covered with napalm. The flamethrower gave him another burst and it still didn't ignite." The Japanese soldier's eyes went wide with fear. A third burst still failed to ignite, whereupon one of the Marines said, "This is nonsense," and shot the terrified man dead.[41]

PFC Gabe Vertucci, a tough kid from Amsterdam, New York, nearly lost his life clambering up rugged hills in vegetation so tangled it was often easier to crawl underneath than try to push through. Edging his way down a narrow path, he was startled to hear a baby cry just off to his right. He turned his head to find himself looking directly into the eyes of a uniformed Japanese soldier pointing a rifle at his head at point-blank range. Before he could react, the world exploded. "It happened so fast," he recalled. The rifle was so close that the muzzle blast burned Vertucci's neck, but the simple act of turning his head to look to the right saved his life. The slug went through the back of his helmet, grazing his hair but somehow missing his skull.

The Japanese worked his rifle bolt, chambering another round, but before he could fire again, Vertucci dropped to one knee and shot him twice in the chest. The Japanese—his uniform indicated he was a member of the Special Naval Landing Force—fell on his face, but Vertucci wasn't taking any chances. "I put a bullet in the side of his head and the whole top of his head come off from the ears up," he remembered. The brain lay in the top of the skull "like it was setting in a bowl," he observed. He suddenly realized his left leg was shaking uncontrollably. As he gathered himself, another Marine came up, studied the gory scene, and remarked thoughtfully, "Boy, Gabe, you really equalized him."

It turned out that the Japanese had been with a group of civilians—including a baby—hiding in a camouflaged shelter by the side of the path. Vertucci had been at arm's length and never saw it. If not for the baby's squall, he never would have turned his head. "That baby saved my life," he said years later.[42]

While most Americans on Saipan were intent on killing Japanese, Lt. Bob Sheeks was in the business of persuading enemy soldiers and civilians to give themselves up. The son of a Ford Motor executive, Sheeks was born in Shanghai, China, in 1922 and lived there until he was thirteen years old. Already able to speak some Chinese when he went into the service, he was sent to language school in Colorado to learn Japanese and ended up with the 2nd Marine Division as an interpreter. Though he took the job seriously, his presence evoked some skepticism in the line units. "Everybody thought the Japanese were fanatics who would never give up, but I thought under the right circumstances that some would," he said. "For one thing, they didn't know about raising a white flag to surrender—they were never taught. It was important to show them how to do it."[43]

Using battery-powered loudspeakers, Japanese linguists tried with mixed success to talk Japanese soldiers and civilians out of the caves, promising them water and repeating phrases like *shimpai shinaide* (don't be afraid) and *te o age* (put your hands up). Sometimes someone would answer. Sometimes there would be silence or explosions from inside the cave as the occupants killed themselves with hand grenades. If no one came out, the Marine demolition teams would move in.

Sheeks observed that the Marines demonstrated some sympathy for civilians but seemed almost bemused by his exertions to persuade Japanese soldiers to give up. They would stand around waiting for him to complete his pitch. When it failed, as it so often did, they would go about their deadly business and move in and burn out the cave and its stubborn occupants. They showed no compassion for the enemy, nor did they seem particularly interested in making Sheeks's job any easier. "They often thought I was really just delaying their work," he observed.[44]

Fear, caution, an inability to communicate, enemy recalcitrance, the insistence by too many cornered Japanese to try to kill one more enemy, all contributed to the American reluctance to show mercy. "We learned early on not to get close to one lying on the ground unless you could see his brains or his guts," remarked PFC John Pope. "No matter if you had the best of intentions; if alive he would kill you as he draws his last breath."[45] Lee Weber, a lieutenant with the 2nd Marine Division, said bluntly, "We would never take a Japanese prisoner . . . We'd shoot them all. . . ."[46]

Pvt. Frank Borta's outfit ran into a Japanese sniper who killed one Marine and wounded another before he was shot out of a tree. He looked to be about fourteen or fifteen years old. Wounded and crying, he was dragged off for interrogation. "At the command post there was a chaplain," recalled Borta. "He gave the prisoner some water." When the chaplain turned to leave, the terrified prisoner crawled after him, grabbing at his leg. "Don't worry," the chaplain reassured him. "You'll be all right." As soon as the chaplain was out of sight the Marines took the prisoner into the bush and killed him.[47]

By the end of the first week only seventy-one military POWs had been taken by the entire landing force.[48] It is indicative of the Japanese aversion to surrender—as much as the American aversion to take chances—that this number could be considered encouraging in light of previous campaigns. One of the lucky ones was Superior Private Kawamura Kazuo, a member of the Black Leopard Unit, *150th Infantry Regiment*, which had been stranded on Saipan in April. Acting as a messenger, the twenty-one-year-old draftee was wounded in the foot, leg, and buttocks by shell fragments the night of June 19. By the time he dragged himself back to the cave serving as his unit's headquarters, everyone was gone. Over the next few days he hobbled aimlessly from place to place in hopes of escaping the incessant naval gunfire. It seemed that even a lighted cigarette or the mere flash of metal from an aluminum box of *kanpan* (dried biscuits) was enough to draw attention from the ships off shore. "Order broke down among the soldiers," he recalled. "During the night we dodged bullets and moved from cave to cave and hole to hole."

Kawamura came down with amoebic dysentery. He lost track of the days. His wounds began to fester and smell and it became difficult for him to move. At some point he lost his rifle. He retained a hand grenade to use on himself if he were about to be captured. One day, lying in a cave in a near stupor, he awoke to loud voices speaking English and found himself looking at the muzzle of a rifle and the boots of three or four American soldiers. "Through a hole in my pants they could see my buttocks and my wound, which was full of maggots," he said. A voice demanded, "Stand up! Stand up!" Kawamura resigned himself to death, hoping only that they would at least kill him quickly.

His captors roughly checked him for weapons. His grenade fell out when one of them tore open his jacket pocket. They took his watch and soldier's handbook. Finally he was hauled off and put on a jeep. He found the words of the *Senjinkun* (Instructions for the Battlefield) drifting in and out of his mind. *Ikite ryoushu no hazukashime wo ukezu* (A soldier must never suffer the disgrace of being captured alive). He knew he should kill himself, but made no effort to do so. "I had been taught to expect the worst from the Americans, but it didn't happen," he recalled. A medic at a field hospital cleaned his body with alcohol and doctors treated his wounds. "In response to their kind treatment, I had a feeling of gratitude," he said. "Near my bed at the field hospital, I remember seeing three dead American soldiers who looked like wax figures."

Kawamura eventually ended up in a POW camp in Wisconsin. He was repatriated in January 1947, after two and a half years as a prisoner, returning to his parents' home in Azumino. The local newspaper printed a small item titled "Soul of a Departed Soldier Returns Home." It was an appropriate observation; he felt like a man who had come back from the dead. One of only a handful of survivors from his unit, he quietly returned to his peacetime occupation as a rice farmer and descended into obscurity.[49]

Dogged by shellfire, Saburo Arakaki and Sergeant Aoki made their way north after fleeing the Donnay hospital charnel house. There was no respite from the Americans. Even the night was set alight by flares. The trails were crowded with desperate refugees. The dead lay where they fell, stripped of any useful belongings by the living. Fights broke out over canteens and precious water. One morning, in the half light of dawn, Saburo was awakened by voices. He stiffened apprehensively before realizing they were speaking Japanese. Three soldiers passed by. Saburo spoke up, asking if they knew where food might be found. One replied that there was a provisions warehouse at Matansa on the western shore. "Try there," he said.

Saburo and Aoki trudged up the roadway leading north from Garapan, accompanied by scores of others, moving like sleepwalkers in the night. They located the naval provisions warehouse to find it had been destroyed in the shelling. The stench of rotting food and the corpses of military personnel lying about offered little hope of succor, but Saburo burrowed into the rubble and miraculously came up with hard tack, some canned crab, and canned red bean rice. They stuffed their shoulder bags and pockets with all the food they could carry, filled their canteens from the muddy dregs of a demolished water tank, and resumed their journey north toward Marpi Point. After that, there would be nowhere to go.

The futility of their trek was not lost on them. They talked it over briefly. If they stayed where they were, they'd be killed. If they kept heading north, they were just delaying the inevitable. "Saburo," said Sergeant Aoki finally, "if it has come to this, let's just try to survive as long as we can." They gathered their meager belongings and started walking.[50]

CHAPTER XXI

Rabbit Hunt

WITH THE STALEMATE IN THE DEATH VALLEY FINALLY BROKEN, THE long-delayed push through Garapan began the morning of July 2. Supported by tanks, the 3rd Battalion, 2nd Marines ventured cautiously into the rubble of the once tidy little coastal city. The division historian compared the onetime "Little Tokyo" to "a crushed anthill under a carpet of autumn leaves"—the leaves being the litter of corrugated metal roofing strewn thickly over the ground.[1]

An intelligence assessment issued on June 28 expressed concern that Garapan might be a Japanese trap. According to that report, POWs claimed that "artillery and mortars have been registered on every point in GARAPAN and the city left open to BLUE advance with the obvious purpose of annihilating our troops as they occupied the city in force."[2] Fortunately, that ominous warning was not borne out. "Moving out, we found the city lightly defended initially . . . ," observed Lt. James L. Fawcett, advancing with K Company. Fawcett's platoon came upon the Garapan post office, a substantial concrete building that was still relatively intact. "We moved up rapidly, stormed the double door, threw in two hand grenades, and followed up right after they exploded, entering a large room," said Fawcett. "Two enemy lay on the floor, victims of our hand grenades. The men raced up the stairs to the next floor, found one more of the enemy, and shot him dead."[3]

Ducking sniper fire, the Marines advanced warily along the rubble-choked streets, past the occasional bloated dead cow, investigating holes and the shattered remnants of buildings littered with the now somehow incongruous possessions of former residents. A gutted shop contained a Singer sewing machine; phonograph records lay strewn about, some the product of Nipponphone Company of Kawasaki, others by the Teitoku Gramophone Company. During a pause on a street corner, some Marines amused themselves playing Bach and Wagner on a salvaged phonograph. Other records produced strange and grating—to Western ears—Asian musical arrangements. A store mannequin—yellow-haired and thoroughly occidental—lay in the street, naked except for her brown shoes. Papers and photographs of somber-faced schoolchildren, formal family portraits, and even photos of Japanese baseball teams were scattered about. Among the few relatively intact items in the ruins of Garapan's Catholic church was a statute of Christ on the Cross.[4]

By noon, the advance had made about 700 yards through the battered city. In the foothills to the east, the Marines enveloped Flametree Hill—the incongruously beautiful red blossoms looking over the putrefying corpses of enemy soldiers killed in an artillery trap three days before. Hoping to eradicate the position without direct assault, on June 29 the division had put down artillery fire on the hill as if preceding an infantry attack. When the barrage lifted, the Marines opened up with small arms and when the Japanese came out of their shelters to repel the "attack," brought the artillery crashing back down. Evidence indicated the deception had worked well.

After exterminating a few last defenders, the advance continued north toward the day's objective—a forested knob, dubbed Sugarloaf Hill, located about 1,000 yards inland from Garapan center. Shaped like its namesake loaf, the limestone hill rose up like a small "Pacific Gibraltar," noted the division historian. Marine halftracks pocked the sides of the height with their 75mm guns, while Japanese fired back from hollowed-out caverns in the limestone. A private raised his head too high and a bullet struck him in the left eye, sending his helmet tumbling and spattering a nearby sergeant with blood. The sergeant had had enough. He stood up and yelled at a nearby Marine, "Goddamn it, Mac. Let's go up and get these bastards!" The Marines got moving, pushing up into the rocks against withering machine-gun fire. As they came over the crest, about twenty Japanese rose up out of their holes in a desperate effort to sweep them off the hill. The Marines gunned them down.[5]

The 6th Marines had an easier time with flat-topped Observatory Hill, surmounted by a 50-foot, copper-roofed lighthouse built in 1934 to assist ships navigating into Tanapag Harbor. Armed with drum-fed machine guns originally designed for use in aircraft, the Japanese made a stand in the white concrete lighthouse and attached one-story light keeper's quarters, but were quickly cleaned out.

Still farther inland, the 8th Marines were finally descending from the hills that had caused them so much grief in the preceding days. Remarking on the effect of unrelenting combat on his platoon, PFC Rick Spooner observed, "They were lean and mean and obviously looked it. Dungarees were tattered and worn and faded with perspiration stains. They seemed held together by little more than bloodstains, dirt and dried mud. The men's tempers had grown short and their language was colorful and somewhat bizarre. [They] had reverted to using profanity to a marked degree and were practically unaware of it. It was not second nature but had nearly progressed to the point where it was an art form." They traveled light: a spoon, mess gear, a change of socks, poncho, two canteens of water (if they could get it), bandoleers of ammo, rations, combat knife, first-aid kit, and shovel—always a shovel. Almost every infantryman also had a dirty toothbrush sticking out of his breast pocket. It was used to clean his weapon, not his teeth.[6] Catching a break for once, the 8th Marines swept ahead nearly a mile on July 1 and 2, bringing the waters of Tanapag Harbor north of Garapan into view.

The following day, Maj. Harold Thronesen's 3rd Battalion, 2nd Marines jumped off soon after dawn from the intersection of "27th and Broadway" and pushed into Garapan's former business district. Just to the east, the 1st Battalion moved through residential areas on the eastern edge of town, prowling past the vacant homes of the island's wealthier Japanese with their ornamental gardens and artful concrete bridges over tiny burbling brooks. Tropical fish floated belly up on the clouded waters of decorated ponds. By late afternoon, the battalion had reached the shoreline north of Garapan while Thronesen emerged from Garapan and swept north to seize the burned-out Japanese barracks complex at Mutcho Point.

The booty there included three 140mm guns still loaded on railroad cars for delivery; three 5-inch coast defense guns (tubes and carriages); thirty-two 120mm dual-purpose guns (tubes and carriages); and six 200mm mortars (complete)—mute testimony to the surprise achieved by the American landing on June 15. A couple of shot-up buses and about twenty burned-out trucks, all bearing naval insignia, sat around the former motor pool. Storage areas contained hundreds of rolls of unused barbed wire and about twenty big searchlights, while a blockhouse yielded cases of canned crab meat "packed for the Evers Company, Hamburg."

A few of the men paused to rinse their grimy hands and faces in the lapping ocean. "Son of a bitch," said a Marine private to no one in particular. "Tomorrow's the Fourth of July."[7]

That same night—as the Japanese prepared to move their combined headquarters north yet again—Major Hirakushi approached Generals Igeta and

Saito with disastrous news. What was left of the so-called defense line was in a state of collapse. Igeta did not respond to Hirakushi's report. "Are we going to start for the new headquarters as planned?" asked Hirakushi.

"Yes," replied Igeta. "Everything on schedule as stated."

General Saito said nothing.

Delayed by U.S. naval gunfire, the headquarters detachment left about a half an hour after midnight. "There were about thirty of us," recalled Hirakushi. "The moon was shining brightly; men in single file, dragging along, shadows reflected on the ground. Even to me, a miserable scene. No equipment, only pistols and grenades. No food, no water."[8]

What would prove to be their final destination was a cave in a narrow ravine about 1,000 yards east of Makunsha Village. The Americans would dub the ravine "Paradise Valley." The Japanese, having a different perspective, called it "the Valley of Hell." Arriving some three hours later, the men were so exhausted they simply collapsed on the ground. Though tired and frustrated, Igeta and Saito resisted urgings from some officers that they authorize a final charge so they might all die gloriously in battle. For the moment, they would continue to hope against hope that a dogged defense would "chew the American forces to pieces."[9]

The following day—Independence Day—the U.S. advance secured the remainder of Mutcho Point and the Japanese naval installation at Tanapag, beating the bushes in what one Marine described as a "rabbit hunt."[10] The hulks of eight huge Kawanishi four-engine flying boats like the one in which Admiral Koga had met his death months before lay broken on the pitted concrete apron of the seaplane base. Two amphibious tanks were found hidden in a couple of nondescript buildings, apparently abandoned by their crews, but except for a couple of snipers, the base was deserted.

Bands of Japanese soldiers moved haphazardly along the coastal plain and in the foothills after dark. Most were stragglers who had been cut off by the advance and were trying to make their way north. A group of Japanese officers blundered into the 6th Marines. Challenged, they tried to run, but were clearly visible in the moonlight. "We could see them holding their sabers as they ran," said PFC Clarence Hargis. "Seven were in the group. All were dead the next morning. Two had jumped in a hole and committed hara kiri by holding grenades to their heads. They were headless when we saw them the next morning. We had thought that when they were tapping the grenades on their helmets that they would throw them. Some of the

Marines in the command post got sprinkled with the skulls and debris."[11] Two other Japanese burst into a 27th Division company perimeter the night of July 3 shouting, "American soldier die!" but it was they who did the dying. One was shot and the other, an officer, blew himself up with a grenade.[12]

In the early morning hours of July 4, the long-suffering 27th Division got a small measure of revenge on the architects of their travails. At about 0130, GIs manning the perimeter of the 165th Infantry command post observed half a dozen figures approaching in the rainy darkness. A larger group trailed behind, clearly unaware of their peril. The night exploded as the Americans opened fire. Some of the shadowy figures dropped, others scattered. At daylight, GIs found twenty-seven dead Japanese—including a sizeable number of officers—lying sprawled in the rain. Among the dead was Col. Yukimatsu Ogawa, commanding officer of the *136th Infantry Regiment*. A sheaf of operational orders and message books were retrieved from the colonel's body, one of which turned out to be a field order dated July 2, accompanied by a sketch map. The order included detailed instructions from General Saito on plans to form a new defense line extending from north of Garapan through Radar Hill and Hill 112 to the eastern coast. Complying with these orders, Colonel Ogawa had ordered the remnants of his bypassed regiment to withdraw the night of July 3. He was apparently on his way to a new command post about 500 meters east of Radar Hill when he was killed.[13]

As Major Hirakushi had already deduced, Japanese hopes of forming a new line were doomed. Probably few of the *136th Regiment* survivors and assorted stragglers from other units were able to get to the assembly area. Those who did had no time to dig in or organize and were quickly overrun. It was pretty much the same story along the entire front. Orders were to "defend to the end" and the end was clearly near. With no shovels to dig fighting holes, the men used their helmets. The survivors of the *135th Infantry* from Tanapag had "dumped everything . . . some even their rifles," observed Hirakushi. "Men were like refugees."[14] The breakdown was apparent to the GIs and Marines. "Although there were considerable numbers of enemy encountered," commented the 27th Division G-3 Periodic Report, "they appeared to be very much disorganized and confused."[15] An Army intelligence memo reported, "Six (6) Japs were found at TA 204X at 1235 who had committed suicide by taking their shoes off and pulling the trigger with their toes."[16]

By July 4, the axis of the drive by the 27th Division and 4th Marine Division had taken a more northwesterly direction toward the coast, threatening to cut off Japanese forces hoping to mount a defense in the Tanapag area. On the far right of the advance, the 4th Marine Division had emerged from the open Kagan Peninsula to tackle a series of hills, the most notable being Hill 721, Hill 767, and Hill 221, the latter dubbed Radar Hill due to the enemy radar installation rising from its summit like a derelict bedspring. A fourth prominence, a sort of nose protruding from the southeastern face of Hill 721, was dubbed "Fourth of July Hill."

As the 27th Division closed on the Flores Point, large numbers of Japanese began fleeing along the coastal plain to escape the rapidly closing trap. There was no organization to their movement—it was a rout. "Some of them merely ran along in the open as far and as fast as they could go," reported 27th Division historian Edmund Love. "Others moved from cover to cover."[17] Some isolated groups fired on the GIs coming down from the hills, but most seemed intent only on escaping the pocket. Gratified by the number of targets after more than two weeks of fighting an often invisible enemy, the GIs lined the ridge overlooking the plain. By mid-afternoon the whole division front was engaged, pot-shooting at Japanese below.

Accompanying a battalion of the 105th Infantry into the gutted naval installations on Flores Point, S/Sgt. Louis S. Doddo bagged a member of *5th Special Naval Base Force* commander Rear Adm. Takeshita Tsujimura's staff when Navy Cmdr. Jiro Saito emerged from a bunker and gave up. Interrogators described Saito, the highest-ranking enemy officer captured to date, as "intelligent, talking easily, but seems to be withholding information and evasive." Originally in charge of keeping track of convoys sailing in and out of Saipan, Saito had been left in command of the defense sector near Tanapag after Admiral Tsujimura and other staff withdrew to the north the previous day. He claimed he had been knocked unconscious by a near miss from a naval shell and awakened the morning of July 4 to find himself alone. He then sought refuge in a bunker where he remained until the arrival of Sergeant Doddo and the prospect of sharing his hideout with a live hand grenade. The Japanese plan, he said, was to "fight a delaying action, attacking if possible." The morale of the Base Force units was good, he declared, and they would "fight to the death."

Apparently ruminating on his own failure to fight to the death, Commander Saito belatedly asked to be returned to his own lines or shot. He seemed genuinely disappointed when both requests were refused. An Army photographer took a shot of the prisoner—sitting shirtless and looking malnourished and dejected—under the rifle and watchful eye of twenty-nine-year old Sergeant Doddo, who in happier times had been a carpenter in his home-town of Norwalk, Connecticut. Despite his objections, Commander Saito would survive the war. Sergeant Doddo was not so lucky. At the time of the triumphant photo, he had less than three days to live.[18]

As organized Japanese resistance crumbled, thousands of terrified—often starving—civilians were in desperate straits. Among the refugees hiding in Saipan's caves and thickets, Gregorio Muna Quintugua's family had exhausted their food two weeks after fleeing inland. They tried to assuage their hunger by chewing on sugar cane scavenged from a nearby farm, but they were starving. Scavenging in the jungle, Gregorio found a dead Jap-anese soldier with an unopened bag of *kamenpo*, a type of Japanese hard cracker, still clutched in his hand. The soldier had been dead for at least a couple of days. His gas-distended stomach strained against his uniform shirt, ready to burst. Thousands of flies covered the stinking corpse, but Gre-gorio could not resist the bag of crackers. He pried the bag out of the dead man's swollen hand and brought it back to the cave where his prize was greeted as a feast fit for kings.[19]

The plight of innocent civilians moved even the more callous Marines and GIs. PFC Gardner A. Browning recalled a man in his outfit named Monroe. "He was a big, loudmouthed fellow . . . who weighed 260 pounds and had played on the Marine football team," said Browning. "One time we hit a cave, and we heard somebody crying and out came a teenage girl with no clothes on. Monroe took his jacket off and wrapped it around her. She went to a little shrine near the cave and prayed. Then she came back and kissed Monroe's boots."[20]

Twelve-year-old David Sablan and about three dozen others had taken shelter in a cave, surviving mostly on scavenged sugar cane. Their prospects looked bleak. "In school our teachers told us the Americans will kill all men and take our girls to the U.S.," he recalled. "We had visions of Americans as being 8 feet tall in pressed white shorts and white short-sleeve shirts and wearing white stockings and nothing can ever get them dirty." Juan Cama-cho Diaz had similar fears. "The Japanese had told us Americans are the very worst enemy," he observed. "They will cut off your nose and ears and maybe poke out your eyes. Don't be captured by the Americans."

In the end, David Sablan's life was saved by a crying baby. Unable to quiet the infant as Marines approached their hideout, the Chamor-ros retreated into the far corners of their cave and began praying. What sounded to Sablan's youthful ears like a "terrible voice" yelled something into the mouth of the cave. Sablan's father jumped up and ran out with his hands in the air. Seconds later he called to the others to come out. Bracing for death, young David followed his mother out into the sunlight to find three sweaty Marines in dirty green uniforms. "The Americans gave us water, treated our wounds and were very nice to us," remembered Sablan. One of the Marines was wearing a crucifix around his neck. "We all kissed it and felt better because we now knew that the three men were Christian," observed Sablan. They later learned that the Marines had been about to throw a grenade into the cave when they heard the baby cry.[21]

Other encounters ended less happily. Mariana Sablan's family was captured by Americans checking caves in the Tanapag area on July 4. Mariana's father went back into the cave to get a Japanese civilian who was afraid to come out, but the man refused to move. Mariana's father finally gave up and emerged without him. An American soldier threw a hand grenade into the cave and killed the recalcitrant Japanese, who was apparently more terrified than threatening.[22] In a more horrific incident, a corpsman in Albert Ouellette's outfit went into a cave to help a Japanese woman in childbirth. The delivery was a success, but when he turned his back, the mother strangled the newborn. The Marines were shocked, but the incident was a sign of things to come as frightened Japanese civilians grew more and more desperate.[23]

In an effort to spare civilians pushed into the northern end of the island, NTLF planned to air drop leaflets addressed to General Saito at dawn on July 7, offering a "last chance to save the lives of non-combatants on Saipan island." The leaflet observed that "If the Japanese troops want to sacrifice their lives uselessly, that is their affair, but the American forces do not want to kill non-combatants." It directed non-combatants to come down the Banadero Road toward Tanapag at nine o'clock on Friday, July 7. "They will come unarmed and carrying white flags held high. If they do this, the American forces will receive them and save their lives . . . as human beings let us save the lives of the innocent."[24]

Tragically, events would dictate otherwise.

The end finally appeared to be within reach by July 5. Disorganized Japanese forces had been pushed into the northern end of the island. The 2nd Marine Division was pinched out of the advance on July 4, leaving the 27th Infantry Division and 4th Marine Division to move up the island side by side. Descending from the hills, Sgt. John Domanowski's company found an abandoned hospital located by a large cave. "There are a lot of wounded enemy lying on the ground," he wrote. "Some are on dirty blankets, and all are in a lot of pain. Most of them are too weak to do anything. I can hear a lot of death cries coming from below . . . We leave them and push on."[25]

Captured documents indicated two principal areas of resistance remaining: one near the Marpi Airfield at the northern end of the island in the 4th Marine Division's zone and the other centered on Paradise Valley facing the 27th Infantry Division. Of the original 30,000 Japanese troops, it was estimated that 5,000 to 7,000 were left, supported by one battalion of 77mm guns and perhaps as many as twenty tanks. Prisoner interrogations and other intelligence indicated a complete breakdown of enemy communications, a shortage of food and water, and abominable medical facilities. A few trucks were left, but there was little gasoline to operate them. Small arms also appeared to be in short supply.[26]

As Japanese morale sagged, the number of prisoners—a total of 172 Japanese and 237 Koreans was reported by NTLF as of July 6—began to rise, though surrenders remained the exception rather than the rule. A superior private from the *135th Infantry* estimated there were only 1,500 effectives capable of resistance on the northern end of the island.[27] Another captured private said half his unit had been killed; a few of the survivors had rifles but most were unarmed. Each man had been given a grenade with which to commit suicide. "Apparently the enemy feels that, since its fleet is so long overdue, there is no longer any hope," noted a 27th Division translator. "Many report that there would be more surrenders but that the officers threaten to kill them." Some POWs said the older men would be willing to give up, but the officers and younger soldiers were determined to continue the fight.[28]

A POW captured by the 24th Marines on July 5 said "he does not believe there would be a final 'Banzai charge' because remaining units are too scattered and disorganized." Four Korean POWs estimated that "more than half" of the remaining enemy in the north end of the island were "too sick or wounded to be effective."[29] Periodic Report No. 22, recorded by Task Force 56 on July 6, observed, "The enemy's ability to offer effective resistance has been eliminated; his freedom of movement is restricted, his centers of resistance are contained . . . The end of the SAIPAN operation is in view." A report of enemy air activities at Marpi Airfield the night of July 5—including a plane that apparently took off from the field in the early morning hours of July 6—led to speculation the Japanese "were probably attempting the evacuation of key personnel."[30]

But if there was cause for optimism, there was also reason for caution as the enemy grew increasingly desperate. Reporting on July 3 that enemy morale appeared to be sagging, 27th Division intelligence felt compelled to add a warning: "NOTE: In previous engagements it has not been unusual for the Jap to launch counterattacks at the time when his morale appears broken."[31] A Japanese army lieutenant captured the next day by the 2nd Marine Division lent credence to that caution, telling his captors he believed "the remainder of the garrison would fight to the last man with a probable all-out Banzai charge of all ambulatories in the final stage."[32]

Twenty-two-year-old Marine sergeant William Rogal entertained no doubts that the enemy would fight to the last gasp; he came across a prime example around July 5. "This Jap was lying on his stomach and he must have heard my footsteps because he turned over and he had a pistol," recounted Rogal. "I of course put a couple rounds into him and I looked at his face. He was blind. He was completely blind. And he was fighting, going to kill one more American if he could."[33]

Isolated in his headquarters cave in the side of Paradise Valley southeast of Makunsha, General Saito was showing the strain as his command disintegrated. "General Saito was feeling very poorly because for several days he had neither eaten nor slept well and was overstrained," recalled Major Hirakushi. "He was wearing a long beard and was a pitiful sight."[34]

The general had been wounded in the arm when American artillery pounded his headquarters area on July 4, though not so seriously that he could not continue. That same afternoon, Major Hirakushi saw men moving along the height across from the cave. They began to dig foxholes and he assumed they were Japanese preparing defenses. But when he took a closer look through his field glasses, he realized they were Americans. Soon afterward, the headquarters area came under fire from heavy automatic weapons. "At that time I felt we were entirely surrounded and had lost all hope," observed Hirakushi.[35]

Grasping at evaporating hopes, Igeta and Saito once again sent Major Hirakushi into the field to check the defensive line. He found no one: no soldiers, no bodies. He ran north along the beach. Nothing. The defenders had left so hurriedly, they hadn't even taken the time to carve up the carcasses of newly killed water buffalos to assuage their hunger. Returning to the headquarters, the major reported that there was no effective defense. All units were in a state of disorganization or retreat. The Americans could not be stopped.

After a moment of silence, General Igeta said, "Tomorrow morning we will begin assembling all remaining troops in the area for the final attack. Let us end this battle."

Generals Saito and Igeta went into a private conference with their staff officers to decide on a course of action. Though not privy to the discussion, Major Hirakushi later observed, "This final decisive action had to be simply one of two courses. First, to remain as we were and starve to death or secondly, to make a last attack and fight to the finish."[36] According to the Japanese military mindset, such a choice was a simple one: self-destruction, or *gyokusai*. Translated literally as "breaking the jewel," a *gyokusai* was an attack that would end only with complete self-annihilation. On July 5, General Saito advised Imperial General Headquarters in Tokyo, "I have issued the following order: On the 7th—the day after tomorrow—we will advance to attack the American forces and all will die an honorable death. Each man will kill ten Americans."[37]

Learning of the decision, Major Hirakushi asked about the fate of the thousands of Japanese civilians that had been pushed into the northern part of the island with fleeing military personnel. "There is no longer any distinction between civilians and troops," replied Saito. "It would be better for them to join in the attack with bamboo spears than be captured. Write out instructions to that effect."[38]

Three hundred copies of the attack order were mimeographed for distribution. Before they could be sent out, a messenger from the naval communications cave located to the north arrived. A dispatch from Tokyo had arrived, apparently crossing with Saito's communique. The messenger told the army officers that Tokyo wanted the battle to be continued in order to "gain time." Reinforcements were promised. "Hang on and try to check enemy. We are trying to send you reinforcements." Navy officers were prepared to obey that directive, but the army staff officers dissented: "The arrow has been shot," said one officer. Voices were raised. Relations between the army and navy, never warm to begin with, degenerated into name calling with army officers dismissing the navy as "cowards." The argument went on all night among staff officers. Igeta, Saito, and Nagumo said nothing.[39]

Despite navy objections, the *gyokusai* would go forward. "After issuing the orders, it seemed that the work of headquarters was finished," observed Hirakushi. "Everybody put his personal belongings in order." The headquarters group indulged in a farewell "feast" with the last of their food—a can of crab meat and a rice ball for each man. Major Hirakushi produced two cigarettes, all that remained from a pack that had been given to him in Japan by Prince Kaya Tsunenori, a first cousin to the empress, as a memento. The officers passed them around, smoking them down until they were too small to hold.[40]

About 2 miles down the coast from General Saito's headquarters cave, Sgt. Ronald L. Johnson and his best friend, twenty-four-year-old Sgt. Ervin D. "Dale" Deadmond, were sitting in the rubble of the former Japanese naval base at Flores Point sipping looted Scotch whiskey from canteen cups. Their unit, the 1st Battalion, 105th Infantry, was in reserve and the campaign seemed to be nearing an end. Deadmond had made it no secret that he expected to be killed on Saipan. Now, as they enjoyed the spoils of victory, Johnson good-naturedly chided him a bit. The worst was over, he observed. They were almost to the end of the island. "Don't you feel you're going to make it?" he asked.

To his surprise, Deadmond "kinda laughed, smiled" and replied, "I don't think I'm going to make it."[41]

Within a few hours, Dale Deadmond and much of the 1st Battalion would be dead.

The American shelling in the vicinity of General Saito's headquarters resumed at dawn. A sentry posted at the entrance to the cave reported that an enemy tank was visible on the edge of the cliff above. Saito, who had been conferring quietly with General Igeta, summoned Major Hirakushi. The *gyokusai* was set for the night of July 6 or 7 depending on how quickly troops could be assembled. As for himself, he and General Igeta had decided to die at ten o'clock, he confided, adding, "Excuse us for going first." The general then read aloud a message he wished conveyed to all army troops:

> *I am addressing the officers and men of the Imperial Army on Saipan.*
>
> *For more than twenty days since the American devils attacked, the officers, men and civilian employees of the Imperial Army and Navy on this island have fought well and bravely. Everywhere they have demonstrated the honor and glory of the Imperial Forces. I expected that every man would do his duty.*
>
> *Heaven has not given us an opportunity. We have not been able to utilize fully the terrain. We have fought in unison up to the present time but now we have no materials with which to fight and our artillery for*

attack has been completely destroyed. Our comrades have fallen one after another. Despite the bitterness of defeat, we pledge "Seven lives to repay our country."

The barbarous attack of the enemy is being continued. Even though the enemy has occupied only a corner of Saipan, we are dying without avail under the violent shelling and bombing. Whether we attack or whether we stay where we are, there is only death. However, in death there is life. We must utilize this opportunity to exalt true Japanese manhood. I will advance with those who remain to deliver still another blow to the American devils and leave my bones on Saipan as a bulwark of the Pacific.

As it says in the Senjinkun (Battle Ethics), "I will never suffer the disgrace of being taken alive," and "I will offer up the courage of my soul and calmly rejoice in living by the eternal principle."

Here I pray with you for the eternal life of the Emperor and the welfare of the country and I advance to seek out the enemy.

Follow me![42]

Major Hirakushi accompanied Generals Saito and Igeta to a smaller cave near the headquarters. The two generals and a third high-ranking staff officer intended to cut open their stomachs as the first step in *seppuku*—ritual suicide—said Saito. Officers standing behind them would then shoot each of them in the back of the head to speed the process. The three officers sat cross-legged on the floor with their swords. Hirakushi turned away to find some water to wash their faces, but was distracted by a naval officer who called out that his group intended to head north in defiance of General Saito's orders. As Hirakushi moved to stop him, there were three shots. He turned to find Igeta, Saito, and the third staff officer sprawled on the floor of the cave, shot dead by the aides as they committed *seppuku*. Exhausted by events of the past few days, Hirakushi could not go on. Returning to the command cave, he collapsed and fell into a deep sleep.[43]

That same morning, in a cave serving as temporary naval headquarters just inland from Matansa, Admiral Nagumo, the onetime hero of Pearl Harbor, remarked to his staff, "Shall we go?" He then put a pistol to his head and squeezed the trigger. His chief of staff, Adm. Hideo Yano, also committed suicide. Nagumo's remains were hastily buried in an unmarked grave to prevent them from falling into the hands of the Americans.[44]

CHAPTER XXII

My Life Is Fluttering Away

WITH THE 2ND MARINE DIVISION PINCHED OUT OF THE LINE, THE 27TH Division GIs now held down the American left, extending from the water's edge, across 800 yards of coastal plain and into the hills to the east. The plain, which forty-eight hours earlier had been swarming with fleeing Japanese, now seemed strangely deserted.

As the attack resumed at 0905 on July 6, General Griner received orders from NTLF that seemed to let his division off the hook. The 4th Marine Division had been making faster progress just inland to the east. Gen. Holland Smith directed the Marine division, which was already ahead of the GIs, to continue the drive north alone. The GIs would finish up by pushing some 2,500 yards farther, charged only with cleaning out the coastal pocket in front of them. With the Japanese apparently in a state of collapse, Griner's headquarters felt this final mission could be quickly accomplished.

Jumping off from below Tanapag Village, a cluster of deserted houses by the shoreline, the 2nd Battalion, 105th Infantry advanced 600 yards to a large coconut grove. Beyond the grove, a dirt track meandered eastward across the plain from Road Junction 2 before disappearing into the hills. Battalion commander Maj. Edward A. McCarthy sent his men up the shoreline, skirting the edge of a minefield before fanning out again. All seemed to be going well until supporting artillery fire shifted off to the east. Almost immediately a Japanese machine gun opened up on the advance, accompanied by a fusillade of small arms fire. The GIs went to ground in the foot-high grass. McCarthy tried to get the men moving, loping up and down the line yelling, "Up and at 'em!," but the first two men who got up were hit and killed and the others showed little enthusiasm to follow their example.

Three and a half hours later, the battalion remained stalled and McCarthy still wasn't sure where all the fire was coming from. Finally, an E

Company private noticed movement along a drainage ditch or dry creekbed to their front. The ditch ran from the shore all the way across the plain to the mouth of a ravine called Harakiri Gulch. Sgt. William H. Allen led his squad in a rush toward the ditch. Taken under fire, the squad dove for cover. Allen, not realizing no one was following him, jumped into the ditch amid about eight Japanese soldiers. He shot two and rammed his bayonet into a third, but was himself hit in the leg by a bullet. Belatedly realizing he was alone and greatly outnumbered, he scrambled out of the ditch and made his way back to his company. Unfazed by his narrow escape or his leg wound, he wanted to take his squad back to clean out the remaining enemy—he thought there were only five left—but by now McCarthy realized the ditch was held in large numbers and was the source of the fire that had been holding him down all morning. It was now an hour past noon.

Meanwhile, a bizarre scene unfolded a few hundred yards to the right as the Japanese launched a counterattack against elements of the 3rd Battalion. Gathered in the coconut grove, facing the same ditch that was holding up McCarthy, the GIs were about to assault an enemy machine gun positioned on a knoll to their front when large numbers of Japanese suddenly streamed down from the high ground. Sgt. Arthur A. Gilman looked up to see two Japanese charging directly at him. Before he could react, there was a tremendous explosion and the two soldiers were blasted skyward amid a geyser of dirt and debris. Knocked flat by concussion, Gilman saw the first man's body—or what was left of it—soar at least a hundred feet in the air. One of the Japanese had apparently stepped on the horn of a large, spherical sea mine—one of a series that had been set out as an antitank barrier. The detonation set off nearby mines—perhaps even the whole field—in an earth-shaking explosion. Japanese gun crews were hurled from their weapons. The counterattack disintegrated. "For some time afterwards troops could see random Japanese soldiers picking themselves up off the ground and wandering back up into the cliffs in a dazed manner," observed a subsequent U.S. Army study of the action around Tanapag. "All firing from the enemy virtually ceased and, for over an hour afterward American troops wandered around in the open without having a shot fired at them."[1]

McCarthy got a lift at about 1530 when Lt. Willis K. "Bill" Dorey clattered up to the 2nd Battalion with three light tanks. Without waiting for the infantry, Dorey's tank "Jeanie" and the two accompanying Stuarts charged the gully which, as McCarthy had suspected, was crammed with Japanese infantry. The tanks wheeled and started down the ditch, guns blazing. They had just gotten underway when an enemy infantryman threw a magnetic mine against the tank commanded by twenty-four-year-old Sgt. Joseph Allocco. The explosion blew off a track and the tank clanked to a halt.

Leaving his third tank to cover Allocco's stricken Stuart, Dorey pressed on alone. For more than a half an hour "Jeanie" rolled back and forth along the ditch as far east as Harakiri Gulch blasting the occupants with canister and machine-gun fire. "We were in a ditch running down Japs and we had cleaned up a hell of a lot of them when we winged a single," recalled Dorey. "The Jap, an officer, crawled to a stump and braced himself against it. He drew his Samurai sword and turned over and held it high, then drew it right across his belly, then held his head in his hands for a moment, finally folded his arms across his chest and died."[2]

Despite the carnage in the ditch, there were plenty of live Japanese left. When McCarthy's infantry attacked, they again came under fire. The assault bogged down about 50 yards from Allocco's stricken tank. As the GIs fell back, Dorey pulled up to the immobilized tank and tried unsuccessfully to raise Allocco on the radio. He then opened his hatch as small arms fire spanged off the armor and tried to shout over the din to the other crew to evacuate the tank. Japanese infantry was already closing in, using the ditch as cover. Neither Dorey nor the third tank, commanded by Sgt. Emanuel Mavrikas, could depress their guns far enough to put fire onto the attackers. Dorey grabbed a Thompson submachine gun from inside his tank and popped up and down in the open hatch, firing short bursts at the Japanese, but the enemy showed no sign of backing off.

While unable to hear Dorey, Allocco's crew had come to realize they had to get out, but the bottom escape hatch was blocked by the broken tread, forcing them to emerge from the top hatches in full view of the Japanese. Driver John Proden and bow gunner Harry V. Magilton threw open the front hatches. Magilton lobbed two grenades at the Japanese outside and Proden scrambled out, firing into the ditch with a submachine gun. Magilton, armed with a tommy gun, followed. Dropping to the ground, they kept up the fire while the gunner and Sergeant Allocco bailed out, then they all made a break for Mavrikas's tank. Allocco insisted that the others go first. As Proden crawled under the tank to enter the escape hatch, he felt Allocco fall across his legs. The sergeant was dead. As Magilton turned and fired a burst from his tommy gun toward the ditch, he too was shot and killed. Proden and the gunner scrambled up through the emergency hatch and both tanks withdrew, leaving the stricken tank and two dead crewmen behind.[3]

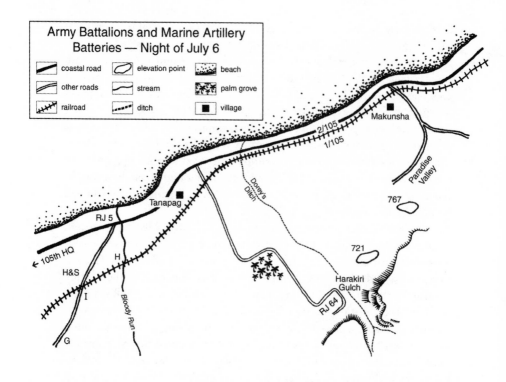

Stopping by 27th Division headquarters on July 6, Bob Sherrod chatted with assistant chief of staff Lt. Col. Oakley Bidwell, who estimated that the campaign would drag on for another five to seven days. "Of course it looks easier back at corps headquarters," he observed in an apparent shot at Holland Smith's staff; "you just move a blue pencil mark forward on a map."[4]

Still hoping to get some momentum going as late afternoon drew near, General Griner telephoned Col. Leonard A. Bishop, commanding the 105th Infantry, at 1520 and ordered him to commit his 1st Battalion to the push. Bishop argued that it was too late in the day and the battalions would not have time to put together a proper perimeter defense for the night, but Griner was not interested in excuses. Bishop was overruled.

The 1st Battalion, commanded by forty-four-year-old Col. William J. "Obie" O'Brien, arrived on the line at 1645. A bantam rooster of a man, O'Brien was a lead-from-the-front officer who had risen from the ranks—a fighter by nature—but he was not enthusiastic about his present mission.

Like Bishop, he was concerned about the late timing of the movement. Briefing his company commanders, the longtime Guardsman seemed on edge. "It's the old end run all over again," he remarked. "Whenever they get a job nobody else can do, we have to do it. Sooner or later we're going to get caught, and this may be it." He told the company commanders to keep pushing; they had to reach the objective before dark. "Whatever you do, don't stop—keep moving, keep moving!" he emphasized.

The 1st and 2nd Battalions moved off in line at 1715. Thanks largely to Dorey and his tanks, the once formidable Japanese cross-plain ditch defense was a shambles. The GIs found as many as 150 Japanese corpses sprawled along the makeshift trench. "We had to walk across that ditch on dead Japs," remarked Sgt. Angelo Nicoletti. "There were so many of them you couldn't find the ground. I must have stepped on about ten of them myself."[5] Despite coming under increasing fire from the hills on the right, the GIs pressed on up the plain. It appeared that Griner's decision to commit O'Brien's battalion was paying off. Watching from the 165th Infantry command post on Hill 721, Lt. Col. Leslie R. Rock, assistant operations officer with the 4th Marine Division, reported, "The 105th has broken through. They're going a mile a minute up the island and if they go as fast as they are now, they'll be in Makunsha in about twenty minutes. They're all over the place. This looks like the end."[6]

Colonel Rock's optimism was premature. Company A continued for 500 yards beyond the ditch, but slowed as resistance stiffened. At the same time, machine-gun fire from the hills held up Capt. Richard F. Ryan's Company B on the right of the line. Ryan, a University of California ROTC graduate and lawyer who had requested a combat assignment, was so tall and beanpole thin that some of his men joked that he could never be hit. Now he directed machine-gun fire at the hillside, but this only seemed to stir up more trouble. Return fire intensified and two of Ryan's machine gunners were hit. He was assembling a patrol to try to knock out the nearest enemy machine gun when the battalion operations officer, Capt. Emmett Catlin, came running up from the coconut grove to demand an explanation for the delay. He insisted that B Company get moving. The words were no sooner out of his mouth than Ryan, standing at his side, was shot in the head and killed. His death did not alter the urgency of the advance. B Company, now under the command of a lieutenant, continued forward.[7]

Taro Kawaguchi, a member of the *43rd Division's* medical unit, was lucky to be alive. Slightly wounded in the leg by artillery fire on June 30, he only narrowly survived the fighting on July 6. He recorded the details of his escape in his diary:

> *Received artillery barrage during the morning and took cover among the rocks. As each round approached nearer and nearer, I closed my eyes and waited. Rifle reports and tanks seemed nearer and everybody took cover within the forest and waited for the enemy to approach. Soon the voice of the enemy could be heard and machine gun bullets could be heard over our heads. I thought this was the end and was ready to charge out with a hand grenade when ordered to take cover by the captain. When I looked from the side of the rock, I could see the hateful bearded face of the enemy shining in the sunlight. With a terrific report, the rock in front of my eyes exploded and the sergeant that joined us last night was killed. Also the corporal received wounds in his left thigh. However I could not treat the wounds even though I wanted to. Everybody hugged the ground and kept quiet, waiting for an opening in the enemy. As I stood up to get the rifle from one of the dead, a bullet hit between my legs and I thought sure I was hit but after glancing down, to my happiness, nothing was wrong. A report was heard and as I looked back it was my friend Corporal Ito lying on his back with a rifle in his hand. Oh! Corporal Ito who has been in my section since Magoya had died.*

To Kawaguchi's relief, the Americans withdrew. He went over to the unfortunate Corporal Ito "who had a bullet hole through his left temple with his eyes half open and lips tightly clenched." Promising revenge, he took Ito's rifle from his hands. Corporal Yasuhiro had been wounded in both legs and was begging, "Please kill me." Kawacuchi wrote later, "So 1st Lieutenant Matsuma beautifully cut his head off. The corporal pleaded before being cut to the lieutenant, 'Please cut skillfully.' The lieutenant with sweat pouring down his head, took one stroke, two strokes, and on the third stroke, he cut his head off."[8]

As day waned, there were indications that something unusual was going on out in the bush. Sgt. Thurlby A. Colyer, a crewman on a self-propelled gun with the 105th Infantry, took his vehicle into the mouth of Harakiri Gulch at about 1600 to bring out a wounded man. "We picked this guy up and he said, 'There's something big going on here. There's really something big happening here. I've been shooting them all day and they don't even bother with me. They've got tanks down there and there's hundreds of Japs in that gully.'" Colyer's gun crew passed the information on to an infantry captain before pulling back for the night.[9]

Activity in Harakiri Gulch was of particular concern to Capt. Frank H. Olander's Company G, 2nd Battalion, 105th Infantry. Olander's company had been attached to the 3rd Battalion earlier in the afternoon, tasked with sealing off the mouth of the gulch while the rest of his battalion continued up the coastal plain. Olander had reason to be nervous. There had been bitter fighting along the gulch over the past few days as Japanese defenders held GIs and Marines to a standstill, knocking out tanks with magnetic mines and ambushing American units that ventured into the steep-sided corridor. Diehard Japanese even climbed into a derelict American tank and turned its guns on the GIs.

Somewhat to the disconcertion of his men, the thirty-two-year-old Olander decided to embark on a personal reconnaissance up the gulch. Darkness was approaching when the lieutenant led a patrol past a burned out U.S. tank and literally walked into a group of enemy soldiers hiding in a brush-choked depression by the roadway. A hand-to-hand struggle ensued when Sgt. Edward J. Wojcicki stepped squarely on the back of one of the hidden Japanese and the rest boiled up all around. Machine guns opened up, grenades exploded, and men burst out in all directions.

Emptying his carbine, Olander used it as a club until it broke, then grabbed a sword from one of the fallen Japanese. Two of the GIs were killed. Sgt. Benjamin J. Drenzek, wounded four times, was grabbed by enemy soldiers who tried to drag him away. Three times Wojcicki's men killed Japanese trying to drag Drenzek up into the gulch before the surviving GIs broke free. Rejoining the company, Olander ordered all platoons to pull out of the gulch. Obviously something was going on with the enemy. Raising 3rd Battalion commander Col. Edward Bradt on the radio, Olander said he didn't think it would be feasible to build a line across the mouth of the gulch for the night as had been planned. However, he felt he could control the entrance from a nose of higher ground overlooking the roadway. Bradt gave permission to dig in up on the nose and Olander moved his company across the road and up onto the higher ground. Subsequent events would indicate that the decision probably saved his company from annihilation.[10]

Late afternoon found Major McCarthy's 2nd Battalion (less Olander's G Company)—the troublesome ditch now well behind them—digging in between the sugar cane company railroad tracks and the coast road about 1,200 yards short of Japanese-held Makunsha. According to the 1:20,000 maps then in use, the road was located 50 yards inland from the beach with the railroad tracks running parallel about 50 yards farther east. However, subsequent testimony by a battalion commander from the 106th Infantry maintained that the maps were wrong and the railroad was actually about 200 yards from the water.[11] Just ahead of the battalion, an open swale extended about 75 yards toward Makunsha before ending in a tangle of bushes and low trees. The ground behind the battalion was open and rolling and largely devoid of cover.

McCarthy set up an oval-shaped perimeter between the road and the railroad tracks with the top end facing north. His three antitank guns were sited to cover the northern approach to the perimeter—one gun overlooking the coastal road to Makunsha and the others facing Paradise Valley to the northeast—under the assumption that any Japanese attack would come from one or both directions. The antitank guns were supported on each flank by the battalion's machine guns.

Obie O'Brien's 1st Battalion pulled up to McCarthy's perimeter about a half an hour before dark. Though originally supposed to dig in on McCarthy's left between the roadway and the shore, O'Brien didn't like the spot. The corridor was choked with underbrush that would limit his fields of fire. After some discussion with McCarthy, he placed his battalion on McCarthy's right, setting up along the rail line. Company A tied in with the 2nd Battalion at the railroad tracks with B Company digging in on A Company's right. This "circle the wagons defense" left a 500- to 600-yard gap between O'Brien's right flank and elements of the 165th Infantry in the hills. O'Brien covered the hole with his three antitank guns and all four of his heavy machine guns. As darkness fell, Companies A and B were still digging in. Slowed by harassment from the hills, C Company did not arrive until 2100 and dug in a hundred yards behind the battalion front line.

Also arriving in the area late in the day were two artillery battalions from the 10th Marines. Though part of the 2nd Marine Division, the 3rd and 4th Battalions had been sent forward to provide support for the 4th Division in its drive to the top of the island. Rolling up the coast road from Garapan, the artillery went into position about 1,200 yards southeast of the O'Brien/McCarthy perimeter. Unbeknownst to the artillerymen, they were right in the middle of the undefended gap between the Army battalions and the high ground to the east.[12]

Major Hirakushi awoke after dark. Outside the cave, men armed with everything from rifles and machine guns to swords and bamboo spears were milling around. Officers divided them into groups and shepherded them toward the coastal plain below. To the dejected Hirakushi they looked like "spiritless sheep being led to the slaughter" and their officers "guides to the Gates of Hell."

Hirakushi made his way to the cave where Generals Saito and Igeta lay and ordered the two guards to burn the bodies, using 10 liters of gasoline that had been previously put aside. They were also to burn the regimental flags of the *135th* and *136th Infantry* regiments, which had been left with division headquarters for safekeeping. Leaving them to their task, the major gathered about a dozen men and started toward the beach to join the *gyokusai*.[13]

Another group of officers from the headquarters cave had other plans. Rather than commit suicide or sacrifice himself in the *gyokusai*, forty-six-year-old Maj. Gen. Masatake Kimihira had decided to escape from the island, ostensibly so that he could personally report to Tokyo on the failed defense and lessons learned. It was only by bad luck that Kimihira was on Saipan at all. As the vice chief of staff of the *8th Area Army*, he had been returning to Rabaul after a conference in Tokyo when his plane was forced to land on Saipan due to U.S. air activity. During the fighting Kimihira had filled in as General Igeta's deputy chief of staff. Now, accompanied by seven other officers and enlisted men, he struck out in the darkness over the hills toward the east coast in hopes of securing a boat.[14]

The survivors of Taro Kawaguchi's medical detachment joined the stream of men heading south. Kawaguchi had already come to the realization that he was doomed, writing in his diary, "My foxhole is my grave . . . Heard that the orders were issued by the Commander in Chief for all men to take part in the last assault." The survivors of his unit bid each other farewell and "promised to meet at the Yasukuni Shrine after death." Two men whose severe wounds left them unable to participate in the *gyokusai* committed suicide.[15]

Also joining the procession was Yeoman Second Class Mitsuharu Noda and about twenty members of the naval headquarters group. After sending out a final message that all was lost, they destroyed their radio and headed out to join the final attack. Word circulated that the *gyokusai* had been ordered by the emperor himself, the directive dropped from a friendly plane to the commanders of the Saipan garrison.

Noda was not a warrior. Earlier in the war he had served as a clerk in Adm. Isoroku Yamamoto's headquarters staff. After Admiral Yamamoto was killed in an American aerial ambush over Bougainville in April 1943, Noda was assigned as a paymaster for Admiral Nagumo's headquarters staff, charged with seeing that troops throughout the Central Pacific were paid. Earlier in the morning he had witnessed Admiral Nagumo's suicide at the navy headquarters cave. Now he and his comrades drank a bottle of Suntory whiskey they had hoarded until the last minute. They smoked their last tobacco—Hikari brand. Noda knew he was about to go to his death, but rather than fear, he felt a strange sense of superiority.[16]

About an hour after dark, GIs from the 105th Infantry found a Japanese seaman sleeping—or pretending to sleep—near the road by the 3rd Battalion command post. Under preliminary interrogation, the seaman, who said he was from the *55th Keibitai* (Naval Guard Force), revealed that an attack was imminent. At 2030, Regimental Headquarters was advised, "Prisoner says that his unit has been ordered to attack at 2000 tonight. That all men alive at 1500 on July 7 must commit suicide."[17] The seaman was escorted down to Garapan where he ended up in front of Lt. Benjamin Hazard, the 27th Division language officer.

Hazard was already worried. This was not the first his interrogation team had heard of a *gyokusai*: On July 4 a Japanese civilian who had been employed painting the hulls of flying boats at Tanapag stated that a mass assault was planned for July 7. Hazard recognized the significance of the date. July 7 was the seventh day of the seventh month, marking the Tanabata Festival when the spirits of the dead are supposed to return to earth. It was considered a particularly auspicious time to die and join one's ancestors. He had tried to explain the significance of the date to his commanding officer, Lt. Col. William M. Van Antwerp, the division intelligence chief, but to no avail. The colonel "said it was nonsense," recalled Hazard, but there were other indications of trouble ahead.[18] On July 6 a POW stated there were approximately 2,000 Japanese near Makunsha. Division observation posts and air surveillance confirmed considerable activity in the area and all along the shoreline. "All of this force could be employed on the Division front within a short period of time," acknowledged 27th Division intelligence.[19]

Holland Smith visited his division commanders during the day, dropping in at Griner's headquarters late in the morning. A notation in the NTLF war diary for July 6 observed: "Based on intelligence information, the Commanding General visited the Division CP's this date and warned

Division Commanders to prepare for and be particularly alert for a hostile counterattack."[20] Despite these warnings, at least one Army officer—Lt. William H. Fulton of the 773rd Amphibian Tractor Battalion—recalled that NTLF seemed to share the general perception that the Japanese were beaten. In conversation with Fulton, an assistant in the NTLF intelligence section dismissed concerns about Japanese troop concentrations as alarmist, saying something to the effect, "The Army is excited. The 27th Division G-2 has called me several times this afternoon telling me that Japs are massing around Makunsha."[21]

Now the prisoner from the *55th Keibitai* confirmed to Hazard that an all-out attack had been ordered by all Japanese still capable of bearing arms. The attack was to start at 2000 hours from a road junction near Matansa village, northeast of Makunsha. Despite some discrepancies and the fact that the supposed hour for the assault had passed, Hazard was convinced the man was telling the truth and that an attack was imminent. "We knew the roof was about to fall in," he recalled.[22] He advised Van Antwerp, who personally called the assistant division commander and acting chief of staff Brig. Gen. Ogden J. Ross. It was now 2100. Ross promptly put division artillery on alert and notified the infantry regiments to prepare for a possible counterattack.[23]

With his battalion quite likely in harm's way, Colonel O'Brien contacted the 105th Regiment's executive officer, Lt. Col. Leslie Jensen. He told Jensen he was worried about the gap on the 1st Battalion's right and asked if there were any units available to fill it. O'Brien's radioman, Sgt. Ron Johnson, recalled that the feeling from higher up seemed to be that "expected resistance was minimal" and there was no reason for undue concern.[24] In any case, Jensen said there were no troops available; O'Brien would have to cover the hole as best he could. Nevertheless, Jensen called the division command post and passed O'Brien's concerns on to Colonel Van Antwerp. Van Antwerp took the matter seriously enough to awaken the division operations officer—Lt. Col. Frederic H. Sheldon—and inform him about the gap. Sheldon said there was nothing he could do. There were no reserves available.[25]

For over two weeks Sgt. Takeo Yamauchi had seen nothing but death as American artillery and airpower decimated any gathering of Japanese. His company commander disappeared; Yamauchi heard the man had gone mad. On July 3, he and two other stragglers made their way through a ravine filled with blackened corpses down to the beach area where they found shelter in a dugout. On the night of July 6, they heard men passing by. Yamauchi asked where they were going. To attack the Americans, they replied.

His two companions asked what they should do. Yamauchi told them there was no reason to die there on Saipan. Japan was going to lose the war anyway. "Squad Leader! You're talking like a traitor," they admonished him. "Behave like a military man." Yamauchi, the university man, had been rebuked by a farmer and a city man who merely finished elementary school. "They were unflinching," he observed. He was the aberration. Still, he made no effort to leave his shelter.[26]

Saburo Arakaki and Sergeant Aoki joined a mixed mob of soldiers, sailors, and civilians near Marpi Airfield as word was passed to gather round. A commissioned officer addressed them, shouting, "Today both Navy Vice Admiral Nagumo and Army Lieutenant General Saito, at the combined headquarters at Hell Valley, made the decision to die an honorable death!" As a spontaneous groan arose from the crowd, the officer proceeded to read aloud General Saito's final attack order. Saburo could hear only bits and pieces until the officer raised his voice even further. "I give you this command! The Saipan garrison shall mount an attack on the American devils tomorrow July 7, with each man killing ten Americans and fighting to an honorable death!" A stir went through the soldiers and the shout went up, "Death for honor! Death for honor!"[27]

Officers near Saburo began to organize the men into two attack groups to join the column heading south. They represented the survivors of nearly every unit that had defended the island. American intelligence would later find dead soldiers and sailors from the *118th*, *135th*, and *136th Infantry* regiments; *43rd Division Headquarters*; *43rd Division Hospital*; *3rd Independent Mountain Artillery Regiment*; *16th Shipping Engineer Regiment*; *9th Tank Regiment*; *55th Naval Guard Force*; *1st Yokusuka Special Landing Force*; and a polyglot of others. Numbers of civilians also joined, including at least one woman whose corpse was found afterwards. Many of the civilian workers were drunk, having consumed great quantities of sake and beer. Years later, the bottles still littered the field where they gathered.[28] Any wounded who could not walk were killed or committed suicide. The others hobbled along with the rest. A soldier who was subsequently taken prisoner told his American interrogators that his *135th Infantry Regiment* was able to muster only 113 "effectuals" for the assault and that 107 badly wounded men who remained behind were given grenades so they could commit suicide.[29]

Without sufficient rifles and machine guns to go around, the men were armed with whatever came to hand—bamboo spears, bayonets lashed to poles, even pitchforks. Officers gave away their pistols, keeping only their swords. The Japanese naval troops started south from Marpi Point just after dark. The long column—three and four men abreast—wended its way down the road to be at the assembly point by 2200 as ordered. As the column passed, other groups and individuals joined the march—so many that it was estimated that when the head of the column neared Makunsha, the tail was still leaving Marpi Point.[30] Assigned to the second attack group, Saburo, carrying a sharpened stick as a weapon, trudged along with the rest. "They knew at the outset they had no hope of succeeding," admitted Maj. Takashi Hirakushi. "They simply felt it was better to die that way and to take some of the enemy with them than to be holed up in caves and be killed."[31]

Hirakushi arrived at the beach to see the offshore reef shining whitely in the moonlight. Thick clouds gathered overhead. One cloud looked to him like a mother carrying a baby on her back. Stripping off his uniform, he waded into the water and bathed. As he put his uniform back on he could hear men shouting the battle cry "*Wa! Wa!*" in the distance. He discarded his binoculars and dispatch case, keeping only his pistol and his sword.

Command of the *gyokusai* fell to Col. Takuji Suzuki of the *135th Infantry Regiment*. Despite the hopelessness of their situation, Suzuki was not about to just throw himself blindly on the enemy. As the attackers organized, he sent out patrols to probe the American lines. It did not take them long to discover the 500-yard gap next to Obie O'Brien's 1st Battalion.

A heavy rain blew across Saipan in the early morning hours, soaking Japanese and Americans alike. Wet and miserable, his stomach upset from indulging in too much liberated Scotch whiskey, Sgt. Ron Johnson sat in his hole by Colonel O'Brien's command post staring sleeplessly toward the hills to the east. After a while, he noticed "shadows or silhouettes," as if people were moving through the gap east of the perimeter. Preoccupied with his own discomfort, he put it from his mind and finally drifted off into an uneasy sleep.[32]

Despite Johnson's personal disinterest, the GIs on the forward perimeter were becoming aware of building activity out beyond the open swale. 1st Sgt. Mario Occhinerio was talking with A Company commander Capt. Louis F. Ackerman when they became conscious of a curious droning sound. "While he was talking, we began to hear this buzz," recalled Occhinerio. "It was the damnedest noise I ever heard. I think you could describe it as a great big hive of bees. It kept getting louder and louder and then it began to sound like I guess the old Indian war dances did, sort of like a chant. All at once a couple of Japs busted out of the bushes to our front. Somebody shot them. That's when things got going in earnest."[33]

Major McCarthy called for artillery fire on the mounting activity around Makunsha. He also shifted his machine guns to give them fields of fire up the railroad tracks as Japanese, screened by the tangle of bushes on the far side of the swale, yelled and sang and generally raised hell. More convinced than ever that a major attack was imminent, Ben Hazard spent considerable time on the phone with Van Antwerp, his intelligence chief. Further interrogation had revealed that the naval POW was one of the messengers sent out to pass the word to General Saito's scattered forces to assemble for the mass attack. Van Antwerp contacted the 27th Reconnaissance Troop, which had an outpost on Hill 767, and told them to be alert for activity on the plain below. On two occasions between 2100 and 2300 the outpost reported seeing large groups of Japanese moving in and out of Paradise Valley. At 2330 Van Antwerp contacted NTLF headquarters. "Though vague and contradictory in places, there seems to be something in the air," he cautioned. "All units should be particularly alert."[34]

Hazard's recollection of Van Antwerp's reaction to the developing situation was rather different. As Hazard recalled it later, the division intelligence chief did not fully share his concern about an imminent attack. As midnight came and went, the colonel seemed inclined to dismiss Hazard's fears. Since the Japanese hadn't attacked by midnight, they probably wouldn't, he reassured the twenty-four-year-old language officer.[35]

The vanguard of Japanese had been gathering in Makunsha since nightfall, but due to American artillery fire and general disorganization, it was not until about 0400—nearly an hour before sunrise—that the mob started south in the rain. While subsequent estimates of their numbers varied, it appears that between 3,000 and 4,000 Japanese participated. They ranged from disciplined soldiers and fragments of military units to civilians and labor force personnel.

A Korean POW from a Navy construction unit later told interrogators that naval troops—mostly Special Naval Landing Force personnel—had been ordered by a vice admiral to gather in the Banadero [Marpi Field] area and formed a large proportion of the assault. The objective was to reach southern Garapan by 0340 and, if possible, to push on to the Aslito Air-field, claimed the POW. However, it was already 0330 when they reached Matansa just northeast of Makunsha. There they were told to continue on and "drive recklessly" into the U.S. troops.[36]

Somewhere out beyond the American lines, Taro Kawaguchi conscien-tiously jotted a last lengthy entry in his diary. "While shivering from wet-ness, orders to move were issued," he wrote. Facing the dawn, he bowed reverently to the Imperial Palace and bid farewell to his parents and relatives before emerging from the forest and heading down toward the coastal plain. "I am only 26 years [old]," he wrote. "Thanks to the Emperor, both of my parents and my aunt. I have lived to this day and I am deeply gratified. At the same time it is deeply regrettable that I have nothing to report when my life is fluttering away like a flower petal to become a part of the soil. Since the enemy landing, [I] have fought against the enemy endeavoring my utmost power in carrying out my duty and thus become a war god. I am very happy. It is only regrettable that we have not fought enough and that the American devil is stomping on the Imperial Soil. I, with my sacrificed body, will become the white-caps of the Pacific and will stay on this island when the friendly forces come to reclaim the soil of the Emperor." He offered last best wishes to family members and concluded, "I am happy that I can die on the 7th anniversary of the Sino-Japanese incident. I believe the enemy will be annihilated and will pray for certain victory of the Imperial land."[37]

On the beach, Major Hirakushi heard rifle shots signaling the attack. He and his twelve men joined the mob rushing down the shoreline toward the Americans. Suddenly there was a great explosion. Hirakushi felt as if he was entering a great column of bursting fire. "I'm dead," he thought, and then everything went black.[38]

GIs from the 27th Division wade ashore after heavy fighting on Saipan forces postponement of the operation to seize Guam. (U.S. ARMY)

Marines take cover behind a medium tank during the push north. (USMC)

Weary Marines carry one of their dead buddies back toward the beach for burial. (USMC)

A flamethrower operator burns out a Japanese position near a farmhouse. (USMC)

Marines await developments after lobbing a smoke grenade into an underground cave position. (USMC)

GIs from the 27th Division head for the front lines. The division saw tough fighting in the aptly named Death Valley. (U.S. ARMY)

Maj. Gen. Ralph Smith (left) congratulates fellow officers after the capture of Aslito Airfield. The title "Conroy Field" would prove short-lived. (U.S. ARMY)

An infantryman looks over a Japanese 6-inch coastal defense gun following the capture of Nafutan Point. This gun was put out of action by naval bombardment. (U.S. ARMY)

Accompanied by tanks, infantrymen venture into the lower end of Death Valley, dominated by the Tapotchau cliffs in the background. (U.S. ARMY)

A self-propelled gun fires on the cliff-face in Death Valley. The 27th Division lost numerous tanks to enemy guns in the deadly corridor. (U.S. ARMY)

Early in the battle the Japanese were careful to remove their dead, but as they were forced to fall back, they began to leave stark evidence of their losses. (USMC)

Every cane field seemed to claim a Marine or two. (USMC)

Two Marines tend to a wounded buddy. (USMC)

A crew operates a 37mm gun. Note the bullet holes through the gun shield. (USMC)

A Japanese machine-gun crew lies where they fell defending a trench position. (USMC)

A Marine attempts to talk a civilian family out of hiding. (USMC)

Civilians wait under guard for the trucks that will transport them to the internment camp. (U.S. ARMY)

Civilian survivors included large numbers of children whose parents were killed or committed suicide. (USMC)

Marines try to comfort
a crying child behind
the barbed wire at the
civilian internment camp.
(U.S. COAST GUARD)

Marines set up a
defensive perimeter
after seizing the
summit of Mount
Tapotchau, the
highest point on
Saipan. (USMC)

A civilian burial
party maneuvers
the body of a GI
onto a stretcher
to be brought to
the 27th Divi-
sion cemetery.
(U.S. ARMY)

Three 27th Division casualties lie on the blood-spattered floor of a battalion aid station. (U.S. ARMY)

Dead GIs of the 27th Division await burial. (U.S. ARMY)

Garapan lies in ruins after extended bombardment and street fighting during the U.S. advance up the coast. (USMC)

Once celebrated as "Little Tokyo," Garapan was completely destroyed by naval gunfire when it appeared the Japanese military was using the city as a staging area. (U.S. NAVY)

Two of the thousands of civilians who fled inland on D-day, only to be killed in the course of the battle. (U.S. ARMY)

Searching for snipers, Marines move carefully from house to house in the ruins of Garapan. (USMC)

A Marine pauses before a shrine. Hundreds of years of Spanish occupation left the Saipan's native Chamorros devoutly Catholic. (USMC)

Dodging enemy fire, two Marines head past a burning building in Garapan. (USMC)

Weapons at the ready, Marines go about the task of flushing the enemy out of a hidden position. (USMC)

While most Japanese refused to surrender, the number of military POWs increased as General Saito's defense collapsed and hope of rescue faded. (U.S. ARMY)

Two Japanese attempt to surrender to approaching Marines. (USMC)

This superior private was among the relatively few Japanese military personnel who chose to surrender. (U.S. ARMY)

An Army translator interrogates a wounded Japanese POW. (U.S. ARMY)

Wrecked flying boats
litter the area at the
Japanese naval facility at
Tanapag Harbor. (USMC)

The strain of combat
shows on the faces
of these weary
27th Division GIs.
(U.S. ARMY)

Marines enlist some less
than enthusiastic outside
help to carry their gear.
(USMC)

PFC Harold C. Agerholm
(Medal of Honor) (USMC)

Sgt. Thomas A. Baker
(Medal of Honor) (U.S. ARMY)

PFC Harold G. Epperson
(Medal of Honor) (USMC)

Sgt. Grant F. Timmerman
(Medal of Honor) (USMC)

G/Sgt. Robert H. McCard
(Medal of Honor) (USMC)

Col. William J. O'Brien
(Medal of Honor) (U.S. ARMY)

Capt. Ben L. Salomon
(Medal of Honor) (U.S. ARMY)

Gen. Holland Smith (standing) with Admirals King (passenger seat) and Nimitz on a tour of Saipan. (USMC)

Generals Holland M. Smith, Harry Schmidt, and Graves Erskine (seated, left to right) during an outdoor briefing. (USMC)

Lt. Col. William J. O'Brien (center) confers with his officers as his battalion prepares to relieve another unit. (U.S. ARMY)

Dead Japanese lie along the beach following the mass attack that overran two battalions of the 27th Division the morning of July 7. (U.S. ARMY)

Marines patrol along the coast past heaps of Japanese corpses left in the wake of the mass attack on the 105th Infantry. (USMC)

A Japanese sailor killed in the *gyokusai* lies in the shallows. He may have been a member of the 55th Naval Guard Force. (U.S. ARMY)

The tank knocked out by Battery H, 10th Marines, before their position was overrun the morning of July 7. (U.S. ARMY)

Killed during the *gyokusai*, a Japanese soldier lies next to his weapon, a bayonet tied to a pole. The Marines called these weapons "idiot sticks." (U.S. ARMY)

Two light tanks bogged down when they ventured into the shallows in an effort to protect GIs who had fled out to the reef during the *gyokusai*. (U.S. ARMY)

Marines pick cautiously through the litter of dead the day after the *gyokusai*. (USMC)

A Marine unit files through the ruins of Garapan as the campaign draws to a close. (USMC)

Bulldozers scrape out a mass grave for Japanese killed in the *gyokusai*. (U.S. ARMY)

General Saito's charred remains are ceremoniously laid to rest in an area reserved for Japanese officers in the 27th Division cemetery. (USMC)

Capt. Sakae Oba surrenders his sword to Lt. Col. Howard G. Kirgis on December 1, 1945, nearly four months after the end of the war. (USMC)

CHAPTER XXIII

Overrun

LT. COL. LEWIS B. ROCK AWOKE BEFORE SUNRISE TO THE POUNDING OF artillery fire. "I realized at once that it was heavier than normal and could not possibly be our usual morning softening up," he recalled. "I looked down in the valley below me and from the Japanese lines I could see thousands of red tracer bullets cutting the morning sky, all headed in our direction. From our lines, other thousands of tracers were pouring back into the enemy." Red, green, yellow—even occasional blue—trails floated through the darkness overhead. "It was a strangely beautiful and fascinating sight," recalled Rock.[1]

Down on the plain, Obie O'Brien's battalion intelligence officer, Lt. Luke Hammond, awoke in his soggy foxhole to the rising din of gunfire from the perimeter. It was 0430. Calls were coming in from the companies for artillery support. He could hear O'Brien yelling back and forth with the artillery forward observer, twenty-nine-year-old Capt. Bernard "Bernie" Toft, who had dug in on the other side of the railroad tracks. He heard Toft call for "normal barrage" and the shells began arriving steadily, but rather slowly, on an area 300 to 400 yards to the northeast. As the crack of small arms fire intensified, it sounded to Hammond like they "were tearing the Japs apart." From a nearby hole, Capt. Emmett T. Catlin called out, "Say Luke, let's go up to the front line where we can get a shot at these bastards." Hammond demurred, but remained complacent despite all the noise, thinking, "We had the firepower and were giving them hell."[2]

Dug in with B Company, Sgt. John Domanowski had already endured an eerie few hours. All night long he had been on edge listening to what sounded like babies crying. "They never shut up," he said. "It sounded like there were about twenty of them. We found out later that the crying was done by goats." In the early morning he made out a figure running toward his position. The man was running, then falling, all the while calling, "Medic! Medic!" Not sure if he was a GI or a Japanese, Domanowski was close to

385

pulling the trigger on him, but the figure fell down again and he lost track of him. By now, small arms fire was passing overhead. "At times you can hear them pop over your head," he recalled. "Other times you don't hear them at all." As it grew lighter, Sgt. Jay B. Hollifield, who was dug in nearby, raised his head a little too high and took a slug in the eye. "He cried a little and stopped when his gunner gave him first aid," said Domanowski.

Now Domanowski saw the Japanese approaching in the gray light of dawn. "[T]hey [were] running toward us in groups, all the while yelling and screaming at the top of their lungs."[3] Toft adjusted artillery fire on the enemy swarm. It was not enough. As the pressure mounted, Capt. Louis F. Ackerman, commanding Company A, raised Toft on the radio. "For God's sake, Bernie, get that artillery in closer," he pleaded. Toft replied he was already bringing in fire within 150 yards of Ackerman's line. Ackerman told him to pull it in to 75; he would take his chances. Toft brought the fire in closer, but it didn't stop the Japanese.[4] They swarmed into the American foxholes. "When they hit us there were so many of them we couldn't shoot fast enough," said Sgt. Frederick W. Stilz.[5]

Survivors would later refer to the *gyokusai* with remarkable understatement simply as "the Raid." News accounts would dub it the "Saipan Banzai." It was more than a raid, more than a banzai. "This was not a banzai attack," observed Lt. Ben Hazard; "this was something completely different . . . The Japanese knew they were going to die. They came in singing. You could hear them in the distance."[6]

The attack down the plain followed three general routes. The main force streamed down the railroad tracks. Another column advanced into the gap on the 1st Battalion's right. The third and smallest column moved south along the beach at the water's edge. Another group of perhaps as many as 400 Japanese, accompanied by two tanks, emerged from Harakiri Gulch, streaming past Capt. Frank Olander's G Company, which—to its great good fortune—had dug in the night before on the high ground above the gulch instead of across its mouth. "In the darkness we could hear a lot of people running," recalled a GI. "There were so many of them that the ground rumbled." Dawn revealed the whole plain below was crowded with people; it "looked like a circus had just gotten out."[7]

Down on the plain, PFC Sam Dinova was crowded in a shallow foxhole with two other GIs. Figuring they were going to move out in the morning, they hadn't bothered to dig in very deeply. Now bedlam reigned. "The sky lit up. It was like daylight," recalled Dinova. "It was like twelve o'clock in the afternoon. You could see kids, women, soldiers, they had bamboo poles with bayonets on them, shovels, picks, pitchforks, they had everything. These are civilians with soldiers too . . . There were so many of them . . . I couldn't get out of my hole because [the gunfire] was raking the dirt; it was going in my hole." His two companions disappeared. Dinova had no idea where they'd gone. "I grabbed my carbine," he remembered. "Everybody was screaming and hollering. I didn't know what the hell was going on. Kids hollering, women screaming, machine guns firing, rifles firing."[8]

As Sergeant Domanowski raised his rifle, he heard a loud noise as if a firecracker had gone off near his ear. His rifle went flying. A bullet had torn through his left bicep, spattering him with blood and flesh. "It looked like chopped meat," he said. His broken arm dangled uselessly like the pendulum on a clock, white bones poking through a hole the size of a tennis ball. Oddly enough, his first thought was, "There goes my baseball." A medic rushed up and started to put a bandage on the wound, but fell with a bullet in the head before he could finish. PFC Ralph J. Carpenter, a heavy-set twenty-five-year-old from Michigan, called out from a nearby foxhole that he had been hit. Domanowski yelled at him to get down, but Carpenter remained upright an instant too long and was eviscerated by a burst of machine-gun fire. "I can't explain the look on his face as he fell," said Domanowski. "I knew he was going to die soon. No one could help him."[9]

Battalion commander McCarthy later compared the onslaught to cattle stampedes as pictured in movies about the old Wild West. "We were the cameramen. These Japs just kept coming and coming and didn't stop. It didn't make any difference if you shot one; five more would take his place. We would be in the foxholes looking up, as I said, just like those cameramen used to be. The Japs ran right over us."[10]

Sgt. Felix Giuffre of A Company woke in his foxhole to the din of small arms fire. The machine guns on the company perimeter were blasting away, punctuated by the two antitank guns directing canister at the advancing horde. They could scarcely miss. Each canister round leveled twenty-five or thirty attackers, but the Japanese kept coming. The two machine gunners were killed. Japanese seemed to be running all over the place. Two of them came after Giuffre. When he went to shoot, his M1 jammed. Giuffre ran, but was shot in the leg before he could get very far. Crawling along, he came across PFC William A. Priddy. Armed with a BAR, Priddy had three Japanese soldiers cornered in a ditch, but for some reason he didn't shoot. Giuffre grabbed the BAR and mowed them down.[11]

Dug in with A Company along the railroad track, Pvt. David M. Boynton had been seriously wounded by a Japanese grenade about an hour before the main attack. Now, as the Japanese swarmed through the area, he was last seen standing in his hole, blood streaming down his face, squeezing off shots and shouting defiance. His body was found later in the foxhole.

An Able Company radioman, Corp. Ralph T. Ross, took cover in a hole near Colonel O'Brien, but as the line began to come apart, Ross inexplicably jumped up and ran into the midst of the enemy. His body was found two days later near that of his assistant radioman, PFC Olin H. Duncan, who still had their radio. Apparently Ross had seen Duncan go down and ran out in an effort to retrieve the radio. Also killed was Sgt. Edward A. Bogan. Wounded in the right shoulder, he switched the rifle to his left shoulder and kept firing until his position was overrun.[12]

A Japanese officer jumped into Sgt. Robert W. Smith's foxhole, his sword half-drawn from the scabbard. Before he could pull it all the way out, Smith drove his bayonet into the officer's midsection. As he pulled the bayonet back, the officer "half jumped, half stumbled away." Smith shot him and put him down for good.[13]

In B Company, the entire eight-man squad commanded by Sgt. Barney S. Stopera went down fighting. Their ammo exhausted, the twenty-three-year-old sergeant led them in hand-to-hand fighting as the Japanese kept coming. All eight were later found dead in a single group surrounded by thirty dead Japanese. Five of the eight had been members of Company B's undefeated touch football team at Schofield Barracks in 1943. They were among twenty-one B Company men killed in the fighting at the original perimeter that morning.[14]

"All type of weapons were being fired," recalled Sgt. W. Taylor Hudson, a member of the antitank platoon dug in with the 2nd Battalion. "Just over our heads tracers were passing and these were all colors of the rainbow. Huge parachute flares kept the scene as bright as day." As the situation deteriorated, one of the cannoneers called out to 2nd Lt. Robert D. Young, "Rip, our guys are falling back." Young told his men to stay put while he went forward to check on the other squads. The platoon never saw him again; he was killed somewhere in the confusion. Of the thirty-four men in the antitank platoon who came up the night of July 6 to support the 2nd Battalion, ten were killed and twelve wounded so seriously that they never returned to the unit.[15]

As the perimeter collapsed, Japanese soldiers paused to bayonet GIs wounded too badly to flee. Alone and out of ammunition, with his companions dead, Pvt. Erytell W. "Bill" Lynch started to run back through the chaos in B Company's area, but quickly decided his best chance was to try to lie low. He jumped into the nearest hole and landed squarely on top of two Japanese. Before he could react, one of them shot him in the chest. As he lay there stunned, the Japanese bayoneted him multiple times, one thrust piercing his neck and coming out through the ear on the opposite side of his head. They then shot Lynch again before leaving him for dead.[16]

In the 2nd Battalion, E Company alone lost sixteen killed in what was almost a matter of minutes. The machine guns were a prime target for the enemy, who overran guns and then turned them to fire wildly in all directions. In F Company, Lt. John E. Titterington, a twenty-seven-year-old Guardsman from Schenectady, New York, struggled to keep his machine guns in action as man after man went down. Wounded early in the attack, Titterington dashed from one position to another as the gunners were hit, taking over the gun and firing at the enemy until someone else jumped in to take over. Urged to have his wound tended to, Titterington refused, apparently realizing their position was hopeless. "I've got to go, I guess, but if I do go, I'm going to take a lot of those sons of bitches with me," he said grimly. He finally died on one of the precious machine guns. Twenty-three other F Company men also died trying to preserve the battalion perimeter.[17]

As the Japanese kept coming, the machine guns could not keep up. D Company lost every gunner and assistant gunner on the air-cooled Brownings. Trying to hold the line with C Company, PFC Sam Dinova saw two of his best friends killed when their machine guns quit, either overheated or out of ammunition. Before they could get out, they were beheaded by sword-wielding Japanese. In another gun pit with PFC Frank Dagliere, Sgt. Salvatore S. Ferino jumped up and ran when their machine gun got so hot it seized up. He called to Dagliere to follow, but Dagliere waited too long. Hit by small arms fire, he was left helpless. A sword-wielding Japanese decapitated him.[18]

Colonel O'Brien struggled to keep control of his hard-hit battalion. Left-handed, the colonel typically carried a pistol in a shoulder holster under his right armpit. At some point during the confusion he had picked up another .45. Shadowed by his radioman, he stalked around, a .45 in each hand, offering encouragement and taking an occasional shot at the enemy. A bullet slammed into the back of his right shoulder near the spine, but he refused to pause long enough to allow medic Walter Grigas to take care of the wound. As Japanese swarmed into the perimeter, the colonel went down on his right knee, firing his pistol with his left hand, exhorting nearby GIs, "Don't give them a damn inch!" Grigas finally managed to slap a quick bandage over the colonel's shoulder wound when O'Brien paused to use the radio. It was 0507. Unable to get through to regiment, his radioman made contact with the 3rd Battalion up on the high ground, which relayed O'Brien's hurried report to regiment. He asked for help, but it was already too late.[19]

By now the antitank guns had been overrun. Many of the GIs had run out of ammunition, and scores were wounded and stumbling around looking for aid. Back in the command post area, Luke Hammond's complacency had evaporated. Red and blue tracers from Japanese machine guns floated down the roadway about 3 feet off the ground. "At least a half hour must have elapsed by now, and we could see objects 20–30 yards away," he recalled. "Suddenly I beheld a ghostly spectacle. Our front lines were falling back. Men were fleeing across the field." Startled, he sat up in his foxhole, blurting aloud, "What the hell is this?!"[20]

O'Brien saw it too and knew his battalion was on the brink of disaster. "Hold that line and stay up there!" he shouted, throwing down the phone. It was no use. Organized resistance collapsed, dissolving into a melee of individual combats. An A Company soldier stumbled past O'Brien toward the rear. "Where the hell are you going?" yelled O'Brien. The man gestured helplessly. "I have no weapon!" he exclaimed, and kept on going.[21]

Hammond crawled from his foxhole and joined a handful of GIs in a shallow concrete cistern. About 15 feet square and 3 feet deep, it provided more substantial protection than his foxhole. He peered over the wall. "Fifty yards away I saw a mass of people—I heard yells of thousands," he recalled. "I wondered if they were all Japs . . . They were Japs, all right—thousands of them—I remember their helmets in the dawn's early light." The men in the cistern readied themselves. Word passed around, "Let's hold here!" Out in front, not 30 yards away, Hammond saw two Japanese "jumping among our dead and wounded, slashing their sabers for all their beastly worth." Both became a priority target for any American with a rifle and were quickly shot down.

Hammond was about to open up with his carbine when he spotted a light machine gun someone had abandoned with a nearly full belt of ammunition. The gun was muddy, but the barrel was still hot and burned his hand as he picked it up and moved to the edge of the cistern. He tried to feed the belt, but the bolt was stuck and defied all efforts to move it. Hammond gave up, grabbed his carbine, and began to pick out targets from the onrush of enemy. A bullet smashed into the wall in front of his chest, pelting him with concrete fragments. As he resumed firing, another bullet slammed into his helmet. Staggered, he felt no pain but was aware of blood streaming down from under his helmet. A battalion cook slapped a bandage on his head. The next thing Hammond remembered was a Japanese light machine gun not 20 yards away, pouring a stream of bullets into the cistern.[22]

His battalion shattered, O'Brien gave what was probably his last order, directing 1st Sgt. Charles J. Stephani to gather up the walking wounded and establish a new line about 100 yards to the rear. O'Brien himself stayed. He jumped into a foxhole, grabbed a rifle from a badly wounded man, and emptied it at the waves of Japanese washing over them. Throwing the weapon aside, he ran to one of the jeeps parked in the perimeter for the night and climbed up behind the .50-caliber machine gun mounted on the rear. There were Japanese all around now. One of the last things Stephani saw as he pulled back was the diminutive colonel firing the machine gun at the advancing mob of Japanese.[23]

Over in the 2nd Battalion, an unlikely hero emerged in the person of the regimental dentist, Capt. Ben Salomon, who was acting battalion surgeon that morning. A graduate of UCLA dental school, Salomon had been shanghaied into the Dental Corps after previously serving as a sergeant in the infantry where he had led a machine-gun squad and qualified as an expert rifle and pistol shot. He had set up his medical tent the night before about 50 yards behind the front line. Within minutes of the attack, over two dozen wounded crowded into the tent. A Japanese soldier suddenly burst in and bayoneted a wounded GI lying on a stretcher. Salomon grabbed a rifle and killed the intruder, then shot two more as they pushed through the front entrance of the tent. Four other Japanese crawled under the tent walls. Salomon went after them. He kicked a knife out of one man's hand, shot another, and bayoneted a third. He butted the fourth in the stomach, stunning him long enough for one of the wounded GIs to finish the intruder off with a bullet.

Looking outside the tent, Salomon saw total mayhem with Japanese and GIs fighting hand to hand. Realizing the area was about to be completely overrun and the wounded massacred, he ordered every casualty who could still walk to try to escape back to the regimental aid station, about three-quarters of a mile back down the coast. Then he picked up a rifle and ran outside. A survivor later reported seeing the captain down on one knee squeezing off shots. As four men manning a nearby machine gun were killed one after the other, Salomon dashed over, settled in behind the gun, and started shooting. He was still firing away when last seen.[24]

Twenty-eight-year-old Sgt. Thomas A. Baker had charge of a squad on the front line near the railroad. In civilian life, Baker had been a boiler tender at the YMCA in his hometown of Troy, New York. Over the past two weeks on Saipan, he had earned a reputation as a seemingly fearless combat soldier. During the fighting at Nafutan Point on June 19, he had walked into an open field under heavy fire, shouldered a bazooka, and taken on a Japanese dual-purpose gun, knocking it out with the second round. On July 3, he volunteered to mop up bypassed enemy positions near Tanapag. Over the course of an hour, he killed eighteen Japanese—at one point walking directly into a concrete pillbox and shooting four occupants before they could get off a shot in return.

The Japanese attack on the 1st Battalion had scarcely gotten underway when a grenade exploded in Baker's foxhole and blew his foot nearly off. Despite the grievous injury, he kept shooting until he ran through his last clip. Unable to walk, he crawled out in search of more ammunition. PFC Frank Zielinski, who was also wounded, saw Baker crabbing along on the ground. He picked the sergeant up and started to carry him to the rear. They had gone about 150 yards when Zielinski was shot in the hip and had to put Baker down. As he did, Baker was hit again, this time shot in the chest.

Artillery observer Capt. Bernie Toft came down along the railway and saw Baker lying on the ground. He picked him up and carried him down the tracks for about 30 yards, before suddenly doubling over, shot in the midsection. Sgt. Robert W. Smith stopped to help the captain. Smith told the wounded officer he would be all right, but Toft demurred. "I felt it hit me in the back," he told Smith. "I'm dying." He asked Smith to make sure the Japanese didn't take him alive. Smith stayed by his side until Toft died, then continued his flight to the rear.

Baker had had enough. When a third GI came along and tried to help him, the sergeant brusquely refused any assistance. "I've caused enough trouble already," he told his would-be benefactor. "I'll stay here and take my chances." He asked to be propped up so he could see. The GI pulled him into a sitting position against a slender telephone pole. "I'm done for," Baker observed calmly. He asked for a cigarette and the GI lit one and handed it to him before continuing toward the rear. Baker spotted Sgt. Carlos Patricelli and called out, asking if Patricelli had an extra weapon. As it happened, Patricelli had just picked up a .45-caliber pistol. He handed it over to the wounded sergeant, first checking that it was fully loaded with seven cartridges in the magazine and an eighth in the chamber. When he left, Baker was sitting propped up against the pole with the cigarette in one hand and the pistol in the other. "He was as cool as a cucumber," recalled Patricelli. Two days later Patricelli and 1st Sgt. Mario Occhinerio were sent forward to help identify the dead. They found Baker still slumped against the pole where Patricelli had last seen him. The now empty .45 pistol was still in his hand. Eight Japanese lay dead in front of him.[25]

John Domanowski picked up his rifle with his good right hand and decided it was time to get out. As he stood up, some men from his company drifted by. One called out, "Come with me, John." As they started back, Domanowski saw a line of Japanese running by in single file, each man with his hand on the shoulder of the man in front. "They weren't in uniform, but had tattered clothes and had bandanas on their foreheads," he remembered. "They looked mean." At about the same time, he noticed streaks of light passing close by his body. It took him a few seconds to realize the streaks were from tracers being fired from a machine gun behind him—probably one of the company weapons overrun on the perimeter. The fire suddenly stopped, but he later found holes in his jacket.[26]

Dug in toward the rear of the 1st Battalion oval, C Company was also overrun as a mixed mob of Japanese and fleeing Americans descended on them. PFC Robert Jones shot five Japanese almost as fast as he could pull the trigger, but others were swarming right past him. He heard someone yell, "We've got to stop these sons-of-bitches before they cut us off!"[27] It was too late. Twenty-three-year-old Sgt. Nick Grinaldo, a Guardsman from Troy, New York, saw Japanese all around. They were "like cockroaches coming out of the woodwork," he recalled. Grinaldo's platoon leader, twenty-eight-year-old 2nd Lt. Charles P. Gower, ordered him to take the men back to some abandoned Japanese positions where they would have better protection. "Nick, get the men back to the Jap trenches," he ordered. "Dig in down there in the Jap trenches." Gower had scarcely finished his instructions when a bullet hit him in the face. "He took a bullet and it blew the bottom part of his jaw right off," recalled Grinaldo. "He had no bottom jaw." The men went to help him, but Gower resisted, somehow managing to mumble, "No, leave me. I don't want to go back. Just leave me. Just take the men back to the trenches." With the Japanese swarming at them, the GIs didn't have time to argue. They turned to run, leaving Gower. "We didn't get ten feet—boom—he blew his brains out," said Grinaldo.[28]

By 0600 both battalions were broken, the survivors fleeing south, individually and in small groups, trying to get away as best they could. There was no semblance of order. It was a rout. "Japs were all around us," recalled Grinaldo. "We had them running right alongside of us. I had one running right alongside of me. Christ he wasn't five feet from me."[29] Watching from the hills as the sky lightened, Lieutenant Colonel Rock could see thousands of Japanese streaming down the coastal plain. In the van billowed a huge, red-rayed naval battle flag, moving inexorably forward. It was like "a throwback to medieval battle scenes, gripping and dramatic," observed the colonel.[30]

The plain teemed with running men: Japanese armed with everything from machine guns and rifles to bayonets lashed to poles, some hobbling along on crutches trying to keep up with comrades; Americans fleeing along paths, sometimes alone, sometimes helping a wounded comrade, everyone was mixed together in a confused mass. As Grinaldo ran for his life, his rifle suddenly fell from his hand. He paused to pick it up and discovered he could not close his hand. He noticed a trickle of blood on his right shoulder and realized he had been shot. Sgt. Tony Simons, a medic from C Company, stopped to help. Grinaldo protested, "Not here; Jesus Christ, not here," he retorted. Simons ignored him. "Here, you're hurt bad!" he said. An instant later, Simons was shot and killed. "While he's standing in front of me he took one [bullet] right in the back that was intended for me," observed Grinaldo.[31]

Sam Dinova finally got out of his foxhole as the position was overrun. "I grabbed my carbine [and] ran back with the other guys," he recalled. "Somebody hollered, 'Let's stop and form a line!' We did that and they overran us . . . there was too many of them." Dinova ran down the railroad tracks. There were Japanese all over. "They kept coming, and I'm shooting at them," he said. "And I run down by the ocean. I could see different guys running." Dinova recognized one of his unit's medical officers. "I could see the back of his shirt; it was all blood," he recalled. "Everybody was for themselves. You couldn't help your brother if you had to. You had to leave him."[32]

Lt. John B. Mulhearn was running back when he spotted nineteen-year-old Pvt. Anthony J. LaSorta lying on the ground calling to him. LaSorta had been hit in the thigh by a burst of machine-gun fire. His leg was broken. Mulhearn picked him up and slung him over his back, but had only taken a

394

few steps when the machine gun opened fire again. The burst literally blew LaSorta apart. Mulhearn did not receive a scratch.[33]

Also unwilling to abandon a comrade, PFC Gerald D. Ostrum was struggling back with Sgt. Louis S. Doddo, the captor of Navy Cmdr. Jiro Saito at the Tanapag naval base two days earlier. Doddo had been badly wounded earlier in the morning and Ostrum was carrying him fireman-style on his back. As he labored along. he suddenly heard footsteps behind him, followed by a loud *swish*. A Japanese had run up with a sword and with one stroke cut off Doddo's head. Ostrum dropped Doddo's body and fired his carbine from the hip, killing the enemy officer.[34]

Bleeding from his head wound, Lt. Luke Hammond had somehow managed to escape the cistern fortress and was making his way back along the railroad tracks. He noticed a medic working on a wounded GI and asked where he could find an aid station. "There's an aid station at regiment," the medic replied. He examined Hammond's head wound and tied on a new bandage. When Hammond put his helmet back on, the pressure, in combination with the new bandage, seemed to stop the bleeding. Continuing along the tracks, he could plainly see hundreds of Japanese soldiers rushing down the plain to his left. In their mad rush forward, they seemed completely unconcerned with the Americans withdrawing along the tracks. Hammond spotted a platoon from C Company in full flight east of the railroad. Half crying, he begged their platoon sergeant to stop them. "Hold your men here and wait for the rest of the battalion," he urged the noncom; "they're still up front fighting like hell." The sergeant listened noncommittedly. Hammond walked on. When he glanced back, he saw the platoon had picked up and was continuing its flight to the rear.[35]

Manning a machine-gun position providing security for the gun line of H Battery, 10th Marines about 500 yards southeast of Tanapag Village, PFCs Ben Hokit and James Dent could hear the rattle of gunfire in the distance, but all seemed quiet on the artillery battery's perimeter. The battery had only arrived the evening before and was supposed to be well behind the infantry line. Nevertheless, Dent was uneasy. He told Hokit he thought he heard noises from a dry streambed just behind them. The gully, about 5 feet deep and 12 feet across, lay between them and the H Battery howitzers. Hokit suggested that Dent fire his carbine toward the sounds. Dent did and they were stunned to glimpse numbers of Japanese moving down the gully.[36]

Hundreds of Japanese were on the move into the area, having poured through the gap between the Army battalions and the hills. H Battery was set up just east of the Tanapag Road with its four 155mm howitzers pointed roughly north/northeast in anticipation of providing support for the 23rd Marines. The battery had positioned all four of its .50-caliber machine guns on the other side of some trees to cover the open plain and the coastal road.

At about 0300 the artillerymen heard a surge of small arms and machine-gun fire. "We knew that some kind of attack was in progress," observed Lt. David Cox. "But this commotion increased and we could hear our machine guns firing in front of our battery . . . We had the gunners level the tubes." The gunners cut time fuses to 4/10 of a second—the shortest setting—in preparation for close-in fire. It was now 0515. "We could see people out there coming in," said Cox. "And we didn't want to fire on them because we thought they might be Army troops." Cox studied the approaching men through his field glasses and realized they were Japanese.[37] Obie O'Brien's fears about the gap were about to be realized, and H Battery was going to pay a good part of the price.

As Dent and Hokit opened fire with their carbines on the Japanese in the streambed behind them, the third member of their crew, PFC Richard Hopkins, swung the .50-caliber around and sprayed the ditch with machine-gun fire. As the enemy returned fire, Hopkins was shot in the head and killed. Hokit took over the machine gun, but soon noticed the tracers were curving off out of line. Shortly afterward, the gun froze up. A Japanese grenade plunked in next to him. Hokit pushed the grenade into the bottom of the muddy hole with his carbine butt and held the stock over it as it exploded, somehow escaping injury.[38]

Manning another of the battery's .50s, PFCs Donald Holzer and Harold Hoffman heard gunfire to their right and rear. As they peered around, wondering what was going on, three Japanese suddenly appeared behind them. Another group materialized off to the right. The two Marines dove into some weeds behind their position, hoping to escape notice, but a passing Japanese spotted Holzer. When Holzer went to shoot him, his carbine jammed. Before the Japanese could react, Holzer clubbed him to death with the malfunctioning rifle. He and Hoffman killed two more Japanese with their combat knives, but came up short when they found the streambed separating them from the battery position was full of Japanese. They decided to make a run for it. A bullet slammed into Holzer's shoulder, but he managed to keep going. Hoffman was hit in the back and killed.[39]

By now the Japanese advancing on the gun line from the north were within 400 yards and clearly identifiable as enemy. Battery executive officer 1st Lt. Arnold C. Hofstetter estimated their numbers at somewhere between 400 and 500. The Marine crews opened up on them with time and ricochet fire. The rounds tore into the front ranks, but the Japanese kept coming. "They were coming in droves," recalled PFC Gene "Tex" Douglas. "We were cutting fuses to 4/10th of a second and we began to bounce the shells in front of them. One Jap was in front of our gun and several fired their rifles at him and he fell and Corporal Divert said, 'Tex, watch him and if he moves, shoot him again,' but he did not move."[40]

Manning an outlying security position, Corp. Earl Shoenker heard a tank on the roadway. He assumed it was a U.S. tank coming forward to help repulse the enemy attack. But as the tank pulled up directly behind the gun position, the Marines realized the men sitting on the deck were speaking Japanese. Then Shoenker looked out toward the front of the gun line and saw what seemed like thousands of Japanese approaching.[41]

Unequipped for an infantry fight, the artillerymen manning the guns did what they could, but the Japanese began to break through the wooded area to the battery's left. Small arms fire became so heavy the gunners were forced to crawl as they served the howitzers. As cannoneers were shot down, it became impossible to service the pieces. Orders came to abandon gun No. 1 on the right of the firing line as Japanese closed in. Corp. Ellis Oscar "E. O." Palm pulled the firing lock from the howitzer and started toward gun No. 2 when he was intercepted by Sgt. Robert Pace. The sergeant, a twenty-five-year-old prewar enlistee from southeastern Illinois coal country, ordered the crew back to the gun. A Japanese light tank—presumably one of the two tanks that had emerged from Harakiri Gulch—had taken up position on the road behind the gun line. The other howitzers were blocked by trees—only gun No. 1 had a reasonably clear shot at the tank.

Palm balked. They didn't have a chance in hell, he protested, but Pace wasn't taking no for an answer. He led Palm, PFC Eric Johnson, and Corp. Clifford Doggett back to the abandoned howitzer. They replaced the lock and swung the gun around to face the road. In the gathering light, they could see there were actually two enemy tanks. Ducking small arms fire, they sent half a dozen shells at the tanks at point-blank range—about 50 yards—and thought they knocked out both. In actuality, only one tank was destroyed—its turret blown completely off—but the other soon clattered off down the road. As the crew went to abandon the gun for the second time,

Johnson was shot and killed and Sergeant Pace was shot in the chest and right leg. The sergeant managed to stagger away, but the wound was fatal.

Assigned to security at the left rear of the battery position the night before, PFC Henry Basford and two other Marines had dug a foxhole in a small clearing and covered it with a shelter half to keep the rain off. In the early morning, they saw figures approaching. "Nine or ten Japanese came into the clearing," recalled Basford. "They were real close before we realized that they were Japanese, for it was just getting light and we really weren't expecting Japanese."

The three Marines immediately opened fire on the intruders, who responded with a machine gun, and a flurry of well-aimed grenades. In those few frantic moments, Basford managed to throw back two grenades that landed among them, but the third rolled to the back of the hole under the shelter half. Basford got a hand on it just as it exploded. His hand disappeared. The other two men in the hole suffered minor wounds. Basford's wound seemed to have been cauterized in the explosion and he continued to help as best he could, but they quickly realized there were too many Japanese flooding in. They jumped out of the hole and ran for the gun line, only to find it had been overrun. The survivors fell back in such haste that they failed to remove breech blocks and firing locks from the abandoned howitzers. As they joined the fleeing crews, Basford's wound began bleeding heavily. Another Marine took off his web belt and tied off the stump, tightening the makeshift tourniquet with his Ka-bar before they stumbled on.

"We were being overrun and [battery commander] Captain [Harold E.] Nelson gave the order to fall back to the battery position behind us," remembered PFC Gene Douglas. "We went across the road. The radio man (I do not remember his name) was on my left and the captain was on my right. We came to a clearing. The radio man was hit. I knew he was dead . . . Then someone called my name. I looked over and saw some of my buddies . . . were motioning for me to come over where they were. As I turned I was hit in my shoulder."

Lt. Hal Lanes looked back toward the gun line as he pulled out and saw the Japanese closing in "waving rifles over their heads, yelling and screaming." Most of the surviving artillerymen crossed the road and made their way about 150 yards into a brushy, wooded area where they came upon an abandoned Japanese airplane parts dump. The dump was littered with airplane wings and a large number of crates, some containing aircraft engines.

Shot in the hip, Captain Nelson turned command over to Hofstetter. The Marines piled up crates as a makeshift barricade and prepared to make a stand. "This was about 0700," recalled Hofstetter. "We held out there with carbines, one BAR, one pistol and eight captured Jap rifles. Japs got behind us and around us in considerable strength."

Despite his shoulder wound, Gene Douglas also made it to the machinery dump. "I was told to get over to where there were some more who were wounded." Among them was PFC Burton Sayer, a twenty-year-old farm kid from upstate New York who had a sucking wound to the chest. "I could hear Burton Sayer saying, 'I can't breathe.' He kept saying he could not breathe," remembered Douglas. "All of our corpsmen had been killed and no one knew what to do for him. He died about that time."[42]

Though H Battery took the brunt of the assault, the rest of the 3rd Battalion did not escape unscathed. Set up among some trees and tall grass across the road and a little to the south of the H Battery position, H&S Battery was quickly overrun. Led by Maj. Bill Crouch, H&S was the battalion's command center; it had no artillery and only a forward command post had been established. Two large tents, one serving as the Fire Direction Control Center and the other as the Battalion Aid Station, had been set up the evening before. Fire from an enemy tank on the road—probably the one that eluded Sergeant Palm—and from Japanese troops filtering through the underbrush raked the position, decimating the Marines around the aid station and riddling the fire control tent. Many of the survivors took to the bush. Fortunately, the tank did not press the attack and eventually clanked off down the road.

The 3rd Battalion's other two batteries—I and G—also got into the fight. Item Battery, located about 250 yards southeast of H Battery, came under attack by Japanese advancing down the railroad tracks. Unable to lower their howitzer muzzles for fear of hitting Marines to their front, the crews held off the Japanese until 0650 when they ran out of small arms ammo. Battery commander Capt. John M. Allen ordered the firing locks removed from the howitzers and the artillerymen fell back on Battery G to its rear.

Marines at G Battery had heard the outbreak of gunfire to the north. P/Sgt. Michael J. Scott organized some men and intercepted a group of Japanese moving along the railroad berm. The Marines killed most of them, but lost one man who was shot in the stomach and died within minutes. As they took stock, a Japanese tank lurched across the berm, spraying the area with its machine gun. Sergeant Scott stood up—probably to take a shot or lob a grenade—just as the tank cut loose with its main gun. The shell decapitated the sergeant. The turret turned toward PFC Bill Zachary, who was close enough to see a crewman's eyes peering at him through the firing slit. Fortunately, the tank was unable to depress the main gun enough to get a shot at the horrified Marine, but the enemy machine gunner did manage to cut down PFC Robert Burchfield as he bolted for cover.

Finally the enemy tank commander made a fatal mistake. Attempting to get a better line of fire on G Battery positions higher on the slope, he directed the tank up a small knoll, a maneuver that exposed the vulnerable underside of the vehicle. Manning a .50-caliber machine gun on the perimeter, PFC Edmund Sargis poured fire into the unarmored tank bottom. If any crewmembers survived the hail of bullets ripping through the vehicle, they died soon after as the tank caught fire and subsequently blew up.[43]

Here and there in the chaos following the collapse of the two Army battalions, surviving officers tried to regain control over the fleeing men. 1st Lt. Seymour P. Drovis, a twenty-four-year-old former UCLA light heavyweight boxer, made an early effort to establish a holding position at a small railroad cut just behind the original perimeter. As a platoon leader, Drovis had been awarded a Silver Star for bravery during the Makin landing seven months before, but now, loping back and forth in an attempt to organize a defense, he was shot in the head and killed. The railroad cut defense held out a mere fifteen minutes before coming apart.[44]

Following the railroad tracks south toward Road Junction 2, Luke Hammond encountered Lt. Hugh King, who had inherited B Company after Captain Ryan's death the day before. King and Sgt. James F. Rhodes had stopped not far from the edge of Tanapag Village, looking for a place to make a stand. Rhodes was killed by a grenade that exploded in his face, but King, a longtime Guardsman whose grandfather had been a brigadier general, remained undaunted. "You think we ought to set up a line here, Luke?" he asked Hammond.

Hammond agreed, but before they could get organized, a group of GIs approached from the south, returning from what should have been the greater safety of the rear area. They brought ominous news. The Japanese were already behind them. Enemy troops were roaming the area between Tanapag and regimental headquarters, picking off stragglers and the walking wounded. "The Japs are all along back there," one of them reported.[45]

Hammond hardly had time to digest this news when the GIs were hit by the first in what was to be a series of "friendly" fire mishaps over the course of the day. Located in the hills to the east, Cannon Company of the 165th Infantry had been firing its self-propelled 105mm howitzers at the mob of Japanese moving down the plain. Now, attracted by the activity along the coastal area, they turned their fire on the GIs congregated on the railroad tracks. "I heard a close shell, and looking back, beheld the black puff of smoke slightly to our rear," remembered Hammond. "Well, the next one must have been right over us, for suddenly the ground in front of me was literally sprayed with shrapnel." Hammond picked himself out of the dirt after the blast, but the soldier next to him remained on the ground. "I'll have to stay here," he told Hammond calmly. "My foot is cut off."

"You can't make it any farther?" said Hammond.

"No," replied the GI.[46]

Hugh King had already begun to stem the pell-mell rush of men fleeing down the railroad tracks, directing them across the road into the cluster of houses and abandoned trenches along the western edge of Tanapag Village. A moment later F Company commander Capt. Earl White, who had been seriously wounded in the leg, hobbled up and joined King. It was now about 0700. The two officers were exhorting their rag-tag force to dig in and form a new defense line when a mortar shell scored a direct hit on King, killing him instantly.

Nevertheless, the thirty-one-year-old lieutenant had already contributed greatly to stemming the tide of fleeing GIs. A hasty perimeter had begun to take shape in the village to exhortations of "We'll hold here. Get on a line back to the beach over there. Let's don't be leaving now." Men were "dashing madly to and fro," recalled Hammond, but they were prepared to make a fight of it. Major McCarthy arrived and extended the defense—subsequently dubbed the "Second Perimeter" to distinguish it from the battalion's original position before the *gyokusai*—so that it encompassed most of Tanapag Village.[47]

Men too injured to fight were placed in the houses. A few of the buildings were concrete and provided good protection from enemy small arms fire. Others were wood, but were built up off the ground, leaving space enough to crawl underneath. Even so, there was room for only about a third of the wounded. The others, and the GIs still able to bear arms, took shelter in shallow trenches originally dug by the Japanese, deepening them during lulls. Japanese directed fire at them from the fringes of the village.

Hammond saw one man hit in the head. "I knew he was dead. Seconds later another soldier walking near the same spot doubled up and fell without uttering a word. At least fifteen men saw what happened. They looked at each other in a fearful, helpless sort of way. It was indeed a queer feeling."[48]

Among those filtering in to the Second Perimeter was Sgt. Walter T. Hudson, who had no idea of how he got there or how he managed to acquire a dent the size of a baseball in the side of his helmet. His first memory after being overrun that morning was trudging along with several other GIs until an officer stopped them. "Men, let's try to form a defense line behind this rise in the ground," he said. They moved into a grove of trees along the beach where a wounded enlisted man seemed to be in charge. It appeared to Hudson that the GI "seemed to be not only on top of the situation but enjoying himself." He told the newcomers, "All of you with rifles, get on the line. The rest of you get in the center of the grove. Pass any rifle ammo up to us. Give the medics any first aid stuff you have."[49]

John Domanowski ended up with the wounded in the grove. His left arm was useless and the pain was intense. Swarms of flies descended on the wound. As more and more wounded were brought in, men were practically lying on top of each other. One young GI—he looked to be about nineteen years old—lay next to Domanowski. The youngster's foot had been half shot off and was covered with flies. Though he had to be in great pain, he never uttered a sound. Other men had lost arms or legs. There was no morphine. Bandages were in short supply. "Soon we [were] using anything to wrap the wounds, even burlap bags that [were] found on the beach," Domanowski observed.[50]

Survivors continued to trickle in to the new perimeter. In one strange encounter, Sgt. John Sidur was confronted by a pair of Japanese soldiers as he helped two wounded men—one of whom had an arm blown off—back toward the Second Perimeter. The Japanese pointed their rifles at them, but for some reason didn't shoot. Sidur pushed past them and they never did shoot. Reaching the perimeter, he and another GI jumped into a trench. "This Jap jumped up, he must have been lying there," recalled Sidur. "He jumped up on the top [of the trench] and he was pointing [his rifle] at me and then the other guy. Back and forth. If he wanted to have killed us he could have killed us right away." The enemy soldier was still vacillating when Sidur's companion shot him dead.[51]

The Second Perimeter defense was largely in place by 0800, but it was far from airtight. "One [Japanese] ran bewildered right into our midst, staring at [a] soldier who was firing at him as if he wondered who he was," recalled Hammond. When the Japanese paused, the GI took careful aim and killed him. On at least three occasions, Hammond saw individual Japanese wander in among the Americans, only to blow themselves up with their own hand grenades.[52]

PFC Willie Hokoana, a twenty-eight-year-old native Hawaiian who had worked as a driver before the war, took up a spot by the shoreline. Weeks earlier, during the fight for Nafutan Point, Hokoana had picked up a damaged BAR and decided to keep it. He'd been lugging the thing around ever since, gradually scavenging parts from other damaged Brownings. By July 6 he had a working weapon, though part of the assembly was held in place with a nail. Now, noticing small groups of enemy trying to slip in along the shoreline, Hokoana rested the BAR in the fork of a small tree overlooking the beach and started shooting.

Hokoana was joined by Sgt. William Baralis, the former pitcher for A Company's baseball team. While Hokoana used his BAR to good advantage, Baralis pitched grenades, resupplied by a bucket brigade of wounded men who gathered all available grenades and passed them forward. It was later estimated that Baralis threw 150 grenades and killed about a hundred Japanese in the course of the day, but his luck finally ran out during the afternoon when a bullet hit him in the spine. The twenty-five-year-old ballplayer survived the night only to die the next day. Hokoana, who stuck to his exposed position all day, suffered only one small wound. He was later credited with killing over 140 Japanese.[53]

Sgt. Frank Mandaro chronicled the fate of a machine gun some stubborn GIs had managed to lug back from the First Perimeter. As Japanese began emerging from a small grove of trees near the beach, the machine gunners held their fire, leaving the defense to the riflemen. "In a few minutes, however, they had to begin shooting," recalled Mandaro. "I'd never seen so many Japs. As the machine guns opened up, the Japs fell like ten-pins, but others kept coming. They ran, they crawled, they tried to get close enough to toss grenades." Mandaro saw a handful of Japanese jump into one of the machine-gun pits. The gun went silent as the crew fought them hand-to-hand. They soon resumed firing, but the break allowed other Japanese to close within grenade range. There was a shower of explosions around the gun. "One of the gunners, his face bloody, continued firing until he toppled over," recalled Mandaro. "Another man took his place. Then several grenades exploded all around and inside the gun position, and the Japs swarmed in."[54]

The battalions had been out of contact with regimental headquarters since Colonel O'Brien's initial message shortly after 0500. The survivors in the perimeter had no communication with the outside world until later in the morning when PFC J. C. Baird showed up lugging his heavy SCR-300 radio. As the C Company radio operator, Baird had been asleep at the rear of the company perimeter when the attack washed over the battalion. Awakening to find the Japanese all around, he feigned death until the enemy moved on, then shouldered the 38-pound radio and made his way back to the Second Perimeter. The radio had been damaged, but Baird was able to get it working intermittently, which allowed the 1st Battalion operations officer, Capt. Emmett Catlin, to get a call through to regimental headquarters at 0905. Caitlin advised regiment that O'Brien's battalion had been overrun and virtually wiped out. About a hundred survivors of the two battalions were holding out in the vicinity of Road Junction 2, but they needed help quickly. Major McCarthy then got on the radio and reiterated the plea for help. They needed tanks, ammunition, and medical supplies, he told the 105th's executive officer, Lt. Col. Leslie Jensen. Jensen promised to do what he could, but then Baird's radio quit, cutting them off once again.[55]

Though McCarthy could not know it, Jensen had problems of his own as the *gyokusai* began to wash up against the regimental command post, leaving the survivors of the 1st and 2nd Battalions at Tanapag Village like an island in its wake. Though Col. Leonard A. Bishop had nominal command of the regiment, he had seemed to suffer from a certain lassitude over the past several days. "He had seemed unable to exert pressure on his units or move about physically himself and maintain complete control over his men," observed the division historian later. It was later found the colonel had been concealing a severe case of diabetes, which may have been a factor in his shortcomings.[56] Now, as the regiment faced potential annihilation, it was left to Jensen, a forty-seven-year-old World War I veteran who had been a Guardsman since he was eighteen, to handle the emerging crisis.

As early as 0530 Jensen reported to Lieutenant Colonel Van Antwerp at Division Headquarters that the sound of gunfire was drawing near to the regimental command post, located in a former concrete air raid shelter about a half-mile below Tanapag. At 0615, Jensen informed division that the CP was "pinned down by rifle fire."[57] Some of the Japanese had come down the coast by boat, landing just north of the command post, but most were remnants of the human tide that had overwhelmed the 1st and 2nd Battalions and Marine artillery batteries.

Edward H. Redfield, a member of the Regimental Reconnaissance Platoon, encountered living evidence of the disaster unfolding to the north when he spotted a lone GI staggering toward the headquarters area early that morning. As Redfield ran to help him, the soldier collapsed, dropping his rifle. "He was seriously wounded in several body areas," observed Redfield. "He seemed delirious and kept calling for his rifle." As Redfield tried to assist him, his hand slipped into a massive hole in the GI's back. How the man—whom Redfield believed was from the 1st Battalion—had managed to come as far as he did seemed almost miraculous. The GI was taken back for medical attention. Redfield never found out who he was or what happened to him, but it seemed unlikely he could have survived his severe wounds.[58]

CHAPTER XXIV

The Killing Fields

AT 27TH DIVISION HEADQUARTERS, SET IN A CLUSTER OF TENTS OFF THE coastal road north of Garapan, General Griner was attempting to sort through the confusion. There had been no word from the 1st or 2nd Battalions since Colonel O'Brien's brief contact at about dawn, but Griner had already begun to act on what little information was available. He alerted 106th Infantry commander Col. Albert K. Stebbins to ready two of his battalions to move out and directed the 762nd Tank Battalion to rush all available tanks to the support of the 105th Infantry. Griner also telephoned NTLF chief of staff Graves Erskine to apprise him of the situation.[1]

Two platoons of light tanks and a platoon of mediums rolled north shortly after 0530. Drawing abreast of the 105th Infantry CP about thirty minutes later, three light tanks commanded by Lt. Hugh J. Guffey continued 400 yards up the coast road to a creek subsequently dubbed "Bloody Run." Peering out from the third tank in line, Sgt. Oliver Hendricks noticed large numbers of people moving along the creekbed below the level of the roadway. Hendricks held his fire, unable to determine in the poor light whether they were friendly or enemy. That question was resolved an instant later when an explosion rocked Sgt. Joseph Kernoschak's tank just in front of him. The troops in the gully were Japanese, and one of them had thrown a magnetic mine against Kernoschak's tank, blowing off a track and tearing a hole in the fuel tank.

Hendricks swept the gully with his machine guns as Japanese swarmed around Kernoschak's tank, apparently hoping to ignite the spilled fuel and immolate the crew. Kernoschak managed to pull the damaged Stuart away from the spreading puddle of fuel, but the tank wasn't going any farther. As the Japanese pressed their attacks, Guffey feared his tanks—lacking infantry support—were in danger of being overrun. He raised Kernoschak on the radio and ordered him to bail out of the damaged tank while he still could.

The crew scrambled out the bottom escape hatch and slipped into some heavy brush on the edge of the road where they found four Marines from the overrun artillery battalion. One of the Marines, "a mere boy," observed the tankers, had been badly wounded. After some discussion, they decided their best chance was to try and make it back down the coast to friendly lines. One of the Marines, "a large man who looked as if he might be a Mexican," observed one of the tank crewmen, slung the wounded youth over his shoulder and they worked their way toward the ocean and then south along a winding trench running along the beach. They had not gone far when the wounded Marine died. Bringing up the rear, twenty-eight-year-old Pvt. Thomas Veneziano spotted trouble. "For God's sake, hurry up!" he shouted. "Japs are following us down the trench!" An instant later, Veneziano was shot and killed. The next man in line, another of the tank crew, was also shot and seriously wounded, but the Marines grabbed him and they managed to break free.

Back at the bridge crossing, Lieutenant Guffey had run into still more trouble. As the tanks turned around to head back to the CP, Hendricks's Stuart slid off the road and got hung up. Guffey radioed the crew to bail out, but with Japanese infantry swarming all around, the tankers decided to stay put. Guffey clanked back down the road to get help, leaving Hendricks to fend for himself. To the crew's relief, the mob moving along the streambed momentarily seemed to lose interest in the tank. However, trouble soon arose again as several dozen Japanese, led by a sword-brandishing officer, headed for them. Just as the officer swept his sword forward to signal an apparent charge, gunner Phillip L. Peterson let loose with a canister round from the tank's 37mm gun. The shotgun-type round sent 122 ⅜-inch steel balls tearing through the massed Japanese. The enemy officer sagged to his knees; then, apparently by sheer force of will, he slowly straightened himself up to his full height. Placing the point of the sword against his abdomen, he fell forward on it, driving the blade entirely through his body.

Fighting off a series of lesser attacks, Hendricks had begun to run low on ammunition when four Shermans and a platoon of Stuarts finally clanked up to the rescue. As the tanks swept the area with fire, the crew bailed out of their tank under cover of a couple of smoke grenades and hustled back down the road on foot. Despite badly jangled nerves, the only injury was to the gunner, who had burned his hand while extracting hot shell casings from the tank's 37mm gun.[2]

A greater sense of the disaster unfolding to the north arrived at the 105th Infantry command post at 0720 when the Marines accompanying the survivors of Kernoschak's tank crew stumbled in to report that H Battery had been overrun. Colonel Jensen, who had hastily thrown together a defense line of headquarters personnel, clerks, typists, mess sergeants, and other rear-echelon personnel, messaged Division: "H Btry of 3d Bn, 10th Marines, 400 yds fwd of 105 CP rptd overrun by En; Japs have their guns."[3] The report was followed soon after by news that H&S Battery had also been overrun.

Alarmed, General Griner ordered the 2nd Battalion, 106th Infantry under Maj. Almerin O'Hara to recapture the artillery batteries. O'Hara, who had already started to position his battalion to go to the aid of the 105th Infantry, objected that he would have to reorient his entire movement. Griner insisted. "You will attack at once, in any formation you deem advisable, with the mission of recapturing the Japanese-held artillery positions, and then make contact with the 105th on your left," he ordered.[4]

Up on the high ground overlooking the plain, the 165th Infantry had a bird's-eye view of the chaos below. The regiment had logged a frantic radio message, probably sent over PFC Baird's salvaged radio, shortly before 0800: "There are only 100 men left from the 1st and 2nd Battalions of the 105th. For God's sake get us some ammunition and water and medical supplies right away."[5] At 0935 observers reported they could see what appeared to be the motor pool of either the 1st or 2nd Battalion. "In it they can see 15 vehicles, 4 on fire," noted the division journal.[6]

Despite the scene unfolding below, the 165th made no effort to assist the two shattered battalions. Griner later remarked with thinly veiled disgust that they preferred to "stand where they were and shoot Japs without any effort to move forward."[7] The 3rd Battalion, 105th Infantry also failed to act and "never moved from its pre-attack position," observed a subsequent report.[8]

At 0920, Griner called Colonel Stebbins and directed him to attack up the railroad tracks with his 1st Battalion. Despite the previous alert of the 106th Infantry, it took until 1000 to get the battalion deployed and underway. Even then the GIs seemed oblivious to the direness of the situation—they moved forward at a snail's pace despite an almost complete lack of opposition. It would take them another two hours merely to reach Colonel Jensen at the 105th Infantry command post.

While Griner took steps to contain the *gyokusai*, there was little indication that anyone at NTLF Headquarters in Charan Kanoa understood the extent of the disaster taking place up the coast. Ironically, Holland Smith had already begun plans for a victory ceremony. As GIs fought for their lives near Tanapag, the 106th Infantry logged a message from division, advising: "CG NT&LF advises that American flag will be hoisted at his CP when conquest of SAIPAN is completed. You have been selected to furnish one private as member of color guard for this occasion. Further notice will be given of hour set for ceremony and uniform to be worn."[9]

Attending a routine briefing at 0830, news correspondents learned that night fighters had shot down a couple of enemy bombers, one near Rota, the other near Guam; there had been some artillery fire from Tinian directed at Aslito Airfield; and a couple of hundred civilians had come into U.S. lines the day before. The major giving the briefing added there had been a report that "one of our gun positions in the 10th Marines' area" had been overrun earlier in the morning, but the 106th Infantry had sent a battalion and fifteen tanks to recapture the guns. The officer was so nonchalant that Bob Sherrod decided to head out to do a feature piece about black Marines in the field depot companies. He wouldn't realize the magnitude of the *gyoku-sai* until later in the morning.[10]

The makeshift defense at the Second Perimeter had been holding out for more than three hours when yet another disaster befell the beleaguered GIs—this one at the hands of their own artillery. "We got to the Jap trenches all right, and all of sudden we started to get hit with artillery fire," recalled Sgt. Nick Grinaldo. "Real bad, and it was our own. They had to be 155mm howitzers, and they poured them into us. . . ."[11]

The misdirected barrage slammed in at about 1130. Sgt. Attilio W. Grestini was manning a rifle position when there was a massive explosion and he found himself sprawled on the ground like a slaughtered calf. A shell had blown his left arm completely off and mangled his left leg at the hip. The twenty-three-year-old sergeant lay there silently, biting his lips to keep from crying out. Two GIs discovered him and dragged him to the center of the perimeter where he received some rudimentary medical treatment. Presumably doomed, he lay quietly, a tourniquet on the remnant of his arm and another on his leg as the battle continued around him.[12]

Another victim of the errant barrage was PFC Mark W. Winters. Seriously wounded when the battalions were overrun, the twenty-five-year-old Californian was hit again shortly after getting into the Second Perimeter. Nevertheless, he insisted that his buddies prop him up in a firing position and proceeded to pick away with his carbine all morning at encroaching Japanese. When another GI remonstrated with him for unnecessarily exposing himself, Winters shrugged him off. "I'll stay here and fire until I get the last Jap or they get me," he replied. But it wasn't the Japanese that finally got him. He was killed by an American artillery shell.[13]

Some of the indiscriminate shelling came from division artillery, some from the 165th Infantry's Cannon Company, firing from the hills to the east. Nick Grinaldo later estimated that half the casualties suffered in the Second Perimeter that morning were caused by friendly artillery fire. Luke Hammond heard shouts, "Pass the word back, artillery falling in our front lines!" He wondered where "the word" was being passed back to; he was not aware of any radio communication with the rear or other contact with outside units. "We felt completely deserted," said Hammond. No one seemed to be in charge. "It seemed that we were doomed."[14]

Major McCarthy was still alive, though he does not appear to have been a forceful presence up to this point. But at noon, with no outside rescue in sight, McCarthy decided he had to do something. His plan, born of desperation, was to assemble a "flying wedge" of volunteers to fight their way back to the regimental command post and secure help. As Sgt. Walter T. Hudson remembered it, he was hunkered down in a trench when an officer—he thought it was a lieutenant—came along and said, "Some of you fellows come with me and let's try to get back to the Regimental P.C. to tell them what's happening here."[15]

Dozens of men gathered for the attempted breakout, but such was the confusion that other GIs had no idea what was going on. Luke Hammond believed they were simply fleeing in panic. As the "flying wedge" started off, other GIs shouted at them, "Where the hell are you going? Come back here!" Still others, anxious to escape—or fearful they were being abandoned—rushed to join the flight to the rear.

The commotion caught the attention of the 165th Infantry's Cannon Company, which once again opened fire on their own people. The barrage landed on the edge of the flying wedge, sending panicked survivors fleeing south along the roadway. Instead of salvation, they ran into yet another barrage, this one delivered by division artillery. Any semblance of order vanished. Observers on the high ground saw men splashing into the lagoon, fleeing the artillery only to come under fire from Japanese on shore. About seventy men swam and waded out to the reef some 250 yards from shore. Some were from the original flying wedge; others saw the flight into the water and followed for no other reason than it seemed like a good idea at the time. John Domanowski saw about forty men rush into the shallow water as if trying to hide. "The Japs [saw] them in the water, and open[ed] fire at them with machine guns. You could hear the bullets hitting their skulls." Domanowski yelled angrily at the panicked GIs to stay and fight, but if anyone heard him, they paid no attention.[16]

"We all started to run and we got hit again by some big stuff and then everyone headed for the water, me right along with them," recalled twenty-two-year-old PFC Marcus H. Itano. "I ended up on the beach and some of the men ahead of me were already in the water swimming but I could see bullets hitting the water all around them and I figured they'd all be killed. I figured my best chance might be to try for our lines alone by cutting down the beach, so I did."

Itano ran about 50 yards along the shoreline, before noticing about twenty men up ahead of him. "They were laying prone on the beach with their backs to me and were pretty busy watching something farther on ahead," he recalled. "I couldn't see their faces. I took another look and thought they were some of our own men who were hiding from the Japs so I thought I'd join them. I ran right smack into the center of the group and laid down. Nobody paid any attention to me. I must have laid there for two or three minutes and then I poked the man next to me to find out what they were looking at. When he turned towards me, I found myself looking right into the face of a Jap. The Jap was surprised, but not as surprised as I was. I had a grenade on my shoulder strap and as I jumped to my feet I pulled this off and yanked the pin. Then I dropped it and ran like hell. I'm telling you, I stepped on heads and backs and everything else getting out of there."[17]

About twenty-five survivors of the flying wedge fiasco made it as far as Bloody Run where they stopped and settled in to what became known later as the "Little Perimeter." Stragglers trickled in for the rest of the day until there were as many as seventy-five GIs holed up. They had no contact with the Second Perimeter or with regimental headquarters only 400 yards to the south, but they would eventually be relieved without much fanfare.

Back in the village, PFC Sam Dinova had made it to the beach and was lying low. "The guys were running out in the ocean to get away from the Japs," he recalled. Two GIs with Dinova panicked. "These guys got up and they ran. I heard they got killed after," he said. There was a sudden explosion, probably another U.S. artillery shell. "I remember seeing the black dirt, sand and everything in the air," he recalled. "Next thing, I don't remember nothing. I got hit in the leg. When I got hit in the leg I got knocked out . . . When I came to, there was guys all around me that were still fighting. The Japs were all around where I was. They were fighting them off."[18]

Nick Grinaldo had been hit in the shoulder earlier in the morning and then in the hip, but was still able to move around. "[T]he Japs started coming along, the beach," he recalled. "And I started to holler for some BAR fire from down there. There were a lot of them." Lying helpless on the sand, Sam Dinova recognized Grinaldo's voice—the two Guardsmen came from the same neighborhood in Troy, New York—and he called out to him. Grinaldo shouted to Dinova, "Sammy, stay where you are!" He started after Dinova a couple of times, but had to duck back as bullets kicked up the sand around him. Finally, he managed to worm his way down to Dinova, who was in agony from a huge hole in his left thigh. He'd also been hit in the right leg and had a wound in his back. "I'm not gonna make it," he told Grinaldo. "I'm gonna die. Tell my father and mother . . ."

"You're not going anywhere, you're too friggin' miserable to die," snapped Grinaldo. He extended his unwounded leg and told Dinova to grab his ankle. Dinova latched on and Grinaldo dragged him into the shelter of some coconut trees.[19]

Corp. William Bowsh had been trying to clear his jammed carbine when U.S. artillery descended on Major McCarthy's flying wedge. Shoving the assembly in his pocket, he scrambled under a nearby house where he found five wounded GIs hiding out. Bowsh bandaged two of the more seriously wounded men with his undershirt, as another GI reassembled his carbine for him, pausing momentarily in his task to lob a grenade out from under the house, killing two Japanese. "There were Japs prowling around all over the place and if you didn't watch out they crawled right in with you," remarked Bowsh.

At about 1230, almost an hour after the artillery concentrations first slammed into the Second Perimeter, the GIs were astonished to see a jeep careening down the road from the direction of the overrun First Perimeter. The driver turned out to be twenty-nine-year-old 1st Lt. Bernard A. Tougaw. A longtime Guardsman who had been decorated for taking over a disorganized platoon in the Marshalls campaign the previous year, Tougaw had reached the Second Perimeter earlier in the morning and helped organize the defense. How he now came to be driving down the road toward them in a jeep was a mystery to the GIs. The most likely explanation is that he had run north to escape the artillery barrage on the northeast corner of the perimeter and found the jeep—emblazoned with the name "Lena Horne"—abandoned in the overrun area beyond.

Tougaw raced down the road, running a gauntlet of enemy fire into the Second Perimeter, and announced he was going to try to get back to the regimental command post. Anybody who wanted to risk it was welcome to pile aboard. Bowsh and one of the wounded men crawled out from under the house and jumped in as Tougaw put the jeep into gear and took off down the road in the direction of regimental headquarters. The Japanese didn't even fire on them for the first hundred yards. "Everybody was just too surprised, I think," speculated Bowsh. "The road was littered with dead Japs and that jeep sure bumped along over them just like we were riding on ties on a railroad track." A few more GIs had piled on the jeep along the way, but they did not get far. Coming to a tree lying across the road, Tougaw put the jeep in low and pushed through the branches but as he emerged on the other side, he was shot between the eyes. The jeep lurched and rolled off the road into a ditch. The passengers scattered, leaving the dead lieutenant slumped at the wheel.

Bowsh dove into a ditch alongside the road, landing almost on top of two Japanese. "I pulled up my carbine to shoot them and the damned thing wouldn't go off," he recalled. "I just squeezed the trigger and nothing happened." As the Japanese scrambled to bring their own weapons to bear, another GI appeared on the roadway overhead and killed them both. Bowsh paused to examine his malfunctioning carbine and found he had neglected to take the safety off.

Continuing cautiously down the ditch, he saw a GI walking along the road ahead of him. "This guy is walking along the middle of the road as big as life," he recalled. "He was wounded and limping and had a cane." As Bowsh followed along, a Japanese officer jumped out of a ditch on the other side of the road and confronted the injured GI. "He was yelling and hollering and waving a pistol under the American's nose," remarked Bowsh. Making sure the safety was off, Bowsh raised his carbine and dropped the officer in the road with two shots. "You know that other American just kept right on walking down the road like nothing had happened," observed Bowsh. "I never saw him again."

With only a few rounds left for his carbine, Bowsh ventured up onto the roadway to retrieve the dead officer's pistol, but changed his mind as an enemy machine gun opened up in his direction. He jumped for the ditch again, but this time he looked before he leaped. "It was a damned good thing

I did look first, too because there was another Jap in there right where I was going to jump." As Bowsh landed in the ditch, the Japanese turned around, took one look at him and shouted, "Suwendah! Suwendah!"

Bowsh retorted, "Suwendah, hell!" and shot him three times.

He finally found shelter in a concrete structure, which turned out to be a Japanese air raid shelter. Three more GIs ducked inside soon after he arrived. One of them had a BAR he had picked up, but only one full magazine. After some discussion, the four men decided to head south toward the regimental command post. "This guy with the BAR went first and just as he poked his head out the door, two Japs came in the door just as big as life," recalled Bowsh. "This guy with the BAR got excited. He had it on full auto and he just pulled the trigger and cut those Japs right square in two." They waited a few minutes—the BAR was now empty and Bowsh had only two rounds for his carbine—and when no more Japanese showed up, they made a dash for the regimental command post. They ran about 75 yards and suddenly there were GIs all around them. "It sure felt good," admitted Bowsh. They were among the first men to make it back from the two overrun battalions, though others—including one GI, naked except for his helmet, who staggered out of the ocean—would continue to straggle in during the afternoon.[20]

Lying in the sand among the litter of corpses at the overrun First Perimeter, Yeoman Second Class Mitsuharu Noda was surprised to find himself still alive that morning. He had been racing along with the others when two bullets slammed into his torso. "I didn't suffer pain," he recalled. "None at all. But I couldn't stand, either. I was lying on my back. I could see tracer bullets passing overhead." There were bodies everywhere. He quenched his thirst with a canteen taken from a dead GI and watched with some curiosity as his own blood pooled around him. "This is it," he thought.

Four other wounded Japanese huddled nearby. One of them clasped a grenade in his hand. The man with the grenade called out to Noda, "Hey, sailor, there! Won't you come with us?"

Noda replied politely, "I have a grenade. Please go ahead."

One of the four cried out, "Long live the Emperor!" The grenade exploded almost simultaneously. Noda looked over at them, appalled by the destruction the grenade had wrought on their bodies. "Their heads were all cracked open and smoke was coming out," he recalled. As he lay there alone in his own pooling blood, his mind began to wander to incidents of his youth and he lapsed into unconsciousness.[21]

Survivors of the overrun Marine artillery batteries hung on in small pockets throughout the morning, fighting off repeated Japanese efforts to annihilate them. The largest concentration of holdouts consisted of roughly forty H Battery men who had barricaded themselves in the Japanese machinery dump not far from the coast road.

By mid-morning the wounded were becoming desperate with thirst. Rainwater that had puddled up on the tarps covering the crates provided some relief—one ingenious Marine used the cellophane from a cigarette pack as a makeshift cup—but it was not nearly enough. Two volunteers ventured back to the H Battery position to retrieve jerry cans from the abandoned jeeps. The metal containers had been shot full of holes, but some water remained. Clutching the precious cans, the two volunteers dashed back to the barricades followed by a few random rifle shots.[22]

Dozens of other Marines from the overrun batteries owed their lives to nineteen-year-old PFC Harold Agerholm, an artilleryman with the regiment's 4th Battalion, dug in just to the southeast. Located beyond the main thrust of the *gyokusai*, the battalion killed about eighty-five Japanese during the morning, but was never seriously threatened. However, as small numbers of wounded Marines trickled into the perimeter and the 3rd Battalion's plight became increasingly apparent, Agerholm obtained permission to take an ambulance jeep out to search for survivors.

He had not traveled far when he began to encounter wounded men, alone and in knots of two or three, often with one supporting another. Loading as many wounded onto the jeep as possible, Agerholm drove them to safety, dodging groups of marauding Japanese. Then he went back. The identity of all those he saved will never be known, such was the confusion of that morning. One of them may have been Pvt. Armand Masse, who, though severely wounded, was able to hobble south along the roadway with the help of another Marine. A third Marine in their party died of his injuries before Masse and his buddy were finally spotted by someone in a jeep and were taken to safety. Another survivor was Pharmacist's Mate Frederick Barrows. Hit seven times, he last remembered lying down and looking up at the sun, expecting to die. He regained consciousness on a hospital ship with no idea of how he got there.[23]

Over a period of three hours that morning, Agerholm—whose family later remembered his boyhood penchant for bringing home stray pets and captured turtles—single-handedly evacuated at least forty-five wounded men. His luck finally ran out when he spotted two casualties lying in the open under enemy fire. Vaulting out of the jeep, he ran out to get them and was shot dead.[24]

Not far from H battery's makeshift fortress, Marines holding out in the H&S Battery area thought help might be at hand when U.S. tanks appeared on the coastal road. The battalion commander, Maj. William Crouch, hurriedly ducked out of a hole in the side of the riddled command tent and struck out across an open field toward the tanks, which had pulled up a couple of hundred yards away by the bridge at Bloody Run. He had made it about halfway across the field when he was shot in the back. Witnesses saw the major's helmet fly off; he dropped his carbine, but staggered along another 20 yards before collapsing.[25]

The tanks also caught the attention of the men barricaded at the airplane parts dump. PFC Rod Sandburg volunteered to try to get their help. Avoiding the open field, he made his way to the crossing at Bloody Run and found four tanks, one of which appeared to be stuck. They were all tightly buttoned up. Sandburg pounded on the side of one of the tanks with his rifle butt, but got no response. In frustration, he stood back and fired his rifle at the armor, then took off his helmet to reveal his blonde hair lest anyone mistake him for an especially suicidal Japanese. The turret hatch popped open and a crewman emerged to ask Sandburg what he thought he was doing. Sandburg told him about the besieged artillerymen and asked for help. The tank commander disappeared back inside to radio for instructions. When he finally reemerged, it was to tell Sandburg he could not help; the tanks were supposed to move north.[26]

Fortunately, help was on the way—albeit very slowly–as the 2nd Battalion, 106th Infantry, under Major O'Hara, neared the Marine gun positions late in the morning. Accompanying the GIs, an exasperated Bob Sherrod jotted in his notebook: "Machine guns fire millions of rounds through the cane field. Once in a while a rifleman fires. We halt . . . Nobody has seen a live Jap. No return fire. What are these infantrymen waiting for?"[27] At 1115, the battalion notified division it had reached I Battery. Twenty minutes later, O'Hara reported that his men were in the process of securing H&S Battery. Many of the Japanese were now fleeing north, back across the plain.[28]

Combat correspondent William Worden saw a prisoner being escorted to the rear. He did not look particularly fearsome. "He walked with bloodless hands clutching his wounded side," observed Worden. "His trousers dragged on the ground, his buttocks exposed. He said nothing. The American guard walking behind him said nothing." Corpses littered the fields around the Marine battery positions. Some of the Japanese dead lay under farmhouses where they had crawled "like sick dogs," he observed. Some had died of wounds; some were suicides who had eviscerated themselves with hand grenades. "It may have been an honorable death, but it wasn't pretty," remarked Worden.[29]

The approaching GIs stepped around the body of Major Crouch. In his final moments the stricken officer had pulled a sheaf of letters from home from his pocket. They were still clutched in his hand. Dead Marines lay around the H&S Battery tents. A jeep still burned, flames licking out from the gas tank. A dead corpsman sprawled a few feet away, his face in the dirt. Beside him lay the man he had been trying to help, his features, in death, still contorted with pain. Nine dead Japanese sprawled in a nearby ditch. One of them, armed only with a bayonet tied to a stick, had been shot through the head. A Japanese officer with a fancy belt lay on his back, staring sightlessly into the afternoon sky.[30] Most of the dead Japanese wore caps with the navy anchor, but a few had helmets bearing the army star.

As the afternoon wore on, the Marine holdouts in the airplane parts dump heard the squeal and clatter of an approaching tank. To their relief, it was American. The Sherman knocked out a Japanese machine gun south of the perimeter and a skirmish line of GIs approached the makeshift barricade. "[B]y the time we were rescued there were only nineteen of us that could still shoot a weapon," remembered PFC Robert A. Olsen.[31]

Compared to the rest of the 106th Infantry, O'Hara's advance was a veritable *blitzkrieg*. Due to a series of delays—including sitting on its heels after somehow mistaking Road Junction 4, which was well to the south, for Road Junction 2—Lt. Col. Winslow Cornett's 1st Battalion finally arrived at the 105th Infantry command post at 1410, four hours after setting out in its push up the coastal rail line and despite having encountered virtually no resistance. In the meantime, Colonel Jensen's clerks, truck drivers, cooks, and supply men—holding down hurriedly organized positions—had killed scores of Japanese as the *gyokusai*, greatly reduced by casualties and gradually losing momentum, lapped up against the regimental command post. Cornett's arrival evoked both relief and annoyance among 105th Infantry officers who were disgusted by the slow pace of the 106th's advance. Apparently oblivious to their irritation, the colonel promptly halted his forward movement, such as it was, and sent out patrols.[32]

Showing more initiative, Lt. Jack Lansford pushed up the road with two medium tanks, harassed only by sniper fire and an occasional Molotov cocktail. Continuing on about a quarter of a mile past Bloody Run, the Shermans came upon a wooded area with a couple of partly demolished houses visible back in the trees. Lansford was still taking it all in when a mob of GIs—many of them wounded—suddenly emerged, running up to beat frantically on the side of the tanks with their rifle butts. Though Lansford didn't realize it, he had broken through to the Second Perimeter at Tanapag Village. "The men thought their deliverance was at hand and were overjoyed," observed Luke Hammond. A fellow lieutenant, who had also narrowly escaped the overrun First Perimeter, broke down. "He was half crying—wouldn't say anything."[33] Major McCarthy borrowed Lansford's radio to report to the 105th Infantry command post. Word circulated that trucks would be sent up for the wounded.

But deliverance would have to wait. The celebration had scarcely begun when Lansford received orders to go to the aid of three light tanks that had bogged down after venturing into the lagoon to fire on Japanese shooting the GIs who had fled out to the reef. As the tanks headed back down the road, McCarthy and about thirty-five men followed behind. The major arrived at the regimental command post at 1500 hours to find Jensen, Colonel Cornett, and Brig. Gen. Ogden J. Ross from Division Headquarters conferring on their next move. Ushered in, he provided them with a detailed summary of the current situation and the disaster that had befallen the 1st and 2nd Battalions.[34]

Oblivious to events on shore, the destroyer USS *Heywood L. Edwards* was cutting through the waves about a mile off Tanapag Harbor when crew members spotted knots of men waving frantically from the reef. "At first glance they appeared to be having a swimming party, but this seemed odd as enemy positions were only a short distance away," observed the ship's war diary.

An explanation arrived as a light observation plane circling the reef buzzed over the destroyer and dropped a note reporting that the "swimmers" had been cut off from their lines and were in need of help. Capt. Joseph W. Boulware sent a motor whaleboat to investigate. It came back loaded with wounded soldiers. Boulware promptly dispatched more boats and radioed an alert to other destroyers in the area. The boats eventually picked up about 135 GIs, along with one Japanese POW who had joined them on the reef.[35] The GIs were in tough shape. "It seemed every one of the men was wounded," recalled Boulware. "Some were naked, for they had to swim at one time or another." A pharmacist's mate aboard the *Edwards* treated wounds as best he could; the ship's crew fed the men and gave them clothing. A patrol boat soon arrived to transfer the wounded to a larger ship with better medical facilities. "That was the last I saw of them," remarked Boulware.[36]

An hour after Major McCarthy's arrival at 105th Infantry headquarters, the first concerted efforts got underway to rescue the men still waiting in the Second Perimeter. Two supply officers, Lt. Herman Schroeder and Lt. Francois Albanese, organized a convoy of trucks and DUKWs loaded with medical supplies and ammo and at 1600 made a dash up the road. Though the *gyokusai* had spent its force, the area was still crawling with armed Japanese. Albanese saw abandoned jeeps with dead American soldiers slumped inside. Some of his trucks were knocked out, and Albanese was wounded by a hand grenade that exploded under his jeep. Schroeder was also wounded, but managed to get three of his trucks through to the GIs. He loaded the trucks with the most seriously wounded men and dashed back down the highway to the regimental command post.[37]

While Schroeder made his dash to the Second Perimeter, Major Cornett's lollygagging 1st Battalion finally reached Bloody Run after working through a maze of entrenchments along the beach area. Instead of continuing the push, Cornett now halted for the day still 300 to 400 yards from the survivors in the Second Perimeter. Liaison officer Maj. Regan Fuller reported to NTLF—and later to Griner himself—that the advance could have easily been continued; there was virtually no opposition. Questioned later by an annoyed Griner, Colonel Stebbins admitted the decision to halt the advance was his own and had been made over the protests of his battalion commander. He explained that although enemy fire was not heavy, he feared the advance had bypassed large numbers of Japanese that could threaten his rear and that "mopping up of the area already gained consumed the remaining period of daylight."[38]

Giving up on the 106th Infantry, Griner arranged to evacuate the survivors by water, using LVTs from the 773rd Amphibian Tractor Battalion. The 773rd's executive officer, twenty-eight-year-old Maj. James B. Bartholomees, reported to the 105th Infantry command post to find that most of the staff had left upon arrival of the 106th Infantry. The regimental operations officer sat beside a phone of dubious utility, assisted by "three or four men lying around eating K rations," recalled Bartholomees. The officer told Bartholomees he thought the division G-1, Lt. Col. Oakley M. Bidwell, would be along in a few minutes. "Then he unhooked his phone, and followed by his men, headed toward the rear," recalled Bartholomees. Bidwell arrived a few minutes later and Bartholomees learned that the survivors of the two battalions—believed to number anywhere from 100 to 600 men— were holed up in Tanapag Village just up the coast.

Bartholomees had eight tractors available with seven more on the way. It was now nearing dusk. His first action was to send his eight tractors under the command of Lt. Erik R. Fredericksen north by water to locate the stranded GIs. He also sent his jeep back with a messenger to summon ambulances and medical personnel to care for the large number of wounded he anticipated would be arriving. The regimental surgeon of the 105th Infantry soon showed up with several aid men and began to set up an aid station in an open field.[39]

On the edge of the Second Perimeter, a bloody Nick Grinaldo saw Fredericksen's landing craft making their way up the coast toward the beach. He turned and shouted, "Here comes our salvation! We're gonna be taken out!" A lieutenant Grinaldo didn't recognize started to chew him out: "What do you mean giving these guys false hope? What's the matter with you? Keep your mouth shut!"

But as the LVTs drew closer, it became clear that Grinaldo was right. Grinaldo dragged himself down to the water to warn the little flotilla there were mines on the beach. "And I started waving them off," he recalled. "And the guy, coxswain I guess, he had a horn. He said, 'What's wrong?' I says, 'The mines are all over the place, back off.' He says, 'Can you guide me in?' 'Yeah, I can guide you in.' So I did." Safely ashore, the coxswain looked at Grinaldo, all bedraggled and bloody, and blurted, "My God, man, you're wounded." He told Grinaldo to get aboard the LVT. "You're the first man out of here."[40]

Lying up under some coconut trees, Sam Dinova was still alive despite his three wounds. Now, as the amtracs arrived, the survivors were rushing to get aboard. "Guys were running out," recalled Dinova. "The guys were all jumping in." Fearful he would be left behind, Dinova grabbed at a passing GI and pleaded, "Get me out of here!" Two GIs dragged him down to one of the LVTs, but there was no more room inside the jammed troop bay, so they laid Dinova over the engine compartment. The metal was hot, but someone tucked a field jacket under him to provide some insulation. Dinova was not about to complain. "As we pulled out they were shooting at us," he recalled of the Japanese still lurking throughout the area.[41]

John Domanowski made his way over to one of the tractors. During the afternoon he had relocated to a new tree, only to be shot in his right elbow by a Japanese hiding in the branches. Someone dropped the sniper at his feet. Berserk with pain, Domanowski kicked the corpse savagely in the head before passing out. He had no idea how long he was unconscious. Now he stood by the tractor with two broken arms. There was room for one more man but he was unable to climb aboard. A couple of men saw his predicament and gave him a boost. Moments later, with a lurch, the tractor headed out into the water.[42]

As Bartholomees's seven remaining amtracs arrived near the former 105th Infantry command post and prepared to head out to pick up more GIs, Fredericksen was already returning with a load of survivors—an estimated twenty men per vehicle. "The few unwounded were sitting or standing where there was room," observed Bartholomees. "There was not a sound from any one of those men. They were so tired and so relieved at being pulled out of an impossible situation that the unwounded merely got to the ground and helped unload the wounded. Then they gathered in small knots and just waited. Not a man had had a drink of water or a thing to eat all day and yet they were not interested in food or water. They had no ammunition whatsoever; their only resupply for 24 hours of constant firing had been what they could get off the bodies of their comrades."[43]

Back at the perimeter, Luke Hammond helped carry stretchers out onto the tractors as they arrived. Finally someone gave Hammond a closer look and said, "You better get on, Mac." Hammond waded out into the shallow water and climbed aboard. The tractor crew opened up a rusty can of grapefruit juice and passed it among the wounded. "It was wonderful," he recalled. As the tractor pulled out, a Japanese machine gunner in a bunker loosed one long last burst, then blew himself up with a grenade. As darkness approached, the amtracs made a third trip for the remainder of the survivors. Just to be sure, two LVTs went back for a final look. The crews boldly snapped on their headlights as they searched the area in the dark, but found no one else.[44]

Medical personnel began sorting out the wounded as they came ashore. Someone gave Sam Dinova a shot of morphine and he was strapped onto a jeep next to another casualty. "Next thing I know, we come to this big area, it looked like three football fields," he recalled. Though everything seemed blurry, he saw that medical personnel were operating from the back of a big truck. "They were operating right out of there with a light."[45]

The first thing Luke Hammond did after coming safely ashore was to stop on the beach to move his bowels. Then he climbed aboard a truck, joining the convoy of wounded bound for the 31st Field Hospital where rows of patients lay on litters awaiting medical attention.[46] Among the casualties was Corp. Eddie Beaudoin. Earlier in the afternoon, the twenty-two-year-old medic had wandered into the beach area, disoriented and covered with blood, but still clutching his rifle. Two Japanese soldiers suddenly charged out of the brush, one carrying a flag and one armed with a rifle. Beaudoin snapped off a shot and killed the man with the flag, but the Japanese with the rifle fired back, hitting Beaudoin in the head. Beaudoin collapsed in the water. He was conscious but unable to move. A soldier dragged him out of the water to find he was still alive. A medic pushed the exposed brain matter back into Beaudoin's skull and covered it with a bandage. He was still breathing at nightfall when he arrived at the field hospital.[47]

Sunrise over the rolling coastal plain revealed a horrific mess of stinking corpses—Japanese and American—already rapidly decomposing in Saipan's cloying heat and attracting swarms of flies. The 1st and 2nd Battalions of the 105th Infantry had been virtually wiped out. Of the approximately 1,200 officers and men who dug in below Makunsha at dusk the previous night, at least 406 were now dead and another 512 wounded.[48] The 3rd Battalion, 10th Marines lost forty-five killed and eighty-two wounded.[49]

As the magnitude of the disaster became more clear, Holland Smith ordered the 2nd Marine Division to relieve the GIs. Griner protested that he had the situation in hand, but Smith was adamant. In his mind, the Army had once again failed. "They're yellow," he told Bob Sherrod. "They are not aggressive. They've held up the battle and caused my Marines casualties. I'm sending the 2nd Marine Division through them tomorrow and I hope the 2nd doesn't get into a fight passing through. I'm afraid they'll say, 'You yellow bastards,' as they pass through."[50]

After wiping out a second attack by *gyokusai* remnants earlier in the morning at Bloody Run, the 106th Infantry had already begun pursuit in what one officer later described as "probably the greatest souvenir hunt of the Pacific war."[51] The Marines caught up to the GIs about a quarter of a mile north of Bloody Run. Accompanied by tanks and halftracks, they fixed bayonets, formed a line extending inland from the beach, and trudged forward through the litter of rapidly decomposing corpses. NTLF had been reporting that between 300 and 400 Japanese were involved in the *gyokusai*.

The battlefield gave lie to that estimate. Thousands of dead lay in heaps on the coastal plain, clogging ditches and sprawled grotesquely along the road and rail line. "The whole area seemed to be a mass of stinking bodies, spilled guts and brains," observed Sherrod.[52]

A count by the 27th Division later tallied over 4,300 Japanese dead in the general battle area. Fleet Marine Headquarters put the number of enemy bodies actually counted in the area of the attack at 3,190.[53] "They were dead, one on top of the other," recalled Sgt. Hoichi Kubo.[54] The smell was indescribable. "We checked them over carefully to make sure that they were dead. If there was any doubt, we made sure that they were," remarked Corp. Roy Roush.[55] Occasionally a survivor would rise out of the carrion in a futile charge. One officer charged a halftrack with his sword. He got to within a few yards when the halftrack fired its 75mm gun. The officer simply disintegrated, sword and all. Now and again, a Marine would pause and direct a round or two into a hole or ditch. "It's like killing rats now," remarked a company commander.[56]

Translator Lt. Ben Hazard followed the skirmish line picking its way through the heaps of dead and clouds of buzzing flies. "I could tell how long a Japanese had been dead by the color of his skin," he recalled. "They were dark brown when they were alive. When dead they turned green, then black." Walking along a trench near the site of the original perimeter, he noticed a couple of bodies that looked less than dead. Suspicious, he paused. "Come on out!" he ordered in Japanese.

There were two of them—an officer and an enlisted man—who had covered themselves with corpses. As they pushed their way free, Hazard demanded their surrender. The officer shouted, "*Tenno heika, banzai!*" (Long live the emperor). He sat down with his sword, obviously preparing to commit ritual suicide. The enlisted man made no move; Hazard suspected he was waiting for the officer to kill himself so he could surrender. He didn't get a chance to find out if his hunch was correct. There was a sudden blast of gunfire as an American sergeant cut down both of the Japanese with a burst from his Thompson submachine gun. Hazard started to chew him out, but the sergeant was unmoved. "Well sir, I wasn't going to give them the pleasure of committing suicide," he replied unapologetically.[57]

Clanking along in support of the infantry, "Bonita," a Sherman tank commanded by twenty-five-year-old Sgt. Grant Timmerman, lurched through brush and debris, belching exhaust. One of the few Marines who wore glasses, Timmerman had served in China before the war—his tank was named after his White Russian girlfriend from those days. To the green youngsters in his outfit, the "old China hand" was someone to look up to. "We were just kids," recalled one of his men. "He was an old man. But he took care of us."[58]

Timmerman was standing in the open hatch when a Japanese soldier appeared out of nowhere and lobbed a grenade up at him. "[Danny Brown in a nearby tank] said he was looking right at it when it happened," said tanker Robert Thompson. "This guy, the Japanese, was under a piece of tin out there. He came out and threw this grenade up there. Danny saw it going and he killed him, but that grenade had already been thrown."

As the grenade rattled into the open hatch, Timmerman turned and trapped it between his chest and the side of the tank to keep it from dropping on the crew below. "He just grabbed it, and of course it blew his whole chest area out," said Thompson. Timmerman sagged down into the tank, killed instantly. "I think his gunner got a fragment, but nobody else in the tank was seriously hurt," observed Thompson.[59]

The concentration of corpses increased as the skirmish line entered the abandoned First Perimeter. A 37mm gun pointed silently northward. A pile of Japanese cut down by canister lay about a hundred yards beyond. Eleven dead Americans remained sprawled around the gun. As one died, the others had dragged the body aside in order to keep serving the gun. It appeared they had continued until there was no one left.[60] In another spot, Roy Roush saw a pile of five bodies—American and Japanese—tangled together in a trench.[61]

Colonel O'Brien's battered remains lay near the jeep where he had died. Not far distant from the riddled aid tent in the 2nd Battalion's area, Capt. Ben Salomon was found dead beside his machine gun, a fan-shaped array of dead Japanese in front of the muzzle. An examination subsequently revealed seventy-six wounds to Salomon's body; a doctor opined that as many as twenty-four of those wounds had been suffered before Salomon died. A trail of blood indicated he had moved the machine gun four times to obtain new fields of fire before finally succumbing.[62]

There was at least one miracle. Picking through the dead strewn around the B Company foxholes, Marines heard the sound of labored breathing. It was nineteen-year-old Pvt. Bill Lynch, still clinging to life despite having been shot twice and bayoneted multiple times. He would survive to return to his native South Carolina. Also found alive was an unidentified B Company cook. Deeply traumatized, the man could scarcely talk, observed Bob

Sherrod. He munched on a cracker from a C ration and observed slowly, "Don't know where my outfit is; guess I'm the only one left."[63]

Lying half-conscious on the beach, Mitsuharu Noda heard foreign voices drawing near. Someone kicked him in the side and he groaned. He felt himself being rolled onto a litter and had time to see Americans kicking the dead—not discriminating between Japanese and American—before he sank back into darkness. Of the fifty men in naval headquarters, Noda was the lone survivor.[64]

Maj. Takashi Hirakushi, whose last memory was being engulfed in an explosion, awoke to see white walls. He was on a naval vessel offshore, lying naked on a bed with a blanket over him, his left hand manacled to the bedframe. "I'm alive!" he thought in wonder. He had been wounded in the right shoulder and forehead. His right eye was covered. But he was alive. "It was a second life. I didn't think about what to do next. Nor that it was a great disgrace or anything else. Only I'm alive!" That night an American sailor brought him a hamburger. It was wonderful, recalled Hirakushi.[65]

On the reef off shore, scores of other Japanese—remnants of the *gyokusai*—awaited death. Trapped, their situation hopeless, the majority refused to surrender. "They are naked and just will not give up," wrote Lt. Col. Russell Lloyd, serving with the 6th Marines. "They refuse to be taken aboard the boats we have sent out there for them so after they repeat their refusals a couple of times there is only one thing left to do."[66]

About two dozen riflemen from the 6th Marines, commanded by twenty-seven-year-old 1st Lt. Kenneth J. Hensley, boarded amtracs with orders "to pick up all enemy military prisoners that we could and to destroy those who would not surrender," Hensley recalled. They had some small successes, but as the LVTs motored on toward a small islet occupied by six Japanese enlisted men and an officer, the enemy officer drew his sword and motioned to his men to approach him one by one. As each man stepped up and bowed, the officer swung his sword in a high arc and cut off his head. "We had then closed the range to about 200 yards and the Jap officer brandished his sword at us and chopped the water in front of him," reported Hensley. The LVTs opened fire, mowing down the officer and the two remaining soldiers.[67]

With organized resistance at an end, the 4th Marine Division finished the push toward Marpi Point and the final objective—the long anticipated O-9 line—on July 9, sweeping over the unfinished northern airfield, past Mount

Marpi and finally to Marpi Point overlooking the ocean to the north. The 25th Marines raised the Stars and Stripes over the airfield at 1405. Two hours and ten minutes later, all three regiments on the line reported they were on the O-9. At virtually the same moment, Expeditionary Force commander Adm. Kelly Turner declared the island secure.

A handful of bemused Marines with the 2nd Battalion, 24th Marines heard Turner's announcement over a tank radio. The general consensus was that if Saipan was secure, someone had neglected to tell the Japanese. Among the continuing stream of casualties was Roy Roush's best friend since boot camp, PFC Edward J. Runyon, who ended his combat career in a cane field when a Japanese soldier shot him in the left leg below the knee. The bullet completely shattered the bone and the leg had to be amputated. "But Runyon said that he managed to get a shot at the son-of-a-bitch and blow the top of his head off," observed Roush with undisguised satisfaction.[68] Observing that the island had been formally declared secure, a Marine joked darkly, "It means if you get shot now, you were hit in your own rear areas."[69]

Over in Bob Cary's artillery outfit, a few Marines were lounging around a radio jeep listening to Tokyo Rose. After a couple of musical numbers, Rose broke in with her soft seductive voice: "You Marines of the 2nd and 4th Divisions may think you won a great victory on Saipan, but the fight is not over. A huge naval task force with thousands of Japanese troops is steaming toward the island at this very moment and will sweep you into the sea. Sorry to say, but none of you Marines will ever get home for another Christmas."

Cary's hard-bitten sergeant took a slow pull on a cigar he had salvaged from someplace, thoughtfully exhaled an impressive cloud of smoke and addressed the radio: "Send 'em down, Rose. We just laid out 25,000 of your best troops and we'll lay out another 25,000 if they land here."[70]

CHAPTER XXV

The Suicide Cliffs

SADLY, THE DYING WAS FAR FROM OVER—ONLY NOW IT WAS ESPECIALLY pointless. Interpreter Bob Sheeks started the morning of July 10 trying to coax some Japanese soldiers out of a hole in the ground up by Marpi Point where thousands of stragglers and civilians remained in hiding. He pleaded with the occupants, telling them they would be treated well and assuring them they would not be shot. A murmur of discussion from below was followed by a defiant shout of refusal. Moments later, an explosion sent smoke and rocks spewing from the hole as the occupants blew themselves up.

Sheeks and his assistant were contemplating the mess below when they heard shouts from the nearby cliffs overlooking the ocean. Heading off to investigate, they found themselves on the edge of a 300-foot drop with a spectacular view of the surf pounding against the rocks below. A half a dozen men were peering down the cliff line toward Marpi Point. "There goes another one!" someone shouted. Sheeks saw a figure plummet through the air to smash onto the rocks below. About 200 yards away, a woman appeared at the cliff edge with several children in tow. One by one she hurled the children into the abyss, then threw herself after them. Several more civilians made their way to the precipice and leaped to their deaths. Persuaded by propaganda that torture, rape, and death awaited them at the hands of the Americans, and with nowhere left to flee, hundreds of terrified Japanese civilians were now choosing suicide.

Sheeks retrieved a portable megaphone from his jeep as still more civilians appeared. Leaning over the edge of the cliff, he attempted to dissuade them from jumping, but if they could hear his pleas over the roar of the surf, they paid no attention. They seemed determined to die, caught up in what Sheeks could only describe as a strange sense of urgency. No one hesitated or paused for long at the brink. One after another, they leaped into space and plummeted to their deaths on the rocks below.[1]

The unfolding tragedy centered on two towering cliffs: the subsequently named 265-foot "Banzai Cliff" and 800-foot "Suicide Cliff" just to the east. "I remember this one woman," said Field Music First Class John Des Jarlais of an encounter on the cliffs. "She was about fifty yards away running toward the cliff with a baby clutched in her arms. I wanted to stop her, but we were still taking sniper fire, so I kept low and motioned for her to stop. She ran up to the edge, turned and looked at me with such hate in her eyes. Then she and her baby disappeared over the cliff."[2]

Patrolling cautiously along the base of the cliffs, two platoons led by 1st Lt. Lewis Meyers found dead and dying Japanese scattered among the rocks. One enemy soldier had hanged himself with a neckerchief. Drowned babies floated in tidal pools. A few hundred yards away, Meyers could see movement on a point extending about 50 yards into the water. Drawing closer, the Marines saw that the low promontory was crowded with civilians and soldiers. The Marines began to receive some rifle fire. "A few minutes later someone in the rocks and bushes blew himself up, and a helmet and assorted fragments flew through the air," said Meyers. Some of the people on the point seemed to be singing in unison.

A linguist had set up a loudspeaker on a cliff overlooking the scene, but his attempts to persuade the civilians to give up were largely ignored. "Many of them were making the inevitable preparations of changing clothes, bathing in the pools among the rocks, and binding their heads," observed Meyers. "The men out on the end of the point took the lead in these activities and soon were ready in G-strings and spotless headbands. Then the people began to jump into the sea. Whole families plunged off the point together, some of the women with babies strapped on their backs. The ocean was dotted with black heads floating in the water, most of them swimming slowly around. For a few minutes the scene resembled a bathing beach on a busy holiday, until the heads began to disappear beneath the surface and did not come up again ... A BAR man jumped in and pulled out three women who had changed their minds and were struggling against death in the sea. Some others swam ashore when we waved them in. But many had disappeared and the men and boys for the most part swam away from shore and gradually dropped from sight."[3]

Bob Sherrod heard talk of the mass suicides on the afternoon of July 11. The next day he drove up to Marpi Point. He stood on the cliff just beyond the unfinished Japanese airfield and looked out to sea. On the rocks below, a Japanese boy in knee-length black trousers walked uncertainly back and forth by the water's edge. He sat down, then got up. He sat down again. When a high wave broke on the rocks, the boy allowed himself to be washed away. "At first he lay face down, inert on the surface of the water," wrote Sherrod. "Then his arms flailed frantically, as if an instinct stronger than his willpower bade him live. Then he was quiet. He was dead."[4]

G/Sgt. Keith Renstrom came upon a Japanese man and his family—wife, little girl, and two little boys—at the edge of the cliffs. As Renstrom watched in horror from about 50 yards away, the man took a baby from the woman's arms and threw it over the cliff. He tried to push one of the little boys over, but the child clung to his father's legs in terror. Finally, the father hit the child and threw him over, then the girl and finally the other boy. He and his wife stood by the edge of the cliff and bowed to each other. When she hesitated, he pushed her over the edge, then jumped himself.[5]

Marines watched as three women sat on the rocks by the water, carefully combing their long black hair. Then they joined hands and walked slowly out into the sea to their deaths. Sherrod saw a body in a red print dress bobbing on the swells. Closer to the rocks, a child's body in a white shirt drifted by, followed by a woman, then a man. A group of Japanese soldiers stripped off their clothes and bathed in the sea, then spread out a large meatball flag on the rocks. The leader distributed hand grenades. One by one they blew themselves apart. Another circle of about fifty Japanese, including several small children, tossed grenades to each other. Six Japanese soldiers suddenly ran out of a cave, struck martial poses in front of the civilians, and blew themselves up. Thus encouraged, the civilians then followed suit.

Al Perry and Paul Scanlon stumbled into the human tragedy by accident while looking for a way down to the ocean. They had been wearing the same clothes for three weeks and were desperate for a saltwater bath. "Our clothes were filthy," remarked Perry. "We couldn't stand ourselves." A short walk brought them to the base of the northern cliffs. Perry noticed what seemed to be hundreds of round objects on the surface of the ocean. He belatedly realized they were the heads of people swimming out to sea. Pushing through the brush and trees to the water's edge for a closer look, he found a mob of people: civilians, men in uniform, women and babies sick from drinking seawater. Dozens were turning and wading out into the ocean to intentionally drown themselves. They milled around the lone Marine seemingly oblivious to his presence in their focus on self-destruction. It was madness.

Perry and Scanlon gave what water they had to desperately thirsty civilians. A little girl, so parched she had foamy spittle on her mouth from drinking seawater, opened a suitcase she had been clutching and tried to give them a clock in gratitude. Scanlon went back to their company for more water, which also soon ran out. As they stood helplessly watching, another group of Marines arrived on the scene. They were wearing new dungarees and looked like they were right out of boot camp, recalled Perry. He heard rifle fire break out. The new arrivals were shooting at the heads of people out in the water. Perry confronted them. The newcomers ignored him and kept shooting. One of them said something about "getting a Jap before he had to go home." The absurdity of the nightmare was not lost on Perry. "War is crazy," he admitted years later of his efforts to defend Japanese intent on killing themselves. "One day we are killing each other and the next day we are trying to save them."[6]

Still aboard the USS *Harris*, his arm in a sling from the grenade fragment wound suffered on D-day, Sgt. Bob Webster saw evidence of the tragedy drifting past the ship. "We started seeing these bodies floating in the water and we didn't know what they were because they didn't have any heads or hands and they were all swelled up like rubber dolls or something," he remembered. "They were swollen and it looked like the fish had eaten all exposed flesh. It was a terrible sight."[7] Lt. Emery Cleaves, serving aboard the minesweeper USS *Chief*, observed, "Part of the area is so congested with floating bodies we simply can't avoid running them down. I remember one woman in khaki trousers and a white polka dot blouse with her black hair streaming in the water. . . . Here was another one, nude, who had drowned herself while giving birth to a baby. The baby's head had entered this world, but that was all of him. A small boy of four or five had drowned with his arm firmly clenched around the neck of a Jap soldier; the two bodies rocked crazily in the waves. I've seen literally hundreds in the water."[8]

Up in the rugged cliff area by Marpi Point, fourteen-year-old Ryoko Okuyama and her family—father, mother and three siblings—were part of a rag-tag group of civilians and soldiers who had been hiding out in isolated caves. Ryoko and her two brothers and sister were sunbathing on a ledge with their shoes off. A plump, baby-faced soldier sat nearby, cleaning his rifle. The soldier suddenly looked up with a start. "Enemy!" he shouted, pointing toward the top of the cliff. He shouldered his rifle and fired. Other Japanese soldiers emerged from nearby caves and also opened fire as grenades started to rain down on them from above.

"Get away!" someone shouted.

Ryoko heard a soldier shout, "*Tenno heika banzai!*" The baby-faced soldier suddenly fell on his back. Her parents rushed her and her siblings into a small natural cave. A Japanese sergeant and a correspondent from the Asahi newspaper also crowded in. An abandoned baby girl started to wail. Ryoko's mother picked her up and tried to soothe her, but as the gunfire increased, the infant began to scream. "Quiet it!" whispered the sergeant. "Any way!"

Mrs. Okuyama tried to nurse the baby at her breast, but it continued to shriek. At the sergeant's insistence, she finally stifled its cries with her skirt, pressing the material down over the baby's mouth. The crying stopped. The baby was dead. American voices could be heard outside the cave.

The sergeant handed Mr. Okuyama a hand grenade and kept another for himself. "We are all going to a nice place together," Mrs. Okuyama reassured Ryoko's four-year-old brother Yoshitada. "We are going to die," thought Ryoko, but she wasn't afraid. Her little brother was smiling happily and looking around. The sergeant removed the pin on his grenade and struck the detonator against a rock to start the fuse. Ryoko's father followed suit. Ryoko heard a *shuh! shuh!* sound and was aware of an acrid smell as the fuses ignited. An instant later a terrific blast threw her against the wall of the cave.

Ryoko awoke to find herself smeared with blood and fragments of flesh. It took her a moment to realize she was uninjured. The sergeant, still wearing his helmet, sat cross-legged, across from her, leaning against a rock. Through a gaping hole in his abdomen, Ryoko could see his internal organs, all still neatly in place. There was no blood. They looked beautiful, she thought. They reminded her of the human model from her biology class. Sprawled nearby, Ryoko's six-year-old sister, Tatsuko, no longer had a face. "From her neck down she looked just as usual," observed Ryoko. "The flesh from her face had blown off, the skull showing, looking like a white candle with its color and texture." Her father and two younger brothers were also dead.

Ryoko was startled by a touch on her shoulder. Her mother had also survived, but she was dying, her legs shattered from the knees down. Ryoko tried to tend to the wounds but her mother told her it was useless. "Only you are alive," she said.

An almost inaudible whisper intruded. It was the Asahi correspondent, horribly wounded, but still alive. "Kill me," he pleaded. "Please." Mrs. Okuyama told him she could not move. She could not help him. She was dying too. In his agony, the correspondent began to slam his head against a rock. Again and again he hit his head on the rocks, each time uttering a strange groan. Finally his bloody head fell for the last time. He was dead.

Holding her daughter's hand, Mrs. Okuyama told Ryoko to leave the cave at nightfall. She must live. Ryoko begged her not to die. Her mother smiled and nodded and then she was gone. She was thirty-four years old. Ryoko's father, a tailor in happier days, was thirty-seven. Leaving the horrific scene in the cave, Ryoko eventually gave up to the Americans, the lone survivor of her family.[9]

Shizuko Miura also survived, but the remnants of her medical detachment all perished when they were discovered by American soldiers in the Valley of Hell. The chief surgeon, a captain, urged her to surrender. "Save yourself!" agreed his lieutenant. As Shizuko hesitated, fearful she would be raped, the captain shot himself with his pistol. The lieutenant slashed his own throat with a knife and collapsed over Shizuko, his blood pumping out onto her legs. Shizuko shook off her paralysis and picked up a grenade. She tried to call out for her mother, but her voice failed her as she pulled the pin and struck the detonator on a rock to activate it. That was all she remembered until she awoke to strange voices and found herself in an American medical facility. By some fluke, the grenade explosion had only wounded her. She would fully recover. When she asked about the others, she was told they were all dead.[10]

Lt. Edmund J. Lyga, executive officer of B Battery, 531st Field Artillery, was in his foxhole by the gun line south of Charan Kanoa about three days after the *gyokusai* when he became conscious of a terrific stench in the air. "I looked out of my foxhole and American trucks were coming into our area with bodies with rigor mortis set in—arms and legs sticking out," he recalled. The dead were GIs from the 105th Infantry overrun on July 7. The trucks were taking them to the nearby 27th Division Cemetery for burial.[11]

The Army's mortuary system was overwhelmed by the number of dead left in the wake of the *gyokusai*. Burial details picked through the carnage, looking for dead GIs. "The difficulties of locating American bodies among the thousands of Japanese dead, of recovering bodies from shell holes which had filled with water, and the collection of bodies which had been badly shattered by mortar fire made it impossible to complete collection of these dead in less than 4½ days, notwithstanding the amount of personnel and transportation involved," reported the Quartermaster Corps. One result of the delay was that numerous GIs were recorded as having been killed days after their actual date of death.[12]

Graves Registration also noted that an estimated 90 percent of all American bodies had been looted, presumably by other Americans. Of seventy-four bodies recovered by the 105th Infantry burial detail on July 9 "almost all had been found with pockets slashed open and all articles of value missing," observed the 27th Division G-1 journal for the day. Bodies were loaded into trucks and brought to an LVT landing point. There they were transferred to amphibious tractors and taken by water to Yellow Beach 3 where the tractors proceeded directly to the cemetery. Not incidentally, the roundabout route minimized the exposure of other troops to the demoralizing sight. As it was, a subsequent report noted, "This delay in evacuating our dead is believed to have had a depressing effect on the morale of troops in the area and was the subject of adverse comment by individual Marines."[13]

The thousands of decomposing Japanese were disposed of with less ceremony. Sgt. Roland Fronheiser and some men from the 33rd Coast Artillery were among the idle hands ordered to pitch in with the cleanup. "After the banzai charge we were given the dirty job of burying fifty dead Japs," he recalled. "We put them in a pile and tried to burn them. That didn't work and few of us ate dinner that night. A colonel came by and saw what we were doing and gave us proper hell. He then had a bulldozer come, dig a trench and push the smoking, stinking mess into the trench."[14]

A couple of hundred civilian internees were impressed to carry or drag the rotting corpses of their countrymen to central points. Bulldozers scooped out deep trenches; the bodies were pushed in, sprayed with a sodium arsenite solution, then covered up. Their only memorials were markers indicating the approximate number of dead interred below. Traffic along the coastal roadway passed long mass graves with signs noting; "95 Enemy Dead Buried here" or "176 dead Japs."[15]

Meanwhile, Americans and Japanese continued to die in so-called "mopping up" operations. Sgt. Keith Renstrom's unit was patrolling in the Marpi Point area on July 10 when there was a shot and PFC Frank Gaboda went down. Renstrom yelled over to him, "Gaboda, are you hit?"

"Not really," Gaboda shouted back. "Just in the arm."

Sgt. Mike Plasha ran out to get Gaboda. "Just before he reached him, the Japs cut Mike in two with a Nambu machine gun," recalled Renstrom. By the time the others knocked out the machine gun and got to Gaboda, he was dead of chest wounds. Stunned by shock, he knew he had been hit in the arm, but didn't realize he'd also been shot in the chest. "The poor guy probably didn't even know he was dying," observed Renstrom.[16] New

Jersey–raised Gaboda was twenty-one years old. Plasha, the son of Yugo-slavian immigrants who settled in the coal-mining town of Kingston, West Virginia, was nineteen. They were buried beside each other in Plot 5, Row 4, Graves 971 and 972 in the 4th Marine Division cemetery.[17]

Dug in on tiny Maniagassa, a 300-yard-long geological apostrophe of an islet off Tanapag Harbor, Adachi Genji and a handful of comrades continued to await the arrival of the Americans following the fall of the main island. Their wait ended on July 13 when the 3rd Battalion, 6th Marines ground ashore in their LVTs. It took the Marines only an hour to eradicate the thirty-one-man garrison centered around a light machine gun housed in a pillbox.

The fire was terrific, remembered Genji. "The four of us in the trench were pinned to the wall and unable to move. Almost all of those above us seemed to have been hit." Unlit fuel from a flamethrower sprayed in on them as death drew near. "Come out!" ordered a voice in barely intelligible Japanese.

Adachi had retained a grenade to commit suicide. He looked at his comrades, believing his time had come. His sergeant major, one thumb practically detached from a wound to his hand, intervened. "I'll take responsibility," he said. "There's always a time to die. Let's go out." Adachi obliged due to "my cowardly feelings," though he knew how dishonorable surrender was. "I wanted a drink of water," he confessed years later. "I wanted to live."[18] He was one of fifteen prisoners—ten of them Koreans—taken that morning. Sixteen Japanese were killed.

While surrenders by military personnel remained the exception, the numbers were higher than in previous campaigns. As of July 13, a total of 657 Japanese military personnel had been captured (the number would rise to nearly 900 by the end of the month). The captures included sixteen officers. The highest ranking were Maj. Takashi Hirakushi and Navy Cmdr. Jiro Saito. Others included four army lieutenants, two navy lieutenants, three navy ensigns (including a Navy Air Corps officer), three probationary officers, one warrant officer, and a civilian officer with the equivalent rank of captain.[19]

One extremely lucky Japanese was Senior Flight Petty Officer Yoshi-hisa Imanishi. Imanishi had been co-pilot of the crashed seaplane carrying Admiral Fukudome and the Z Plan to Cebu months earlier and was among the Japanese captured and later released by Filipino guerrillas. Trapped on Saipan when U.S. forces landed, he had been wounded and unable to take part in the *gyokusai* of July 7. A comrade carried him to a cave, where they resolved to commit suicide, but their one remaining grenade turned out to be a dud. And so Imanishi had the dubious distinction of becoming probably the only Japanese prisoner of the war to be captured twice.[20]

Maj. Gen. Masatake Kimihira was less fortunate. His attempt to escape Saipan came to an abrupt end on July 10 when he and three companions stumbled into the perimeter of the 27th Division's 105th Artillery Regiment. An alert machine-gun crew cut down two of the intruders. Examining their victims at daylight, the GIs were astonished to find one of them wearing the single-starred, yellow-gold insignia of a Japanese major general. Intelligence personnel identified the victim as General "Kajima" through documents found on the body, though his presence on Saipan presented a bit of a mystery since his name did not appear on any order of battle. Based on a message to the commanding officer on Pagan found on the general's body, U.S. intelligence speculated he may have been stranded on Saipan during an inspection tour.[21]

It was later learned, apparently from one or both of the only two survivors—a fisherman and a soldier—that after leaving General Saito's headquarters cave the night of July 6, General Kimihira's group made its way east to Tsukimi Island located in an inlet on Saipan's northeast coast. A number of engine-equipped Daihatsu barges had been cached on the east side of the island and the escapees hoped to commandeer one of them to cross the nearly 200 miles of open water to Pagan. To their dismay, they found all the boats had been destroyed.

Still hopeful, they spent a day assembling a raft out of oil drums and wood and commandeered the fisherman as a pilot. Though pessimistic about their chances, they launched the raft. As they had feared, they were pushed back to shore by strong tides and prevailing east winds. Abandoning the effort, they had been trying to make their way back to the area of General Saito's last headquarters when they wandered into the American perimeter.[22]

Sgt. Yamauchi Takeo's journey came to a happier end. After avoiding the *gyokusai* on July 7, he had hidden in the hills in what he later described as almost a "catatonic state" of mind, one of only three survivors from his 250-man company. Finally, hearing the broadcast appeals to surrender, he attached himself to a small group of civilians and gave himself up. "Will peace come soon?" he asked one of his captors, an American sergeant.

"I hope so," answered the sergeant.[23]

Four days after the *gyokusai*, a detachment led by Lt. Richard L. Sullivan, a liaison officer with the intelligence section of the 4th Marine Division, located General Saito's final headquarters during a search of the caves in the upper end of Paradise Valley. The patrol was accompanied by what a subsequent report described only as "a captured Japanese intelligence officer." The officer was none other than Maj. Takashi Hirakushi, whose wounds had turned out to be relatively minor. Though cooperating with his captors, the major did engage in one bit of deception: Instead of providing his true name, he identified himself as General Saito's intelligence chief, Maj. Kiyoshi Yoshida, who had been killed during the battle. American intelligence would not learn of Hirakushi's fabrication until after the war.[24]

Drawn by the "indescribable smell of the place," Sullivan's detachment stopped in front of a cliffside cave about 50 yards off a roadway. Inside they found four charred bodies lying on an upper ledge. Despite the condition of the remains, the Japanese "intelligence officer" identified one of the bodies as General Saito. "We didn't know we had Saito's body until we found his personal effects," Sullivan said. "The bodies were burned beyond recognition."[25]

Though years later Hirakushi would claim that General Igeta and Admiral Nagumo had died with Saito in the cave, he told a different story to American intelligence immediately after his capture. According to that account, General Saito had been shot by his adjutant after drawing blood with his sword. "After that," noted a U.S. report, "the Adjutant committed suicide followed by two other Shamboes (Japanese staff officers)." If the other bodies in the cave were in fact those of General Igeta and Admiral Nagumo, "Major Yoshida" did not reveal their identities to his captors.[26]

Adding to the confusion as to Vice Admiral Nagumo's end, Yeoman Mitsuharu Noda told interrogators that Nagumo and Rear Adm. Hideo Yano committed suicide in another location "at the temporary headquarters located inland from Matansa" just under a mile northeast of General Saito's final command post in Paradise Valley. "Prisoner states that he personally witnessed the suicide of Vice Admiral Nagumo . . ." noted the report.[27]

A twelve-man patrol led by two lieutenants from the V Amphibious Corps Reconnaissance Battalion returned the next morning to recover the general's remains and ended up in a firefight with Japanese stragglers outside the cave. "We were firing rifles and pitching grenades and the Japs using mostly grenades," reported Lt. Russell Corey. "I guess it was two hours before they quit firing and we figured it was safe to go in. We found eight fresh-killed Japs in the cave. The last one was on his hands and knees before a little ledge in the back end. And up on the ledge was the general." It appeared that new efforts had been made to burn the body by lighting a fire on top of it, but without noticeable success. The patrol maneuvered the general's charred remains into a mattress cover brought along for that purpose and lugged him back to Holland Smith's headquarters in Charan Kanoa.[28]

On July 13, General Saito was buried with full military honors in a plot reserved for enemy officers in the 27th Division cemetery. Unlike the dead Marines and GIs who were buried wrapped in blankets or ponchos, the general rated a 6-foot-long wooden coffin, which also required a larger than standard grave.[29] It was raining as the "mourners" gathered. Four Marines acted as pallbearers. "They carried the coffin, covered with a Japanese flag, to the graveside with as much ease as if it were filled only with cotton," observed Associated Press correspondent Rembert James. "A Marine bugler blew taps. The pall-bearers lowered the coffin into the grave. A Marine rifle squad fired the traditional salute."[30]

That same day, Admiral Nimitz announced that Vice Admiral Nagumo, who had led the carrier attack on Pearl Harbor in December 1941, had died on Saipan six days earlier. Neither the admiral's body, nor General Igeta's remains, were recovered. Whether they were overlooked, burned beyond recognition, or hidden after the suicides to keep them out of American hands remains a mystery. They joined the approximately 30,000 Japanese army and navy personnel who died in defense of Saipan, most of whom would have no marked grave.

On July 18, an American patrol operating southeast of Makunsha found Corp. Taro Kawaguchi's diary containing his last prayer "for certain victory for the Imperial land."[31]

That same morning, a thousand miles away, General Tojo assembled his cabinet and wearily informed them that he had decided to step down. "I must ask you all to resign," he added.[32]

The Japanese public learned of the loss of Saipan on July 19 when the morning papers reported: "All Members of Our Forces on Saipan Meet Heroic Death/Remaining Japanese Civilians Seem to Share Fate." A bulletin from Imperial Headquarters acknowledged that Japanese forces on the island had made a "last attack" on July 7 and that remnants had fought on for at least another nine days before "attaining heroic death."[33]

Despite the defiant rhetoric, news of the disaster in the Marianas rocked the Japanese home front. The shocking revelation was followed by a statement from Prime Minister Tojo, who observed, "Our empire has entered the most difficult state in its entire history. But these developments have also provided us with the opportunity to smash the enemy and win the war. The time for decisive battle has arrived."[34] Others were less sanguine. "Hell is upon us," said Fleet Adm. Osami Nagano, supreme naval advisor to the emperor, of the defeat.[35]

As word of the defeat spread, Hideki Tojo's wife began to receive anonymous telephone calls inquiring if her husband had committed suicide yet. Military dissidents conspired to assassinate the prime minister—one plot called for throwing a hydrocyanic bomb at Tojo's car, another involved a machine-gun ambush. Hoping to hang on to power, Tojo offered to reshuffle his Cabinet, but was unable to appease political opponents. The fall of Saipan was too great a disaster. Even the emperor, who had long been among Tojo's supporters, had come to the conclusion that it was time for him to go.[36] Less than twenty-four hours after conferring with his Cabinet, the man most Americans saw as the face of Japanese aggression stepped down from office.

The fall of Saipan and Tojo's subsequent demise encouraged a nascent movement toward peace in the Japanese government. While hardliners were prepared to fight to the bitter end, realists in the military and government began to ponder ways to terminate the conflict.[37] On June 30, soon-to-be-named Navy Minister Mitsumasa Yonai admitted to Rear Adm. Sokichi Takagi, "I don't know the details, but the war is lost. We're really beaten."[38] Toshikuzo Kase observed that "these circumstances suggested that the time was approaching when a new and rationally minded cabinet could work for an early cease fire."[39] But that realization did not necessarily translate into action. In early July, Prince Fumimaro Konoe conceded privately, "The Army and Navy have both concluded that defeat is unavoidable. But today they are at the stage where they don't have courage to say so publicly."[40]

So shaken were those in the higher circles of government by the loss of Saipan that there was actually discussion about a possible imperial abdication. Under that scenario, Hirohito would step down to be succeeded by the eleven-year-old crown prince. A regent would then attempt to broker a peace that preserved the imperial system.[41] Though such talk reflected general despair, there was no appetite for unconditional surrender. Determined to preserve the imperial system and the sacred nation itself, the emperor and military continued to pin their hopes on a decisive victory against the American juggernaut elsewhere—perhaps in the Philippines—still thinking a major win would lead to a negotiated end to the war. It was a delusion that completely underestimated American rage and determination that had started with the attack on Pearl Harbor and only hardened in succeeding years.

A textbook demonstration of the Japanese reluctance to confront unwelcome realities—and the tendency to view events through the lens of wishful thinking—appeared less than a month after the fall of Hideki Tojo's Cabinet, and it turned the disaster at Saipan on its head. The harbinger was an article titled "The Heroic Last Moments of Our Fellow Countrymen on Saipan/Sublimely Women Too Commit Suicide on Rocks in Front of the Great Sun Flag/Patriotic Essence Astounds the World," which appeared in the newspaper *Asahi Shimbun*. The article was inspired, ironically enough, by a story about the Marpi Point suicides by Robert Sherrod in the August 7 issue of *Time* magazine. Titled "The Nature of the Enemy," Sherrod's stunning account of the Marpi Point suicides implied that the enemy's obsession with self-destruction boded ill for any future invasion of the Japanese home islands. It appeared, the article suggested, that every last Japanese was prepared to die rather than surrender.[42]

The fears expressed in Sherrod's article, based on the experience of Saipan, were soon to be reflected in U.S. operational planning and expectations. The number of casualties suffered by the invasion force had been sobering. Planners anticipated that 3.5 million Japanese troops would be available to defend against an invasion of the home islands. Using the so-called "Saipan Ratio" as a model, American casualties would be catastrophic. Then there was the probability—again suggested by the experience of Saipan—that the civilian population would join the military and sacrifice itself against any invasion.

The Japanese propaganda machine took this horrific assessment— which helped shape the decision several months later to deploy the most terrible weapon in the American arsenal against Japan—and recast it as "an unprecedented orgy of glorification of death," as Haruke Taya Cook was to observe fifty-one years later in her essay, "The Myth of the Saipan Suicides." The *Asahi Shimbun* published a report from a correspondent on August 17 noting, "It has been reported that noncombatants, women, and children have chosen death rather than to be captured alive and shamed by the demonlike American forces. The world has been astounded by the strength of the fighting spirit and patriotism of the entire people of Japan."[43] A day later the newspaper *Mainichi* reported that the Japanese women had donned their best apparel, prayed to the Imperial palace and then proceeded to "sublimely" commit suicide in front of the American devils, sacrificing themselves "for the national exigency together with the brave men." There was no suggestion that anyone—soldier or civilian—on Saipan had willingly given up; all had seemingly chosen death over the shame of surrender. The Japanese poet Ryu Saito was even moved to compose laudatory verse urging all Japanese women to be prepared for "a beautiful death."[44]

The poet might have profited from a chat with Lt. Bob Sheeks, who witnessed one of those "beautiful deaths" along a dusty road on northern Saipan one afternoon. It was a woman who had been severely burned by a flamethrower. What remained of her clothing hung in charred strips from her body. Her skin had been seared red and black; her face had been mostly burned away. Looking down on her as she lay by the side of the road, Sheeks could not even discern eyes in the ruined face. But incredibly, she continued to breathe, her chest still heaving as she gasped for air through the hole that had once been her mouth. Horrified, Sheeks injected her with his own morphine syrette as well as two others from nearby Marines. The pathetic figure before him seemed to relax, the breathing slowed and then stopped as she was released from her agonies.[45] This was not poetry, it was the stuff of nightmares, and the nightmare was soon to appear in the skies over Japan in the form of the new long-range B-29 Superfortress.

Out of the line at last, John Pope sprawled on the ground, using his buddy Jim Rainey's stomach as a pillow. The two pals from just outside Atlanta, Georgia, had joined the Marines together—Rainey routinely, if falsely, accused Pope of sweet-talking him into enlisting. Now, somehow, they had survived Saipan together. The seizure of tiny Maniagassa islet off Tanapag on July 13 marked the end of the battle for the Marines. The 2nd and 4th Marine Divisions were withdrawn to rest and refit. The respite would be all too brief: The two divisions were scheduled to seize Tinian, just 3 miles off Saipan's southern tip, on July 24.

"Rainey, your breath stinks," complained Pope as they lay there waiting for word on what to do next. "Turn your head the other way."

"Since you talked me into joining this outfit I'm damn lucky to have any breath at all," retorted Rainey.[46]

Rainey wasn't far wrong. "We were . . . to say the least, we were badly hurt," said Al Perry of his unit. "We had lost over forty percent of our company and were down to approximately 155 men. I was personally exhausted from our fighting on Saipan. I had lost thirty pounds and seen many of my good friends killed or wounded."⁴⁷ Bob Cary's artillery battalion was also beaten down. "Along with our casualties there were a number of victims of dengue fever, numerous recurring malaria cases and a lot of dysentery," he observed. "Still, we had time to wash our clothes, shave, shower, eat a few meals of real food, re-build our ammunition supply and replace missing or broken equipment."⁴⁸ Some of the wounded began to come back. It was indicative of the unanticipated number of casualties on Saipan—and a lack of sufficient preparation—that some of the returnees arrived unarmed and clothed only in pajama bottoms or in some cases just in boxer shorts.⁴⁹

Sgt. Rowland Lewis's company of the 23rd Marines ended up on the south end of the island. "When I took my shoes off for the first time since D-day, 25 days ago, there were only a few threads of my socks left," he observed. "I'm sure we all smelled rather ripe, but we were all in the same fix so no one noticed!" They spent the next week and a half without any particular duties. "We received mail from home and were allowed to just rest. I don't recall what we did about security but I believe we could sleep through the night without being awakened to stand watch every two hours."⁵⁰

One bureaucratic snafu was uncovered with joyful results for one family and sorrow for another. C Company, 23rd Marines, carried two men by the name of Charles Jones on the roster—Charles Jones Jr. and Charles D. Jones Jr. Charles Jones was killed on July 4. Through some mix-up, Charles D.'s family was notified that he had been killed. While the company was recouping on the southern end of the island, Charles D.'s brother, who was with an Army unit, visited the company to ask about the circumstances of his death. The first person he saw was his supposedly dead brother.⁵¹

John Eardley's company was ferried back to a transport. He finally discarded the filthy Japanese army blanket hanging in tatters from his mud-encrusted pack. His socks had to be peeled from his feet like an extra layer of skin. The hot navy chow was too much for most of the men who had been living for weeks on C-rations. "Most of our company came down with a bad case of diarrhea," remembered Eardley. "It was so bad that men were lined up around the ship waiting to go to the head. Some of the men just couldn't wait for their turn so they ran ahead and defecated in the urinals. It was a really bad situation." The corpsmen treated the outbreak with large doses of paregoric, which slowed the dysentery down—and in Eardley's case "stopped me up for a week." A showing of the movie *Holiday Inn* with Bing Crosby aboard ship was followed a couple of days later by the burial at sea of thirteen Marines who had succumbed to wounds.⁵²

"I can never forget how amazed the sailors on the ship were at the way we and our clothes stank," said S. G. Silcox. "Even the flies followed us aboard ship."[53] PFC Roy Roush was standing against the ship's railing with a cup of coffee when a Navy cook grabbed the cup and tried to throw the contents overboard. Roush asked him what he thought he was doing and the cook replied, "Hell man. You can't drink that! It has flies in it." It was all Roush could do not to laugh. "Of course it had flies in it," he remarked. "But there were only two or three." He hadn't had a cup of coffee—or much of anything else—without flies in it since landing on June 15.[54]

PFCs Bob Tierney and Carl Matthews would not be making the Tinian assault. Both were aboard the hospital ship USS *Samaritan*. After slogging through the entire campaign since coming ashore on June 15, Tierney had been shot by a sniper only twenty minutes after word was passed that the island was secure. The bullet hit him in the back, passed through his ribs, and shattered the bone in his left arm. There were about 1,200 wounded Marines on board the ship, estimated Tierney. Doctors had been operating for seventy-two hours with just short breaks. "The next morning I heard the bugler playing taps; a nurse informed me that ten Marines had died overnight and the ceremony on deck was for burials at sea," recalled Tierney. At 0200 the following morning, he went into surgery to have his arm amputated. He awoke from the anesthetic to discover he still had his arm—contrary to expectations, the doctors had managed to save the limb.[55]

Also aboard the hospital ship, Carl Matthews suffered from blast concussion as well as wounds of a less physical nature. On July 6, a Japanese machine gunner had killed his platoon leader, twenty-two-year-old Lt. James S. Leary. One moment Leary and Matthews had been standing side by side, the next moment Leary was dead. Matthews, who had been severely concussed by a shell days before but had stayed with his unit, had been completely devoted to Leary and the officer's death shattered him. He had little memory of what followed, only regaining his senses eight days later on the *Samaritan*. But his nerves were shot—so emotionally spent that the loud clang of a heavy weight dropped on the deck above frightened him to the point that he trembled all over and began to vomit.[56]

Matthews thus joined the over 16,500 casualties suffered by U.S. ground forces in the seizure of Saipan. According to an NTLF summary dated August 10, 1944, ground force casualties to date totaled 3,126 killed, 13,160 wounded, and 326 missing in action for a total of 16,612. The 4th Marine Division recorded the most casualties with 966 killed, 5,505 wounded, and

141 missing for a total of 6,612. The 2nd Marine Division lost 1,150 killed, 4,914 wounded, and 106 missing for a total of 6,170. The 27th Infantry Division reported 960 killed, 2,493 wounded, and 73 missing for a total of 3,526 casualties. Remaining casualties in the grand total were suffered by various corps and attached units. Those numbers, while subject to some later upward revision, represented about 20 percent of the combat troops committed to the battle, roughly the same percentage of losses suffered at Tarawa and later at Peleliu, though the latter two are better remembered for their horrific casualty rates.[57]

As would be expected, line units suffered the most. In the 2nd Marine Division, the 3rd Battalion, 6th Marines led the grim tally with 513 casualties, but the other infantry battalions were not far behind. In the 4th Marine Division the dubious honor went to the 3rd Battalion, 24th Marines, which listed 464 dead and wounded. The 27th Division's casualties for Saipan were highest by far among the two battalions overrun in the *gyokusai*: The 1st Battalion, 105th Infantry reported 521 dead, wounded or missing; the 2nd Battalion reported 486.[58] More than a third of the men wounded during the *gyokusai* had been hit two or more times and as many as thirty-five had been wounded three or more times. Of the men who had dug in at the original two-battalion perimeter on July 6, only 189 answered a roll call on July 9. "Where is everyone?" asked a GI returning to the battalion after being wounded earlier in the campaign.

"They're all gone," replied a survivor.[59]

Evacuated after the *gyokusai*, Nick Grinaldo survived a bout with gangrene and returned to service guarding Italian prisoners of war. His buddy Sam Dinova was evacuated to the USS *Solace* and then to the 29th General Hospital in New Caledonia and finally to Hawaii. He kept his leg, but his Army days were over; he was eventually discharged from the service and returned to Troy, New York. Corp. Eddie Beaudoin miraculously recovered from his horrific head wound after a long hospitalization.[60] Attilio W. Grestini, his arm blown off and left leg mangled at the hip, also survived. PFC Tom Biondi, who lost his right arm in the Japanese tank attack the morning of June 17, ended up in the naval hospital in San Diego where he dictated letters home to New Jersey while learning to write with his left hand. Such were the numbers of casualties following the *gyokusai* that Luke Hammond did not receive medical attention for his head wound until July 10. He was subsequently able to return to his unit where he learned that most—if not all—of the men who had held out in the cistern the morning of the attack had been killed.[61]

John Domanowski was operated on the day after the *gyokusai*. He fully expected to lose his left arm, but when he awoke, it was to find both arms encased in plaster. He was loaded onto a plane for evacuation to Hawaii. Also aboard was PFC Richard Tessnear from his company. Tessnear had lost a leg. Domanowski wanted to talk to him, but the twenty-one-year-old farm kid from rural Ellensboro, North Carolina, was not lucid. Tessnear made it to Johnson Island, but died during the final hop to Hawaii. In Hawaii, a nurse came into Domanowski's hospital ward and asked if anyone knew anything about Lt. Seymour Drovis. She said they had been married just before he left for Saipan. Domanowski was certain Drovis had been killed, but he could not bring himself to tell her.[62]

Of the thousands of deaths on Saipan, two in particular attracted the attention of war crimes investigators. A week after the island was declared secure, the onetime accused Palauan thief, Neratus, led an American intelligence officer, Maj. Owen Durham, to the courtyard of the Garapan jail and pointed out the place where he had burned the bodies of two American flyers the night of June 14 as the American armada prepared to invade the island. Durham found two mounds of sand at the spot. Asking around, he learned that a Marine medical detachment bivouacked by the jail had found the charred remains and covered them.

Durham returned the following day with a couple of medical officers and some Chamorros and exhumed the "partly decomposed, partly burned bodies of two men," which had been covered with 6 to 8 inches of dirt. The remains were removed to the 369th Station Hospital, where autopsies were performed. The results supported the Palauan's story. One body was found to have suffered "[p]artial amputation of head through body of fourth cervical vertebra, [p]uncture wounds [to the] posterior dorsal and dorso lumbar region [and] amputation of [the] right arm" by a sharp instrument. The second body, the skull of which was still covered with blonde, curly hair, apparently died as the result of a .50-caliber projectile "found lying against the psoas muscle, on the right side of the fifth lumbar vertebra."

The identity of the victims remained unknown. The one substantial clue was a leather flying jacket marked to "J.J. Perry" that was found in the cell occupied by the blonde-haired flyer. Military records indicated that a T/Sgt. Joseph J. Perry had been a radioman on a B-24 Liberator bomber "Baby Sandy 2" from the 431st Bombardment Squadron that crash-landed off Majuro on December 29, 1943, after suffering battle damage in a raid against Japanese-held Maloeope. Eight crewmen, including Perry, were known to have survived the water landing, but were captured the next day by Japanese forces. They were believed to have been transferred to Kwajalein and executed prior to the U.S. landings in the Marshalls the following February. How Perry, or his flying jacket, came to be in a jail cell on Saipan months later—if in fact it was Perry—was a mystery.

The autopsy findings and Neratus's testimony led the War Crimes Branch of the Judge Advocate Section to request an investigation into the whereabouts of four Japanese policemen known as Nitta, Kinashi, Yamashita, and Yokota, "who were alleged to have committed, or were suspected of complicity in, this incident." None was registered at the Japanese civilian internment camp and an investigation revealed that all four had apparently died during the battle for the island. They had last been seen between June 20 and 30 in the Tapotchau area "and were never heard from again," reported Durham. Investigators concluded, "it is believed to be highly unlikely that further information can be obtained in this case or any of the suspects brought to justice." No one was charged in the murder and, despite the evidence of the flying jacket, the identity of the two aviators was never positively established.[63]

CHAPTER XXVI

The Whirlwind

As the victory flag celebrating the seizure of Saipan rose over Holland Smith's headquarters in Charan Kanoa, another battle—this one between the Marine Corps and the U.S. Army—was just heating up. Holland Smith's relief of Gen. Ralph Smith on June 24 had not been well received at General Richardson's headquarters in Hawaii. The incident was about to degenerate into one of the most volatile interservice squabbles of the war.

Reporting to Richardson on June 27, Ralph Smith was directed to compile a record of what had transpired on Saipan. His sixteen-page account with eighteen pages of annexes covering the period June 15–24 was completed on July 11. In the meantime, Richardson appointed an all-Army board to investigate the circumstances of Ralph Smith's relief. Headed by Lt. Gen. Simon B. Buckner and consisting of Maj. Gen. John Hodge, Brig. Gen. Henry Holmes Jr., and Brig. Gen. Roy Blount, the so-called "Buckner Board" met nine times between July 7 and July 26 to examine documents and reports and question witnesses.[1]

Their 2-inch-thick report, issued in August, concluded that Holland Smith had been within his rights as a commander to relieve Ralph Smith on June 24. However, the board also opined that the relief had not been justified by the facts. Holland Smith's charge that Ralph Smith had twice issued an illegal order to a unit no longer under his command—this involving Army units that fell under NTLF control at Nafutan Point after the rest of the 27th Division moved north—was dismissed as resulting from a communications failure and was not a deliberate disobedience of orders or disregard for the chain of command. In fact, it appeared the charge was merely a weak construct intended to bolster a flimsy case against Ralph Smith—a case of throwing mud against the wall to see what might stick.

Holland Smith's criticisms regarding the actions of the 27th Division at Nafutan Point and in Death Valley were also viewed as having little substance. It was the opinion of the investigating officers that Holland Smith and his staff had been largely oblivious to the reality of what the 27th Division faced in Death Valley. Holland Smith, observed the report, "was not aware of the strength of the position and expected the 27th Division to overrun it rapidly." When Ralph Smith initiated a maneuver to outflank the position, rather than make frontal attacks, "the delay incident to this situation was mistaken by Lt. Gen. Holland M. Smith as an indication that the 27th Division was lacking in aggressiveness and that its commander was inefficient."[2]

The report then went on the offensive, raising questions about Holland Smith's exercise of command and the competency of his staff. Witnesses testified that Smith and his staff openly scorned Army forces as cowards who could not or would not fight; that no Army unit under Holland Smith's command could hope to be treated fairly or expect its accomplishments to be recognized; that his headquarters demonstrated shoddy staff work; orders were issued too late and were poorly drafted; and Holland Smith and his senior officers failed to visit the front lines and thus had no concept of the horrific terrain or nature of the opposition confronting the 27th Division GIs.[3]

While the Buckner Board examined only Army witnesses, some of these same complaints would be echoed in classified special action reports submitted by Marine units following the campaign. Marine officers complained that NTLF often failed to consider factors of time and space in its insistence on pushing the attack as rapidly as possible. The 24th Marines noted "higher echelon's" failure to pass orders down in a timely manner. "Plans on which to base reconnaissance the next day were seldom received until late the night before, and too early an hour was generally set for the jump off," reported the regiment. Commanders were compelled to start attacks with no opportunity to properly brief subordinate units. Assignments and "many queries as to why troops were not advancing more rapidly" from "higher echelon" were "indicative of their lack of reconnaissance and on-the-ground appreciation of the terrain," observed the regiment's special action report, which concluded somewhat bitterly, "It is much easier to advance troops over the map [than] it is over the ground."[4] Added one regimental commander, "Progress through heavy cane fields, through dense underbrush, and over extremely rough terrain, such as was encountered, cannot be made at 'book' speed."[5] Holland Smith himself subsequently conceded that his chief of staff, Gen. Graves Erskine, had been "tied to his desk" and unable to get away "more frequently" to visit the front. "For nearly two weeks, his personal knowledge of Saipan was limited to the area immediately adjacent to our quarters," he wrote later.[6]

But the Army reserved its greatest venom for Holland Smith personally. Ralph Smith, who had refrained from making a fuss during his relief, was candid in his evaluation to Richardson. He recommended that no Army troops ever again be permitted to serve under Holland Smith's command. "So far as the employment of Army troops is concerned, he is prejudiced, petty and unstable," he wrote. In an observation echoed by others, he opined that Holland Smith had "an apparent lack of understanding of the accepted Army doctrines for the tactical employment of larger units." General Blount, who visited Saipan in the course of the investigation, came away feeling the Buckner report was too generous to Holland Smith, whom he described as "a stupid egomaniac! A perfect ass if one ever lived."[7]

The final report exonerated Ralph Smith, who was given command of another division and eventually transferred to Europe. And there things might have rested—albeit uncomfortably—had it not been for the *gyokusai* of July 7. Unaware at first of the magnitude of the attack, Holland Smith's headquarters reported that the GIs had been overrun by a mere 300 to 400 Japanese and that the 27th Division had ignored warnings of a possible counterattack.[8] A widely repeated story circulated that as the panicked GIs fled, the *gyokusai* had been almost single-handedly halted by a small band of valiant Marine artillerymen firing their howitzers at point-blank range into the advancing horde.[9]

Infuriated by these claims, General Griner ordered a careful count of enemy dead and their locations. That survey revealed 4,311 Japanese dead, 2,295 of which were located in the area fought over by the 1st and 2nd Battalions.[10] Another 322 enemy dead were found in and around the positions held by the 10th Marines, while 1,694 were counted in the vicinity of the 105th Infantry command post and area swept by the 106th Infantry on the morning of the attack.[11]

When NTLF scoffed at those numbers, Griner snapped, "I submit that my personal observations be given more credence than is indicated by the record."[12] Admiral Spruance was moved to dispatch a two-man commission to establish the facts. Examining the site of the *gyokusai* on July 9, their investigation estimated that between 1,500 and 3,000 Japanese had been killed in the attack. Holland Smith eventually relented, reluctantly agreeing to the 1,500 number, though he grumbled that he thought it was too generous. Actually, in retrospect, it appears that Spruance's commission erred on the low side. The number of Japanese involved in the attack was likely between 3,000 and 4,000.[13]

If the Army suffered from unfair accusations and outright distortions, the Marines were not immune from similar injustices. The 27th Division G-1, Col. M. Oakley Bidwell, contributed a couple of the more inflammatory—and frankly suspect—tales in a letter to a would-be author after the war. Bidwell, a onetime advertising executive, claimed that after the *gyokusai* he was accosted by a near hysterical Marine lieutenant colonel who accused the GIs of allowing his gun battery to be slaughtered. The Marine officer then supposedly led Bidwell to a "sickening sight" in the battery position. "Slung between trees were dozens of green Marine Corps jungle hammocks," claimed Bidwell. "Most contained the bodies of young men whose throats had been cut. Nearby were the battery's 105mm guns. I did not see a single empty shell case. The guns had never been fired."[14]

Despite Bidwell's claims, it does not appear that the artillerymen even had possession of, never mind used jungle hammocks.[15] Muster roll records indicate that virtually all of the Marine fatalities were the result of small arms fire, not some mass orgy of throat cutting.[16] Finally, there is no doubt that H Battery fired its guns during the attack—the tank they destroyed is concrete evidence of that—though it would be a gross overstatement to say they stopped the *gyokusai*.

In the same letter, Bidwell claimed that Gen. Graves Erskine visited the scene of the *gyokusai* a day or so later, emerged from his staff car, "took two steps, a long breath," glanced at Bidwell and an enlisted man who were nonchalantly enjoying their K-ration lunch in the shade of a pile of dead Japanese, and "promptly and efficiently lost his breakfast." According to Bidwell's tale, Erskine then hurried back into his car and sped off. Curiously, the Erskine anecdote, though enthusiastically cited by later authors on the basis of Bidwell's questionable postwar letter, is not mentioned in a brief existing account by the enlisted man said to have been dining alongside the colonel. Erskine, a survivor of hand-to-hand combat with the Marine Brigade during some of the bloodiest battles of World War I, including Belleau Wood and Soissons, had his faults, but it is doubtful that a weak stomach was among them.[17]

Aware early on that the interservice catfight was getting out of control, Kelly Turner attempted to keep the squabble in-house. On July 11, a memo went out observing: "Vice Admiral Turner has directed that under no circumstances will any story submitted by either civilian or service correspondents be released when [it] emphasizes [the] merits of the Marines or Navy against the Army. In this connection all articles detailing Japanese attack against [the] 105th Infantry at dawn 7 July East Longitude Time have been killed."[18]

Obviously piqued, General Richardson stoked the flames when he flew into Saipan on July 12 to present a number of valor awards to 27th Division GIs. The demonstration was not well received by Admirals Turner and Spruance or by Holland Smith. Turner and Spruance questioned Richardson's authority to interfere with an Army unit that was presently under Navy command. Richardson defiantly told Turner that he was in command of all Army troops in the Pacific and he did not have to answer to the admiral for anything. Holland Smith recounted a still more venomous confrontation in which Richardson chastised him for relieving Ralph Smith, warning "you can't push the Army around the way you have been doing" and referring to the Marines as "a bunch of beach runners."[19] Asked by Admiral Nimitz to explain his actions, Richardson claimed he had merely visited Saipan to present awards. He flatly denied Holland Smith's claims.[20]

The quarrel had already started to go public thanks to a July 8 article in the *San Francisco Examiner* about Ralph Smith's relief. The story cast Ralph Smith as a conscientious Army general trying to get the job done while keeping casualties to a minimum, only to be unjustly maligned by a Marine general with no qualms about squandering the lives of young Americans. The *Examiner*, a Hearst paper, had an agenda behind this distortion: The chain had long lobbied to have General MacArthur named Supreme Commander in the Pacific Theater and was quick to seize on any supposed shortcomings by the Navy or Marines. A few days later, the Hearst-owned *New York Journal* editorialized that Americans were shocked by the "staggering casualties" on Saipan and even more so by the revelation that an Army general had been relieved for advocating "more cautious tactics."[21]

In yet another effort to calm the waters, Admiral Nimitz forbade a rebuttal to these claims, but his efforts came to naught when *Time* magazine published an article by Bob Sherrod declaring that Ralph Smith's relief "had nothing to do with tactics." He was relieved, wrote Sherrod, because "he had long ago failed to get tough enough to remove incompetent subordinate officers." What's more, stated Sherrod, the 27th Division had "bogged down," its men "lacked confidence in their officers," and "froze in their foxholes."[22]

In the towns surrounding Albany and Troy, New York, home to many of the onetime Guardsmen, whole neighborhoods were still reeling from seemingly endless telegrams announcing the dead and wounded when Sherrod's article appeared. One grieving widow expressed fears that her officer husband had died uselessly. Morale in the 27th Division, then refitting in the New Hebrides, plummeted and the division never really recovered.[23] The article infuriated the Army and sparked a firestorm extending all the way up to Admiral Nimitz and Secretary of the Navy James Forrestal.[24] An angry Nimitz damned such divisive stories as "contrary to the best interests of the nation,"[25] and Sherrod narrowly avoided having his press credentials revoked. Events finally moved on, but the 27th Division Saipan controversy and its impact on interservice relations was far from over.

Largely disinterested in the squabbles of generals and admirals, the human detritus of the Saipan campaign had scattered across the Pacific. Suffering from his leg wound in a fleet hospital in the Russell Islands, Joe Fiore took a turn for the worse and was placed in isolation. He overheard doctors talking about taking his leg off. "What do you think his chances are?" someone asked. The other replied, "He'll be dead by morning." Fiore hung on. "I was in tough shape there for eighteen days . . . I was out of it," he recalled. "I was receiving morphine every twelve hours—at noon and midnight. It would wear off at 10 o'clock, right on the dot, and I'd beg the nurse for another shot, and she'd say, 'No way.'" In the end, he walked out of the hospital and returned to his unit, his life and leg saved by a miracle called penicillin.[26]

Mike Masters came off the USS *Bolivar* on a stretcher at Pearl Harbor. He and the other non-ambulatory wounded were loaded into ambulances and rushed up the hill to Aiea Naval Hospital, sirens blaring. "The hospital complex was huge," consisting of more than a dozen two-story buildings connected in six wings, he recalled. Each ward could accommodate up to one hundred men. Masters was placed on a pushcart, irreverently dubbed "the meat wagon," and rushed to the "ass ward" for patients wounded from the waist down. Doctors repaired the large hole in his left buttock as best they could, but it was five months before Masters was able to get around on crutches. He considered himself lucky. "At the entrance to our ward, just across from the nurses' desks were two glass enclosed quiet rooms, where dying patients were enclosed in oxygen tents with life-sustaining tubes attached to their arms. When I became ambulatory, I noticed that other Marines would stop in from time to time, trying to console these men as if they were conscious. Some mornings we found the beds empty and knew they had passed on during the night."[27]

Carl Matthews ended up in a military hospital in Queensland, Australia. Some earlier casualties from Saipan were already there when he arrived. A nurse was taking down names, ranks, and information for registration when a voice from a bed across the aisle asked, "Matthews, is that you?" Matthews looked over to see a patient whose head and eyes were wrapped in bandages. It turned out to be Winfred Moore, a corpsman he knew from the 24th Marines. A bullet had pierced Moore's helmet and entered his head between and above the eyes, leaving him permanently blind. Moore, not yet twenty-one years old, seemed to accept his condition with remarkable equanimity. The "spark of the ward," he laughed and joked that he had just retired.[28]

Jack Claven encountered another example of do or die spirit in Naval Hospital MOB #5 in Noumea, New Caledonia. The ward had one room that was reserved for patients who wanted to read, write letters, or whatever. The room was usually open, but when Claven went down one day to do some ironing, he found the door closed. He opened it to find a fellow Marine patient "doing a number on one of our nurses on a gurney." The Marine had his right leg in a full cast to the hips and his right arm in a similar cast to his shoulders, but that didn't seem to bother him in the least, laughed Claven.[29]

Sadly, pain and tragedy were more common. Among those wounded in the last days of the campaign was Maj. Roger G. B. Broome, a Marine Reservist and University of Virginia Law School graduate, who was shot on July 8. Dragged to safety, he dictated a letter to a fellow officer to send to his wife Jane, who was then pregnant with their second child. "I was hit in the thigh yesterday afternoon and sustained a pretty bad fracture of the femur," he observed. He was doing all right, he assured her, and said he expected to be in the hospital the next day and back in the States in probably a month.

On July 16 a chief pharmacist's mate at U.S. Naval Hospital #10 in Hawaii sent Jane Broome an official Navy Speed Letter advising her that her husband had been admitted to the hospital July 15 with a fracture of the left femur and was "seriously ill." The medical report on Broome painted a grim picture, observing he had been hit through the left hip by a rifle bullet, adding: "A cast was applied, and he was transferred here. Examination showed him to be critically ill. He was incontinent with a small wound of entrance over the sacrum, and a very large foul, destructive wound of exit on the left thigh. The bullet went through the acetabulum (the cup-shaped area where the leg attaches to the hip at the pelvis) and shattered the head of the femur and the proximal [sic] third of the shaft of the femur. Laboratory examination showed positive culture for clostridium welchii [bacteria], and a non-protein nitrogen of 165. He was given intensive penicillin and support therapy."

Jane Broome received another letter on July 24 advising her that her husband's condition was critical. This was followed by a letter dated July 26 noting that his condition was "much improved but still considered serious." But Broome's condition took a sudden turn for the worse and on July 30 doctors performed a guillotine amputation at the hip of his left leg. On September 7, incontinent and confined to a stretcher, Major Broome was flown by plane to the U.S. Naval Hospital at Treasure Island, California, and then to the East Coast, arriving at Bethesda Naval Hospital on September 20. By now his condition had deteriorated further. Doctors removed what was left of his leg up to the hip socket and also took out a kidney. Over the next four months, Broome clung to life, buoyed somewhat by regular visits from his wife and family and fellow officers.

On January 18, Jane Broome was giving her newborn daughter Katy a bottle at 6:30 in the morning when the phone rang. The voice on the line said, "I'm calling to tell you your husband just died."

Roger Broome was buried beside his grandparents in the cemetery of St. John's in Green Springs, Virginia. He was twenty-nine years old.[30]

Meanwhile, the military machine that would bring the Japanese Empire to its knees continued to grind on with hardly a pause. Marines and GIs stormed Guam on July 21, moving inland after initial hard fighting on the beaches. Three days later, the 2nd and 4th Marine Divisions, following an all-too-brief rest, assaulted Tinian. Landing over two small rocky beaches on the island's northwest coast, the Marines duped the Japanese who had concentrated their defense along the wide sandy expanses near Tinian Town Harbor in the southwest. In sharp contrast to the bitterly contested Saipan landings, U.S. casualties the first day at Tinian were only fifteen killed and 225 wounded.[31] The island was declared secure on August 1. U.S. casualties totaled 328 killed and 1,571 wounded. The 9,000-man Japanese garrison was virtually wiped out: Only 252 military prisoners were taken.[32] Among the dead was Adm. Kakuji Kakuta, who had consistently misled Admiral Ozawa regarding the strength of his land-based air forces a month and a half earlier.

Massive construction on Saipan, Guam, and Tinian began to transform cane fields into airfields for the huge B-29 bombers that would be sent to devastate Japanese cities. The four-engine behemoths—99 feet long with a 141-foot wingspan—required a runway 8,500 feet long and 200 feet wide and taxiways almost the size of a fighter strip. Engineers on Saipan also began building a road network that within a year would total 230 miles of hard surfaced highway. U.S. crews erected Quonset huts, movie theaters, repair shops, post exchanges, chapels, parking lots, hundreds of warehouses, and seven hospitals with 11,500 beds and surgical wards. A radio station, WXLD, went on the air on August 10.[33]

The number of civilians streaming into the 600-acre internment camp at Susupe peaked during July following the Marpi Point suicides. By July 15, the number of civilian internees had soared to 13,289, including 2,258 Chamorros, 782 Carolinians, 9,091 Japanese, and 1,158 Koreans.[34] How many civilians had perished during the battle would never be known with any certainty as precise wartime population figures for the island do not exist. Japanese-prepared population figures for 1936 indicate a total of 23,819 inhabitants: 2,339 Chamorros, 893 Carolinians, 20,293 Japanese, 280 Koreans, and fourteen other foreigners (probably Catholic clergy). Figures for 1943 indicate about 30,000 inhabitants, of whom about 25,000 were Japanese; the estimate as of January 1944 was about 32,000 total residents. Beginning in March 1944 between 3,000 and 5,000 Japanese civilians, mostly women and children connected with the South Seas Development Company, were evacuated to Japan.[35]

Those rough figures can be compared to the number of civilians known to have survived. By August 1945 the number of internees at Camp Susupe totaled 18,400, which included 13,373 Japanese, 1,365 Koreans, 810 Carolinians, and 2,426 Chamorros.[36] Even assuming 5,000 Japanese were evacuated prior to the battle, casualties among that element of the population were obviously severe—and, of course, many of the evacuees escaped the island only to perish in submarine attacks. Despite the shocking sensationalism of the Marpi Point suicides, the vast majority of civilian deaths were "collateral" to the actual fighting, victims of artillery fire, reduction of caves, and nighttime encounters with American defensive positions.

Though the island was now well in hand, enemy holdouts—both military and civilian—remained a nuisance, dodging patrols, stealing food from American supply dumps, and occasionally killing an unwary Marine or soldier who unwisely went off for a solitary swim or ventured into the bush to scavenge for souvenirs. Shortly after midnight on July 30, a small Japanese raiding party slipped into the boat basin at Tanapag Harbor and blew up a dump containing 84 tons of boxed dynamite. The massive explosion left a crater 210 feet long and 120 feet wide and completely obliterated the two Seabee guards. Also killed in the blast were three Japanese, including an officer, who apparently misjudged the margin of safety when they set off the blast. Their bodies were found about 75 feet from the edge of the crater.[37] On September 10, in another daring foray, a Coronado patrol plane moored off the west shore of Saipan was holed and sunk by two Japanese boarders. The seaplane's crew escaped without injury. The Japanese were killed.[38]

The most organized group roaming the hinterlands was led by Capt. Sadae Oba, who had opted not to waste his life in General Saito's *gyokusai* and slipped off into the hills to wage guerrilla warfare and await the return of the Japanese navy. Oba eventually accumulated about fifty men—including Saburo Arakaki, who had walked away from the *gyokusai* the night of July 6 after a naval officer announced the Imperial Navy was on its way. Arakaki's companion, Sergeant Aiko, drowned when they tried to swim south along the coast to avoid American units. The captain was soon identified by American intelligence, who nicknamed him "the Fox" for his ability to elude sweeps and patrols. His group also received assistance and food from Japanese civilians in the internment camp, but as a practical matter Oba's so-called guerrilla war was primarily a struggle for self-preservation and more of an embarrassment than a serious threat to the American occupation.[39]

The first B-29 Superfortresses arrived at Saipan on October 12. Others followed at a rate of three to five a day until by November there were roughly 120 of the monstrous silver aircraft crowding the airfields, accompanied by thousands of Army Air Force personnel.

The first actual strike against Japan set out on November 24 when 111 B-29s, led by "Dauntless Dotty," took off from Isley Field for the sixteen-hour, 2,700-mile round-trip, targeting the Musashino aircraft plant near Tokyo. In addition to the tons of bombs intended for the enemy, the tail gunner on "Lucky Lynn" brought along a harmonica, a girl's picture, and a pair of panties for luck and to keep him company on the long flight.[40]

As Emperor Hirohito had feared, the long-range bombers soon began to lay waste to Japanese cities. Early bombing raids were largely ineffective, but a switch to low-level attacks using incendiaries in March 1945 wreaked havoc on densely packed urban areas. On March 9, a swarm of 282 B-29s burned out 16 square miles of Tokyo—an estimated 267,000 buildings—creating a firestorm so intense that small canals actually boiled. Aircrews at the tail of the attack gagged at the reek of burning flesh as they passed thousands of feet over the conflagration. Upwards of 100,000 people died. A million more were left homeless. The attacks continued, day after day, week after week, month after month. On March 11 it was Nagoya; on March 13 Osaka. By June, all but a handful of Japan's major cities lay in ashes. By one calculation, the firebombing campaign ultimately destroyed 180 square miles of sixty-seven cities and killed more than 300,000 people.[41]

The Japanese made an effort to strike back at the airfields in the Marianas. Only three days after the first B-29 raid on Tokyo from Saipan, two twin-engine Mitsubishi "Betty" bombers from Iwo Jima raced in for a low-level early morning attack on Isley Field, destroying one B-29 and damaging eleven others. Surprise was so complete that construction lights were still on at the airfield as the Bettys came in. Hours later, eleven Zeros strafed the field, destroying three B-29s and damaging two. Hiding under his jeep during the attack, XXI Bomber Command chief Gen. Haywood S. Hansell saw a Zero coming in with its wheels down. To his astonishment, the plane rolled to a stop on the airstrip and the pilot climbed out, pistol in hand. This suicidal individual fired away at ground crews until someone on the flight line picked him off with a rifle.[42]

A total of more than eighty Japanese aircraft were sent on raids against Saipan and Tinian between November 1944 and February 1945. The raids destroyed eleven B-29s, seriously damaged eight, and caused minor damage to another thirty-five. American casualties were forty-five dead and over 200 wounded. About thirty-seven Japanese aircraft fell victim to U.S. fighters and/or antiaircraft fire. For all of the effort, the impact on the U.S. bombing program was negligible and the devastating air offensive against Japan continued.[43]

In desperation, the Japanese decided to launch a commando raid on Saipan's air bases. About 125 specially trained paratroopers from the Japanese army's *1st Raiding Regiment* were assembled in December to prepare for a suicide mission. The troops would be carried to the airfields on Mitsubishi K-21 "Sally" bombers. The bombers would crash-land on the fields and the commandos would emerge to destroy the B-29s with explosive charges. The raid, scheduled to take place in January, was subsequently canceled due to damage to the airfields at Iwo Jima where the Sallys were scheduled to refuel. However, as the B-29s continued to devastate the Japanese home islands, plans for an even more ambitious raid began to take shape. This raid would involve sixty aircraft carrying 300 naval commandos from the *101st*

Kure Special Naval Landing Force and 300 Army commandos from the *1st Raiding Regiment.*

Twenty aircraft would crash land at Aslito Airfield on Saipan, twenty at Guam, and the remainder at Tinian where they would destroy as many bombers as possible before survivors disappeared into the bush to carry out guerrilla operations. Captured American bomber crews were interrogated for information about their home bases and the commandos rehearsed on full-scale mockups of B-29s. The raiders were also issued replica uniforms intended to disguise them as American Army Air Force ground personnel in order to sow confusion. In perhaps the most ambitious—some might say ludicrous—part of the plan, the commandos hoped to capture a B-29 and fly it back to Japan. The Japanese had recovered a flight manual from a Superfortress crash site near Nagoya and felt confident they would be able to operate the massive aircraft. The attack was set to take place between August 19 and 23, but larger events would intervene.[44]

While the commandos trained, more sinister plans contemplated employing biological agents against the U.S. air bases. The Japanese had been experimenting with weaponized biological agents since before the war; reports of mysterious epidemics of cholera, typhoid, anthrax, and bubonic plague had been coming out of China for years. Horrific tests were routinely carried out on Chinese captives and the civilian population. Among the results of these experiments was the so-called "Uji" bomb, which was designed to burst hundreds of feet above the ground and rain bubonic plague–carrying fleas on population centers below.

The American military was not oblivious to the danger. As early as June 23, eight days into the battle for Saipan, NTLF issued a directive to ordnance units, "Requesting immediate notification if Bacillus Bomb is located." Units in the field were further advised: "Appears that Japs are [manufacturing] a bacillus bomb probably marked with green tip, purple band gray body, purple tail or tail struts. Probably marked TUSHO type 13 Experimental 1 kg."[45]

Information uncovered after the war indicated a ship carrying a biological warfare unit had been sent to Saipan two months before the U.S. landings, but most of the personnel—and their containers of plague-infected fleas—were lost when their ship was sunk. Another report, which, may have been a variation on the other, claimed that in late June or early July, as it became apparent that Saipan was lost, Gen. Ishii Shiro, the director of the Japanese biological weapons program, sent a team of seventeen officers out by ship to raid the American airfield. The plan was to plant porcelain bombs containing millions of plague-infected fleas in the vicinity of the airfield. The plan reportedly failed when the ship was sunk en route by a submarine, losing the plague bombs and all but one of the biological warfare team.[46]

It is unclear how much, if anything, the U.S. military knew of such plans at the time, but a directive issued on August 5, less than a month after Saipan was secured, indicates that the high command was aware of the general threat and that the potential for a biological attack was a matter of grave concern. The bulletin stressed the importance of recognizing "indications of Japanese plans to carry on bacteriological warfare." Such indications could include low-flying planes engaging in "spraying of any sort," death or illness of numbers of troops for no apparent cause, the deaths of rodents or domestic animals in large numbers, and "odd types of containers or bombs made of plastic or glass from which powder or liquid can be sprayed." Prisoners were to be asked about recent vaccinations. Personnel were advised to be alert for any changes in enemy gas masks.[47]

Previous tests had indicated that the issue U.S. gas mask gave poor protection against simulated biological agents. This led the Chemical Warfare Service to develop a special outlet-valve filter for the masks. U.S. command felt the threat was serious enough that some 425,000 of the upgraded masks were rushed to Saipan under special security conditions. Fortunately, they were never needed. Probably due more to logistical obstacles than any moral qualms, the Japanese never employed biological agents against U.S. troops in the Marianas.[48]

In any case, time was about to run out on the Empire.

At 0245 on August 6, a B-29 named *Enola Gay* in honor of the pilot's mother lumbered into the air from Tinian just 5 nautical miles from Saipan's southern shore. Loaded down with a 5-ton atom bomb incongruously nicknamed "Little Boy," the Superfortress turned toward Japan and a rendezvous with unsuspecting Hiroshima. The bomb run began 12 miles from the city, *Enola Gay* approaching the release point at 328 miles per hour. Bombardier Thomas Ferebee took over the plane from Col. Paul Tibbetts two minutes out from target. The city sprawl was clearly visible 31,600 feet below. At 0915, Ferebee hit the bomb release and less than one minute later the world changed forever as Little Boy detonated 2,000 feet over the city. Three days later, the B-29 *Bocks Car* dropped a second device, "Fat Man," on Nagasaki. On August 10 Japan sued for peace. Many in Japanese government and high military circles had considered this moment to be inevitable—sentiment for terminating the war had been gaining momentum since the fall of Saipan—but no one had imagined hostilities would end in a radioactive cloud.[49]

Five days later, at Tokyo's Omori Prison Camp where Capt. Loren Stoddard had been held since being shot down off Saipan in May, one of the friendlier Japanese took some of the prisoners aside and tried to give them a message without being overheard by the other guards. The man could speak no English and the prisoners were able to make out only two words, *Senso warri*. It finally dawned on them that he was telling them the war was over.

On August 21, the Japanese camp commander called a formation of all the prisoners and officially announced the end of the war. He said the prisoners were free to roam the camp—located on a small island in Tokyo Bay—as they pleased, but were to stay within the fence. Four days later, U.S. planes appeared overhead. The planes circled and parachutes began to blossom out. It was food: B rations, C rations, D rations, and K rations, later followed by steel drums of peaches, chocolate, sugar, fruit salad, and other food the starving Americans had begun to think existed only in their dreams. Stoddard at one point had declined to a mere 92 pounds—so thin that his tailbone protruded.

On the afternoon of August 29, while the prisoners were still feasting, five U.S. landing craft appeared in the waters off the island. They pulled in at the back gate where the garbage and supply boats normally docked. The front ramps dropped and armed men emerged accompanied by a naval officer. Smiling broadly, the officer surveyed the waiting prisoners and exclaimed, "Boys! Let's go home!"

Loren Stoddard's long ordeal was finally over.[50]

In the Japanese internment camp on Saipan, Shizuko Miura heard the emperor's rescript broadcast on the radio. Though the high-pitched voice and formal imperial phrasing was difficult to understand, it was soon clear to her that the war was over. Japan had capitulated.

Not all of the Japanese in the camp were convinced. Many believed the announcement was a hoax. An internee who cooperated with American efforts to persuade the others that the war was indeed over was assassinated by a member of Captain Oba's band who infiltrated into the camp with the assistance of Japanese civilians. Still up in the hills, Oba dismissed American broadcasts and leaflets reporting the surrender as outright lies. A former Japanese soldier who agreed to go into the bush to reason with the holdouts was murdered. Finally, in late November 1945, after much back and forth between American officers and the diehards, Captain Oba was presented with written orders issued by Major General Umahachi Amau, former commander of Japanese forces on Pagan in the Northern Marianas, authorizing him to surrender.

On the morning of December 1, the forty-seven Japanese soldiers in Oba's band shaved, cleaned their weapons, and marched down from the hills. They reportedly came out singing "*Ho hei no honryo*" ("The Heart of the Infantry"). Preceded by a large rising sun flag provided by one of the Camp Susupe internees, the ragged band marched, somewhat incongruously, into the parking lot of the Stateside Theater, an outdoor stage in Charan Laulau on the east coast by Magicienne Bay. Captain Oba brought his men to attention in two orderly ranks, then stepped forward and surrendered his sword to Lt. Col. Howard G. Kirgis, commanding officer of the 18th Marine Antiaircraft Battalion. The Japanese troops then laid down their rifles and marched quietly off to the POW stockade.[51]

So ended the last organized resistance of Japanese forces on Saipan.

Epilogue

Loose Ends

THE END OF THE WAR FOUND CHARLES TOTH SOMEHOW STILL ALIVE, HAVing gone from Saipan to Tinian to fearsome combat on Iwo Jima over the course of only seven months. On Saipan he had narrowly missed being killed by a Japanese officer with a sword. "He hit me somehow, knocked my head open . . . they said I had this big hole in my helmet and whatever happened, I don't know," said Toth. "It was a scramble, but they said I killed him. I guess I was a little faster than he was. I guess I cut his throat with a knife."

Back in Hawaii, he and some buddies sneaked off to town and got drunk. They were caught on their return. "We all got court-martialed," remarked Toth. "I was busted down to private." He didn't much care at that point. "Captain Rogers," he told his company commander at the court-martial, "let me tell you something right now. I'm on my way home. The war is over. I don't give a goddamn about the Marine Corps and I don't give a damn about anything, because where I'm going to, my rank ain't going to give me a promotion."

The captain, himself a combat veteran, just looked at him a moment and said, "So long, Totie."[1]

And that should have been it. But it wasn't. Not for Toth or for thousands upon thousands of others.

Call them loose ends. They are the memories, the agonies, the physical and emotional scars, the ramifications and the detritus—both human and material—of the battle for Saipan.

In May 1952, nearly eight years after the U.S. landings on Saipan, some Chamorros who had ventured into the jungle to catch bats emerged with a wild tale about a naked man they had seen scrambling up the side of a cliff. A party of constables and American officials hiked out to the site and discovered two wraith-thin Japanese standing on top of the rock face. Ordered

465

to surrender, the men bobbed their heads and held up their hands. The pair turned out to be Kamigawara Toshiji, thirty-one, and Toshiyoshi Ide, thirty-seven, both former members of the Japanese garrison. Toshiji arrived on Saipan on March 20, 1944, while his companion Ide had arrived only three days before the U.S. landings. Certain they would be killed if the Americans found them, they had spent the last eight years hiding in what newspapers somewhat generously referred to as their clifftop "eagle's nest," living on smoked land snails, fresh water eels, rats, breadfruit, mangoes, and papayas. Their only diversion was catching and breeding wild canaries.

Severely malnourished, the two former soldiers were hospitalized on Saipan and later on Guam for a month before being repatriated to Japan. Mentally shaken, weak and in shock, they were placed in a Tokyo psychiatric ward. One of the two was reported to be almost incoherent, saying nothing but "Thank you" any time he was spoken to. He suspected his relatives of being spies and refused to take either food or medicine. The two eventually disappeared from the news columns and faded into oblivion, the last hold-outs from Saipan's doomed garrison.[2]

Fifty-three years later, on a rainy, overcast day in June 2005, Japan's Emperor Akihito—the seventy-one-year-old son of the wartime emperor, Hirohito—stood atop the cliffs at Saipan's Marpi Point, the scene of so much tragedy decades before. His father had died of natural causes in 1989, having managed to retain the throne after Japan's defeat. Gen. Hideki Tojo was also dead. Tried as a war criminal, the popular face of Japanese aggression had been executed by hanging two days before Christmas, 1948. Sadae Oba had died in Japan in 1992. On the American side, most of the major participants were also dead: Holland Smith in 1967, Ray Spruance in 1969, Ralph Smith in 1998, and Gen. Robert Richardson in 1954.

"Our hearts ache when we think of those people who fought at a place where there was no food, no water, no medical treatment for the wounded," Emperor Akihito observed prior to his visit. Now, bowing deeply under an intermittent rain, the emperor offered his prayers for all those who had perished in the struggle for the island six decades before.[3]

It was the first trip by a Japanese monarch to a World War II battle site outside Japan, but the Saipan Emperor Akihito visited was far removed from the Saipan of 1944. Now a U.S. territory, all the thousands of Japanese internees held in Camp Susupe—including Shizuko Miuro and Ryoko Okuyama—had been repatriated to Japan after the war, returning to a homeland many had never really known. The sugar cane industry had gone with them, leaving fewer than 3,000 Chamorros in possession of Saipan with little idea of what came next. The imposing statute of "Sugar King" Haruji Matsue in Central Park at Garapan and a carefully restored sugar cane locomotive remained among the few reminders of that prewar way of life.

Fueled, ironically, by money from a booming 1980s Japanese economy, by the time of Emperor Akihito's visit luxury hotels had replaced gun positions along the beaches where the Marine divisions stormed ashore six decades earlier. Today, tourism brochures tout the scuba diving off the picturesque lagoon where Cmdr. Bill Martin narrowly escaped with his life and his two crewmembers died when their TBF was shot down on D minus 2. A rebuilt Garapan and Charan Kanoa boast a Taco Bell, Kentucky Fried Chicken, a casino, and other attractions never dreamed of in 1944. Japanese honeymooners stroll hand in hand along the beaches and enjoy golf on greens laid out over old battlegrounds. The Mariana Country Club with its manicured golf course lies just to the south of the Marpi Point cliffs where so many chose death.

Memorials abound. A park and long line of monuments at Marpi Point—virtually all inscribed in Japanese—commemorate the dead and plead for peace. One represents a mother kneeling, facing south, mourning her dead sons. Another depicts a kneeling child facing the cliff itself. The most prominent include the Okinawa Peace Monument and Korean Peace Memorial, the latter built in remembrance of all the Koreans forced into slavery and killed during World War II. The many monuments have become a place of pilgrimage where visiting Japanese often leave prayer boards before returning to the white sand beaches and luxury hotels touted in the travel brochures. Another popular attraction is an old Japanese bunker erroneously titled "last command post" of General Saito. Few if any visitors probably know that Saito died in a nondescript cave some distance to the south.

The American cemeteries on the southwest coast are gone—the dead returned to their hometowns or the National Cemetery of the Pacific in Hawaii—the former gravesites now occupied by developments. The dead are commemorated by the World War II Saipan American Memorial located near the beach overlooking Tanapag Harbor. Dedicated on June 15, 1994, the fiftieth anniversary of the American landings, the Memorial Court of Honor and Flag Circle consists of twenty-six granite panels inscribed with the names of 5,204 service personnel who perished. Also on the site is the Marianas Memorial, dedicated on June 13, 2004, in memory of indigenous Chamorros and Carolinians of the northern Marianas who died from the beginning of the American aerial bombardment on June 11, 1944, to the closure of civilian camps on July 4, 1946. The memorial consists of ten granite panels listing 929 names.

A less visible relic of Saipan is the continuing discussion among military historians over what has become known as "Smith vs. Smith"—though it might be more properly termed "Howlin' Mad vs. the Army" or perhaps even "the Army vs. Howlin' Mad." The relief of Gen. Ralph Smith by Gen. Holland M. Smith and whether or not that action was justified remains a sometimes contentious subject over seventy years after a messenger handed the Army general an envelope along the roadway by Purple Heart Ridge and then hastily sped away. It was a controversy the highest echelons had hoped to defuse—an "exonerated" Ralph Smith was given new duties in Europe after his relief, while H. M. Smith was kicked upstairs to an administrative command that would keep him well away from the U.S. Army.

Unfortunately, like some stubborn Hydra, the issue reemerged—once again threatening to shake interservice cooperation to its foundations—when H. M. Smith, now retired, published his intemperate memoir, *Coral & Brass*, parts of which were serialized in the *Saturday Evening Post* in 1948. Recognizing the numerous flaws, inaccuracies, and inflammatory tone of Smith's memoir, friends and high-ranking officers urged him not to publish, but he went ahead anyway. Sadly, his friends were right. The book did nothing to enhance Smith's legacy; it only added to his reputation as a loudmouthed bully who could never admit he was wrong. This was unfortunate, for despite his personal shortcomings, Smith's contribution to the evolution of amphibious warfare was enormous and his administrative talents considerable.[4]

But was he wrong to relieve Ralph Smith? Adm. Ray Spruance did not think so. In a personal letter to Admiral Nimitz on July 4, 1944, Spruance observed, "The relief of Ralph Smith from command of the 27th Division was regrettable but necessary. He has been in command of that division for a long time and cannot avoid being held responsible for its fighting efficiency or lack thereof."[5] Graves Erskine dismissed the idea that Holland Smith acted out of personal pique. Smith recognized the potential fireworks his decision would ignite, he said, but "Holland Smith was a man who didn't worry about the consequences to himself when he thought he was right."[6]

On the other hand, it seems evident that H. M. Smith grossly underestimated the daunting problems the GIs faced in Death Valley. In retrospect it would appear that his decision to relieve Ralph Smith was too hasty, the product of his frustration with the 27th Division and his anxiousness to conclude the seizure of Saipan—which was already well past the anticipated schedule—as quickly as possible. While not admitting that it affected his competence, Smith conceded in his memoir, "I was 62 when we attacked Saipan, and many times during that month I felt like a tired old man under the strain of directing a campaign which required so much nervous and physical energy." Ironically, Ralph Smith's removal came just as the Army general was formulating a practical method to counter the strong defenses he faced in Death Valley.

Ralph Smith's departure did little to improve the division's performance. While individual GIs repeatedly demonstrated great courage, there seemed to be a systemic lack of initiative—even an air of confusion—in the overall organization, almost like a machine that had the right parts but lacked the proper lubrication. Even the Buckner Report, compiled by Army officers who might be expected to be generous toward one of their own, conceded that the 27th failed to perform as would be "expected from a well-trained division, as evidenced by poor leadership on the part of some regimental and battalion commanders, undue hesitancy to bypass snipers, with a tendency to alibi because of lack of reserves to mop up," poor march discipline, and lack of reconnaissance.[7] Captured ground was given up, only to be reoccupied by the enemy; minor casualties brought advances to a standstill; at times officers did not seem to know what their units were doing or even where they were. The official Army historian Philip A. Crowl wrote, with praiseworthy professional objectivity, "Although Army troops in Death Valley sustained fairly heavy casualties, the two Marine divisions on the flanks suffered greater ones." Yet the Marines—even the 2nd Division struggling through the almost impassable ground of Mount Tapotchau and its surrounds—"made considerable advances while the 165th Infantry registered only small gains and the 106th Infantry made almost none at all."[8]

Defenders of the 27th Division maintained that the Army preferred to take a more methodical approach in the field, which required more time but reduced the number of casualties. For their part, Marines argued that maintaining offensive momentum shortened the campaigns, which meant that the supporting naval vessels were vulnerable for a shorter period of time. A widely cited case in point was the loss of the escort carrier USS *Liscomb Bay* at Makin. Forced to remain off shore in support while the GI invasion force plodded along for four long days, the carrier was torpedoed by an enemy submarine only hours after the island was declared secure. Of the 961 crewmen, only 272 survived.

In a study of U.S. Army doctrine during World War II, historian Edward J. Drea suggests the 27th's problems may have been systemic of a larger issue in Army divisions in general. Drea cites an Army officer in the Southwest Pacific, who observed, "In too many instances, either due to lack of training or poor leadership, or to a combination of both, our troops did not have the will to close with and kill the enemy. Troops seemed to think they should be able to stand off at a distance and kill the enemy, or have our aircraft, tanks, artillery, mortars, or machine guns do the killing for them, and were reluctant to believe that it was their duty to go forward and kill the Japs themselves."[9]

Unfortunately, the Smith vs. Smith controversy and the ensuing public debate cast an aspersion on the many good soldiers in the division. Whatever its shortcomings may have been as an organization, the 27th Division suffered no lack of brave men. The actions of so many GIs during the *gyokusai*—men who fought to the death and men who risked their lives to save their injured comrades—is proof of that. As the great naval historian Samuel Eliot Morison observed, "The Saipan battle weeded out the unfit, but it also killed many of the brave and true."[10]

Still livid years later, a former Army sergeant, now an old man, spoke for many of his comrades when he referred to H. M. Smith as "just a contemptible bastard, anxious to get one more battle star, and one more chance to make the Army look bad compared to his beloved Corps . . . They don't care how many bodies pile up, as long as they're on schedule. I've taken the position for many years that the Army could do anything the Marine Corps could do, with a lot less loss of life, and just a little more time. I will give the Marine Corps one thing: They have the most powerful and smoothest running propaganda machine of any branch of the service."[11]

In fact, the reality of what occurred on Saipan was more complicated than either side would ever be willing to concede—an unfortunate mix of personality, circumstance, conflicting doctrine, leadership lapses, and failure—that created the storm known as Smith vs. Smith.

More than 3,200 Marines and soldiers died in the struggle for Saipan. Except for a notice in their hometown newspapers, most of them died anonymously, known only to their buddies, their families, and to Graves Registration. Many of them were returned home after the war to be buried in family plots. Others were interred in the National Cemetery of the Pacific on Oahu. Still others, like twenty-three-year-old Pvt. William Yawney, just disappeared.

Born in eastern Pennsylvania coal country, Yawney was the fourth oldest of eight children. His father, who had come to the United States from the Ukraine around 1908, worked in the mines and later tried his hand at farming. He died a week before Will's twelfth birthday, making a tough life even tougher. The dark-haired youngster left high school after his freshman year, going to work at a silk mill and then at Bethlehem Steel as an unskilled laborer to help support his mother and siblings. He enjoyed sports and played softball and basketball.

Caught up in the draft, Yawney had been in the Army for less than a year when the 27th Division mounted out for Saipan. His family was close and he was a conscientious letter writer, but after July his letters abruptly stopped. Yawney's mother Katherine and his siblings continued to write to him hopefully—his mother in her native Ukrainian, always prefacing her letters "Glory to Jesus Christ!" Setting pen to paper yet again that fall as B-29s began to arrive at Saipan for the bombing campaign against Japan, she pleaded, "Dear my son, if you are still alive write me back. Write me those nice words you always tell me . . . I had dreams about you twice. Once you fought the Japanese and once you had long hair. My son, I ask you to give me a sign of you."[12] But Will Yawney, a member of Company D, 2nd Battalion, 105th Infantry, would never write back to his mother in tiny Freemansburg, Pennsylvania. The third of Katherine Yawney's five sons was dead, killed July 7 when the *gyokusai* overran his battalion.

The Yawney family contacted the War Department and the Red Cross in hopes of getting some information. The latter replied that the family shouldn't worry, Will was "in the best of health." Not until December, when one of Yawney's buddies came home, did the family learn the truth. Will was dead. The buddy knew this to be true because he had been there when it happened. "He was shot by a sniper in a tree, then they [Japanese] came down and hacked him to death—that's the story I got," Yawney's nephew, John, later told a newspaper reporter.[13]

Soon afterward, the family received a package of letters they had sent over the months, each stamped "undeliverable" and marked with the "date" of Will's death—dates variously noted as June, August, and September. Another package arrived with a couple of military ribbons and some photographs, apparently from his personal effects. "I remember my grandmother crying," John Yawney said later. "She cried until 1948."[14]

A subsequent letter from Will's commanding officer mentioned his ready smile and his adept play on the unit's softball team. The officer said he had been killed by a sniper, his remains buried on the island with a Catholic chaplain in attendance and a bugler sounding "Taps." The officer presumably had the best of intentions. But after the war, when it came time to bring the dead home, William Yawney's grave was nowhere to be found. The War Department notified the family in December 1949 that Will's remains were "unrecoverable." He was one of thirty-nine members of the 27th Infantry Division—virtually all of them from the overrun 105th Infantry—listed as missing in action on Saipan.

For years the Yawneys persisted, writing to congressmen and various officials, in hopes that someone could locate Will's grave. Decades passed. Katherine Yawney died in 1983 without answers. But before she died, she had Will's name engraved alongside her own on the family marker in the Ukrainian cemetery against the day when he would be found. She lay at rest for nearly thirty years before that day arrived. In 2011, Will's younger brother Harry was contacted by government officials. They told him that Kuentai-Japan, a private organization devoted to searching for the remains of Japanese war dead in order to return them to Japan, had discovered remains that might be his brother. Found under 3 feet of clay in an old bunker on the site of the July 7 *gyokusai*, the skeletal remains bore Will Yawney's dog tag.

The remains were passed on to JPAC—the Joint POW/MIA Accounting Command based in Hawaii—which is tasked with accounting for the nation's war dead. Dental records indicated the remains were indeed Will Yawney. A DNA sample from Harry confirmed it. Subsequent digs in the area where Will was found turned up four more sets of remains, along with dog tags, a high school ring, and other items. Three of the four, all from Yawney's D Company, were identified as PFC William Corneal of Paducah, Kentucky, PFC Bernard Gavrin of Brooklyn, New York, and PFC Richard Bean of Manassas, Virginia.

William Yawney was laid to rest beside his mother at St. John the Baptist Ukrainian Cemetery in Northampton, Pennsylvania, on a Saturday, two days before Memorial Day, 2013. An unseasonably blustery wind plucked at the clothes of mourners—most of whom had never met the deceased—as a firing squad fired a volley and a bugler played "Taps." Nearly seventy years after his death on Saipan, Will Yawney was finally home.[15]

In the summer of 1960, American theater marquees announced the arrival of a new movie starring heartthrob Jeffrey Hunter as a Japanese-speaking

Mexican-American who secures the surrender of hundreds of Japanese troops during the battle for Saipan. Titled *Hell to Eternity*, the bio-pic was based on the life and self-proclaimed wartime exploits of Guy Gabaldon.

Gabaldon, who acquired a rudimentary knowledge of spoken Japanese while living with a Nisei family in Los Angeles before the war, arrived on Saipan with the 2nd Marine Division. According to his own accounts, he almost immediately disappeared into the bush as a self-styled " lone wolf" and began persuading Japanese soldiers and civilians to give themselves up. Later dubbed "The Pied Piper of Saipan," he claimed to have brought in 1,500 enemy soldiers and civilians over the course of the campaign. This effort supposedly culminated on July 8, following the *gyokusai*, when he claimed to have talked a veritable Army of some 800 Japanese soldiers into surrendering.

While it appears indisputable that Gabaldon did bring in numbers of civilians during the campaign, his supposed military captures do not match up with the record and his claims have been described by skeptics as "one of the great fish stories of World War II."[16] But Gabaldon proved to be an accomplished self-promoter and his stories gained traction with the public after he appeared in 1957 on the popular TV show *This Is Your Life*. The movie with Jeffrey Hunter followed and helped build a movement seeking the Medal of Honor for the former Marine. Public pressure was intense enough that the military eventually upgraded Gabaldon's Silver Star medal to a Navy Cross in 1960, though it resisted decades of continued efforts to bestow the Medal of Honor for his "deeds." Gabaldon died in 2006 without obtaining the nation's highest military decoration, leaving some feeling he was a spurned hero and victim of racism and others equally convinced he was an unabashed phony of the first magnitude.

Meanwhile, efforts were also underway by former members of the 27th Infantry Division to recognize Capt. Ben Salomon's heroic stand in defense of wounded GIs during the *gyokusai*. Two other heroes of the *gyokusai* had received posthumous awards of the Medal of Honor: The widows of Col. William O'Brien and Sgt. Tom Baker accepted the awards from Undersecretary of War Robert J. Patterson in a dual ceremony on May 27, 1945, on the campus of Rensselaer Polytechnic Institute in their hometown of Troy, New York. But a similar recommendation for Salomon following the battle, complete with eyewitness affidavits, was returned without action, accompanied by a note from General Griner observing, "I am deeply sorry that I cannot approve the award of this medal to Captain Salomon, although he richly deserves it. At the time of his death, this officer was in the medical service and wore a Red Cross brassard upon his arm. Under the rules of the Geneva Convention, to which the United States subscribes, no medical officer can bear arms against the enemy." Despite pleas, Griner refused to reconsider.

Sporadic efforts to recognize Captain Salomon continued over the next fifty-five years, hampered by the passage of time and key witnesses, including 2nd Battalion commander Maj. Edward McCarthy, who committed suicide in 1953. However, those efforts received a major boost in 1970 when a legal review concluded that under the 1929 Geneva Convention, medical personnel were permitted to bear arms in self-defense and in defense of the wounded. Nevertheless, it was not until 2002 that the award was finally authorized.

By now, those who had been closest to Ben Salomon were all gone. The twenty-nine-year-old Jewish dentist had been an only child. His mother had died in 1946. When his father died in 1970 and was laid to rest beside his wife and son in Forest Lawn Memorial Park in Glendale, California, there was no one left. Those who had worked so hard to ensure that Salomon received the recognition he so justly deserved—including division historian Edmund Love and Doctors John Ingle and Robert West of the University of Southern California School of Dentistry—had never personally met the man. They knew him only through college photos showing what one writer later described as "a young man with a shy smile, dark, curly hair and wire-rimmed glasses," and the testimony of the GIs who bore witness to his courage.

On May 1, 2002, in a ceremony in the White House Rose Garden, President George W. Bush presented Captain Salomon's Medal of Honor to Dr. Robert West, representing the USC School of Dentistry. And so it was that a long injustice was made right.[17]

No longer young, former Army private Marty Mestre sat at his dining room table sixty years after the war, holding a Japanese bayonet, the 18-inch blade still sharp and gleaming when pulled from its metal sheath. It was a memento of a fear-filled night of his youth, taken from an enemy soldier who came within feet of killing him on Saipan. "At night one of us would sleep in the hole while the other one kept watch," he related. "This particular night, I spotted a Jap crawling up to our hole. I emptied my carbine on him."[18]

For Marine Corps veteran Bernard Ruchin, the memories accompanied souvenirs dumped from the cardboard box where they had rested largely undisturbed for decades. There was a red-tasseled Japanese bugle retrieved from the carnage of the *gyokusai*; a cigarette case taken from the body of a Japanese officer; a 3-inch-tall doll found inside a soldier's helmet.[19]

But some things don't fit conveniently into a box. "There are things you want to forget," Saipan veteran Bob Hoichi Kubo said of his experiences. "You want to make them vague. But some things you cannot forget." Among those things was the smell of death. "I hate the smell of old flesh," observed Kubo. "There's a stench to it because of the maggots. But the fresh killed ones, there's a sweet smell to it."[20]

There were faces from long ago that old men would carry to the grave. Aloysius T. Rolfes, who entered the Army as an enlisted man and ended the war as a captain in command of a company, remembered a man in his platoon on Saipan who wrote the most beautiful letters—letters Rolfes had to read as part of the censorship procedure. "You got to know their families pretty well," he observed about screening the unit's outgoing mail. "I remember we had a guy by the name of Smith and he was just a nice young man, a very simple sort of guy, but he wrote the most beautiful letters, I don't care if it was for his mother or his sweetheart or his aunt or his uncle. And he got hit by me one day. Just feet from me and got killed instantly. I often wondered whatever happened to that family after[wards]."[21]

For former lieutenant Richard Langhinrichs, it was "Louie," a nineteen-year-old Marine from Peoria, Illinois, who was severely wounded by a grenade on their second day on Saipan. All officers had morphine syrettes, but had been carefully instructed not to use them for certain kinds of heavily bleeding wounds as the morphine would cause or hasten death. "Louie was in agonizing pain, screaming and begging for morphine, but he had the kind of wound that prohibited the use of morphine," remembered Langhinrichs. "This went on for about an hour. I did not give him the morphine and still, to this day, I have nightmares about that decision. I know that if I had given him the morphine, he would have died—which he did anyhow. I can still hear him screaming."[22]

Sergeant Thurlby Amos Colyer's self-propelled gun crew was looking for a sniper when a bullet directed at the open-top armored vehicle snapped just over his head and hit the crewman behind him, taking the top off the man's skull in a torrent of blood. "It was just like dumping water out of a boot when he went down in the bottom of that tank and right down between his knees his head went," said Colyer. "I grabbed a handkerchief that was dirty and then I grabbed a clean one and laid it over his head. I held it a half hour to 45 minutes. You can't do nothing, but you try to do something. So I held his head . . . He lived for hours."[23]

Having survived the *gyokusai*, Nick Grinaldo seemed all right for a while. His wounds had healed and he had been reassigned as a guard watching over Italian prisoners of war. He was still in the Army when his troubles began. "I guess what I went through started catching up with me, and I got the shakes pretty good. I could not even hold a canteen cup in my hand," he recalled. "I would spill it. I turned in to the medics. They put me in a hospital, they put me behind bars. I was there one night. And they are yelling and screaming. These guys were cuckoo, you know. I said to this colonel the next morning, 'You better get me the hell out of here, I will be worse than these guys if you don't.' I did not sleep all night, they put me in another ward. I was there until the Japanese capitulated . . . They got me down for 'Tension, state, severe, and combat fatigue,' they called it back then."

Discharged from the Army, he went home to Troy, New York. He couldn't seem to hold a job. "I sure as hell was not that way when I went away," he said. "My wife put up with me for years. I'd go into these fits and spasms, rip sheets, pillow cases. I told her, 'Don't come near me, if I go into a tantrum, get the hell away from me fast.'" He eventually improved—for years he operated a shoe store in Troy—but as late as 2001, having managed to get through an interview about his experiences on Saipan, he admitted, "I did not know how I would hold up. I shook a little bit. I just don't like to think too much about it. For the simple reason, that I get these shakes. . . ."[24]

Some men got involved in veterans groups; some never did. One day former Marine Al Perry received a phone call from his friend Jim Jackson. "I am not going to another of these damned reunions unless you attend with me," declared Jackson. "There are no riflemen, there are only guys who were behind the lines. I have nothing in common with them; in talking to them I wonder if we were on the same island." All of what happened on the front lines was "totally incomprehensible" to those who were a few yards away. Trying to explain combat to someone who had never heard a shot fired in anger was like trying to explain nuclear physics to an orangutan. It wasn't their fault, but there was just no basis for understanding.[25]

Charlie Toth, a confirmed Catholic and former altar boy, came home to Allentown, Pennsylvania, in late 1945 with a new cynicism about God. His mother, grateful that all four of her sons had survived the war, was greatly disturbed by his attitude. "All you boys came home," she told Charlie, "thank God. But you're the only one that don't believe anymore."

Toth replied it seemed to him that God had died a long time ago. If there were a God, he must be a very miserable deity to allow even a fraction of the cruelty that goes on in the world.

His mother insisted that he go to confession.

"I said, 'What for?'" recalled Toth.

His mother retorted, "You're going to go to confession, Charlie. Maybe this will help you."

"So I went," observed Toth, "and Father Nagy said, 'Well son, what's up?'"

"Father, I was away almost four years. I think I have committed every crime that's known to the human race," said Toth.

"Son," said the priest, "I know. You're forgiven. Your country forgives you. You've done your job. You're home."

But Toth didn't feel forgiven. He married in 1946. His wife, appalled by his inner torments, burned his old uniform, but the gesture had little effect. "If I started telling you what I have seen, I would never sleep again," Toth told a newspaper reporter six decades after walking off Saipan. "See, I go to a psychiatrist once in a while because I still get my nightmares. She said, 'Charlie, we can help you, but it's going to go to the grave with you.' And she's right."[26]

Not everyone suffered the same—or even at all. There were also some grim beginnings that enjoyed happy endings. Lt. James L. Fawcett was talking with his company commander one day on Saipan when a Japanese machine gun opened up on them. "[T]he skipper screamed," recalled Fawcett. "I believe he jumped ten feet into the air and he just crumpled." Fawcett moved him out of the line of fire and injected him with morphine. "I later learned he had been shot in the testicles," he observed. "God! What a place to get shot! He had been married only weeks before being shipped overseas...."

Years later, Fawcett received a birth announcement from the former captain and his wife. They'd had a baby girl. At the bottom of the announcement the captain had written, "It only takes one!" Fawcett puzzled over this for a while before it finally dawned on him: "He had lost only one testicle!"[27]

In 1999 Joe Fiore, former corporal, U.S. Marine Corps, and holder of two Purple Hearts, traveled to Hawaii to pay a call on Warren "Bob" Ackerman, the buddy who had pulled him to safety when he was wounded on Mount

Tapotchau so many years before. After his discharge, Fiore had returned to Glens Falls, New York, and ended up taking over his father's liquor store; he married and had five children, and served on the County Board of Supervisors and as director of the County Veterans Service Agency.

Ackerman had no family. He had been raised in a New York orphanage. When he was killed by enemy small arms fire a few days after Fiore was evacuated from Saipan, his next of kin was listed as Miss Eleanor W. Gordon, State Charities Aid Association.

Fiore found his friend's gravesite among the thousands of others in the National Cemetery of the Pacific—"The Punchbowl"—the flat stone markers all the same except for the names. The one he had come so far to see identified the occupant as WARREN R ACKERMAN/NEW YORK/ PFC 18 MARINES 2 MARINE DIV/WORLD WAR II/NOV 6 1921 JULY 8 1944.

Looking down at the name on the stone, Fiore spoke quietly to the buddy who had quite probably saved his life: "Bob, it took over fifty years to get here. Here I am."

And then he added simply, "Thanks."[28]

NOTES

INTRODUCTION

1. D. M. Giangreco, "Casualty Projections for the U.S. Invasions of Japan, 1945–1946: Planning and Policy Implications," *Journal of Military History, Vol. 61* (July 1997), 521–82, http://tigger.uic.edu/~rjensen/invade.htm.
2. Oscar E. Gilbert, *Marine Tank Battles in the Pacific* (Conshohocken, PA: Combined Publishing, 2001), 139.
3. Richard W. Johnston, *Follow Me! The Story of the Second Marine Division in World War II* (New York: Random House, 1948), 175.
4. Patrick O'Sheel and Gene Cook (eds.), *Semper Fidelis: The U.S. Marines in the Pacific—1942–1945* (New York: William Sloane Associates, Inc., 1947), 199–200.
5. Oliver North, *War Stories II: Heroism in the Pacific* (Washington, DC: Regnery Publishing, Inc., 2004), 256.

CHAPTER I: FATEFUL DECISIONS

1. Edward J. Drea, *In the Service of the Empire: Essays on the Imperial Japanese Army* (Lincoln: University of Nebraska Press, 1998), 187–91.
2. Noriko Kawamura, *Emperor Hirohito and the Pacific War* (Seattle: University of Washington Press, 2015), 125.
3. Kenryo Sato, Dai Toa, "War Memoir (Great Eastern War Memoirs)," Undated, Toland Papers, Franklin D. Roosevelt Library, Hyde Park, NY (henceforth FDRL); John Toland, *The Rising Sun: The Decline and Fall of the Japanese Empire 1936–1945* (New York: Random House, 1970), 594–95.
4. Toland, *Rising Sun*, 596; Sato memoir.
5. Many military studies cite Saipan's area as 72 square miles, but modern surveys cite the island's land area as roughly 45.5 square miles.
6. Charan Kanoa is actually "Chalon Kanoa," but as the town was referred to as Charan Kanoa in all U.S. military references, that will be the name used here in order to avoid confusion.
7. D. Colt Denfeld, *Hold the Marianas: The Japanese Defense of the Mariana Islands* (Shippensburg, PA: Mane Publishing Company, 1997), 1–2.

8. Denfeld, 5; the description of Saipan is based largely on Philip A. Crowl, *United States Army in World War II: The War in the Pacific. Campaign in the Marianas* (Office of the Chief of Military History, Department of the Army: Washington, DC, 1960) and Maj. Carl Q. Hoffman, *Saipan: The Beginning of the End* (Washington, DC: Historical Division, Headquarters, U.S. Marine Corps, 1950).

9. Bruce M. Petty, *Saipan: Oral Histories of the Pacific War* (Jefferson, NC: McFarland & Company, Inc., 2002), 22.

10. Samuel Eliot Morison, *History of United States Naval Operations in World War II, Volume VII Aleutians, Gilberts, Marshalls: June 1942–April 1944* (Boston: Little, Brown and Company, 1951), 71.

11. Denfeld, 6–7; Crowl, 53–55.

12. Crowl, 23–24.

13. Douglas Westfall and Ryozo Kimihira, *Taking Saipan: Two Sides to Every Battle in WWII* (Orange, CA: The Paragon Agency Publishers, 2014), 4.

14. Katharyn Tuten-Puckett, *"We Drank Our Tears:" Memories of the Battles for Saipan and Tinian as Told by Our Elders* (Saipan: Pacific STAR Center for Young Writers, June 2004), 79.

15. Westfall, 21–28.

16. Petty, *Saipan*, 25–26.

17. Grace P. Hayes, *The History of the Joint Chiefs of Staff in World War II—The War Against Japan* (Annapolis, MD: Naval Institute Press, 1982), 280–81, 403, 431.

18. Hayes, 422–23; Crowl, 10; E. B. Potter, *Nimitz* (Annapolis, MD: Naval Institute Press, 1976), 279.

19. Potter, *Nimitz*, 280.

20. Crowl, 13.

21. Hayes, 545–47; Crowl, 13.

22. Hayes, 546–47.

23. Potter, *Nimitz*, 280–81.

24. Hayes, 547; Crowl, 14.

25. Crowl, 14; Toland, *Rising Sun*, 592.

26. Ibid.

27. Hayes, 547.

28. Potter, *Nimitz*, 281–82.

29. Hayes, 549; Toland, *Rising Sun*, 592.

30. Potter, *Nimitz*, 283.

31. Hayes, 550.

32. Ibid, 551–52, 559.

33. Hayes, 559–60; Crowl, 19; Thomas B. Buell, *Master of Sea Power: A Biography of Fleet Admiral Ernest J. King* (Boston: Little, Brown and Company, 1980), 417–25.

34. Petty, *Saipan*, 35.

35. Don Jones, *Oba: The Last Samurai* (Novato, CA: Presidio Press, 1986), 6–14. Jones's account, while based on Oba's experiences, is highly fictionalized in places and must be used with care.

36. Theodore Roscoe, *United States Submarine Operations in World War II* (Annapolis, MD: United States Naval Institute, 1949), 317.

37. Jones, *Oba*, 18.

CHAPTER II: SHARPENING THE SPEAR

1. Norman V. Cooper, *A Fighting General: The Biography of Gen Holland M. "Howlin' Mad" Smith* (Quantico, VA: The Marine Corps Association, 1987), 155; Capt. John C. Chapin, *Breaching the Marianas: The Battle for Saipan* (Washington, DC: History and Museums Division, Headquarters, U.S. Marine Corps, 1994), 4.

2. S. L. A. Marshall, *Bringing Up the Rear: A Memoir* (San Rafael, CA: Presidio, 1979), 69.

3. Cooper, 155.

4. Harry A. Gailey, *Howlin' Mad vs. the Army: Conflict in Command Saipan 1944* (Novato, CA: Presidio, 1986), 32.

5. Holland Smith and Percy Finch, *Coral & Brass* (New York: Charles Scribner's Sons, 1949), 115–16; Cooper, 134–35; Gailey, 84–85.

6. *Coral & Brass*, 125.

7. Anne C. Venzon, *From Whaleboats to Amphibious Warfare: Lt. Gen. "Howlin' Mad" Smith and the U.S. Marine Corps* (Westport, CT: Praeger, 2003), 87–89, 99.

8. Samuel Eliot Morison, *History of United States Naval Operations in World War II, Volume VIII New Guinea and the Marianas* (Boston: Little, Brown and Company, 1959), 12.

9. Denfeld, *Hold the Marianas*, 19.

10. Toshikazu Kase, *Journey to the Missouri* (New Haven, CT: Yale University Press, 1950), 73.

11. Ibid, 57.

12. Jones, *Oba*, 18–20.

13. Ibid, 59–62.

14. Ryoko Okuyama, "Surviving on the Island of Suicide," Toland Papers, FDRL.

15. Petty, *Saipan*, 46.

16. Headquarters, Expeditionary Troops Task Force Fifty-Six, Report on Marianas (henceforth TF-56 Report) Enclosures D, G-2, 31 August, 1944; Hoffman, 25–26.

17. Action Report, Photographic Reconnaissance Mission to Saipan, Tenian and Aguijan of 18 April 1944, Air Force Fleet Air Photographic Squadron Three, 19 April 1944.

18. Operations Rpt., Saipan CG, 4th Mar Div., 3 October, 1944, Annex B, Intelligence (henceforth 4th Mar. Div. Ops. Rpt.).

19. TF-56 Report. G-2.

20. Ibid.

21. Johnston, *Follow Me!*, 166.

22. Mike A. Masters, *Once A Marine Always A Marine* (Privately printed, 1988), 169.

23. William Banning (ed.), *Heritage Years: Second Marine Division Commemorative Anthology 1940–1949* (Paducah, KY: Turner Publishing Company, 1988), 84.

24. Chapin, *Breaching the Marianas*, 9; Cooper, 164.

25. USS *Nautilus*. Report of War Patrol number eight, 21 March 1944.

26. Denfeld, *Hold the Marianas*, 17.

27. Carl LaVo, *Slade Cutter: Submarine Warrior* (Annapolis, MD: Naval Institute Press, 2003), 152–53; Dave Bouslog, *Maru Killer* (Placentia, CA: Cline Publishing, 1996), 146–47.

28. USS *Seahorse* (SS 304), Report of Fourth War Patrol, 11 May 1944.

29. Ibid.

30. Ibid.

31. Ibid; Bouslog, 147–72; LaVo, 153–63.

32. Roscoe, 550.

33. Ibid, 554–55.

34. Hoffman, 9.

35. Roscoe, 320–23.

36. Interview notes with Maj. Takashi Hirakushi (Toland Papers, FDRL); Major Hirakushi also wrote a memoir, *Saipan nikudansen: Gyokusaisen kara seikanshita sanbǒ, no shǒ,gen*, published in 2006.

37. Haruko Taya Cook and Theodore F. Cook, *Japan at War: An Oral History* (New York: The New Press, 1992), 282. Takeo Yamauchi also wrote a memoir, *Kyōheiki: Saipan tōkōhei no shuki*, published in Tokyo in 1984.

38. USSBS Interrogations I, 212.

39. Hirakushi.

40. TF-56 Report, G2 Periodic Report, August 3, 1944.

41. Cooper, 163–64.

42. Paul Harper, *Growing Up in the Marine Corps 1942–1945* (Essex, CT: The Granite Ledge Press, 1997), 48.

43. Al Perry, "A Personal History of the Fourth Marine Division in WWII" (unpublished).

44. Harry A. Pearce, *Star Shells, Condoms, & Ka-Bars* (Leawood, KS: Leathers Publishing, 2004), 52.

45. John E. Lane, *This Here Is "G" Company* (Great Neck, NY: Brightlights Publications, 1997), 39.

46. Carl Matthews, *The War Years*, self-published memoir.

47. Ibid.

48. Ibid.

49. Hoffman, 31.

50. Dick Bailey, "Barracks Ballads, Sea Stories and War: One Marine's Memoirs," http://marinememoir.homestead.com/IndexBailey.html.

51. John C. Chapin undated memoir, Quantico, VA, USMC University (henceforth USMCU), 7, 46.

52. Commander Task Force 52.2, 23 August 1944 p. 12 Enclosures (A) to CTG 52.2 Serial 0226.

53. Roy W. Roush, *Open Fire!* (Apache Junction, AZ: Frontline Press, 2003), 388–89.

54. Commander Joint Expeditionary Force Marianas, Report of Amphibious Operations for the capture of the Marianas Islands (Enclosure A) August 25, 1944; Gene Eric Salecker, *The Second Pearl Harbor: The West Loch Disaster, May 21, 1944* (Norman: University of Oklahoma Press, 2014), 14; Hoffman, 32–33.

55. Paul Chambers (ed.), *The Third Battalion, Twenty-Fifth Marines: An Oral History by Colonel Justice Marion Chambers, USMCR, Ret.* (unpublished, 1987), 70–71.

CHAPTER III: ACTS OF MAN OR GOD

1. USSBS Interrogations II, 522.

2. USSBS Campaigns, 519; Toland, *Rising Sun*, 601; Greg Bradsher, "The Z Plan Story," *Prologue Magazine*, Fall 2005; Steven Trent Smith, *The Rescue* (New York: John Wiley & Sons, Inc., 2001), 141 (hereafter *Rescue*).

3. USSBS Campaigns, 221; Bradsher.

4. *Rescue*, 265; USSBS Campaigns, 221–22.

5. USSBS II Interrogations, 520.

6. Toland, *Rising Sun*, 602; Bradsher.

7. *Rescue*, 150.

8. USSBS Interrogations II, 520–21.

9. *Rescue*, 152–54.

10. Ibid, 157.

11. Bradsher; *Rescue*, 240.

12. *Rescue*, 184–85, 244–46.

13. Ibid, 160.

14. USSBS Campaigns (Combined Fleet Ultra Secret Dispatch 041213), 233; Toland, *Rising Sun*, 606; *Rescue*, 268–69.

15. Dick Bailey memoir.

16. William L. C. Johnson, *The West Loch Story* (Seattle, WA: West Loch Publication, 1986), 13 (hereafter *West Loch*); Salecker, *Second Pearl Harbor*, 46–51.

17. *West Loch*, 33.

18. Ibid; Salecker, *Second Pearl Harbor*, 51.

19. Salecker, *Second Pearl Harbor*, 52–59.

20. *West Loch*, 35.

21. Ibid, 51–55.

22. Ibid, 99–100, 155.

23. Ibid, 127–28.

24. Ibid, 69–70.

25. Ibid, 49.

26. Ibid, 144–45.

27. Pearce, 63; Salecker, *Second Pearl Harbor*, 76.

28. Salecker, 120.

29. *West Loch*, 147–48.
30. Ibid, 135–40.
31. Ibid, 96–97.
32. Pearce, 64.
33. Arthur J. Rath, "Secret at West Loch," *Honolulu Star-Bulletin*, May 20, 2007.
34. *West Loch*, 158–59.
35. Salecker, *Second Pearl Harbor*, 131–32, 138, 160–61.
36. Arthur W. Wells, *The Quack Corps* (Chico, CA: DolArt, 1992), 110.
37. *West Loch*, 161–63.
38. Hoffman, 33–34; Morison VIII, 171.
39. *West Loch*, 145–46.
40. Salecker, *Second Pearl Harbor*, 195.
41. *West Loch*, 64–65; Salecker, *Second Pearl Harbor*, 60–69.
42. Ibid, 67.
43. Salecker, 196–200.
44. Henry I. Shaw, Bernard C. Nalty, and Edwin T. Turnbladh. *Central Pacific Drive: History of U.S. Marine Corps Operations in World War II. Vol. III* (Washington, DC: Historical Branch, G-3 Division, Headquarters, U.S. Marine Corps, 1966), 253.
45. Lt. Charles W. Goe, *Is War Hell?* (W. Los Angeles, CA: Charles Goe, 1947), 76–77.
46. *2nd Armored Amphibian Battalion USMC WWII: Saipan, Tinian, Iwo Jima* (2nd Armored Amphibian Battalion Association, 1991), 37 (henceforth *2nd Armored*).

CHAPTER IV: ON TO THE WESTWARD

1. Loren and Helen Joe Stoddard, *One Flesh* (Salt Lake City, UT: Privately printed, 2013), 131.
2. Aircraft Action Report, Photographic Squadron Four, Photographic Reconnaissance Saipan of 29 May 1944, dated May 30, 1944.
3. Missing Air Crew Rpt. 42-73499, Headquarters Seventh Air Force, 431st Bomb Sq (H), 11th Bomb Gr (H), 11 June 1944; Stoddard, 150.
4. Ibid; ibid, 132.
5. Stoddard, 174.
6. Ibid, 132–33, 149.
7. Petty, *Saipan*, 35–36.
8. Stoddard, 139, 151–52.
9. Ibid, 152.
10. 27th Division, G-2 Journal, G-2 Periodic Rpt., July 6, 1944.
11. Stoddard, 140, 152–53.
12. Northern Troops and Landing Force Report of Marianas Operation, Phase 1 [Saipan] (henceforth *NTLF Report*), G-2 Rpt., 12 August 1944.
13. TF 56 Special G-2 Summary of the Enemy Situation on 13 June 1944.
14. USSBS Interrogations II, 429.

15. NTLF Report, G-2 Summary No. 20, 24 May 1944.
16. Crowl, 51; Shaw, 246.
17. Crowl, 65; Denfield, *Hold the Marianas*, 19–20; Shaw, 257.
18. Denfield, *Hold the Marianas*, 31.
19. TF 56 G-2 Summary of Enemy Situation, 13 June 1944.
20. The size of the tank force on Saipan is difficult to pin down. According to tables of organization, the companies of the *9th Tank Regiment* present at Saipan should have been equipped with forty-eight medium and light tanks. A POW from the regiment later claimed there were also two smaller army independent tank units, one with nine tanks and the other with eleven, but those units, if they existed, do not seem to have found their way into U.S. order of battle reports. It is possible the POW was referring to survivors of the *3rd* and *4th Independent Tank Companies*, though their tanks were reportedly lost when their ship was sunk in a torpedo attack. Naval forces reportedly had a company (about a dozen) land tanks and three or more amphibious tanks. The 27th Infantry Division subsequently claimed to have destroyed between forty-one and forty-seven tanks; the 2nd Marine Division claimed about forty and the 4th Marine Division reported knocking out six. Considering Japanese tables of organization, those numbers may be somewhat inflated.
21. Mark Peattie, *Naj'yo: The Rise and Fall of the Japanese in Micronesia, 1885–1945* (Honolulu: University of Hawaii Press, 1988), 281.
22. Crowl, 63.
23. Ibid, 64.
24. Edmund G. Love, *The 27th Infantry Division in World War II* (Nashville, TN: Battery Press, 2001), 119.
25. Hirakushi.
26. *2nd Armored*, 69.
27. Albert Greg Sutcliffe, interviewed by Harry Ziegler, Albert Greg Sutcliffe Collection (AFC/2001/001/16857), Veterans History Project, American Folklife Center, Library of Congress.
28. Rick Spooner, *The Spirit of Semper Fidelis: Reflections from the Bottom of an Old Canteen Cup* (Williamstown, NJ: Phillips Publications, 2004), 6.
29. Masters, 182.
30. Spooner, 7.
31. Goe, 75.
32. John Domanowski, Untitled Recollections, O'Brien Papers, New York State Military Museum, Saratoga Springs, NY (henceforth NYSMM).
33. S. G. Silcox, *A Hillbilly Marine* (n.p., 1977), 90.
34. NTLF Report, Narrative Assault on Saipan.
35. Ibid.
36. Hoffman, 27–29.
37. Lt. Russell A. Gugeler, "Army Amphibian Tractor and Tank Battalions in the Battle of Saipan, 15 June–9 July 1944," Manuscript Office of the Chief of Military History, 20 January 1945, 3.

38. NTLF Report Annex "King" to Operation Plan No. 3-44, 4.
39. Graves Erskine, interviewed by Benis Frank, 1970, USMCU, 336.
40. Leo J. Dougherty III, "Lest We Forget: General Graves B. Erskine, USMC (1897–1973)," *Marine Corps Gazette*, April 1997.
41. Hoffman, 51–52.
42. Masters, 181.
43. Wilbur Jones, *Gyrene: The World War II United States Marine* (Shippensburg, PA: White Mane Books, 1998), 140.
44. *2nd Armored*, 68.
45. Pearce, 68.
46. *Heritage Years*, 102.
47. Hoffman, 275; NTLF, Operation Plan No. 3-44.
48. Erskine interview, 342–44.
49. Wood Kyle, interviewed by Benis Frank (USMCU, 1969), 72.
50. Gene Adkins, *Where Angels Die* (n.p., 2004), 24.
51. Carl Conover interviewed by Chase Osborne, April 12, 2012, https://www.youtube.com/watch?v=SDdLvzKA6jQ, accessed November 11, 2017.
52. Ibid, 277.
53. Ibid; NTLF Operation Plan Change No. 1 to Operation Plan No. 3-44.
54. Hoffman, 278.
55. Kyle interview, 81.
56. Hoffman, 276.

CHAPTER V: OPENING MOVES

1. *We Drank Our Tears*, 175.
2. Hoffman, 35; Morison VIII, 174.
3. Barrett Tillman, *Clash of the Carriers: The True Story of the Marianas Turkey Shoot of World War II* (New York: NAL Caliber, 2005), 55.
4. Morison VIII, 174.
5. Hirakushi.
6. VT-10 Aircraft Action Reports Nos. 36-41 and 43-67, Air Operations Against the Marianas, June 11–30, 1944.
7. Shizuko Sugano (nee Miura), "The End at Saipan," translator unknown, draft manuscript c. 1959, Toland Papers, FDRL.
8. Aircraft Action Report USS *Lexington*, CAG-16 Rpt. of Attack on Marianas, June 11–19, 1944.
9. William T. Y'Blood, *Red Sun Setting: The Battle of the Philippine Sea* (Annapolis, MD: Naval Institute Press, 1981), 42.
10. USSBS Interrogations II, 429.
11. Sugano memoir.
12. W. D. Dickson, *The Battle of the Philippine Sea, June 1944* (London: Ian Allen, Ltd., 1975), 59.

13. Stephen L. Moore, *The Buzzard Brigade: Torpedo Squadron Ten at War* (Missoula, MT: Pictorial Histories Publishing Co.), 1996, 190 (hereafter *Buzzard Brigade*).

14. USS *Enterprise* Action Rpt. 3 July 1944, Commander William I. Martin, Account of Being Shot Down and Rescued at Saipan; E. T. Wooldridge (ed.), *Carrier Warfare in the Pacific: An Oral History Collection* (Washington, DC: Smithsonian Institute Press, 1993), 135; *Buzzard Brigade*, 191–98.

15. Fred Gwynn, "Torpedo 16," www.rb-29.net/HTML/81lexingtonstys/Fred GwynnSty/09.04.04gwynn.htm, accessed November 6, 2017.

16. USS *Lexington* CAG 16 Aircraft Action Rpt., June 12, 1944.

17. Ibid.

18. Robert Sherrod, *On to Westward: War in the Central Pacific* (New York: Duell, Sloan and Pearce, 1945), 42; Hoffman, 44.

19. Dickson, 53; Bob Hackett and Sander Kingsepp, "OPERATION TAN NO. 2: The Japanese Attack on Task Force 58's Anchorage at Ulithi," www.combinedfleet .com/Tan%20No.%202.htm, accessed December 10, 2017.

20. Ryonusuke Kusaka, "The Combined Fleet: Memoirs of Former Chief of Staff Kusaka," Manuscript, Toland Papers, FDRL, 65.

21. Crowl, 72–73.

22. David C. Evans, *The Japanese Navy in World War II in the Words of Former Japanese Naval Officers* (Annapolis, MD: Naval Institute Press, 1986), 310.

23. USSBS Campaigns, 21; Adm. Matome Ugaki, *Fading Victory: The Diary of Admiral Matome Ugaki* (Pittsburgh, PA: University of Pittsburgh Press, 1991), 418–19.

24. Kusaka, 113; Morison VIII, 215–16.

25. Evans, 312.

26. Hirakushi.

27. Jay Gluck, *Ukiyo: Stories of the Floating World of Post War Japan* (Ashiya, Japan: Personally Oriented, Ltd., 1963), 12.

28. Kusaka, 110.

29. USS *Redfin* Patrol report May 1944 to July 1944.

30. Y'Blood, 9.

31. Kusaka, 113.

32. *Rescue*, 261–62, 264–69; Edwin T. Layton, *And I Was There* (New York: William Morrow and Company, 1985), 485.

33. John Winton, *Ultra in the Pacific* (London: Leo Cooper, 1993), 163–64.

34. Cook and Cook, 283.

35. Ibid.

36. Hoffman, 36.

37. Cook and Cook, 283.

38. Ibid.

39. David Lippman, "Combat History on Saipan," *World War II History Magazine*, February 2014.

40. James J. Fahey, *Pacific War Diary: 1942–1945* (Boston: Houghton Mifflin Co., 1963), 166.
41. Hirakushi.
42. Hoffman, 36–37.
43. Sugano memoir.
44. Crowl, 75.
45. Ibid, 79.
46. HQ 27th Division, POW Interrogation Rpt., 14 August 1944.
47. Morison VIII, 182.
48. John T. Mason Jr. (ed.), *The Pacific War Remembered: An Oral History Collection* (Annapolis, MD: Naval Institute Press, 1986), 237; Douglas Fane and Don Moore, *The Naked Warriors* (New York: Appleton-Century-Crofts, Inc., 1956), 87.
49. Ibid, 71.
50. Elizabeth Kauffman Bush, *America's First Frogman: The Draper Kauffman Story* (Annapolis, MD: Naval Institute Press, 2004), 138; Fane, 98.
51. Fane, 95.
52. Ibid, 98.
53. Hoffman, 45.
54. Mason, 243; Bush, 133.
55. NTLF Report, G-2 Rpt. of Interrogation of POW taken from USS *Cony*, 15 June 1944.
56. Chapin memoir, 48.
57. Pamela Wood (ed.), *Fourth Marine Division* (Paducah, KY: Turner Publishing Company, 1992), 17.
58. John M. Eardley, *You'll Be Sorry: A Marine's Memoir of the War in the Pacific* (Privately published, 2009), 71.
59. Philip W. Clemmons, *Island-Hopping With L-3-6* (Knoxville, TN: Tennessee Valley Publications, 2004), 91.
60. Lane, 48.
61. James Campbell, *The Color of War* (New York: Crown Publishers, 2012), 141, 167.
62. *Heritage Years*, 92.
63. Adkins, 42.
64. Robert E. Everett Sr., *World War II: Battle of Saipan* (n.p., 1996), 4.
65. Campbell, 170.
66. Sherrod, *On to Westward*, 43.
67. Ibid, 34–39.
68. NTLF Report, G2 Rpt.
69. TF 56 Report, G-2 Periodic Rpt. No. 27.
70. Petty, *Saipan*, 37.
71. War Crimes Office Judge Advocate General's Office, Headquarters Army Garrison Force Office of the AC of S, G-2, 1 August 1944, investigation of atrocities, statement of Neratus.

CHAPTER VI: ACROSS THE REEF

1. *2nd Armored*, 102.
2. Spooner, 40.
3. Sherrod, *On to Westward*, 40.
4. *2nd Armored*, 93.
5. Clemmons, 273.
6. North, 258.
7. Sherrod, *On to Westward*, 44–45.
8. *2nd Armored*, 109.
9. Spooner, 40.
10. Sherrod, *On to Westward*, 45.
11. Clemmons, 252–53.
12. Army Life War Dept. Pamphlet 21-13, 1944.
13. Eardley, 119.
14. Sherrod, *On to Westward*, 44, 47.
15. Orvel Johnson, WWII Company C, Memories, www.c123rd.com/our-wwii-marines/johnson-orvel/memories.
16. Joseph Fiore interview, 2004, NYSMM.
17. Lane, 55.
18. Ibid, 56.
19. Despite Roush's vivid recollection, there is no record that any of the amtanks sank upon exiting an LST.
20. Roush, 399–400.
21. *2nd Armored*, 103.
22. Ibid, 102.
23. Ibid, 103.
24. Masters, 183.
25. Clemmons, 302.
26. Hoffman, 47.
27. *2nd Armored*, 109.
28. Wayne Terwilliger, *Terwilliger Bunts One* (Guilford, CT: Globe Pequot Press, 2006), 24–25.
29. *2nd Armored*, 102.
30. Ibid, 95.
31. *2nd Armored*, 92.
32. Ibid, 92–93.
33. Ibid, 94.
34. Ibid, 89.
35. Cook and Cook, 283.
36. Mitsuharu Noda interview transcript, Toland Papers, FDRL.
37. Goe, 88.
38. USS *Frederick Funston* (APA 89)—Operation Saipan—report on, 26 June 1944.

39. Sherrod, *On to Westward*, 50.

40. Hoffman, 48; NTLF Report, G-2 Rpt., Special Interrogation of Major Yoshida; the *135th Infantry* was already short its 1st Battalion which had been training on Tinian and was stranded by the U.S. landing.

41. *2nd Armored*, 95.

42. Ibid, 100.

43. Ibid, 105.

44. Ibid, 94.

45. Ibid, 90–92.

46. Recollections on 2nd Armored Battalion website, http://2ndarmoredamphibian battalion.com/saipan/.

47. *2nd Armored*, 102.

48. *Heritage Years*, 92.

49. Roush, 400.

50. Adkins, 45–46.

51. Roush, 400–401.

52. Ibid, 402.

53. Clemmons, 218–19.

54. Ibid, 253.

55. H. William Johnson, *On to Saipan* (Privately printed, 2012), 48.

56. Clemmons, 230–31.

57. Roush, 408.

58. USS *Funston* War Diary.

59. Sherrod, *On to Westward*, 50–51.

60. Stanford Joseph Slama interview, Veterans History Project, State Historical Society of North Dakota.

61. Masters, 185–88.

62. Carl W. Hoffman interview by Lt. Gen. Alpha L. Bowser, USMCU.

63. Henry P. Crowe interview by Benis Frank, 1979, USMCU.

64. Warren Jack O'Brien, Memoir, *Colorado War Stories*, August 13, 2007.

65. Hoffman interview, 36.

66. Russ Hofvendahl, "God and a Good Marine," *Leatherneck*, November 1983.

67. Hoffman, 54; Hoffman interview, 36.

68. Crowe interview.

69. Bernard Lee Riggs, "EI KIE MALINGY A Story About a Legendary Combat Intelligence Section" (n.p., 1995).

70. Frank X. Tolbert, "Crowe's Feats," *Leatherneck*, October 1944.

CHAPTER VII: FAILED *BLITZKRIEG*

1. Robert Graf, *Easy Company: My Life in the United States Marine Corps during World War II* (Self-published, 1986), 200.

2. Matthews memoir.

3. Gugeler, 49–50.

4. Graf, 200.

5. Keith Renstrom interview by Geoffrey Panos, Eccles Broadcast Center, Salt Lake City, UT.

6. Graf, 200.

7. Matthews memoir.

8. Paul K. McDevitt, *All Came Home* (Privately printed, 2015), 192; USS *Leon* Action Report, Saipan Operation, 1 July 1944.

9. Sutcliffe interview.

10. Gugeler, 6.

11. Richard H. Hicks, interview, Richard H. Hicks Collection, (AFC/2001/001/56815), Veterans History Project, American Folklife Center, Library of Congress.

12. Graf, 201.

13. "Andy Fancher Presents Carl Matthews," https://www.youtube.com/watch?v=tVPVssio9ac.

14. Matthews memoir.

15. Gugeler, 6.

16. Hoffman, 60.

17. Gugeler, 6–7; Dombrowski was awarded the Distinguished Service Cross for his efforts to save his fellow crewmembers.

18. Ibid, 16.

19. Robert T. Webster Jr. interview, Robert T. Webster Jr. Collection (AFC/2001/001/66330), Veterans History Project, American Folklife Center, Library of Congress.

20. Hoffman, 55.

21. Gugeler, 9.

22. Sgt. Bill Dvorak, "Marine Captain Leads Assault Group on Saipan," undated newspaper clipping.

23. James A. Hatcher, "Herbert Lewis Kiser: An American Life Well Lived," 2013, http://jeff560.tripod.com/kiser.html.

24. Bernard Nalty, *The Right to Fight: African-American Marines in World War II* (Washington, DC: Marine Corps Historical Center, 1995), 20; Kenneth Tibbs, "Understanding Sacrifice," an ABMC and NCA Education Project, https://abmc education.org/understandingsacrifice/soldier/kenneth-tibbs.

25. Donald Boots interview by Dr., Ronald E. Marcello. May 17, 2001, University of North Texas Oral History Collection Number 1405, 96.

26. Gugeler, 10–11.

27. Lane, 58.

28. Ibid, 57.

29. Renstrom interview; Henry Berry, *Semper Fi, Mac: Living Memories of the U.S. Marines in World War II* (New York: Arbor House, 1982), 216.

30. Griffin, Navy Cross Citation.

31. Jeff Smith, "Decorated Marine Veteran Honored in 9-11 Ceremony at California Base," *Sentinel-Record* (Hot Springs, AR), November 11, 2010.
32. Lane, 59.
33. Ibid, 59, 104.
34. Wood, *Fourth Marine Division*, 46.
35. Lane, 57; Hoffman, 59.
36. Graves Erskine later said, "I have always felt that if they had pushed a little harder we would have been in a much better position in the early phase of that operation," though he conceded, "But we might have lost many amtracs on the deal." (Erskine interview, 186)
37. Hoffman, 59.
38. Ibid, 7–8.
39. Ibid, 14–15.
40. Lane, 62.
41. Eardley, 122.
42. Adkins, 52.
43. Berry, 217.
44. Sutcliffe interview.
45. Bob Cary, *Fear Was Never an Option* (Westminster, MD: Heritage Books, Inc., 2005), 138.

CHAPTER VIII: INTO THE MAELSTROM

1. William Curran, "Saipan Remembered," *Leatherneck*, June 1984.
2. Hugh Lessy, "Saved by Wounded Comrade," *Daily Press Newport News*, July 3, 2011.
3. Jack Powell, "Remember Our Sacrifice at Saipan," *Birmingham* (AL) *News*, June 12, 1994.
4. Sherrod, *On to Westward*, 55, 77; Hoffman, 53.
5. William K. Jones, "The Battle of Saipan-Tinian," *Marine Corps Gazette*, June 1988.
6. Edward F. Bailey memoir.
7. Jack Pepper, "Saipan Is a Story of Mortar Shells, Foxholes and Dead Buddies," *Daily Oklahoman*, August 13, 1944.
8. Jones, "Battle of Saipan-Tinian."
9. Edward F. Bailey memoir.
10. *2nd Armored*, 105, 108.
11. Hoffman, 65.
12. Roush, 404.
13. Roush, 404–5; Keiningham Silver Star Citation, General Orders: Commanding General, Fleet Marine Force Pacific: Serial 22939.
14. William Hoover Memoir, 2nd Armored Amphibian Battalion, William B. Hoover Collection (AFC/2001/001/24397), Veterans History Project, American Folklife Center, Library of Congress.

15. NTLF Report, G-2 Ser. 0024A.

16. Cook and Cook, 284.

17. Michael H. Rogers (ed.), *Answering Their Country's Call: Marylanders in World War II* (The Johns Hopkins University Press: Baltimore, 2002), 154.

18. O'Sheel, 50–51.

19. Task Group 52.2 War Diary, Report of Saipan Operation, June 14–July 9, 1944 (henceforth TG-52.2).

20. Shaw, 269.

21. Hoffman, 69.

22. Special Action Report, 23rd Marines Saipan.

23. Masters, 187–90.

24. USS *Bolivar* Action Report—Saipan, 15–22 June 1944.

25. Carl Bertil Carlson interview, State Historical Society of North Dakota.

26. Harold Banks (ed.), *Second Marine Division 1940–1999* (Paducah, KY: Turner Publishing Company, 1999), 37–38.

27. Mason, 243; Bush, 134.

28. Gilbert, 145.

29. Robert M. Neiman and Kenneth W. Estes, *Tanks on the Beaches: A Marine Tanker in the Pacific War* (College Station: Texas A&M University Press, 2003), 95–97.

30. Hoffman, 61–62.

31. NTLF Report, G-2 Rpt. Serial 0634A; Crowl, 93; 4th Marine Division Operations Rpt., G-2.

32. *Buzzard Brigade*, 200.

33. Harper, 13, 57–58.

34. Ibid, 59–60.

35. Harper, 60–61.

36. Hoffman, 66.

37. Crowl, 92.

38. Chapin, 2.

39. Sherrod, *On to Westward*, 59–61.

40. Hoffman, 70–71; Shaw, 271.

41. Crowl, 90.

42. Hoffman, 68.

43. Ibid.

44. USS *Enterprise* Aircraft Action Report VF(N) 101, 1 July 1944.

45. USS *Lexington* War Diary, 1–30 June, 1944, account of Japanese shore based aircraft attack on Task Group 58.3, June 15, 1944.

46. Henry Murowsky, Henry Stanley Murowsky Collection, (AFC/2001/001/65284), Veterans History Project, American Folklife Center, Library of Congress.

47. Everett, 5.

48. Sherrod, *On to Westward*, 22.

CHAPTER IX: UNDER THE GUN

1. Crowl, 95.
2. Hoffman, 76.
3. Cook and Cook, 284–85.
4. Roush, 409.
5. Ibid.
6. Warren Smith interview by Paul Loeffler, September 13, 2014, *Hometown Heroes* radio show.
7. Petty, *Saipan*, 106.
8. Sutcliffe interview.
9. Cary, 146.
10. Dwayne Epstein, *Lee Marvin: Point Blank* (Tucson, AZ: Schaffner Press, 2013), 49.
11. Tibor Torok, *Stepping Stones Across the Pacific: A Collection of Short Stories from the Pacific War* (New York: Vantage Press, 1999), 15.
12. Thomas J. Smith interview, New York State Military Museum, Saratoga Springs, NY.
13. Harry Toland, *Ben's Will* (n.p.: Furness Press, 1998), 116–18.
14. *Heritage Years*, 93–94.
15. Ibid.
16. Ibid, 94.
17. Hoffman, 72.
18. Jack Keiningham Navy Cross citation.
19. Crowl, 96.
20. Cook and Cook, 285–86.
21. Sugano memoir.
22. Harry S. Bowman Navy Cross citation; Hoffman, 73.
23. Hoffman, 73.
24. Frank Borta, Oral History Monologue, National Museum of the Pacific War, Fredericksburg, TX, Digital Archive (henceforth Borta interview); Petty, *Saipan*, 100; Campbell, 183–84.
25. Chapin memoir, 58.
26. Harry Toland, *Ben's Will*, 118–19; Ben Toland eventually returned to his unit. He was killed on Iwo Jima.
27. Westfall, 60, 66.
28. *Heritage Years*, 94.
29. Roush, 432–33.
30. Hoffman, 279; NTLF Report, G-2.
31. Ugaki, 400.
32. Morison VIII, 231.
33. 27 Div. G-3 Forager Journal, June 16; USS *Flying Fish*, Report of Tenth War Patrol, 5 July, 1944.

34. Morison VIII, 237–40.
35. Thomas Buell, *The Quiet Warrior: A Biography of Admiral Raymond A. Spruance* (Boston: Little Brown and Company, 1974), 262.
36. Ibid, 263.
37. Chambers, 80–81.
38. Gilbert, 149.
39. Ibid, 149–51; Neiman, 100–102.
40. Garland Dankworth interview by author.
41. Edward Bollard interview by author.
42. Dankworth interview.
43. McCard was awarded the Medal of Honor for sacrificing himself in an effort to save his crew.
44. Chambers memoir, 83–84.
45. Lane, 68.
46. Ibid, 66.
47. John C. Pope, *Angel on My Shoulder* (Privately printed, 2013).
48. Sherrod, *On to Westward*, 64.
49. Goe, 97.
50. USS *Knox* (APA-46) Action Report: Amphibious Operation—Saipan.
51. Eli Silverman interview, *Combat Stories from World War II, Witness to War*, www.witnesstowar.org/combat_stories/WWII/543.
52. Wells, 132–33.
53. Emil L. Bonnot, "The USS *Fremont* and the Invasion of Saipan," www.uss fremont.org/bonnot.html.
54. Lane, 104.
55. Hatcher, "Herbert Lewis Kiser."
56. USS *Monrovia* Rpt. Operations Saipan.

CHAPTER X: TANKS!

1. Pope, *Angel on My Shoulder.*
2. Matthews memoir.
3. Borta interview; Campbell, 192; Petty, *Saipan*, 101.
4. Donald B. McLean, *Japanese Tanks, Tactics & Antitank Weapons* (Wickenburg, AZ: Paramount Technical Publications, 1973).
5. Hoffman, 87; Hirakushi.
6. Hoffman, 91.
7. Powell, "Remember Our Sacrifice"; Hoffman, 89.
8. Ibid.
9. NTLF Report, Annex Able to NTLF Memorandum 9-44.
10. Powell, "Remember Our Sacrifice."
11. H. M. Mason, "Patrol in Paradise," *Leatherneck*, October 2001.
12. Hoffman, 89.

13. Ibid.
14. Ibid.
15. "Saipan D Day Plus 2," *Leatherneck*, September 1944.
16. Silcox, 98.
17. James A. Donovan Jr., "Saipan Tank Battle," *Marine Corps Gazette*, October 1944; Herbert J. Hodges Navy Cross citation; Johnston, 121; Jack Pepper, "Ingenious Marine Finds Sure Way of Ripping Tank," *Miami Oklahoma Daily News Record*, July 21, 1944.
18. Hoffman, 90.
19. Donovan.
20. NTLF Report.
21. William Curran, "Saipan Remembered," *Leatherneck*, June 1984.
22. Lewis Michelony interview by John Daniels, May 2, 1993, University of North Texas Oral History Collection, Denton, TX.
23. William Jefferies, Recollections on website "Tarawa Talk," September 20, 2008.
24. *Heritage Years*, 110.
25. Hoffman, 90.
26. Powell, "Remember Our Sacrifice."
27. Hoffman, 90; Donovan.
28. Hoffman, 90.
29. Clemmons, 187.
30. *Heritage Years*, 110.
31. Hirakushi.
32. NTLF Report, G-2 Periodic Rpt. No. 3, 17 June 1944; TF-56 Report; the estimate of twenty-nine tanks destroyed is probably on the high side.
33. Eardley, 126.
34. Mason, "Patrol in Paradise."
35. Curran, "Saipan Remembered."
36. Sherrod, *On to Westward*, 68.
37. *Coral & Brass*, 164; Hoffman, 85.
38. Gailey, 35–42.
39. Erskine interview, 319.
40. Marshall, 62.
41. Gailey, 48.
42. Love, 116; Gailey, 106–7; Crowl, 41–42.
43. Francis A. O'Brien, *Battling for Saipan* (New York: Ballantine Books, 2003), 87.
44. O'Brien, 88–92; Hoffman, 86.
45. Alexander Vraciu interview by Ronald E. Marcello, October 9, 1994, Admiral Nimitz Foundation and University of North Texas Oral History Collection, 69–70.
46. Roscoe, 381; Y'Blood, 75.
47. Y'Blood, 83.
48. USSBS Campaigns, 212.

49. Y'Blood, 61; Adm. J. J. Clark, "The Marianas Turkey Shoot," in Stephen W. Sears, *Eyewitness to World War II: The Best of American Heritage* (Boston: Houghton Mifflin Company, 1991), 195–96.
50. Clark, 195.
51. Ibid, 195–96.
52. Ibid, 193–96; Y'Blood, 61; Taylor, *The Magnificent Mitscher* (Annapolis, MD: Naval Institute Press, 1954), 212–13.

CHAPTER XI: TOWARD THE AIRFIELD

1. Orvel Johnson memoir.
2. Wood, *Fourth Marine Division*, 60.
3. Edwin J. Donley interview, Edwin John Donley Collection (AFC/2001/001/56648), Veterans History Project, American Folklife Center, Library of Congress.
4. Keith Rogers, "Veterans Parade Highlights Vegas Patriotism," *Las Vegas Review-Journal*, November 5, 2014; 4th Mar Div Ops, Special Action Rpt., Fourth Tank Battalion, 20 August 1944.
5. Borta interview; Petty, *Saipan*, 101.
6. Everett, 14.
7. Richard J. Lynes Navy Cross citation.
8. Campbell, 213.
9. Jesse Boyce Holleman interview by Orley B. Caudill, University of Southern Mississippi Libraries Oral History, 1976; USS *Gambier Bay*, VC-10 Aircraft Action Rpt., June 17, 1944.
10. Sherrod, *On to Westward*, 68.
11. 4th Mar Div Ops, Annex B (Intelligence).
12. Love, 155; Crowl, 101–6; Hoffman, 95.
13. Hoffman, 95.
14. David Moore, "The Battle of Saipan—The Final Curtain," 2003, www.battleofsaipan.com/seabee.htm.
15. *Coral & Brass*, 183.
16. Jeffrey M. Moore, *Spies for Nimitz: Joint Military Intelligence in the Pacific War* (Annapolis, MD: Naval Institute Press, 2004), 110; Edwin T. Layton, *And I Was There* (New York: William Morrow and Company, 1985), 487.
17. NTLF Report, G-2.
18. Silcox, 99.
19. Goe, 104.
20. Sherrod, *On to Westward*, 72.
21. Ibid, 99.
22. Sugano; Toland, *Rising Sun*, 619–21.
23. Ibid.

24. USSBS Interrogations I, 10; Evans, 319.

25. Evans, 314.

26. Morison VIII, 233.

27. Potter, *Nimitz*, 299; Evans, 305; Y'Blood, 73.

28. Morison VIII, 232.

29. Y'Blood, 74.

30. USSBS, Campaigns, 263.

31. Mark D. Tate, "Operation Forager: Air Power in the Campaign for Saipan," master's degree thesis, U.S. Army Command and General Staff College, (Fort Leavenworth, KS, 1995), 41; Evans, 13; USSBS, 7–8; Morison, 235.

32. James F. Dunnigan and Albert A. Nofi, *Victory at Sea: World War II in the Pacific* (New York: William Morrow and Company, Inc., 1995), 50–52.

33. Y'Blood, 24–25.

34. Dickson, 54–55; Y'Blood, 64–65.

35. Buell, *Quiet Warrior*, 267; Y'Blood, 78; TF-58 Report, Enclosure B.

36. Buell, *Quiet Warrior*, 264; Mason, 209.

37. Sherrod, *On to Westward*, 116.

38. USS *Cavalla* (SS 244), Report of War Patrol Number One, 3 August 1944.

39. Capt. Walter Karig, *Battle Report: The End of an Empire* (New York: Rinehart and Company, Inc., 1948), 235.

40. Chambers, 87.

41. Robert E. Tierney, "My Marine Corps Experience," https://www.ancestry.com/mediaui-viewer/tree/33605091/person/18502464331/.

CHAPTER XII: A GATHERING OF EAGLES

1. Albert J. Harris Interview, Oral History Collection, NYSMM.

2. E. B. Potter, *Admiral Arleigh Burke: A Biography* (New York: Random House, 1990), 141.

3. Mason, 210; Buell, *Quiet Warrior*, 267–69; *Rescue*, 261–62.

4. Morison VIII, 244; Taylor, 218.

5. USSBS Interrogations I, 11; Y'Blood, 74; Morison 244.

6. Mason, 211; Y'Blood, 82, 90; Vice Adm. E. P. Forrestel, *Admiral Raymond A. Spruance, USN: A Study in Command* (Washington, DC: U.S. Government Printing Office. 1966), 137.

7. Y'Blood, 83.

8. TF-56 Report, Medical Rpt., 9 September 1944.

9. Report of Operations of USS *Sheridan* during Amphibious Assault on Saipan (Medical).

10. War Diary, USS *Solace*, June 1, 1944 to June 30, 1944.

11. Jan K. Herman, *Battle Station Sick Bay: Navy Medicine in World War II* (Annapolis, MD: Naval Institute Press, 1997), 171.

12. *Heritage Years*, 101–2.

13. Hirakushi.
14. Action Report of USS LCI (G) 458, Marianas Operation, Saipan.
15. War Diary LCI (G) Flotilla Three, 12 August 1944.
16. NTLF Report, G-2 Rpt.
17. Hoffman, 101.
18. Love, 154–55; Crowl, 112.
19. 27th Division, G-3 Journal, June 18, 1944.
20. NTLF Report, G-2 Summary, Enclosure D.
21. Francis O'Brien, 105.
22. 27th Division, G-2 Journal, Periodic Rpts., 44, 45; Petty, *Saipan*, 144.
23. Hoffman, 108.
24. Hoffman, 104.
25. Hoffman, 101; Crowl, 116–17.
26. Crowl, 117.
27. Ibid; Shaw, 295.
28. Shaw, 292.
29. Ibid.
30. Hoffman, 101.
31. Ibid, 107.
32. Arthur E. Abney, *Wings Over Illinois* (Carbondale: Southern Illinois University Press, 2007), 49.
33. Ibid, 49–50.
34. Tillman, *Clash of Carriers*, 94; *Buzzard Brigade*, 202.
35. Ibid.
36. Tillman, *Clash of Carriers*, 109.
37. Tillman, *Clash of Carriers*, 95; Y'Blood, 83.
38. Y'Blood, 84–85.
39. Evans, 321; Toland, *Rising Sun*, 626; Y'Blood, 85–86.
40. Tillman, *Clash of Carriers*, 102; USSBS Interrogations I, 10–11; Y'Blood, 87.
41. Ikuhiko Hata and Yashuho Zawa, *Japanese Naval Aces and Fighter Units in World War II* (Annapolis, MD: Naval Institute Press, 1989), 178–79.
42. Evans, 317; Y'Blood, 87, 97–98.
43. Morison VIII, 219.
44. Dickson, 79.
45. Potter, *Nimitz*, 300; Tillman, *Clash of Carriers*, 96.
46. Forrestel, 137.
47. Mason, *Pacific War Remembered*, 211; Wooldridge, 161–63; Forrestel, 132.
48. Buell, *Quiet Warrior*, 270; Forrestel, 137–38.
49. Taylor, 219–22; Y'Blood, 93; Morison VIII, 252; CinPac Monthly Analysis, June 1944, 81.
50. Taylor, 222; Potter, *Admiral Arleigh Burke*, 151.
51. Tillman, *Clash of Carriers*, 108.
52. Ibid, 126.

53. Abney, 50–51, 125–26; Y'Blood, 94–95; VP-16 War Diary, 30 June 1944.
54. Y'Blood, 95.
55. Ibid, 102–3.
56. Ibid, 103.
57. Ibid, 103–4.
58. Gluck, 12–14.
59. Ibid, 303.
60. Armoured Aircraft Carriers in World War II (www.armouredcarriers.com/japanese-aircraft-carrier-taiho-armoured-flight-decks/).
61. Morison VIII, 280.
62. Roscoe, 382–84; USS *Albacore* Report of Ninth War Patrol; Morison, 278–80.
63. Eric Hammel, *Aces Against Japan II* (Pacifica, CA: Pacifica Press, 1996), 202.
64. Ibid, 204; Aircraft Action Report, Air Group 15, USS *Essex*, June 19, 1944.

CHAPTER XIII: SHOWDOWN

1. Y'Blood, 104–5.
2. Hammel, *Aces II*, 209–10.
3. Aircraft Action Report, VF-15, June 19, 1944.
4. Ibid; Y'Blood, 108–9.
5. Thomas Cleaver, *Fabled Fifteen: The Pacific Saga of Carrier Air Group 15* (Philadelphia: Casemate Publishers, 2014), 102–3; Aircraft Action Report, VF-15, June 19, 1944.
6. Air Group 15 Aircraft Action Report, June 19, 1944; VF-15 Aircraft Action Report; Tillman, *Clash of Carriers.*
7. Hammel, *Aces II*, 210.
8. Eric Hammel, *Aces Against Japan I* (New York, Pocket Books, 1992), 220–22.
9. Y'Blood, 112.
10. Aircraft Action Report, Air Group 25, June 19, 1944.
11. USS *Cowpens*, Report of Actions During the Period 6 June 1944 to 6 July 1944.
12. Hammel, *Aces II*, 210–11.
13. Y'Blood, 115–17; VF-15 Aircraft Action Report June 19, 1944.
14. Vraciu interview, 73–74.
15. Ibid, 74.
16. Ibid, 75.
17. Tillman, *Clash of Carriers*, 165, 173.
18. Hammel, *Aces II*, 207–8.
19. USS *Yorktown* Report of Operations in Support of the Occupation of the Marianas, June 3, 1944 to July 21, 1944, ACA Reports; Y'Blood, 121.
20. *Yorktown* Report.
21. Ibid.
22. Cleaver, 107.

23. *Yorktown* Report.
24. Ibid.
25. Ibid.
26. Ibid.
27. Y'Blood, 123–25.
28. USS *Bunker Hill* War Diary, June 1944; Y'Blood, 125–26.
29. Y'Blood, 119–20.
30. *Yorktown* Report; Tillman, *Clash of Carriers*, 173–74.
31. Kusaka, 112; Toland, *Rising Sun*, 606.
32. Kusaka, 137–38.
33. Kusaka, 127; Toland, *Rising Sun*, 627.
34. Gluck, 14.
35. USS *Cavalla* Report; Sherrod, *On to Westward*, 117–18.
36. Sherrod, *On to Westward*, 118.
37. Anthony Tully, Jon Parshall, and Richard Wolff, "The Sinking of Shokaku— An Analysis," www.combinedfleet.com/shoksink.htm.
38. *Cavalla* Report.
39. Tully, "Sinking of Shokaku."
40. Ibid.
41. Ibid.
42. Gluck, 15.
43. Sherrod, *On to Westward*, 118.
44. Roscoe, 381–82.
45. Y'Blood, 130; Tillman, *Clash of Carriers*, 176.
46. Tillman, *Clash of Carriers*, 179.
47. Tillman, *Clash of Carriers*, 180–81; USS *Wasp* Anti-Aircraft Action Summary—19 June 1944.
48. Hammel, *Aces I*, 230–33.
49. Ibid, 232.
50. Ibid, 233.
51. Aircraft Action Report, USS *Hornet*, June 19, 1944.
52. Y'Blood, 137–38.
53. Hammel, *Aces I*, 230–35; Tillman, *Clash of Carriers*, 185.
54. Hideo Kobayashi, "Sinking of the Aircraft Carrier *Taiho* Caused by One Hit of a Torpedo," Tokyo Institute of Technology, 2005, www.shippai.org/fkd/en/hfen/ HB1011023.pdf, 1–3.
55. Toland, *Rising Sun*, 628–29.
56. Y'Blood, 127–29.
57. Morison VIII, 132.
58. Morison, 281–82; Kobayashi.
59. Tillman, *Clash of Carriers*, 195, 198–99.
60. Ibid, 194; Y'Blood, 128.
61. Tillman, *Clash of Carriers*, 196.

62. Evans, 324–25.
63. Ibid, 326.
64. Wooldridge, 164; Y'Blood, 139.

CHAPTER XIV: MISSION INTO DARKNESS

1. Buell, *Quiet Warrior*, 275; Mason, *Pacific War Remembered*, 213; Forrestel, 140.
2. Morison VIII, 287; Evans, 325; Y'Blood, 142–43; USSBS Interrogations I, 9.
3. Y'Blood, 143.
4. Aircraft Action Reports, Form ACA-1, of the Commanding Officer of CAG-16 (Rescue of F6F Pilot After Water Landing).
5. *Buzzard Brigade*, 206.
6. Ibid, 205; Aircraft Action Report, VT-10, June 20, 1944.
7. J. Bryan and Philip Reed, *Mission Beyond Darkness* (New York: Duell, Sloan and Pearce, 1945), 3; Y'Blood, 147.
8. Y'Blood, 145.
9. Ibid, 145–46.
10. *Buzzard Brigade*, 206–7; Tillman, *Clash of Carriers*, 207–8; Y'Blood, 147–48.
11. Narrative by Lt. Nelson, June 20, 1944, VT-10 Aircraft Action Reports.
12. Y'Blood, 150.
13. Bryan, 15.
14. Ibid, 16.
15. Ronald Drez, *Twenty-Five Yards of War* (New York: Hyperion, 2001), 155.
16. Bryan, 17–22.
17. *Buzzard Brigade*, 205.
18. Y'Blood, 150–51.
19. Bryan, 23; Taylor, 233; Y'Blood, 151.
20. James Ramage and Don Gordon, "Operation Forager: The Marianas Campaign," CV6.ORG, www.cv6.org/1944/marianas.
21. Y'Blood, 151.
22. *Buzzard Brigade*, 207.
23. Y'Blood, 150.
24. Ibid, 152–53.
25. Tillman, *Clash of Carriers*, 212.
26. Aircraft Action Report, VT-24, USS *Belleau Wood*, June 20, 1944.
27. War Diary, USS *Bunker Hill*, June 1944.
28. Aircraft Action Report, USS *Belleau Wood*; Y'Blood, 161–63.
29. Toland, *Rising Sun*, 630.
30. Statement of Ens. M. H. Barr, Aircraft Action Report, USS *Belleau Wood*, June 20, 1944.
31. Bryan, 29.
32. Ibid, 31.
33. Wooldridge, 177–78.

34. Y'Blood, 169.
35. Ramage.
36. *Buzzard Brigade*, 212; Aircraft Action Report, VT-10, Narrative of Lt. (j.g.) Lawton, June 20, 1944.
37. Eason survived; *Buzzard Brigade*, 214; Lawton narrative.
38. Bryan, 49.
39. Ramage.
40. Bryan, 50–51.
41. Harold Buell, *Dauntless Helldivers: A Dive-Bomber Pilot's Epic Story of the Carrier Battles* (New York: Dell Publishing, 1991), 297–300.
42. Morison VIII, 298.
43. Gluck, 16.
44. Ibid, 16–17.
45. USSBS, Campaigns, 245–46.
46. Y'Blood, 154.
47. Bryan, 51–57; Observations of Flight Personnel Rescued from Locality of Action, CAG 16, USS *Lexington* Aircraft Action Report, June 20, 1944; Experience of Lt. (j.g.) Warren E. McLellan of Torpedo Squadron Sixteen, CAG 16, June 20, 1944; The Warren McLellan Story, www.rb-29.net/HTML/81lexingtonstys/05.01mclellan.htm.

CHAPTER XV: WINNERS AND LOSERS

1. Aircraft Action Report, USS *Belleau Wood*, June 20, 1944.
2. Vraciu interview.
3. Bryan, 32–33, 57–58, 61.
4. Gluck, 17.
5. Anthony Tully, "Last Hours of Aircraft Carrier *Hiyo*: A Look at Discrepancies," 1997, www.combinedfleet.com/atully02.htm.
6. Toland, *Rising Sun*, 630.
7. Tully, "Last Hours of Aircraft Carrier *Hiyo*."
8. Gluck, 17–18.
9. USS *Bunker Hill*, Report of Air Attack on Japanese Task Force on June 20, 1944.
10. Y'Blood, 179.
11. Bryan, 63–64.
12. Peter Mersky, *The Grim Reapers: Fighting Squadron Ten in WWII* (Mesa, AZ: Champlin Museum Press, 1986), 92.
13. Taylor, 234; Y'Blood, 180.
14. Bryan, 73.
15. Buell, *Dauntless Helldivers*, 301–4.
16. Ramage.
17. VT-10 Aircraft Action Report June 20, 1944, Lawton Narrative.
18. Ibid; *Buzzard Brigade*, 216.

19. Ibid, 80–81; CAG-16 Aircraft Action Report, June 20, 1944.
20. Buell, *Dauntless Helldivers*; Bryan, 75–78.
21. USS *San Jacinto*, Action Report: Operations against Saipan, Tinian, and Guam, June 10, 1944; Y'Blood, 188.
22. Bryan, 86–87, 92.
23. Ibid, 194–95.
24. Wooldridge, 185; Ramage.
25. USSBS Interrogations I, 10; Y'Blood, 177–78.
26. Y'Blood, 193.
27. Bryan, 118.
28. Mersky, 93.
29. Ibid, 118–21; Warren McLellan Story; the aircraft McLellan mentions may have been a U.S. PBM.
30. *Buzzard Brigade*, 220–23; VT-10 Aircraft Action Reports, Narrative of Lt. Nelson, June 21, 1944.
31. *Buzzard Brigade*, 223.
32. Y'Blood, 194–97.
33. Bryan, 121–26; McLellan Story.
34. Elmont Waite, "Five American Fliers Saved: Airmen Parachuted Down in Midst of Jap Fleet in Pacific," *Ardmore* (OK) *Daily Ardmoreite*, June 28, 1944.
35. Statement of Ens. M. H. Barr, Aircraft Action Report, USS *Belleau Wood*, June 20, 1944.
36. USS *Eaton*, Report of Action(s) in Saipan-Tinian Area, 20–24 June; USS *Eaton* War Diary, June 1–30, 1944; TF-56 Report, G-2 Periodic Report, No. 10, 24 June 1944.
37. Y'Blood, 193; Sharp did not survive the war. Shot down October 12, 1944, in an air attack on enemy installations on Formosa, he and his radioman, James R. Langiotti, drifted ashore in their raft. Captured by the Japanese, they were subsequently executed.
38. Buell, *Quiet Warrior*, 277; Taylor, 237.
39. Dickson, 175.
40. Commander in Chief, U.S. Pacific Fleet and Pacific Ocean Areas, Operations in Pacific Ocean Areas—June 1944; Potter, *Nimitz*, 303.
41. Ibid; Buell, *Quiet Warrior*, 180; Morison VIII, 315; Y'Blood, 205.
42. Buell, *Quiet Warrior*, 280.
43. Kusaka, 128.
44. Y'Blood, 203–13; Morison VIII, 319.
45. Toland, 576.

CHAPTER XVI: DEAD MEN, FLIES, AND THIRST

1. Josh McAuliffe, "Despite Injuries, Blakely Marine Officer Kept Leading Men into WWII Battles," *Times Tribune* (Scranton, PA), June 30, 2013.
2. Chambers, 118.

3. Joint Expeditionary Force (TF 51), Office of the Commander, Report of Amphibious Operations for the Capture of the Marianas Islands (Saipan Operation), August 25, 1944.

4. Domanowski, Recollections.

5. Samuel Dinova interview, New York State Military Museum Oral History Collection.

6. Letter home from Luther Hammond, August 15, 1944, O'Brien Papers, NYSMM.

7. Domanowski, Recollections.

8. Dinova interview.

9. Love, 221–22; Crowl, 137.

10. Love, 160–66.

11. Sgt. Gilbert Bailey, "Battle for Saipan Was a Test of Yanks' Courage, Endurance," *Palladium-Item* (Richmond, IN), July 13, 1944.

12. Chapin memoir, 97.

13. Report of Intelligence Activities, 27th Division, Saipan Operation, G-2 Journal, July 1, 1944.

14. Harper, 66–68.

15. Renstrom interview; Berry, 217.

16. Matthews memoir.

17. Hoffman, 114.

18. NTLF Report, G2 Serial 0024A; Hoffman, 110–11.

19. Chambers, 91–92.

20. Ibid, 92.

21. Wood, *Fourth Marine Division*, 20.

22. Chambers, 93.

23. Wood, *Fourth Marine Division*, 20.

24. Chambers, 93.

25. NTLF Report, G-2.

26. Harper, 73.

27. Petty, *Saipan*, 18–19.

28. Report of Intelligence Activities, 27th Division, G2 Periodic Report. No. 19.

29. Frank Waldron, interview, NYSMM.

30. Beatrice Trefalt, "After the Battle for Saipan: the Internment of Japanese Civilians at Camp Susupe, 1944–1946," *Japanese Studies, Vol. 29, Issue 3*, 2009, 337–52.

31. Petty, *Saipan*, 159.

32. 318th Fighter Group at Saipan, http://home.earthlink.net/~atdouble/~318th FighterGroup.Saipan.html.

33. Chapin memoir, 96.

34. Albert J. Harris interview, NYSMM.

35. Howard Handleman, "Order Succeeds Chaos as Men Force Jap Surrender at Saipan," *Palladium-Item* (Richmond, IN), Aug. 9, 1944.

36. Perry memoir.

37. Chapin memoir, 97–98.
38. Ibid.
39. NTLF Report G-2, 19 June 1944.
40. Perry memoir.
41. Gail Chatfield, *By Dammit, We're Marines!* (San Diego, CA: Merthvin Publishing, 2008), 70.
42. Orvel Johnson memoir.
43. Borta interview; Petty, *Saipan*, 102–3.
44. Everett, 30.
45. Ibid, 11–12.
46. Cary, 172.
47. Vincent Perrone, Transcript of Diary, USS *Fremont*, www.ussfremont.org/diaries.html.
48. Cary, 173–74.
49. USSBS Campaigns, Mobile Fleet Classified No. 1048 (5 September 1944), Detailed Battle Report of Ago Operations; Drea, 192–93.
50. Toland, *Rising Sun*, 631–32.
51. Kase, 73–74.
52. Anthony Tully, *Battle of Surigao Strait* (Bloomington: Indiana University Press, 2014), 34–35.
53. Kase, 74.
54. Evans, 330–32.
55. Translation by D-2 Section, 4th Marine Division, of a diary received at hospital, NTLF, June 27, 1944.
56. Love, 172–73.
57. Ibid, 173.
58. Ibid, 168–69.
59. Hoffman, 121.
60. NTLF Report, G-2 Periodic Report, June 21, 1944.
61. Love, 187; Gailey, 139; Crowl, 149.
62. Gailey, 144–45.
63. Ibid, 140.
64. Gailey, 145–46; Hoffman, 131; Love, 194–95.
65. Hoffman, 133.
66. NTLF Report, G-2 Serial 0024A.
67. Hoffman, 120.
68. NTLF Report, G-2 Periodic Report, 20–21 June 1944.
69. Capt. Frederic A. Stott, *Saipan Under Fire* (Andover, MA: Self-published, 1945).
70. Hoffman, 126.
71. Chambers, 96.
72. Ibid.
73. Michael Blankfort, *The Big Yankee: The Life of Carlson of the Raiders* (Boston: Little, Brown and Company, 1947), 341; Sgt. Ellsworth Shiebler, "Youth's Life Saved by Col. Carlson," *Marine Corps Chevron*, September 23, 1944.

74. Howard Kerr interview, Howard Matthew Kerr Collection (AFC/2001/001/65492), Veterans History Project, American Folklife Center, Library of Congress.

75. "First Battalion, 24th Marines: The History of the Men of 1/24 in World War II and Beyond," https://1stbattalion24thmarines.com/the-battles/saipan/saipan.

CHAPTER XVII: HOLLAND SMITH VS. THE ARMY

1. Gailey, 161.

2. Maj. Charles H. Hallden, "The Operations of Company L, 3rd Battalion, 106th Infantry (27th Infantry Division) in the Battle of Death Valley, Saipan, 23 June–28 June 1944 (Western Pacific Campaign. Personal Experience of a Company Commander)," n.d., 7–8; Crowl, 172.

3. Chambers, 100–101.

4. Love, 228.

5. Crowl, 173; Love, 228–30.

6. Shaw, 313–14; Maj. Martin E. Nolan, "The Operations of the 3d Battalion, 165th Infantry (27th Infantry Division) in the Assault of the Eastern Slopes of the Mt. Tapotchau Hill Mass, Saipan, Marianas Islands, 24–28 June 1944 Central Pacific Theater (Personal experience of a Battalion Operations Officer)," Advanced Infantry Officers Course 1949–50, Staff Department, The Infantry School, Fort Benning, GA, n.d., 9.

7. Ibid, 167.

8. Crowl, 176–77.

9. Love, 231–32, 235–38.

10. Roy Edgar Appleman, "Army Tanks in the Battle for Saipan," n.p., 1945, U.S. Army Heritage and Education Center, Carlisle, PA, 34.

11. Ibid, 34–35.

12. Erskine, 322.

13. Francis O'Brien, 128–29; Gailey, 142, 154–56; Love, 655; Crowl, 151; Hoffman, 122–23, 132.

14. Robert E. Hogaboom, Interviewed by Benis Frank, 1972, USMCU, 208–9.

15. Gailey, 175.

16. Ibid, 175–76; *Coral & Brass*, 173–74; Love, 246; Crowl, 178.

17. *Coral & Brass*, 171–72; Gailey, 176; Cooper, 178; Hoffman, 135–36; Crowl, 179.

18. Crowl, 178; Gailey, 180; Hoffman 144; NTLF Report, Dispatch, 24 June 1944.

19. Special Action Report, 25th Marines.

20. TF-56 Report.

21. Hoffman, 141.

22. Ibid, 148.

23. NTLF Report, G-2 Report.

24. Evans, 331.

25. Haruko Taya Cook, "The Meaning of 'Saipan' in Creating Japanese War Memory: The Use and Abuse of a Wartime Myth," Northern Marianas Humanities Council, May 19, 2015, https://www.youtube.com/watch?v=JGiP9W1-a6M.
26. Drea, 193.
27. Love, 243–44.
28. Love, 243–44; Hallden, 11–12; Crowl, 179–80.
29. Love, 253–54.
30. Journal Forager Operation, G-3 (27th Division), June 24, 1944; Crowl, 181; Headquarters 106th Infantry Forager Operations Report, June 24, 1944; Gailey, 186; Cooper, 178.
31. Love, 254.
32. Hallden, 15.
33. Love, 254–55; Crowl, 184.
34. Love, 257–58.
35. Crowl, 186.
36. Cooper, 179.
37. Gailey, 190; Love, 263.
38. *Coral & Brass*, 172–73; Gailey, 180–83.
39. Buell, *Quiet Warrior*, 283.
40. Ibid, 281–86; Venzon, 106–8.
41. Gailey, 188.
42. Love, 263–64.
43. Gailey, 190.
44. Ibid, 189, 191; Love, 264.
45. Gailey, 191.
46. Ibid; Love, 264.

CHAPTER XVIII: INTO THE VALLEY

1. Author interviews with Malcolm Jonah; Bailey memoir.
2. NTLF Report, G-2.
3. Leigh M. Trowbridge, *Operation Leap Frog* (Privately printed. 2004), 122–23.
4. Gailey, 197; Crowl, 206.
5. Nolan, 15.
6. Love, 271–75; Gailey, 193–94; Crowl, 206–7.
7. Chapin memoir, 99.
8. NTLF Report, G-1, "Replacements"; TF-56 Report.
9. Johnston, 201.
10. Everett, 35; Hoffman, 151–53.
11. Everett, 36.
12. Borta interview; Petty, *Saipan*, 102; Campbell, 242–44; Everett, 50.
13. Everett, 34.

14. Goe, 132.

15. Chapin, 17.

16. Torok, 22.

17. Pope, *Angel on My Shoulder.*

18. Pearce, 114.

19. Chambers, 101–2.

20. Sherrod, *On to Westward,* 94–95.

21. Guy Gabaldon, *Saipan: Suicide Island* (Privately printed, 1990), 90–91.

22. Love, 278–86; Crowl, 208–9.

23. Cooper, 181–82.

24. Crowl, 207; *Coral & Brass,* 174; Gailey, 198; Cooper, 182.

25. Cooper, 181–82; Crowl, 216.

26. Hoffman, 158.

27. Cooper, 182.

28. Ibid; *Coral & Brass,* 174.

29. Hoffman, 145.

30. Ibid, 170.

31. 27th Division, G-3 Journal, June 24, 1944.

32. After Action Report, 762nd Tank Bn., 30 May–25 August 1944.

33. Appleman, 50–51.

34. Love, 298–99.

35. Appleman, 24–27.

36. Crowl, 156.

37. Translation by the D-2 Section, 4th Marine Division of a Diary Received at Hospital, NTLF, June 27, 1944.

38. USS *Winged Arrow,* AP-170 Saipan Operation Report, July 30, 1944.

39. Love, 219–20.

40. Hoffman, 162–63; Crowl, 159.

41. Love, 221.

42. 318th Fighter Group at Saipan, http://home.earthlink.net/~atdouble/~318thFighterGroup.Saipan.html.

43. Chambers, 103.

44. Special Action Report, 25th Marines.

45. Chambers, 103–4.

46. George E. Doying, *War on Japan's Doorstep: The Battle for Saipan,"* *Leatherneck,* September 1944.

47. Wood, *Fourth Marine Division,* 21.

48. Chambers, 103.

49. Ibid, 105.

50. Love, 315–16.

51. "Plan Last Rites for Brother Heroes," *Daily News* (Huntington and Mount Union, PA), December 2, 1948.

CHAPTER XIX: EVERY SOLDIER MUST
STAND HIS GROUND

1. Dorothy E. Richard, *United States Naval Administration of the Trust Territory of the Pacific Islands, Vol. 1* (Washington, DC: Office of the Chief of Naval Operations, 1957), 434.
2. 27th Division, G-2 Journal, Periodic Report #68.
3. Petty, *Saipan*, 21.
4. Ibid, 158.
5. Trefalt, "After the Battle."
6. H. W. Johnson, 57.
7. Everett, 38.
8. Borta interview; Everett, 38; Petty, *Saipan*, 103; Campbell, 247–48.
9. Pope, *Angel on My Shoulder.*
10. Cary, 185–86.
11. Trowbridge, 123.
12. Harper, 74.
13. Lane, 76; Hicks interview.
14. Torok, 23–24.
15. Love, 293.
16. Hallden, 19–20.
17. Love, 300.
18. Hallden, 21.
19. Ibid, 21–27; Crowl, 216–18; Love, 300–307.
20. Hirakushi.
21. Shaw, 323.
22. Crowl, 211; Hoffman, 157.
23. TF 56 Report, G-2, Enclosure D.
24. NTLF Report, G-2, Serial 0024A.
25. Hoffman, 168.
26. Ibid, 177.
27. NTLF Report, G-2 Periodic Reports.
28. Crowl, 213.
29. Ibid, 124.
30. Morison VIII, 324.
31. Hirakushi.
32. Hoffman, 156–57.
33. Crowl, 218–19; Love, 310.
34. 27th Division, G-1 Journal, June 26, 1944.
35. Crowl, 222–24.
36. Hallden, 29–30.
37. Love, 321.
38. Ibid, 322.

39. Ibid, 324.
40. Ibid.
41. Ibid, 324–25; Hallden, 30–33.
42. Love, 316.
43. Crowl, 227.
44. Love, 330–33.
45. Ibid, 333–35.
46. Crowl, 228.
47. Love, 356.
48. NTLF Report, G-2 Report.
49. Tsuneyuki Mohri, *Rainbow Over Hell* (Nampa, ID: Pacific Press Publishing Association, 2006), 46.
50. Sugano memoir.
51. Ibid; Toland, *Rising Sun*, 638–39.

CHAPTER XX: BEYOND THE VALLEY

1. Hoffman, 185.
2. 27th Division, G-2 Periodic Report, July 1, 1944.
3. Ryoko Okuyama, "A Lone Survivor at Saipan—An Isle of Death," undated, Toland Papers, FDRL.
4. NTLF Report, Dispatch Summary, Serial No. 00104-3, June 27, 1944.
5. Goe, 148.
6. 4th Mar. Div. Ops. Rpt., Appendice 5 to Annex Dog to Division Final Report-Saipan (Medical Report).
7. "First Battalion, 24th Marines: The History of the Men of 1/24 in World War II and Beyond, https://1stbattalion24thmarines.com/the-battles/saipan/saipan.
8. Rogers, *Answering Their Country's Call*, 55–56.
9. Dean Ladd interview, Bristol Productions Ltd., Olympia, WA, undated, www.wwiihistoryclass.com/education/transcripts/Ladd_D_125.pdf.
10. Chambers, 144–45.
11. H. W. Johnson, 87.
12. Trowbridge, 137.
13. Eardley, 142.
14. Brian E. Albrecht, "Facing Banzai Charges in Saipan Fight," *Plain Dealer* (Cleveland, OH), June 26, 1994.
15. Tierney memoir.
16. Roush, 447.
17. Clemmons, 262.
18. Berry, 252.
19. Johnston, 206.
20. Lane, 73.
21. Albrecht, "Facing Banzai Charges."

22. E. R. McElveen, "Never Forgotten," *Marine Corps Gazette*, November 1998.
23. Campbell, 192.
24. Col. Joseph H. Alexander, "World War II: 50 Years Ago: Saipan's Bloody Legacy," *Leatherneck*, June 1994.
25. Rogers, *Answering Their Country's Call*, 155.
26. O'Sheel, 152–53.
27. Fiore interview.
28. *Heritage Years*, 103.
29. Fiore interview.
30. Sherrod, *On to Westward*, 119–21.
31. Ibid, 120–23.
32. Masters, 191.
33. Eardley, 135.
34. Annex "I" Headquarters 27th Infantry Division Report of Medical Inspector— Saipan Operation.
35. 27th Division, G-1, Forager Operation, Graves Registration and Burial.
36. Petty, *Saipan*, 148.
37. Love, 346.
38. Tierney memoir.
39. David Venditta, "Don't Be Afraid to Die, the Officers Told Us," *Morning Call* (Allentown, PA), May 29, 2006.
40. Matthews memoir.
41. Harvey Hunt interview, Harvey B. Hunt Collection (AFC/2001/001/66868), Veterans History Project, American Folklife Center, Library of Congress.
42. Gabriel J. Vertucci interview, NYSMM.
43. Eileen Clegg, "Marine's Mission on Saipan: Save Lives," *Press Democrat* (Santa Rosa, CA), August 14, 1999.
44. Rex Alan Smith and Gerald A. Meehl, *Pacific War Stories in the Words of Those Who Survived* (New York: Abbeville Press, 2004), 191–93.
45. Pope, *Angel on My Shoulder*.
46. Benjamin P. Hegi, "Extermination Warfare? The Conduct of the Second Marine Division at Saipan," Thesis Prepared for the Degree of Master of Arts, University of North Texas, May 2008, 77.
47. Borta interview; Petty, *Saipan*, 104.
48. NTLF Report, G-2.
49. Karen Ann Takizawa, "War Stories (1): The Battle of Saipan (June 15–July 9, 1944," *Shakai Shiri -Hosei Journal of Sociology and Social Sciences*, July 2012), 5–14; Kawamura is a pseudonym she used to protect the soldier's privacy.
50. Mohri, 40–44.

CHAPTER XXI: RABBIT HUNT

1. Johnston, 216.
2. TF 56 Report.

3. James L. Fawcett, *Their Way* (New York: Vantage Press, 1989), 102–4.
4. Johnston, 219–20; Sherrod, *On to Westward*, 125–27; Hoffman, 196.
5. Johnston, 218.
6. Spooner, 87.
7. Johnston, 224.
8. Hirakushi.
9. Ibid; Denfeld, *Hold the Marianas*, 81.
10. Hoffman, 200.
11. *Heritage Years*, 47.
12. 106th Infantry Narrative Report.
13. Crowl, 241–42; 27th Division G-2 Journal.
14. Hirakushi.
15. Hoffman, 201.
16. Report of Intelligence Activities, 27th Infantry Division: Saipan Operation, 2 July 1944.
17. Ibid, 372.
18. NTLF Report, G-2 Periodic Report No. 21.
19. *Drank Our Tears*, 139.
20. Pat Hammond, "America's Other D-Day Was a Massive Assault on Saipan in the Pacific," *New Hampshire Sunday News* (Manchester, NH), June 12, 1994.
21. *Heritage Years*, 96–97.
22. *Drank Our Tears*, 24.
23. Wood, *Fourth Division*, 19.
24. NTLF Report, Japanese Text No. 3, G-2.
25. Domanowski.
26. NTLF Report, G-2 Periodic Report No. 21.
27. TF 56 Report.
28. 27th Division G-2 Journal.
29. NTLF Report, G2 Periodic Rpt. No. 21.
30. Ibid, Periodic Report No. 22; Hoffman, 212.
31. 27th Div G-2 Intelligence Journal, July 3, 1944.
32. NTLF Report.
33. William Rogal, interview in "Pacific: The Lost Evidence. Saipan" History Channel TV Miniseries, 2006.
34. Hoffman, 283.
35. Ibid; Hirakushi.
36. Hirakushi; Toland, *Rising Sun*, 640; Hoffman, 284.
37. Saburo Hayashi and Alvin D. Coox, *Kogun: The Japanese Army in the Pacific War* (Quantico, VA: The Marine Corps Association, 1959), 108.
38. Hirakushi; Toland, *Rising Sun*, 640.
39. Ibid; ibid.
40. Hirakushi.
41. Ronald Johnson, transcription of recorded memoirs, O'Brien Papers, NYSMM.

42. NTLF Report, G-2 Report, "Message to Officers and Men Defending Saipan."
43. Hirakushi; Toland, *Rising Sun*, 641–42.
44. Morison VIII, 337; TF 56 Report, G-2 Periodic Report No. 25, 9 July 1944, Yeoman testimony; Noda interview in Toland Papers. There is considerable uncertainty regarding the suicides of General Saito and Admiral Nagumo. Historian John Toland maintains, based on an "eyewitness account" by Major Hirakushi, that the two officers committed suicide together. Subsequent historians have repeated that scenario, but this writer is skeptical. Hirakushi told interrogators immediately after his capture that he had not witnessed the suicides, though he offered a speculative account of what "probably" occurred. In a later memoir, he claimed to be a witness. Even had Hirakushi been lying to interrogators in 1944 (which later events indicate is unlikely), his subsequent account is contradicted by Admiral Nagumo's chief yeoman, who claimed to have personally witnessed the suicides of Admirals Nagumo and Yano in the naval cave north of Saito's headquarters. Historian Samuel Eliot Morison cites another survivor who claimed to have helped bury Nagumo's body after he shot himself at naval headquarters. Given that testimony, the legendary lack of cooperation between army and navy, and Nagumo's apparent lack of participation in the defense of Saipan, it seems more likely that the suicides were committed at two different times and at different locations as maintained by Admiral Nagumo's yeoman.

CHAPTER XXII: MY LIFE IS FLUTTERING AWAY

1. Ibid, 84.
2. "Kansan Is Decorated on Saipan," *Hutchinson* (KS) *News-Herald*, November 9, 1944.
3. Appleman, 101–11.
4. Sherrod, *On to Westward*, 131.
5. Francis O'Brien, 204–11.
6. Jim G. Lucas, "Jap Banzai Assault on Saipan Described," *Evening Independent* (Massillon, OH), August 5, 1944.
7. Francis O'Brien, 208.
8. William H. Stewart, *Saipan in Flames* (Saipan: Economic Service Council, 1993), 20–21.
9. Thurlby Amos Colyer, Interviewed by Michael Russert and Wayne Clark, August 23, 2005, Oral History Collection, NYSMM; the captain was quite possibly Frank Olander.
10. Love, 418–19.
11. O'Hara, "Report of Japanese Counterattack at Saipan on Morning of 7 July 1944," Nast Papers, USAMH.
12. Francis O'Brien, 215–19; Love, 420–29.
13. Hirakushi; Toland, *Rising Sun*, 642.

14. Westfall, 89, 91.
15. *Saipan in Flames*, 21.
16. Haruko Taya Cook, "The Myth of the Saipan Suicides," *MHQ: The Quarterly Journal of Military History*, Spring 1995, 15; Noda interview; Commander, 5th Fleet War Diary, June 9, 1944.
17. 27th Division, G-2 Journal, July 6, 1944; O'Brien, 225; Crowl, 256–57.
18. Petty, *Saipan*, 137–38.
19. 27th Division, G-2 Periodic Rpt. No. 20, 6 July 1944.
20. NTLF Report, July 6, 1944; *Coral & Brass*, 194; Hoffman, 222.
21. Maj. James B. Bartholomees, "Operations of the 773d Amphibian Tractor Battalion (attached to 27th Division) in the Operation on Tanapag Plains Saipan 7–8 July, 1944," Staff Department, The Infantry School, Fort Benning, GA, n.d.
22. Petty, *Saipan*, 138.
23. Crowl, 256–57.
24. Ronald Johnson memoir.
25. Love, 436–37; Crowl, 257.
26. Cook and Cook, 286–89.
27. Mohri, 52–53.
28. Love, 438.
29. NTLF Report, G-2 Periodic Rpt. No. 23, July 8, 1944.
30. Love, 438.
31. NTLF Report, G-2.
32. Ronald Johnson memoir.
33. Love, 438.
34. 27th Division, G-2 Periodic Rpt., July 6, 1944.
35. Petty, *Saipan*, 138.
36. NTLF Report, G-2 Rpt., July 7, 1944.
37. *Saipan in Flames*, 21.
38. Hirakushi.

CHAPTER XXIII: OVERRUN

1. Jim G. Lucas, "Jap Banzai Assault on Saipan Described," *Evening Independent* (Massillon, OH), August 5, 1944.
2. Luther Hammond, Japanese "Gyokusai," O'Brien Papers, NYSMM.
3. Domanowski memoir.
4. Love, 462.
5. Sherrod, *On to Westward*, 138.
6. Petty, *Saipan*, 138.
7. Love, 479.
8. Dinova interview.
9. Domanowski memoir.
10. Love, 443.

11. Francis O'Brien, 235.
12. Love, 455.
13. Francis O'Brien, 241.
14. Ibid, 244.
15. W. Taylor Hudson, "Four Years and a Week," O'Brien Papers, NYSMM.
16. Love, 456.
17. Ibid, 456–57.
18. Francis O'Brien, 246.
19. Ibid, 239.
20. Hammond, "Gyokusai."
21. Francis O'Brien, 236.
22. Hammond, "Gyokusai."
23. Francis O'Brien, 239.
24. Ibid, 248–49.
25. Love, 454; O'Brien, 240–41.
26. Domanowski memoir.
27. Luther Hammond, "The Last Resting Place," O'Brien Papers, NYSMM.
28. Nicholas H. Grinaldo, Interviewed by Michael Aikey, September 26, 2001, Oral History Collection, NYSMM.
29. Ibid.
30. Lucas, "Jap Banzai Assault."
31. Grinaldo interview.
32. Dinova interview.
33. Love, 461.
34. Ibid.
35. Hammond, "Gyokusai."
36. Brad Gates, *The Last Great Banzai* (n.p., c. 1994), 61–62.
37. Ibid.
38. Ibid, 62.
39. Ibid, 62–63.
40. Gene W. Douglas, Interviewed by Robert Lewis, Gene W. Douglas Collection (AFC/2001/001/15767), Veterans History Project, American Folklife Center, Library of Congress.
41. Gates, 66.
42. Douglas interview.
43. Gates, 85–93.
44. Love, 459.
45. Hammond, "Gyokusai."
46. Ibid.
47. Ibid; Love, 460.
48. Hammond, "Gyokusai."
49. Hudson, "Four Years."
50. Domanowski memoir.

51. Andrew Beam, "WWII Soldier Gets Purple Heart Decades After Battle," SpotlightNEWs.com, Delmar, NY, August 31, 2010.
52. Hammond, "Gyokusai."
53. Love, 463–65.
54. O'Brien, 284.
55. Ibid, 447–48.
56. Love, 486.
57. 27th Division Journal Forager Operation, G-2, No. 11, July 6, 1944.
58. Edward Redfield, "Recollections of One Brief Incident on Saipan, 7 July 1944," O'Brien Papers, NYSMM.

CHAPTER XXIV: THE KILLING FIELDS

1. Love, 487–88; Hoffman, 227.
2. Appleman, 109–10.
3. 27th Division, G-2 Periodic Rpt. No. 18, July 7, 1944.
4. Maj. A. C. O'Hara narrative, Nast Papers, USAHEC.
5. Love, 447.
6. 27th Division Journal Forager Operation, No. 29, July 7, 1944.
7. Love, 475.
8. Commander Fifth Fleet, "Report on Japanese Counterattack at SAIPAN on morning of 7 July 1944," Nast Papers, USAHEC; Hoffman, 235.
9. 106th Infantry Journal, Rpt. 1066, July 7, 1944.
10. Sherrod, *On to Westward*, 133–34.
11. Grinaldo interview.
12. Love, 465–66.
13. Ibid, 466.
14. Hammond, "Gyokusai."
15. Hudson memoir.
16. Domanowski memoir.
17. Love, 470–71.
18. Dinova interview.
19. Grinaldo interview.
20. Love, 467–70.
21. Mitsuharu Noda interview, Toland Papers, FDRL; Cook, "Myth of Saipan Suicides," 15.
22. Gates, 94–97, 99.
23. Ibid, 83.
24. Agerholm Medal of Honor Citation; Johnston, 232–33; Agerholm's Medal of Honor was awarded to his mother in Racine, Wisconsin, almost a year later.
25. Gates, 82.
26. Ibid, 97–98.
27. Cooper, 188.

28. 106th Infantry Journal, July 7, 1944.
29. William Worden, "Japs Died in 3 Waves in Last Bid for Saipan," *Courier-Journal* (Louisville, KY), July 17, 1944.
30. Ibid; Sherrod, *On to Westward*, 136–37.
31. Johnston, 230.
32. Love, 490–93.
33. Hammond, "Gyokusai."
34. Love, 495–96.
35. USS *Heywood L. Edwards* (DD663) War Diary, July 1944; NTLF Report, Mailbrief, 7 July 1944, Serial No. 00180-3.
36. Francis O'Brien, 291–92.
37. Francois V. Albanese 105th Infantry, Interviewed by Francis A. O'Brien, O'Brien Papers, NYSMM.
38. Hoffman, 228; *Coral & Brass*, 196–97.
39. Bartholomees, 7–11.
40. Grinaldo interview.
41. Dinova interview.
42. Domanowski memoir.
43. Bartholomees, 11.
44. Ibid, 11–12.
45. Dinova interview.
46. Hammond, "Gyokusai."
47. Charles Edward Beaudoin, Interviewed by Francis A. O'Brien, O'Brien Papers, NYSMM.
48. Crowl, 261.
49. Maj. David N. Bucker, *A Brief History of the 10th Marines* (Washington, DC: History and Museums Division, Headquarters, U.S. Marine Corps, 1981), 77.
50. Cooper, 188.
51. Love, 501.
52. Sherrod, *On to Westward*, 140.
53. Headquarters, Fleet Marine Force Pacific, Report of the Marianas Operation.
54. De Tran, "American's Tale of Two Islands Veterans: Decorated Nisei Soldier 'Cannot Forget' Test of Loyalty, Courage," *San Jose Mercury News*, December 25, 1994.
55. Roush, 482.
56. Sherrod, *On to Westward*, 142.
57. Petty, *Saipan*, 139–40; Ulrich Straus, *The Anguish of Surrender: Japanese POWs of World War II* (Seattle: University of Washington Press, 2003), 87–88.
58. James Fisher, "Bravery Concluded Love Story," *Kansas City Star*, July 12, 1994.
59. Gilbert, 165–66; Timmerman's Medal of Honor was presented to his parents in Emporia, Kansas, on July 8, 1945, a year to the day after his death.
60. Petty, *Saipan*, 140.
61. Roush, 486.

62. Col. William T. Bowers, "Ben Salomon," Medal of Honor recipients: United States Army Medical Department, Office of Medical History, Office of the Surgeon General, http://history.amedd.Army.mil/moh/Salomon.html, retrieved 2017.
63. Sherrod, *On to Westward*, 143.
64. Toland, *Rising Sun*, 645; Noda interview, Toland Papers, FDRL.
65. Hirakushi.
66. Hegi, 89.
67. Hoffman, 233; NTLF Report, "Statement of 1st LT Kenneth J. Hensley, USMC, G Co 2d Bn 6 Mar."
68. Roush, 490.
69. Hoffman, 243.
70. Cary, 192.

CHAPTER XXV: THE SUICIDE CLIFFS

1. Gerald A. Meehl, *One Marine's War: A Combat Interpreter's Quest for Humanity in the Pacific* (Annapolis, MD: Naval Institute Press, 2012), 176–77.
2. Terry Wilson, "Ex-Marines Storm Beach of Brutal Memories," *San Diego Union Tribune*, November 9, 1997.
3. Lewis Meyers, "Japanese Civilians in Combat Zones," *Marine Corps Gazette*, February 1945.
4. Sherrod, *On to Westward*, 145.
5. Renstrom interview.
6. Perry memoir.
7. Webster interview.
8. Sherrod, *On to Westward*, 147.
9. Okuyama, "A Lone Survivor at Saipan—An Isle of Death," Toland Papers, FDRL.
10. Sugano memoir.
11. Petty, *Saipan*, 155.
12. Alvin P. Stauffer, *United States Army in World War II. The Technical Services. The Quartermaster Corps: Operations in the War Against Japan* (Washington, DC: Center of Military History United States Army, 1990), 255; 27th Division, G-1 Rpt., Graves Registration and Burial.
13. Stauffer, 255; 27th Division, G-1 Rpt., Graves Registration and Burial.
14. Petty, *Saipan*, 148.
15. Jim G. Lucas, "Saipan Soaked with Blood by Banzai Attack," *East Liverpool* (OH) *Review*, August 4, 1944.
16. Berry, 218.
17. Muster Rolls, 2nd Btn., 25th Marines, July 1944.
18. Frank Gibney, *Senso: The Japanese Remember the Pacific War* (Armonk, NY: M.E. Sharpe, Inc., 1995), 134–35.

19. TF 56 Report, G-2 Periodic Rpts.
20. Straus, 158.
21. 27th Division, G-2 Journal, #8, #10, July 10, 1944.
22. Westfall, 89.
23. Cook, *Japan at War*, 290–91.
24. NTLF Report, G-2 Periodic Rpt., July 12, 1944; Crowl, 131, 258.
25. United Press, "Body of Saipan Chief Is Found," *Mason City Globe-Gazette*, December 15, 1944.
26. NTLF Report.
27. Commander, 5th Fleet, War Diary, 9 July 1944.
28. Keith Wheeler, "Marines Get Jap General But They Have to Kill His Bodyguards," *Pittsburgh* (PA) *Press*, July 23, 1944.
29. 27th Division, G-1 Journal, July 12, 1944.
30. Rembert James, "Disclose How Marines Buried Jap Officer Killed on Saipan, *Palladium-Item and Sun-Telegram* (Richmond, IN), September 10, 1945.
31. *Saipan in Flames*, 21.
32. Toland, *Rising Sun*, 658.
33. Cook, "Myth of Saipan Suicides," 15–16.
34. Ben-Ami Shillony, *Politics and Culture in Wartime Japan* (Oxford: Clarendon Press, 1981), 67.
35. USSBS Interrogations II, 356.
36. Hoyt, *Warlord: Tojo Against the World* (Lanham, MD: Scarborough House, 1993), 193, 201–2.
37. Hoffman, 260.
38. Drea, 194.
39. Kase, 82.
40. Cook, "Myth of Saipan Suicides," 19.
41. Drea, 198; Hoyt, 192–93; Shillony, 61.
42. Cook, "Myth of Saipan Suicides," 17–18.
43. Ibid, 17.
44. Ibid, 16.
45. Meehl, 173.
46. Pope, *Angel on My Shoulder*.
47. Perry memoir.
48. Cary, 192.
49. 23rd Marines Special Action Report.
50. WWII Company C, 1st Battalion, 23rd Marines, "Our WWII History," www .c123rd.com/our-wwii-history.
51. Ibid.
52. Eardley, 145; Eardley recalled the movie as *White Christmas* (1954), apparently confusing it with *Holiday Inn* (1942), where Bing Crosby's classic song "White Christmas" first appeared.
53. Silcox, 119.

54. Roush, 490.
55. Tierney memoir.
56. Matthews memoir.
57. NTLF Report, G-1 Rpt., August 10, 1944; Crowl, 265.
58. Hoffman, 268–69.
59. Francis O'Brien, 313–14.
60. Beaudoin died of natural causes in 2001, leaving a wife, four children, and eight grandchildren.
61. Hammond letter.
62. Domanowski memoir.
63. War Crimes Office, Judge Advocate General's Office, Headquarters Army Garrison Force Office of the AC of S, G-2, 1 August 1944, Investigation of atrocities. At least one writer has erroneously identified one of the aviators as Lt. Woodie L. McVay Jr. In fact, the remains of McVay, who had been lost over Tanapag Harbor during the raid on February 22, were recovered from a shallow grave in the Catholic cemetery at Garapan where he had been buried by some Chamorros. An autopsy indicated McVay had died of massive injuries suffered in the crash of his Hellcat, Report of autopsy on Body of Unknown Aviator, JAG Case Files, Pacific Atrocities on Island of Saipan; "Home at Last" (Naval History, United States Naval Institute, June 2015).

CHAPTER XXVI: THE WHIRLWIND

1. Crowl, 193.
2. Crowl, 194; Gailey, 224.
3. Ibid, 192; ibid, 232–34; Maj. William Bland Allen IV, *Sacked at Saipan*, (Fort Leavenworth, KS: School of Advanced Military Studies, United States Army Command and General Staff College, 2012), 31.
4. 24th Marines Special Action Report, Tactical: Comments and Recommendations.
5. Shaw, 348.
6. *Coral & Brass*, 184.
7. Venzon, 114–15; Crowl, 192, 194; Gailey, 222.
8. Hoffman, 235.
9. 27th Division, G-2 Journal, July 6, 1944; Love, 484.
10. Letter from Gen. George W. Griner to editor, *Time* magazine, September 28, 1944, NAST Papers, USAHEC.
11. Hoffman, 225, 233–34.
12. Ibid, 233–34; Gailey, 217.
13. Hoffman, 233–35.
14. Letter from Lt. Col. Oakley C. Bidwell to Dr. June Hoyt, July 30, 1984, O'Brien Papers, NYSMM; Gailey, 211.

15. Love makes the only contemporary mention of hammocks, claiming that "at least two Marines were found dead the next morning in hammocks which had been slung between two adjacent trees," Love, 429.
16. Muster Rolls, 10th Marines, July 1944.
17. Bidwell letter; letter from Steve Burns to Dr. June Hoyt, July 21, 1984, O'Brien Papers, NYSMM.
18. CinPac memo, July 1944, Nast Papers.
19. *Coral & Brass*, 176–78; Gailey, 227.
20. Gailey, 228.
21. Ibid, 4–5.
22. Cooper, 214.
23. Love, 669.
24. Letter from Admiral Nimitz to Commander in Chief, United States Fleet, October 27, 1944, Nast Papers, USAHEC.
25. Letter from James Forrestal to Lt. Col. Charles C. Nast, October 10, 1944, Nast Papers, USAHEC.
26. Fiore interview.
27. Masters, 195.
28. Matthews memoir.
29. Wood, *Fourth Marine Division*, 46–47.
30. Kathleen Broome Williams, *The Measure of a Man: My Father, the Marine Corps and Saipan* (Annapolis, MD: Naval Institute Press, 2013), 137–51.
31. Shaw, 383.
32. Maj. Carl Q. Hoffman, *The Seizure of Tinian* (Historical Division, Headquarters, U.S. Marine Corps, 1951), 122, 156.
33. Stanford L. Opotowsky, "Saipan, D+200," *Leatherneck*, March 1945.
34. NTLF Report, Civil Affairs Rpt.
35. Bill Miller, "Beachhead Government," *Marine Corps Gazette*, November 1944.
36. NTLF Report, Civil Affairs.
37. Lt Cdr. C. H. Howe, "Report of Investigation of Dynamite Explosion at Tanapag Harbor Saipan, Marianas Island, July 30, 1944."
38. War Diary of Commander Forward Area Central Pacific from 1 September to 30 September 1944.
39. Mohri, 56–57, 65.
40. Steve Birdsall, *Saga of the Superfortresses* (Garden City, NY: Doubleday & Company, 1980), 116.
41. Sahr Conway-Lanz, *Collateral Damage: Americans, Noncombatant Immunity and Atrocity After World War II* (New York: Routledge, 2006), 1.
42. Birdsall, 123; Hata, 117; Barrett Tillman, *Whirlwind: The Air War Against Japan 1942–1945* (New York: Simon & Schuster, 2010), 87.
43. Wesley Frank Craven and James Lea Cate, *The Army Air Forces in World War II: The Pacific, Matterhorn to Nagasaki, June 1944 to August 1945, Vol. V* (Chicago: University of Chicago Press, 1953), 582.

44. Osamu Tagaya, *Mitsubishi Type 1 Rikko "Betty" Units of World War 2* (Oxford, England: Osprey Publishing, 2001), 95–100.
45. 27th Division, G-2 Journal, Periodic Rpt. #102.
46. Peter Williams and David Wallace, *Unit 731: Japan's Secret Biological Warfare in World War II* (New York: The Free Press, 1989), 81; Yuki Tanaka, *Hidden Horrors: Japanese War Crimes in World War II* (Boulder, CO: Westview Press, 1996), 188–89.
47. 27th Division, G-2, August 5, 1944.
48. Frederick Sidel, Ernest Takafuji, and David Franz, *Medical Aspects of Chemical and Biological Warfare* (Washington, DC: Office of the Surgeon General, 1997), 43.
49. Birdsall, 296–302.
50. Stoddard, 196.
51. Mohri, 93; Jones, *Oba*, 236–41; Bob Sarni, "Capt Oba Surrenders Diehard Saipan Jap 'Garrison' of Two Officers, 45 Men; About Ten Still At Large," *Saipan Target*, December 2, 1945.

EPILOGUE: LOOSE ENDS

1. David Venditta, "Don't Be Afraid to Die, the Officers Told Us," *Morning Call* (Allentown, PA), May 29, 2006.
2. "Island Hideout Yields 2 Japs," *News Journal* (Wilmington, DE), May 15, 1952; Beatrice Trefalt, *Japanese Army Stragglers and Memories of the War in Japan 1950–1975* (London: Routledge Studies in the Modern History of Asia, 2006), 62.
3. James Brooke, "Visiting Saipan, Japan's Emperor Honors Dead," *New York Times*, June 28, 2005; "Imperial Couple Forges Ahead Despite Rain," Saipan Tribune.com, June 28, 2005.
4. Venzon, 133–34; Cooper, foreword.
5. Buell, *Quiet Warrior*, 287.
6. Erskine interview, 323.
7. Crowl, 195.
8. Ibid, 201.
9. Drea, 67.
10. Morison VIII, 333.
11. Joseph W. Winter, "Recollections of MSG Joseph W. Winter," Blodgett's Historical Consulting, blodgetthistoricalconsulting/the-invasion-of-saipan/recollections-of-msg-joseph-w-winter.
12. Matt Assad, "Remembering Pvt. Yawney: For Family, 70-Year War Is Over," *Morning Call* (Allentown, PA), May 26, 2013; Daniel Patrick Sheehan, "A Soldier Almost Home," *Morning Call*, January 9, 2013.
13. Sheehan, "A Soldier Almost Home."
14. Ibid.
15. Assad; Sheehan, "A Soldier Almost Home."

16. James Burbeck, "Guy Gabaldon: An Interview and Discussion," *War Times Journal*, 1998; Gabaldon, *Suicide Island*.

17. Bowers, "Ben Salomon"; Patricia Ward Biederman, "A Heroic World War II Dentist Finally Gets His Due," *Los Angeles Times*, May 5, 2002.

18. Don Moore, "He Fought at Saipan and Okinawa: Pvt. Marty Mestre Was in the 27th Division," *DeSoto Sun* (Arcadia, FL), November 1, 2005.

19. Hammond, "Terrible Loss of Life."

20. De Tran, "American's Tale."

21. Aloysius T. Rolfes interview, Aloysius Theodore Rolfes Collection, (AFC/2001/001/55273), Veterans History Project, American Folklife Center, Library of Congress.

22. Ruth Imler Langhinrichs, *Atheist in a Foxhole: One Man's Quest for Meaning: Reflections, Insights, and Legacy of Richard Alan Langhinrichs (1921–1990)* (Bloomington, IN: iUniverse, 2015).

23. Colyer interview.

24. Grinaldo interview.

25. Perry memoir.

26. Venditta, "Don't Be Afraid to Die."

27. Fawcett, 107.

28. Fiore interview.

Bibliography

FDRL: Franklin Delano Roosevelt Presidential Library, Hyde Park, NY
USAHEC: U.S. Army Heritage and Education Center, Carlisle, PA
USMCU: U.S. Marine Corps University, Quantico, VA
NYSMM: New York State Military Museum and Research Center, Saratoga
Springs, NY

ORAL HISTORIES AND INTERVIEWS

Albanese, Francois V., 105th Infantry. Interviewed by Francis A. O'Brien. O'Brien
Papers, NYSMM.
Beaudoin, Charles Edward. Interviewed by Francis A. O'Brien. O'Brien Papers,
NYSMM.
Boots, Donald. Interviewed by Dr. Ronald E. Marcello. May 17, 2001. University
of North Texas Oral History Collection Number 1405.
Borta, Frank. Oral History Monologue. National Museum of the Pacific War,
Fredericksburg, TX, Digital Archive.
Carlson, Carl Bertil. Interview. State Historical Society of North Dakota.
Chambers, Paul (ed.) "The Third Battalion, Twenty-Fifth Marines: An Oral His-
tory by Colonel Justice Marion Chambers, USMCR, Ret.," 1987.
Colyer, Thurlby Amos. Interviewed by Michael Russert and Wayne Clark. August
23, 2005. Oral History Collection, NYSMM.
Conover, Corp. Carl. Interviewed by Chase Osborne. April 12, 2012. https://www
.youtube.com/watch?v=SDdLvzKA6jQ, accessed November 11, 2017.
Cox, David. Interviewed by Albert Winkler. May 4, 2001. L. Tom Perry Special
Collections, Harold B. Lee Library. Brigham Young University.
Crowe, Henry P. Interviewed by Benis Frank, 1979, USMCU.
Dinova, Samuel. Interview. Oral History Collection, NYSMM.
Donley, Edwin J. Edwin John Donley Collection (AFC/2001/001/56648), Veter-
ans History Project, American Folklife Center, Library of Congress.
Douglas, Gene W. Interviewed by Robert Lewis. Gene W. Douglas Collection
(AFC/2001/001/15767), Veterans History Project, American Folklife Center,
Library of Congress.
Erskine, Graves. Interviewed by Benis Frank, 1970, USMCU.

Fiore, Joseph. Oral History Collection, NYSMM.
Gabaldon, Guy. "An Interview and Discussion." *War Times Journal*, 1996, http://
www.wtj.com/articles/gabaldon/.
Grinaldo, Nicholas H. Interviewed by Michael Aikey. September 26, 2001. Oral
History Collection, NYSMM.
Hanson, Joseph H. Interview. State Historical Society of North Dakota.
Harris, Albert J. Interview. Oral History Collection, NYSMM.
Hicks, Richard H. Interview. Richard H. Hicks Collection
(AFC/2001/001/56815), Veterans History Project, American Folklife Center,
Library of Congress.
Hirsbrunner, Paul A. Oral History Interview, 1996. Wisconsin Veterans Museum
Research Center.
Hoffman, Carl W. Interviewed by Lt. Gen. Alpha L. Bowser. USMCU.
Hogaboom, Robert E. Interviewed by Benis Frank, 1972. USMCU.
Holleman, Jesse Boyce. Interviewed by Orley B. Caudill, August 9, 20 and Octo-
ber 19, 1976. University of Southern Mississippi Libraries Oral History
Collection.
Hoover, William. Memoir 2nd Armored Amphibian Battalion. William B. Hoover
Collection (AFC/2001/001/24397), Veterans History Project, American
Folklife Center, Library of Congress.
Hunt, Harvey. Interviewed by Ryan Fairfield. Harvey B. Hunt Collection
(AFC/2001/001/66868), Veterans History Project, American Folklife Center,
Library of Congress.
Johnson, Ronald. Transcription of recorded memoirs. 1984. O'Brien Papers,
NYSMM.
Kerr, Howard. Interview. Howard Matthew Kerr Collection
(AFC/2001/001/65492), Veterans History Project, American Folklife Center,
Library of Congress.
Kyle, Wood. Interviewed by Benis Frank, 1969. USMCU.
Ladd, Dean. Interview. Bristol Productions Ltd., Olympia, WA, Undated, www
.wwiihistoryclass.com/education/transcripts/Ladd_D_125.pdf.
Michelony, Lewis. Interviewed by John Daniels. May 2, 1993. University of North
Texas Oral History Collection, Denton, TX.
Miller, William "Ken." Interviewed by Paul Loeffler, June 21, 2014. *Hometown
Heroes* radio show.
Murowsky, Henry. Henry Stanley Murowsky Collection (AFC/2001/001/65284),
Veterans History Project, American Folklife Center, Library of Congress.
Noda, Mitsuharu. Interview transcript. Toland Papers. FDRL.
O'Brien, Warren Jack. Written reminiscences. *Colorado War Stories*, August 13,
2007.
Oliver, Dale E. World War II Experiences of Dale E. Oliver, 773rd Amphibious
Tractor Battalion, Saipan, Tinian, Okinawa. Interviewed by Justin Engleman.
Barton County Community College, Great Bend, KS, 2002.

Renstrom, Keith. Interviewed by Geoffrey Panos. December 16, 2005 and January 24, 2006. Eccles Broadcast Center, Salt Lake City, UT.

———. Interview. National World War II Museum, New Orleans, LA, 2015.

———. Interview. Remember WWII Lecture Series. Utah Education Network, 2008.

———. Interview. Keith Arnold Renstrom Collection (AFC/2001/001/40781), Veterans History Project, American Folklife Center, Library of Congress.

Riggs, Bernard Lee. Interviewed by Robert Markman. Bernard Lee Riggs Collection (AFC/2001/001/39607), Veterans History Project, American Folklife Center, Library of Congress.

Rogal, William. Interview in "Pacific: The Lost Evidence. Saipan." The History Channel TV Miniseries, 2006.

Rolfes, Aloysius T. Aloysius Theodore Rolfes Collection (AFC/2001/001/55273), Veterans History Project, American Folklife Center, Library of Congress.

Silverman, Eli. Interview. Combat Stories From World War II. Witness to War. www.witnesstowar.org/combat_stories/WWII/543.

Slama, Stanford Joseph. Interview. Veterans History Project. State Historical Society of North Dakota.

Smith, Thomas J. Interview. Oral History Collection, NYSMM.

Smith, Warren. Interviewed by Paul Loeffler. September 13, 2014. *Hometown Heroes* radio show.

Sutcliffe, Albert Greg. Interviewed by Harry Ziegler. Albert Greg Sutcliffe Collection (AFC/2001/001/16857), Veterans History Project, American Folklife Center, Library of Congress.

Tierney, Robert E. Interviewed by John K. Driscoll. Wisconsin Veterans Museum, 2005.

Vertucci, Gabriel J. Interview. Oral History Program, NYSMM.

Vraciu, Alexander. Interviewed by Ronald E. Marcello. October 9, 1994. Admiral Nimitz Foundation and University of North Texas Oral History Collection.

Waldron, Frank. Interviewed by Joseph Waldron. Oral History Collection, NYSMM. Project.

Webster Jr., Robert T. Interview. Robert T. Webster Jr. Collection (AFC/2001/001/66330), Veterans History Project, American Folklife Center, Library of Congress.

Williams, Bob. Interview. Veteran Voices of Pittsburgh Oral History Project, March 14, 2014.

Winkler, Albert. Interview with David Raymond Cox, May 4, 2001. L. Tom Perry Special Collections, 20th Century Western & Mormon Manuscripts, 1130 Harold B. Lee Library, Brigham Young University, Provo, UT.

Winter, Joseph W. "Recollections of MSG Joseph W. Winter," 1999. Blodgett's Historical Consulting, blodgetthistoricalconsulting/the-invasion-of-saipan/recollections-of-msg-joseph-w-winter.

BOOKS AND ARTICLES

Abney, Arthur E. *Wings Over Illinois*. Carbondale: Southern Illinois University Press, 2007.
Adkins, Gene. *Where Angels Die*. Privately published, 2004.
Albrecht, Brian E. "Facing Banzai Charges in Saipan Fight." *Plain Dealer* (Cleveland, OH), June 26, 1994.
Alexander, Col. Joseph H. "World War II: 50 Years Ago: Saipan's Bloody Legacy." *Leatherneck*, June 1994.
Assad, Matt. "Remembering Pvt. Yawney: For Family, 70-Year War Is Over." *Morning Call* (Allentown, PA), May 26, 2013.
Astor, Gerald. *Wings of Gold: The U.S. Naval Air Campaign in World War II*. New York: Ballantine Books, 2004.
Bailey, Sgt. Gilbert P. "Battle for Saipan Was a Test of Yanks' Courage, Endurance." *Palladium-Item* (Richmond, IN), July 13, 1944.
Banks, Harold (ed.). *Second Marine Division 1940–1999*. Paducah, KY: Turner Publishing Company, 1999.
Banning, William (ed.). *Heritage Years: Second Marine Division Commemorative Anthology 1940–1949*. Paducah, KY: Turner Publishing Company, 1988.
Barenblatt, Daniel. *A Plague Upon Humanity*. New York: Harper Collins Publishers, 2004.
Barreveld, Dirk Jan. *Cushing's Coup*. Philadelphia, PA: Casement, 2015.
Barrington, Rudolph. "I Will Never Forget, Marine Speaks About Saipan and Iwo Jima." *USMC Life*, August 15, 2015.
Berry, Henry. *Semper Fi, Mac: Living Memories of the U.S. Marines in World War II*. New York: Arbor House, 1982.
Biederman, Patricia Ward. "A Heroic World War II Dentist Finally Gets His Due." *Los Angeles Times*, May 5, 2002.
Birdsall, Steve. *Saga of the Superfortresses*. Garden City, NY: Doubleday & Company, 1980.
Blankfort, Michael. *The Big Yankee: The Life of Carlson of the Raiders*. Boston: Little, Brown and Company, 1947.
"Body of Saipan Chief Is Found." *Mason City* (IA) *Globe-Gazette*, December 15, 1944.
Bouslog, Dave. *Maru Killer*. Placentia, CA: Cline Publishing, 1996.
Bradsher, Greg. The "Z Plan Story." *Prologue Magazine*, Fall 2005.
Brooke, James. "Visiting Saipan, Japan's Emperor Honors Dead." *New York Times*, June 28, 2005.
Bryan, J., and Philip Reed. *Mission Beyond Darkness*. New York: Duell, Sloan and Pearce, 1945.
Bucker, Maj. David N. *A Brief History of the 10th Marines*. Washington, DC: History and Museums Division, Headquarters, U.S. Marine Corps, 1981.
Buell, Harold L. *Dauntless Helldivers: A Dive-Bomber Pilot's Epic Story of the Carrier Battles*. New York: Dell Publishing, 1991.

Buell, Thomas B. *Master of Sea Power: A Biography of Fleet Admiral Ernest J. King.* Boston: Little, Brown and Company, 1980.

———. *The Quiet Warrior: A Biography of Admiral Raymond A. Spruance.* Boston: Little Brown and Company, 1974.

Burbeck, James. "Guy Gabaldon: An Interview and Discussion." *War Times Journal,* 1998.

Bush, Elizabeth Kauffman. *America's First Frogman: The Draper Kauffman Story.* Annapolis, MD: Naval Institute Press, 2004.

Campbell, James. *The Color of War.* New York: Crown Publishers, 2012.

Cary, Bob. *Fear Was Never an Option.* Westminster, MD: Heritage Books, Inc., 2005.

Chapin, Capt. John C. *Breaching the Marianas: The Battle for Saipan.* Washington, DC: History and Museums Division, Headquarters, U.S. Marine Corps, 1994.

Chatfield, Gail. *By Dammit, We're Marines!* San Diego, CA: Merthvin Publishing, 2008.

Chihaya, Masataka, Donald Goldstein, and Catherine Dillon (eds.). *Fading Victory: The Diary of Admiral Matome Ugaki, 1941–45.* Pittsburgh: University of Pittsburgh Press, 1991.

Clark, Adm. J. J., "The Marianas Turkey Shoot," in Sears, Stephen W. *Eyewitness to World War II: The Best of American Heritage.* Boston: Houghton Mifflin Company, 1991.

Cleaver, Thomas M. *Fabled Fifteen: The Pacific Saga of Carrier Air Group 15.* Philadelphia: Casemate Publishers, 2014.

Clegg, Eileen. "Marine's Mission on Saipan: Save Lives." *Press Democrat* (Santa Rosa, CA), August 14, 1999.

Clemmons, Philip W. *Island-Hopping With L-3-6.* Knoxville, TN: Tennessee Valley Publications, 2004.

Conway-Lanz, Sahr. *Collateral Damage: Americans, Noncombatant Immunity and Atrocity After World War II.* New York: Routledge, 2006.

Cook, Haruko Taya. "The Myth of the Saipan Suicides." *MHQ: The Quarterly Journal of Military History,* Spring 1995.

Cook, Haruko Taya and Theodore Cook. *Japan at War: An Oral History.* New York: New Press, 1992.

Cooper, Norman V. *A Fighting General: The Biography of Gen Holland M. "Howlin' Mad" Smith.* Quantico, VA: The Marine Corps Association, 1987.

Craven, Wesley Frank, and James Lea Cate. *The Army Air Forces in World War II: The Pacific: Guadalcanal to Saipan August 1942 to July 1944, Vol. IV.* Washington, DC: Office of Air Force History, 1951.

———. *The Army Air Forces in World War II: The Pacific, Matterhorn to Nagasaki, June 1944 to August 1945, Vol. V.* Chicago: University of Chicago Press, 1953.

Crowl, Philip A. *United States Army in World War II: The War in the Pacific. Campaign in the Marianas.* Washington, DC: Office of the Chief of Military History, Department of the Army, 1960.

Croziat, Victor J. *Across the Reef: The Amphibious Tracked Vehicle at War*. Quantico, VA: Marine Corps Association, 1989.

Curran, William. "Saipan Remembered." *Leatherneck*, June 1984.

Dempsey, Sgt. David. "Fight Rages All Night 24-Hour Charan Kanoa Battle One of War's Fiercest." *Chevron*, July 8, 1944.

Denfeld, D. Colt. *Hold the Marianas: The Japanese Defense of the Mariana Islands*. Shippensburg, PA: Mane Publishing Company, 1997.

———. *Japanese Fortifications and Other Structures in the Central Pacific*. Saipan: Micronesian Archaeological Survey Reports, No. 9, 1992.

De Viana, Augusto V. "The Capture of the Koga Papers and Its Effect on the Plan to Retake the Philippines in 1944." *Micronesian Journal of the Humanities and Social Sciences*, December 2005.

Dickson, W. D. *The Battle of the Philippine Sea June 1944*. London: Ian Allen, Ltd., 1975.

Dingman, Roger. *Deciphering the Rising Sun*. Annapolis, MD: Naval Institute Press, 2009.

Dockery, Kevin. *Navy Seals: A History. Part I: The Early Years*. Garden City, NY: The Military Book Club, 2002.

Donovan, James A., Jr. "Saipan Tank Battle." *Marine Corps Gazette*, October 1944.

Dougherty, Leo J., III. "Lest We Forget: General Graves B. Erskine, USMC (1897–1973)." *Marine Corps Gazette*, April 1997.

Doying, George E. "War On Japan's Doorstep: The Battle for Saipan." *Leatherneck*, September 1944.

Drea, Edward J. *In the Service of the Empire: Essays on the Imperial Japanese Army*. Lincoln: University of Nebraska Press, 1998.

Drez, Ronald J. *Twenty-Five Yards of War*. New York: Hyperion, 2001.

Dunnigan, James F., and Albert A. Nofi. *Victory at Sea: World War II in the Pacific*. New York: William Morrow and Company, Inc., 1995.

Dyer, Vice Adm. George C. *The Amphibians Came to Conquer: The Story of Admiral Richmond Kelly Turner*. 2 vols. Washington, DC: Department of the Navy, 1972.

Eardley, John M. *You'll Be Sorry: A Marine's Memoir of the War in the Pacific*. Privately printed, 2009.

11th Bombardment Group (H): The Grey Geese. Paducah, KY: Turner Publishing Company, 1996.

Epstein, Dwayne. *Lee Marvin: Point Blank*. Tucson, AZ: Schaffner Press, 2013.

Evans, David C. *The Japanese Navy in World War II in the Words of Former Japanese Naval Officers*. Annapolis, MD: Naval Institute Press, 1986.

Everett, Robert E., Sr. *World War II: Battle of Saipan*. Self-published, 1996.

Fahey, James J. *Pacific War Diary: 1942–1945*. Boston: Houghton Mifflin Co., 1963.

Fane, Douglas, and Don Moore. *The Naked Warriors*. New York: Appleton-Century-Crofts, Inc., 1956.

Fawcett, James L. *Their Way*. New York: Vantage Press, 1989.

Fisher, James. "Bravery Concluded Love Story." *Kansas City Star*, July 12, 1994.

Forrestel, Vice Admiral E. P. *Admiral Raymond A. Spruance, USN: A Study in Command.* Washington, DC: U.S. Government Printing Office, 1966.

Fuller, Richard. *Shokan: Hirohito's Samurai.* London: Arms and Armour Press, 1992.

Gabaldon, Guy. *Saipan: Suicide Island.* Privately printed, 1990.

Gailey, Harry A. *Howlin' Mad vs. the Army: Conflict in Command Saipan 1944.* Novato, CA: Presidio, 1986.

Gates, Brad. *The Last Great Banzai.* Privately printed, c. 1994.

Giangreco, D. M. "Casualty Projections for the U.S. Invasions of Japan, 1945–1946: Planning and Policy Implications." *Journal of Military History*, July 1997.

Gibney, Frank (ed.). *Senso: The Japanese Remember the Pacific War.* Armonk, NY: M.E. Sharpe, Inc., 1995.

Gilbert, Oscar E. *Marine Tank Battles in the Pacific.* Conshohocken, PA: Combined Publishing, 2001.

Gluck, Jay. *Ukiyo: Stories of the Floating World of Post War Japan.* Ashiya, Japan: Personally Oriented, Ltd., 1963.

Goe, Lt. W. Charles. *Is War Hell?* Los Angeles, CA: Charles Goe, 1947.

Going, Robert N. *Where Do We Find Such Men?* Amsterdam, NY: George Street Press, 2013.

Goldberg, Harold J. *D-Day in the Pacific.* Bloomington: Indiana University Press, 2007.

Graf, Robert. *Easy Company: My Life in the United States Marine Corps during World War II.* Self-published, 1986.

Hammel, Eric. *Aces Against Japan.* New York, Pocket Books, 1992.

———. *Aces Against Japan II.* Pacifica, CA: Pacifica Press, 1996.

Hammond, Pat. "A Terrible Loss of Life." *New Hampshire Union Leader*, February 19, 2009.

———. "America's Other D-Day Was a Massive Assault on Saipan in the Pacific." *New Hampshire Sunday News* (Manchester, NH), June 12, 1994.

Handleman, Howard. "Order Succeeds Chaos as Men Force Jap Surrender at Saipan." *Palladium-Item* (Richmond, IN), August 9, 1944.

Harper, Paul. *Growing Up in the Marine Corps 1942–1945.* Essex, CT: The Granite Ledge Press, 1997.

Harries, Meiron, and Susie Harries. *Soldiers of the Sun: The Rise and Fall of the Imperial Japanese Army.* New York: Random House, 1992.

Hata, Ikuhiko, and Yasuho Zawa. *Japanese Naval Aces and Fighter Units in World War II.* Annapolis, MD: Naval Institute Press, 1989.

Hatcher, Gardner N. (ed.). *Heritage Years: Second Division Commemorative Anthology 1940–1949.* Paducah, KY: Turner Publishing Co., 1988.

Hayashi, Saburo, and Alvin D. Coox. *Kogun: The Japanese Army in the Pacific War.* Quantico, VA: The Marine Corps Association, 1959.

Hayes, Grace P. *The History of the Joint Chiefs of Staff in World War II (The War Against Japan).* Annapolis, MD: Naval Institute Press, 1982.

Herman, Jan K. *Battle Station Sick Bay: Navy Medicine in World War II.* Annapolis, MD: Naval Institute Press, 1997.

Hoffman, Maj. Carl Q. *Saipan: The Beginning of the End.* Washington, DC: Historical Division, Headquarters, U.S. Marine Corps, 1950.

———. *The Seizure of Tinian.* Washington, DC: Historical Division, Headquarters, U.S. Marine Corps, 1951.

Hofvendahl, Russ. "God and a Good Marine." *Leatherneck,* November 1983.

Hornfischer, John D. *The Fleet at Flood Tide: America at Total War in the Pacific, 1944–1945.* New York: Bantam Books, 2016.

Hoyt, Edwin P. *McCampbell's Heroes.* New York: Van Nostrand Reinhold, 1983.

———. *Warlord: Tojo Against the World.* Lanham, MD: Scarborough House, 1993.

Isely, Jeter A., and Philip A. Crowl. *The U.S. Marines and Amphibious War.* Princeton, NJ: Princeton University Press, 1951.

James, Rembert. "Disclose How Marines Buried Jap Officer Killed on Saipan." *Palladium-Item and Sun-Telegram* (Richmond, IN), September 10, 1945.

Johansen, Herbert O. "Bulldozers and Bullets." *Air Force,* October 1944.

Johnson, H. William. *On to Saipan.* Privately printed, 2012.

Johnson, William L. C. *The West Loch Story.* Seattle, WA: West Loch Publication, 1986.

Johnston, Richard W. *Follow Me! The Story of the Second Marine Division in World War II.* New York: Random House. 1948.

Jones, Don. *Oba: The Last Samurai.* Presidio Press: Novato, CA, 1986.

Jones, Wilbur. *Gyrene: The World War II United States Marine.* Shippensburg, PA: White Mane Books, 1998.

Jones, William K. "The Battle of Saipan-Tinian." *Marine Corps Gazette,* June 1988.

Karig, Capt. Walter. *Battle Report: The End of an Empire.* New York: Rinehart and Company, Inc., 1948.

Kase, Toshikazu. *Journey to the Missouri.* New Haven: Yale University Press, 1950.

Kawamura, Noriko. *Emperor Hirohito and the Pacific War.* Seattle: University of Washington Press, 2015.

Keene, R. R. "Please Apologize Deeply to the Emperor." *Leatherneck,* June 2004.

———. "The Orphan Battalion That Took Mount Tapotchau." *Leatherneck,* June 1994.

King, Ernest J., and Walter Muir Whitehill. *Fleet Admiral King: A Naval Record.* New York: W.W. Norton & Company, Inc., 1952.

Lacey, Sharon Tosi. *Pacific Blitzkrieg: World War II in the Central Pacific.* Denton, TX: University of North Texas Press, 2013.

Ladd, Dean. *Faithful Warriors.* Spokane, WA: Teen-Aid, Inc., 1993.

Lane, John E. *This Here Is "G" Company.* Great Neck, NY: Brightlights Publications, 1997.

Langhinrichs, Ruth Imler. *Atheist in a Foxhole: One Man's Quest for Meaning: Reflections, Insights, and Legacy of Richard Alan Langhinrichs (1921–1990).* Bloomington, IN: iUniverse, 2015.

LaVo, Carl. *Slade Cutter: Submarine Warrior*. Annapolis, MD: Naval Institute Press, 2003.

Layton, Edwin T. *"And I Was There."* New York: William Morrow and Company, 1985.

Leckie, Robert. *Strong Men Armed: The United States Marines Against Japan*. New York: Random House, 1962.

Lippman, David. "Combat History on Saipan." *World War II History Magazine*, February 2014.

Love, Edmund G. *The 27th Infantry Division in World War II*. Nashville, TN: Battery Press, 2001.

Lucas, Jim G. "Jap Banzai Assault on Saipan Described." *Evening Independent* (Massillon, OH), August 5, 1944.

———. "Saipan Soaked with Blood by Banzai Attack." *East Liverpool* (OH) *Review*, August 4, 1944.

Marshall, S. L. A. *Bringing Up the Rear: A Memoir*. San Rafael, CA: Presidio, 1979.

Mason, H. M. "Patrol in Paradise." *Leatherneck*, October 2001.

Mason, John T., Jr. (ed.) *The Pacific War Remembered: An Oral History Collection*. Annapolis, MD: Naval Institute Press, 1986.

Masters, Mike A. *Once a Marine Always a Marine*. Privately printed, 1988.

Matthews, Carl. *The War Years*. Self-published.

McAuliffe, Josh, "Despite Injuries, Blakely Marine Officer Kept Leading Men into WWII Battles." *Times Tribune* (Scranton, PA), June 30, 2013.

McClure, Glenn E. *Saipan Then and Now: Photos of World War II and Today, Maps, Interesting Facts*. Self-published, 1989.

McDevitt, Paul K. *All Came Home*. Privately printed, 2015.

McElveen, E. R. "Never Forgotten." *Marine Corps Gazette*, November 1998.

McLean, Donald B. *Japanese Tanks, Tactics & Antitank Weapons*. Wickenburg, AZ: Paramount Technical Publications, 1973.

Meehl, Gerald A. *One Marine's War: A Combat Interpreter's Quest for Humanity in the Pacific*. Annapolis, MD: Naval Institute Press, 2012.

Mersky, Peter. *The Grim Reapers: Fighting Squadron Ten in WWII*. Mesa, AZ: Champlin Museum Press, 1986.

Meyers, 1st Lt. Lewis. "Japanese Civilians in Combat Zones." *Marine Corps Gazette*, February 1945.

Miller, Bill. "Beachhead Government." *Marine Corps Gazette*, November 1944.

Mohri, Tsuneyuki. *Rainbow Over Hell*. Nampa, ID: Pacific Press Publishing Association, 2006.

Moore, Don. "He Fought at Saipan and Okinawa: Pvt. Marty Mestre Was in the 27th Division." *DeSoto Sun* (Arcadia, FL), November 1, 2005.

Moore, Jeffrey M. *Spies for Nimitz: Joint Military Intelligence in the Pacific War*. Annapolis, MD: Naval Institute Press, 2004.

Moore, Stephen L. *The Buzzard Brigade: Torpedo Squadron Ten at War*. Missoula, MT: Pictorial Histories Publishing Co., 1996.

Morison, Samuel Eliot. *History of United States Naval Operations in World War II, Volume VII Aleutians, Gilberts, Marshalls: June 1942–April 1944.* Boston: Little, Brown and Company, 1951.

———. *History of United States Naval Operations in World War II, Volume VIII New Guinea and the Marianas.* Boston: Little, Brown and Company, 1959.

Nalty, Bernard C. *The Right to Fight: African-American Marines in World War II.* Washington, DC: Marine Corps Historical Center, 1995.

North, Oliver. *War Stories II: Heroism in the Pacific.* Washington, DC: Regnery Publishing, Inc., 2004.

O'Brien, Francis A. *Battling for Saipan.* New York: Ballantine Books, 2003.

Opotowsky, Stanford L. "Saipan, D+200." *Leatherneck,* March 1945.

O'Sheel, Patrick, and Gene Cook (eds.) *Semper Fidelis: The U.S. Marines in the Pacific 1942–1945.* New York: William Sloane Associates, Inc., 1947.

Pearce, Harry A. *Star Shells, Condoms, & Ka-Bars.* Leawood, KS: Leathers Publishing, 2004.

Peattie, Mark R. *Naj'yo: The Rise and Fall of the Japanese in Micronesia, 1885–1945.* Honolulu: University of Hawaii Press, 1988.

Pepper, Jack. "Ingenious Marine Finds Sure Way of Ripping Tank." *Miami* (OK) *Daily News Record,* July 21, 1944.

———. "Saipan Is a Story of Mortar Shells, Foxholes and Dead Buddies." *Daily Oklahoman,* August 13, 1944.

Petty, Bruce. "Home at Last." *Naval History* (United States Naval Institute), June 2015.

———. *Saipan: Oral Histories of the Pacific War.* Jefferson, NC: McFarland & Company, Inc., 2002.

Pope, John C. *Angel on My Shoulder.* Privately printed, 2013.

Potter, E. B. *Admiral Arleigh Burke: A Biography.* New York: Random House, 1990.

———. *Nimitz.* Annapolis, MD: Naval Institute Press, 1976.

Powell, Jack. "Remember Our Sacrifice at Saipan." *Birmingham* (AL) *News,* June 12, 1994.

Proehl, Carl W. *The Fourth Marine Division in World War II.* Washington, DC: Infantry Journal Press, 1946.

Richard, Dorothy E. *United States Naval Administration of the Trust Territory of the Pacific Islands (Vol. 1).* Washington, DC: Office of the Chief of Naval Operations, 1957.

Riggs, Bernard Lee. *EI KIE MALINGY: A Story About a Legendary Combat Intelligence Section.* Self-published, 1995.

Rogers, Keith. "Veterans Parade Highlights Vegas Patriotism." *Las Vegas Review-Journal,* November 5, 2014.

Rogers, Michael H. (ed.). *Answering Their Country's Call: Marylanders in World War II.* Baltimore: The Johns Hopkins University Press, 2002.

Roscoe, Theodore. *United States Submarine Operations in World War II.* Annapolis, MD: United States Naval Institute, 1949.

Roush, Roy W. *Open Fire!* Apache Junction, AZ: Frontline Press, 2003.

Russell, Scott. *Operation Forager: The Battle for Saipan.* Commemoration of the 50th Anniversary, Saipan: Division of Historic Preservation, June 1994.

Salaberria, Sister Maria Angelica. *A Time of Agony: Saipan 1944.* Guam: Micronesian Research Center, University of Guam, 1994.

Salecker, Gene Eric. *Rolling Thunder Against the Rising Sun: The Combat History of U.S. Army Tank Battalions in the Pacific in World War II.* Mechanicsburg, PA: Stackpole Books, 2008.

——. *The Second Pearl Harbor: The West Loch Disaster, May 21, 1944.* Norman: University of Oklahoma Press, 2014.

Samuelsen, Lewis N. "Handling Enemy Civilians." *Marine Corps Gazette*, April 1945.

2nd Armored Amphibian Battalion USMC WWII: Saipan, Tinian, Iwo Jima. 2nd Armored Amphibian Battalion Association, 1991.

Shaw, Henry I., Bernard C. Nalty, and Edwin T. Turnbladh. *Central Pacific Drive: History of U.S. Marine Corps Operations in World War II. Vol. III.* Washington, DC: Historical Branch, G-3 Division, Headquarters, U.S. Marine Corps, 1966.

Sheehan, Daniel Patrick. "A Soldier Almost Home." *Morning Call* (Allentown, PA), January 9, 2013.

Sherrod, Robert. "Battalion on Saipan." *Marine Corps Gazette*, October 1944.

——. *On to Westward: War in the Central Pacific.* New York: Duell, Sloan and Pearce, 1945.

——. "The Nature of the Enemy." *Time*, August 7, 1944.

Shiebler, Sgt. Ellsworth. "Youth's Life Saved by Col. Carlson." *Marine Corps Chevron*, September 23, 1944.

Shillony, Ben-Ami. *Politics and Culture in Wartime Japan.* Oxford: Clarendon Press, 1981.

Sidel, Frederick, Ernest Takafuji, and David Franz (eds.). *Medical Aspects of Chemical and Biological Warfare.* Washington, DC: Office of the Surgeon General, 1997.

Silcox, S. G. *A Hillbilly Marine.* Privately printed, 1977.

Sims, Edward. *Greatest Fighter Missions.* New York: Ballantine Books, 1963.

Small Unit Actions: The Fight on the Tanapag Plain. Washington, DC: Historical Division, War Department, 1946.

Smith, Holland, and Percy Finch. *Coral & Brass.* New York: Charles Scribner's Sons, 1949.

Smith, Jeff. "Decorated Marine Veteran Honored in 9-11 Ceremony at California Base." *Sentinel-Record* (Hot Springs, AR), November 11, 2010.

Smith, Rex Alan, and Gerald A. Meehl. *Pacific War Stories in the Words of Those Who Survived.* New York: Abbeville Press, 2004.

Smith, Steven Trent. *The Rescue.* New York: John Wiley & Sons, Inc., 2001.

Spooner, Rick. *The Spirit of Semper Fidelis: Reflections from the Bottom of an Old Canteen Cup.* Williamstown, NJ: Phillips Publications, 2004.

Stauffer, Alvin P. *United States Army in World War II. The Technical Services. The Quartermaster Corps: Operations in the War Against Japan.* Washington, DC: Center of Military History United States Army, 1990.

Stewart, William H. *Saipan in Flames.* Saipan: Economic Service Council, 1993.

Stoddard, Loren and Helen Joe. *One Flesh.* Salt Lake City, UT: Privately printed, 2013.

Stott, Capt. Frederic A. *Saipan Under Fire.* Andover, MA: Self-published, 1945.

Straus, Ulrich. *The Anguish of Surrender: Japanese POWs of World War II.* Seattle: University of Washington Press, 2003.

Tagaya, Osamu. *Mitsubishi Type 1 Rikko "Betty" Units of World War 2.* Oxford: Osprey Publishing, 2001.

Takizawa, Karen Ann. "War Stories: The Battle of Saipan. War Stories (1)—The Battle of Saipan (June 15–July 9, 1944)" (experiences of Kawamura Kazuo). *Shakai Shirin-Hosei Journal of Sociology and Social Sciences,* July 2012.

Tanaka, Yuki. *Hidden Horrors: Japanese War Crimes in World War II.* Boulder, CO: Westview Press, 1996.

Taylor, Theodore. *The Magnificent Mitscher.* Annapolis, MD: Naval Institute Press, 1954.

Terwilliger, Wayne. *Terwilliger Bunts One.* Guilford, CT: Globe Pequot Press, 2006.

Tillman, Barrett. *Clash of the Carriers: The True Story of the Marianas Turkey Shoot of World War II.* New York: NAL Caliber, 2005.

———. *Hellcat Aces of World War II.* London: Osprey Publishing, 1996.

———. *TBF/TBM Avenger Units of World War 2.* London: Osprey Publishing, 1999.

———. *Whirlwind: The Air War Against Japan 1942–1945.* New York: Simon & Schuster, 2010.

Toland, Harry. *Ben's Will.* n.p: Furness Press, 1998.

Toland, John. *The Rising Sun: The Decline and Fall of the Japanese Empire 1936–1945.* New York: Random House, 1970.

Tolbert, Frank X. "Crowe's Feats." *Leatherneck,* October 1944.

Torok, Tibor. *Stepping Stones Across the Pacific: A Collection of Short Stories from the Pacific War.* New York: Vantage Press, 1999.

Tran, De. "America's Tale of Two Islands Veterans: Decorated Nisei Soldier Cannot Forget Test of Loyalty, Courage." *San Jose Mercury News,* December 25, 1994.

Trefalt, Beatrice. "After the Battle for Saipan: the Internment of Japanese Civilians at Camp Susupe, 1944–1946." *Japanese Studies, Vol. 29, Issue 3,* 2009.

———. *Japanese Army Stragglers and Memories of the War in Japan 1950–1975.* London: Routledge Studies in the Modern History of Asia, 2006.

Trowbridge, Leigh M. *Operation Leap Frog.* Privately printed, 2004.

Tully, Anthony P. *Battle of Surigao Strait.* Bloomington: Indiana University Press, 2014.

Tuten-Puckett, Katharyn (Director). *"We Drank Our Tears:" Memories of the Battles for Saipan and Tinian as Told by Our Elders.* Saipan: Pacific STAR Center for Young Writers, 2004.

U.S. Army. Japanese Monograph, Operations in the Central Pacific. Vol. 48. Washington, DC: Historical Section, G-2, 1946.
———. Japanese Monograph, The "A-Go" Operation May-June 1944. Vol. 90. Washington, DC: Historical Section, G-2, 1947.
———. Japanese Monograph. The "A-Go" Operations Log, Supplement May–June 1944, Vol. 91. Washington, DC: Historical Section, G-2, c. 1947.
United States Strategic Bombing Survey [Pacific]. *The Campaigns of the Pacific War.* Naval Analysis Division. Washington, DC: Government Printing Office, 1946.
United States Strategic Bombing Survey [Pacific] *Interrogations of Japanese Officials.* 2 vols. Naval Analysis Division. Washington, DC: Government Printing Office, 1946.
U.S. War Dept. Hist. Div. *Small Unit Actions.* Washington, DC: Government Printing Office, 1946.
Venditta, David. "Don't Be Afraid to Die, the Officers Told Us." *Morning Call* (Allentown, PA), May 29, 2006.
Venzon, Anne C. *From Whaleboats to Amphibious Warfare: Lt. Gen. "Howlin' Mad" Smith and the U.S. Marine Corps.* Westport, CT: Praeger, 2003.
Waite, Elmont. "Five American Fliers Saved: Airmen Parachuted Down in Midst of Jap Fleet in Pacific." *Ardmore* (OK*) Daily Ardmoreite,* June 28, 1944.
Wells, Arthur W. *The Quack Corps: A Marine's War—Pearl Harbor to Okinawa.* Chico, CA: DolArt, 1992.
Westfall, Douglas, and Ryozo Kimihira. *Taking Saipan: Two Sides to Every Battle in WWII.* Orange, CA: The Paragon Agency Publishers, 2014.
Wheeler, Keith. "Marines Get Jap General But They Have to Kill His Bodyguards." *Pittsburgh* (PA) *Press,* July 23, 1944.
Wheeler, Richard. *A Special Valor: The U.S. Marines and the Pacific War.* New York: Harper and Row Publishers, 1983.
Williams, Kathleen Broome. *The Measure of a Man: My Father, the Marine Corps and Saipan.* Annapolis, MD: Naval Institute Press, 2013.
Williams, Peter, and David Wallace. *Unit 731: Japan's Secret Biological Warfare in World War II.* New York: The Free Press, 1989.
Wilson, Terry. "Ex-Marines Storm Beach of Brutal Memories." *San Diego Union Tribune,* November 9, 1997.
Winton, John. *Ultra in the Pacific.* London: Leo Cooper, 1993.
Wood, Pamela (ed.). *Fourth Marine Division.* Paducah, KY: Turner Publishing Company, 1992.
Woods, Jim. "Tokyo Rose's Dire Warnings Struck Marine in Heart." *Columbus* (OH) *Dispatch,* June 15, 1994.
Wooldridge, E. T. (ed.) *Carrier Warfare in the Pacific: An Oral History Collection.* Washington, DC: Smithsonian Institute Press, 1993.
Worden, William. "Japs Last Saipan Assault Described." *Lincoln* (NE) *Evening Journal,* July 17, 1944.

———. "Japs Died in 3 Waves in Last Bid for Saipan." *Courier-Journal* (Louisville, KY), July 17, 1944.
Y'Blood, William T. *Red Sun Setting: The Battle of the Philippine Sea.* Annapolis, MD: Naval Institute Press, 1981.
Yeide, Harry. *The Infantry's Armor: The U.S. Army's Separate Tank Battalions in World War II.* Mechanicsburg, PA: Stackpole Books, 2010.

UNPUBLISHED

Adams, Maj. Richard E. "The Operations of Company B, 715th Amphibian Tractor Battalion During the Assault Landing on Saipan Island, 15 June 1944. (Personal Experiences of Company Commander)." Staff Department, The Infantry School, Fort Benning, GA, n.d.
Allen, Maj. William Bland IV. "Sacked at Saipan." School of Advanced Military Studies, United States Army Command and General Staff College, Fort Leavenworth, KS, 2012.
Appleman, Roy Edgar. "Army Tanks in the Battle for Saipan." Typescript. USAHEC.
Bailey, Dick. "Barracks Ballads, Sea Stories and War: One Marine's Memoirs." http://marinememoir.homestead.com/IndexBailey.html.
Bailey, Edward, Unpublished memoir of Saipan and death of Harold Epperson. Author's collection, undated.
Bartholomees, Maj. James B. "Operations of the 773d Amphibian Tractor Battalion (attached to 27th Division) in the Operation on Tanapag Plains Saipan 7–8 July, 1944." Staff Department, The Infantry School, Fort Benning, GA, n.d.
Bidwell, Lt. Col. Oakley C. Letter to Dr. June Hoyt, July 30, 1984. O'Brien Papers, NYSMM.
Bonnot, Emile L. "The USS *Fremont* and the Invasion of Saipan." www.ussfremont.org/bonnot.html, accessed November 29, 2017.
Chapin, John C. Undated memoir, USMCU.
Cook, Haruko Taya . "The Meaning of 'Saipan' in Creating Japanese War Memory: The Use and Abuse of a Wartime Myth." Northern Marianas Humanities Council, May 19, 2015, https://www.youtube.com/watch?v=JGiP9W1-a6M.
Domanowski, John. Untitled recollections. O'Brien Papers, NYSMM.
Everett, Robert E., Sr. *World War II: Battle of Saipan.* 1996, USMCU.
The Fighting Fourth of World War II. www.fightingfourth.com/saipan.htm.
"First Battalion, 24th Marines: The History of the Men of 1/24 in World War II and Beyond." https://1stbattalion24thmarines.com/the-battles/saipan/saipan.
Gugeler, 1st Lt. Russell A. "Army Amphibian Tractor and Tank Battalions in the Battle of Saipan, 15 June–9 July 1944." Manuscript, 20 January 1945, USAHEC.
Gwynn, Fred. "Torpedo 16." www.rb-29.net/HTML/81lexingtonstys/FredGwynnSty/09.04.04gwynn.htm, accessed November 6, 2017.

Hackett, Bob, and Sander Kingsepp. "OPERATION TAN NO. 2: The Japanese Attack on Task Force 58's Anchorage at Ulithi." www.combinedfleet.com/Tan%20No.%202.htm, accessed December 10, 2017.

Hallden, Maj. Charles H. "The Operations of Company L, 3rd Battalion, 106th Infantry (27th Infantry Division) in the Battle of Death Valley, Saipan, 23 June–28 June 1944 (Western Pacific Campaign. Personal Experience of a Company Commander)." Infantry Officers Advanced Course, Fort Benning, GA, 1947–48.

Hammond, Luther. "Intelligence Activities—Saipan, June 17–26, 1944 O'Brien Papers, NYSMM.

———. Japanese "Gyokusai" Attack. O'Brien Papers, NYSMM.

———. Letter home. August 15, 1944. O'Brien Papers, NYSMM.

———. "The Last Resting Place." O'Brien Papers, NYSMM.

Hegi, Benjamin P. "Extermination Warfare? The Conduct of the Second Marine Division at Saipan." Thesis Prepared for the Degree of Master of Arts. University of North Texas, May 2008.

Hensley, 1st Lt. Kenneth J. "Statement of 1st Lt. Kenneth J. Hensley, USMC, G Co. 2d Bn. 6th Mar." NTLF Report of Marianas Operation, Phase I (Saipan).

Hirakushi, Maj. Takashi. Interview notes. Toland Papers, FDRL.

Hooker, Maj. Howard C. "Amphibian Tank Battalion of Saipan." United States Army Armor Center, Fort Knox, The Armored School, May 1, 1948.

Hudson, Walter Taylor. "Four Years and a Week: The Experiences of Walter Taylor Hudson in the Army of the United States." O'Brien Papers, NYSMM.

"IJN Taiho: Armoured Aircraft Carriers in World War II." www.armouredcarriers.com/.

Jefferies, William. Recollections on website "Tarawa Talk," September 20, 2008.

Johnson, Orvel. Memories. www.c123rd.com/our-wwii-marines/johnson-orvel/memories.

Kaune, Charles S. "National Guard in War: An Historical Analysis of the 27th Infantry Division (New York National Guard) in World War II." A thesis presented to the Faculty of the U.S. Army Command and General Staff College in partial fulfillment of the requirement for the degree Master of Military Art and Science, Fort Leavenworth, KS, 1990.

Kobayashi, Hideo. "Sinking of the Aircraft Carrier Taiho Caused by One Hit of a Torpedo." Tokyo Institute of Technology, 2005. www.shippai.org/fkd/en/hfen/HB1011023.pdf.

Kusaka, Ryonusuke. "The Combined Fleet: Memoirs of Former Chief of Staff Kusaka." Manuscript. Toland Papers, FDRL.

Langston, Jack W. "As I Remember." Unpublished memoir. c. 2007. http://disc.yourwebapps.com/discussion.cgi?disc=149620;article=17865.

Moore, Cmdr. David. "The Battle of Saipan: The Final Curtain." 2003. Recollections of CDR David Moore. www.battleofsaipan.com/seabee.htm.

Nast, Charles C. Charles C. Nast Papers, 1944–1948. USAHEC.

Nolan, Maj. Martin E. "The Operations of the 3d Battalion, 165th Infantry (27th Infantry Division) in the Assault of the Eastern Slopes of the Mt. Tapotchau Hill Mass, Saipan, Marianas Islands, 24–28 June 1944 Central Pacific Theater (Personal experience of a Battalion Operations Officer)." Advanced Infantry Officers Course 1949–50, Staff Department, The Infantry School, Fort Benning, GA. n.d.

Okuyama, Ryoko. "Surviving on the Island of Suicide." Undated. Toland Papers, FDRL.

———. "A Lone Survivor at Saipan—An Isle of Death." Undated. Toland Papers, FDRL.

Perrone, Vincent, Transcript of Diary USS *Fremont*. www.ussfremont.org/diaries .html.

Perry, Al. "A Personal History of the Fourth Marine Division in WWII." www .semper-fi.us/history_of_fourth_division_final.htm.

Ramage, James, and Don Gordon. "Operation Forager: The Marianas Campaign." CV6.ORGwww.cv6.org/1944/marianas.

Redfield, Edward H. "Recollections of One Brief Incident on Saipan 7 July 1944." O'Brien Papers, NYSMM.

Sato, Kenryo. Dai Toa: "War Memoir (Great Eastern War Memoirs)." Undated. Toland Papers, FDRL.

2nd Armored Amphibian Battalion. http://2ndarmoredamphibianbattalion.com/ saipan/.

Sugano (nee Miura), Shizuko. "The End at Saipan." Translator unknown. Draft manuscript, c. 1959. Toland Papers, FDRL.

Tate, Lt. Cmdr. Mark D. "Operation Forager: Air Power in the Campaign for Saipan." Master's degree thesis. U.S. Army Command and General Staff College: Fort Leavenworth, KS, 1995.

318th Fighter Group at Saipan. http://home.earthlink.net/~atdouble/~318thFighter Group.Saipan.html.

Tierney, Robert E. "My Marine Corps Experience." https://www.ancestry.com/ mediaui-viewer/tree/33605091/person/18502464331/.

Tully, Anthony, Jon Parshall, and Richard Wolff. "The Sinking of *Shokaku*—An Analysis. www.combinedfleet.com/shoksink.htm.

Tully, Anthony. "Last Hours of Aircraft Carrier *Hiyo*: A Look at Discrepancies." 1997. www.combinedfleet.com/atully02.htm.

———. "IJN *Hiyo*: Tabular Record of Movement." 2006. www.combinedfleet.com/ hiyo.htm.

Understanding Sacrifice. An ABMC and NCA Education Project. https://abmc education.org/understandingsacrifice/soldier/kenneth-tibbs.

Warren McLellan Story (from a presentation that Warren McLellan made to a school group in Fort Smith, Arkansas, November 11, 2002). www.rb-29.net/ HTML/81lexingtonstys/05.01mclellan.htm.

WWII Company C, 1st Battalion, 23rd Marines. "Our WWII History." www
.c123rd.com/our-wwii-history.

WAR DIARIES AND AFTER-ACTION REPORTS

Action Reports and War Diaries of battleships *Alabama, Indiana, Iowa, New Jersey, North Carolina, South Dakota, Washington.*
Action Reports and War Diaries of the carriers *Bataan, Belleau Wood, Bunker Hill, Cabot, Cowpens, Enterprise, Essex, Hornet, Langley, Lexington, Monterey, Princeton, San Jacinto, Wasp, Yorktown.*
ACA Reports of Air Groups, 1, 2, 8, 14, 15, 16, 25, 27, 28, 50.
ACA Reports of VFs 1, 2, 8, 10, 14, 15, 16, 24, 25, 27, 28, 31, 532, 0, 51, 77; VBs 8, 10, 14, 15, 16, 25, 27; and VTs 1, 2, 8, 10, 14, 16, 24, 28, 31, 51.
Air Force Fleet Air Photographic Squadron Three, Action Report, Photographic Reconnaissance Mission to Saipan, Tinian and Aguijan of 18 April 1944.
Battle Experience: Supporting Operations for the Capture of the Marianas Islands (Saipan, Guam and Tinian) June–August 1944. Secret Information Bulletin No. 20. United States Fleet, Headquarters of the Commander in Chief.
Commander in Chief Pacific. Report of Operations in Pacific Ocean Areas, June 1944.
Fifth Fleet. ComFifthFleet War Diary for Month of June 1944.
Fourth Marine Division, Operations Report—Saipan, 18 September, 1944.
Headquarters 106th Infantry "Forager" Narrative Report: The 106th Infantry and the Battle of Saipan 19 June 1944–5 August 1944.
Headquarters 106th Infantry "Forager" Regimental Journal.
Information Bulletin #20 Battle Experience Support Ops for the Capture of the Marianas.
Missing Air Crew Rpt. 42-73499. Headquarters Seventh Air Force, 431st Bomb Sq. (H), 11th Bomb Gr. (H) 11 June 1944.
Northern Troops and Landing Force Operations Report, Phase I (Saipan).
Photographic Squadron Four. Aircraft Action Report, Photographic Reconnaissance Saipan of 29 May 1944.
Report of Canadian Officers Attached to the 2, United States Army, for the Saipan Operation. n.p. [1945?], USAHEC.
Report of Intelligence Activities, 27th Division, Saipan Operation.
Report of Intelligence Activities, 27th Infantry Division, Saipan Operation. September 15, 1944.
Report of Investigation of Dynamite Explosion at Tanapag Harbor, Saipan Island, Marianas, July 30, 1944.
Report on Japanese Defensive Plan for the Island of Saipan Southern Marianas prepared by Engineer, Expeditionary Troops (Task Force 56) July 1944.
715th Amphibious Tractor Battalion. After Action Report. 26 March–30 June, 1944.

762nd Tank Battalion. After Action Report. 30 May–25 August, 1944.

773rd Amphibious Tractor Battalion. After Action Report, 25 May–4 August, 1944.

Sylvester, E. W. Untitled narrative. Recorded July 18, 1944. Remarks at the U.S. Navy's Bureau of Ships. Office of Naval Records and Library, National Archives and Records Administration.

Task Force 51. Report of Amphibious Operations for the Capture of the Marianas Islands, August 25, 1944.

Task Force 56. Report of Commanding General Expeditionary Troops, Task Force 56, Marianas, August 1944.

Task Group 52.2, War Diary Report of Saipan Operation, June 14–July 9, 1944.

Task Group 58.3, Report of Operations During the Period June 6, 1944 to July 6, 1944 in Support of Marianas Operations Including Air Engagement Against the Japanese Fleet.

27th Division Journal. Forager Operation. May 31, 1944–August 6, 1944.

USS *Cavalla* (SS 244), Report of War Patrol Number One, 3 August 1944.

USS *Flying Fish*. Report of Tenth War Patrol. 5 July, 1944.

USS *Heywood L. Edwards* (DD663), War Diary, July 1944.

USS *Knox*. Report of Operations in the Invasion of Saipan Island, Marianas, June 15–22, 1944.

USS LCI(G) 468. Action Report, June 17, 1944.

USS *Mercury*. War Diary, May 1 to July 31, 1944.

USS *Monrovia*. Report of Operations in the Invasion of Saipan Island, Marianas, June 15–22, 1944.

USS *Nautilus*. Report of War Patrol number eight, March 21, 1944.

USS *Redfin*. Patrol Report, May 1944 to July 1944.

USS *Seahorse* (SS 304). Report of Fourth War Patrol, May 11, 1944.

USS *Sheridan*, APA 51. Saipan Action Report, June 15–22, 1944.

VD-4 Aircraft Action Report. Photographic Reconnaissance Saipan of 29 May 1944.

WWII JAG Case Files, Pacific-Army Atrocities on Island of Saipan. Files of Pacific Area War Crimes Trials, 1944–1949.

INDEX